RESTORATION COMEDY

Restoration Comedy

EDITED BY

A. NORMAN JEFFARES

Professor of English Literature
University of Leeds

Volume 3

THE FOLIO PRESS
LONDON
ROWMAN AND LITTLEFIELD
TOTOWA, NEW JERSEY
1974

© Copyright The Folio Society Limited 1974

First published in the United States 1974
by Rowman and Littlefield, Totowa, N.J.

Folio Press ISBN 0 85067 030 6

Library of Congress Cataloging in Publication Data
Jeffares, Alexander Norman, comp. Restoration comedy.
'A Folio Press publication.'
CONTENTS: *v. 1*. Killigrew, T. The parson's wedding –
Sedley, C. The mulberry garden – Etherege, G.
She would if she could. (etc.)
1. English drama (Comedy) 2. English drama – Restoration.
I. Title.
PRI248.J4   822'.052   73–19769
Rowman and Littlefield ISBN 0–87471–476–1

PRINTED IN GREAT BRITAIN
by W & J Mackay Limited, Chatham

COMPLETE CONTENTS

COMPLETE ILLUSTRATIONS

Volume 1
Thomas Killigrew
Sir Charles Sedley
A Scene from *She Would If She Could*
A Scene from *Sir Martin Mar-All*
William Wycherley
A Scene from *The Man of Mode*

Volume 2
Thomas Durfey
A Scene from *The Plain Dealer*
Mrs Aphra Behn
John Dryden
Mrs Elizabeth Barry
Anthony Leigh

Volume 3
Thomas Betterton
Thomas Shadwell
William Congreve
Colley Cibber
Sir John Vanbrugh
Mrs Anne Bracegirdle

Volume 4
Robert Wilks as Sir Harry Wildair in *The Constant Couple*
A Scene from *The Way of the World*
Colley Cibber as Lord Foppington
A Scene from *The Recruiting Officer*
George Farquhar
Sir Richard Steele

CONTENTS OF VOLUME THREE

ILLUSTRATIONS IN
VOLUME THREE

A GENERAL NOTE ON THE TEXT

In this edition the base texts are those of the first editions, the only exception being *The Constant Couple* where, since Farquhar incorporated additional material, the text of the third edition has been used in preference. Spelling has been regularized and modernized throughout, but the original punctuation has been retained to as large an extent as possible because the natural breaks in speech were often indicated more clearly by playwrights and their contemporary typesetters in the early editions than by subsequent texts with punctuation regularized to accord with later practice. Any additions, as opposed to emendations, made by the present editor for the sake of clarification are clearly differentiated by being enclosed within ⟨ ⟩.

Catchwords and the long 's' have been abandoned, as have the heavy capitalization and the italics of the originals. Full points after terms such as Mr, Mrs and St have been omitted. Contracted past tenses of verbs have been expanded, as have contracted names in stage directions and speech prefixes. Similarly the form '*Ex.*' has been printed '*Exit*' or '*Exeunt*' in full, but superfluous directions such as '*Manet*' and '*Manent*' have been omitted. '*Exit*' has been amended to '*Exeunt*' where necessary. Some variant spellings have been made consistent: 'hark'ee' for 'harky', 'hark'e' or 'heark'e'; 'd'ye' for 'd'ee', 'de'e' or 'd'e'; 'aye' for 'ay', 'ey' or 'I'; 'o'clock' for 'a'clock' or 'a clock'; 'Egad' for 'I gad', 'I'gad' or 'I ga'd', and similarly with 'Ecod'; 'pshaw' for 'p'shaw' or 'p'sha', 's'death' for ''sdeath', and the same for parallel exclamations. 'I'faith' has been adopted as the normal spelling, 'bye' for 'b'w'y' and 'than', where necessary, for 'then'. 'W' replaces the occasional 'VV' of some copy texts. The form 'O' has been used where there is no following punctuation, otherwise the form 'Oh'. The punctuation and capitalization of 'Ha! Ha! Ha!' or 'ha, ha, ha.' and the like have been regularized, even where it involves amending a preceding punctuation mark to a full point. The copy texts' use of capital or lower case initial letters after dashes (which are sometimes preceded by a comma, semi-colon or colon) has been followed as closely as possible, except that, where the meaning or general direction of a speech alters after a dash, a capital letter is used: where the sense runs on, lower case is adopted.

At times the copy texts' use of exclamation marks precludes their being followed by a capital letter. On these occasions lower case has been adopted, as in *The Mulberry Garden* (Vol. I, p. 173): 'But who, alas! such love, or health can show?' In some cases the copy text has been followed where a capital letter succeeds a colon or semi-colon, but when a sentence which closes a speech ends with a comma, semi-colon or colon, a full stop has generally been silently substituted. Dashes preceding speeches have been omitted. Reported speech has normally been indicated by single inverted commas and the use of hyphens has been regularized. Expressions such as 'a foot' or 'no body', which originally appeared as two words, are printed as one. The spelling of French phrases, except where clearly intended to indicate eccentricity, has been regularized. The occasional use of the form 'Act the First' has been amended to 'Act I', and, in the instances where 'End of the First Act' has been printed (apparently haphazardly), it has been omitted. Marginal brackets indicating triple rhymes have also been deleted.

The form 'Dramatis Personae' has been used throughout for the lists of characters, and, since they do not appear in all plays, the names of the original actors, where they were printed, have been omitted, though reference is made to outstanding performers in the individual introductions. The positioning of preliminary matter has been made consistent, the present editor's introduction being followed, where relevant, by dedication, author's preface, dramatis personae, prologue and text. Epilogues, where occasionally placed at the beginning of plays, have been moved to the end.

Only in the positioning of stage directions has some liberty been taken. In the original texts, these were often printed in the right-hand margin or, particularly in the case of directions such as *'aside'*, at the end of the speech to which they refer. In this edition, such directions have been moved to their relevant place. In the textual notes the line numbering includes all headings, stage directions, etc.

A note on the text of each play is provided, and where departures (including changes in punctuation or major re-positioning of stage directions) other than silent corrections of the kind described above, have been made from the copy text, these are recorded. Where the present editor's emendations have been anticipated by other editors, these are also recorded in the textual notes by way of acknowledgement (even though such emendations do not have authorial authority), and details of the editions consulted for such alterations are listed in the 'Abbreviations' cited.

Footnotes have been supplied where meanings seemed difficult or ambiguous, or where amplification seemed called for, but these have been kept to a minimum.

The editor wishes to record his appreciation of the help he has received from Mr David I. Masson of the Brotherton Collection, University of Leeds, as well as from Mr D. G. Neill of the Bodleian Library, Professor Shirley Strum Kenny, Professor Carl J. Stratman CSV, and Mr Brian Rawson, Editorial Director of the Folio Society. He has also received valuable advice and aid from colleagues in the School of English at the University of Leeds: Miss Audrey Stead, Mr Brian Scobie and Mr John Horden, Director of the Institute of Bibliography in the School. He also wishes to thank the Keeper of the Brotherton Collection, University of Leeds, and the Trustees of the British Library for permission to use the copy texts employed in this edition.

THE LUCKY CHANCE
by Mrs Aphra Behn

INTRODUCTION

The Lucky Chance contrasts youth and age. It blends two plots, similarly centred on the differences between young lovers and old husbands, with a third, the rivalry between Bredwell and Bearjest for Diana. The play's two old men, aptly named Sir Feeble Fainwould and Sir Cautious Fulbank, are City aldermen, apt for being cuckolded. They are mixtures of cunning and credulity, caution and cupidity: they have to learn the facts of the play's life, that they were, in Sir Cautious's words, a couple of old fellows indeed to think at their age to cozen two lusty young fellows of their mistresses. They are not shown in any attractive light: they are mean, they have a grasping desire for money, and they are unscrupulous. And, of course, they are ridiculous. Sir Feeble's absurdity as the old man turned doting husband, an 'impatient dotard' as Leticia characterises him, is brilliantly, even cruelly, exposed in the bedchamber scene in the fifth act where he talks amorously to Leticia. And the cupidity of Sir Cautious is exposed in the gambling scene where he gambles with Gayman with stakes of three hundred pounds or a night with Lady Fulbank.

The action of the play moves fast and there are elements of suspense and surprise, as well as farce and melodrama, as the young men pursue their loves. Belmont's predicament is clear at the beginning: he has been proscribed, and Sir Feeble is about to marry Leticia who has resisted his advances for a time, unlike Julia who chose to marry Sir Cautious. Belmont seizes the opportunity of pretending to be Sir Feeble's nephew and thus introduced into the household can attempt to disrupt the progress of Sir Feeble towards a consummation of his marriage. Gayman, on the other hand, has different difficulties: he is in a perilous financial state, and the opening of the second act shows us his miserable room in Alsatia (comedy of a kind we find later in Goldsmith's 'Description of an author's bedchamber'), matched by the sordid yet kindly landlady from whom he borrows funds to redeem a sword and a suit. Gayman is well and truly ready to accept Bredwell's anonymous gift of gold – given on condition he visits the Shades below, a prospect hardly worse than kissing his landlady. This assignation of his with the devil, the anonymous donor, provides scope for difficulties between Gayman and Julia, who has sent the money via Bredwell. Gayman can get himself into silly situations, unlike Belmont, whose role has more romance in it.

The first two acts set the scene – there is irony in the discussion between the aldermen about methods of preventing their wives cuckolding them – while the third increases the tension, with the wedding scenes in Sir Feeble Fainwould's house and the introduction of Gayman into Sir Cautious Fulbank's house which he begins to think is not Hades after all, but a real London house. Mrs Behn obviously enjoyed farcical business, and introduced an apparent appearance of the devil into the play at this stage. The fourth act drags somewhat. Gayman's explanation to Julia of how he got his money from the apparent devil works well dramatically, as he describes her as deformed, old and ugly, 'a canvas bag of wooden ladles', a phrase Julia hurls back at him later. The scene between Gayman and Sir Cautious is less well done, and the relationships of Bredwell and Bearjest to Diana where Bredwell makes love to her apparently on Bearjest's behalf, are not very convincing. But the gambling scene ends off the act with some tension, and this is caught up again in the comedy of the fifth act.

The final pulling together of the three plots is hastily contrived. Diana is off to her wedding, Sir Feeble's attempts to consummate his marriage are interrupted and Bredwell is carried into the Fulbank house in a chest. The play ends with explanations, Diana is married, Sir Feeble pardons Belmont and Leticia, and Gayman hears of his inheritance of two thousand pounds a year. This may imply divorce, but from the point of view of comedy the play has run its course with Bearjest deprived of Diana and with the punishment of the aldermen who have been defeated by sexual potential and prowess: though they have laid themselves open to this by their avarice and their earlier lack of scruple, the conclusion is hardly edifying. But then this comedy is a high-spirited romp, an extravaganza, not to be taken too seriously but enjoyed for its suspense, for the knockabout nature of its battle between youth and age, and for Mrs Behn's delight in fulfilling the amorous desires of the lovers. It was as if she anticipated and obliged Yeats's later injunction:

> Throw likely couples into bed
> And knock the others down.

Thomas Betterton who played Gayman in the first performance of The Lucky Chance

The
Lucky Chance

or

an Alderman's Bargain

A COMEDY

As it is acted by Their Majesties'
Servants. Chas. Walmesley.

Written by Mrs A. Behn

This may be printed, 23 April 1686. R. P.

LONDON

Printed by R. H. for W. Canning, at his shop in
Vine Court, Middle Temple.

1687

THE EPISTLE DEDICATORY

To the Right Honourable Laurence, Lord Hyde, Earl of Rochester,* one of His Majesty's most honourable Privy Council, Lord High Treasurer of England, and Knight of the Noble Order of the Garter.

My Lord,

When I consider how ancient and honourable a date plays have born, how they have been the peculiar care of the most illustrious persons of Greece and Rome, who strove as much to outdo each other in magnificence, (when by turns they managed the great business of the stage, as if they had contended for the victory of the universe:) I say, my lord, when I consider this, I with the greater assurance most humbly address this comedy to your lordship, since by right of ancient custom, the patronage of plays belonged only to the great men, and chiefest magistrates. Cardinal Richelieu, that great and wise statesman, said, that there was no surer testimony to be given of the flourishing greatness of a state, than public pleasures and divertisements – for they are, says he – the schools of virtue, where vice is always either punished, or disdained. They are secret instructions to the people, in things that 'tis impossible to insinuate into them any other way. 'Tis example that prevails above reason or divine precepts. (Philosophy not understood by the multitudes) 'tis example alone that inspires morality, and best establishes virtue. I have myself known a man, whom neither conscience nor religion could persuade to loyalty, who with beholding in our theatre a modern politician set forth in all his colours, was converted, renounced his opinion, and quitted the party.

The Abbot of Aubignac,† to show that plays have been ever held most important to the very political part of government, says, the philosophy of Greece, and the majesty and wisdom of the Romans, did equally concern their great men in making them venerable, noble and magnificent: venerable, by their consecration to their

* Laurence, Lord Hyde: second son (1641–1701) of Edward Hyde, 1st Earl of Clarendon. He was dismissed from Court in 1687 for his refusal to be received into the Church.
† The Abbot of Aubignac: François Hédelin (1604–76), a critic who championed the theatre.

gods: noble, by being governed by their chiefest men; and their magnificency was from the public treasury, and the liberal contributions of their noble men.

It being undeniable then, that plays and public diversions were thought by the greatest and wisest of states, one of the most essential parts of good government, and in which so many great persons were interested; suffer me to beg your lordship's patronage for this little endeavour, and believe it not below the grandeur of your birth and state, the illustrious places you so justly hold in the kingdom, nor your illustrious relation to the greatest monarch of the world, to afford it the glory of your protection; since it is the product of a heart and pen, that always faithfully served that royal cause, to which your lordship is by many ties so firmly fixed. It approaches you with that absolute veneration, that all the world is obliged to pay you; and has no other design than to express my sense of those excellent virtues, that make your lordship so truly admired and loved. Amongst which we find those two so rare in a great man and a statesman, those of gracious speech and easy access, and I believe none were ever sent from your presence dissatisfied. You have an art to please even when you deny; and something in your look and voice has an air so greatly good, it recompences even for disappointment, and we never leave your lordship but with blessings. It is no less our admiration, to behold with what serenity and perfect conduct, that great part of the nation's business is carried on, by one single person; who having to do with so vast numbers of men of all quality, interests and humours, nevertheless all are well satisfied, and none complain of oppression, but all is done with gentleness and silence, as if (like the first creator) you could finish all by a word. You have, my lord, a judgment so piercing and solid, a wisdom so quick and clear, and a fortitude so truly noble, that those fatigues of state, that would even sink a spirit of less magnitude, is by yours accomplished without toil, or any appearance of that harsh and crabbed austerity, that is usually put on by the busy great. You, my lord, support the globe, as if you did not feel its weight; nor so much as seem to bend beneath it: your zeal for the glorious monarch you love and serve, makes all things a pleasure that advance his interest, which is so absolutely your care. You are, my lord, by your generous candour, your unbiased justice, your sweetness, affability and condescending goodness (those never-failing marks of greatness) above that envy which reigns in courts, and is aimed at the most elevated fortunes and noblest favourites of princes: and when they consider your lordship, with all the ability and wisdom of a great counsellor, your unblemished virtue, your unshaken loyalty, your constant industry for the public good, how all things under your part of sway have been refined and purged from those grossnesses, frauds, briberies, and grievances, beneath which so many of His Majesty's subjects groaned, when we see merit established and preferred, and vice discouraged; it imposes silence on malice itself, and compels 'em to bless His Majesty's choice of such a pillar of the state, such a patron of virtue.

Long may your lordship live to remain in this most honourable station, that His Majesty may be served with an entire fidelity, and the nation be rendered perfectly happy. Since from such heads and hearts, the monarch reaps his glory, and the kingdom receives its safety and tranquility. This is the unfeigned prayer of

my lord,

Your lordship's most humble,

and most obedient servant.

A. BEHN.

PREFACE

The little obligation I have to some of the witty sparks and poets of the Town, has put me on a vindication of this comedy from those censures that malice, and ill nature have thrown upon it, though in vain: the poets I heartily excuse, since there is a sort of self-interest in their malice, which I should rather call a witty way they have in this age, of railing at everything they find with pain successful, and never to show good nature and speak well of anything; but when they are sure 'tis damned, then they afford it that worse scandal, their pity. And nothing makes them so through-stitched an enemy as a full third day, that's crime enough to load it with all manner of infamy; and when they can no other way prevail with the Town, they charge it with the old never failing scandal – That 'tis not fit for the ladies: as if (if it were as they falsely give it out) the ladies were obliged to hear indecencies only from their pens and plays and some of them have ventured to treat 'em as coarsely as 'twas possible, without the least reproach from them; and in some of their most celebrated plays have entertained 'em with things, that if I should here strip from their wit and occasion that conducts 'em in and makes them proper, their fair cheeks would perhaps wear a natural colour at the reading them: yet are never taken notice of, because a man writ them, and they may hear that from them they blush at from a woman – But I make a challenge to any person of commonsense and reason – that is not wilfully bent on ill nature, and will in spite of sense wrest a double *entendre* from everything, lying upon the catch for a jest or a quibble, like a rook for a cully; but any unprejudiced person that knows not the author, to read any of my comedies and compare 'em with others of this age, and if they find one word that can offend the chastest ear, I will submit to all their peevish cavils; but right or wrong they must be criminal because a woman's; condemning them without having the Christian charity, to examine whether it be guilty or not, with reading, comparing, or thinking; the ladies taking up any scandal on trust from some conceited sparks, who will in spite of nature be wits and beaus; then scatter it for authentic all over the Town and Court, poisoning of others' judgements with their false notions, condemning it to worse than death, loss of fame. And to fortify their detraction,

charge me with all the plays that have ever been offensive; though I
wish with all their faults I had been the author of some of those they
have honoured me with.

For the farther justification of this play; it being a comedy of
intrigue, Dr Davenant* out of respect to the commands he had from
Court, to take great care that no indecency should be in plays, sent
for it and nicely looked it over, putting out anything he but imagined the critics would play with. After that, Sir Roger l'Estrange†
read it and licensed it, and found no such faults as 'tis charged with:
then Mr Killigrew,‡ who more severe than any, from the strict
order he had, perused it with great circumspection; and lastly the
master players, who you will I hope in some measure esteem judges
of decency and their own interest, having been so many years
prentice to the trade of judging.

I say, after all these supervisors the ladies may be convinced, they
left nothing that could offend, and the men of their unjust reflections on so many judges of wit and decencies. When it happens
that I challenge any one, to point me out the least expression of
what some have made their discourse, they cry, 'That, Mr Leigh§
opens his nightgown, when he comes into the bride-chamber', if he
do, which is a jest of his own making, and which I never saw, I hope
he has his clothes on underneath? And if so, where is the indecency?
I have seen in that admirable play of *Oedipus*,‖ the gown opened wide,
and the man shown in his drawers and waistcoat, and never thought
it an offence before. Another cries, 'Why we know not what they
mean, when the man takes a woman off the stage, and another is
thereby cuckolded'; is that any more than you see in the most celebrated of your plays? As the *City Politics*,¶ the Lady Mayoress, and

---

* Dr Davenant: Charles Davenant (1656–1714), eldest son of Sir William
Davenant. He was appointed, along with the Master of the Revels, to license
plays.

† Sir Roger L'Estrange (1616–1704), a Tory pamphleteer and censor also, who
supported James II.

‡ Mr Killigrew: Charles Killigrew (1655–1729). Appointed Master of the
Revels in 1683; he became a patentee of Drury Lane in 1683.

§ Mr Leigh: Antony Leigh who played Sir Feeble Fainwould.

‖ *Oedipus*: the version by Dryden and Lee was produced in 1679. The reference is to II, i.

¶ *City Politics*: a comedy by Crowne, satirising the Whigs.

the Old Lawyer's Wife, who goes with a man she never saw before, and comes out again the joyfullest woman alive, for having made her husband a cuckold with such dexterity, and yet I see nothing unnatural nor obscene: 'tis proper for the characters. So in that lucky play of *The London Cuckolds,** not to recite particulars. And in that good comedy of *Sir Courtly Nice,*† the Tailor to the young Lady – in the famed *Sir Fopling,*‡ Dorimant and Bellinda, see the very words – In *Valentinian,*§ see the scene between the Court Bawds. And Valentinian all loose and ruffled a moment after the rape, and all this you see without scandal, and a thousand others. The *Moor of Venice*|| in many places. The *Maid's Tragedy*¶ – see the scene of undressing the bride, and after between the King and Evadne – All these I name as some of the best plays I know; if I should repeat the words expressed in these scenes I mention, I might justly be charged with coarse ill manners, and very little modesty, and yet they so naturally fell into the places they are designed for, and so are proper for the business, that there is not the least fault to be found with them; though I say those things in any of mine would damn the whole piece, and alarm the Town. Had I a day or two's time, as I have scarce so many hours to write this in (the play, being all printed off and the press waiting) I would sum up all your beloved plays, and all the things in them that are passed with such silence by; because written by men: such masculine strokes in me, must not be allowed. I must conclude those women (if there be any such) greater critics in that sort of conversation than myself, who find any of that sort in mine, or anything that can justly be reproached. But 'tis in vain by dint of reason or comparison to convince the obstinate critics, whose business is to find fault, if not by a loose and gross imagination to create them, for they must either find the jest, or make it; and those of this sort fall to my share, they find faults of another kind for the men writers. And this one thing I will

---

* *The London Cuckolds*: Ravenscroft's play, see volume 2, pp. 441–552.
† *Sir Courtly Nice*: Crowne's play, see volume 2, pp. 560–650.
‡ *Sir Fopling*: *The Man of Mode, or, Sir Fopling Flutter* by Etherege.
§ *Valentinian* by the Earl of Rochester, produced in 1684.
|| *The Moor of Venice*: *Othello* was often performed after the Restoration.
¶ *The Maid's Tragedy* by Beaumont and Fletcher: a reference to II, i, and III, i, of that play.

venture to say, though against my nature, because it has a vanity in it: that had the plays I have writ come forth under any man's name, and never known to have been mine; I appeal to all unbiased judges of sense, if they had not said that person had made as many good comedies, as any one man that has writ in our age; but a devil on't the woman damns the poet.

Ladies, for its further justification to you, be pleased to know, that the first copy of this play was read by several ladies of very great quality, and unquestioned fame, and received their most favourable opinion, not one charging it with the crime, that some have been pleased to find in the acting. Other ladies who saw it more than once, whose quality and virtue can sufficiently justify anything they design to favour, were pleased to say, they found an entertainment in it very far from scandalous; and for the generality of the Town, I found by my receipts it was not thought so criminal. However, that shall not be an encouragement to me to trouble the critics with new occasion of affronting me, for endeavouring at least to divert; and at this rate, both the few poets that are left, and the players who toil in vain, will be weary of their trade.

I cannot omit to tell you, that a wit of the Town, a friend of mine at Will's coffee house,* the first night of the play, cried it down as much as in him lay, who before had read it and assured me he never saw a prettier comedy. So complaisant one pestilent wit will be to another, and in the full cry make his noise too; but since 'tis to the witty few I speak, I hope the better judges will take no offence, to whom I am obliged for better judgments; and those I hope will be so kind to me, knowing my conversation not at all addicted to the indecencies alleged, that I would much less practice it in a play, that must stand the test of the censuring world. And I must want common sense, and all the degrees of good manners, renouncing my fame, all modesty and interest for a silly saucy fruitless jest, to make fools laugh, and women blush, and wise men ashamed; myself all the while, if I had been guilty of this crime charged to me, remaining the only stupid, insensible. Is this likely, is this reasonable to be believed by anybody, but the wilfully blind? All I ask, is the privilege for my masculine part the poet in me, (if any such you will allow me) to tread in those successful paths my predecessors have so long

* Will's coffee house: No 1, Bow Street, Covent Garden.

thrived in, to take those measures that both the ancient and modern writers have set me, and by which they have pleased the world so well. If I must not, because of my sex, have this freedom, but that you will usurp all to yourselves; I lay down my quill, and you shall hear no more of me, no not so much as to make comparisons, because I will be kinder to my brothers of the pen, than they have been to a defenceless woman; for I am not content to write for a third day* only. I value fame as much as if I had been born a hero; and if you rob me of that, I can retire from the ungrateful world, and scorn its fickle favours.

* third day: the profits of this day usually went to the author.

DRAMATIS PERSONAE

MEN

Sir Feeble Fainwould	An old alderman to be married to Leticia.
Sir Cautious Fulbank	An old banker married to Julia.
Mr Gayman	A spark of the Town, lover of Julia.
Mr Belmour	Contracted to Leticia disguised, and passes for Sir Feeble's nephew.
Mr Bearjest	Nephew to Sir Cautious, a fop.
Captain Noisy	His companion.
Mr Bredwell	Prentice to Sir Cautious, and brother to Leticia, in love with Diana.
Rag	Footman to Gayman.
Ralph	Footman to Sir Feeble.
Dick	Footman to Sir Cautious.
Gingle	A music master.

WOMEN

Lady Fulbank	In love with Gayman, honest and generous.
Leticia	Contracted to Belmour, married to Sir Feeble, young and virtuous.
Diana	Daughter to Sir Feeble, in love with Bredwell – virtuous.
Pert	Lady Fulbank's woman.
Gammer Grime	Landlady to Gayman, a smith's wife in Alsatia.
Susan	Servant to Sir Feeble.
Phillis	Leticia's woman.

A Parson, Fiddlers, Dancers and Singers.

The scene London.

PROLOGUE

Spoken by Mr Jevon ⟨Bearjest⟩

Since with old plays you have so long been cloyed
As with a mistress many years enjoyed;
How briskly dear variety you pursue;
Nay though for worse ye change, ye will have new.
Widows take heed, some of you in fresh youth
Have been the unpitied martyrs of this truth.
When for a drunken sot, that had kind hours,
And taking their own freedom, left you yours;
'Twas your deliberate choice your days to pass
With a damned, sober self-admiring ass;
Who thinks good usage for the sex unfit,
And slights ye out of sparkishness and wit.
But you can fit him – Let a worse fool come,
If he neglect, to officiate in his room.
Vain amorous coxcombs everywhere are found,
Fops for all uses, but the stage abound.
Though you should change them oftener than your fashions,
There still would be enough for your occasions:
But ours are not so easily supplied,
All that could e'er quit cost, we have already tried.
Nay, dear some times have bought the frippery stuff.
This, widows, you – I mean the old and tough –
Will never think, be they but fool enough.
    Such will with any kind of puppies play;
But we must better know for what we pay:
We must not purchase such dull fools as they.
Should we show each her own particular dear,
What they admire at home, they would loathe here.
Thus, though the Mall, the Ring, the pit is full,
And every coffee-house still swarms with fool:
Though still by fools all other callings live,
Nay our own women by fresh cullies thrive.
Though your intrigues which no lampoon can cure,
Promise a long succession to ensure,

And all your matches plenty do presage:
Dire is the dearth and famine on the stage.
Our store's quite wasted, and our credit's small,
Not a fool left to bless ourselves withal.
We're forced at last to rob, (which is great pity,
Though 'tis a never-failing bank) the City.
    We show you one today entirely new,
And of all jests, none relish like the true.
Let that the value of our play enhance,
Then it may prove indeed the Lucky Chance.

ACT ONE

SCENE I

The street at break of day

Enter Belmour disguised in a travelling habit.

BELMOUR Sure 'tis the day that gleams in yonder east,
The day that all but lovers blessed by shade
Pay cheerful homage to:
Lovers! And those pursued like guilty me
By rigid laws, which put no difference
'Twixt fairly killing in my own defence,
And murders bred by drunken arguments,
Whores, or the mean revenges of a coward.
– This is Leticia's father's house – [*looking about*]
And that the dear balcony
That has so oft been conscious of our loves;
From whence she's sent me down a thousand sighs,
A thousand looks of love, a thousand vows!
O thou dear witness of those charming hours,
How do I bless thee, how am I pleased to view thee
After a tedious age of six months' banishment.

Enter ⟨Mr Gingle and⟩ several with music.

FIDDLER But hark ye Mr Gingle, is it proper to play before the wedding.
GINGLE Ever while you live, for many a time in playing after the first night, the bride's sleepy, the bridegroom tired, and both so out of humour, that perhaps they hate anything that puts 'em in mind they are married. [*they play and sing*]

> Rise Cloris, charming maid arise!
>   And baffle breaking day,
> Show the adoring world thy eyes
>   Are more surprising gay;
> The gods of love are smiling round,
>   And lead the bridegroom on,

And Hymen has the altar crowned,
  While all thy sighing lovers are undone.

To see thee pass they throng the plain;
  The groves with flowers are strown,
And every young and envying swain
  Wishes the hour his own.
Rise then, and let the god of day,
  When thou dost to the lover yield,
Behold more treasure given away
  Than he in his vast circle e'er beheld.

Enter Phillis in the balcony, throws 'em money.

BELMOUR Hah, Phillis, Leticia's woman!

GINGLE Fie Mrs Phillis, do ye take us for fiddlers that play for hire? I came to compliment Mrs Leticia on her wedding-morning because she is my scholar.

PHILLIS She sends it only to drink her health.

GINGLE Come lads let's to the tavern then – [*Exit Music*]

BELMOUR Hah! Said he Leticia? – Sure I shall turn to marble at this news – I harden – and cold damps pass through my senseless pores – Hah – who's here –

Enter Gayman wrapped in his cloak.

GAYMAN 'Tis yet too early, but my soul's impatient and I must see Leticia – [*goes to the door*]

BELMOUR Death and the divel – the bridegroom – Stay Sir, by heaven you pass not this way – [*goes to the door as he is knocking, pushes him away, and draws*]

GAYMAN Hah! What art thou that durst forbid me entrance? – Stand off. [*they fight a little, and closing view each other*]

BELMOUR Gayman!

GAYMAN My dearest Belmour.

BELMOUR O thou false friend, thou treacherous base deceiver!

GAYMAN Hah, this to me dear Harry?

BELMOUR Whither is honour, truth and friendship fled?

GAYMAN Why there ne'er was such a virtue. 'Tis all a poet's dream.

BELMOUR I thank you Sir.

GAYMAN I am sorry for't, or that ever I did anything that could deserve it: put up your sword – an honest man would say how he's offended, before he rashly draws.

BELMOUR Are not you going to be married Sir?

GAYMAN No Sir, as long as any man in London is so, that has but a handsome wife Sir.

BELMOUR Are not you in love Sir?

GAYMAN Most damnably, – and would fain lie with the dear jilting gypsy.

BELMOUR Hah – who would you lie with Sir?

GAYMAN You catechise me roundly – 'tis not fair to name, but I am no starter,* Harry; just as you left me you find me, I am for the faithless Julia still, the old alderman's wife. – 'Twas high time the City should lose their charter, when their wives turn honest: but pray Sir answer me a question or two?

BELMOUR Answer me first. – What make you here this morning?

GAYMAN Faith to do you service. Your damned little jade of a mistress has learned of her neighbours the art of swearing and lying in abundance, and is –

BELMOUR [*sighing*] To be married!

GAYMAN Even so, God save the mark; and she'll be a fair one for many an arrow besides her husband's, though he an old Finsbury hero† this threescore years.

BELMOUR Who mean you?

GAYMAN Why thy cuckold that shall be, if thou be'st wise.

BELMOUR Away – Who is this man? – thou dalliest with me.

GAYMAN Why an old knight, and alderman, here o'th'City, Sir Feeble Fainwould, a jolly old fellow, whose activity is all got into his tongue, a very excellent teaser; but neither youth nor beauty can grind his dudgeon‡ to an edge.

BELMOUR Fie what stuff's here.

GAYMAN Very excellent stuff, if you have but the grace to improve it.

* starter: a milksop, but also a weathercock or changeable person.
† Finsbury hero: Finsbury Fields were kept open for citizens to practise archery in.
‡ dudgeon: dagger.

BELMOUR You banter me – but in plain English tell me what made you here thus early, entering yon house with such authority?

GAYMAN Why your mistress Leticia – your contracted wife, is this morning to be married to old Sir Feeble Fainwould, induced to't I suppose by the great jointure he makes her, and the improbability of your ever gaining your pardon for your high duel – Do I speak English now Sir?

BELMOUR Too well, would I had never heard thee.

GAYMAN Now I being the confident in your amours, the jack-go-between – the civil pimp, or so – you left her in charge with me at your departure –

BELMOUR I did so.

GAYMAN I saw her every day – and every day she paid the tribute of a shower of tears, to the dear lord of all her vows, young Belmour; till faith at last, for reasons manifold, I slacked my daily visits.

BELMOUR And left her to temptation – was that well done?

GAYMAN Now must I afflict you and myself with a long tale of causes why; or be charged with want of friendship.

BELMOUR You will do well to clear that point to me.

GAYMAN I see you're peevish, and you shall be humoured. – You know my Julia – played me e'en such another prank as your false one is going to play you, and married old Sir Cautious Fulbank here i'th'City; at which you know I stormed, and raved, and swore, as thou wo't now, and to as little purpose. There was but one way left, and that was cuckolding him.

BELMOUR Well that design I left thee hot upon.

GAYMAN And hotly have pursued it. Swore - wept – vowed – wrote, upbraided, prayed and railed; then treated lavishly – and presented high – till between you and I Harry, I have presented the best part of eight hundred a year into her husband's hands, in mortgage.

BELMOUR This is the course you'd have me steer, I thank you.

GAYMAN No no, pox on't, all women are not jilts. Some are honest, and will give as well as take; or else there would not be so many broke i'th'City. – In fine Sir, I have been in tribulation, that is to say, moneyless, for six tedious weeks, without either clothes – or equipage to appear withal; and so not only my own love affair lay neglected – but thine too – and I am forced to pretend to my lady, that I am i'th'country with a dying uncle – from whom if he were indeed dead, I expect two thousand a year.

BELMOUR But what's all this to being here this morning?

GAYMAN Thus have I lain concealed like a winter fly, hoping for some blessed sunshine to warm me into life again, and make me hover my flagging wings; till the news of this marriage (which fills the Town) made me crawl out this silent hour – to upbraid the fickle maid.

BELMOUR Did'st thou? – Pursue thy kind design. Get me to see her, and sure no woman even possessed with a new passion, grown confident even to prostitution; but when she sees the man to whom she's sworn so very – very much, will find remorse and shame.

GAYMAN For your sake though the day be broke upon us, and I'm undone if seen – I'll venture in – [*throws his cloak over*]

Enter Sir Feeble Fainwould – Sir Cautious Fulbank – Bearjest and Noisy. ⟨They⟩ pass over the stage and go in.

– Hah – see – the bridegroom! And with him my destined cuckold, old Sir Cautious Fulbank. – Hah – what ail'st thou man?

BELMOUR The bridegroom! Like Gorgon's head he 'as turned me into stone –

GAYMAN Gorgon's head – a cuckold's head – 'twas made to graft upon –

BELMOUR By heaven I'll seize her even at the altar! And bear her thence in triumph.

GAYMAN Aye, and be born to Newgate in triumph, and be hanged in triumph – 'twill be cold comfort celebrating your nuptials in the Press Yard, and be waked next morning like Mr Barnardine* in the play – Will you please to rise and be hanged a little Sir?

---

* Mr Barnardine: a criminal. See *Measure for Measure*, IV. 3 where Pompey's three speeches run: 'You must rise and be hanged, Master Barnardine' . . . 'You must be so good, Sir, to rise, and be put to death' . . . 'Pray, Master Barnardine, awake till you are executed, and sleep afterwards'. The reference might be to *The Law against Lovers*, an adaptation by Sir William Davenant (1606–68) of *Measure for Measure* and *Much Ado about Nothing* first staged in 1662 and published in 1673.

BELMOUR What would'st thou have me do?

GAYMAN As many an honest man has done before thee – Cuckold him – Cuckold him.

BELMOUR What – and let him marry her! She that's mine by sacred vow already? By heaven it would be flat adultery in her!

GAYMAN She'll learn the trick, and practise it the better with thee.

BELMOUR O heavens! Leticia marry him! And lie with him? – – Here will I stand and see this shameful woman, see if she dares pass by me to this wickedness.

GAYMAN Hark ye Harry – in earnest have a care of betraying yourself – and do not venture sweet life for a fickle woman, who perhaps hates you.

BELMOUR You counsel well – but yet to see her married! – How every thought of that shocks all my resolution – But hang it I'll be resolute and saucy, despise a woman who can use me ill, and think myself above her.

GAYMAN Why now thou art thyself – a man again. But see they're coming forth, now stand your ground.

Enter Sir Feeble, Sir Cautious, Bearjest, Noisy, Leticia sad, Diana, Phillis. ⟨They⟩ pass over the stage.

BELMOUR 'Tis she, support me Charles, or I shall sink to earth. – Methought in passing by she cast a scornful glance at me: such charming pride I've seen upon her eyes, when our love-quarrels armed 'em with disdain – – I'll after 'em, if I live she shall not scape me. [*offers to go*]

GAYMAN Hold, remember you're proscribed, [*Gayman holds him*] and die if you are taken –

BELMOUR I've done and I will live, but he shall ne'er enjoy her. – Who's yonder, Ralph, my trusty confident?

Enter Ralph.

Now though I perish I must speak to him. – Friend, what wedding's this?

RALPH One that was never made in heaven Sir, 'tis Alderman Fainwould, and Mrs Leticia Bredwell.

BELMOUR Bredwell – I've heard of her – she was mistress –

RALPH To fine Mr Belmour Sir, – aye there was a gentleman – But rest his soul – he's hanged Sir. [*weeps*]

BELMOUR How! Hanged?

RALPH Hanged Sir, hanged – at the Hague in Holland.

GAYMAN I heard some such news, but did not credit it.

BELMOUR For what said they was he hanged?

RALPH Why e'en for high treason Sir, he killed one of their kings.

GAYMAN Holland's a commonwealth, and is not ruled by kings.

RALPH Not by one Sir, but by a great many; this was a cheese-monger – they fell out over a bottle of brandy, went to snicker-snee,* – Mr Belmour cut his throat, and was hanged for't, that's all Sir. –

BELMOUR And did the young lady believe this?

RALPH Yes, – and took on most heavily, – the doctors gave her over – and there was the divel to do to get her to consent to this marriage – but her fortune was small, and the hope of a ladyship, and a gold chain at the Spital sermon† did the business, – and so your servant Sir. –   [*Exit Ralph*]

BELMOUR So – here's a hopeful account of my sweet self now.

Enter Postman with letters.

POSTMAN Pray Sir which is Sir Feeble Fainwould's?

BELMOUR What would you with him, friend?

POSTMAN I have a letter here from the Hague for him.

BELMOUR From the Hague! Now have I a curiosity to see it – I am his servant – give it me –   [⟨*Postman*⟩ *gives it him and exit*]

– Perhaps here may be the second part of my tragedy. I'm full of mischief, Charles – and have a mind to see this fellow's secrets. For from this hour I'll be his evil genius, haunt him at bed and board, he shall not sleep nor eat – disturb him at his prayers, in his embraces; and tease him into madness. Help me invention, malice, love, and wit. [*opening the letter*] Ye gods, and little fiends instruct my mischief. [*reads*] 'Dear brother, according to your

---

* snickersnee: the practice of fighting, or a fight with cut-and-thrust knives, a word of Dutch origin.

† Spital sermon: one of the sermons preached on Easter Monday and Tuesday at St Mary Spital, later at St Bride's and then at Christ Church in the City. Spital: hospital.

desire I have sent for my son from St Omer's, whom I have sent
to wait on you in England, he is a very good accountant and fit for
business, and much pleased he shall see that uncle to whom he's
so obliged, and which is so gratefully acknowledged by – Dear
brother, your affectionate brother Francis Fainwould.'
– Hum – hark ye Charles, do you know who I am now?

GAYMAN Why I hope a very honest friend of mine, Harry Belmour.

BELMOUR No Sir, you are mistaken in your man.

GAYMAN It may be so.

BELMOUR I am d'ye see Charles, this very individual, numerical
young Mr – what ye call'um Fainwould, just come from Saint
Omer's into England – to my uncle the alderman. I am, Charles,
this very man.

GAYMAN I know you are, and will swear't upon occasion.

BELMOUR This lucky thought has almost calmed my mind. And
if I don't fit you my dear uncle – May I never lie with my aunt.

GAYMAN Ah rogue – but prithee what care have you taken about
your pardon? 'Twere good you should secure that.

BELMOUR There's the divel Charles, – had I but that – but I have
had a very good friend at work, a thousand guineas, that seldom
fails; but yet in vain, I being the first transgressor since the Act
against duelling. But I impatient to see this dear delight of my
soul, and hearing from none of you this six weeks, came from
Brussels in this disguise – for the Hague I have not seen, though
hanged there – but come – let's away and complete me a right
Saint Omer's spark, that I may present myself as soon as they come
from church.   [*Exeunt*]

SCENE II

Sir Cautious Fulbank's house

Enter Lady Fulbank, Pert, and Bredwell. Bredwell gives her a letter.

LADY FULBANK [*reads*] 'Did my Julia know how I languish in this
cruel separation, she would afford me her pity, and write oftener.
If only the expectation of two thousand a year kept me from you,

ah! Julia how easily would I abandon that trifle for your more valued sight, but that I know a fortune will render me more agreeable to the charming Julia, I should quit all my interest here, to throw myself at her feet, to make her sensible how am I entirely her adorer, Charles Gayman.'
– Faith Charles you lie – you are as welcome to me now, now when I doubt thy fortune is declining, as if the universe were thine.

PERT That Madam is a noble gratitude. For if his fortune be declining, 'tis sacrificed to his passion for your ladyship. – 'Tis all laid out on love.

LADY FULBANK I prize my honour more than life, yet I had rather have given him all he wished of me, than be guilty of his undoing.

PERT And I think the sin were less.

LADY FULBANK I must confess, such jewels, rings, and presents as he made me must needs decay his fortune.

BREDWELL Aye Madam, his very coach at last was turned into a jewel for your ladyship. Then Madam what expenses his despairs have run him on – As drinking and gaming to divert the thought of your marrying my old master.

LADY FULBANK And put in wenching too. –

BREDWELL No assure yourself Madam –

LADY FULBANK Of that I would be better satisfied – [*to Bredwell*] and you too must assist me as e'er you hope I should be kind to you in gaining you Diana.

BREDWELL Madam, I'll die to serve you.

PERT Nor will I be behind in my duty.

LADY FULBANK O how fatal are forced marriages!
How many ruins one such match pulls on –
Had I but kept my sacred vows to Gayman
How happy had I been – how prosperous he!
Whilst now I languish in a loathed embrace,
Pine out my life with age – consumptious coughs,
– But dost thou fear that Gayman is declining?

BREDWELL You are my lady, and the best of mistresses – therefore I would not grieve you, for I know you love this best – but most unhappy man.

LADY FULBANK You shall not grieve me – prithee on –

BREDWELL My master sent me yesterday to Mr Crap his scrivener, to send to one Mr Wastall, to tell him his first mortgage was out, which is two hundred pounds a year – and who has since engaged five or six hundred more to my master; but if this first be not redeemed he'll take the forfeit on't, as he says a wise man ought.

LADY FULBANK That is to say, a knave according to his notion of a wise man.

BREDWELL Mr Crap being busy with a borrowing lord, sent me to Mr Wastall; whose lodging is in a nasty place, called Alsatia,* at a blacksmith's.

LADYFULBANK But what's all this to Gayman?

BREDWELL Madam, this Wastall was Mr Gayman.

LADY FULBANK Gayman? Saw'st thou Gayman?

BREDWELL Madam, Mr Gayman, yesterday.

LADY FULBANK When came he to Town?

BREDWELL Madam, he has not been out of it.

LADY FULBANK Not at his uncle's in Northamptonshire?

BREDWELL Your ladyship was wont to credit me.

LADY FULBANK Forgive me – you went to a blacksmith's –

BREDWELL Yes Madam; and at the door encountered the beastly thing he calls a landlady; who looked as if she'd been of her own husband's making, composed of moulded smith's dust. I asked for Mr Wastall, and she began to open – and did so rail at him, that what with her Billingsgate, and her husband's hammers, I was both deaf and dumb – at last the hammers ceased, and she grew weary, and called down Mr Wastall; but he not answering – I was sent up a ladder rather than a pair of stairs; at last I scaled the top, and entered the enchanted castle; there did I find him, spite of the noise below, drowning his cares in sleep.

LADY FULBANK Whom foundst thou Gayman – ?

BREDWELL He Madam, whom I waked – and seeing me, heavens what confusion seized him! Which nothing but my own surprise could equal. Ashamed – he would have turned away, but when he saw by my dejected eyes, I knew him, he sighed, and blushed, and heard me tell my business. Then begged I would be secret: for he

---

* Alsatia: a cant name for Whitefriars, a refuge for those wishing to avoid creditors and bailiffs.

vowed, his whole repose and life, depended on my silence. Nor had I told it now, but that your ladyship, may find some speedy means to draw him from this desperate condition.

LADY FULBANK Heavens is't possible!

BREDWELL He's driven to the last degree of poverty – Had you but seen his lodgings, Madam!

LADY FULBANK What were they?

BREDWELL 'Tis a pretty convenient tub Madam. He may lie along in't, there's just room for an old joined stool besides the bed, which one cannot call a cabin, about the largeness of a pantry bin, or a usurer's trunk, there had been dornex★ curtains to't in the days of yore; but they were now annihilated, and nothing left to save his eyes from the light, but my landlady's blue apron, tied by the strings before the window, in which stood a broken six-penny looking-glass, that showed as many faces, as the scene in *Henry the Eighth*,† which could but just stand upright, and then the comb-case filled it.

LADY FULBANK What a lewd description hast thou made of his chamber!

BREDWELL Then for his equipage, 'tis banished to one small monsieur, who (saucy with his master's poverty) is rather a companion than a footman.

LADY FULBANK But what said he to the forfeiture of his land?

BREDWELL He sighed, and cried, 'Why farewell dirty acres. It shall not trouble me, since 'twas all but for love!'

LADY FULBANK How much redeems it?

BREDWELL Madam, five hundred pounds.

LADY FULBANK Enough – you shall in some disguise convey this money to him, as from an unknown hand: I would not have him think it comes from me, for all the world; that nicety and virtue I've professed, I am resolved to keep.

PERT If I were your ladyship, I would make use of Sir Cautious his cash: pay him in his own coin.

BREDWELL Your ladyship would make no scruple of it, if you

★ dornex: worsted fabric for curtains, sometimes called dornick, made in Tournai.

† *Henry the Eighth*: a reference to Davenant's famous lavish production of the play in 1663 and later.

knew how this poor gentleman has been used by my unmerciful master.

LADY FULBANK I have a key already to his counting-house; it being lost, he had another made, and this I found and kept.

BREDWELL Madam, this is an excellent time for't, my master being gone to give my sister Leticia at church.

LADY FULBANK 'Tis so, I'll go and commit the theft, whilst you prepare to carry it, and then we'll to dinner with your sister the bride.

[*Exeunt*]

SCENE III

The house of Sir Feeble

Enter Sir Feeble, Leticia, Sir Cautious, Bearjest, Diana, Noisy.
Sir Feeble sings and salutes 'em.

SIR FEEBLE Welcome Joan Sanderson,★ welcome, welcome, [*kisses the bride*] Od's bobs, and so thou art sweetheart. [*so do the rest*]

BEARJEST Methinks my lady bride is very melancholy.

SIR CAUTIOUS Aye, aye, women that are discreet, are always thus upon their wedding-day.

SIR FEEBLE Always by daylight, Sir Cautious.
But when bright Phoebus does retire –
To Thetis' bed to quench his fire,
And do the thing we need not name,
We mortals by his influence do the same.
Then then the blushing maid lays by
Her simpering, and her modesty;
And round the lover clasps and twines
Like ivy, or the circling vines.

SIR FEEBLE Here Ralph, the bottle rogue, of sack ye rascal, hadst thou been a butler worth hanging, thou wouldst have met us at the door with it – Od's bobs sweetheart thy health.

BEARJEST Away with it, to the bride's *haunce in kelder*.†

★ Joan Sanderson: the air to which the cushion dance was performed, to be found in Playford's *Dancing Master* (1686). The dance itself was also called Joan Sanderson.

† *haunce in kelder*: Jack in the cellar, or the unborn babe in the womb.

SIR FEEBLE God so, go to rogue, go to, that shall be, knave, that shall be, by the morrow morning, he – od's bobs, we'll do't sweetheart; here's to't – [*drinks again*]

LETICIA I die but to imagine it, would I were dead indeed.

SIR FEEBLE Hah – hum – how's this? Tears upon your weddingday? Why – why – you baggage you, ye little ting, fool's-face – away you rogue, you're naughty, you're naughty, [*patting, and playing, and following her*] Look – look – look now, – buss it – buss it – and friends, did'ums, did'ums, beat its none silly baby – away you little hussy, away, and pledge me – [*she drinks a little*]

SIR CAUTIOUS A wise discreet lady, I'll warrant her, my lady would prodigally have took it off all –

SIR FEEBLE Dear's its nown dear fubs; buss again, buss again, away, away – od's bobs, I long for night – look – look Sir Cautious; what an eye's there –

SIR CAUTIOUS Aye, so there is brother, and a modest eye too.

SIR FEEBLE Adad, I love her more and more, Ralph – call old Susan hither – Come Mr Bearjest, put the glass about. Od's bobs, when I was a young fellow, I would not let the young wenches look pale and wan – but would rouse 'em, and touse 'em, and blowze 'em, 'till I put a colour in their cheeks, like an apple John★ assacks – Nay, I can make a shift still, and pupsey shall not be jealous –

Enter Susan, Sir Feeble whispers her, she goes out.

LETICIA Indeed not I Sir. I shall be all obedience.

SIR CAUTIOUS A most judicious lady; would my Julia had a little of her modesty; but my lady's a wit.

⟨*Re-*⟩*enter Susan with a box.*

SIR FEEBLE Look here my little puskin, here's fine playthings for its n'own little coxcomb – go – get ye gone – get ye gone and off with this Saint Martin's trumpery,† these playhouse glass baubles, this necklace, and these pendants, and all this false ware; od's bobs I'll have no counterfeit gear about thee, not I. See – these are

★ apple John: an apple said to keep two years and be ideal when shrivelled.
† Saint Martin's trumpery: cheap jewellery was sold in the parish of St Martin-le-grand. St Martin's ware meant a forgery.

right as the blushes on thy cheeks and these – as true as my heart
my girl. Go – put 'em on and be fine – [*gives 'em her*]

LETICIA Believe me Sir I shall not merit this kindness.

SIR FEEBLE Go to – More of your love, and less of your ceremony
– give the old fool a hearty buss and pay him that way – he ye
little wanton tit, I'll steal up – and catch ye and love ye – adod I
will – get ye gone – get ye gone –

LETICIA Heavens what a nauseous thing is an old man turned
lover.

[*Exeunt Leticia and Diana*]

SIR CAUTIOUS How steal up Sir Feeble – I hope not so; I hold it
most indecent before the lawful hour.

SIR FEEBLE Lawful hour! Why I hope all hours and are lawful
with a man's own wife.

SIR CAUTIOUS But wise men have respect to times and seasons.

SIR FEEBLE [*singing and dancing*] Wise young men Sir Cautious,
but wise old men must nick their inclinations, for it is not as
'twas wont to be, for it is not as 'twas wont to be –

Enter Ralph.

RALPH Sir here's a young gentleman without would speak with you.

SIR FEEBLE Hum – I hope it is not that same Belmour come to
forbid the bans – if it be, he comes too late – therefore bring me
first my long sword, and then the gentleman.   [*Exit Ralph*]

BEARJEST Pray Sir use mine it is a travelled blade I can assure you
Sir.

SIR FEEBLE I thank you Sir –

Enter Ralph and Belmour disguised, gives him a letter; he reads.

– How – my nephew – Francis Fainwould? [*embraces him*]

BELMOUR ⟨*aside*⟩ I am glad he has told me my Christian name.

SIR FEEBLE Sir Cautious know my nephew – 'tis a young Saint
Omer's scholar – but none of the witnesses.

SIR CAUTIOUS Marry Sir, the wiser he – for they got nothing
by't.

BELMOUR Sir I love and honour you because you are a traveller.

SIR FEEBLE A very proper young fellow, and as like old Frank
Fainwould as the devil to the collier; but Francis you are come

into a very lewd town Francis for whoring and plotting and roaring and drinking, but you must go to church Francis, and avoid ill company, or you may make damnable havoc in my cash Francis – what you can keep merchants' books?

BELMOUR 'T has been my study Sir.

SIR FEEBLE And you will not be proud but will be commanded by me Francis?

BELMOUR I desire not to be favoured as a kinsman Sir, but as your humblest servant.

SIR FEEBLE Why thou'rt an honest fellow Francis – and thou'rt heartily welcome – and I'll make thee fortunate! But come Sir Cautious let you and I take a turn i'th' garden, and beget a right understanding between your nephew Mr Bearjest and my daughter Dye.

SIR CAUTIOUS Prudently thought on Sir, I'll wait on you –
[Exeunt Sir Feeble and Sir Cautious]

BEARJEST You are a traveller Sir, I understand –

BELMOUR I have seen a little part of the world Sir.

BEARJEST So have I Sir thank my stars, and have performed most of my travels on foot Sir.

BELMOUR You did not travel far then I presume Sir.

BEARJEST No Sir, it was for my diversion indeed; but I assure you I travelled into Ireland a-foot Sir.

BELMOUR Sure Sir, you go by shipping into Ireland?

BEARJEST That's all one Sir, I was still a-foot – ever walking on the deck –

BELMOUR Was that your farthest travels Sir?

BEARJEST Farthest – why that's the end of the world – and sure a man can go no further.

BELMOUR Sure there can be nothing worth a man's curiosity?

BEARJEST No Sir? I'll assure you there are the wonders of the world Sir; I'll hint you this one. There is a harbour which since the creation was never capable of receiving a lighter, yet by another miracle the King of France was to ride there with a vast fleet of ships, and to land a hundred thousand men.

BELMOUR This is a swinging wonder – but are there store of madmen there Sir –?

BEARJEST That's another rarity to see a man run out of his wits.

NOISY Marry Sir, the wiser they I say.

BEARJEST Pray Sir what store of miracles have you at St Omer's?

BELMOUR None Sir since that of the wonderful Salamanca doctor,*
who was both here and there, at the same instant of time.

BEARJEST How Sir! Why that's impossible.

BELMOUR That was the wonder Sir, because 'twas impossible.

NOISY But 'twas a greater Sir that 'twas believed.

Enter Lady Fulbank and Pert, Sir Cautious and Sir Feeble.

SIR FEEBLE Enough, enough, Sir Cautious we apprehend one
another, Mr. Bearjest, your uncle here and I have struck the
bargain, the wench is yours with three thousand pound present,
and something more after death: which your uncle likes well.

BEARJEST Does he so Sir, I'm beholding to him, then 'tis not a pin
matter whether I like or not, Sir.

SIR FEEBLE How Sir not like my daughter Dye?

BEARJEST O Lord Sir – die or live 'tis all one for that Sir – I'll
stand to the bargain my uncle makes.

PERT [*aside*] Will you so Sir, you'll have very good luck if you do –

BEARJEST Prithee hold thy peace, my lady's woman.

LADY FULBANK Sir I beg your pardon for not waiting on you to
church – I knew you would be private –

Enter Leticia fine in jewels.

SIR FEEBLE You honour us too highly now Madam – [*presents his
wife, who salutes her*]

LADY FULBANK Give you joy my dear Leticia! I find Sir you were
resolved for youth wit and beauty.

SIR FEEBLE Aye Madam to the comfort of many a hoping coxcomb but Lette – rogue Lette – thou wo't not make me free
o'th'City a second time, wo't thou entice the rogues with the
twire† and wanton leer – the amorous simper that cries 'Come kiss
me' – then the pretty round lips are pouted out – he rogue how I
long to be at 'em! – well she shall never go to church more – that
she shall not.

---

* the Salamanca doctor: Titus Oates pretended to have a D.D. of that university.

† twire: a sly, saucy glance.

LADY FULBANK How Sir, not to church, the chiefest recreation of a City lady?

SIR FEEBLE That's all one Madam, that tricking and dressing and prinking and patching, is not your devotion to heaven, but to the young knaves that are licked and combed – and are minding you more than the parson – od's bobs there are more cuckolds destined at church than are made out of it.

SIR CAUTIOUS Ha, ha, ha, he! [*to his lady*] Tickles ye i'faith ladies.

BELMOUR Not one chance look this way – and yet I can forgive her lovely eyes – Because they look not pleased with all this ceremony; and yet methinks some sympathy in love might this way glance their beams – I cannot hold – Sir, is this fair lady my aunt?

SIR FEEBLE O Francis! Come hither Francis. Lette, here's a young rogue has a mind to kiss thee. [*puts them together, she starts back*] – Nay start not, he's my own flesh and blood. My nephew – baby – look – look how the young rogues stare at one another, like will to like, I see that.

LETICIA There's something in his face, so like my Belmour it calls my blushes up, and leaves my heart defenceless –

Enter Ralph.

RALPH Sir, dinner's on the table.

SIR FEEBLE Come, come – let's in then – gentlemen and ladies –
And share today my pleasures and delight
But –
Add's bobs they must be all mine own at night.

ACT TWO

SCENE I

Gayman's lodging

Enter Gayman in a night-cap, and an old campaign coat tied about him. Very melancholy.

GAYMAN Curse on my birth! Curse on my faithless fortune!
Curse on my stars, and cursed be all – but love!
That dear, that charming sin, though t'have pulled
Innumerable mischiefs on my head,
I have not, nor I cannot find repentance for.
No let me die despised, upbraided, poor:
Let fortune, friends and all abandon me –
But let me hold thee thou soft smiling god
Close to my heart while life continues there.
Till the last pantings of my vital blood
May the last spark of life and fire be love's!

Enter Rag.

– How now Rag, what's o'clock?

RAG My belly can inform you better than my tongue.

GAYMAN Why you gormandizing vermin you, what have you done with the threepence I gave you a fortnight ago.

RAG Alas Sir that's all gone, long since.

GAYMAN You gutling rascal, you are enough to breed a famine in a land. I have known some industrious footmen, that have not only gotten their own livings, but a pretty livelihood for their masters too.

RAG Aye, till they came to the gallows Sir.

GAYMAN Very well sirrah, they died in an honourable calling – but hark'ee Rag – I have business – very earnest business abroad this evening, now were you a rascal of docity,* you would invent a way – to get home my last suit that was laid in lavender† – with the appurtenances thereunto belonging, as periwig, cravat – and – so forth –

* docity: gumption.   † laid in lavender: pawned.

RAG Faith master I must deal in the Black Art then, for no human means will do't – and now I talk of the Black Art master, try your power once more with my landlady –

GAYMAN Oh! Name her not, the thought on't turns my stomach – a sight of her is a vomit, but he's a bold hero that dares venture on her for a kiss, and all beyond that sure is hell itself – yet there's my last, last refuge – and I must to this wedding – I know not what – but something whispers me – this night I shall be happy – and without Julia 'tis impossible! –

RAG Julia; who's that? My Lady Fulbank Sir?

GAYMAN Peace Sirrah – and call – a – no – pox on't come back – and yet – yes – call my fulsome landlady.   [*Exit Rag*]
– Sir Cautious knows me not, by name or person. And I will to this wedding, I'm sure of seeing Julia there. And what may come of that – but here's old nasty coming. I smell her up – hah my dear landlady –

Enter Rag and Landlady.

Quite out of breath – A chair there for my landlady –

RAG Here's ne'er a one Sir.

LANDLADY More of your money and less of your civility good Mr Wastall.

GAYMAN Dear landlady –

LANDLADY Dear me no dears Sir, but let me have my money – Eight weeks' rent last Friday. Besides taverns, ale-houses, chandlers, laundresses, stores, and ready money out of my purse; you know it Sir.

GAYMAN Aye but your husband does not; speak softly.

LANDLADY My husband! What do you think to fright me with my husband – I'd have you to know I am an honest woman and care not this – for my husband. Is this all the thanks I have for my kindness, for patching, borrowing, and shifting for you; 'twas but last week I pawned my best petticoat, as I hope to wear it again it cost me six and twenty shillings besides making; then this morning my new Norwich mantua followed, and two 'postle spoons, I had the whole dozen when you came first; but they dropped and dropped, till I had only Judas left for my husband.

GAYMAN Hear me good landlady –

LANDLADY Then I've passed my word at the George Tavern for forty shillings for you, ten shillings at my neighbour Squabs for ale; besides seven shillings to Mother Suds for washing, and do you fob me off with my husband? –

GAYMAN Here Rag – Run and fetch her a pint of sack – There's no other way of quenching the fire in her slabber chops; [*Exit Rag*] – but my dear landlady have a little patience.

LANDLADY Patience? I scorn your words Sir – Is this a place to trust in, tell me of patience that used to have my money beforehand; come, come pay me quickly – or old Gregory Grimes's house shall be too hot to hold you.

GAYMAN Is't come to this, can I not be heard!

LANDLADY No Sir, you had good clothes when you came first, but they dwindled daily, till they dwindled to this old campaign – with tanned-coloured lining – once red – but now all colours of the rainbow, a cloak to skulk in a-nights, and a pair of piss-burned chamois breeches. Nay your very badge of manhood's gone too.

GAYMAN How landlady, nay then i'faith no wonder if you rail so.

LANDLADY Your silver sword I mean – transmogrified to this two-handed basket hilt – this old Sir Guy of Warwick★ – which will sell for nothing but old iron. In fine I'll have my money Sir, or i'faith Alsatia shall not shelter you.

Enter Rag.

GAYMAN Well landlady – if we must part – let's drink at parting, here landlady, here's to the fool – that shall love you better than I have done. [*sighing drinks*]

LANDLADY Rot your wine – d'ye think to pacify me with wine Sir. [*she refusing to drink he holds open her jaws, Rag throws a glass of wine into her mouth*] – What will you force me – no – give me another glass, I scorn to be so uncivil to be forced, my service to you Sir – but this shan't do Sir – [*she drinks, he embracing her sings*]

> Ah Cloris 'tis in vain you scold,
> Whilst your eyes kindle such a fire.
> Your railing cannot make me cold,
> So fast as they a warmth inspire.

★ Sir Guy of Warwick: slang name for a rapier.

LANDLADY Well Sir you have no reason to complain of my eyes nor my tongue neither, if rightly understood. [*weeps*]

GAYMAN I know you are the best of landladies. As such I drink your health – [*drinks*] – But to upbraid a man in tribulation – fie – 'tis not done like a woman of honour, a man that loves you too. [*she drinks*]

LANDLADY I am a little hasty sometimes, but you know my good nature.

GAYMAN I do and therefore trust my little wants with you. I shall be rich again – and then my dearest landlady –

LANDLADY Would this wine might ne'er go through me, if I would not go as they say through fire and water – by night or by day for you. [*she drinks*]

GAYMAN And as this is wine – I do believe thee – [*he drinks*]

LANDLADY Well – you have no money in your pocket now I'll warrant you – here – here's ten shillings for you old Greg'ry knows not of. [*opens a great greasy purse*]

GAYMAN I cannot in conscience take it, good faith I cannot – besides the next quarrel you'll hit me in the teeth with it.

LANDLADY Nay pray no more of that, forget it, forget it. I own I was to blame – here – Sir you shall take it.

GAYMAN Aye – but what should I do with money in – these – damned breeches? – No put it up – I can't appear abroad this – no I'll stay at home and lose my business.

LANDLADY Why, is there no way to redeem one of your suits?

GAYMAN None – none – I'll e'en lay me down and die –

LANDLADY Die – marry heavens forbid – I would not for the world – let me see – hum – what does it lie for?

GAYMAN Alas! Dear landlady a sum – a sum.

LANDLADY Well, say no more, I'll lay about me –

GAYMAN By this kiss but you shall not – *Assafoetida* by this light.

LANDLADY Shall not? That's a good one i'faith: shall you rule – or I?

GAYMAN But should your husband know it.

LANDLADY Husband – marry come up, husbands know wives' secrets? No sure the world's not so bad yet – Where do your things lie? And for what?

GAYMAN Five pounds equips me – Rag can conduct you – but I say you shall not go – I've sworn –

LANDLADY Meddle with your matters – let me see, the caudle cup that Molly's grandmother left her will pawn for about that sum – I'll sneak it out – well Sir you shall haveyour things presently – trouble not your head, but expect me. [*Exeunt Landlady and Rag*]

GAYMAN Was ever man put to such beastly shifts? S'death, how she stunk – my senses are most luxuriously regaled – there's my perpetual music too – [*knocking of hammers on an anvil*] The ringing of bells is an ass to't.

Enter Rag.

RAG Sir there's one in a coach below would speak to you.

GAYMAN With me – and in a coach, who can it be?

RAG The devil I think, for he has a strange countenance.

GAYMAN The devil, show yourself a rascal of parts, sirrah, and wait on him up with ceremony.

RAG Who the devil, Sir?

GAYMAN Aye the devil Sir, if you mean to thrive. [*Exit Rag*] – Who can this be – But see he comes to inform me – withdraw –

Enter Bredwell dressed like a devil.

BREDWELL I come to bring you this – [*gives him a letter*]

GAYMAN [*reads*] 'Receive what love and fortune present you with, be grateful and be silent, or 'twill vanish like a dream, and leave you more wretched than it found you. Adieu.' [⟨*Bredwell*⟩ *gives him a bag of money*] – hah –

BREDWELL Nay view it Sir, 'tis all substantial gold.

GAYMAN [*aside*] Now dare not I ask one civil question for fear it vanish all – But I may ask how 'tis I ought to pay for this great bounty.

BREDWELL Sir all the pay is secrecy –

GAYMAN And is this all that is required Sir?

BREDWELL No you're invited to the Shades below.

GAYMAN Hum, Shades below? – I am not prepared for such a journey Sir.

BREDWELL [*in feigned heroic tone*] If you have courage, youth, or love, you'll follow me,

When night's black curtains drawn around the world,
And mortal eyes are safely locked in sleep,
And no bold spy dares view when gods caress:
Then I'll conduct thee to the banks of bliss.
– Durst thou not trust me?
GAYMAN [*hugs the bag*] Yes sure on such substantial security.
BREDWELL Just when the day is vanished into night,
And only twinkling stars inform the world,
Near to the corner of the silent wall
In fields of Lincoln's Inn thy spirit shall meet thee.
– Farewell –   [*Goes out*]
GAYMAN Hum – I am awake sure, and this is gold I grasp.
I could not see this devil's cloven foot,
Nor am I such a coxcomb to believe,
But he was as substantial as his gold.
Spirits, ghosts, hobgoblins, furies, fiends, and devils
I've often heard old wives fright fools and children with,
Which once arrived to common sense they laugh at.
– No, I am for things possible and natural,
– Some female devil old, and damned to ugliness,
And past all hopes of courtship and address,
Full of another devil called desire,
Has seen this face – this – shape – this youth
And thinks it worth her hire. It must be so.
I must moil on in the damned dirty road,
And sure such pay will make the journey easy;
And for the price of the dull drudging night,
All day I'll purchase new and fresh delight.   [*Exit*]

SCENE II

Sir Feeble's house

Enter Leticia pursued by Phillis.

PHILLIS Why Madam do you leave the garden, for this retreat to melancholy?
LETICIA Because it suits my fortune and my humour. And even thy presence would afflict me now.

PHILLIS Madam, I was sent after you, my Lady Fulbank has challenged Sir Feeble at bowls, and stakes a ring of fifty pound against his new chariot.

LETICIA Tell him I wish him luck in everything
But in his love to me –
Go tell him I am viewing of the garden.   [*Exit Phillis*]

Enter Belmour at a distance behind her.

– Blessed be this kind retreat, this 'lone occasion
That lends a short cessation to my torments.
And gives me leave to vent my sighs and tears!

BELMOUR And doubly blessed be all the powers of love,
That gives me this dear opportunity. [*weeps*]

LETICIA Where were you all ye pitying gods of love,
That once seemed pleased at Belmour's flame and mine,
And smiling joined our hearts, our sacred vows
And spread your wings, and held your torches high.

BELMOUR O –

LETICIA [*she starts, pauses*] Where were you now! When this un-
equal marriage,
Gave me from all my joys, gave me from Belmour:
Your wings were flagged, your torches bent to earth;
And all your little bonnets veiled your eyes.
You saw not, or were deaf and pitiless.

BELMOUR O my Leticia!

LETICIA Hah, 'tis there again; that very voice was Belmour's:
Where art thou, o thou lovely charming shade?
For sure thou can'st not take a shape to fright me.
– What art thou – speak! [*not looking behind her yet for fear*]

BELMOUR [*approaching nearer*] Thy constant true adorer.
Who all this fatal day has haunted thee
To ease his tortured soul.

LETICIA [*speaking with signs of fear*] My heart is well acquainted with
that voice,
But O my eyes dare not encounter thee.

BELMOUR Is it because thou'st broken all thy vows?
– Take to thee courage and behold thy slaughters.

LETICIA Yes, though the sight would blast me I would view it.
[*turns*]
– 'Tis he – 'tis very Belmour? Or so like –
I cannot doubt but thou deservest this welcome. [*embraces him*]

BELMOUR O my Leticia!

LETICIA I'm sure I grasp not air; thou art no phantom.
My arms return not empty to my bosom,
But meet a solid treasure.

BELMOUR A treasure thou so easily threw'st away?
A riddle simple love ne'er understood.

LETICIA Alas I heard, my Belmour, thou wert dead.

BELMOUR And was it thus you mourned my funeral?

LETICIA I will not justify my hated crime.
But O remember I was poor and helpless.
And much reduced, and much imposed upon.

BELMOUR [*weeps*] And want compelled thee to this wretched
marriage – did it?

LETICIA 'Tis not a marriage, since my Belmour lives:
The consummation were adultery.
I was thy wife before, wo't thou deny me?

BELMOUR No by those powers that heard our mutual vows,
Those vows that tie us faster than dull priests.

LETICIA But O my Belmour, thy sad circumstances
Permit thee not to make a public claim.
Thou art proscribed, and diest if thou art seen.

BELMOUR Alas!

LETICIA Yet I would wander with thee o'er the world,
And share thy humblest fortune with thy love.

BELMOUR Is't possible Leticia thou wouldst fly
To foreign shores with me?

LETICIA Can Belmour doubt the soul he knows so well?

BELMOUR Perhaps in time the king may find my innocence, and
may extend his mercy: meantime I'll make provision for our flight.

LETICIA But how 'twixt this and that can I defend myself from the
loathed arms of an impatient dotard, that I may come a spotless
maid to thee?

BELMOUR Thy native modesty and my industry
Shall well enough secure us.

Feign you nice virgin-cautions all the day:
Then trust at night to my conduct to preserve thee.
– And wilt thou yet be mine! O swear a-new,
Give me again thy faith, thy vows, thy soul:
For mine's so sick with this day's fatal business,
It needs a cordial of that mighty strength;
Swear, – swear, so as if thou break'st –
Thou mayst be – anything – but damned Leticia.

LETICIA [*kneels*] Thus then, and hear me heaven!

BELMOUR [*kneels*] And thus – I'll listen to thee.

Enter Sir Feeble, Lady Fulbank, Sir Cautious.

SIR FEEBLE Lette, Lette, Lette, where are you little rogue Lette. – Hah – hum – what's here – [*Belmour snatches her to his bosom as if she fainted*]

BELMOUR O heavens, she's gone, she's gone!

SIR FEEBLE Gone – whither is she gone? – It seems she had the wit to take good company with her – [*the women go to her, take her up*]

BELMOUR She's gone to heaven Sir, for ought I know.

SIR CAUTIOUS She was resolved to go in a young fellow's arms I see.

SIR FEEBLE Go to Francis – go to.

LADY FULBANK Stand back Sir, she recovers.

BELMOUR Alas, I found her dead upon the floor, – should I have left her so – if I had known your mind –

SIR FEEBLE Was it so – was it so – God so, by no means Francis. –

LETICIA Pardon him Sir; for surely I had died, but for his timely coming.

SIR FEEBLE Alas poor pupsey – was it sick – look here – here's a fine thing to make it well again. Come buss, and it shall have it – O how I long for night. Ralph, are the fiddlers ready?

RALPH They are tuning in the hall Sir.

SIR FEEBLE That's well, they know my mind. I hate that same twang, twang, twang, fum, fum, fum, tweedle, tweedle, tweedle, then screw go the pins, till a man's teeth are on edge; then snap says a small gut, and there we are at a loss again. I long to be in bed – [*dancing and playing on his stick, like a flute*] with a hey tredodle,

tredodle, tredodle – with a hey tredool, tredodle, tredo –

SIR CAUTIOUS A prudent man would reserve himself – Good-sacks I danced so on my wedding day, that when I came to bed, to my shame be it spoken, I fell fast asleep, and slept till morning.

LADY FULBANK Where was your wisdom then, Sir Cautious? But I know what a wise woman ought to have done.

SIR FEEBLE Od's bobs, that's wormwood, that's wormwood – I shall have my young hussy set agog too; she'll hear there are better things in the world than she has at home, and then od's bobs, and then they'll ha't, adod they will, Sir Cautious. Ever while you live, keep a wife ignorant, unless a man be as brisk as his neighbours.

SIR CAUTIOUS A wise man will keep 'em from bawdy christen-ings then, and gossipings.

SIR FEEBLE Christenings, and gossipings; why they are the very schools that debauch our wives, as dancing-schools do our daugh-ters.

SIR CAUTIOUS Aye, when the overjoyed good man invites 'em all against that time twelve month: 'O he's a dear man', cries one – 'Marry,' cries another, 'here's a man indeed – my husband – God help him –'

SIR FEEBLE Then she falls to telling of her grievance till (half maudlin) she weeps again: 'Just my condition' cries a third, so the frolic goes round, and we poor cuckolds are anatomized, and turned the right sides outwards; od's bobs we are Sir Cautious.

SIR CAUTIOUS Aye, aye, this grievance ought to be redressed, Sir Feeble, the grave and sober part o'th'nation are hereby ridi-culed, – Aye, and cuckolded too, for ought I know.

LADY FULBANK Wise men, knowing this, should not expose their infirmities, by marrying us young wenches; who, without instruction, find how we are imposed upon.

Enter Fiddles playing, Mr Bearjest and Diana dancing;
Bredwell, Noisy, &c.

LADY FULBANK So cousin, I see you have found the way to Mrs Dye's heart.

BEARJEST Who I, my dear lady aunt, I never knew but one way to a woman's heart, and that road I have not yet travelled; for my uncle, who is a wise man, says matrimony is a sort of a – kind of a – as it were d'ye see of a voyage, which every man of fortune is bound to make one time or other – and Madam – I am as it were – a bold adventurer.

DIANA And are you sure, Sir, you will venture on me?

BEARJEST Sure? – I thank you for that – as if I could not believe my uncle: for in this case a young heir has no more to do, but to come and see, settle, marry, and use you scurvily.

DIANA How Sir, scurvily?

BEARJEST Very scurvily, that is to say, be always fashionably drunk, despise the tyranny of your bed, and reign absolutely – keep a seraglio of women, and let my bastard issue inherit: be seen once a quarter, or so, with you in the Park for countenance, where we loll two several ways in the gilt coach like Janus, or a-spreadeagle.

DIANA And do you expect I should be honest the while?

BEARJEST Heaven forbid, not I, I have not met with that wonder in all my travels.

LADY FULBANK How Sir, not an honest woman?

BEARJEST Except my lady aunt – Nay as I am a gentleman and the first of my family – you shall pardon me, here – [*kneels to her*] Cuff me, cuff me soundly.

Enter Gayman richly dressed.

GAYMAN This love's a damned bewitched thing – now though I should lose my assignation with my devil, I cannot hold from seeing Julia tonight: hah – there, and with a fop at her feet – O vanity of woman! [*softly pulls her*]

LADY FULBANK O Sir, you're welcome from Northamptonshire.

GAYMAN [*aside*] Hum – surely she knows the cheat.

LADY FULBANK You are so gay, you save me Sir the labour of asking if your uncle be alive.

GAYMAN [*aside*] Pray heaven she have not found my circumstances! But if she have, confidence must assist me – And Madam you're too gay, for me to enquire whether you are that Julia, which I left you?

LADY FULBANK Oh, doubtless Sir –

GAYMAN But why the devil do I ask – Yes, you are still the same;

one of those hoiting ladies, that love nothing like fool and fiddle; crowds of fops; had rather be publicly, though dully, flattered, than privately adored; you love to pass for the wit of the company, by talking all and loud.

LADY FULBANK Rail on! Till you have made me think my virtue at so low ebb, it should submit to you.

GAYMAN What – I'm not discreet enough,
I'll babble all in my next high debauch,
Boast of your favours, and describe your charms
To every wishing fool?

LADY FULBANK Or make most filthy verses of me –
Under the name of Cloris – you Philander,
Who in lewd rhymes confess the dear appointment;
What hour, and where, how silent was the night,
How full of love your eyes, and wishing, mine.
Faith no; if you can afford me a lease of your love,
'Till the old gentleman my husband depart this wicked world,
I'm for the bargain.

SIR CAUTIOUS Hum – what's here, a young spark at my wife?
[*goes about 'em*]

GAYMAN Unreasonable Julia, is that all,
My love, my sufferings, and my vows must hope?
Set me an age – say when you will be kind,
And I will languish out in starving wish.
But thus to gape for legacies of love,
'Till youth be past enjoyment,
The devil I will as soon – farewell – [*offers to go*]

LADY FULBANK Stay, I conjure you stay –

GAYMAN [*aside*] And lose my assignation with my devil.

SIR CAUTIOUS 'Tis so, aye, aye, 'tis so – and wise men will perceive it; 'tis here – here in my forehead, it more than buds; it sprouts, it flourishes.

SIR FEEBLE So, that young gentleman has nettled him, stung him to th' quick: I hope he'll chain her up – the gad bee's* in his quonundrum† – in charity I'll relieve him – come my Lady

---

* gad bee: a big bee, or horse fly; a 'gad-bee in the brain' was like a 'bee in the bonnet'.

† quonundrum: conundrum, a whim.

Fulbank, the night grows old upon our hands, to dancing, to jiggeting – Come shall I lead your ladyship?

LADY FULBANK No Sir, you see I am better provided – [*takes Gayman's hand*]

SIR CAUTIOUS Aye, no doubt on't, a pox on him for a young handsome dog. [*they dance all*]

SIR FEEBLE Very well, very well, now the posset, and then – od's bobs, and then –

DIANA And then we'll have t'other dance.

SIR FEEBLE Away girls, away, and steal the bride to bed; they have a deal to do upon their wedding-nights; and what with the tedious ceremonies of dressing and undressing, the smutty lectures of the women, by way of instruction, and the little stratagems of the young wenches – od's bobs, a man's cozened of half his night: come gentlemen, one bottle, and then – we'll toss the stocking.

[*Exeunt all but Lady Fulbank, Bredwell who are talking, and Gayman*]

LADY FULBANK But dost thou think he'll come?

BREDWELL I do believe so Madam –

LADY FULBANK Be sure you contrive it so, he may not know whither, or to whom he comes.

BREDWELL I warrant you Madam for our parts.

[*Exit Bredwell stealing out Gayman*]

LADY FULBANK How now, what departing?

GAYMAN You are going to the bride-chamber.

LADY FULBANK No matter, you shall stay –

GAYMAN I hate to have you in a crowd.

LADY FULBANK Can you deny me – will you not give me one lone hour i'th'garden?

GAYMAN Where we shall only tantalize each other with dull kissing, and part with the same appetite we met – no Madam, besides I have business –

LADY FULBANK Some assignation – is it so indeed?

GAYMAN Away; you cannot think me such a traitor; 'tis most important business.

LADY FULBANK O 'tis too late for business – let tomorrow serve.

GAYMAN By no means – the gentleman is to go out of Town.

LADY FULBANK Rise the earlier then –

GAYMAN But Madam, the gentleman lies dangerously – sick – and should he die –

LADY FULBANK 'Tis not a dying uncle, I hope Sir?

GAYMAN Hum –

LADY FULBANK The gentleman a-dying, and to go out of Town tomorrow!

GAYMAN Aye – ah – he goes – in a litter – 'tis his fancy Madam – Change of air may recover him.

LADY FULBANK So may your change of mistress do me Sir – farewell.   [*Goes out*]

GAYMAN Stay Julia – Devil be damned – for you shall tempt no more,
I'll love and be undone – but she is gone –
And if I stay the most that I shall gain
Is but a reconciling look, or kiss.
No my kind goblin –
I'll keep my word with thee, as the least evil,
A tantalizing woman's worse than devil.

ACT THREE

SCENE I

Sir Feeble's house

A Song made by Mr Cheek★

No more Lucinda, ah! expose no more
    To the admiring world those conqu'ring charms:
In vain all day unhappy men adore,
    What the kind night gives to my longing arms.
Their vain attempts can ne'er successful prove,
Whilst I so well maintain the fort of love.
Yet to the world with so bewitching arts,
    Your dazzling beauty you around display,
And triumph in the spoils of broken hearts,
    That sink beneath your feet, and crowd your way:
Ah! Suffer now your cruelty to cease,
And to a fruitless war prefer a peace.

Enter Ralph with Light, Sir Feeble, and Belmour sad.

SIR FEEBLE So, so; they're gone – come Francis, you shall have the honour of undressing me for the encounter, but 'twill be a sweet one, Francis.

BELMOUR [*undressing all the while*] ⟨*aside*⟩ Hell take him, how he teases me?

SIR FEEBLE But is the young rogue laid Francis – is she stolen to bed? What tricks the young baggages have to whet a man's appetite?

BELMOUR Aye Sir – ⟨*aside*⟩ Pox on him – he will raise my anger up to madness, and I shall kill him, to prevent his going to bed to her.

SIR FEEBLE A pise of those bandstrings† – the more haste the less speed.

BELMOUR ⟨*aside*⟩ Be it so in all things, I beseech thee Venus?

★ Mr Cheek: Thomas Cheek, who wrote the words for a song in Southerne's *The Wives' Excuse* and for one in Southerne's *Oroonoko*. He also wrote the Prologue for Boyer's *Achilles* (1699).
† bandstrings: for fastening his bands or collar.

SIR FEEBLE Thy aid a little Francis [*pinches him by the throat*] O – O – thou chokest me. 'Sbobs, what dost mean –

BELMOUR You had so hampered 'em Sir – [*aside*] the devil's very mischievous in me.

SIR FEEBLE Come, come quick, good Francis, adod I'm as yare★ as a hawk at the young wanton – nimbly good Francis, untruss, untruss –

BELMOUR ⟨*aside*⟩ Cramps seize ye – what shall I do – the near approach distracts me!

SIR FEEBLE So, so, my breeches, good Francis. But well Francis, how dost think I got the young jade my wife?

BELMOUR With five hundred pounds a year jointure Sir.

SIR FEEBLE No, that would not do, the baggage was damnably in love with a young fellow, they call Belmour, a handsome young rascal he was they say, that's truth on't, and a pretty estate, but happening to kill a man, he was forced to fly.

BELMOUR That was great pity Sir.

SIR FEEBLE Pity, hang him rogue, 'sbobs, and all the young fellows in the Town deserve it; we can never keep our wives and daughters honest for rampant young dogs; and an old fellow cannot put in amongst 'em, under being undone, with presenting, and the devil and all. But what dost think I did, being damnably in love – I feigned a letter as from the Hague, wherein was a relation of this same Belmour's being hanged.

BELMOUR Is't possible Sir, could you devise such news?

SIR FEEBLE Possible man? I did it, I did it; she swooned at the news, shut herself up a whole month in her chamber; but I presented high; she sighed and wept, and swore she'd never marry. Still I presented, she hated, loathed, spit upon me, still adod I presented! Till I presented myself effectually in church to her; for she at last wisely considered her vows were cancelled since Belmour was hanged.

BELMOUR Faith Sir, this was very cruel to take away his fame, and then his mistress.

SIR FEEBLE Cruel? Thou'rt an ass, we are but even with the brisk rogues, for they take away our fame, cuckold us, and take away our wives. – So, so, my cap Francis.

★ yare: eager.

BELMOUR And do you think this marriage lawful Sir?

SIR FEEBLE Lawful; it shall be when I've had livery and seizin* of her body – and that shall be presently rogue – quick – besides this, Belmour dares as well be hanged as come into England.

BELMOUR If he gets his pardon Sir –

SIR FEEBLE Pardon, no, no, I have took care for that, for I have you must know got his pardon already.

BELMOUR How Sir, got his pardon, that's some amends for robbing him of his wife.

SIR FEEBLE Hold honest Francis; what dost think 'twas in kindness to him? No you fool, I got his pardon myself, that nobody else should have it, so that if he gets anybody to speak to His Majesty for it, His Majesty cries he has granted it, but for want of my appearance, he's defunct, trussed up, hanged Francis.

BELMOUR This is the most excellent revenge I ever heard of.

SIR FEEBLE Aye, I learned it of a great politician of our times.

BELMOUR But have you got his pardon? –

SIR FEEBLE I've done't, I've done't; pox on him, it cost me five hundred pounds though! Here 'tis, my solicitor brought it me this evening. [*gives it him*]

BELMOUR ⟨*aside*⟩ This was a lucky hit – and if it 'scape me, let me be hanged by a trick indeed.

SIR FEEBLE So, put it into my cabinet – safe Francis, safe.

BELMOUR Safe I'll warrant you Sir.

SIR FEEBLE My gown, quick, quick – t'other sleeve man – so now my night-cap; well I'll in, throw open my gown to fright away the women, and jump into her arms – [*Exit Sir Feeble*]

BELMOUR He's gone, quickly O love inspire me!

Enter a Footman.

FOOTMAN Sir, my master Sir Cautious Fulbank left his watch on the little parlour-table tonight, and bid me call for't.

BELMOUR Hah – the bridegroom has it Sir, who is just gone to bed, it shall be sent him in the morning.

FOOTMAN 'Tis very well Sir – your servant – [*Exit Footman*]

BELMOUR Let me see – here is the watch, I took it up to keep for him – but his sending has inspired me with a sudden stratagem,

* livery and seizin: livery of seisin, a law term for the delivery of property.

that will do better than force, to secure the poor trembling Leticia – who I am sure is dying with her fears. [*Exit Belmour*]

SCENE ⟨II⟩

Changes to the bedchamber; Leticia in an undressing, by the women at the table

Enter to them Sir Feeble Fainwould.

SIR FEEBLE What's here? What's here? The prating women still. Od's bobs, what not in bed yet? For shame of love Leticia.

LETICIA For shame of modesty Sir; you would not have me go to bed before all this company.

SIR FEEBLE What the women; why they must see you laid, 'tis the fashion.

LETICIA What with a man? I would not for the world. O Belmour, where art thou, with all thy promised aid?

DIANA Nay Madam, we should see you laid indeed.

LETICIA First in my grave Diana.

SIR FEEBLE Od's bobs, here's a compact amongst the women – High treason against the bridegroom – therefore ladies withdraw, or adod I'll lock you all in. [*throws open his gown, they run all away, he locks the door*] So, so, now we're alone Leticia – Off with this foolish modesty, and nightgown, and slide into my arms, [*she runs from him*] Hey my little puskin – what fly me my coy Daphne, [*he pursues her. Knocking*] Hah – who's that knocks – who's there? –

BELMOUR 'Tis I Sir, 'tis I, open the door presently.

SIR FEEBLE Why, what's the matter, is the house o-fire?

BELMOUR Worse Sir, worse –

He opens the door, Belmour enters with the watch in his hand.

LETICIA 'Tis Belmour's voice!

BELMOUR O Sir, do you know this watch?

SIR FEEBLE This watch?

BELMOUR Aye Sir, this watch.

SIR FEEBLE This watch – why prithee, why dost tell me of a

watch, 'tis Sir Cautious Fulbank's watch, what then, what a pox dost trouble me with watches. [*offers to put him out, he returns*]

BELMOUR 'Tis indeed his watch Sir, and by this token he has sent for you, to come immediately to his house Sir.

SIR FEEBLE What a devil! Art mad Francis, or is his worship mad, or does he think me mad – go prithee tell him I'll come to him tomorrow. [*goes to put him out*]

BELMOUR Tomorrow Sir, why all our throats may be cut before tomorrow.

SIR FEEBLE What say'st thou, throats cut?

BELMOUR Why, the City's up in arms Sir, and all the aldermen are met at Guildhall; some damnable plot Sir.

SIR FEEBLE Hah – Plot – the aldermen met at Guildhall? – hum – why let 'em meet, I'll not lose this night to save the nation.

LETICIA Would you to bed Sir, when the weighty affairs of state require your presence?

SIR FEEBLE Hum – met at Guildhall? – my clothes, my gown again Francis, I'll out – out, what upon my wedding night? [*putting on his gown pausing, pulls it off again*] No – I'll in.

LETICIA For shame Sir, shall the reverend Council of the City debate without you?

SIR FEEBLE Aye, that's true, that's true, come truss again Francis, truss again – yet now I think on't Francis, prithee run thee to the Hall, and tell 'em 'tis my wedding-night, d'ye see Francis; and let somebody give my voice for –

BELMOUR What Sir?

SIR FEEBLE Adod I cannot tell; up in arms say you, why, let 'em fight dog, fight bear; mun, I'll to bed – go –

LETICIA And shall His Majesty's service and his safety lie unregarded for a slight woman Sir?

SIR FEEBLE Hum, His Majesty! – come, haste Francis, I'll away, and call Ralph, and the footmen, and bid 'em arm; each man shoulder his musket, and advance his pike – and bring my artillery implements quick – and let's away: pupsey – bye pupsey, I'll bring it a fine thing yet before morning, it may be – let's away; I shall grow fond, and forget the business of the nation – come follow me Francis –

[*Exit Sir Feeble; Belmour runs to Leticia*]

BELMOUR Now my Leticia, if thou e'er didst love!
If ever thou design'st to make me blest –
Without delay fly this adulterous bed!
SIR FEEBLE [*within*] Why Francis – where are you knave?
BELMOUR I must be gone, lest he suspect us – I'll loose him, and
return to thee immediately – get thyself ready –   [*Exit Belmour*]
– Old man forgive me – thou the agressor art,
Who rudely forced the hand without the heart.
She cannot from the paths of honour rove,
Whose guide's religion, and whose end is love.   [*Exit*]
LETICIA I will not fail my love.

SCENE ⟨III⟩

Changes to a wash-house, or out-house

Enter with dark-lanthorn Bredwell disguised like a devil, leading
Gayman.

BREDWELL Stay here, till I give notice of your coming.
                    [*Exit Bredwell, leaves his dark-lanthorn*]
GAYMAN Kind light, a little of your aid – now must I be peeping
though my curiosity should lose me all – hah – Zouns, what's
here – a hovel or a hog-sty? Hum, see the wickedness of man, that
I should find no time to swear in, but just when I'm in the devil's
clutches.

Enter Pert, as an old woman with a staff.

OLD WOMAN Good even to you, fair Sir.
GAYMAN Ha – defend me! If this be she, I must rival the devil,
that's certain.
OLD WOMAN Come young gentleman, dare not you venture?
GAYMAN He must be as hot as Vesuvius, that does – I shall never
earn my morning's present.
OLD WOMAN What do you fear, a longing woman Sir?
GAYMAN The devil I do – this is a damned preparation to love.
OLD WOMAN Why stand you gazing Sir, a woman's passion is
like the tide, it stays for no man when the hour is come –

GAYMAN I'm sorry I have took it at the turning. I'm sure mine's ebbing out as fast.

OLD WOMAN Will you not speak Sir – will you not on?

GAYMAN I would fain ask – a civil question or two first.

OLD WOMAN You know, too much curiosity lost paradise.

GAYMAN Why there's it now.

OLD WOMAN Fortune and love invite you if you dare follow me.

GAYMAN This is the first thing in petticoats that ever dared me in vain. Were I but sure she were but human now – for sundry considerations she might down – but I will on –

[She goes, he follows; both go out]

SCENE ⟨IV⟩

A chamber in the apartment of Lady Fulbank

Enter ⟨Pert disguised as an⟩ old woman followed by Gayman in the dark. Soft music plays, she leaves him.

⟨GAYMAN⟩ – Hah, music – and excellent!

SONG

Oh! Love, that stronger art than wine,
Pleasing delusion, witchery divine,
Want to be prized above all wealth,
Disease that has more joys than health.
Though we blaspheme thee in our pain,
And of thy tyranny complain,
We all are bettered by thy reign.

What reason never can bestow
We to this useful passion owe.
Love wakes the dull from sluggish ease,
And learns a clown the art to please.
Humbles the vain, kindles the cold,
Makes misers free, and cowards bold.
'Tis he reforms the sot from drink,
And teaches airy fops to think.

When full fruit appetite is fed,
And choked the glutton lies, and dead:
Thou new spirits does dispense,
And fine'st the gross delights of sense.
Virtue's unconquerable aid,
That against nature can persuade:
And makes a roving mind retire
Within the bounds of just desire.
Cheerer of age, youth's kind unrest,
And half the heaven of the blest.

Ah Julia, Julia! If this soft preparation
Were but to bring me to thy dear embraces;
What different motions would surround my soul,
From what perplex it now.

⟨*Re-enter Pert, still disguised.*⟩ *Enter Nymphs and Shepherds, and dance.
Then two dance alone. All go out but Pert and a Shepherd.*

If these be divels, they are obliging ones.
I did not care if I ventured on that last female fiend.

Shepherd sings
Cease your wonder, cease your guess,
Whence arrives your happiness.
Cease your wonder, cease your pain,
Human fancy is in vain. [*gives him* ⟨*Gayman*⟩ *gold*]

⟨*Re-enter Nymphs and Shepherds.*⟩

CHORUS   'Tis enough you once shall find,
Fortune may to worth be kind;
And love can leave off being blind.

Pert sings
You, before you enter here –
On this sacred ring must swear. [*puts it on his finger,*
By the figure which is round,   *holds his hand*]
Your passion constant and profound.
By the adamantine stone,

To be fixed to one alone.
By the lustre which is true,
Ne'er to break your sacred vow.
Lastly by the gold that's tried
For love all dangers to abide.

They all dance about him ⟨Gayman⟩, while those same two sing.

SHEPHERD Once about him let us move,
      To confirm him true to love.   [*bis*]
PERT Twice with mystic turning feet,
      Make him silent and discreet.   [*bis*]
SHEPHERD Thrice about him let us tread,
      To keep him ever young in bed. [*bis*]

Gives him ⟨Gayman⟩ another part ⟨of gold⟩.

Forget Aminta's proud disdain,
Taste here, and sigh no more in vain.
The joy of love without the pain.

PERT That god repents his former slights,
      And fortune thus your faith requites.

BOTH Forget Aminta's proud disdain,
      Then taste, and sigh no more in vain,
      The joy of love without the pain.
      The joy of love without the pain. [*Exeunt all dancers*]

GAYMAN [*looks on himself and feels about him*] What the devil can all this mean? If there be a woman in the case – Sure I have not lived so bad a life, to gain the dull reputation of so modest a coxcomb, but that a female might down with me, without all this ceremony. Is it care of her honour? – that cannot be – this age affords none so nice: nor fiend, nor goddess can she be, for these I saw were mortal! No – 'tis a woman – I am positive. Not young nor handsome, for then vanity had made her glory to have been seen. No – since 'tis resolved a woman – she must be old and ugly, and will not baulk my fancy with her sight. But baits me more with this essential beauty.

Well – be she young or old, woman or devil.
She pays, and I'll endeavour to be civil.

SCENE ⟨V⟩

In the same house

*The flat scene of the hall. After a knocking, enter Bredwell in his
masking habit, with his vizard in one hand and a light in t'other
in haste.*

BREDWELL Hah, knocking so late at our gate – [*opens the door*]

*Enter Sir Feeble dressed and armed cap-a-pie with a broad waist-belt
stuck round with pistols, a helmet, scarf, buffcoat and half pike.*

SIR FEEBLE How now, how now, what's the matter here?
BREDWELL Matter, what is my lady's innocent intrigue found
out? – Heavens Sir what makes you here in this warlike equipage?
SIR FEEBLE What makes you in this showing equipage Sir?
BREDWELL I have been dancing among some of my friends.
SIR FEEBLE And I thought to have been fighting with some of
my friends. Where's Sir Cautious? Where's Sir Cautious?
BREDWELL Sir Cautious – Sir, in bed.
SIR FEEBLE Call him, call him – quickly good Edward.
BREDWELL Sure my lady's frolic is betrayed and he comes to
make mischief. However I'll go and secure Mr Gayman.

[Exit Bredwell]

Enter Sir Cautious and Boy ⟨Dick⟩ with light.

DICK Pray Sir go to bed, here's no thieves; all's still and well.
SIR CAUTIOUS This last night's misfortune of mine Dick, has
kept me waking and methought all night I heard a kind of a
silent noise. I am still afraid of thieves, – mercy upon me to lose
five hundred guineas at one clap Dick. – Hah – bless me! What's
yonder! Blow the great horn Dick – Thieves – Murder, murder.
SIR FEEBLE Why what a pox are you mad? 'Tis I, 'tis I man.
SIR CAUTIOUS I, who am I? Speak – declare – pronounce.
SIR FEEBLE Your friend old Feeble Fainwould.

SIR CAUTIOUS How, Sir Feeble! At this late hour, and on his
wedding night – why what's the matter Sir – is it peace or war
with you?

SIR FEEBLE A mistake – a mistake – proceed to the business good
brother, for time you know is precious.

SIR CAUTIOUS [aside] Some strange catastrophe has happened
between him and his wife tonight, that makes him disturb me
thus – Come sit good brother, and to the business as you say –

*They sit one at one end of the table, the other at the other, Dick sets
down the light and goes out – both sit gaping and staring and expecting
when either should speak.*

SIR FEEBLE As soon as you please Sir. Lord how wildly he stares!
He's much disturbed in's mind – well Sir let us be brief –

SIR CAUTIOUS As brief as you please Sir, – well brother – [*pausing
still*]

SIR FEEBLE So Sir.

SIR CAUTIOUS How strangely he stares and gapes – some deep
concern!

SIR FEEBLE Hum – hum –

SIR CAUTIOUS I listen to you, advance –

SIR FEEBLE Sir?

SIR CAUTIOUS [aside] A very distracted countenance – pray
heaven he be not mad, and a young wife is able to make any old
fellow mad, that's the truth on't.

SIR FEEBLE ⟨aside⟩ Sure 'tis something of his lady – he's so loath
to bring it out – ⟨to Sir Cautious⟩ I am sorry you are thus disturbed Sir.

SIR CAUTIOUS No disturbance to serve a friend –

SIR FEEBLE I think I am your friend indeed Sir Cautious, or I
would not have been here upon my wedding night.

SIR CAUTIOUS [aside] His wedding night – there lies his grief
poor heart! Perhaps she has cuckolded him already – ⟨to Sir
Feeble⟩ – Well come brother – many such things are done –

SIR FEEBLE Done – hum – come out with it brother – what
troubles you tonight.

SIR CAUTIOUS Troubles me – [aside] Why, knows he I am
robbed?

SIR FEEBLE I may perhaps restore you to the rest you've lost.

SIR CAUTIOUS The rest, why have I lost more since? Why know you then who did it? O how I'll be revenged upon the rascal?

SIR FEEBLE [*aside*] 'Tis – Jealousy the old worm that bites – ⟨*to Sir Cautious*⟩ Who is it you suspect?

SIR CAUTIOUS Alas I know not whom to suspect, I would I did; but if you could discover him – I would so swinge him. –

SIR FEEBLE I know him – what do you take me for a pimp Sir? I know him – there's your watch again Sir, I'm your friend, but no pimp Sir – [*rises in rage*]

SIR CAUTIOUS My watch, I thank you Sir – but why pimp Sir?

SIR FEEBLE O a very thriving calling Sir – and I have a young wife to practice with. I know your rogues?

SIR CAUTIOUS [*aside*] A young wife – 'tis so, his gentlewoman has been at hot-cockles without her husband, and he's horn mad upon't. I suspected her being so close in with his nephew – in a fit with a pox – ⟨*to Sir Feeble*⟩ Come come Sir Feeble 'tis many an honest man's fortune.

SIR FEEBLE I grant it Sir – but to the business Sir I came for.

SIR CAUTIOUS With all my soul – [*they sit gaping and expecting when either should speak*]

Enter Bredwell and Gayman at the door. Bredwell sees them and puts Gayman back again.

BREDWELL Hah – Sir Feeble – and Sir Cautious there – what shall I do? For this way we must pass, and to carry him back would discover my lady to him, betray all and spoil the jest – ⟨*to Gayman*⟩ retire Sir; your life depends upon your being unseen.

[⟨*They*⟩ *go out*]

SIR FEEBLE Well Sir, – do you not know that I am married Sir? And this my wedding-night?

SIR CAUTIOUS Very good Sir.

SIR FEEBLE And that I long to be in bed!

SIR CAUTIOUS Very well Sir –

SIR FEEBLE Very good Sir, and very well Sir – why then what the devil do I make here Sir! [*rises in a rage*]

SIR CAUTIOUS Patience brother – and forward –

SIR FEEBLE Forward – lend me your hand good brother – let's feel your pulse – how has this night gone with you?

SIR CAUTIOUS Ha, ha, ha – this is the oddest conundrum – sure he's mad – and yet now I think on't, I have not slept tonight, nor shall I ever sleep again till I have found the villain that robbed me. [*weeps*]

SIR FEEBLE [*aside*] So – now he weeps – far gone – this laughing and weeping is a very bad sign! ⟨*to Sir Cautious*⟩ Come let me lead you to your bed.

SIR CAUTIOUS Mad – stark mad – no – now I'm up 'tis no matter – pray ease your troubled mind – I am your friend – out with it – what was it acted? Or but designed?

SIR FEEBLE How Sir?

SIR CAUTIOUS Be not ashamed – I'm under the same premunire* I doubt, little better than a – but let that pass –

SIR FEEBLE Have you any proof?

SIR CAUTIOUS Proof of what, good Sir?

SIR FEEBLE Of what, why that you're a cuckold – Sir a cuckold if you'll ha't.

SIR CAUTIOUS Cuckold Sir – do ye know what ye say?

SIR FEEBLE What I say?

SIR CAUTIOUS Aye, what you say, can you make this out?

SIR FEEBLE I make it out –

SIR CAUTIOUS Aye Sir – if you say it and cannot make it out – you're a –

SIR FEEBLE What am I Sir? What am I?

SIR CAUTIOUS A cuckold as well as myself Sir, and I'll sue you for *Scandalum Magnatum*, I shall recover swinging damages with a City jury.

SIR FEEBLE I know of no such thing Sir.

SIR CAUTIOUS No Sir?

SIR FEEBLE No Sir.

SIR CAUTIOUS Then what would you be at Sir?

SIR FEEBLE I be at Sir – what would you be at Sir?

SIR CAUTIOUS Ha, ha, ha – why this is the strangest thing – to see an old fellow, a magistrate of the City, the first night he's

* premunire: a predicament, from the writ by which a sheriff is charged to prosecute the accused.

married forsake his bride and bed, and come armed cap-a-pie, like Gargantua,* to disturb another old fellow and banter him with a tale of a tub;† and all to be-cuckold him here – in plain English what's your business?

SIR FEEBLE Why what the devil's your business and you go to that?

SIR CAUTIOUS My business with whom?

SIR FEEBLE With me Sir, with me, what a pox do ye think I do here.

SIR CAUTIOUS 'Tis that I would be glad to know Sir.

Enter Dick.

SIR FEEBLE Here Dick, remember I've brought back your master's watch, next time he sends for me o'er night I'll come to him in the morning.

SIR CAUTIOUS Ha, ha, ha – I send for you? Go home and sleep Sir – ad and ye keep your wife waking to so little purpose you'll go near to be haunted with a vision of horns.

SIR FEEBLE Roguery – Knavery to keep me from my wife – Look ye this was the message I received – [*tells him seemingly*]

Enter Bredwell to the door – in a white sheet like a ghost speaking to Gayman who stands within.

BREDWELL Now Sir we are two to two, for this way you must pass or be taken in the lady's lodgings – I'll first adventure out to make you pass the safer. And that he may not, if possible, see Sir Cautious, whom I shall fright into a trance I am sure. [*aside*] And Sir Feeble the devil's in't if he know him.

GAYMAN A brave kind fellow this –

Enter Bredwell stalking on as a ghost by them.

SIR CAUTIOUS O – undone – undone – help help – I'm dead, I'm dead – [*falls down on his face, Sir Feeble stares – and stands still*]

---

* Gargantua: originally a giant in French folklore, later character in Rabelais' *La vie très horrifique du grand gargantua*, 1534.
† a tale of a tub: probably suggested by Swift's preface to *A Tale of a Tub* where he states it is the practice of seamen when they meet a whale to throw him out an empty tub to distract him from attacking their ship.

BREDWELL [*aside*] As I could wish – [*turns*] – Come on thou ghastly thing and follow me –

Enter Gayman like a ghost with a torch.

SIR CAUTIOUS O Lord, O Lord –

GAYMAN Hah – old Sir Feeble Fainwould – why where the devil am I? – 'Tis he – and be it where it will I'll fright the old dotard for cozening my friend of his mistres – [*stalks on*]

SIR FEEBLE [*trembling*] O guard me – guard me – all ye powers!

GAYMAN Thou call'st in vain fond wretch – for I am Belmour, Whom first thou rob'st of fame and life.
And then what dearer was – his wife –
[*Goes out shaking his torch at him*]

SIR CAUTIOUS O Lord – O Lord!

Enter Lady Fulbank in an undress, and Pert undressed.

LADY FULBANK Heavens what noise is this? – So he's got safe out I see – [*sees Sir Feeble armed*] hah what thing art thou –

SIR FEEBLE Stay Madam stay – 'tis I, 'tis I, a poor trembling mortal –

LADY FULBANK Sir Feeble Fainwould? – rise – are you both mad? –

SIR CAUTIOUS No no – Madam we have seen the devil.

SIR FEEBLE Aye and he was as tall as the Monument.

SIR CAUTIOUS With eyes like a beacon – and a mouth – Heaven bless us like London Bridge at a full tide.

SIR FEEBLE Aye, and roared as loud –

LADY FULBANK Idle fancies, what makes you from your bed? And you Sir from your bride?

Enter Dick with sack.

SIR FEEBLE Oh! That's the business of another day, a mistake only Madam.

LADY FULBANK Away, I'm ashamed to see wise men so weak, the phantoms of the night, or your own shadows, the whimsies of the brain for want of rest, or perhaps Bredwell your man – who being wiser than his master played you this trick to fright you both to bed.

SIR FEEBLE Hum – adod and that may be, for the young knave
when he let me in tonight, was dressed up for some waggery –
SIR CAUTIOUS Ha, ha, ha, 'twas even so sure enough brother –
SIR FEEBLE Add's bobs but they frighted me at first basely –
but I'll home to pupsey, there may be roguery, as well as here –
Madam I ask your pardon, I see we're all mistaken.
LADY FULBANK Aye, Sir Feeble; go home to your wife.

[Exeunt severally]

SCENE ⟨VI⟩

The street

*Enter Belmour at the door, knocks, and enter to him
from the house Phillis.*

PHILLIS O are you come Sir, I'll call my lady down.
BELMOUR O haste, the minutes fly – leave all behind. And bring
Leticia only to my arms. *[a noise of people]* – Hah – what noise is
that? 'Tis coming this way – I tremble with my fears – hah –
Death and the devil – 'Tis he –

Enter Sir Feeble and his men armed, goes to the door, knocks.

Aye 'tis he – and I'm undone – what shall I do to kill him now?
Besides the sin would put me past all hopes of pardoning.
SIR FEEBLE A damned rogue to deceive me thus –
BELMOUR Hah – see by heaven Leticia! O we are ruined!
SIR FEEBLE Hum – what's here two women? – *[stands a little off]*

Enter Leticia and Phillis softly undressed with a box.

LETICIA Where are you my best wishes? Lord of my vows – and
charmer of my soul? Where are you?
BELMOUR O heavens! – *[draws his sword hal fway]*
SIR FEEBLE *[aside]* Hum, who's here? My gentlewoman – She's
monstrous kind of the sudden. But whom is't meant to?
LETICIA Give me your hand my love, my life, my all – Alas! where
are you?
SIR FEEBLE ⟨aside⟩ Hum – no, no, this is not to me – I am jilted,
cozened, cuckolded, and so forth – *[groping she takes hold of Sir
Feeble]*

LETICIA O are you here, indeed you frighted me with your silence
– here take these jewels and let us haste away.

SIR FEEBLE [*aside*] Hum – are you thereabouts mistress, was I
sent away with a sham-plot for this! – She cannot mean it to me.

LETICIA Will you not speak – will you not answer me? Do you
repent already? – Before enjoyment are you cold and false?

SIR FEEBLE Hum – before enjoyment – that must be me? Before
enjoyment – Aye, aye 'tis I – I see a little. [*merrily*] Prolonging a
woman's joy, sets an edge upon her appetite.

LETICIA What means my dear? Shall we not haste away?

SIR FEEBLE Haste away? There 'tis again – no – 'tis not me she
means. What at your tricks and intrigues already – yes yes I am
destined a cuckold –

LETICIA Say, am I not your wife; can you deny me?

SIR FEEBLE Wife! [*merrily*] Adod 'tis I she means – 'tis I she means –

LETICIA Oh, Belmour, Belmour! [*Sir Feeble starts back from her hands*]

SIR FEEBLE Hum – what's that – Belmour?

LETICIA Hah! Sir Feeble! – He would not, Sir, have used me thus
unkindly.

SIR FEEBLE O – I'm glad 'tis no worse – Belmour quotha; I
thought the ghost was come again.

PHILLIS Why did you not speak, Sir, all this while – my lady
weeps with your unkindness.

SIR FEEBLE I did but hold my peace to hear how prettily she
prattled love: but fags you are naught* to think of a young
fellow – add's bobs you are now.

LETICIA I only said – he would not have been so unkind to me.

SIR FEEBLE But what makes ye out at this hour, and with these
jewels?

PHILLIS Alas Sir, we thought the City was in arms, and packed up
our things to secure 'em, if there had been a necessity for flight.
For had they come to plundering once, they would have begun
with the rich aldermen's wives, you know Sir.

SIR FEEBLE Add's bobs and so they would – but there was no
arms – nor mutiny – where's Francis?

BELMOUR Here Sir.

SIR FEEBLE Here Sir – why what a story you made of a meeting in

* naught : naughty.

the Hall and – arms and – a – the divel of anything was stirring, but a couple of old fools, that sat gaping and waiting for one another's business –

BELMOUR Such a message was brought me Sir.

SIR FEEBLE Brought, thou'rt an ass Francis – but no more – come, come, let's to bed. –

LETICIA To bed Sir? What by daylight – for that's hasting on – I would not for the world – the night would hide my blushes – but the day – would let me see myself in your embraces.

SIR FEEBLE Embraces, in a fiddlestick, why are we not married?

LETICIA 'Tis true Sir, and time will make me more familiar with you, but yet my virgin modesty forbids it. I'll to Diana's chamber, the night will come again.

SIR FEEBLE For once you shall prevail; and this damned jaunt has pretty well mortified me: – a pox of your mutiny Francis – Come I'll conduct thee to Diana, and lock thee in, that I may have thee safe rogue –
We'll give young wenches leave to whine and blush,
And fly those blessings which – add's bobs they wish.

ACT FOUR

SCENE I

Sir Feeble's house

Enter Lady Fulbank, Gayman fine, gently pulling her back by the
hand; and Ralph meets 'em.

LADY FULBANK How now Ralph – Let your lady know I am
come to wait on her.   [*Exit Ralph*]

GAYMAN O why this needless visit –
Your husband's safe, at least till evening safe.
Why will you not go back?
And give me one soft hour, though to torment me.

LADY FULBANK You are at leisure now I thank you Sir.
Last night when I with all love's rhetoric pleaded,
And heaven knows what last night might have produced,
You were engaged! False man, I do believe it,
And I am satisfied you love me not. [*walks away in scorn*]

GAYMAN Not love you!
Why do I waste my youth in vain pursuit,
Neglecting interest, and despising power!
Unheeding, and despising other beauties.
Why at your feet is all my fortune laid,
And why does all my fate depend on you?

LADY FULBANK I'll not consider why you play the fool,
Present me rings and bracelets; why pursue me,
Why watch whole nights before my senseless door,
And take such pains to show yourself a coxcomb –

GAYMAN Oh! Why all this?
By all the powers above! By this dear hand,
And by this ring, which on this hand I place,
On which I've sworn fidelity to love;
I never had a wish or soft desire
To any other woman,
Since Julia swayed the empire of my soul!

LADY FULBANK [*aside*] Hah, my own ring I gave him last night.
– Your jewel Sir, is rich,

Why do you part with things of so much value
So easily, and so frequently?

GAYMAN To strengthen the weak arguments of love.

LADY FULBANK And leave yourself undone?

GAYMAN Impossible, if I am blessed with Julia.

LADY FULBANK Love's a thin diet, nor will keep out cold,
You cannot satisfy your dunning tailor,
To cry – 'I am in love!'
Though possible you may your seamstress.

GAYMAN Does ought about me speak such poverty?

LADY FULBANK I am sorry that it does not, since to maintain
this gallantry, 'tis said you use base means, below a gentleman.

GAYMAN Who dares but to imagine it's a rascal, a slave, below a
beating – what means my Julia?

LADY FULBANK No more dissembling, I know your land is gone
– I know each circumstance of all your wants, therefore – as e'er
you hope that I should love you ever tell me – where 'twas you
got this jewel Sir.

GAYMAN [*aside*] Hah – I hope 'tis no stolen goods;
⟨*to Lady Fulbank*⟩ Why on the sudden all this nice examining ?

LADY FULBANK You trifle with me, and I'll plead no more.

GAYMAN Stay – why – I bought it Madam –

LADY FULBANK Where had you money Sir? You see I am no
stranger to your poverty.

GAYMAN This is strange – perhaps it is a secret.

LADY FULBANK So is my love, which shall be kept from you.
[*offers to go*]

GAYMAN [*sighing*] Stay Julia – your will shall be obeyed! –
Though I had rather die, than be obedient,
Because I know you'll hate me, when 'tis told.

LADY FULBANK By all my vows, let it be what it will,
It ne'er shall alter me from loving you.

GAYMAN I have – of late – been tempted –
With presents, jewels, and large sums of gold.

LADY FULBANK Tempted! By whom?

GAYMAN The devil, for ought I know.

LADY FULBANK Defend me heaven! The divel?
I hope you have not made a contract with him?

GAYMAN No, though in the shape of woman it appeared.

LADY FULBANK Where met you with it?

GAYMAN By magic art I was conducted – I know not how,
To an enchanted palace in the clouds,
Where I was so attended –
Young dancing – singing fiends innumerable!

LADY FULBANK Imagination all.

GAYMAN But for the amorous devil, the old Proserpine.

LADY FULBANK Aye she – what said she? –

GAYMAN Not a word! Heaven be praised, she was a silent devil –
but she was laid in a pavilion, all formed of gilded clouds, which
hung by geometry,* whither I was conveyed, after much ceremony, and laid in bed with her; where much ado, and trembling
with my fears – I forced my arms about her.

LADY FULBANK And sure that undeceived him –

GAYMAN But such a carcase 'twas – deliver me – so rivelled,† lean,
and rough – a canvas bag of wooden ladles were a better bedfellow.

LADY FULBANK Now though I know that nothing is more distant than I from such a monster – yet this angers me.
Death could you love me and submit to this?

GAYMAN 'Twas that first drew me in –
The tempting hope of means to conquer you,
Would put me upon any dangerous enterprise
Were I the lord of all the universe,
I am so lost in love,
For one dear night to clasp you in my arms,
I'd lavish all that world – then die with joy.

LADY FULBANK [*walking in a fret*] S'life after all to seem deformed,
old, ugly –

GAYMAN I knew you would be angry when you heard it. [*he
pursues her in a submissive posture*]

Enter Sir Cautious, Bearjest, Noisy and Bredwell.

SIR CAUTIOUS How, what's here – my lady with the spark
that courted her last night – hum – with her again so soon – well

* geometry: magic, in this context.   † rivelled: wrinkled, shrivelled.

this impudence and importunity undoes more City wives than all their unmerciful finery.

GAYMAN But Madam –

LADY FULBANK O here's my husband – you'd best tell him your story – [*aside angrily*] What makes him here so soon –

SIR CAUTIOUS Me his story – I hope he will not tell me he's a mind to cuckold me!

GAYMAN A devil on him, what shall I say to him?

LADY FULBANK [*to Gayman*] What – so excellent at intrigues, and so dull at an excuse?

GAYMAN Yes Madam, I shall tell him –

Enter Belmour.

LADY FULBANK Is my lady at leisure for a visit Sir?

BELMOUR Always to receive your ladyship.   [*She goes out*]

SIR CAUTIOUS With me Sir, would you speak?

GAYMAN With you Sir, if your name be Fulbank?

SIR CAUTIOUS Plain Fulbank, methinks you might have had a Sirreverence* under your girdle Sir, I am honoured with another title Sir – [*goes talking to the rest*]

GAYMAN With many Sir, that very well become you – [*pulls him a little aside*] I've something to deliver to your ear.

SIR CAUTIOUS ⟨*aside*⟩ So, I'll be hanged if he do not tell me, I'm a cuckold now. I see it in his eyes; ⟨*to Gayman*⟩ my ear Sir, I'd have you to know I scorn any man's secrets Sir – For ought I know you may whisper treason to me Sir. [*aside*] Pox on him, how handsome he is, I hate the sight of the young stallion.

GAYMAN I would not be uncivil Sir, before all this company.

SIR CAUTIOUS ⟨*aside*⟩ Uncivil – Aye, aye, 'tis so, he cannot be content to cuckold me, but he must tell me so too.

GAYMAN But since you'll have it Sir – you are – a rascal – a most notorious villain Sir, d'ye hear –

SIR CAUTIOUS [*laughing*] Yes, yes, I do – hear – and am glad 'tis no worse.

GAYMAN Griping as hell – and as insatiable – worse than a broker-ing Jew, not all the twelve tribes harbours such a damned extortioner.

* Sirreverence: a colloquialism, a form of apology.

SIR CAUTIOUS [*pulling off his hat*] Pray under favour Sir – who are you?

GAYMAN One whom thou hast undone –

SIR CAUTIOUS [*aside smiling*] Hum – I'm glad of that however.

GAYMAN Racking me up to starving want and misery, then took advantages to ruin me.

SIR CAUTIOUS [*aside smiling*] So, and he'd revenge it on my wife –

GAYMAN Do you not know one Wastall Sir?

Enter Ralph with wine, sets it on a table.

SIR CAUTIOUS Wastall – ha, ha, ha – if you are any friend to that poor fellow – you may return and tell him Sir – d'ye hear – that the mortgage of two hundred pound a year is this day out, and I'll not bate him an hour Sir – ha, ha, ha – what do you think to hector civil magistrates?

GAYMAN Very well Sir, and is this your conscience?

SIR CAUTIOUS Conscience – what do you tell me of conscience? Why what a noise's here – as if the undoing a young heir were such a wonder; ods so I've undone a hundred without half this ado.

GAYMAN I do believe thee – and am come to tell you – I'll be none of that number – for this minute I'll go and redeem it – and free myself from the hell of your indentures.

SIR CAUTIOUS How redeem it, sure the devil must help him then! – Stay Sir – stay – Lord Sir what need you put yourself to that trouble, your land is in safe hands Sir, come come sit down – and let us take a glass of wine together Sir –

BELMOUR Sir my service to you. [*drinks to him*]

GAYMAN Your servant Sir. ⟨*aside*⟩ Would I could come to speak to Belmour which I dare not do in public, lest I betray him. I long to be resolved where 'twas Sir Feeble was last night – if it were he – by which I might find out my invisible mistress.

NOISY Noble Mr Wastall – [*salutes him; so does Bearjest*]

BELMOUR Will you please to sit Sir?

GAYMAN I have a little business Sir – but anon I'll wait on you – your servant gentlemen – I'll to Crap the scriveners. [*goes out*]

SIR CAUTIOUS [*to Noisy*] Do you know this Wastall Sir! –

NOISY Know him Sir, aye too well –

BEARJEST The world's well amended with him Captain, since I

lost my money to him and you at the George★ in White Friars.

NOISY Aye poor fellow – he's sometimes up and sometimes down, as the dice favour him –

BEARJEST Faith and that's pity; but how came he so fine o'th'sudden? 'Twas but last week he borrowed eighteen pence of me on his waist-belt to pay his dinner in an ordinary.

BELMOUR Were you so cruel Sir to take it?

NOISY We are not all one man's children; faith Sir, we are here today and gone tomorrow –

SIR CAUTIOUS I say 'twas done like a wise man Sir – but under favour gentlemen this Wastall is a rascal –

NOISY A very rascal Sir, and a most dangerous fellow – He cullies in your prentices and cashiers to play – which ruins so many o'th'young fry i'th'City –

SIR CAUTIOUS Hum – does he so? – do ⟨you⟩ hear that Edward? –

NOISY Then he keeps a private press and prints your Amsterdam and Leiden libels.†

SIR CAUTIOUS Aye and makes 'em too I'll warrant him; a dangerous fellow –

NOISY Sometimes he begs for a lame soldier with a wooden leg.

BEARJEST Sometimes as a blind man sells switches in Newmarket Road.

NOISY At other times he runs the country like a gypsy – tells fortunes and robs hedges, when he's out of linen.

SIR CAUTIOUS Tells fortunes too – nay I thought he dealt with the devil – well gentlemen you are all wide o'this matter – for to tell you the truth – he deals with the devil gentlemen – otherwise he could never have redeemed his land.

BELMOUR How Sir, the devil?

★ The George: a tavern in Dogwell Court.

† Amsterdam and Leiden libels: to avoid English laws on libel, pamphlets were printed in Amsterdam. In the period 1679–85 the printers were virtually free from surveillance because Parliament failed to re-enact the licensing measures of 1662. But the laws on libel could be invoked to prosecute printed matter. The concept of obscene libel was recognised in Common Law in 1727 when Edmund Curll was prosecuted, the case of Sir Charles Sedley (the notorious affair at the Cock Tavern in 1663) being cited for precedent. At Curll's trial it was established that libel in the phrase 'obscene libel' derived from *libellus*, a little book.

SIR CAUTIOUS I say the devil. Heaven bless every wise man from the devil.

BEARJEST The devil, sha! There's no such animal in nature. I rather think he pads.*

NOISY O Sir he has not courage for that – but he's an admirable fellow at your lock.

SIR CAUTIOUS Lock! My study lock was picked – I begin to suspect him –

BEARJEST I saw him once open a lock with the bone of a breast of mutton, and break an iron bar asunder with the eye of a needle.

SIR CAUTIOUS Prodigious – Well I say the devil still.

Enter Sir Feeble.

SIR FEEBLE Who's this talks of the devil – A pox of the devil I say, this last night's devil has so haunted me –

SIR CAUTIOUS Why have you seen it since brother?

SIR FEEBLE In imagination Sir.

BELMOUR How Sir a devil?

SIR FEEBLE Aye, or a ghost.

BELMOUR Where good Sir?

BEARJEST Aye where? I'd travel a hundred mile to see a ghost –

BELMOUR Sure Sir 'twas fancy?

SIR FEEBLE If 'twere a fancy, 'twas a strong one, and ghosts and fancies are all one, if they can deceive. I tell you – if ever I thought in my life – I thought I saw a ghost – Aye and a damnable inpudent ghost too; he said he was a – a fellow here – they call Belmour.

BELMOUR How Sir!

BEARJEST Well I would give the world to see the devil, provided he were a civil affable devil, such an one as Wastall's acquaintance is –

SIR CAUTIOUS He can show him too soon, it may be. I'm sure as civil as he is, he helps him to steal my gold I doubt – and to be sure – Gentlemen you say he's a gamester – I desire when he comes anon, that you would propose to sport a dye† or so – and we'll fall to play for a teaster,‡ or the like – and if he sets any money – I shall go near to know my own gold, by some

* pads: is a highwayman.   † sport a dye: play at dice.
‡ teaster: tester, a sixpence.

remarkable pieces amongst it; and if he have it, I'll hang him,
and then all his six hundred a year will be my own which I have
in mortgage.

BEARJEST Let the captain and I alone to top upon him* – meantime Sir I have brought my music – to entertain my mistress with
a song.

SIR FEEBLE Take your own methods Sir – they are at leisure –
while we go drink their healths within. Adod I long for night, we
are not half in kelter,† this damned ghost will not out of my head
yet.   [*Exeunt all but Belmour*]

BELMOUR Hah – a ghost! What can he mean? A ghost, and
Belmour's.
– Sure my good angel, or my genius,
In pity of my love, and of Leticia –
But see Leticia comes, but still attended –

Enter Leticia, Lady Fulbank, Diana.

[*aside to her passing by*] – Remember – O remember to be true [*Goes
out*]

LADY FULBANK I was sick to know with what Christian patience
you bore the martyrdom of this night.

LETICIA As those condemned bear the last hour of life. A short
reprieve I had – and by a kind mistake. Diana only was my bedfellow – [*weeps*]

DIANA I wish for your repose you ne'er had seen my father. [*weeps*]

LETICIA And so do I, I fear he has undone me –

DIANA And me, in breaking of his word with Bredwell –

LADY FULBANK So – As Trincolo says‡ would you were both
hanged for me, for putting me in mind of my husband. For I have
e'en no better luck than either of you –
– Let our two fates warn your approaching one:
I love young Bredwell and must plead for him.

DIANA I know his virtue justifies my choice.
But pride and modesty forbids I should unloved pursue him.

* to top upon him: to cheat him.   † in kelter: in order.
‡ As Trincolo says: Stephano's remark in Dryden and Davenant's *The Tempest*
(1667), III, i 'Would you were both hanged for putting me in thought of mine'.

LETICIA Wrong not my brother so who dies for you –
DIANA Could he so easily see me given away
    Without a sigh at parting?
    For all the day a calm was in his eyes,
    And unconcerned he looked and talked to me.
    In dancing never pressed my willing hand,
    Nor with a scornful glance reproached my falsehood.
LETICIA Believe me that dissembling was his masterpiece.
DIANA Why should he fear, did not my father promise him?
LETICIA Aye that was in his wooing time to me.
    But now 'tis all forgotten –

    Music at the door. After which enter Bearjest and Bredwell.

LADY FULBANK How now cousin! Is this high piece of gallantry
    from you?
BEARJEST Aye Madam, I have not travelled for nothing –
LADY FULBANK I find my cousin is resolved to conquer, he
    assails with all his artillery of charms; we'll leave him to his
    success Madam –   [*Exeunt Leticia and Lady Fulbank*]
BEARJEST O Lord Madam you oblige me – look Ned you had a
    mind to have a full view of my mistress, Sir, and – here she is.
    [*he stands gazing*] Go – salute her – look how he stands now, what a
    sneaking thing is a fellow who has never travelled and seen the
    world! – Madam – this is a very honest friend of mine, for all he
    looks so simply.
DIANA Come he speaks for you, Sir.
BEARJEST He Madam, though he be but a banker's prentice
    Madam, he's as pretty a fellow of his inches as any i'th'City –
    he has made love in dancing schools, and to ladies of quality in
    the middle gallery,★ and shall joke ye – and repartee with any
    foreman within the walls – prithee to her – and commend me,
    I'll give thee a new point cravat.
DIANA He looks as if he could not speak to me.
BEARJEST Not speak to you? – Yes gad Madam and do anything to
    you too.
DIANA [*in scorn*] Are you his advocate Sir?
BEARJEST For want of a better – [*stands behind him pushing him on*]
    ★ in the middle gallery: usually frequented by women of the Town.

BREDWELL An advocate for love I am,
  And bring you such a message from a heart –
BEARJEST Meaning mine dear Madam.
BREDWELL That when you hear it, you will pity it.
BEARJEST Or the devil's in her –
DIANA Sir I have many reasons to believe
  It is my fortune you pursue, not person?
BEARJEST There's something in that I must confess. [*behind him*]
  But say what you will Ned –
BREDWELL May all the mischiefs of despairing love
  Fall on me if it be.
BEARJEST That's well enough –
BREDWELL No were you born an humble village maid,
  That fed a flock, upon the neighbouring plain;
  With all that shining virtue in your soul,
  By heaven I would adore you – love you – wed you.
  Though the gay world were lost by such a nuptial. [*Bearjest looks on him*]
  – This – [*recollecting*] I would do were I my friend the squire.
BEARJEST Aye if you were me – you might do what you pleased;
  but I'm of another mind.
DIANA Should I consent, my father is a man whom interest sways
  not honour, and whatsoever promises he's made you, he means to
  break 'em all, and I am destined to another.
BEARJEST How another – his name, his name Madam – here's
  Ned and I fear ne'er a single man i'th'nation. What is he? – What
  is he? –
DIANA A fop, a fool, a beaten ass – a blockhead.
BEARJEST What a damned shame's this, that women should be
  sacrificed to fools, and fops must run away with heiresses –
  whilst we men of wit and parts – dress and dance, and cock, and
  travel, for nothing but to be tame keepers.
DIANA But I by heaven will never be that victim. But where my
  soul is vowed 'tis fixed forever.
BREDWELL Are you resolved, are you confirmed in this? O my
  Diana speak it o'er again. [*runs to her and embraces her*]
  Bless me and make me happier than a monarch.
BEARJEST Hold, hold dear Ned – that's my part I take it.

BREDWELL Your pardon Sir, I had forgot myself. – But time is short – what's to be done in this?

BEARJEST Done, I'll enter the house with fire and sword d'ye see, not that I care this – but I'll not be fobbed off – what do they take me for a fool – an ass?

BREDWELL Madam, dare you run the risk of your father's displeasure, and run away with the man you love?

DIANA With all my soul –

BEARJEST That's hearty – and we'll do't – Ned and I here – and I love an amour with an adventure in't like *Amadis de Gaula** – Hark'ee Ned – get a coach and six ready tonight when 'tis dark at the back gate –

BREDWELL And I'll get a parson ready in my lodging, to which I have a key through the garden by which we may pass unseen.

BEARJEST Good – Mun here's company –

Enter Gayman with his hat with money in't, Sir Cautious in a rage – Sir Feeble, Lady Fulbank, Leticia, Captain Noisy, Belmour.

SIR CAUTIOUS A hundred pound lost already! O coxcomb, old coxcomb, and a wise coxcomb – to turn prodigal at my years, whe' I was bewitched!

SIR FEEBLE Sho, 'twas a frolic Sir, I have lost a hundred pound as well as you. My lady has lost, and your lady has lost, and the rest – what old cows will kick sometimes, what's a hundred pound?

SIR CAUTIOUS A hundred pound, why 'tis a sum Sir – a sum – why what the devil did I do with a box and dice? –

LADY FULBANK Why you made a shift to lose Sir? And where's the harm of that? We have lost, and he has won, anon it may be your fortune.

SIR CAUTIOUS Aye, but he could never do it fairly, that's certain. Three hundred pound! Why how came you to win so unmercifully Sir?

GAYMAN O the devil will not lose a gamester of me – you see Sir.

SIR CAUTIOUS The devil! – Mark that gentlemen –

* *Amadis de Gaula*: a Spanish or Portuguese romance written by Garcia de Montalvo in the second half of the fifteenth century, printed early in the sixteenth century.

BEARJEST The rogue has damned luck sure, he has got a fly★ –

SIR CAUTIOUS And can you have the conscience to carry away all our money Sir?

GAYMAN Most assuredly, unless you have the courage to retrieve it. I'll set it at a throw, or any way, what say you gentlemen?

SIR FEEBLE Od's bobs you young fellows are too hard for us every way, and I am engaged at an old game with a new gamester here – who will require all an old man's stock.

LADY FULBANK Come cousin will you venture a guinea – Come Mr Bredwell –

GAYMAN Well if nobody dare venture on me I'll send away my cash –

They all go to play at the table but Sir Cautious, Sir Feeble and Gayman.

SIR CAUTIOUS [*aside*] Hum – must it all go? – a rare sum, if a man were but sure the devil would but stand neuter now – – Sir I wish I had anything but ready money to stake – three hundred pound – a fine sum!

GAYMAN You have moveables Sir, goods – commodities –

SIR CAUTIOUS That's all one Sir; that's money's worth Sir; but if I had anything that were worth nothing –

GAYMAN You would venture it, – I thank you Sir, – I would your lady were worth nothing –

SIR CAUTIOUS Why so Sir?

GAYMAN Then I would set all this against that nothing.

SIR CAUTIOUS What set it against my wife?

GAYMAN Wife Sir, aye your wife –

SIR CAUTIOUS Hum, my wife against three hundred pounds? – What all my wife Sir?

GAYMAN All your wife. Why Sir, some part of her would serve my turn.

SIR CAUTIOUS [*aside*] Hum – my wife – why, if I should lose, he could not have the impudence to take her –

GAYMAN Well, I find you are not for the bargain, and so I put up –

SIR CAUTIOUS Hold Sir – why so hasty – my wife? No – put up your money Sir – what lose my wife, for three hundred pounds! –

GAYMAN Lose her Sir – why she shall be never the worse for my

★ a fly: a familiar.

wearing Sir – ⟨*aside*⟩ the old covetous rogue is considering on't I think – ⟨*to Sir Cautious*⟩ what say you to a night? I'll set it to a night – there's none need know it Sir.

SIR CAUTIOUS [*aside*] Hum – a night! – three hundred pounds for a night! Why what a lavish whoremaster's this: we take money to marry our wives, but very seldom part with 'em, and by the bargain get money – ⟨*to Gayman*⟩ for a night say you? – gad if I should take the rogue at his word, 'twould be a pure jest.

SIR FEEBLE You are not mad brother.

SIR CAUTIOUS No, but I'm wise – and that's as good; let me consider –

SIR FEEBLE What whether you shall be a cuckold or not?

SIR CAUTIOUS Or lose three hundred pounds – consider that; a cuckold – why, 'tis a word – an empty sound – 'tis breath – 'tis air – 'tis nothing – but three hundred pounds – Lord, what will not three hundred pounds do! You may chance to be a cuckold for nothing Sir –

SIR FEEBLE It may be so – but she shall do't discreetly then.

SIR CAUTIOUS Under favour, you're an ass brother, this is the discreetest way of doing it, I take it.

SIR FEEBLE But would a wise man expose his wife?

SIR CAUTIOUS Why, Cato was a wiser man than I, and he lent his wife to a young fellow they called Hortensius,* as story says; and can a wise man have a better precedent than Cato?

SIR FEEBLE I say Cato was an ass Sir, for obliging any young rogue of 'em all.

SIR CAUTIOUS But I am of Cato's mind; well, a single night you say.

GAYMAN A single night – to have – to hold – possess – and so forth at discretion.

SIR CAUTIOUS A night – I shall have her safe and sound i'th'morning.

SIR FEEBLE Safe no doubt on't – but how sound? –

GAYMAN And for non-performance, you shall pay me three hundred pounds, I'll forfeit as much if I tell –

SIR CAUTIOUS Tell? – Why make your three hundred pounds

---

* Hortensius: Cato was reputed to have handed over his wife Marcia to Hortensius in 56 BC and taken her back at Hortensius's death in 50 BC.

six hundred, and let it be put into the *Gazette*, if you will man –
but is't a bargain? –

GAYMAN Done – Sir Feeble shall be witness – and there stands my
hat. [*puts down his hat of money, and each of 'em take a box and dice,
and kneel on the stage, the rest come about 'em*]

SIR CAUTIOUS – He that comes first to one and thirty wins –
[*they throw and count*]

LADY FULBANK What are you playing for?

SIR FEEBLE Nothing, nothing – but a trial of skill between an old
man and a young – and your ladyship is to be judge.

LADY FULBANK I shall be partial Sir.

SIR CAUTIOUS [*throws – and pulls the hat towards him*] Six and five's
eleven –

GAYMAN Cater tray* – pox of the dice –

SIR CAUTIOUS Two fives – one and twenty –

GAYMAN [*sets up, pulls the hat nearer*] Now luck – doubles of sixes –
nineteen.

SIR CAUTIOUS [*draws the hat to him*] Five and four – thirty –

SIR FEEBLE Now if he wins it, I'll swear he has a fly indeed –
'tis impossible without doubles of sixes –

GAYMAN Now fortune smile – and for the future drown. [*throws*]

SIR CAUTIOUS Hum – two sixes – [*rises and looks dolefully round*]

LADY FULBANK How now? What's the matter you look so like
an ass, what have you lost?

SIR CAUTIOUS A bauble – a bauble – 'tis not for what I've lost –
but because I have not won –

SIR FEEBLE You look very simply Sir – what think you of Cato
now?

SIR CAUTIOUS A wise man may have his failings –

LADY FULBANK What has my husband lost? –

SIR CAUTIOUS Only a small parcel of ware that lay dead upon my
hands, sweetheart.

GAYMAN But I shall improve 'em, Madam, I'll warrant you.

LADY FULBANK Well, since 'tis no worse, bring in your fine
dancer cousin, you say you brought to entertain your mistress
with.   [*Bearjest goes out*]

GAYMAN Sir, you'll take care to see me paid tonight?

* Cater tray : cater or quatre, the four; tray, the three.

SIR CAUTIOUS Well Sir – but my lady you must know Sir, has the common frailties of her sex, and will refuse what she even longs for, if persuaded to't by me.

GAYMAN 'Tis not in my bargain to solicit her Sir, you are to procure her – or three hundred pounds Sir; choose you whether.

SIR CAUTIOUS Procure her? With all my soul Sir; alas you mistake my honest meaning, I scorn to be so unjust as not to see you a-bed together; and then agree as well as you can, I have done my part – in order to this Sir – get you but yourself conveyed in a chest to my house, with a direction upon't for me, and for the rest –

GAYMAN I understand you –

SIR FEEBLE Ralph get supper ready.

Enter Bearjest with Dancers. All go out but Sir Cautious.

SIR CAUTIOUS Well, I must break my mind, if possible, to my lady – but if she should be refractory now – and make me pay three hundred pounds – why sure she won't have so little grace – Three hundred pounds saved, is three hundred pounds got – by our account – could all –
Who of this City-privilege are free,
Hope to be paid for cuckoldom like me;
Th'unthriving merchant, whom grey hair adorns,
Before all ventures would ensure his horns;
For thus, while he but lets spare rooms to hire,
His wife's racked credit keeps his own entire.

ACT FIVE

SCENE I

Sir Cautious his house

Enter Belmour alone sad.

BELMOUR The night is come, O my Leticia!
  The longing bridegroom hastens to his bed;
  Whilst she with all the languishment of love,
  And sad despair, casts her fair eyes on me,
  Which silently implore, I would deliver her.
  But how! Aye there's the question – hah [*pausing*] –
  I'll get myself hid in her bed-chamber –
  And something I will do – may save us yet –
  If all my arts should fail – [*draws a dagger*] I'll have recourse
  To this – and bear Leticia off by force.
  – But see she comes –

*Enter Lady Fulbank, Sir Cautious, Sir Feeble, Leticia, Bearjest,
Noisy, Gayman. Exit Belmour.*

SIR FEEBLE Lights there Ralph, and my lady's coach there –
BEARJEST [*goes to Gayman*] Well Sir, remember you have promised
  to grant me my diabolical request, in showing me the devil –
GAYMAN I will not fail you Sir.
LADY FULBANK Madam, your servant; I hope you'll see no more
  ghosts, Sir Feeble.
SIR FEEBLE No more of that, I beseech you Madam: prithee Sir
  Cautious take away your wife – Madam your servant –
                                    [*All go out after the light*]
  – Come Lette, Lette; hasten rogue, hasten to thy chamber, away,
  here be the young wenches coming –   [*Puts her out, he goes out*]

Enter Diana, puts on her hood and scarf.

DIANA So – they are gone to bed; and now for Bredwell – the coach
  waits, and I'll take this opportunity.
  Father farewell – if you dislike my course,
  Blame the old rigid customs of your force.   [*Goes out*]

SCENE ⟨II⟩

A bedchamber

Enter Sir Feeble, Leticia and Phillis.

LETICIA Ah Phillis! I am fainting with my fears, hast thou no comfort for me?

SIR FEEBLE [*he undresses to his gown*] Why what art doing there – fiddle faddling – adod you young wenches are so loathe to come to – but when your hands in, you have no mercy upon us poor husbands.

LETICIA Why do you talk so Sir?

SIR FEEBLE Was it an-angered, at the fool's prattle; tum-a me, tum-a me, I'll undress it, effags I will – roguey.

LETICIA You are so wanton Sir, you make me blush – I will not go to bed, unless you'll promise me –

SIR FEEBLE No bargaining my little hussey – what you'll tie my hands behind me, will you?

LETICIA What shall I do? – [*she goes to the table*] Assist me gentle maid, thy eyes methinks put on a little hope!

PHILLIS Take courage Madam – you guess right – be confident.

SIR FEEBLE No whispering gentlewoman – and putting tricks into her head, that shall not cheat me of another night – [*as she is at the toilet he looks over her shoulder, and sees her face in the glass*] Look on that silly little round chitty-face – look on those smiling roguish loving eyes there – look – look how they laugh, twire and tempt – he rogue – I'll buss 'em there, and here and everywhere – Od's bobs – away, this is fooling and spoiling of a man's stomach, with a bit here, and a bit there – to bed – to bed –

LETICIA Go you first Sir, I will but stay to say my prayers, [*aside*] which are that heaven would deliver me.

SIR FEEBLE Say thy prayers? – What art thou mad, prayers upon thy wedding-night? A short thanksgiving or so – but prayers quotha – S'bobs you'll have time enough for that – I doubt –

LETICIA I am ashamed to undress before you Sir, go to bed –

SIR FEEBLE What was it ashamed to show its little white foots, and its little round bubbies – well I'll go, I'll go – I cannot think on't, no I cannot – [*going towards the bed*]

*Belmour comes forth from between the curtains, his coat off, his shirt
bloody, a dagger in his hand, and his disguise off.*

BELMOUR Stand –

SIR FEEBLE Hah –

LETICIA and PHILLIS [*squeak*] O heavens –

⟨LETICIA⟩ [*aside to Phillis*] Why is it Belmour?

BELMOUR Go not to bed, I guard this sacred place,
   And the adulterer dies that enters here.

SIR FEEBLE O – why do I shake – sure I'm a man? What art
   thou?

BELMOUR I am the wronged, the lost, and murdered Belmour.

SIR FEEBLE O Lord! It is the same I saw last night – Oh! –
   Hold thy dread vengeance – pity me, and hear me – Oh! A
   parson – a parson – what shall I do – Oh! Where shall I hide myself.

BELMOUR I'th'utmost borders of the earth I'll find thee –
   Seas shall not hide thee, nor vast mountains guard thee.
   Even in the depth of hell, I'll find thee out,
   And lash thy filthy and adulterous soul –

SIR FEEBLE Oh! I am dead, I'm dead, will no repentance save me –
   'twas that young eye that tempted me to sin; oh! –

BELMOUR See fair seducer, what thou'st made me do.
   Look on this bleeding wound, it reached my heart,
   To pluck my dear tormenting image thence,
   When news arrived that thou had'st broke thy vow.

SIR FEEBLE O Lord! Oh! – I'm glad he's dead though.

LETICIA O hide that fatal wound, my tender heart faints with a
   sight so horrid! [*seems to weep*]

SIR FEEBLE ⟨*aside*⟩ So she'll clear herself and leave me in the
   devil's clutches.

BELMOUR You've both offended heaven, and must repent or die.

SIR FEEBLE Ah – I do confess I was an old fool – bewitched with
   beauty, besotted with love, and do repent most heartily.

BELMOUR No, you had rather yet go on in sin. Thou wouldst
   live on, and be a baffled cuckold.

SIR FEEBLE Oh, not for the world Sir: I am convinced and
   mortified.

BELMOUR Maintain her fine, undo thy peace to please her, and

still be cuckolded on – believe her – trust her, and be cuckold
still.

SIR FEEBLE I see my folly – and my age's dotage – and find the
devil was in me – yet spare my age – ah! Spare me to repent.

BELMOUR If thou repentest, renounce her, fly her sight; –
Shun her bewitching charms, as thou wouldst hell;
Those dark eternal mansions of the dead –
Whither I must descend.

SIR FEEBLE O – would he were gone! –

BELMOUR Fly – begone – depart, vanish for ever, from her to
some more safe and innocent apartment.

SIR FEEBLE O that's very hard – [*he goes back trembling, Belmour
follows in with his dagger up; both go out*]

LETICIA Blessed be this kind release, and yet methinks it grieves
me to consider how the poor old man is frighted.

Belmour re-enters, puts on his coat.

BELMOUR He's gone, and locked himself into his chamber –
And now my dear Leticia let us fly –
Despair till now, did my wild heart invade,
But pitying love has the rough storm allayed.   [*Exeunt*]

SCENE III

Sir Cautious his garden

*Enter two Porters and Rag bearing Gayman in a chest. Set it down;
he comes forth with a dark lanthorn.*

GAYMAN Set down the chest behind yon hedge of roses – and
then put on those shapes I have appointed you – and be sure you
well-favouredly bang both Bearjest and Noisy; since they have a
mind to see the devil.

RAG O Sir leave 'em to us for that, and if we do not play the devil
with 'em, we deserve they should beat us. But Sir we are in Sir
Cautious his garden, will not he sue us for a trespass?

GAYMAN I'll bear you out; be ready at my call.   [*Exeunt*]

– Let me see – I have got no ready stuff to banter with – but no
matter any gibberish will serve the fools – 'tis now about the
hour of ten – but twelve is my appointed lucky minute, when all
the blessings that my soul could wish shall be resigned to me.

Enter Bredwell.

– Hah who's there, Bredwell?

BREDWELL O are you come Sir – and can you be so kind to a poor
youth, to favour his designs and bless his days?

GAYMAN Yes, I am ready here with all my devils, both to secure
you your mistress, and to cudgel your captain and squire, for
abusing me behind my back so basely.

BREDWELL 'Twas most unmanly Sir, and they deserve it – I
wonder that they come not?

GAYMAN How durst you trust her with him?

BREDWELL Because 'tis dangerous to steal a City heiress, and let
the theft be his – so the dear maid be mine – Hark – sure they
come –

Enter Bearjest; runs against Bredwell.

– Who's there, Mr Bearjest?

BEARJEST Who's that, Ned? – Well I have brought my mistress
– hast thou got a parson ready – and a license?

BREDWELL Aye, aye – but where's the lady?

BEARJEST In the coach, with the captain at the gate. I came before
to see if the coast be clear.

BREDWELL Aye Sir – but what shall we do – here's Mr Gayman
come on purpose to show you the devil, as you desired.

BEARJEST Shoh! A pox of the devil man – I can't intend to speak
with him now.

GAYMAN How Sir? D'ye think my devil of so little quality to
suffer an affront unrevenged?

BEARJEST Sir I cry his devilship's pardon: I did not know his
quality – I protest Sir I love and honour him, but I am now just
going to be married Sir, and when that ceremony's past, I'm ready
to go to the devil as soon as you please.

GAYMAN I have told him your desire of seeing him, and should you
baffle him?

BEARJEST Who I Sir? Pray let his worship know, I shall be proud
of the honour of his acquaintance; but Sir my mistress and the
parson wait in Ned's chamber.

GAYMAN If all the world wait Sir, the prince of hell will stay for
no man.

BREDWELL O Sir rather than the prince of the infernals shall be
affronted, I'll conduct the lady up, and entertain her till you
come Sir.

BEARJEST Nay I have a great mind to kiss his – paw Sir, but I
could wish you'd show him me by daylight Sir.

GAYMAN The prince of darkness does abhor the light. But Sir I
will for once allow your friend the captain to keep you company.

Enter Noisy and Diana.

BEARJEST I'm much obliged to you Sir, O Captain – [*talks to him*]

BREDWELL Haste dear; the parson waits,
To finish what the powers designed above.

DIANA Sure nothing is so bold as maids in love!   [*They go out*]

NOISY Pshaw! He conjure – he can fly as soon.

GAYMAN Gentlemen you must be sure to confine yourselves to
this circle, and have a care you neither swear, nor pray.

BEARJEST Pray, Sir? I dare say neither of us were ever that way
gifted. [*a horrid noise*]

GAYMAN Cease your horror, cease your haste,
And calmly as I saw you last,
Appear! Appear!
By thy pearls and diamond rocks,
By thy heavy money box.
By thy shining petticoat,
That hid thy cloven feet from note.
By the veil that hid thy face,
Which else had frightened human race.
Appear, that I thy love may see,
Appear kind fiends, appear to me!
⟨*aside*⟩ A pox of these rascals why come they not.

*Four enter from the four corners of the stage to music that plays, they
dance, and in the dance, dance round 'em, and kick, pinch, and beat 'em.*

BEARJEST O enough, enough! Good Sir lay 'em and I'll pay the music –

GAYMAN I wonder at it – these spirits are in their nature kind, and peaceable – and you have basely injured somebody – and then they will be satisfied –

BEARJEST O good Sir take your Cerberusés off – I do confess the captain here and I have violated your fame.

NOISY Abused you – and traduced you, – and thus we beg your pardon –

GAYMAN Abused me? 'Tis more than I know gentlemen.

BEARJEST But it seems your friend the devil does.

GAYMAN By this time Bredwell's married.
– Great Pantamogan hold for I am satisfied. [*Exeunt devils*] And thus undo my charm – [*takes away the circle, they run out*] – so – the fools are gone, and [*going*] now to Julia's arms.   ⟨*Exit*⟩

SCENE ⟨IV⟩

Lady Fulbank's antechamber

She discovered undressed at her glass. Sir Cautious undressed.

LADY FULBANK But why tonight? Indeed you're wonderous kind methinks.

SIR CAUTIOUS Why I don't know – a wedding is a sort of an alarm to love; it calls up every man's courage.

LADY FULBANK Aye but will it come when 'tis called?

SIR CAUTIOUS I doubt you'll find it to my grief – But I think 'tis all one to thee, thou carest not for my compliment; no, thou'dst rather have a young fellow.

LADY FULBANK I am not used to flatter much; if forty years were taken from your age, 'twould render you something more agreeable to my bed, I must confess.

SIR CAUTIOUS Aye, aye, no doubt on't.

LADY FULBANK Yet you may take my word without an oath, were you as old as time, and I were young and gay as April flowers,

Which all are fond to gather;
My beauties all should wither in the shade,
E'er I'd be worn in a dishonest bosom.
SIR CAUTIOUS Aye but you're wondrous free methinks – sometimes, which gives shrewd suspicions.
LADY FULBANK What, because I cannot simper – look demure, and justify my honour when none questions it.
– Cry 'fie', and 'out upon the naughty women',
Because they please themselves – and so would I.
SIR CAUTIOUS How, would, what cuckold me?
LADY FULBANK Yes, if it pleased me better than virtue Sir.
But I'll not change my freedom and my humour,
To purchase the dull fame of being honest.
SIR CAUTIOUS Aye but the world, the world –
LADY FULBANK I value not the censures of the crowd.
SIR CAUTIOUS But I am old.
LADY FULBANK That's your fault Sir, not mine.
SIR CAUTIOUS But being so, if I should be good-natured and give thee leave to love discreetly? –
LADY FULBANK I'd do't without your leave Sir.
SIR CAUTIOUS Do't – what – cuckold me?
LADY FULBANK No, love discreetly Sir, love as I ought, love honestly.
SIR CAUTIOUS What in love with anybody, but your own husband?
LADY FULBANK Yes.
SIR CAUTIOUS Yes quotha – is that your loving as you ought? –
LADY FULBANK We cannot help our inclinations Sir,
No more than time, or light from coming on –
But I can keep my virtue Sir entire.
SIR CAUTIOUS What! I'll warrant this is your first love Gayman?
LADY FULBANK I'll not deny that truth, though even to you.
SIR CAUTIOUS Why in consideration of my age and your youth,
I'd bear a conscience – provided you do things wisely.
LADY FULBANK Do what thing Sir?
SIR CAUTIOUS You know what I mean –
LADY FULBANK Hah – I hope you would not be a cuckold Sir?
SIR CAUTIOUS Why – truly in a civil way – or so. –

LADY FULBANK There is but one way Sir to make me hate you; and that would be tame suffering.

SIR CAUTIOUS Nay and she be thereabouts, there's no discovering –

LADY FULBANK But leave this fond discourse – and if you must – Let us to bed –

SIR CAUTIOUS Aye, aye – I did but try your virtue, mun – dost think I was in earnest?

Enter Servant.

SERVANT Sir here's a chest directed to your worship.

SIR CAUTIOUS Hum – 'tis Wastall – now does my heart fail me – a chest say you? – to me? – so late – I'll warrant it comes from Sir Nicholas Smuggle – some prohibited goods that he has stolen the Custom of, and cheated His Majesty – well he's an honest man, bring it in –   [*Exit servant*]

LADY FULBANK What into my apartment Sir, a nasty chest!

SIR CAUTIOUS By all means – for if the searchers come – they'll never be so uncivil to ransack thy lodgings – and we are bound in Christian charity to do for one another – Some rich commodities I am sure – and some fine knick-knack will fall to thy share I'll warrant thee – [*aside*] Pox on him for a young rogue, how punctual he is! –

Enter with the chest.

– Go my dear, go to bed – I'll send Sir Nicholas a receipt for the chest, and be with thee presently –   [*Exeunt severally*]

Gayman peeps out of the chest, and looks round him wondering.

GAYMAN Hah, where am I? By heaven my last night's vision – 'Tis that enchanted room and yonder the alcove! Sure 'twas indeed some witch, who knowing of my infidelity – has by enchantment brought me hither – 'tis so – I am betrayed – [*pauses*] Hah! Or was it Julia! That last night gave me that lone opportunity – but hark I hear some coming – [*shuts himself in*]

Enter Sir Cautious.

SIR CAUTIOUS [*lifting up the chest lid*] So you are come I see – [*goes and locks the door*]

GAYMAN [*aside*] Hah – he here, nay then I was deceived, and it was Julia that last night gave me the dear assignation.

Sir Cautious peeps into the bedchamber.

LADY FULBANK [*within*] Come Sir Cautious – I shall fall asleep and then you'll waken me –

SIR CAUTIOUS Aye my dear I'm coming – she's in bed – I'll go put out the candle, and then –

GAYMAN Aye I'll warrant you for my part –

SIR CAUTIOUS Aye – but you may over-act your part and spoil all – but Sir I hope you'll use a Christian conscience in this business.

GAYMAN O doubt not Sir, but I shall do you reason.

SIR CAUTIOUS Aye Sir, but –

GAYMAN Good Sir no more cautions, you unlike a fair gamester will rook me out of half my night – I am impatient –

SIR CAUTIOUS Good Lord are you so hasty; if I please you shan't go at all.

GAYMAN With all my soul Sir, pay me three hundred pound Sir –

SIR CAUTIOUS Lord Sir you mistake my candid meaning still. I am content to be a cuckold Sir – but I would have things done decently, d'ye mind me?

GAYMAN As decently as a cuckold can be made Sir. – But no more disputes I pray Sir.

SIR CAUTIOUS I'm gone – I'm gone – [*going out, returns*] but hark'ee Sir – you'll rise before day?

GAYMAN Yet again –

SIR CAUTIOUS I vanish Sir – but hark'ee – you'll not speak a word? But let her think 'tis I?

GAYMAN Begone I say Sir – [*he runs out*] I am convinced last night I was with Julia. O sot – insensible and dull –

Enter softly Sir Cautious.

SIR CAUTIOUS So – the candle's out – give me your hand.
[*Leads him softly in*]

SCENE ⟨V⟩

Changes to a bedchamber

Lady Fulbank supposed in bed. Enter Sir Cautious and Gayman by dark.

SIR CAUTIOUS [*leads him to the bed*] Where are you my dear?
LADY FULBANK Where should I be – in bed, what are you by
dark?
SIR CAUTIOUS Aye the candle went out by chance.
[*Gayman signs to him to be gone, he makes grimaces*
as loath to go, and exit]

SCENE ⟨VI⟩

Draws over and represents another room
in the same house

Enter Parson, Diana, and Pert dressed in Diana's clothes.

DIANA I'll swear Mrs Pert you look very prettily in my clothes;
and since you Sir have convinced me that this innocent deceit is
not unlawful, I am glad to be the instrument of advancing Mrs
Pert to a husband, she already has so just a claim to.
PARSON Since she has so firm a contract, I pronounce it a lawful
marriage – but hark they are coming sure –
DIANA Pull your hoods down – and keep your face from the light.
[*Diana runs out*]

Enter Bearjest, and Noisy disordered.

BEARJEST Madam I beg your pardon – I met with a most divellish
adventure, – your pardon too Mr Doctor, for making you wait –
but the business is this Sir, – I have a great mind to lie with this
young gentlewoman tonight, but she swears if I do, the parson of
the parish shall know it –
PARSON If I do Sir, I shall keep counsel.
BEARJEST And that's civil Sir, – come lead the way,
With such a guide, the devil's in't, if we can go astray.

SCENE ⟨VII⟩

Changes to the antechamber

Enter Sir Cautious.

SIR CAUTIOUS Now cannot I sleep! But am as restless as a
merchant in stormy weather, that has ventured all his wealth in
one bottom. – Woman is a leaky vessel – if she should like the
young rogue now, and they should come to a right understanding – why then am I a – wittol* – that's all, and shall be put in
print at Snow Hill† with my effigies o' th'top like the sign of
Cuckolds' Haven‡ – hum – they're damnable silent – pray heaven
he have not murdered her, and robbed her – hum – hark, what's
that? – a noise – he has broke his covenant with me, and shall
forfeit the money – how loud they are? Aye, aye the plot's discovered, what shall I do – Why the devil is not in her sure to be
refractory now and peevish, if she be I must pay my money yet
– and that would be a damned thing – sure they're coming out –
I'll retire and harken how 'tis with them.   [*Retires*]

*Enter Lady Fulbank undressed – Gayman half undressed upon his
knees, following her, holding her gown.*

LADY FULBANK Oh! You unkind – what have you made me do?
Unhand me false deceiver – let me loose –
SIR CAUTIOUS [*aside, peeping*] Made her do? – So, so – 'tis done
– I'm glad of that –
GAYMAN Can you be angry Julia!
Because I only seized my right of love.
LADY FULBANK And must my honour be the price of it?
Could nothing but my fame reward your passion?
– What make me a base prostitute, a foul adulteress,
O – begone, begone – dear robber of my quiet. [*weeping*]
SIR CAUTIOUS O fearful! –
GAYMAN Oh! Calm your rage and hear me, if you are so,

* wittol: a cuckold.
† Snow Hill: a steep highway between Newgate and Holborn Bridge, famous
for sellers of ballads.
‡ Cuckolds' Haven: on the Thames.

You are an innocent adulteress.
It was the feeble husband you enjoyed
In cold imagination, and no more,
Shyly you turned away – faintly resigned.

SIR CAUTIOUS Hum – did she so –

GAYMAN Till my excess of love – betrayed the cheat.

SIR CAUTIOUS Aye, aye that was my fear –

LADY FULBANK Away – begone – I'll never see you more –

GAYMAN You may as well forbid the sun to shine.
    Not see you more! – Heavens! I before adored you
    But now I rave! And with my impatient love,
    A thousand mad, and wild desires are burning!
    I have discovered now new worlds of charms,
    And can no longer tamely love and suffer.

SIR CAUTIOUS So – I have brought an old house upon my head.
    Entailed cuckoldom upon myself.

LADY FULBANK I'll hear no more – Sir Cautious – where's my
    husband?
    Why have you left my honour thus unguarded?

SIR CAUTIOUS Aye, aye, she's well enough pleased I fear for all
    that.

GAYMAN Base as he is, 'twas he exposed this treasure.
    Like silly Indians bartered thee for trifles.

SIR CAUTIOUS O treacherous villain! –

LADY FULBANK Hah – my husband do this?

GAYMAN He by love, he was the kind procurer,
    Contrived the means, and brought me to thy bed.

LADY FULBANK My husband? My wise husband!
    What fondness in my conduct had he seen,
    To take so shameful and so base revenge.

GAYMAN None – 'twas filthy avarice seduced him to't.

LADY FULBANK If he could be so barbarous to expose me,
    Could you who loved me – be so cruel too!

GAYMAN What – to possess thee when the bliss was offered,
    Possess thee too without a crime to thee.
    Charge not my soul with so remiss a flame,
    So dull a sense of virtue to refuse it.

LADY FULBANK I am convinced the fault was all my husband's –

[*kneels*] And here I vow – by all things just and sacred,
To separate for ever from his bed.

SIR CAUTIOUS O I am not able to endure it –
[*he kneels as she rises*] Hold – O hold my dear –

LADY FULBANK Stand off – I do abhor thee –

SIR CAUTIOUS With all my soul – but do not make rash vows.
They break my very heart – regard my reputation!

LADY FULBANK Which you have had such care of Sir already –
Rise, 'tis in vain you kneel.

SIR CAUTIOUS No – I'll never rise again – Alas! Madam I was
merely drawn in, I only thought to sport a die or so – I had only an
innocent design to have discovered whether this gentleman had
stolen my gold – that so I might have hanged him –

GAYMAN A very innocent design indeed.

SIR CAUTIOUS Aye Sir, that's all, as I'm an honest man –

LADY FULBANK I've sworn, nor are the stars more fixed than I.

Enter Servant.

SERVANT How! My lady and his worship up? – Madam, a gentleman, and a lady below in a coach knocked me up, and say they
must speak with your ladyship.

LADY FULBANK This is strange! – Bring 'em up – [*Exit servant*]
Who can it be at this odd time of neither night nor day?

Enter Leticia, Belmour and Phillis.

LETICIA Madam, your virtue, charity and friendship to me, has
made me trespass on you for my life's security, and beg you will
protect me – and my husband – [*points at Belmour*]

SIR CAUTIOUS So – here's another sad catastrophe!

LADY FULBANK Hah – does Belmour live, is't possible?
Believe me Sir, you ever had my wishes:
And shall not fail of my protection now.

BELMOUR I humbly thank your ladyship.

GAYMAN I'm glad thou hast her Harry – but doubt thou durst
not own her; nay, dar'st not own thyself.

BELMOUR Yes friend, I have my pardon –
But hark, I think we are pursued already –
[*a noise of somebody coming in*] But now I fear no force.

LADY FULBANK However step into my bedchamber.

[*Exeunt Leticia, Gayman and Phillis*]

Enter Sir Feeble in an antic manner.

SIR FEEBLE [*coming up in a menacing manner to Sir Cautious*] Hell shall not hold thee – nor vast mountains cover thee, but I will find thee out – and lash thy filthy and adulterous carcase.

SIR CAUTIOUS How – lash my filthy carcase? – I defy thee Satan –

SIR FEEBLE 'Twas thus he said.

SIR CAUTIOUS Let who's will say it, he lies in's throat.

SIR FEEBLE How! The ghostly – hush – have a care – for 'twas the ghost of Belmour – Oh! Hide that bleeding wound, it chills my soul! – [*runs to the Lady Fulbank*]

LADY FULBANK What bleeding wound? – Heavens are you frantic Sir?

SIR FEEBLE No – but for want of rest – I shall e'er morning. – She's gone – she's gone – she's gone – [*he weeps*]

SIR CAUTIOUS Aye, aye, she's gone, she's gone indeed. [*Sir Cautious weeps*]

SIR FEEBLE But let her go – so I may never see that dreadful vision – hark'ee Sir – a word in your ear – have a care of marrying a young wife.

SIR CAUTIOUS [*weeping*] Aye, but I have married one already.

SIR FEEBLE Hast thou? Divorce her – fly her, quick – depart – begone, she'll cuckold thee – and still she'll cuckold thee –

SIR CAUTIOUS Aye brother, but whose fault was that? – Why, are not you married?

SIR FEEBLE Mum – no words on't, unless you'll have the ghost about your ears; part with your wife I say, or else the devil will part ye.

LADY FULBANK Pray go to bed Sir?

SIR FEEBLE Yes, for I shall sleep now, I shall lie alone; [*weeps*] ah fool, old dull besotted fool – to think she'd love me – 'twas by base means I gained her – cozened an honest gentleman – of fame and life –

LADY FULBANK You did so Sir, but 'tis not past redress – you may make that honest gentleman amends.

SIR FEEBLE O would I could, so I gave half my estate –

LADY FULBANK That penitence atones with him and heaven.
– Come forth Leticia, and your injured ghost.

SIR FEEBLE Hah ghost – another sight would make me mad indeed.

BELMOUR Behold me Sir, I have no terror now.

SIR FEEBLE Hah – who's that Francis? – My nephew Francis?

BELMOUR Belmour – or Francis – choose you which you like, and I am either.

SIR FEEBLE Hah, Belmour! And no ghost?

BELMOUR Belmour – and not your nephew Sir.

SIR FEEBLE But art alive? Od's bobs I'm glad on't sirrah, – But are you real Belmour?

BELMOUR As sure as I'm no ghost.

GAYMAN We all can witness for him Sir.

SIR FEEBLE Where be the minstrels, we'll have a dance – adod we will – Ah – art thou there thou cozening little chitsface? – A vengeance on thee – thou madest me an old doting loving coxcomb – but I forgive thee – and give thee all thy jewels, and you your pardon Sir, so you'll give me mine; for I find you young knaves will be too hard for us.

BELMOUR You are so generous Sir, that 'tis almost with grief I receive the blessing of Leticia.

SIR FEEBLE No, no, thou deservest her, she would have made an old fond blockhead of me – and one way or other you would have had her – od's bobs you would –

Enter Bearjest, Diana, Pert, Bredwell and Noisy.

BEARJEST Justice Sir, justice – I have been cheated – abused – assassinated and ravished.

SIR CAUTIOUS How? My nephew ravished –

PERT No Sir, I am his wife.

SIR CAUTIOUS Hum – my heir marry a chambermaid!

BEARJEST Sir, you must know I stole away Mrs Dye, and brought her to Ned's chamber here – to marry her.

SIR FEEBLE My daughter Dye stolen –

BEARJEST But I being to go to the devil a little Sir: whip – what does he, but marries her himself Sir; and fobbed me off, here with my lady's cast petticoat –

NOISY Sir, she's a gentlewoman, and my sister Sir.

PERT Madam, 'twas a pious fraud, if it were one, for I was contracted to him before – see here it is – [*gives it 'em*]

ALL A plain case, a plain case.

SIR FEEBLE [*to Bredwell, who with Diana kneels*] Hark'ee Sir, have you had the impudence to marry my daughter Sir?

BREDWELL Yes Sir, and humbly ask your pardon, and your blessing –

SIR FEEBLE You will ha't, whether I will or not – rise – you are still too hard for us, come Sir forgive your nephew –

SIR CAUTIOUS Well Sir, I will – but all this while you little think the tribulation I am in, my lady has forsworn my bed.

SIR FEEBLE Indeed Sir, the wiser she.

SIR CAUTIOUS For only performing my promise to this gentleman.

SIR FEEBLE Aye, you showed her the difference Sir, you're a wise man. Come dry your eyes – and rest yourself contented, we are a couple of old coxcombs: d'ye hear Sir coxcombs.

SIR CAUTIOUS I grant it Sir, [*to Gayman*] and if I die Sir – I bequeath my lady to you – with my whole estate – my nephew has too much already for a fool.

GAYMAN I thank you Sir – do you consent my Julia?

LADY FULBANK No Sir – you do not like me – a canvas bag of wooden ladles were a better bedfellow.

GAYMAN Cruel tormentor! O I could kill myself with shame and anger!

LADY FULBANK Come hither Bredwell – witness for my honour – that I had no design upon his person, but that of trying of his constancy.

BREDWELL Believe me Sir, 'tis true – I feigned a danger near – just as you got to bed – and I was the kind devil Sir, that brought the gold to you.

BEARJEST And you were one of the devils that beat me, and the captain here Sir?

GAYMAN No truly Sir, those were some I hired – to beat you for abusing me today –

NOISY To make you 'mends Sir, I bring you the certain news of the death of Sir Thomas Gayman your uncle, who has left you two thousand pounds a year –

GAYMAN I thank you Sir – I heard the news before.

SIR CAUTIOUS How's this; Mr Gayman, my lady's first lover? I find Sir Feeble we were a couple of old fools indeed, to think at our age to cozen two lusty young fellows of their mistresses; 'tis no wonder that both the men and the women have been too hard for us, we are not fit matches for either, that's the truth on't.
That warrior needs must to his rival yield,
Who comes with blunted weapons to the field.

⟨*Exeunt*⟩

EPILOGUE

Written by a person of quality, spoken by
Mr Betterton ⟨Gayman⟩

Long have we turned the point of our just rage
On the halfwits, and critics of the age.
Oft has the soft, insipid sonneteer
In Nice and Flutter,* seen his fop-face here.
Well was the ignorant lampooning pack
Of shatterhead rhymers whipped on Craffey's† back;
But such a trouble weed is poetaster,
The lower 'tis cut down, it grows the faster.
Though satire then had such a plenteous crop,
An aftermath of coxcombs is come up:
Who not content false poetry to renew,
By sottish censures would condemn the true.
Let writing like a gentleman – fine appear,
But must you needs judge too *en cavalier*?
These whiffling critics, 'tis our authoress fears,
And humbly begs a trial by her peers:
Or let a pole of fools her fate pronounce,
There's no great harm in a good quiet dunce.
But shield her, heaven! from the left-handed blow
Of airy blockheads, who pretend to know.
On downright dullness let her rather split,
Than be fop-mangled under colour of wit.
   Hear me ye scribbling beaus, –
Why will you in sheer rhyme, without one stroke
Of poetry, ladies' just disdain provoke,
And address songs, to whom you never spoke.
In doleful hymns for dying felons fit,
Why do you tax their eyes, and blame their wit?
Unjustly of the innocent you complain,

---

* Nice and Flutter: typical fops, Sir Courtly Nice, the hero of Crowne's *Sir Courtly Nice*, and Sir Fopling Flutter of Etherege's *The Man of Mode*.
† Craffey: a fop in Crowne's *City Politics*.

Tis bulkers★ give, and tubs† must cure your pain.
Why in lampoons will you yourselves revile?
'Tis true, none else will think it worth their while:
But thus you're hid! Oh, 'tis a politic fetch:
So some have hanged themselves, to ease Jack Ketch.‡
Justly your friends and mistresses you blame,
For being so they well deserve the shame,
'Tis the worst scandal to have born that name.
At poetry of late, and such whose skill   ⎫ See the late
Excels your own, you dart a feeble quill;   ⎬ satire on
Well may you rail at what you ape so ill.   ⎭ poetry.§
With virtuous women, and all men of worth,
You're in a state of mortal war by birth.
Nature in all her atom fights ne'er knew
Two things so opposite as them and you.
On such your Muse her utmost fury spends,
They're slandered worse than any but your friends.
More years may teach you better, the meanwhile,
If you can't mend your morals, mend your style.

★ bulkers: whores.
† tubs: sweating in tubs was a remedy for venereal disease.
‡ Jack Ketch: the hangman of *c.* 1663–87, the name was later attached to all hangmen.
§ satire on poetry: this may be a reference to *An Essay on Poetry* (1682) by John Sheffield, Duke of Buckingham (1648–1721).

NOTES

The copy text used is that of the first edition of 1687 in the Brotherton Collection, University of Leeds.

Abbreviations

Q1   The first quarto edition, 1687
1724 An edition of 1724
S   *The Works of Aphra Behn*, ed. M. Summers, 6 vols, 1925.

Some of the copy text, originally set as verse, has, in this edition, where it is palpably not verse, been set as prose.

18.6   failing / foiling Q1
16.5   passes / presses Q1
19.16   she's/She 'as Q1
20.11   Than/Then Q1
20.12   *Enter Phillis . . .*/ Q1 places before the song
20.13   Phillis, Leticia's / Phillis Leticia's Q1
20.20   news – I / news I Q1
21.31   dudgeon S/dugion Q1
26.2   Omer's/Omers Q1
26.11   'um S/um Q1
26.12   Omer's/Omers Q1
26.26   Omer's/Omers Q1
27.4   am I Q1 / I am S
28.32   me, heavens / me. Heavens Q1
30.15   *kisses / Kiss* Q1
30.16   *so do / So to* Q1
30.25   Then then S/ then thou Q1
31.1   God so / Gots so Q1
31.6   fool's-face / Fools-face Q1
37.10   Julia; who's that? My / Julia; whose that my Q1
42.7   *enter Belmour . . . her* S/Q1 places after 'That lends . . .'
42.25   ; that very / that; very Q1
44.26   God so / got-so Q1
47.35   quonundrum S/qunnundrum Q1
50.4   Q1 *The second song before the entry* omitted here.
50.16   prefer/prefers Q1

51.26   swooned S/swoonded Q1
51.35   Cruel? Thou'rt/Cruel, thou'rt Q1
52.18   done't, I've done't S/don't, I've don't Q1
53.22   Hey/H'e' Q1
54.5   devil! Art/devil art Q1
54.34   bye/b'u'y Q1
56.14   *woman*/ *Women* Q1
57.4   fine'st/fines Q1
57.19   *Shepherd sings*/ *Man sings* Q1
58.30   have S/'ave Q1
65.32   *aside* 1724/Q1 omits
67.7   for S/fot Q1
71.5   *aside angrily*/*angry* Q1
71.9   *to Gayman*/*aside* Q1
73.15   Do you hear/do hear Q1
74.13   *s.p.* Sir Feeble/Q1 omits
77.23   he's/he'as Q1
80.24   precedent/President Q1
82.23   but S/bus Q1
82.24   wife's/wife' Q1
84.18   put/puts Q1
86.21   SCENE III/SCENE II Q1
88.3   wait/waits Q1
88.32   Q1 *soft music ceases* omitted
90.31   What! I'll/What I'll Q1
92.18   with all . . . pound, Sir S/Q1 adds *aside* here
94.8   wittol/wittal Q1
96.23   *Leticia,*/ *Leticia –* Q1
96.25   life's/lifes Q1
101.13 aftermath/an after math Q1/an after match 1724

THE SQUIRE OF ALSATIA
by Thomas Shadwell

INTRODUCTION

Thomas Shadwell (1642?–92) was the son of a lawyer and came from an old Staffordshire family. Educated at Caius College, Cambridge, he then entered the Middle Temple but soon left law for literature. His dramatic career began with *The Sullen Lovers*, based on Molière's *Les Facheux*, which was staged at Lincoln's Inn Fields in 1668. This successful play contained satirical portraits of Sir Robert Howard and his brother Edward, which contributed to its popularity. He wrote fourteen comedies, a tragicomedy, two operas, and adapted Shakespeare's *Timon of Athens* as *The Enchanted Island*.

Shadwell and Dryden, originally friendly, indulged in a fierce quarrel, during which Dryden launched savage and devastating attacks on his contemporary in *The Medal*, in *MacFlecknoe*, and in the second part of *Absalom and Achitophel*. Dryden's comment has remained and damned Shadwell unnecessarily: 'The rest to some faint meaning make pretense/But Shadwell never deviates into sense.' Shadwell's replies in *The Medal of John Bayes* (1682) and his translation of the *Tenth Satire of Juvenal* (1687) did not achieve the same satiric result as Dryden's sharp remarks. In the end, however, Shadwell might have seemed to win the quarrel since he succeeded to Dryden's offices of Poet Laureate and Historiographer Royal when Dryden lost them in 1689.

Shadwell is well worth reading; he could write well; he had a flair for dramatic situations and an ear for good dialogue. He also had a nice sense of humour (rather than wit) backed by a solid common-sensical approach to life. He regarded himself as a follower of Ben Jonson and he certainly shared the earlier dramatist's capacity for ridiculing folly and yet propounding a serious view of life.

The Squire of Alsatia was first produced at Drury Lane in May 1688 and was a triumph, running for thirteen consecutive days. The acting was excellent, according to John Downes in *Roscius Anglicanus* (1708), and no doubt Nokes as the Squire was as impressive a character actor as usual. Anne Bracegirdle played Lucia while Antony Leigh was 'Eminent' as Sir William Belfond and Griffin excelled as Sir Edward Belfond. Cave Underhill, as Lolpoop, portrayed the log-like qualities required. The play continued to hold the stage for nearly eighty years and many prominent actors and actresses appeared in it. It was also very popular in Ireland.

The theme of the play is that of contrasting systems of education: one restrictive, the other liberal, or rather as the *St James Chronicle* put it in its issue of 22 December 1774, while comparing Richard Cumberland's play *The Choleric Man* with Shadwell's *The Squire of Alsatia* and Terence and Molière, 'the different effects of a harsh and severe and a mild and gentle education'. The theme is an old one, and Terence's *Adelphi* the most obvious source. There are, of course, differences. Shadwell's country squire is nearly tricked into marrying a supposed lady of quality, a development Cumberland echoed in *The Choleric Man*. Sir Walter Scott later used *The Squire of Alsatia* for *The Fortunes of Nigel*, and the novel in turn led to two dramatic adaptations in the nineteenth century.

In the play there is much fun to be had out of the use of cant terms, and the squire's rapid adoption of them. The dialogue in general is very lively, not least when Mrs Termagant holds the stage. Shadwell's sense of the contrapuntal emerges constantly, notably in the passage in the second act between Sir William and Sir Edward over the education of the sons, the conflict between 'theoretical' and 'practical' education, with the effects of the two systems being so ironically revealed to us, as the young squire is steadily debauched by the rogues, Cheatly, Hackum and Shamwell. Another reversal is that in which Sir Edward rebukes his brother for setting the mob to pursue Betty, Lolpoop's whore.

The inevitable encounter between Sir William and Belfond senior has its farcical elements but also carries a good deal of commonsense, for Sir William has been unreasonable, indeed stupid in his complacency. He becomes ludicrous in his self-pity later in the fifth act. Belfond Junior is no prig, but he repents his past relationship with Mrs Termagant, has formed ideas about the sanctity of marriage, 'the most solemn vow a man can make', and will be entirely Isabella's. Shadwell's realism emerges in the elder brother's desire to have his own swing at whoring and drinking before he comes to marriage. And the play ends with a denunciation of a situation where the King's writ does not prevail in London while Ireland, Wales and Scotland are respectively conquered, subdued and united, and with Sir Edward's admonition on the need for fathers to make friends of their sons.

Thomas Shadwell

The
Squire of Alsatia

A COMEDY

As it is acted by Their Majesties' Servants

Written by Thomas Shadwell

Creditur, ex medio quia res arcessit, habere
Sudoris minimum, sed habet Comoedia tanto
Plus oneris, quanto veniae minus.★
Horace, Ep. ad Aug. I. lib. 2

LONDON

Printed for James Knapton, at the Queen's Head in
St Paul's Church Yard.

1688

★ *Creditur* . . . *minus*: Horace, *Epistles*, II, 1, 168–70. It is believed that, because it draws its material from everyday things, comedy involves only a little sweat; but in so far as it has less indulgence it is that much more difficult.

DEDICATION

To the Earl of Dorset and Middlesex, etc.

My Lord,

I having had the honour to have lived so many years in your lordship's favour, and to have been always exceedingly obliged by your lordship, ought to be glad of any opportunity of publishing my gratitude. And the offering this comedy to your lordship may not perhaps be thought an improper occasion of doing it; for the first act of it was written at Copt Hall;* and your lordship's approbation of it (whose wit and judgment have ever been unquestioned), encouraged and inspired me to go on: when I had finished it, which was in a month's time, your lordship, upon the perusal of the whole, was pleased to say that you thought it a true, and diverting comedy.

This, I must confess, made me hope for success upon the stage, which it met with, but so great, as was above my expectation (in this age which has run mad after farces) no comedy, for these many years, having filled the theatre so long together: and I had the great honour to find so many friends, that the house was never so full since it was built, as upon the third day of this play; and vast numbers went away, that could not be admitted.

This extraordinary success, the more emboldens me to lay the play at your lordship's feet; in whose service, I should be glad to employ my whole life.

I shall not, according to the custom of dedications, make a long panegyric to your lordship, 'tis superfluous and impertinent to praise him whom all men speak well of, and of whom I never heard any man speak ill: your lordship is the favourite of mankind; and you deserve to be so, for you are ever obliging, and seeking out occasions of doing good, and exerting your charity and generosity, in which you never lose a day.

I must acknowledge myself infinitely obliged to your lordship every way; but particularly, that I have the freedom of being received as one of your family at Copt Hall; where not only the excellence of the air, and regularity of living contribute to my health,

* Copt Hall: Dorset's house near Epping.

but I have the honour of enjoying the conversation which in all the world I would choose.

It is to me, and it must needs be to all who wish your lordship well, an extraordinary satisfaction to observe that you have laid so certain a foundation of solid happiness, for all the remaining part of your life; in retiring from all the unsatisfying pleasures, and noisy troubles of the Town, to so sweet a place, with so admirable a lady, who in beauty is exceeded by none, and has all those qualities of mind besides, which serve to make an excellent lady, an extraordinary governess of a family, and an incomparable wife; whose fruitfulness is like to bless your lordship with a beauteous, noble and numerous issue. And may your lordship and she long enjoy one another, and all the blessings you yourselves can imagine or desire. I am,

My lord,
Your lordship's most humble servant,
THOMAS SHADWELL.

AN EXPLANATION OF THE CANT

Alsatia	Whitefriars.
Prig, Prigster	Pert coxcombs.
Bubble, Caravan	The cheated.
Sealer	One that gives bonds and judgments for goods and money.
A Put	One who is easily wheedled and cheated.
Coal, Ready, Rhino, Darby	Ready-money.
Rhinocerical	Full of money.
Megs	Guineas.
Smelts	Half-guineas.
Decus	A crown-piece.
George	A half-crown.
Hog	A shilling.
Sice	Sixpence.
Scout	A watch.
Tattler	An alarm, or striking watch.
Famble	A ring.
Porker, Tilter	A sword.
A Rum Nab	A good beaver.
Rigging	Clothes.
Blowing, Natural, Convenient, Tackle, Buttock, Pure, Purest Pure	Several names for a mistress, or rather a whore.
To Equip	To furnish one.
A Bolter of Whitefriars	One that does but peep out of Whitefriars, and retire again like a rabbit out of his hole.
To Lug Out	To draw a sword.
To Scamper, To Rub, To Scour	To run away.
Bowsy	Drunk.
Clear	Very drunk.
Smoaky	Jealous.
Sharp	Subtle.

A Sharper	A cheat.
A Tattmonger	A cheat at dice.
Tatts	False dice.
The Doctor	A particular false die, which will run but two or three chances.
Prog	Meat.

DRAMATIS PERSONAE

<MEN>

Sir William Belfond	A gentleman of above £3000 *per annum*, who in his youth had been a spark of the Town; but married and retired into the country, where he turned to the other extreme, rigid, morose, most sordidly covetous, clownish, obstinate, positive and froward.
Sir Edward Belfond	His brother, a merchant, who by lucky hits had gotten a great estate, lives single with ease and pleasure, reasonably and virtuously. A man of great humanity and gentleness and compassion towards mankind; well read in good books, possessed with all gentleman-like qualities.
Belfond Senior	Eldest son to Sir William, bred after his father's rustic, swinish manner, with great rigour and severity; upon whom his father's estate is entailed; the confidence of which makes him break out into open rebellion to his father, and become lewd, abominably vicious, stubborn and obstinate.
Belfond Junior	Second son to Sir William, adopted by Sir Edward and bred from his childhood by him, with all the tenderness, and familiarity, and bounty, and liberty that can be; instructed in all the liberal sciences, and in all gentlemanlike education: somewhat given to women, and now and then to good fellowship; but an ingenious, well-accomplished gentleman; a man of honour and of excellent disposition and temper.
Truman	His friend, a man of honour and fortune.
Cheatly	A rascal, who by reason of debts dares not stir out of Whitefriars, but there inveigles young heirs in tail; and helps 'em to goods and money upon great disadvantages; is bound

	for them, and shares with them, till he undoes them. A lewd, impudent, debauched fellow, very expert in the cant about the Town.
Shamwell	Cousin to the Belfonds, an heir, who being ruined by Cheatly, is made a decoy-duck for others; not daring to stir out of Alsatia, where he lives; is bound with Cheatly for heirs, and lives upon them, a dissolute debauched life.
Captain Hackum	A blockheaded bully of Alsatia; a cowardly, impudent, blustering fellow; formerly a serjeant in Flanders, run from his colours, retreating into Whitefriars for a very small debt; where, by the Alsatians he is dubbed a captain; marries one that lets lodgings, sells cherry brandy, and is a bawd.
Scrapeall	A hypocritical, repeating, praying, psalm-singing, precise fellow, pretending to great piety, a godly knave, who joins with Cheatly and supplies young heirs with goods and money.
Attorney	To Sir William Belfond, who solicits his business, and receives all his packets.
Lolpoop	A north-country fellow, servant to Belfond Senior, much displeased at his master's proceedings.
Termagant	A sharper, brother to Mrs Termagant.
La Mar	French *valet de chambre*.
Roger★	Servant to Belfond Junior
Parson	An indebted Alsatian divine.

⟨WOMEN⟩

Ruth★	A precise governess to Teresia and Isabella.
Teresia	Daughter to Scrapeall, in love with, and beloved by Truman.

★ Not included in *Dramatis Personae* in 1st edition.

Isabella	His niece, in love with, and beloved by Belfond Junior.
Lucia	The attorney's daughter, a young, beautiful girl, of a mild and tender disposition; debauched by Belfond Junior.
Mrs Termagant	A neglected mistress of Belfond Junior, by whom he has had a child: a furious, malicious, and revengeful woman; perpetually plaguing him, and crossing him in all his designs; pursuing him continually with her malice, even to the attempting of his life.
Mrs Hackum	Wife to Captain Hackum.
Mrs Betty	Lolpoop's whore.
Mrs Margaret	His master's whore.

Fiddlers, Constables, Tipstaff, Watch, Sergeant, etc.
Musketeers, Rabble, etc.

PROLOGUE

To *The Squire of Alsatia*. Spoken by
Mr Mountfort ⟨Belfond Junior⟩

How have we in the space of one poor age,
Beheld the rise and downfall of the stage!
When, with our king restored, it first arose,
They did each day some good old play expose;
And then it flourished: till, with manna tired,
For wholesome food the nauseous trash desired.
Then rose the whiffling scribblers of those days,
Who since have lived to bury all their plays;
And had their issue full as numerous been
As Priam's, they the fate of all had seen.
   With what prodigious scarcity of wit
Did the new authors starve the hungry pit?
Infected by the French, you must have rhyme,
Which long, to please the ladies' ears, did chime.
Soon after this came ranting fustian in,
And none but plays upon the fret were seen:
Such roaring bombast stuff, which fops would praise,
Tore our best actors' lungs, cut short their days.
Some in small time did this distemper kill,
And had the savage authors gone on still,
Fustian had been a new disease i'th' bill.
When Time, which all things tries, had laid rhyme dead,
The vile usurper farce reigned in its stead.
Then came machines, brought from a neighbour nation,
O how we suffered under decoration!
If all this stuff has not quite spoiled your taste,
Pray let a comedy once more be graced:
Which does not monsters represent, but men,
Conforming to the rules of Master Ben.★
Our author, ever having him in view,
At humble distance would his steps pursue.
He to correct, and to inform did write:

★ Master Ben: Benjamin Jonson (1572–1637), playwright and poet.

If poets aim at nought but to delight,
Fiddlers have to the bays an equal right.
    Our poet found your gentle fathers kind,
And now some of his works your favour find.
He'll treat you still with somewhat that is new,
But whether good or bad, he leaves to you.
Bawdy the nicest ladies need not fear,
The quickest fancy shall extract none here.
We will not make 'em blush, by which is shown
How much their bought red★ differs from their own.
No fop no beau shall just exceptions make,
None but abandoned knaves offence shall take:
Such knaves as he industriously offends,
And should be very loath to have his friends.
For you who bring good humour to the play,
We'll do our best to make you laugh today.

★ bought red: rouge, artificial as opposed to natural colouring.

ACT ONE

SCENE I

Enter Belfond Senior, meeting Shamwell.

BELFOND SENIOR Cousin Shamwell well met; good morrow to you.

SHAMWELL Cousin Belfond your humble servant: what makes you abroad so early? 'Tis not much past seven.

BELFOND SENIOR You know we were boozy last night: I am a little hot-headed this morning: and come to take the fresh air here in the Temple Walks.

SHAMWELL Well: and what do you think of our way of living here? Is not rich generous wine better than your poor hedge-wine* stummed, or dull March beer? Are not delicate well-bred, well-dressed women better than dairymaids, tenants' daughters, or barefoot strumpets? Streets full of fine coaches, better than a yard full of dung-carts? A magnificent tavern, than a thatched ale-house? Or the society of brave honest, witty, merry fellows, than the conversation of unthinking, hunting, hawking blockheads, or high-shoed peasants and their wiser cattle?

BELFOND SENIOR O yes, a world adad. Ne'er stir, I could never have thought there had been such a gallant place as London: here I can be drunk over-night, and well next morning: can ride in a coach for a shilling as good as a Deputy Lieutenant's; and such merry wags, and ingenious companions. – Well, I vow and swear, I am mightily beholding to you, dear cousin Shamwell: then for the women! Mercy upon us, so civil and well bred. And I'll swear upon a Bible, finer all of them than knight-baronets' wives with us.

SHAMWELL And so kind and pleasant!

BELFOND SENIOR Aye, I vow pretty rogues! No pride in them in the world: but so courteous and familiar, as I am an honest man, they'll do whatever one would have 'em presently; ah sweet rogues: while in the country, a pize† take 'em, there's such a stir

---

* hedge-wine: inferior wine, to be met with by the wayside.
† pize: the origin of this word is uncertain: it may be a substitute for pest or pox.

with 'Pish, fie, nay Mr Timothy, what do you do? I vow I'll squeak, never stir I'll call out, ah hah –'

SHAMWELL And if one of 'em happen to be with child: there's straight an uproar in the country, as if the hundred★ were sued for a robbery!

BELFOND SENIOR Aye so there is: and I am in that fear of my father besides adad, he'd knock me i'th'head, if he should hear of such a thing: to say truth, he's so terrible to me I can never enjoy myself for him: Lord! What will he say when he comes to know I am at London? Which he in all his lifetime would never suffer me to see, for fear I should be debauched forsooth; and allows me little or no money at home neither.

SHAMWELL What matter what he says? Is not every foot of the estate entailed upon you?

BELFOND SENIOR Well, I'll endure it no longer! If I can but raise money; I'll teach him to use his son like a dog, I'll warrant him.

SHAMWELL You can ne'er want that: take up on the reversion: 'tis a lusty one; and Cheatly will help you to the ready: and thou shalt shine and be as gay as any spruce prig that ever walked the street.

BELFOND SENIOR Well: adad, you are pleasant men: and have the neatest sayings with you: 'ready' and 'spruce prig', and abundance of the prettiest witty words. – But sure that Mr Cheatly is as fine a gentleman as any wears a head: and as ingenious; ne'er stir I believe he would run down the best scholars in Oxford, and put 'em in a mouse-hole with his wit.

SHAMWELL In Oxford! Aye, and in London too.

BELFOND SENIOR Godsookers cousin! I always thought they had been wittiest in the Universities.

SHAMWELL O fie cousin: a company of puts! Mere puts.

BELFOND SENIOR Puts, mere puts: very good I'll swear, ha, ha, ha.

SHAMWELL They are all scholar-boys, and nothing else, as long as they live there: and yet they are as confident as if they knew everything; when they understand no more beyond Magdalen Bridge than mere Indians. But Cheatly is a rare fellow; I'll speak

★ the hundred: a sub-division of a shire or county, possessing its own court.

a bold word, he shall cut a sham or banter* with the best wit or poet of'em all.

BELFOND SENIOR Good again! 'Cut a sham or banter!' I shall remember all these quaint words in time: but Mr Cheatly's a prodigy that's certain.

SHAMWELL He is so; and a worthy brave fellow, and the best friend where he takes, and the most sincere of any man breathing.

BELFOND SENIOR Nay, I must needs say, I have found him very frank, and very much a gentleman, and am most extremely obliged to him and you for your great kindness.

SHAMWELL This morning your clothes and liveries will come home, and thou shalt appear rich and splendid like thyself, and the mobile† shall worship thee.

BELFOND SENIOR The mobile! That's pretty.

Enter Cheatly.

Sweet Mr Cheatly, my best friend, let me embrace thee.

CHEATLY My sprightly son of timber and of acres: my noble heir I salute thee: the coal is coming, and shall be brought in this morning.

BELFOND SENIOR Coal? What 'tis summer, I need no firing now. Besides I intend to burn billets.

CHEATLY My lusty rustic, learn and be instructed. Coal is in the language of the witty, money. The ready, the rhino; thou shalt be rhinocerical, my lad, thou shalt.

BELFOND SENIOR Admirable I swear! 'Coal! Ready! Rhino! Rhinocerical!' Lord, how long may a man live in ignorance in the country?

SHAMWELL Aye: but what asses you'll make of the country gentlemen when you go amongst them. 'Tis a providence you are fallen into so good hands.

BELFOND SENIOR 'Tis a mercy indeed. How much coal, ready, and rhino shall I have?

---

* cut a sham or banter: Freeman in Wycherley's *Plain Dealer* remarks 'Shamming is telling you an insipid dull lie, with a dull face, which the sly wag the author only laughs at himself: and making himself believe 'tis a good jest, puts the sham only upon himself'.

† the mobile: the mob.

CHEATLY Enough to set thee up to spark it in thy brother's face: and ere thou shalt want the ready, the darby, thou shalt make thy fruitful acres in reversion to fly, and all thy sturdy oaks to bend like switches! But thou must squeeze* my lad: squeeze hard, and seal my bully. Shamwell and I are to be bound with thee.

BELFOND SENIOR I am mightily beholding to you both I vow and swear; my uncle Sir Edward took my brother when he was a child, and adopted him: would it had been my lot.

SHAMWELL He is a noble gentleman, and maintains him in coach and equipage fit for him.

CHEATLY Thou shalt not see the prig thy brother till thou shalt out-jingle him in ready, out-shine him in thy ornaments of body, out-spark him in thy coach and liveries; and shalt be so equipped that thou shalt dazzle the whole Town with thy outrageous splendour.

BELFOND SENIOR I vow his tongue is rarely hung!

CHEATLY Thy brother's heart shall break with envy at thy gallantry: the fops and beaux shall be astonished at thy brightness. What ogling there will be between thee and the blowings: old staring at thy equipage. And every buttock shall fall down before thee.

BELFOND SENIOR Ha, ha, ha. I vow you are the pleasantest man I ever met with, and I'll swear the best friend I ever had in my life; that I must needs say. I was resolved not to let my brother see me till I was in circumstances d'ye see: and for my father he's in Holland. My mother's brother died and left him sole executor. He'll not be here these six weeks.

SHAMWELL Well, when you see your brother he'll envy you, and rail at those who made you flourish so. We shall be cast off.

BELFOND SENIOR Godsookers cousin! I take it very unkindly that you should say so. I'll cast off all the relations in the world before I'll part with such true, such loving friends, adad.

Enter Captain Hackum.

O noble Captain Hackum, your servant; servant captain.

CAPTAIN HACKUM Your humble trout, good noble squire, you were brave and boozy last night; i'faith you were.

* squeeze: squeeze wax, seal a document.

BELFOND SENIOR Yes really, I was clear:* for I do not remember what I did, or where I was: clear, clear: is not that right?

SHAMWELL Aye, aye: why, you broke windows: scoured, broke open a house in Dorset Court,† and took a pretty wench, a gentleman's natural, away by force.

CHEATLY Very true: and this magnanimous spark, this thunder-bolt of war, Captain Hackum, laid about him like a hero, as did some other of your friends, or else the watch had mauled us: but we made them scour.

BELFOND SENIOR Nay o' my conscience, the captain's mighty valiant; there's terror in that countenance and whiskers: he's a very Scanderberg‡ incarnate. And now you put me in mind, I recollect somewhat of this matter: my shoulders are plaguey sore, and my arms black and blue; but where's the wench, the natural, ha captain?

CAPTAIN HACKUM Ah squire, I led her off. I have her safe for you.

BELFOND SENIOR But does not the gallant thunder and roar for her?

CAPTAIN HACKUM The scoundrel dares not: he knows me, who never knew fear in my life; for my part, I love magnanimity, and honour, and those things; and fighting is one of my recreations. He that wears a brave soul, and dares honestly do, Is a herald to himself, and a godfather too.

BELFOND SENIOR O brave Captain.

CHEATLY The prigster lugged out in defence of his natural; the captain whipped his porker out, and away rubbed§ prigster and called the watch.

BELFOND SENIOR 'Prigster, lugged out, natural, porker, rubbed,' admirable! This is very ingenious conversation: y'are the purest company; who would not keep company with the wits; pox o' the country I say.

CAPTAIN HACKUM But squire, I had damned ill luck afterwards: I went up ⟨to⟩ the gaming ordinary, and lost all my ready; they

* clear: intoxicated.   † Dorset Court: Fleet Street, now Dorset Street.
‡ Scanderberg: Iscander Bey, who renounced Islam and as George Castriota checked the Ottoman advance into Europe.
§ away rubbed: cleared off.

left me not a rag or sock: pox o' the tatts for me: I believe they put the doctor upon me.

BELFOND SENIOR Tatts, and doctor! What's that?

SHAMWELL The tools of sharpers, false dice.

CAPTAIN HACKUM Hark you, prithee noble squire, equip me with a couple of megs, or two couple of smelts.

BELFOND SENIOR 'Smelts!' What shall we bespeak another dish of fish for our dinner?

SHAMWELL No no, megs are guineas, smelts are half-guineas: he would borrow a couple of guineas.

BELFOND SENIOR 'Megs, smelts!' Ha, ha, ha. Very pretty by my troth. And so thou shalt, dear Captain: there are two megs; and I vow and swear I am glad I have 'em to pleasure you, adad I am.

CAPTAIN HACKUM You are so honest a gentleman, quarrel every day and I'll be your second; once a day at least; and I'll say this for you, there's not a finer gentleman this day walks the Friars; no dispraise to any man, let him be what he will.

BELFOND SENIOR Adad you make me proud Sir.

Enter Lolpoop.

O Lolpoop, where have you been all this morning, sirrah?

LOLPOOP Why 'tis but rear* marry, 'tis meet a bit past eight: by'r lady yeow were so drunken last neeght I had thoughten yeow wouden ha been a bed aw th' morn: well, mine eyne ake a-gazing up and down on aw the fine sights; but for aw that send me north to my own county again.

BELFOND SENIOR O silly rogue: you are only fit for cattle. Gentlemen, you must excuse him, he knows no better.

LOLPOOP Marry, better quoth a! By th' mess, this is a life for the deel: to be drunken each night, break windows, roar, sing and swear i'th' streets; go to loggerheads with the constable and the watch, han harlots in gold and silver lace: hea'n bless us, and send me a-whome again.

BELFOND SENIOR Peace, you saucy-scoundrel, or I'll cudgel you to pap: sirrah do not provoke me, I say do not.

LOLPOOP Od's flesh, where's money for aw this? Yeowst be run agraunt soon and you takken this caurse, Ise tell a that.

* rear: early.

BELFOND SENIOR Take that sirrah: I'll teach you to mutter: what, my man become my master?

LOLPOOP Waunds! Give me ten times more and send me whome agen at after. What will awd maaster say to this? I mun ne'er see the face of him I wot.

SHAMWELL Hang him rogue. Toss him in a blanket.

CHEATLY Let me talk with him a little. Come on fellow.

LOLPOOP Talk! Well, what sen ye?

CHEATLY [*bantering*] Your master being in this matter, to deport his countenance somewhat obliquely, to some principles, which others but out of a mature gravity may have weighed, and think too heavy to be undertaken; what does it avail if you shall precipitate or plunge yourself into affairs, as unsuitable to your physiognomy as they are to your complexion.

LOLPOOP Hah, what sen you? Yeow mistaken me: I am not book-learned: I understand a not.

CHEATLY No, 'tis the strangest thing! Why, put the case you are indebted to me £20 upon a *scire facias*:* I extend this up to an outlawry, upon affidavit upon the *nisi prius*:† I plead to all this matter *non est inventus*‡ upon the panel; what is there to be done more in this case, as it lies before the Bench, but to award our execution upon the *posse comitatus*,§ who are presently to issue out a *certiorari*.||

LOLPOOP I understand a little of sizes, nisi-prizes, affidavi, sussurari! But by the mess I cannot tell what to mack of aw this together not I.

BELFOND SENIOR Ha, ha. Puppy! Owl! Loggerhead! O silly country put! Here's a prig indeed: he'll ne'er find out what 'tis to cut a sham or banter: well, I swear Sir you do it the best of any man in the world.

* *scire facias*: a judicial writ.

† *nisi prius*: a writ directing a sheriff to provide a jury at the Court of Westminster unless judges of assize previously come to the county.

‡ *non est inventus*: the sheriff's answer in the return of a writ, when the defendant cannot be found in his bailiwick.

§ *posse comitatus*: the power of the county, citizens who may be summoned by the sheriff to assist in suppressing a riot or executing any legal precept which is being opposed by force.

|| *certiorari*: a writ to expedite justice.

CHEATLY No, no, I swear not I.

BELFOND SENIOR I protest Sir you do it incomparably.

CHEATLY Nay, now you compliment: faith you make me blush.

LOLPOOP Sham and banter are heathen Greek to me: but yeow have cut out fine wark for yoursel last neeght: I went to see the hause yeow had brocken, aw the windows are pood dawne. I askt what was the matter, and by th' mass they haw learnt your nam too; they saiden Squire Belfond had done it, and ravished a wench: and that they hadden gotten the Lord Chief Justice Warren for you, and wooden bring a pawr of actions against yeow.

BELFOND SENIOR Is this true?

LOLPOOP Aye by th' mass.

CHEATLY No matter; we'll bring you off with a wet finger;* trust me for that.

BELFOND SENIOR Dear friend, I rely upon you for everything.

SHAMWELL We value not twenty such things of a rush.

CAPTAIN HACKUM If any of their officers dare invade our privileges, we'll send em to hell without Bail or Mainprize.

LOLPOOP But I can tella a wor news than aw this; I ne'er saw flesh alive, and I saw not your father's man Roger come out oth Temple-Yate een now. Your father's in Town that's certain.

BELFOND SENIOR How! My father say you? 'Tis impossible.

CHEATLY Courage my heir in tail:† thy father's a poor sneaking tenant for life; thou shalt live better than he can: and if we do contract a debt upon thy dirty acres in the north, I have designed for you a fine young lady with a swinging fortune to redeem all; and 'tis impossible my lad to miss her.

BELFOND SENIOR Sir, let me embrace you, and love you; never man embraced a better friend! *Amicus certus in re incerta cernitur,*‡ as the saying is.

LOLPOOP Sir, Sir, let me speak one word with you; od's flesh, I'll die the death of a dog, and aw these yeow seen here, be not rogues, cheats and pickpockets.

BELFOND SENIOR Peace, you rascal; adad I would not have any of

* a wet finger: a trifle.

† in tail: within the limitations of a freehold estate to a person and his heirs, on the failure of whom it reverts to the donor or his heirs.

‡ *Amicus . . . cernitur*: Cicero's quotation of Ennius, *De Amicitiae*, XVII, 64.

'em hear for five hundred pounds; you were a dead man.

LOLPOOP What is the reason they dare not stir out of this privi-
ledged place, but on Sabbath days.

BELFOND SENIOR You blockhead, Mr Cheatly had an alderman's
young wife run away with him, is sued for't, and is in fear of a
substantial jury of City cuckolds. Shamwell's unnatural father lays
wait for him, to apprehend him and run him into the country.
The brave and valiant gentleman, Captain Hackum, who is as
stout as a lion, beat a judge's son t'other day. And now your
questions are fully answered, you put you.

CHEATLY Honest Shamwell, thou art a rare fellow: thy cousin here
is the wealthiest caravan we have met with a long time; the
hopefullest sealer that ever yet touched wax among us: but we
must take off that evil counsellor of his.

SHAMWELL I warrant you.

Enter Tailor with a bundle, a Periwig-maker, Hatter, Shoemaker.

O cousin, here's your tailor, with your clothes and liveries, hatter,
shoemaker, periwig-maker.

CHEATLY All your movables together: go into your lodging and
fit them: your new footmen, and your French *valet de chambre* are
there, I'll wait on you there presently.

LOLPOOP Od's flesh, here's whaint* wark: by'r lady this is fine!
Whaw whaw!

BELFOND SENIOR Get you in, you rogue: an you mutter one
word more, adad I'll mince you, sirrah: well, go in all of you.
Gentlemen, I shall see you presently.   [*Exit*]

CHEATLY Immediately: let us hug ourselves, my dear rascal, in
this adventure you have done very well to engage him last night
in an outrage; and we must take care to put him upon all the
expense we can: we must reduce him to have as much need of us
as possible.

SHAMWELL Tou art i'th'right: but Captain, where's the convenient, the natural?

CAPTAIN HACKUM Why at my house: my wife has wrought her
into a good humour: she is very pretty; and is now pleased to
think the squire will be a better keeper than her former; for he

* whaint: strange, queer.

was but a sharper, a tatmonger, and when he wanted money would kick and beat her most immoderately.

SHAMWELL Well: I'll say that for the captain's wife, she's as good an able discreet woman to carry on an intrigue, as e'er a woman in the Friars! Nay better.

CAPTAIN HACKUM Your servant good Mr Shamwell; she's a very good woman thanks be to heaven, I have great comfort in her; she has a cup of the best cherry brandy in the Friars.

SHAMWELL [*aside*] And commonly a good whore to boot: ⟨*to him*⟩ but prithee Captain, go home and let her and the young girl prepare to dine with us; we must have a great dinner and fiddlers at the George,* to season the squire in his new equipage.

CAPTAIN HACKUM Well, well, it shall be done.   [*Exit*]

SHAMWELL You'll find this fellow a necessary tool in consort with his wife, who is, indeed, a bawd of parts: he is a good ruffian enough: for though he be not stout, he's impudent, and will roar and keep a filthy pother, which is enough to make fools believe he's stout.

CHEATLY Let him, and the small fry pick up the squire's loose crumbs, while we share in the lusty sums.

Enter Scrapeall.

O here comes Mr Scrapeall with all his zeal; our godly accomplice in all designs; leave him to me. [*Exit Shamwell*] O Mr Scrapeall! Have you brought the money for the squire?

SCRAPEALL I come to tell you that my man approacheth with the money and the goods for your squire.

CHEATLY I hope you have not burdened him with too many goods at first?

SCRAPEALL No: but a fourth part: 'tis true the goods are somewhat stale, but I will take them off at small under rates: you know I am not seen in furnishing of the goods and money, but only in the buying of the goods. My lawyer accompanieth my man to testify the writings.

CHEATLY 'Tis as it should be: he is a fat squire; the estate in tail is full £3000 a year. He will yield well.

---

* the George: this tavern was in Dogwell Court. It became a printing press, and was destroyed in a fire in 1713.

SCRAPEALL ⟨*aside*⟩ This squire is to take to wife a niece I have in charge: his father is to give me £5000 out of her fortune; and the squire's lewdness and prodigality will soon let me deep into his reversion. Besides his lighting into these hands, will make his father, when he finds it, hasten to agree with me for his redemption; I like the business well. ⟨*to Cheatly*⟩ I am going to the man you call Crump,* who helpeth solicitors to affidavit men, and swearers, and bail.

CHEATLY His office is next door; his wardrobe for bail and witnesses. Here he comes; let's meet him.   [*Exeunt*]

⟨SCENE II⟩

Enter Sir William Belfond, and an Attorney.

SIR WILLIAM BELFOND Sure I should know the face of that fellow, that's going there into Whitefriars.

ATTORNEY 'Tis a most notorious one; you have seen him often, 'tis that most audacious rogue, Cheatly; who has drawn in so many young heirs, and undone so many sealers: he is a bolter of Whitefriars.

SIR WILLIAM BELFOND It is that villain!

ATTORNEY I am very glad Sir, you have dispatched your business so soon in Holland.

SIR WILLIAM BELFOND I had great success, and finished all six weeks at least ere I expected; and had time to come by the way of Flanders, and see that country which I desired: and from Newport I came to Dover; and riding post from thence, I took a boat at Southwark, and landed just now here at the Temple: but I am troubled you had sent my packet to Holland ere I came.

ATTORNEY I received none from you of late: no packet has arrived this fortnight from Holland.

SIR WILLIAM BELFOND Have you heard no news from my son, nor my steward in the country?

ATTORNEY None these ten or twelve days.

* Crump: the word in cant means one who will 'be bound or swear for anybody', putting on good clothes to make a good appearance 'that bail may be accepted'.

SIR WILLIAM BELFOND That son is all the joy of my life; for him I hurry up and down, take pains, spare and live hard to raise his fortune.

ATTORNEY Indeed, I hear he's a fine gentleman, and understands his country affairs as well as e'er a farmer of them all.

SIR WILLIAM BELFOND I must confess he proves after my own heart: he's a solid young man, a dutiful child as ever man had, and I think I have done well for him in providing him a wife with such a fortune, which he yet knows nothing of. But will not this godly man, this Mr Scrapeall, take a farthing less say you for his niece?

ATTORNEY Not a souse:* I have higgled with him as if I were to buy of a horse-courser, and he will not take a farthing less than £5000 for his niece.

SIR WILLIAM BELFOND He's a strange mixture, a perpetual sermon-hunter, repeats and sings psalms continually, and prays so loud and vehemently, that he is a disturbance to his neighbours; he is so heavenward pious, and seems a very saint of a scrivener.

ATTORNEY He finds the sweet of that, it gets him many a good trust and executorship.

SIR WILLIAM BELFOND Pox on him for a damned godly knave, forsooth, cannot he be contented to sell her, whom his own brother committed to his charge; but he must extort so much for her? Well I must agree with him: I know she has full £20,000 left her: and has been brought up as strictly as my son. Get writings ready: I'll send post for my son Timothy this day.

ATTORNEY They are ready; you may seal in the afternoon if you please.

SIR WILLIAM BELFOND And I will then. I'll detain you no longer: get my writings ready: I am resolved to settle my other boy well: but my Town son afflicts me when e'er I hear him named.

ATTORNEY Your humble servant Sir William Belfond.

[*Exit Attorney*]

Enter Servant to Sir William.

SERVANT Sir, I have been at your brother's house, and they say

* souse: a very small coin, from *sol* or *sou*.

he is come to some lawyer's chamber in the King's Bench Buildings.

SIR WILLIAM BELFOND That's lucky enough: I'll walk here then, and do you watch.

Enter Hackum, and another Bully.

Who are these? Some inhabitants of Whitefriars; some bullies of Alsatia.

CAPTAIN HACKUM I was plaguey boozy last night with Squire Belfond: we had fiddles, whores, scoured, broke windows, beat watches, and roared like thunder.

BULLY Aye, I heard you?

SIR WILLIAM BELFOND [*aside*] What says he?

CAPTAIN HACKUM He drinks, whores, swears, sings, roars, rants and scours with the best of us.

SIR WILLIAM BELFOND Sir, with your favour, are you acquainted with young Belfond?

CAPTAIN HACKUM [*aside*] Yes, that I am. What country put's this?

SIR WILLIAM BELFOND What countryman is he Sir?

CAPTAIN HACKUM Prithee, old prigster, why dost ask? He is a northern man: he has a damned rustic, miserable rascal to his father, who lives a nasty brutal life in the country like a swine: but the squire will be even with him I warrant him.

SIR WILLIAM BELFOND I have something to say to him if I could see him.

CAPTAIN HACKUM You, you old prig, you damned country put: you have somewhat to say to him! I am ready to give you satisfaction: lug out; come you, put: I'll make you scamper.

SIR WILLIAM BELFOND ⟨*draws his sword*⟩ D'ye hear bully rascal, put up and walk your way, or by heaven I'll beat you as long as you are able to be beaten.

BULLY I'll stand by you: you may easily beat this old fellow.

CAPTAIN HACKUM No man e'er gave me such words, but forfeited his life; I could whip thee through the lungs immediately: but I'll desist at present. Who the devil would have thought this put durst have drawn a sword? Well Sir we shall take a time Sir, another time Sir.

SIR WILLIAM BELFOND You lie, you rascal; you will take no time. Here's a fine companion of my sons!   [*Exit Bully*]

Enter Sir Edward Belfond.

SIR EDWARD BELFOND Who's this I see? My brother! Sir William Belfond! Your humble servant. You are welcome into England. I looked not for you these six weeks.

SIR WILLIAM BELFOND I landed at the Temple Stairs* even now: my man has been at your house, and he heard there you were here.

SIR EDWARD BELFOND I hope you have done your business.

SIR WILLIAM BELFOND Beyond my expectation.

SIR EDWARD BELFOND Has your wife's brother done by you in his will, as you would have had him.

SIR WILLIAM BELFOND Truly yes: he has made me sole executor, and left my two sons £5000 apiece, to be paid at each of their days of marriage, or at my death.

SIR EDWARD BELFOND Well brother, you are a happy man; for wealth flows in upon you on every side, and riches you account the greatest happiness.

SIR WILLIAM BELFOND I find that wealth alone will not make happy. Ah brother, I must confess it was a kindness in you, when heaven had blessed you with a great estate by merchandize, to adopt my younger son, and take him and breed him from his childhood: but you have been so gentle to him, he is run into all all manner of vice and riot; no bounds can hold him; no shame can stop him; no laws nor customs can restrain him.

SIR EDWARD BELFOND I am confident you are mistaken: he has as fair a reputation as any gentleman about London: 'tis true he's a good fellow, but no sot; he loves mirth and society, without drunkenness: he is, as all young fellows I believe are, given to women; but 'tis in private; and he is particular: no common whoremaster: and in short, keeps as good company as any man in England.

SIR WILLIAM BELFOND Your over-weening makes you look through a false glass upon him. Company! Why he keeps company for the devil; had you come a minute sooner, you might

* Temple Stairs: one of the principal landing stages on the Thames.

have seen two of his companions; they were praising him for roaring, swearing, ranting, scouring, whoring, beating watches, breaking windows: I but asked one of 'em if he knew him, and said I had somewhat to say to him: the rogue, the most seeming terrible of the two, told me, if I had anything to say to Squire Belfond, he would give me satisfaction.

SIR EDWARD BELFOND What kind of fellow?

SIR WILLIAM BELFOND He came out of Whitefriars: he's some Alsatian bully.

SIR EDWARD BELFOND 'Tis impossible; he never keeps such company.

SIR WILLIAM BELFOND The rogue drew upon me: bid me lug out, called me 'old prig, country put'; and spoke a particular language which such rogues have made to themselves, called canting, as beggars, gypsies, thieves and jailbirds do: but I made his bullies go away very tamely at the sight of my drawn sword.

SIR EDWARD BELFOND I am sure he keeps no such company: it must be some other of his name.

SIR WILLIAM BELFOND You make me mad to excuse him thus: the Town rings of him; you have ruined him by your indulgence: besides, he throws away money like dirt; his infamy is notorious.

SIR EDWARD BELFOND Nay there you wrong him; he does no ungentleman-like things: prithee consider youth a little: what if he does wench a little; and now and then is somewhat extravagant in wine? Where's the great crime? All young fellows that have mettle in 'em will do the first; and if they have wit and good humour in 'em, in this drinking country, they will sometimes be forced upon the latter: and he must be a very dull phlegmatic lump, whom wine will not elevate to some extravagance now and then.

SIR WILLIAM BELFOND Will you distract me? What, are drinking and whoring no faults? His courses will break my heart; they bring tears to my eyes so often.

SIR EDWARD BELFOND One would think you had been drinking and were maudlin: think what we ourselves did when we were young fellows: you were a spark, would drink, scour and wench with the best o'th' Town.

SIR WILLIAM BELFOND Aye, but I soon repented, married and settled.

SIR EDWARD BELFOND And turned as much to the other extreme: and now perhaps I mislike these faults, caused by his heat of youth. But how do you know he may not be reclaimed suddenly?

SIR WILLIAM BELFOND Reclaimed? How can he be reclaimed without severity? You should cudgel him, and allow him no money: make him not dare to offend you thus. Well, I have a son whom by my strictness I have formed according to my heart: he never puts on his hat in my presence; rises at second course, takes away his plate; says grace, and saves me the charge of a chaplain. Whenever he committed a fault, I mauled him with correction: I'd fain see him once dare to be extravagant: no, he's a good youth, and comfort of my age; I weep for joy to think of him. Good Sir, learn to be a father of him that is one: I have a natural care of him you have adopted.

SIR EDWARD BELFOND You are his father by nature, I by choice: I took him when he was a child, and bred him up with gentleness, and that kind of conversation that has made him my friend: he conceals nothing from me, or denies nothing to me. Rigour makes nothing but hypocrites.

SIR WILLIAM BELFOND Perhaps when you begin late; but you should have been severe to him in his childhood: abridged him of liberty and money: and have had him soundly whipped often: he would have blessed you for it afterwards.

SIR EDWARD BELFOND Too much straightness in the minds of youths, like too much lacing the body, will make 'em grow crooked.

SIR WILLIAM BELFOND But no lacing at all, will make them swell and grow monstrous.

SIR EDWARD BELFOND I must govern by love. I had as lief govern a dog as a man if it must be by fear: this I take to be the difference between a good father to children, and a harsh master over slaves.

SIR WILLIAM BELFOND Yes, and see what your government is come to; his vice and prodigality will distract me.

SIR EDWARD BELFOND Why should you be so concerned? He is mine, is he not?

SIR WILLIAM BELFOND Yes, by adoption, but he is mine by nature.

SIR EDWARD BELFOND 'Tis all but custom.

SIR WILLIAM BELFOND Mine is a tender care.

SIR EDWARD BELFOND Your passion blinds you: I have as tender care as you can have: I have been ever delighted with him from his childhood: he is endeared to me by long custom and familiarity. I have had all the pleasure of a father, without the drudgery of getting a son upon a damned wife, whom perhaps I should wish hanged.

SIR WILLIAM BELFOND And will you let him run on in his lewdness and prodigality?

SIR EDWARD BELFOND He is mine: if he offends, 'tis me: if he squanders away money, 'tis mine; and what need you care? Pray take care of your own: if you will take care of this too, what do you but take him from me?

SIR WILLIAM BELFOND This you come to always! I take him from you: no, I'd not be troubled with him. Well, let him run on, and be ruined, hanged and damned – I'll never speak word more about him. Let him go on.

SIR EDWARD BELFOND This heat of youth will be allayed ere long I warrant you.

SIR WILLIAM BELFOND No, no, let him go on, let him go on; I'll take care of my own at home: and happy were this rakehell if he would take example by his brother: but I say no more; I ha' done; let him go on.

SIR EDWARD BELFOND Now you are angry, your passion runs away with you.

SIR WILLIAM BELFOND No no, I have done; what would you have more?

SIR EDWARD BELFOND Let us go and see him: I'll lay my life you'll find him perusing some good author; he ever spends his whole morning in study.

SIR WILLIAM BELFOND I must into the City, the first thing I do, and get my bills accepted; and then if you will we'll see him: and no doubt but we shall find him perusing of some whore or other, instead of a book.

SIR EDWARD BELFOND I am not of your opinion: but I'll carry

you in my coach into the City, and then bring you back to him: he is of so good a disposition: so much a gentleman: and has such worth and honour, that if you knew him as well as I, you'd love him as well as I do.

SIR WILLIAM BELFOND Well, well, I hear you Sir: I must send for my son post: I'll show you a son. Well, heaven bless him, I should be weary of this wicked world: but for the comforts I find in him: come along, I'll show you a son. [*Exeunt ambo*]

ACT TWO

SCENE I

Enter Belfond Junior, and Lucia.

BELFOND JUNIOR Why dost thou sigh? And show such sadness in thy looks, my pretty miss?

LUCIA Have I not reason?

BELFOND JUNIOR Dost thou mislike thy entertainment?

LUCIA Ah cruel Belfond, thou hast undone me.

BELFOND JUNIOR My pretty little rogue, I sooner would undo myself a thousand times.

LUCIA How I tremble to think what I ha' done! I have made myself for ever miserable.

BELFOND JUNIOR O say not so, dear child: I'll kiss those tears from off thy beauteous eyes. But I shall wrong thy cheeks, on which they fall like precious drops of dew on flowers.

LUCIA Heaven! What have I done?

BELFOND JUNIOR No more than what thy mother did before thee: no more than thy whole sex is born to do.

LUCIA O had I thought you would have been so cruel, I never would have seen your face; I swear I would not.

BELFOND JUNIOR I swear thou would'st, I know thou would'st: cruel! No billing turtle e'er was kinder to his tender mate; in billing, cooing, and in gentle murmurs, we expressed our kindness; and cooed and murmured and loved on.

LUCIA The more unhappy fool was I: go go, I hate you now.

BELFOND JUNIOR O my sweet little one; thou canst not sure be so unkind: those pretty tell-tales of thy heart, thy eyes, say better things.

LUCIA Do they so? I'll be revenged on 'em for't: for they shall never see you more.

BELFOND JUNIOR Ah say not so: I had rather much the sun should never shine on me; than thou be hidden from my sight: thou art not sure in earnest?

LUCIA Yes sure, I think I am.

BELFOND JUNIOR No, my sweet love, I think thou art not.

LUCIA O Lord, how shall I look! How shall I bear myself! If

any of my friends shall fix their eyes upon me, I shall look down and blush, and think they know all.

BELFOND JUNIOR How many fair ones daily do the same, and look demurely as any saints?

LUCIA They are confident things I warrant 'em.

BELFOND JUNIOR Let love be made familiar to thee, and thou wilt bear it better: thou must see me every day. Canst thou be so hard-hearted to forbear the sight of me?

LUCIA Perhaps I may desire now and then a look, a sight of thee at some distance: but I will never venture to come near thee more I vow.

BELFOND JUNIOR Let me kiss that vow from off thy lips, while 'tis warm there. I have it here: 'tis gone. Thou wilt not kill me sure? Didst thou not say thou loved'st me?

LUCIA Yes, I loved too much; or this had never happened: I could not else have been undone.

BELFOND JUNIOR Undone; thou art made: woman is but half a creature, till she be joined to man; now thou art whole and perfect.

LUCIA Wicked man! Can I be so confident once to come near thee more?

BELFOND JUNIOR Shouldst thou but fail one day, I never should survive it; and then my ghost will haunt thee. Canst thou look on me pretty creature, and talk thus?

LUCIA Well, go thy ways; that flattering tongue, and those bewitching eyes were made to ruin womankind.

BELFOND JUNIOR Could I but think thou wert in earnest, these arms should clasp thee ever here: I'd never part with thee.

LUCIA No no, now I must be gone: I shall be missed: how shall I get home and not be known? Sure everybody will discover me?

BELFOND JUNIOR Thy mask will cover all: there is a chair below in the entry to carry thee, and set thee down where thou wilt.

LUCIA Farewell, dear cruel man! And must I come tomorrow morning say you? No no.

BELFOND JUNIOR Yes yes; tomorrow and tomorrow, and every morning of our lives; I die else.

Enter Footboy.

FOOTBOY Sir your singing master is coming.

BELFOND JUNIOR My singing master, Mr Solfa is coming.

LUCIA O Lord hide me! He is my master, he'll know me! I shall not be able to go by him for trembling.

BELFOND JUNIOR Pretty miss, into the closet: I'll dispatch him soon. [*goes in*]

Enter Singing Master and his Daughter.

Come master, let your daughter sing the song you promised me.

SOLFA Come Betty. Please to put in a flute Sir.

BELFOND JUNIOR Come on.

[*Song with two flutes and a thorough-bass*]

THE EXPOSTULATION

Still wilt thou sigh, and still in vain
A cold neglectful nymph adore;
No longer fruitlessly complain,
But to thyself thyself restore.
In youth thou caught'st this fond disease,
And shouldst abandon it in age;
Some other nymph as well may please,
Absence or business disengage.

On tender hearts the wounds of love,
Like those imprinted on young trees,
Or kill at first, or else they prove
Larger b'insensible degrees.
Business I tried, she filled my mind;
On others lips my dear I kissed;
But never solid joy could find,
Where I my charming Sylvia missed.

Long absence, like a Greenland night,
Made me but wish for sun the more;
And that inimitable light,
She, none but she, could e'er restore.
She never once regards thy fire,
Nor ever vents one sigh for thee.

I must the glorious sun admire,
Though he can never look on me.

Look well, you'll find she's not so rare,
Much of her former beauty's gone;
My love her shadow larger far
Is made by her declining sun.
What if her glories faded be,
My former wounds I must endure;
For should the bow unbended be,
Yet that can never help the cure.

BELFOND JUNIOR 'Tis very easy and natural: your daughter sings delicately.

Enter Truman.

TRUMAN Belfond, good-morrow to thee: I see thou still tak'st care to melt away thy hours in soft delights.
BELFOND JUNIOR Honest Truman! All the pleasures and diversions we can invent, are little enough to make the farce of life go down.
TRUMAN And yet what a coil they keep: how busy and industrious are those who are reckoned grave and wise, about this life, as if there something in it.
BELFOND JUNIOR Those fools are in earnest, and very solid; they think there's something in't, while wise men know there's nothing to be done here but to make the best of a bad market.
TRUMAN You are mighty philosophical this morning. But shall I not hear one song as well as you?
BELFOND JUNIOR Have you set that ode in Horace?
SOLFA I have.
BELFOND JUNIOR Then I hope you will be encouraged to set more of 'em; we then shall be sure of wit and music together: while you great musicians do often take most pains about the silliest words. Prithee Truman sing it.
TRUMAN [*sings*] *Integer vitae scelerisque purus, etc.*★
BELFOND JUNIOR Very well; you have obliged me: please to

★ *Integer . . . purus*: Horace, Ode XXII, l. 1.

accept of this. And Madam, you shall give me leave to show
my gratitude by a small present.

SOLFA AND DAUGHTER Your servant Sir.   [*Exeunt*]

TRUMAN You are so immoderately given to music; methinks it
should jostle love out of your thoughts.

BELFOND JUNIOR O no! Remember Shakespeare: 'If music be
the food of love, play on'* – There's nothing nourishes that soft
passion like it, it imps† his wings, and makes him fly a higher
pitch. But prithee tell me what news of our dear mistresses? I
never yet was so sincerely in love as with my pretty hypocrite;
there is fire in those eyes that strikes like lightning: what a constant churchman she has made of me!

TRUMAN And mine has made an entire conquest of me: 'tis the
most charming pretty creature, that e'er my eyes beheld.

BELFOND JUNIOR Let us not fall out, like the heroes in *The
Rehearsal*,‡ for not being in love with the same woman.

TRUMAN Nothing could be so fortunate as our difference in this
case: the only one we disagree in.

BELFOND JUNIOR Thou art in the right: mine has so charmed me,
I am content to abandon all other pleasures, and live alone for her;
she has subdued me even to marriage.

TRUMAN Mine has no less vanquished me; I'll render upon
discretion. Ah rogue Belfond, I see by your bed, for all your constant love, you have had a wench this night.

BELFOND JUNIOR Peace peace, man: 'tis dangerous to fast too
long, for fearing of losing an appetite quite.

TRUMAN You are a sincere honest lover indeed.

BELFOND JUNIOR Faith Truman, we may talk of mighty matters; of our honesty and morality; but a young fellow carries that
about him that will make him a knave now and then in spite of
his teeth. Besides, I am afraid 'tis impossible for us profane fellows to succeed in that sanctified family.

* 'If music . . . play on': *Twelfth Night*, I, 1.
† imps: perhaps an echo of *Richard II*, II, 1, 292: 'imp out our drooping country's broken wing'. To imp is to engraft feathers in a damaged wing.
‡ *The Rehearsal*: by George Villiers, 2nd Duke of Buckingham. The reference is
to IV, 2, where Prince Prettyman and Prince Volscius fall out because they are
not in love with the same woman.

TRUMAN You will not say so, when you know what progress I have made in our affairs already.

BELFOND JUNIOR Thou reviv'st my drooping hopes: tell me, are we like to succeed! O if I can but prevail upon my little pretty churchwoman, I am resolved to conform to her for ever.

TRUMAN Look under my coat: am I not well habited? With a plain band, bob peruke,★ and no cuffs.

BELFOND JUNIOR Verily, like one of the pure ones.

TRUMAN Yea; and our frequenting of sermons and lectures, (which heaven knows we did out of no good, but for the sake of these little ones) has used me to their style: thus qualified, I got access into the house, having found that their governante is sister to a weaver† in the west, whom I know; I pretended to be her cousin, and to bring a token sent to her by her brother, and was very welcome to her.

BELFOND JUNIOR Most fortunate: why does he keep 'em so strictly? Never to see the face of man?

TRUMAN Be not troubled at that, 'twill forward our design; they'll be the more earnest to be delivered. But no Italian women are so closely confined; the pure knave intends to sell 'em: even his daughter, who has a good fortune left her by a widow, that was her aunt: and for his niece, he has as good as agreed already with your father for £5000 to marry her to your brother in the country: her uncle gave her £20,000 and this is the reason of confining 'em; for fear of losing the money.

BELFOND JUNIOR With my father say ye?

TRUMAN Most certain: this I learnt out of Madam Governante, at the first interview.

BELFOND JUNIOR This is a very odd accident: 'twill make my difficulty greater.

TRUMAN Not at all: as liars are always readiest to believe lies, I never knew an hypocrite but might easily be cozened by another hypocrite. I have made my way, and I warrant thee a good event. I intend to grow great with the father.

★ bob peruke: with its bottom locks turned up, the opposite to a full bottomed wig.
† a weaver: weavers were traditionally puritanical.

BELFOND JUNIOR Thy sanguine temper makes thee always hope in every enterprise.

TRUMAN You might observe, whenever we stared upon 'em, they would steal a look at us; and by stealth have often twisted eye-beams with us.

BELFOND JUNIOR The sour and devout look indeed seems but put on: there is a pretty warmth and tenderness in their eyes, that now and then gilds o'er the godly look; like the sun's light, when breaking through a cloud, it swiftly glides upon a field of corn.

TRUMAN The air of their faces plainly show they have wit, that must despise those trifling forms; their precise looks most surely are constrained.

Enter Mrs Termagant.

BELFOND JUNIOR How, Madam Termagant here! Then we shall have fine work. What wind blows you hither.

MRS TERMAGANT How dare you think that I of all woman-kind should be used thus?

BELFOND JUNIOR You mean not used; that's your grievance.

MRS TERMAGANT Good Mr Disdain; I shall spoil your scoffing: has my love deserved to be thus slighted? I that have refused princes for your sake? Did not all the Town court me? And must I choose such an ungrateful wretch?

BELFOND JUNIOR When you were first in season, you were a little courted by some of quality: mistresses, like green peas, at first coming are only had by the rich, but afterwards they come to everybody.

MRS TERMAGANT Curse on your saucy similes: was not I yours, and only yours.

BELFOND JUNIOR I had not faith enough for that; but if you were, I never had any that was mine and only mine, but I made 'em all mankind's before I had done.

MRS TERMAGANT Ah traitor! And you must pick me out to make this base example of: must I be left?

BELFOND JUNIOR Left! Yes sure, left! Why you were not married to me: I took no lease of your frail tenement: I was but tenant at my own will.

MRS TERMAGANT Insolent! How dare you thus provoke my

fury! Was ever woman's love like mine to thee? Perfidious man!
[*weeps*]

BELFOND JUNIOR So: after the thunder, thus the heat drops fall.

MRS TERMAGANT No; I scorn that thou shouldst bring tears
into my eyes.

BELFOND JUNIOR Why do you come to trouble me?

MRS TERMAGANT Since I can please no longer, I'll come to
plague thee; and if I die before thee, my ghost shall haunt thee.

BELFOND JUNIOR Indeed your love was most particular with
spitting and scratching, like caterwauling: and in the best of
humours you were ever murmuring and complaining: 'O my head
aches: I am so sick': and jealous to madness too.

MRS TERMAGANT O devil incarnate!

TRUMAN Belfond, thou art the most ungentle knight alive.

MRS TERMAGANT Methinks the pretty child I have had by you
should make you less inhuman.

BELFOND JUNIOR Let me have it; I'll breed it up.

MRS TERMAGANT No, thou shalt never have it while thou
livest. I'll pull it limb from limb ere thou shalt have it.

BELFOND JUNIOR This is so unnatural, that you will make me
so far from thinking it mine, that I shall not believe it yours:
but that you have put a false child upon me.

MRS TERMAGANT Unworthy wretch.

BELFOND JUNIOR When thou art old enough, thy malice and
ill humour will qualify thee for a witch; but thou hadst never
douceurs enough in thy youth to fit thee for a mistress.

MRS TERMAGANT How dare you provoke me thus? For what
little dirty wench am I thus used? If she be above ground I'll
find her, and tear her eyes out. Hah – By the bed I see the devil
has been here tonight – Oh, oh, I cannot bear it. [*falls into a fit*]

TRUMAN Belfond, help the lady, for shame; lay hold on her.

BELFOND JUNIOR No no, let her alone; she will not hurt herself I warrant thee: she is a rare actor: she acts a fit of the mother
the best of any one in England. Ha, ha, ha.

TRUMAN How canst thou be so cruel?

BELFOND JUNIOR What a devil should I do? If a man lies once
with a woman is he bound to do it for ever?

MRS TERMAGANT Oh, oh.

BELFOND JUNIOR Very well faith: admirably well acted.

MRS TERMAGANT Is it so? Devil, devil: I'll spoil your *point de venise* for you. [*flies at him*]

BELFOND JUNIOR Will you force me to make my footman turn you out?

Enter Footman.

FOOTMAN Sir, your father and your uncle are coming hither.

BELFOND JUNIOR S'death my father! 'Tis impossible.

FOOTMAN By heaven, 'tis true; they are coming up by this time.

BELFOND JUNIOR Look you Madam you may if you will ruin me; and put me out of all means of doing for you or your child: try me once more, and get into the bed and cover yourself with the quilt, or I am undone.

MRS TERMAGANT Villain, you deserve to be ruined: but I love my child too well.

TRUMAN For heaven's sake hide yourself in the bed quickly.

MRS TERMAGANT No no, I'll run into the closet.

BELFOND JUNIOR Death and hell! I am ruined: there's a young girl there; she'll make yet a worse uproar.

TRUMAN Peace, let me alone. Madam, whatever happens, ruin not yourself and child inevitably.

Enter Sir William Belfond, Sir Edward, and Servants.

SIR EDWARD BELFOND Ned, good morrow to thee.

BELFOND JUNIOR Your blessing, sir.

SIR EDWARD BELFOND Heaven bless thee. Here's one unexpected.

BELFOND JUNIOR My father! I beg your blessing, sir.

SIR WILLIAM BELFOND Heaven mend you; it can never bless you in the lewd course you are in.

BELFOND JUNIOR You are misinformed, sir; my courses are not so lewd as you imagine.

SIR WILLIAM BELFOND Do you see; I am misinformed: he'll give me the lie.

BELFOND JUNIOR I would first bite my tongue in pieces, and spit it at you: whatever little heats of youth I have been guilty of, I doubt not but in a short time to please you fully.

SIR EDWARD BELFOND Well said, Ned: I dare swear thou wilt.

SIR WILLIAM BELFOND Good brother Credulous; I thank heaven I am not so. You were not drunk last night with bullies, and roared and ranted, scoured, broke windows, beat the watch, broke open a house, and forced away a wench in Salisbury Court. This is a fine life. These he calls heats of youth!

BELFOND JUNIOR I was at home by eight o'clock last night, and supped at home; and never keep such company.

SIR WILLIAM BELFOND No no; you are not called Squire Belfond by the scoundrels your companions? 'Twas not you: no no.

BELFOND JUNIOR Not I upon my faith: I never keep such company, or do such actions: if any one should call me Squire I'd break his head: some rascal has usurped my name.

SIR EDWARD BELFOND Look you brother, what would you have? This must be some mistake.

SIR WILLIAM BELFOND What a devil! You believe this too? Ounds! You make me mad! Is there any of our name in England but ourselves? Does he think to flam me with a lie?

BELFOND JUNIOR I scorn a lie; 'tis the basest thing a gentleman can be guilty of: all my servants can testify I stirred not out last night.

TRUMAN I assure you, Sir, he was not abroad last night.

SIR WILLIAM BELFOND You assure me! Who are you? One of his hopeful companions! No, your clothes are not good enough, you may be his pimp.

TRUMAN You are the father of my friend, an old gentleman, and a little mad.

SIR WILLIAM BELFOND Old! Walk down; I'll try your youth: I'll fight with the bravest ruffian he keeps company with.

SIR EDWARD BELFOND Brother! Are you mad? Has the country robbed you of all good manners, and common sense?

SIR WILLIAM BELFOND I had a bout with two of your bullies in the Temple Walks.

BELFOND JUNIOR Whom does he mean? This is a gentleman of estate and quality; he has above £2000 a year.

SIR EDWARD BELFOND You are a madman: I am ashamed of you. Sir, I beseech you pardon my brother's passion, which transports him beyond civility.

BELFORD JUNIOR I know you will for my sake.

TRUMAN He is the father of my dearest friend; I shall be glad to serve him.

SIR EDWARD BELFOND Will you never be of age of discretion? For shame use me, your son, and everybody better.

SIR WILLIAM BELFOND Well, I must be run down like a tame puppy.

LUCIA [*within*] Murder, murder: help, help; ah, ah!

BELFOND JUNIOR O this damned she devil.

MRS TERMAGANT [*pulls Lucia out by the hair; they part 'em*] I'll make you an example: will you see him whether I will or no, you young whore!

SIR WILLIAM BELFOND Here's a son! Here's a fine son! Here's your breeding! Here's a pretty son! Here's a delicate son! Here's a dainty son!

SIR EDWARD BELFOND If he be mad, will you be madder?

BELFOND JUNIOR Turn out this she-bear; turn her out to the rabble!

MRS TERMAGANT Revenge, you villain, revenge.

                                  [*Exeunt Termagant and Footman*]

BELFOND JUNIOR Dear friend, prithee see this innocent girl safe in the chair, from that outrageous strumpet's fury.

                                  [*Exeunt Truman and Lucia*]

SIR WILLIAM BELFOND Here's a son, here's a son! Very well; make much of him: here's the effect of whoring.

BELFOND JUNIOR No Sir! 'tis the effect of not whoring: this rage is because I have cast her off.

SIR WILLIAM BELFOND Yes yes, for a younger; a sweet reformation! Let me not see your face, nor hear you speak; you will break my heart.

BELFOND JUNIOR Sir, the young girl was never here before; she brought me linen from the Exchange.

SIR WILLIAM BELFOND A fine bawd her mistress in the meantime.

BELFOND JUNIOR This furious wench coming in to rail at me for my leaving her, I was forced to put the other into that closet; and at your coming up, against my will, this run into the same closet.

SIR WILLIAM BELFOND Sirrah, most audacious rogue, do you sham me? Do you think you have your uncle to deal with? Avoid my presence sirrah: get you out sirrah.

BELFOND JUNIOR I am sorry I offended: I obey.

[*Exit Belfond Junior*]

SIR WILLIAM BELFOND I could have found in my heart to have cudgelled him.

SIR EDWARD BELFOND Shame of our family: you behave yourself so like a madman and a fool, you will be begged: these fits are more extravagant than anything he can be guilty of. Do you give your son the words of command you use to dogs?

SIR WILLIAM BELFOND Justify him, do! He's an excellent son! A very pretty son! A delicate son! A virtuous son! A discreet son! He is.

SIR EDWARD BELFOND Pray use me better, or I'll assure you, we must never see one another. Besides, I shall entail my estate for want of issue by this son here, upon another family, if you will treat me thus.

SIR WILLIAM BELFOND [*aside*] What says he? ⟨*to Sir Edward*⟩ Well brother I ha' done: his lewdness distracted me! O my poor boy in the country; I long to see him, the great support of my declining age.

SIR EDWARD BELFOND Let us calmly reason: what has your breeding made of him (with your patience) but a blockhead?

SIR WILLIAM BELFOND A blockhead! When he comes the world shall judge which of us has been the wiser in the education of a son: a blockhead? Why he knows a sample of any grain as well as e'er a fellow in the north: can handle a sheep or bullock as well as any one: knows his seasons of ploughing, sowing, harrowing, laying fallow: understands all sorts of manure: and ne'er a one that wears a head can wrong him in a bargain.

SIR EDWARD BELFOND A very pretty fellow, for a gentleman's baily.

SIR WILLIAM BELFOND For his own baily, and to be a rich –

SIR EDWARD BELFOND Swine, and live as nastily; and keep worse company than beasts in a forest.

SIR WILLIAM BELFOND He knows no vice, poor boy.

SIR EDWARD BELFOND He will have his turn to know it then; as sure as he will have the smallpox; and then he'll be fond on't, when his brother has left it.

SIR WILLIAM BELFOND I defy the omen: he never whores, nor drinks hard, but upon design, as driving a bargain, or so; and that I allow him.

SIR EDWARD BELFOND So: knavish and designing drunkenness you allow; but not good fellowship for mirth and conversation.

SIR WILLIAM BELFOND Now brother, pray what have you made your son good for, with your breeding you so much boast of? Let's hear that now: come on, let's hear.

SIR EDWARD BELFOND First, I bred him at Westminster School, till he was master of the Greek and Latin tongues; then I kept him at the University, where I instructed him to read the noble Greek and Roman authors.

SIR WILLIAM BELFOND Well, and what use can he make of the noble Greek and Latin, but to prate like a pedant, and show his parts over a bottle?

SIR EDWARD BELFOND To make a man fit for the conversation of learned gentlemen is one noble end of study: but those authors make him wiser and honester, Sir, to boot.

SIR WILLIAM BELFOND Wiser! Will he ever get sixpence, or improve or keep his estate by 'em?

SIR EDWARD BELFOND Mean notions: I made him well versed in history.

SIR WILLIAM BELFOND That's a pretty study indeed: how can there be a true history, when we see no man living is able to write truly the history of the last week?

SIR EDWARD BELFOND He by the way read natural philosophy, and had insight enough in the mathematics.

SIR WILLIAM BELFOND Natural philosophy! Knows nothing: nor would I give a fart for any mathematician, but a carpenter, bricklayer, measurer of land, or sailor.

SIR EDWARD BELFOND Some moderate skill in it will use a man to reason closely.

SIR WILLIAM BELFOND Very pretty: reason! Can he reason himself into six shillings by all this?

SIR EDWARD BELFOND He needs it not: but to go on; after three years I removed him from the university (lest he should have too strong a tincture of it) to the Temple; there I got a modest learned lawyer, of little practice, for want of impudence; and there are several such that want, while empty impudent fellows thrive and swagger at the Bar: this man I got to instruct my son in some old Common Law books, the statutes, and the best pleas of the crown, and the constitution of the old true English government.

SIR WILLIAM BELFOND Does he get a shilling by all this? But what a devil made you send him into France, to make an arrant vain coxcomb of him?

SIR EDWARD BELFOND There he did all his manly exercises; saw two campaigns; studied history; civil laws, and laws of commerce; the language he spoke well ere he went. He made the tour of Italy, and saw Germany, and the Low Countries, and returned well skilled in foreign affairs, and a complete accomplished English gentleman.

SIR WILLIAM BELFOND And to know nothing of his own estate, but how to spend it: my poor boy has travelled to better purpose: for he has travelled all about my lands, and knows every acre and nook, and the value of it: there's travel for you! Poor boy.

SIR EDWARD BELFOND And he enjoys so little of that estate he sees, as to be impatient for your death: I dare swear mine wishes my life, next to his own. I have made him a complete gentleman, fit to serve his country in any capacity.

SIR WILLIAM BELFOND Serve his country! Pox on his country: 'tis a country of such knaves, 'tis not worth the serving: all those who pretend to serve it, mean nothing but themselves. But amongst all things, how came you to make him a fiddler, always fluting or scraping? I had as lief hear a jew's-harp.

SIR EDWARD BELFOND I love music: besides I would have young gentlemen have as many helps to spend their time alone as can be; most of our youth are ruined by having time lie heavy on their hands, which makes them run into any base company to shun themselves.

SIR WILLIAM BELFOND And all this gentleman's education is come to drinking, whoring and debauchery.

Enter Servant to Sir William.

SERVANT Sir, Mr Scrapeall is at your attorney's chamber in the Temple, and desires to discourse you.

SIR WILLIAM BELFOND Brother, I must go: I shall tell you when I see you next, what is my business with him.

SIR EDWARD BELFOND Be sure to dine with me.

SIR WILLIAM BELFOND I will –   [*Exeunt*]

⟨SCENE II⟩

Enter Belfond Senior, Shamwell, Cheatly, Hackum,
Lolpoop, French Valet, two Footmen, at the George, in Whitefriars.

CHEATLY Now thou look'st like an heir indeed, my lad: when thou cam'st up thou hadst the scurvy phiz of a mere country put – He did thee a kindness that took thee for a chief constable.

SHAMWELL Now thou shinest, cousin, like a true Belfond! What £3000 a year entailed, and live like a butcher, or grazier, in the country?

CAPTAIN HACKUM Give you joy, noble Sir, now you look like a true gallant squire.

LOLPOOP Like a squire, like a puppy by th' mass: od's flesh, what will the awd man say; he'll be stark wood.*

BELFOND SENIOR Well, I was the fortunat'st man to light upon such true, such real friends: I had never known any breeding or gentility without you.

SHAMWELL You buried all your good parts in a sordid swinish life in the north.

BELFOND SENIOR My father kept me in ignorance, and would have made a very silly blockheadly put of me: why, I never heard a gentleman banter, or cut a sham in my life before I saw you, nor ever heard such ingenious discourse.

CAPTAIN HACKUM Nay, the world knows Mr Cheatly, and Mr

* stark wood: mad with rage.

Shamwell, are as complete gentlemen as ever came within the Friars: and yet we have as fine gentlemen as any in England; we have those here who have broke for a £100,000.

BELFOND SENIOR Well, I protest and vow, I am so very fine, I do not know where to look upon myself first: I don't think my Lord Mayor's son is finer.

CHEATLY He is a scoundrel compared to thee: there's ne'er a prig at Court out-shines thee. Thou shalt strut in the Park, where countesses shall be enamoured on thee.

BELFOND SENIOR I am overjoyed: I can stand no ground: my dear friend Cheatly! My sweet cousin Shamwell! Let me embrace such dear, such loving friends: I could grow to you, methinks, and stick here for ever. [*they embrace*]

LOLPOOP Ah! Dear loving dogs! They love him by'r lady, as a cat loves a mouse.

BELFOND SENIOR What's that you mutter, sirrah? Come hither, sirrah! You are finer than any squire in the country.

LOLPOOP Pox of finery, I say; yeow maken a meer ass, an owl o'mee: here are sleeves fit for nought but a miller to steule with when he takes toll: and damn'd cuffs here, one cannot dip one's meat ith sawce for them: odsflesh, give me my awd cloths againe; would I were a whome in my frock, dressing of my geldings; poor tits, they wanten me dearly, I warrant a.

BELFOND SENIOR Well, there's no making a whistle of a pig's tail; this puppy will never learn any breeding. Sirrah, behold me: here's rigging for you; here's a nab: you never saw such a one in your life.

CHEATLY A rum nab: it is a beaver* of £5.

BELFOND SENIOR Look you there blockhead.

LOLPOOP [*aside*] Look yeow there blockhead I say.

CAPTAIN HACKUM Let me see your porker: here's a porker; here's a tilter: Hah, ha. O how I could whip a prigster through the lungs! Ha, ha. [*thrusts at Lolpoop*]

CHEATLY It cost sixteen louis d'or† in Paris.

CAPTAIN HACKUM Ha, ha. [*he pushes towards Lolpoop*]

* beaver: a *chapeau de port*, an expensive and impressive hat.
† louis d'or: a gold coin, worth about seventeen shillings in England, in circulation from Louis XIII to Louis XVI.

LOLPOOP Hawd you, hawd you: and I tak kibbo★ I'st raddle the
bones o' thee; Ise tell a that: for aw th'art a captain mun.

BELFOND SENIOR Look sirrah, here's a show you rogue: here's a
sight of coal, darby, the ready, and the rhino, you rascal, you
understand me not; you loggerhead, you silly put, you understand me not: here are megs and smelts: I ne'er had such a sight
of my own in my life. Here are more megs and smelts, you rogue;
you understand me not.

LOLPOOP By'r lady not I: I understand not this south-country
speech not I.

BELFOND SENIOR Ah methinks I could tumble in 'em. But d'ye
hear put, put, put, sirrah. Here's a scout: what's o'clock? What's
o'clock sirrah. Here's a tatler; gold, all gold, you rogue. Look on
my finger sirrah, look here: here's a fumble, put, put: you don't
know what a fumble, a scout or a tatler is, you put.

LOLPOOP Fine sights for my awd master! Marry would I were
sent from constable to constable, and whipped whome again by'r
lady.

BELFOND SENIOR Let's whet: bring some wine. Come on: I
love a whet: pray let's huzza: I love huzzaing mightily: but
where's your lady, captain, and the blowing, that is to be my
natural, my convenient, my pure.

Enter Servant with bottles.

CAPTAIN HACKUM They're just coming in. Come Betty.

Enter Mrs Hackum and Mrs Margaret.

MRS HACKUM Come in Mrs Margaret, come.

MRS MARGARET I am so ashamed.

BELFOND SENIOR Madam, your servant; I am very much obliged
to your favours.

MRS HACKUM I shall be proud to do a gentleman, like you, any
service that lies in my power, as a gentlewoman.

BELFOND SENIOR O Lord, Madam, your most humble servant to
command: my pretty blowing let me kiss thee: thou shalt be my
natural: I must manage thee. She is a pure blowing. My pretty
rogue – how happy shall I be? Pox o' the country I say. Madam

★ kibbo: a stick, a Lancashire word.

Hackum, to testify my gratitude, I make bold to equip you with some megs, smelts, decuses and georges.

MRS HACKUM I am your faithful servant, and I shall be glad of any occasion, whereby to express how ready I am to serve any gentleman, or person of quality, as becomes a gentlewoman; and upon honour Sir, you shall never find me tardy.

CHEATLY Come on sirrah, fill up all the glasses; a health to this pretty lady.

BELFOND SENIOR Aye, and i'faith I'll drink it, pretty rogue.

SHAMWELL Let them be facers.

BELFOND SENIOR Facers! What are those? Nay, give the lady and the captain's lady too.

MRS MARGARET No, I cannot drink, I am not dry.

MRS HACKUM Give it me.

SHAMWELL There's a facer for you. [*drinks the glass clear off, and puts it to his face*]

BELFOND SENIOR Excellent adad! Come to our facers. [*all do the like*] It is the prettiest way of drinking: fill again, we'll have more facers. [*fiddles flourish without*] Ha boys! The musicians are come. Ha boys, we'll sing, dance, roar, fling the house out of the windows; and I will manage my pretty natural, my pure blowing here. Huzza: my dear friends, Shamwell and Cheatly, I am transported! My pretty natural: kiss me, kiss me. Huzza.

MRS MARGARET Nay puh, you do so ruffle one's things.

BELFOND SENIOR I'll ruffle thee more, my little rogue, before I have done with thee. Well, I shall never make you amends, my dear friends. Sirrah, Lolpoop, is not this better than the country, sirrah? Give the rogue a facer to my mistress. Come, fill about the facers. Come on, my lads, stand to't. Huzza. I vow 'tis the prettiest way of drinking, never stir!

Enter four Servants with four dishes of meat, who cross the stage.

CHEATLY So here's the prog, here's the dinner coming up; the cloth's laid in the next room: here's a noble dinner.

BELFOND SENIOR Ha boys, we'll sing and roar, and huzza, like devils.

Enter Sir William Belfond at the door.

Ounds! Who's here? My father! Lolpoop, Lolpoop, hide me: give me my Joseph.* Let's sneak into the next room.

SHAMWELL Death! What shall we do? This is the bully's father.

CHEATLY Let me alone: I warrant you.

CAPTAIN HACKUM This is the old fellow I had like to have had a rubbers with in the morning.

SIR WILLIAM BELFOND Is he fallen into these hands? Nay, then he's utterly lost: his estate is spent before he has it.

CHEATLY How now prig, what makes you come into our room?

SIR WILLIAM BELFOND I would speak with Squire Belfond.

CHEATLY Here's no such man.

SIR WILLIAM BELFOND O bully, are you there? And my ungracious kinsman too? Would you bring my son to the gallows! You most notorious seducer of young heirs, I know you too. I warrant you I'll keep my dear boy in the country far enough from your clutches. In short, I would speak with my rebellious Townson, who is here, and bespoke this great dinner.

CHEATLY [*bantering*] Why look you Sir, according to your assertion of things doubtful in themselves, you must be forced to grant that whatsoever may be, may also as well not be, in their own essential differences and degrees.

SIR WILLIAM BELFOND What stuff's this? Where's my son?

CHEATLY Your question consists of two terms: the one *ubi*, where: but of that I shall say nothing, because here is no son, nor anything belonging to you, to be the subject matter of debate, at this time; forasmuch as –

SIR WILLIAM BELFOND Do you hear me Sir, let me see my son; and offer to banter me, or sham me once more, and I will cut your throat, and cudgel your brace of cowards.

CHEATLY Nay, then 'tis time to take a course with you. Help, help; an arrest, an arrest; a baily, a baily.

CAPTAIN HACKUM and SHAMWELL An arrest, an arrest.

SIR WILLIAM BELFOND You dogs? Am I a baily?

CHEATLY You shall be used like one, you old prig. An arrest.

SIR WILLIAM BELFOND Impudent dogs! I must run, or I shall be pulled in pieces. Help, help, an arrest, an arrest.

* Joseph: an old-fashioned cloak.

All cry out 'an arrest:*' Drawers and some of the Rabble come in, and join with the cry, which gets into the street; there they cry out too: he joins the cry, and runs away: Cheatly, Shamwell, Hackum, Drawers follow him, and cry out,* 'Stop, stop, a baily'.

CHEATLY, SHAMWELL, HACKUM [*in the street*] Stop, stop, a baily, a baily.

> [*Sir William runs, the rabble pursue him across the stage*]

ACT THREE

SCENE I

Enter Mrs Termagant and her Brother.

MRS TERMAGANT As I told you, I have had a child by him; he is my husband by contract; and casts me off: has dishonoured me, and made me infamous. Shall you think to game and bully about the Town, and not vindicate the honour of your family?

BROTHER No man shall dare to dishonour our family.

Enter Belfond Junior.

MRS TERMAGANT If you do not cut his throat, you'll be kicked up and down for a damned coward: and besides you shall never see a penny of mine more.

BROTHER I'll fight him an he be above ground.

MRS TERMAGANT There, there's the traitor, walking before his uncle's door: be sure dispatch him: on, I'll withdraw. [*Exit*]

BROTHER Do you hear Sir, do you know Mrs Termagant?

BELFOND JUNIOR What makes you ask such a familiar question Sir?

BROTHER I am her brother.

BELFOND JUNIOR Perhaps so: well, I do? What then Sir?

BROTHER Ours is as ancient a family as any in England, though perhaps unfortunate at present: the Termagants came in with the Conqueror.

BELFOND JUNIOR It may be so: I am no herald.

BROTHER And do you think you shall dishonour this family, and debauch my sister unchastized? You are contracted to her, and have lain with her.

BELFOND JUNIOR Look you Sir, I see what you would be at: she's mad, and puts you upon this: let me advise you, 'tis a foolish quarrel.

BROTHER You debauched her, and have ruined her.

BELFOND JUNIOR 'Tis false; the silliest coxcombly beau in Town had the first of her.

BROTHER You have had a child by her.

BELFOND JUNIOR Then I have added one to your ancient family

that came in with the Normans: prithee do not provoke me to take away one from it.

BROTHER You are contracted to her; and if you will marry her I will save your life.

BELFOND JUNIOR 'Tis a lie; I am not contracted to her: begone, urge me no more.

BROTHER Draw.

BELFOND JUNIOR Have at you. [*Belfond strikes up his heels, and disarms him*]

Enter Sir Edward Belfond.

SIR EDWARD BELFOND Hold, hold: O my son, my son! What's the matter? My dear son, art thou not hurt? Let me see.

BELFOND JUNIOR No Sir, not at all, dear Sir. Here take your sword, and begone: next time you come to trouble me, I'll cut your throat.   [*Exit Brother*]

SIR EDWARD BELFOND What's the matter, dear Ned? This is about some wench I warrant.

BELFOND JUNIOR 'Tis a brother of that furious wench you saw Sir; her violent love is converted to hatred.

SIR EDWARD BELFOND You young fellows will never get knowledge but at your own cost; the precepts of the old weigh nothing with you.

BELFOND JUNIOR Your precepts have been ever sacred to me; and so shall your example be henceforward: you are the best of men; the best of fathers: I have as much honour for you as I can have for human nature: and I love you ten thousand times above my life.

SIR EDWARD BELFOND Dear Ned, thou art the greatest joy I have: and believe thy father, and thy friend, there's nothing but anxiety in vice: I am not strait-laced; but when I was young, I ne'er knew anything gotten by wenching, but duels, claps, and bastards: and every drunken fit is a short madness, that cuts off a good part of life.

BELFOND JUNIOR You have reason★ Sir, and shall ever be my oracle hereafter.

★ you have reason: you're right. *Vous avez raison,* a phrase then regarded as somewhat affected by older folk.

SIR EDWARD BELFOND 'Tis time now to take up, and think of being something in the world: see then, my son, though thou shouldst not be over-busy, to side with parties and with factions, yet that thou takest a care to make some figure in the world, and to sustain that part thy fortune, nature, and thy education fit thee for.

BELFOND JUNIOR Your wise advice I'll strive to follow: but I must confess, I am most passionately in love, and am with your consent, resolved to marry: though I will perish ere I do't without it.

SIR EDWARD BELFOND Be sure to know the humour of the woman; you run a mighty hazard: but if you be valiant enough to venture, (which, I must confess, I never was) I'll leave it to your own choice: I know you have so much honour, you will do nothing below yourself.

BELFOND JUNIOR I doubt not of your approbation; but till I can be sure of obtaining her, pardon me if I conceal her name.

Enter Sir William Belfond.

SIR EDWARD BELFOND Your father comes, retire a little within hearing, till I soften him somewhat: he is much moved, as he always is, I think.   [⟨*Belfond Junior*⟩ *retires*]

SIR WILLIAM BELFOND Now brother, as I was saying, I can convince you, your son, your darling, whom you long have fostered in his wickedness, is become the most profligate of all rascals.

SIR EDWARD BELFOND Still upon this subject.

SIR WILLIAM BELFOND 'Tis very well; my mouth must be stopped, and your ears: 'tis wondrous well. But I have had much ado to escape with life, from him, and his notorious fellow rogues: as I told you when I had found that the rogue was with his wicked associates, at the George in Whitefriars; when they saw I was resolved to see my son, and was rough with 'em, Cheatly and his rogues set up a cry against me: 'An arrest! A baily: an arrest': the mobile, and all the rakehells in the house, and thereabout the streets assembled: I run, and they had a fair course after me into Fleet Street. Thanks to the vigour I have left, my heels have saved my life: your infamous rogue would have suffered me to have been sacrificed to the rabble.

SIR EDWARD BELFOND Ha ha ha, very pretty i'faith; it runs very well: can you tell it over again think you?

SIR WILLIAM BELFOND Ounds! Am I become your scorn? Your laughter?

SIR EDWARD BELFOND Ned, you hear all this?

Belfond Junior appears.

BELFOND JUNIOR Yes; and am distracted to know the meaning of it.

SIR WILLIAM BELFOND Vile patricide! Are you gotten here before me? You are monstrous nimble Sir.

BELFOND JUNIOR By all the powers of heaven! I never was at the George in my life.

SIR WILLIAM BELFOND O then they stay for you, you have not yet been there; you'll lose your dinner, 'tis served up – vile wretch.

BELFOND JUNIOR All this is cross purposes to me: I came to my uncle's house from my own lodgings immediately when you were pleased to banish me your presence, and here have been ever since.

SIR WILLIAM BELFOND Nay, he that will be a thorough villain, must be a complete liar: were not you even now with your associate rascals at the George?

BELFOND JUNIOR No, by heaven! Nor was I ever in the company of any of that gang: I know their infamy too well, to be acquainted with their persons.

SIR WILLIAM BELFOND I am not drunk, nor mad; but you will make me one of 'em.

BELFOND JUNIOR These rascals have gotten somebody to personate me; and are undoubtedly carrying on some cheat in my name.

SIR EDWARD BELFOND Brother it must be.

SIR WILLIAM BELFOND Yes, yes, no doubt it must be so: and I must be in a dream all this while, I must!

SIR EDWARD BELFOND You say yourself, you did not see my son there?

SIR WILLIAM BELFOND No, he was too nimble for me, and got out some back way, to be here before me; so to face down the truth.

BELFOND JUNIOR I'll instantly go thither, and discover this imposture, that I may suffer no longer for the faults of others.

SIR EDWARD BELFOND Dine first: my dinner's ready.

BELFOND JUNIOR Your pardon Sir, I will go instantly: I cannot rest till I have done myself right.

SIR EDWARD BELFOND Let's in, and discourse of this matter: brother, I must say this, I never took him in a lie, since he could speak.

SIR WILLIAM BELFOND Took him: no, nor ever will take him in anything.

SIR EDWARD BELFOND Let's in – and send your own man with him.

SIR WILLIAM BELFOND It shall be so, though I am convinced already. Is there any of the name but you, and I, and my two sons in England?

BELFOND JUNIOR Be pleased to send my footmen out to me, Sir.

SIR EDWARD BELFOND Have a care of a quarrel, and bringing the Alsatians about your ears. Come brother.

[Exeunt Sir Edward and Sir William]

Enter Lucia running, Termagant pursuing her.

LUCIA Help, help, help.

MRS TERMAGANT Now I have found you, you little whore – I'll make you an example.

LUCIA O Lord! Are you here! Save me, save me, this barbarous woman threatens to murder me for your sake.

BELFOND JUNIOR Save thee, dear miss: that I would at the peril of my life: no danger should make me quit thee, cannons, nor bombs.

MRS TERMAGANT Damned false fellow: I'll take a time to slit her nose.

LUCIA O heaven! She'll kill me.

BELFOND JUNIOR Thou devil! In thy properest shape of furious, and malicious woman: resolve to leave off this course this moment, or by heaven I'll lay thee fast in Bedlam: had'st thou fifty brothers, I'd fight 'em all, in defence of this dear pretty miss.

LUCIA Dear kind creature! This sweet love of thine, methinks does make me valiant, and I fear her not so much.

Enter Roger, and his two Footmen.

BELFOND JUNIOR Dear pretty miss: I'll be thy safeguard.

MRS TERMAGANT Thou falsest, basest of thy sex: look to see thy child sent thee in pieces, baked in a pie, for so I will.

BELFOND JUNIOR Though thou hatest everything living besides thyself; yet thou hast too much tenderness for thy own person to bring it to the gallows: offer to follow us one step, and I'll set the rabble upon thee: come my dear child.

[*Exeunt Belfond Junior and Lucia*]

MRS TERMAGANT Thou shalt be dogged; and I'll know who she is: O revenge! Revenge! If thou dost not exceed, thou equall'st all the ecstasies of love.   [*Exit Termagant*]

⟨SCENE II⟩

Enter Cheatly and Shamwell.

CHEATLY Thus far our matters go swimmingly: our squire is as debauched, and prodigal, as we can wish.

SHAMWELL I told you, all England could not afford an heir like this for our purpose, but we must keep him always hot.

CHEATLY That will be easy; we made him so devilish drunk the first two or three days, the least bumper will warm his addle head afresh at any time: he paid a great fine; and may sit at a little rent: I must be gone for a moment; our Suffolk heir is nabbed, for a small business; and I must find him some sham-bail: see the captain performs his charge.   [*Exit*]

Enter Hackum.

SHAMWELL Here he comes. See, Captain, you make that blockhead drunk, and do as we directed.

CAPTAIN HACKUM He's almost drunk, and we are in readiness for him; the squire is retired with his natural, so fond.

SHAMWELL 'Tis well; about your business: I'll be with you soon.   [*Exit Shamwell*]

Enter Lolpoop.

CAPTAIN HACKUM Come on, Mr Lolpoop; you and I'll be merry by ourselves.

LOLPOOP I must needs say Captain, yeow are a civil gentleman, but yeow han given me so many bumpers: I am meet drunken already.

CAPTAIN HACKUM Come on, I warrant you: here's a bumper to the squire's lady.

LOLPOOP With all my heart.

Enter Betty.

CAPTAIN HACKUM O Mrs Betty, art thou come? I sent for this pretty rogue to keep you company: she's as pretty a company-keeper as any's in the Friars.

LOLPOOP Od's flesh, what should I do in company with gentle-women: 'tis not for such fellee's as I.

CAPTAIN HACKUM Have courage man: you shall have her; and never want such a one while I am your friend.

LOLPOOP O Lord I! Don yeow know what yeow saen.

MRS BETTY A proper, handsome gentleman, I swear.

LOLPOOP Who I, no, no; what done yeow mean forsooth?

MRS BETTY I vow, I have not seen a handsomer: so proper, so well shaped!

LOLPOOP O Lord I! I! Yeow jeern me naw.

CAPTAIN HACKUM Why dont you salute her, man?

LOLPOOP Who I? By the mass, I dare not be so bold: what I kiss such a fine gentlewoman?

CAPTAIN HACKUM Kiss, kiss her man: this Town affords us such everywhere? You'll hate the country when you see a little more: kiss her I say.

LOLPOOP I am so hala:* I am ashamed.

MRS BETTY What must I do it to you then?

LOLPOOP O rare! By th' mass! Whoo kisses daintily: and who has a breath like a caw.

CAPTAIN HACKUM Come t'other bumper: to her health let this be: here's to you.

LOLPOOP Thanka forsooth and yeow pleasen. [*drinks to her*]

MRS BETTY Yes, anything that you do, will please me.

LOLPOOP Captain, Captain. What done yeow leave me?

                    [*Hackum steals out and leaves them together*]

    * hala: lean, meagre, a Lancashire word.

MRS BETTY What are you afraid of me?

LOLPOOP Nay, by'r lady: I am ashamed, who's farinely* a pratty lass! Marry.

MRS BETTY A handsome man, and ashamed! [*she edges nearer to him*]

LOLPOOP Who I, a handsome mon! Nay, nay.

MRS BETTY A lovely man, I vow: I cannot forbear kissing you.

LOLPOOP O dear: 'tis your goodness: od's flesh, whoo loves me! Who'll make me stark wood e'en naw: an yeow kissen me, by'r lady, I's kiss yeow.

MRS BETTY What care I?

LOLPOOP Looka there naw! Waunds, whoo's a dainty lass, pure white and red: and most of the London lasses are pure white and red: welly aw alike; and I had her in some nook. Od's flesh, I say no more.

MRS BETTY I'll stay no longer, farewell.   [*She retires*]

LOLPOOP Nay, I's not leave a soo: marry whoo's a gallant lass.

[*Exit following her*]

Enter Hackum.

CAPTAIN HACKUM So, he's caught: this will take him off from teasing his master with his damned good counsel.

Enter Cheatly, and Shamwell.

CHEATLY I have sent our Alsatian attorney, and as substantial bail as can be wished for the redemption of our Suffolk caravan; he's ripe for another judgment, he begins to want the ready much.

SHAMWELL Scrapeall is provided for him: how now Captain, what's become of your blockhead?

CAPTAIN HACKUM He's nibbling at the bait: he'll swallow presently.

CHEATLY But hark you, Shamwell! I have chosen the subtlest and handsomest wench about this town for the great fortune I intend to bestow this kinsman of yours upon: 'tis Mrs Termagant, his brother's cast mistress, who resents her being left to that degree, that though she meditates all the revenge, besides, that woman's nature is capable of against him: yet her heart leaped for

* farinely: very, exceedingly, also a Lancashire word.

joy at this design of marrying his elder brother: if it were for
nothing but to plague the younger, and take place of his wife.

SHAMWELL I have seen her: she will personate a Town lady of
quality admirably, and be as haughty and impertinent as the best
of 'em: is the lodging, and plate, and things ready for her?

CHEATLY It is, she comes there this afternoon; she's set her hand
to a good swinging judgment; and thou and I will divide my lad:
and now, all we have to do, is to preserve him to ourselves from
any other correspondence, and at downright enmity with his
father, and brother: and we must keep him continually hot, as
they do a glass-house, or our work will go backward.

Enter Belfond Senior, Mrs Margaret, Mrs Hackum,
and his Servants.

BELFOND SENIOR O my dear friend and cousin; tread upon my
neck: make me your footstool, you have made me a happy man
to know plenty and pleasure, good company, good wine, music,
fine women: Mrs Hackum and I have been at bumpers hand to
fist: here's my pretty natural, my dear pretty rogue: adad, she's a
rare creature, a delicious creature! And between you and I, dear
friend, she has all her goings as well as e'er a blowing in Christen-
dom: dear Madam Hackum, I am infinitely obliged to you.

MRS HACKUM I am glad, Sir, she gives your worship content, Sir.

BELFOND SENIOR Content: ah my pretty rogue! Pox o' the
country, I say, Captain, Captain here: let me equip you with a
quid.

CAPTAIN HACKUM Noble squire: I am your spaniel dog.

BELFOND SENIOR Pox o' the country, I say: the best team of
horses my father has, shall not draw me thither again.

SHAMWELL Be firm to your resolution, and thou'lt be happy.

CHEATLY If you meet either your father, or brother, or any from
those prigsters, stick up thy countenance, or thou art ruined, my
son of promise, my brisk lad in remainder, when one of 'em
approaches thee, we'll all pull down our hats, and cry 'bow-wow'.

BELFOND SENIOR I warrant you; I am hardened, I knew my
brother in the country, but they shan't sham me, they shall find
me a smoky thief: I vow 'twill be a very pretty way: bow-wow.
I warrant thee I'll do 't.

Enter Belfond Junior, two Footmen, and Roger.

SHAMWELL Who the devil's here! Your brother! Courage.

CHEATLY Courage, be rough and haughty my bumpkin.

BELFOND SENIOR Hey, where are all my servants: call 'em in. [*Captain calls 'em*]

BELFOND JUNIOR Who is that in this house here, who usurps my name, and is called Squire Belfond?

BELFOND SENIOR One who is called so without usurping. Bowwow.

BELFOND JUNIOR Brother, death do I dream! Can I trust my senses! Is this my brother?

BELFOND SENIOR Aye, aye, I know I am. Transmographied: but I am your very brother, Ned.

BELFOND JUNIOR Could you be so unkind, to come to Town, and not see your nearest kindred, your uncle, and myself?

BELFOND SENIOR I would not come to disgrace you, till my equipage was all ready. Hey, La Marr, is my coach at the gate next to the Green Dragon?

VALET *Oui monsieur.*

BELFOND SENIOR But I was resolved to give you a visit tomorrow morning.

BELFOND JUNIOR I should have been glad to have seen you anywhere but here.

BELFOND SENIOR But here! Why 'tis as good a tavern, as any's in Town. Sirrah, fill some bumpers: here brother, here's a facer to you: we'll huzza, call in the fiddlers.

BELFOND JUNIOR I am struck with astonishment: not all Ovid's *Metamorphoses* can show such a one as this.

BELFOND SENIOR I see you wonder at my change: what would you never have a man learn breeding adad? Should I always be kept a country bubble, a caravan, a mere put. I am brave and boozy.

BELFOND JUNIOR S'life! He has got the cant too.

BELFOND SENIOR I shall be clear by and by: t'other bumper, brother.

BELFOND JUNIOR No: I'll drink no more: I hate drinking between meals.

BELFOND SENIOR O Lord! O Lord! Hate drinking between meals! What company do you keep? But 'tis all one. Here brother, pray salute this pretty rogue: I manage her, she is my natural, my pure blowing: I am resolved to be like a gentleman and keep, brother.

BELFOND JUNIOR [*aside*] A thorough-paced Whitefriars man! ⟨*to his brother*⟩ I never refuse to kiss a pretty woman. [*salutes her*]

BELFOND SENIOR This is Mrs Hackum: I am much obliged to her: pray salute her.

BELFOND JUNIOR What a pox! Will he make me kiss the bawd too. [*salutes her*]

BELFOND SENIOR Brother, now pray know these gentlemen here; they are the prettiest wits that are in Town: and between you and I brother, brave gallant fellows, and the best friends I ever had in my life: this is Mr Cheatly, and this my cousin Shamwell.

BELFOND JUNIOR I know 'em, and am acquainted with their worth.

CHEATLY Your humble servant, sweet Sir.

SHAMWELL Your servant, cousin.

BELFOND SENIOR And this is my dear friend Captain Hackum: there is not a braver fellow under the sun.

BELFOND JUNIOR By heaven, a downright Alsatian!

BELFOND SENIOR Come musicians, strike up; and sing the catch the captain gave you, and we'll all join i'faith. We can be merry brother, and we can roar.

CAPTAIN HACKUM 'Tis a very pretty magnanimous military business upon the victory in Hungary.*

> Hark, how the Duke of Lorraine comes,
> The brave victorious soul of war;
> With trumpets and with kettle-drums,
> Like thunder rolling from afar.
>
> On the left-wing the conquering horse
> The brave Bavarian duke does lead;

* the victory in Hungary: a reference to the Battle of Harkány, near Mohács, where the Turks were defeated in 1687.

These heroes with united force,
Fill all the Turkish host with dread.

Their bright caparisons behold;
Rich habits, streamers, shining arms,
The glittering steel and burnished gold;
The pomp of war with all its charms.

With solemn march, and fatal pace,
They bravely on the foe press on;
The cannons roar, the shot takes place,
Whilst smoke and dust obscure the sun.

The horses neigh, the soldiers shout,
And now the furious bodies join,
The slaughter rages all about,
And men in groans their blood resign.

The weapons clash, the roaring drum,
With clangour of the trumpet's sound,
The howls and yells of men o'ercome,
And from the neighbouring hills rebound.

Now, now the infidels give place,
Then all in routs they headlong fly,
Horses in dust pursue the chase,
While deafening clamours rend the sky.

BELFOND SENIOR You see brother, what company I keep: what's
the matter you are melancholy.

BELFOND JUNIOR I am not a little troubled brother, to find you
in such cursed company.

BELFOND SENIOR Hold brother, if you love your life: they are
all stout; but that same captain has killed his five men.

BELFOND JUNIOR Stout say you? This fellow Cheatly is the
most notorious rascal and cheat that ever was out of a dungeon;
this kinsman a most silly bubble first, and afterwards a betrayer
of young heirs, of which they have not ruined less than two

hundred, and made 'em run out their estates before they came to 'em.

BELFOND SENIOR Brother, do you love your life? The captain's a lion!

BELFOND JUNIOR An ass is he not? He is a ruffian, and a cock-bawd to that hen.

CHEATLY If you were not the brother to my dearest friend, I know what my honour would prompt me to. [*walks in a huff*]

SHAMWELL My dear cousin, thou shalt now find how entirely I am thine: my honour will not let me strike thy brother.

CAPTAIN HACKUM But that the punctilios of honour are sacred to me; which tell me nothing can provoke me against the brother of my noble friend, I had whipped him through the lungs ere this.

BELFOND SENIOR Well, never man met with such true, such loving friends.

BELFOND JUNIOR Look you brother, will this convince you, that you are fallen into the hands of fools, knaves, scoundrels, and cowards.

BELFOND SENIOR Fools! Nay there I am sure you are out: they are all deep, they are very deep and sharp; sharp as needles, adad; the wittiest men in England. Here's Mr Cheatly in the first place shall sham and banter with you, or anyone you will bring for £500 of my money.

BELFOND JUNIOR Rascally stuff; fit for no places but Ram Alley, or Pie Corner.

BELFOND SENIOR Persuade me to that: they are the merriest companions, and the truest friends to me: 'tis well for you adad, that they are so; for they are all of 'em as stout as Hector.

BELFOND JUNIOR This is most amazing.

SHAMWELL Did I not tell you he would envy your condition; and be very angry with us that put you into't.

CHEATLY He must needs be a kind brother: we prove ourselves your true friends; and have that respect for your blood, that we will let none of it out, where'er we meet it upon any cause.

BELFOND SENIOR You see brother, how their love prevails over their valour.

BELFOND JUNIOR Their valour! Look you brother, [*kicks Cheatly and Shamwell*] here's valour.

CHEATLY I understand honour and breeding, besides I have been let blood today.

SHAMWELL Nothing shall make me transgress the rules of honour I say.

BELFOND JUNIOR Here! Where are you? Sirrah; kill-cow. [*takes Hackum by the nose, and leads him*]

CAPTAIN HACKUM 'Tis no matter; I know honour: I know punctilios to a hair. You owe your life to your brother: besides, I am to be second to a dear friend, and preserve my vigour for his service: but for all that, were he not your brother –

BELFOND JUNIOR Will not this convince you, brother, of their cowardice?

BELFOND SENIOR No, I think not; for I am sure they are valiant; this convinces me of their respect and friendship to me: my best friends, let me embrace you: a thousand thanks to you.

BELFOND JUNIOR ⟨*aside*⟩ I will redeem him yet from these rascals if I can: ⟨*to his brother*⟩ you are upon the brink of ruin, if you go not off with me, and reconcile yourself to my father; I'll undertake it upon good terms.

BELFOND SENIOR No, I thank you; I'll see no father; he shall use me no more like a dog: he shall put upon me no longer. Look you Sir, I have ready, rhino, coal, darby; look here Sir!

BELFOND JUNIOR Dear brother, let me persuade you to go along with me.

BELFOND SENIOR You love me! And use my best friends thus? Ne'er stir, I desire none of your company: I'll stick to my friends: I look upon what you have done as an affront to me.

CAPTAIN HACKUM No doubt it is so.

SHAMWELL That's most certain; you are in the right, cousin.

CHEATLY We love you but too well, that angers him.

BELFOND JUNIOR Well, I shall take my leave: you are in your cups: you will wish you had heard me. Rogues, I shall take a course with you.

BELFOND SENIOR Rogues! They scorn your words.

BELFOND JUNIOR Fare you well.

BELFOND SENIOR Fare you well Sir, and you be at that sport.

BELFOND JUNIOR Roger, do not discover him to my father yet; I'll talk with him cool in a morning first; perhaps I may redeem him.

ROGER I'll do as you'll have me.

[*Exeunt Belfond Junior, Roger and two Footmen*]

BELFOND SENIOR So now we are free. Dear friends, I never can be grateful enough: but 'tis late, I must show my new coach: come ladies.   [*Exeunt*]

⟨SCENE III⟩

Enter Attorney and Lucia.

ATTORNEY How now, daughter Lucia, where hast thou been?

LUCIA I have been at evening prayers at Saint Bride's,* and am going home through the Temple.

ATTORNEY Thou art my good girl.

Enter Mrs Termagant.

LUCIA O heaven! Who's here!

ATTORNEY What's the matter?

LUCIA I am taken ill on the sudden: I'll run home.

MRS TERMAGANT Stay, stay; thou wicked author of my misfortune.

ATTORNEY How's this? Stay Lucia! What mean you Madam? The girl's strangely disordered.

LUCIA O heaven! I am utterly ruined, beyond redemption.

MRS TERMAGANT Is she your daughter Sir.

ATTORNEY She is.

MRS TERMAGANT Then hear my story: I am contracted with all the solemnity that can be to Mr Belfond, the merchant's son; and for this wicked girl he has lately cast me off: and this morning I went to his lodging, to enquire a reason of his late carriage to me, I found there in his closet this young shameless creature, who had been in bed with him.

ATTORNEY O heaven and earth! Is this true, huswife?

LUCIA O Lord I: I never saw the gentleman nor her in my life: oh, she's a confident thing!

* Saint Bride's: a church on the south side of Fleet Street. The building destroyed in the Great Fire of London was replaced by one designed by Sir Christopher Wren.

MRS TERMAGANT May all the judgments due to perjury fall on me, if this be not true: I tore her by the hair, and pommelled her to some tune; 'till that inhuman wretch Belfond turned me out of doors, and sent her away in a chair.

LUCIA Oh, wicked creature! Are you not afraid the earth should open, and swallow you up? As I hope to be saved, I never saw her!

MRS TERMAGANT Though young in years, yet old in impudence; did I not pursue thee since in the street, till you run into Belfond's arms just before his father's house? Or I had marked thee for a young whore.

LUCIA As I hope to live, Sir, 'tis all false, every word and tittle of it: I know not what she means.

ATTORNEY Have I bestowed so much, and taken so much care in thy education, to have no other fruit but this?

LUCIA O Lord Sir! Why will you believe this wicked woman?

ATTORNEY No, young impudence! I believe you. What made you ready to swoon at the sight of this lady, but your guilt?

LUCIA She mistakes me for some other, as she did today when she pursued me to have killed me; which made me tremble at the sight of her now.

ATTORNEY And yet you never saw her before! I am convinced. Go, wicked wretch, go home: this news will kill thy mother. I'll to my chamber, and follow thee.

LUCIA But if I ever see her, or you either, to be locked from my dear Belfond,★ I shall deserve whatever you can do to me. ⟨*Exit*⟩

ATTORNEY Madam, I beseech you make as few words as you can of this.

MRS TERMAGANT I had much rather for my own honour have concealed it. But I shall say no more, provided you will keep her from him.

ATTORNEY I warrant you, Madam, I'll take a course with her. Your servant.   [*Exit*]

Enter Cheatly.

CHEATLY Madam, your most humble servant: you see I am punctual to my word.

★ The sense is obscure, but probably means if she ever allows anyone to keep her from Belfond.

MRS TERMAGANT You are, sir.

CHEATLY Come, madam, your lodging, furniture, and everything are ready, let's lose no time: I'll wait on you thither, where we will consult about our affairs.

MRS TERMAGANT Come on; it is a rare design; and, if it succeeds, I shall sufficiently be revenged on my ungrateful devil.

CHEATLY I'll warrant the success.   [*Exeunt*]

⟨SCENE IV⟩

Enter Isabella and Teresia.

ISABELLA We must be very careful of this book: my uncle, or our dame gouvernante will burn it if they find it.

TERESIA We cannot have a pleasant or a witty book, but they serve it so: my father loads us with books, such as *The Trial of Man, in the Isle of Man, or Manshire: A Treatise on Sabbath-breakers:* and *Health out-drinking, or Life out-healthing Wretches: A Caustic, or Corrosive, for a Seared Conscience.*

ISABELLA *A Sovereign Ointment for a Wounded Soul: A Cordial for a Sick Sinner: The Nothingness of Good Works: Waxed Boot-Grace, for the Sussex Ways of Affliction*; and a deal of such stuff. But all novels, romances, or poetry, except Quarles and Withers, are an abomination. Well, this is a jewel, if we can keep it.

Enter Ruth behind them.

ISABELLA Anger, in hasty words or blows,
Itself discharges on our foes;
And sorrow too, finds some relief
In tears, which wait upon our grief:
Thus every passion, but fond love,
Unto its own redress does move.

TERESIA 'Tis sweet poetry; there is a pleasing charm in all he writes.

RUTH [*she snatches the book*] Yea, there is a charm of Satan's in it: 'tis vanity and darkness, this book hateth, and is contrary to the light: and ye hate the light.

ISABELLA That's much: and this evening a little before night, thou blamedst us for looking out of the window, and threatened to shut the painted sashes.

TERESIA Now if thou shut'st those: thou hatest the light, and not we.

RUTH Look thee Teresia: thou art wanton, and so is thy cousin Isabella: ye seek temptation: you look out of the casements to pick and cull young men; whereby to feed the lust of the eye: ye may not do it. And look thee Isabel, and Teresia, if you open the casements once more, I will place ye in the back rooms, and lock the fore rooms up.

TERESIA We will obey thee, Ruth.

ISABELLA We will not resist thy power: but prithee leave us that book.

RUTH No, it is wanton and treateth of love: I will instantly commit it to the flames.   [*Exit*]

ISABELLA Shame on this old wall-eyed hypocrite: she is the strictest sort of gaoler.

TERESIA We are as narrowly looked to, as if we had been clapped up for treason, we are kept from books, pen, ink, and paper.

ISABELLA Well, it is a most painful life to dissemble constantly.

TERESIA 'Tis well we are often alone, to unbend to one another, one had as good be a player, and act continually else.

ISABELLA I can never persuade myself, that religion can consist in scurvy out-of-fashion clothes, stiff constrained behaviour, and sour countenances.

TERESIA A tristful aspect, looking always upon one's nose, with a face full of spiritual pride.

ISABELLA And when one walks abroad, not to turn one's head to the right or left, but hold it straight forward, like an old blind mare.

TERESIA True religion must make one cheerful, and affect one with the most ravishing joy which must appear in the face too.

ISABELLA My good mother had the government, and brought me up to better things, as thy good aunt did thee.

TERESIA But we can make no use of our education under this tyranny.

ISABELLA If we should sing or dance, 'twere worse than murder.

TERESIA But of all things: why do they make such a stir to keep us from the conversation of mankind: sure there must be more in it, than we can imagine; and that makes one have more mind to try.

ISABELLA Thou hast been so unquiet in thy sleep of late, and so given to sigh, and get alone when thou art awake: I fancy thou dost imagine somewhat of it.

TERESIA Ah rogue, and I have observed the same in thee: canst thou not guess at love: come, confess, and I'll tell all.

ISABELLA Sometimes in my dreams, methinks I am in love, then a certain youth comes to me; and I grow chill, and pant, and feel a little pain: but 'tis the prettiest thing methinks: and then I wake and blush, and am afraid.

TERESIA Very pretty: and when I am awake, when I see one gentleman, methinks I could look through him: and my heart beats, beats like the drums in the camp.

ISABELLA I dare not ask who 'tis, for fear it should be my man; for there are two come often to our church, that stare at us continually, and one of them is he.

TERESIA I have observed 'em: one, who sat by us at church, knew 'em by their names: I am for one of 'em too.

ISABELLA I will remember it.

TERESIA If it be my man thou lik'st, I'll kill thee.

ISABELLA And if thou lov'st my man, we must not live together.

TERESIA Name him.

ISABELLA Do thou name first.

TERESIA Let's write their names.

ISABELLA Agree: we each have a black-lead pen. [*they write their papers and give 'em to one another at which they both speak together and start*]

TERESIA Truman, mercy on me!

ISABELLA Belfond, O heavens!

TERESIA What's this I see! Would I were blind.

ISABELLA O my Teresia!

TERESIA Get thee from me.

ISABELLA 'Tis as it should be; I wrote the wrong name, on purpose to discover who was your man more clearly; the other's my beloved. Belfond's my heart's delight.

TERESIA Say'st thou so my girl! Good wits jump. I had the same thought with thee. Now 'tis out, Truman for me; and methinks they keep such a staring at us, if we contrive to meet 'em, we need not despair.

ISABELLA Nay, they come not for devotion, that's certain; I see that in their eyes: O that they were ordained to free us from this odious jail.

Enter Ruth, and Truman disguised.

RUTH Go into your chamber; here is a man cometh about business: ye may not see him.

TERESIA We go: come cousin.

RUTH Come friend: let us retire also.   [*Exeunt*]

ACT FOUR

SCENE I

Belfond Junior, and Lucia.

LUCIA I never more must see the face of a relation.

BELFOND JUNIOR I warrant thee, my pretty rogue, I'll put thee into that condition the best of all thy kindred shall visit thee, and make their court to thee; thou shalt spark it in the boxes, shine at the Park, and make all the young fellows in the Town run mad for thee: thou shalt never want, while I have anything.

LUCIA I could abandon all the world for thee; if I could think that thou wouldst love me always.

BELFOND JUNIOR Thou hast so kindly obliged me, I shall never cease to love thee.

LUCIA Pray heaven I do not repent of it: you were kind to Mrs Termagant; and sure it must be some barbarous usage, which thus provokes her now to all this malice.

BELFOND JUNIOR She was debauched by the most nauseous coxcomb, the most silly beau and shape about the Town; and had cuckolded him with several before I had her: she was indeed handsome, but the most froward, ill-natured creature; always murdering or scolding, perpetually jealous and exceptious, ever thinking to work her ends by hectoring and daring.

LUCIA Indeed! Was she such a one? I am sure, you were the first that ever had my heart, and you shall be the last.

BELFOND JUNIOR My dear, I know I had thy virgin heart, and I'll preserve it. But for her, her most diverting minutes were unpleasant: yet for all her malice which you see, I still maintain her.

LUCIA Ungrateful creature! She is indeed a fury. Should'st thou once take thy love from me, I never should use such ways: I silently should mourn and pine away; but never think of once offending thee.

BELFOND JUNIOR Thou art the prettiest, sweetest, softest creature! And all the tenderest joys that wait on love, are ever with thee.

LUCIA Oh, this is charming kindness! May all the joys on earth be still with thee.

BELFOND JUNIOR [*aside*] Now here's a mischief on the other side: for how can a good natured man think of ever quitting so tender, and so kind a mistress, whom no respect, but love has thrown into my arms: and yet I must: but I will better her condition.

Enter Truman.

Oh, how does my friend.

LUCIA O Lord! Who's here?

BELFOND JUNIOR My dear, go to the lodging I have prepared for thee; thou wilt be safe, and I'll wait on thee soon. Who's there?

Enter Servants.

Do you wait on this lady's chair, you know whither.

TRUMAN Thou art a pretty fellow, Belfond, to take thy pleasure thus, and put thy friend upon the damnedst drudgery.

BELFOND JUNIOR What drudgery? A little dissembling.

TRUMAN Why that were bad enough, to dissemble myself an ass; but to dissemble love, nay lust, is the most irksome task a man can undergo.

BELFOND JUNIOR But prithee come to the point: in short, have we any hopes?

TRUMAN 'Tis done; the business is done: whip on your habit; make no words.

BELFOND JUNIOR I'll put it on in my dressing-room. This news transports me.

TRUMAN If you had undergone what I have done, 'twould have humbled you: I have enjoyed a lady; but I had as lief have had a Lancashire witch, just after she had alighted from a broomstaff: I have been uncivil, and enjoyed the governante in most lewd dalliance.

BELFOND JUNIOR Thou art a brave fellow, and makest nothing of it.

TRUMAN Nothing? S'death, I had rather have stormed a half-moon:* I had more pleasure at the Battle of Mons.†

* a half-moon: a crescent formation of men or ships.

† Mons: Mons was blockaded by the French army in 1678; its surrender was

BELFOND JUNIOR But hast thou done our work as well as hers?

TRUMAN I have: for after the enjoyment of her person had led me into some familiarity with her, I proposed, she accepted, for she is covetous as well as amorous: and she has so far wrought for us, that we shall have an interview with our mistresses; whom, she says, we shall find very inclinable; and she has promised this night to deliver 'em into our hands.

BELFOND JUNIOR Thou art a rare friend to me, and to thyself. Now, farewell all the vanity of this lewd Town, at once I quit you all. Dear rogue, let's in.

TRUMAN Come in, in, and dress in your habit.   [*Exeunt*]

⟨SCENE II⟩

Enter Sir William, Sir Edward and Scrapeall.

SCRAPEALL Look ye Sir William, I am glad you like my niece: and I hope also, that she may look lovely in your son's eyes.

SIR EDWARD BELFOND No doubt but he will be extremely taken with her: indeed both she and your daughter are very beautiful.

SIR WILLIAM BELFOND He like her! What's matter whether he like her, or no? Is it not enough for him, that I do? Is a son, a boy, a jackanapes, to have a will of his own? That were to have him be the father, and I the son. But indeed they are both very handsome.

SCRAPEALL Let me tell you both, Sir William and Sir Edward, beauty is but vanity, a mere nothing; but they have that which will not fade; they have grace.

SIR EDWARD BELFOND [*aside*] They look like pretty spirited witty girls.

SCRAPEALL I am sorry I must leave thee so soon: I thought to have bidden thee to dinner, but I am to pay down a sum of money upon a mortgage this afternoon: farewell.

SIR WILLIAM BELFOND Farewell Mr Scrapeall.

SIR EDWARD BELFOND Pray meet my brother at my house at dinner.

prevented by the battle between William of Orange and the Marshal de Luxembourg at St Denys.

SCRAPEALL Thank you Sir Edward, I know not but I may. ⟨*Exit*⟩

SIR EDWARD BELFOND The person of this girl is well chosen for your son, if she were not so precise and pure.

SIR WILLIAM BELFOND Prithee, what matter what she is, has not she fifteen thousand pounds clear?

SIR EDWARD BELFOND For a husband to differ in religion from a wife.

SIR WILLIAM BELFOND What, with fifteen thousand pound?

SIR EDWARD BELFOND A precise wife will think herself so pure, she will be apt to contemn her husband.

SIR WILLIAM BELFOND Aye, but fifteen thousand pound, brother.

SIR EDWARD BELFOND You know how intractable misguided zeal and spiritual pride are.

SIR WILLIAM BELFOND What with fifteen thousand pound!

SIR EDWARD BELFOND I would not willingly my son should have her.

SIR WILLIAM BELFOND Not with fifteen thousand pound?

SIR EDWARD BELFOND I see there's no answer to be given to fifteen thousand pound.

SIR WILLIAM BELFOND A pox o' this godly knave, it should have been twenty.

SIR EDWARD BELFOND Nor would I buy a wife for my son.

SIR WILLIAM BELFOND Not if you could have her a good pennyworth: your son, quoth ye? He is like to make a fine husband. For all your precious son –

SIR EDWARD BELFOND Again, brother?

SIR WILLIAM BELFOND Look you, brother, you fly out so: pray, brother, be not passionate; passion drowns one's parts; let us calmly reason: I have fresh matter; have but patience, and hear me speak.

SIR EDWARD BELFOND Well, brother, go on; for I see I might as soon stop a tide.

SIR WILLIAM BELFOND To be calm and patient; your jewel, though he denied that outrage in Dorset Court, yet he committed it, and was last night hurried before the Lord Chief Justice for it.

SIR EDWARD BELFOND [*aside*] It cannot be, on my certain knowledge. I could convince him, but it is not time.

SIR WILLIAM BELFOND What a devil, are all the world mistaken, but you?

SIR EDWARD BELFOND He was with me all the evening.

SIR WILLIAM BELFOND Why, he got bail immediately, and came to you. Ounds, I never saw such a man in my life!

SIR EDWARD BELFOND I am assured of the contrary.

SIR WILLIAM BELFOND Death and hell, you make me stark mad! You will send me to Bedlam: you will not believe your own senses: I'll hold you a thousand pound.

SIR EDWARD BELFOND Brother, remember passion drowns one's parts.

SIR WILLIAM BELFOND Well, I am tame, I am cool.

SIR EDWARD BELFOND I'll hold you a hundred; which is enough for one brother to win of another.

Enter Attorney.

And here's your own attorney comes opportunely enough to hold stakes. I'll bind it with ten.

SIR WILLIAM BELFOND Done.

SIR EDWARD BELFOND Why, I saw your man Roger, and he says, your son found there a rascal, that went by his name.

ATTORNEY Oh, Sir William, I am undone, ruined, made a miserable man!

SIR WILLIAM BELFOND What's the matter, man?

ATTORNEY Though you have been an exceeding good client to me, I have reason to curse one of your family that has ruined mine.

SIR WILLIAM BELFOND Pray explain yourself.

ATTORNEY Oh, Sir, your wicked son, your most libidinous son.

SIR WILLIAM BELFOND Look you, brother, d'ye hear? D'ye hear? Do you answer?

ATTORNEY He's corrupted, debauched my only daughter, whom I had brought up with all the care and charge I could, who was the hopes, the joy of all our family.

SIR WILLIAM BELFOND Here's a son! Here's a rare son! Here's a hopeful son! And he were mine, I'd lash him with a dog-whip: I'd cool his courage.

SIR EDWARD BELFOND How do you know it is he?

ATTORNEY I have a witness of it, that saw her rise from his bed the other day morning; and last night she ran away to him, and they have lain at a private lodging.

SIR EDWARD BELFOND Be well assured, ere you conclude; for there is a rascal that has taken my son's name, and has swaggered in and about Whitefriars, with Cheatly, and that gang of rogues, whom my son will take a course with.

ATTORNEY Oh, Sir, I am too well assured: my wife tears her hair; and I, for my part shall run distracted.

SIR WILLIAM BELFOND Oh, wicked rascal! Oh, my poor Tim! My dear boy Tim! I think each day a year, till I see thee.

SIR EDWARD BELFOND I am extremely sorry for this, if it be so; but let me beg of you, play the part of a wise man; blaze not this dishonour abroad, and you shall have all the reparation the case is capable of.

SIR WILLIAM BELFOND Reparation, for making his daughter a whore! What, a pox, can he give her her maidenhead again?

SIR EDWARD BELFOND Money, which shall not be wanting, will stop that witness's mouth! And I will give your daughter such a fortune, that were what you believe true and publicly known, she should live above contempt, as the world goes now.

ATTORNEY You speak like the worthy gentleman the world thinks you; but there can be no salve for this sore.

SIR WILLIAM BELFOND Why, you are enough to damn forty sons, if you had 'em; you encourage 'em to whore: you are fit to breed up youth!

SIR EDWARD BELFOND You are mad: but pray Sir, let me entreat you to go home, and I will come and wait upon you; and we will consult how to make the best of this misfortune, in which I assure you, I have a great share.

ATTORNEY I will submit to your wise advice, Sir: my grief had made me forget; here is a letter comes out of the country for you.

[*Exit Attorney*]

SIR WILLIAM BELFOND For me! 'Tis welcome: now for news from my dear boy! Now you shall hear, brother: he is a son indeed.

SIR EDWARD BELFOND [*aside*] Yes, a very hopeful one: I will not undeceive him, till Ned has tried once more to recover him.

SIR WILLIAM BELFOND [*reads*] 'On the tenth of this month, your son, my young master, about two of the clock in the morning, rode out with his man Lolpoop; and notwithstanding all the search and enquiry we can make' (O heaven) 'he cannot be found or heard of'. [*he drops the letter not able to hold it*]

SIR EDWARD BELFOND How's this?

SIR WILLIAM BELFOND Oh, my poor boy! He is robbed and murdered, and buried in some ditch, or flung into some pond. Oh, I shall never see thee more, dear Tim! The joy, and the support of all my life! The only comfort which I had on earth.

SIR EDWARD BELFOND Have patience brother; 'tis nothing but a little ramble in your absence.

SIR WILLIAM BELFOND Oh, no; he durst not ramble: he was the dutifullest child! I shall never see his face again: look you, he goes on. 'We have searched and made enquiry in three adjacent countries, and no tidings can be heard of him.' What have I done, that heaven should thus afflict me?

SIR EDWARD BELFOND What, if after all, this son should be he that has made all this noise in Whitefriars, for which mine has been so blamed?

SIR WILLIAM BELFOND My son, my son play such pranks? That's likely! One so strictly, so soberly educated! One that's educated your way cannot do otherwise.

Enter Roger.

ROGER Sir, Sir, Sir, mercy upon me, here's my young master's man Lolpoop, coming along in the streets with a wench.

Enter Lolpoop leading Betty under the arm.

SIR WILLIAM BELFOND O heaven! What say you?

SIR EDWARD BELFOND [*to himself*] Now it works: ha, ha, ha.

MRS BETTY How now! What have you to say to my friend, my dear?

Sir William lays hold on Lolpoop ere he or she sees him. Sir William and Lolpoop start, and stand amazed at one another; and after a great pause, Sir William falls upon Lolpoop, beats the whore, beats Roger, strikes at his brother, and lays about him like a madman; the rabble get all about him.

SIR WILLIAM BELFOND Sirrah, rogue, dog, villain! Whore! And you rogue, rogue! Confound the world! O that the world were all on fire!

SIR EDWARD BELFOND Brother, for shame be more temperate:
are you a madman?

SIR WILLIAM BELFOND Plague o' your dull philosophy.

SIR EDWARD BELFOND The rabble are gathered together about
you.

SIR WILLIAM BELFOND Villain, rogue, dog, toad, serpent!
Where's my son? Sirrah, you have robbed him, and murdered him.
[*he beats Lolpoop, who roars out murder*]

LOLPOOP Hold, hold; your son is alive, and alive like: he's in
London.

SIR WILLIAM BELFOND What say you, sirrah? In London? And
is he well? Thanks be to heaven for that: where is he sirrah?

LOLPOOP He is in Whitefriars, with Mr Cheatly, his cousin
Shamwell, and Captain Hackum. [*Sir William pauses, as amazed:
then beats him again*]

SIR WILLIAM BELFOND And you rogue, you damned dog, would
you suffer him to keep such company, and commit such villainous actions?

LOLPOOP Hold, hold, hold, I pray you, Sir: I am but a servant,
how could I help it, marry?

SIR WILLIAM BELFOND You could not help being with a whore
yourself; sirrah, sirrah, sirrah. Here honest mob, course this whore
to some purpose. A whore, a whore, a whore. [*She runs out, the
rabble run after, and tear her, crying, 'A whore, a whore'*]

SIR EDWARD BELFOND This is wisely done! If they murder her,
you'll be hanged: I am in commission for Middlesex; I must see
to appease them.

SIR WILLIAM BELFOND Sirrah, rogue, bring me to my son
instantly, or I'll cut your throat.   [*Exeunt*]

⟨SCENE III⟩

Enter Isabella, Teresia, Ruth.

ISABELLA Dear Ruth, thou dost for ever oblige us.

TERESIA And so much, that none but our own mothers could ever
do it more.

RUTH Oblige yourselves, and be not silly, coy, and nice: strike me when the iron's hot, I say. They have great estates, and are both friends, I know both their families and conditions.

Enter Belfond Junior and Truman.

Here they are: welcome friends.

TRUMAN How dost thou?

RUTH These are the damsels, I will retire, and watch, lest the old man surprise us.   [*Exit Ruth*]

BELFOND JUNIOR Look thee, Isabella, I come to confer with thee, in a matter which concerned us both, if thou be'st free.

ISABELLA Friend, 'tis like I am.

TRUMAN And mine with thee is of the same nature.

TERESIA Proceed.

BELFOND JUNIOR Something within me whispereth, that we were made as helps for one another.

TERESIA They act very well, cousin.

ISABELLA For young beginners. Come, leave off your Canaanitish dialect, and talk like the inhabiters of this world.

TERESIA We are as errant hypocrites as the best of you.

ISABELLA We were bred otherwise than you see, and are able to hear you talk like gentlemen.

TERESIA You come to our meeting like sparks and beaux, and I never could perceive much devotion in you.

ISABELLA 'Tis such a pain to dissemble, that I am resolved I'll never do it, but when I must.

BELFOND JUNIOR Dear Madam, I could wish all forms were laid aside betwixt us: but in short, I am most infinitely in love with you, and must be for ever miserable if I go without you.

ISABELLA A frank and hearty declaration, which you make with so much confidence, I warrant you have been used to it.

TRUMAN There is not a difficulty in the world which I would stop at to obtain your love, the only thing on earth could make me happy.

TERESIA And you are as much in earnest now, as you were when you came first to us even now.

ISABELLA That's well urged: cannot you gentlemen counterfeit love, as well as religion?

BELFOND JUNIOR Love is so natural, it cannot be affected.

TRUMAN To show you mine is so, take me at my word: I am
ready to render on discretion.

TERESIA And was this the reason you frequented our parish
church?

BELFOND JUNIOR Could you think our business was to hear
your teacher spin out an hour, over a velvet cushion?★

ISABELLA Profane men! I warrant they came to ogle.

TRUMAN Even so: our eyes might tell you what we came for.

BELFOND JUNIOR In short, dear Madam, our opportunities are
like to be so few, your confinement being so close, that 'tis fit to
make use of this; 'tis not your fortune which I aim at, my uncle
will make a settlement equal to it, were it more; but 'tis your
charming person.

ISABELLA And you would have me a fine forward lady, to love
extempore.

BELFOND JUNIOR Madam, you have but few minutes to make
use of, and therefore should improve those few: your uncle has
sold you for £5000 and for ought I know, you have not this night
good for your deliverance.

TRUMAN Consider, ladies, if you had not better trust a couple of
honest gentlemen, than an old man, that makes his market of you:
for I can tell you, you though his own daughter, are to be sold too.

TERESIA But for all that, our consents are to be had.

BELFOND JUNIOR You can look for nothing, but a more strict
confinement, which must follow your refusal: now, if you have
the courage to venture an escape, we are the knights that will
relieve you.

TRUMAN I have an estate Madam, equal to your fortune: but I
have nothing can deserve your love: but I'll procure your freedom, then use it as you please.

BELFOND JUNIOR If you are unwilling to trust us, you can trust
your governess, whom you shall have with you.

ISABELLA And what would you and the world say of us for this?

BELFOND JUNIOR We should adore you: and I am apt to think
the world would not condemn your choice.

TRUMAN But I am sure, all the world will condemn your delay, in
the condition you are in.

★ a velvet cushion: the pulpit cushion.

Enter Ruth.

RUTH I see Mr Scrapeall coming at the end of the street: begone, I'll bring them to your chamber in the Temple, this evening. Haste, haste out at the back door.

BELFOND JUNIOR This is most unfortunate.

TRUMAN Dear Madam, let me seal my vows.

RUTH Go, go: begone, begone, friends.   [*Exeunt*]

⟨SCENE IV⟩

Enter Scrapeall, crosses the stage; enter Mrs Termagant
and her Brother.

MRS TERMAGANT You see, brother, we have dogged Belfond, till we saw him enter the house of this scrivener with his friend Truman, both in disguises; which, with what we have heard even now, at the neighbouring alehouse, convinces me, that 'tis he is to marry the rich niece.

BROTHER They say she is to be married to the son of Sir William Belfond, and that Sir William gives a great sum of money to her uncle for her; by this it should seem to be the elder son, and not our enemy, who is disguised for her.

MRS TERMAGANT If so, the villain would not at full day go thither.

BROTHER But 'tis in a disguise.

MRS TERMAGANT With that, I suppose the son pretends to be a puritan too, or she would not have him; it must be he. And if you will do as I directed you, I warrant I'll break off his match; and by that work an exquisite piece of revenge.

BROTHER I am wholly at your dispose.

MRS TERMAGANT Now is the time, the door opens; pursue me with a drawn dagger, with all the seeming fury imaginable, now as the old man comes out.

Scrapeall passes over the stage. Brother pursues her with a drawn dagger,
she runs and gets into the house, and claps the door after her.

Enter within, Ruth, Teresia, Isabella, ⟨Mrs⟩ Termagant.

BROTHER Where is the jade? Deliver her to me, I'll cut her in piecemeal: deliver her, I say. Well, you will not deliver her: I shall watch her.

MRS TERMAGANT Oh, oh! Where is the murderer? Where is he? I die with fear, I die.

RUTH Prithee, woman, comfort thyself, no man shall hurt thee here. Take a sup of this bottle. [*she pulls out a silver strong-water bottle*]

TERESIA Thou art safe.

ISABELLA We will defend thee here, as in a castle. But what is the occasion of this man's fury?

MRS TERMAGANT You are so generous, in giving me this succour, and promising my defence, that I am resolved not to conceal it from you: though I must confess, I have no reason to boast of it; but I hope your charity will interpret it as well as you can on my side.

RUTH Go on: thou need'st not fear.

MRS TERMAGANT Know then, I am a gentlewoman, whose parents dying when I was sixteen, left me a moderate fortune, yet able to maintain me like their daughter. I chose an aunt my guardian, one of those jolly widows who love gaming, and have great resort in the evenings at their houses.

RUTH Good: proceed.

MRS TERMAGANT There it was my misfortune to be acquainted with a young gentleman, whose face, air, mien, shape, wit, and breeding, not I alone, but the whole Town admires.

RUTH Very good.

MRS TERMAGANT By all his looks, his gestures, and addresses, he seemed in love with me: the joy that I conceived at this, I wanted cunning to conceal, but he must needs perceive it flash in my eyes, and kindle in my face; he soon began to court me in such sweet, such charming words, as would betray a more experienced heart than mine.

RUTH Humh: very well; she speaks notably.

MRS TERMAGANT There was but little left for him to do, for I had done it all before for him: he had a friend within too ready to give up the fort; yet I held out as long as I could make defence.

RUTH Good lack-a-day! Some men have strange charms, it is confessed.

MRS TERMAGANT Yet I was safe by solemn mutual oaths, in private we were contracted: he would have it private, because he feared to offend an uncle, from whom he had great expectance; but now came all my misery.

RUTH Alack, alack, I warrant he was false.

MRS TERMAGANT False as a crocodile: he watched the fatal minute, and he found it, and greedily seized upon me, when I trusted to his honour and his oaths; he still swore on, that he would marry me, and I sinned on: in short, I had a daughter by him, now three years old, as true a copy as e'er nature drew, beauteous, and witty to a miracle.

RUTH Nay, men are faithless, I can speak it.

TERESIA Poor lady; I am strangely concerned for her.

ISABELLA She was a fool, to be catched in so common a snare.

MRS TERMAGANT From time to time he swore he would marry me: though I must think I am his wife as much as any priest can make me; but still he found excuses about his uncle. I would have patiently waited till his uncle's death, had he been true; but he has thrown me off, abandoned me, without so much as a pretended crime.

RUTH Alack, and well-a-day! It makes me weep.

MRS TERMAGANT But 'tis for an attorney's daughter, whom he keeps, and now is fond of; while he treats me with all contempt and hatred.

ISABELLA Though she was a fool, yet he's a base inhuman fellow.

TERESIA To scorn and hate her, for her love to him.

MRS TERMAGANT By this means, my dishonour, which had been yet concealed, became so public, my brother coming from the wars of Hungary, has heard all, has this day fought with the author of my misery, but was disarmed; and now by accident he spied me by your house, I having fled the place where I had lodged, for fear of him; and here the bloody man would have killed me, for the dishonour done to his family, which never yet was blemished.

RUTH Get the Chief Justice's warrant, and bind him to the peace.

TERESIA She tells her story well.

ISABELLA 'Tis a very odd one; but she expresses it so sensibly, I cannot but believe her.

MRS TERMAGANT [*aside*] If they do not ask me who this is, I have told my tale in vain. ⟨*to them*⟩ Now, ladies, I hope you have charity enough, to pardon the weakness of a poor young woman, who suffers shame enough within.

TERESIA We shall be glad to do you what kindness we can.

MRS TERMAGANT Oh, had you seen this most bewitching person, so beautiful, witty, and well-bred, and full of most gentlemanlike qualities, you would be the readier to have compassion on me.

ISABELLA Pray, who is it?

MRS TERMAGANT Alas, 'tis no secret, it is Belfond, who calls Sir Edward Belfond father, but is his nephew.

ISABELLA What do I hear? Was ever woman so unfortunate as I, in her first love.

TERESIA 'Tis most unlucky.

MRS TERMAGANT ⟨*aside*⟩ That is the niece: I see 'twas he who was to marry her.

ISABELLA But I am glad I have thus early heard it. I'll never see his face more.

RUTH [*aside*] All this is false: he is a pious man, and true professor. This vile woman will break the match off, and undo my hopes.

MRS TERMAGANT [*aside*] 'Tis as I thought. ⟨*to them*⟩ He is a ranting blade, a roister of the Town.

RUTH Come you are an idle woman, and belie him: begone out of the doors; there's the backway, you need not pretend fear of your brother.

MRS TERMAGANT I am obliged enough in the present defence you gave me: I intended not to trouble you long; but heaven can witness what I say is true.

ISABELLA Do you hear cousin! 'Tis most certain, I'll never see him.

RUTH Go, wicked woman, go, what evil spirit sent thee hither? I say begone.

MRS TERMAGANT I go. I care not what she says, it works where I would have it. Your servant ladies.   [*Exit*]

RUTH Go, go, thou wicked slanderer.

TERESIA See him but once, to hear what he can say in his defence.

ISABELLA Yes, to hear him lie, as all the sex will: persuade me not; I am fixed.

RUTH Look thee, Isabella.

ISABELLA I am resolved.   [*Exit Isabella hastily*]

TERESIA Dear Ruth, thou dearest friend, whom once we took for our most cruel gaoler, let's follow, and help me to convince her of her error; but I am resolved, if she be stubborn, to undo herself, she shall not ruin me: I will escape.

RUTH Let us persuade her.   [*Exeunt*]

⟨SCENE V⟩

Enter Belfond Senior and Hackum.

BELFOND SENIOR Captain, call all my servants, why don't they wait?

Enter ⟨Mrs⟩ Margaret, and Mrs Hackum with a candle.

Oh, my pure blowing, my convenient my tackle!

MRS MARGARET How dost thou, my dear?

MRS HACKUM I have brought you a caudle here; there's ambergris in it, 'tis a rare refreshing, strengthening thing.

BELFOND SENIOR What, adad, you take me for a bridegroom; I scorn a caudle, give me some cherry brandy, I'll drink her health in a bumper: do thee eat this, child.

MRS HACKUM I have that at hand – here, Sir. [*she fetches the brandy*]

Enter Captain Hackum, and Servants.

BELFOND SENIOR Come, my dear natural, here's a bumper of cherry brandy to thy health; but first let me kiss thee, my dear rogue.

Enter Sir William.

SIR WILLIAM BELFOND Some thunderbolt light on my head; what's this I see?

BELFOND SENIOR My father!

Enter Cheatly and Shamwell.

SIR WILLIAM BELFOND Hey, here's the whole kennel of hell-hounds.

CHEATLY Bear up to him, bow-wow.

SHAMWELL Do not flinch, bow-wow.

BELFOND SENIOR Bow-wow, bow-wow.

SIR WILLIAM BELFOND Most impudent abandoned rascal; let me go, let me come at him; audacious varlet, how durst thou look on me? [*he endeavours to fly at his son, Footmen hold him*]

BELFOND SENIOR Go strike your dogs, and call them names, you have nothing to do with me, I am of full age; and I thank heaven, am gotten loose from your yoke, don't think to put upon me, I'll be kept no longer like a prigster, a silly country put, fit for nothing but to be a bubble, a caravan, or so.

SIR WILLIAM BELFOND A most perfect downright canting rogue; am I not your father, sirrah? Sirrah, am I not?

BELFOND SENIOR Yes, and tenant for life to my estate in tail, and I'll look to you, that you commit no waste; what-a-pox, did you think to nose me for ever, as the saying is? I am not so dark neither, I am sharp, sharp as a needle, I can smoke now, as soon as another.

SIR WILLIAM BELFOND Let me come at him.

CHEATLY So long as you forbear all violence you are safe; but if you strike here, we command the Friars, and we will raise the posse.

SIR WILLIAM BELFOND O villain! Thou notorious undoer of young heirs: and thou pernicious wretch, thou art no part of me; have I from thy first swaddling nourished thee and bred thee up with care.

BELFOND SENIOR Yes, with care to keep your money from me, and breed me in the greatest ignorance, fit for your slave, and not your son; I had been finely dark if I had stayed at home.

SIR WILLIAM BELFOND Were you not educated like a gentle-man?

BELFOND SENIOR No, like a grazier or a butcher; if I had stayed in the country, I had never seen such a nab, a rum nab, such a modish porker, such spruce and neat accoutrements; here is a tattle; here's a famble, and here's the coal, the ready, the rhino, the darby; I have a lusty cod old prig, I'd have thee know, and

am very rhinocerical, here are megs and smelts good store, decuses and georges, the land is entailed, and I will have my snack of
it while I am young, adad, I will. Hah!

SIR WILLIAM BELFOND Some mountain cover me, and hide my
shame for ever from the world; did I not beget thee, rogue?

BELFOND SENIOR What know I whether you did or not? But
'twas not to use me like a slave; but I am sharp and smoky; I
had been purely bred, had I been ruled by you; I should never
have known these worthy ingenious gentlemen, my dear friends,
all this fine language had been heathen Greek to me, and I had
ne'er been able to have cut a sham or banter while I had lived,
adad. Odsookers, I know myself, and will have nothing to do with
you.

SIR WILLIAM BELFOND I am astonished!

BELFOND SENIOR Shall my younger brother keep his coach and
equipage, and shine like a spruce prig, and I be your baily in the
country? Hi, La Mar; bid my coach be ready at the door; I'll
make him know I am elder brother, and I will have the better
liveries, and I am resolved to manage my natural, my pure blowing, my convenient, my peculiar, my tackle, my purest pure, as
the rest of the young gentlemen of the Town do.

SIR WILLIAM BELFOND [*aside*] A most confirmed Alsatian
rogue! ⟨*to his son*⟩ Thou most ungracious wretch to break from
me, at such a time, when I had provided a wife for you, a pretty
young lady, with fifteen thousand pound down, have settled a
great jointure upon her, and a large estate in present on you, the
writings all sealed, and nothing wanting but you, whom I had
send for post out of the country to marry her!

BELFOND SENIOR Very likely, that you, who have cudgelled me
from my cradle, and made me your slave, and grudged me a
crown in my pocket, should do all this.

CHEATLY Believe him not; there's not one word of truth in't.

SHAMWELL This is a trick to get you in his power.

SIR WILLIAM BELFOND The writings are all at my attorney's
in the Temple; you may go with me, and see'm all; and, if you
will comply, I'll pardon what is past and marry you.

BELFOND SENIOR No, no, I am sharp, as I told you, and smoky;
you shall not put upon me, I understand your shams; but to talk

fairly, in all occurrences of this nature, which either may, or may not be, according to the different accidents which often intervene upon several opportunities, from whence we may collect either good or bad, according to the nature of the things themselves; and forasmuch as whether they be good or bad concerns only the understanding, so far forth as it employs its faculties: now since all this is premised, let us come to the matter in hand.

SIR WILLIAM BELFOND Prodigious impudence! O devil! I'll to my lord Chief Justice, and with his tipstaff I'll do your business, rogues, dogs and villains, I will.   [*Exit in fury*]

CHEATLY This was bravely carried on.

SHAMWELL Most admirably.

BELFOND SENIOR Aye, was't not? Don't I begin to banter pretty well? Ha!

CHEATLY Rarely: but a word in private, my resplendent prig. You see your father resolves to put some trick upon you; be beforehand with him, and marry this fortune I have prepared; lose not time but see her, and treat with her, if you like her, as soon as you can.

BELFOND SENIOR You are in the right; let not my blowing hear a word; I'll to her instantly.

CHEATLY Shamwell and I'll go and prepare her for a visit; you know the place.

BELFOND SENIOR I do, come along. –   [*Exeunt*]

⟨SCENE VI⟩

*Enter Cheatly, Shamwell, and Mrs Termagant, in
her fine lodgings.*

CHEATLY Madam, you must carry yourself somewhat stately, but courteously, to the bubble.

SHAMWELL Somewhat reservedly, and yet so as to give him hopes.

MRS TERMAGANT I warrant you, let me alone; and if I effect this business, you are the best of friends; such friends as I could never yet expect: 'twill be an exquisite revenge.

CHEATLY He comes! Come noble squire.

Enter Belfond Senior.

Madam, this is the gentleman whom I would recommend to your ladyship's favour, who is ambitious of kissing your hand.

BELFOND SENIOR Yes, Madam, as Mr Cheatly says, I am ambitious of kissing your hand, and your lip too, Madam; for I vow to gad, Madam, there is not a person in the world, Madam, has a greater honour for your person: and, Madam, I assure you I am a person –

MRS TERMAGANT My good friend, Mr Cheatly, with whom I entrust the management of my small fortune –

CHEATLY Small fortune! Nay it is a large one –

MRS TERMAGANT He's told me of your family and character: to your name I am no stranger, nor to your estate, though this is the first time I have had the honour to see your person.

BELFOND SENIOR Hold, good Madam, the honour lies on my side; she's a rare lady, ten times handsomer than my blowing: (and here's a lodging and furniture for a queen!) Madam, if your ladyship please to accept of my affection in an honourable way, you shall find I am no put, no country prigster, nor shall ever want the megs, the smelts, decuses and georges, the ready, and the rhino: I am rhinocerical.

MRS TERMAGANT I want nothing Sir, heaven be thanked.

SHAMWELL Her worst servants eat in plate; and her maids have all silver chamber-pots.

BELFOND SENIOR Madam, I beg your pardon, I am somewhat boozy; I have been drinking bumpers and facers till I am almost clear: I have £3000 a year, and £2000 pounds-worth of wood, which I can turn into coal and ready, and my estate ne'er the worse; there's only the encumbrance of an old fellow upon it, and I shall break his heart suddenly.

MRS TERMAGANT This is a weighty matter, and requires advice: nor is it a sudden work to persuade my heart to love. I have my choice of fortunes.

BELFOND SENIOR Very like Madam: but Mr Cheatly and my cousin Shamwell can tell you that my occasions require haste, d'ye see! And therefore I desire you to resolve as soon as conveniently you can.

A noise of a tumult without, and blowing of a horn.

CHEATLY What's this I hear?

SHAMWELL They are up in the Friars: pray heaven the sheriff's officers be not come.

CHEATLY S'life, 'tis so; shift for yourselves; squire let me conduct you – This is your wicked father with officers.   [*Exit*]

Cry without, 'The tipstaff, an arrest; an arrest'; *and the horn blows.*

Enter Sir William Belfond, and a Tipstaff, with the Constable and his Watchmen; and against them the posse of the Friars drawn up, bankrupts hurrying to escape.

SIR WILLIAM BELFOND Are you mad to resist the tipstaff, the king's authority?

They cry out, 'An arrest'. *Several flock to 'em with all sorts of weapons. Women with fire-forks, spits, paring-shovels, etc.*

Enter Cheatly, Shamwell, Belfond Senior and Hackum.

CHEATLY We are too strong for 'em: stand our ground.

SIR WILLIAM BELFOND We demand that same squire, Cheatly, Shamwell and Bully Hackum: deliver them up, and all the rest of you are safe.

CAPTAIN HACKUM Not a man.

SIR WILLIAM BELFOND Nay then, have at you.

TIPSTAFF I charge you, in the king's name, all to assist me.

RABBLE Fall on.

Rabble beat the Constable and the rest into the Temple. Tipstaff runs away. They take Sir William prisoner.

CHEATLY Come on thou wicked author of this broil. You are our prisoner.

SIR WILLIAM BELFOND Let me go, rogue.

SHAMWELL Now we have you in the Temple, we'll show you the pump first.

SIR WILLIAM BELFOND Dogs, rogues, villains.

SHAMWELL To the pump, to the pump.

CAPTAIN HACKUM Pump him, pump him.

BELFOND SENIOR Aye, pump him, pump him, old prig.
RABBLE Pump, pump, to the pump; huzza!

Enter Belfond Junior, Truman, and several Gentlemen,
Porter of the Temple, and Belfond's Footmen.

BELFOND JUNIOR What's the matter here?
TRUMAN The rabble have catcht a bailiff.
BELFOND JUNIOR Death and hell, 'tis my father; 'tis a gentleman, my father. Gentlemen, I beseech you lend me your hands to his rescue.
TRUMAN Come on, rascals: have we caught you? We'll make you an example.
BELFOND JUNIOR Here! Where are the officers of the Temple? Porter, do you shut the gates into Whitefriars.
PORTER I will, Sir.

All draw, and fall upon the Rabble. Belfond Senior runs first away. The
Templars beat 'em and take Cheatly, Shamwell and Hackum prisoners.

BELFOND JUNIOR Here's a guinea among ye. See these three rogues well pumped, and let'em go through the whole course.
CHEATLY Hold, hold, I am a gentleman.
SHAMWELL I am your cousin.
SIR WILLIAM BELFOND Away with 'em. Dear son, I am infinitely obliged to you; I ask your pardon for all that I have said against you: I have wronged you.
BELFOND JUNIOR Good sir, reflect not on that; I am resolved, ere I have done, to deserve your good word.
SIR WILLIAM BELFOND 'Twas ill fortune, we have missed my most ungracious rebel, that monster of villainy.
BELFOND JUNIOR Let me alone with him Sir, upon my honour I will deliver him safe this night. But now let us see the execution.
SIR WILLIAM BELFOND Dear Ned, you bring tears into my eyes. Let me embrace thee, my only comfort now.
BELFOND JUNIOR Good Sir, let's on and see the Justice of this place.   [*Exeunt*]

ACT FIVE

SCENE I

Enter Cheatly, Shamwell, Hackum.

CHEATLY O unmerciful dogs! Were ever a gentleman used thus before? I am drenched into a quartan ague.

SHAMWELL My limbs are stiff and numbed all over: but where I am beaten and bruised, there I have some sense left.

CAPTAIN HACKUM Dry blows I could have borne magnanimously; but to be made such a sop of – Besides, I have had the worst of it, by wearing my own hair; to be shaved all on one side, and with a lather made of channel-dirt, instead of a washball: I have lost half the best head of hair in the Friars; and a whisker, worth fifty pound in its intrinsic value to a commander.

CHEATLY Indeed your magnanimous phiz is somewhat disfigured by it, captain.

SHAMWELL Your military countenance has lost much of its ornament.

CAPTAIN HACKUM I am as disconsolate as a bee that has lost his sting; the other moiety of whisker must follow: then all the terror of my face is gone; that face that used to fright young prigs into submission. I shall now look but like an ordinary man.

CHEATLY We'll swinge these rogues with indictments for a riot, and with actions *sans nombre*.

SHAMWELL What reparation will that be? I am a gentleman, and can never show my face amongst my kindred more.

CHEATLY We that can show our faces after what we have done, may well show 'em after what we have suffered. Great souls are above ordinances, and never can be slaves to fame.

CAPTAIN HACKUM My honour is tender, and this one affront will cost me at least five murders.

CHEATLY Let's not prate and shiver in cold fits here, but call your wife with the cherry brandy, and let's ask after the squire: if they have taken him, 'tis the worst part of the story.

CAPTAIN HACKUM No, I saw the squire run into the Friars at first. But I'll go fetch some cherry brandy, and that will comfort us. [*Steps in for brandy*] Here's the bottle, let's drink by word of mouth. [*drinks*]

CHEATLY Your cherry brandy is most sovereign and edifying. [*Cheatly drinks*]

SHAMWELL Most exceeding comfortable after our Temple-Pickling. [*drinks*]

CHEATLY A fish has a damned life on't: I shall have that aversion to water, after this – that I shall scarce ever be cleanly enough to wash my face again.

CAPTAIN HACKUM Well! I'll to the barber's and get myself shaved; then go to the squire and be new accoutered.

[*Exit Hackum*]

CHEATLY Dear Shamwell, we must not for a little affliction, forget our main business; our caravan must be well managed: he is now drunk, and when he wakes, will be very fit to be married. Mrs Termagant has given us a judgment of £2000 upon that condition.

SHAMWELL The sooner we dispose of him, the better; for all his kindred are bent to retrieve him; and the Temple joining in the war against us, will go near to be too hard for us; so that we must make what we can of him immediately.

CHEATLY If he should be once cool, or irresolute, we have lost him, and all our hopes; but when we have sufficiently dipped* him, as we shall by this marriage and her judgment, he is our own for ever.

SHAMWELL But what shall we do for our Whitefriars chaplain, our Alsatian divine? I was in search of him before our late misfortune, and the rogue is holed somewhere, I could not find him, and we are undone without him.

CHEATLY 'Tis true; pray go instantly and find him out; he dares not stir out of this covert; beat it well all over for him, you'll find him tappesed† in some ale-house, bawdy-house, or brandy-shop.

SHAMWELL He's a brave swinging orthodox, and will marry any couple at any time; he defies licence, and canonical hours, and all those foolish ceremonies.

CHEATLY Prithee look after him, while I go to prepare the lady.

* dipped him: put him in our debt.
† tappesed: hidden away, lying close to the ground.

SHAMWELL You rogue, Cheatly, you have a loving design upon her; you will go to twelve★ with the squire: if you do, I will have my snack.

CHEATLY Go, go, you are a wag.   [*Exeunt severally*]

⟨SCENE II⟩

Enter Ruth, Belfond Junior and Truman at Scrapeall's house.

RUTH She told her tale so passionately, that Isabella believes every word of it; and is resolved, as she says, never to see thee more.

BELFOND JUNIOR Oh, this most malicious, and most infamous of her sex; there is not the least truth in her accusation.

TRUMAN That to my knowledge, he is not a man of those principles.

RUTH I will send them to you, if I can; and in the meantime, be upon the watch.

TRUMAN Take this writing with thee; which is a bond from us, to make good our agreement with thee.

RUTH 'Tis well, and still I doubt not to perform my part.   [*Exit*]

BELFOND JUNIOR Was ever man plagued with a wench like me? Well, say what they will, the life of a whore-master is a foolish, restless, anxious life; and there's an end of it. What can be done with this malicious devil? A man cannot offer violence to a woman.

TRUMAN Steal away her child, and then you may awe her.

BELFOND JUNIOR I have emissaries abroad, to find out the child; but she'll sacrifice that, and all the world, to her revenge.

TRUMAN You must arrest her upon a swinging action, which she cannot get bail for, and keep her till she's humbled.

Enter Teresia.

Madam, I kiss your hand.

TERESIA You have done well, Mr Belfond: here has been a lady, whom you have had a child by, were contracted to, and have deserted, for an attorney's daughter which you keep; my cousin says she will never see you more.

★ go to twelve: share equally.

BELFOND JUNIOR If this be true, Madam, I deserve never to see her more; which would be worse than death to me.

TERESIA I have prevailed with her once more to see you, and hear what you can say to this: come, come, cousin. [*she leads in Isabella*] Look you, cousin, Mr Belfond denies all this matter.

ISABELLA I never doubted that: but certainly it is impossible to counterfeit so lively as she did.

BELFOND JUNIOR Heaven is my witness that her accusation is false: I never was yet contracted to any woman, nor made the least promise, or gave any one the least hope of it; and if I do not demonstrate my innocence to you, I will be content for ever to be debarred the sight of you, more prized by me than liberty, or life.

ISABELLA And yet perhaps these very words were said to her.

TRUMAN Madam, you have not time, if you value your own liberty; to argue any longer: we will carry you to Sir Edward Belfond's, his sister is his housekeeper, and there you may be entertained with safety of your honour.

TERESIA He is esteemed a worthy gentleman; nor could we choose a better guardian.

ISABELLA At least, how could you use a woman ill, you had a child by.

BELFOND JUNIOR Not all the malice of mankind can equal hers. I have been frail, I must confess, as others; and though I have provided for her and her child, yet every day she does me all the most outrageous mischief she can possibly conceive; but this has touched me in the tenderest point.

ISABELLA 'Twould be much for my honour, to put myself into the hands of a known wencher.

BELFOND JUNIOR Into the hands of one, who has abandoned all the thoughts of vice and folly for you.

TRUMAN Besides, Madam, you neither of you trust us; your governess is with you, and yet we are ready to make good our words by the assistance of a parson.

TERESIA That's another point: but I am sure, cousin, there is no dallying about our liberty: if you be in love with your gaol, stay; I, for my part, am resolved to go.

BELFOND JUNIOR My uncle's a virtuous honourable man; my aunt, his sister, a lady of great piety: think if you will not be safer there, than with your uncle, by whom you are sold for £5000 to my knowledge, to one who is the most debauched dissolute fellow this day in London.

TERESIA Liberty, liberty, I say; I'll trust myself, and my governess.

Enter Ruth.

RUTH Haste, and agree: your father has sent to have supper ready in less than half an hour.

TERESIA Away, away; I am ready; cousin, farewell.

BELFOND JUNIOR For heaven's sake, Madam, on my knees I beg you to make use of this occasion, or you have lost yourself; and I too shall for ever lose you for marriage; which alone can keep me from being the most miserable: you may advise, and all things shall be cleared up to your wish.

TERESIA Farewell, dear cousin: let's kiss at parting.

ISABELLA Sure thou hast not the conscience; thou wilt not leave me?

TERESIA By my troth but I will.

ISABELLA By my troth but you shall not; for I'll go with thee.

BELFOND JUNIOR May all the joys of life for ever wait on you.

RUTH Haste! Haste! Begone – [*Exeunt*]

⟨SCENE III⟩

Enter Sir William Belfond.

SIR WILLIAM BELFOND That I should live to this unhappy age! To see the fruit of all my hopes thus blasted: how long, like chemists have I watched and toiled; and in the minute when I expected to have seen projection, all is flown up *in fumo.*

Enter Sir Edward.

Brother! I am ashamed to look on you, my disappointment is so great. O this most wicked recreant! This perverse and infamous son.

SIR EDWARD BELFOND Brother, a wise man is never disappointed. Man's life is like a game at tables; if at any time the cast you most shall need does not come up: let that which comes instead of it be mended by your play.

SIR WILLIAM BELFOND How different have been our fates? I left the pleasures of the Town, to marry, which was no small bondage, had children, which brought more care upon me: for their sakes I lived a rustic, painful, hard, severe, and melancholy life: morose, inhospitable, sparing even necessaries; tenacious, even to griping, for their good: my neighbours shunned me, my friends neglected me, my children hate me, and wish my death: nay, this wicked son in whom I had set up my rest, and principally for whose good I thus had lived, has now defeated all my hopes.

SIR EDWARD BELFOND 'Twas your own choice: you would not learn from others.

SIR WILLIAM BELFOND You have lived ever at ease, indulged all pleasures, and melted down your time in daily feasts, and in continual revels: gentle, complaisant, affable, and liberal, at great expense: the world speaks well of you; mankind embrace you; your son loves you, and wishes your life as much as he can do his own. But I'll perplex myself no more: I look upon this rascal as an excrement, a wen, or gangrened limb, lopped off.

SIR EDWARD BELFOND Rather look on him as a dislocated one, and get him set again: by this time you see, severity will do nothing, entice him back to you by love. In short, give him his liberty, and a good allowance: there now remains no other way to reclaim him; for like a stone-horse★ broke in among the mares, no fence hereafter will contain him.

SIR WILLIAM BELFOND Brother, I look upon you as a true friend, that would not insult upon my folly and presumption, and confess you are nearer to the right than I. Your son I hope will be a comfort to me.

SIR EDWARD BELFOND I doubt it not; but consider, if you do not reconcile yourself, and reclaim yours as I tell you, you lop off the paternal estate, which is all entailed for ever from your family: for, in the course he is, the reversion will be gone in your lifetime.

Enter Belfond Junior, Truman, Isabella, Teresia, and Ruth.

★ stone-horse: a stallion.

BELFOND JUNIOR Here are my father and my uncle: mask your-selves, ladies; you must not yet discover who you are.

SIR EDWARD BELFOND Yonder's Ned, and his friend, with ladies masked: who should they be?

SIR WILLIAM BELFOND Whores, whores, what should they be else? Here's a comfortable sight again! He is incorrigible.

SIR EDWARD BELFOND 'Tis you that are incorrigible: how ready are you with your censures!

BELFOND JUNIOR Sir, pardon the freedom I use with you; I humbly desire protection for these ladies in your house: they are women of honour, I do assure you, and desire to be concealed for some small time; an hour hence I will discover all to you, and you will then approve of what I do.

SIR EDWARD BELFOND Dear Ned, I will trust thy honour; and without any examination, do as you would have me.

SIR WILLIAM BELFOND Why, brother, what a pox, will you pimp for your son? What a devil, will you make your house a bawdy-house?

SIR EDWARD BELFOND What, will the must never be gotten out of your old vessel? Ladies, be pleased to honour my house; and be assured, that while you are there, 'tis yours. [*he waits on the Ladies, and Ruth*]

BELFOND JUNIOR Sir, my friend and I are just now going to do you service: I'll pawn my life to you, Sir, I will retrieve your rebel son, and immediately restore him to you, and bring him, as he ought to come, on's knees, with a full submission.

SIR WILLIAM BELFOND You will oblige me: thou gain'st upon me hourly, and I begin to love thee more and more.

BELFOND JUNIOR There's nothing in the world I aim at now but your love; and I will be bold to say, I shortly will deserve it: but this business requires haste, for I have laid everything ready; 'tis almost bed-time; come friend.   [*Exit with Truman*]

SIR WILLIAM BELFOND Well, I'll say that for him, he is a good-natured boy; it makes me weep, to think how harsh I have been to him. I'll in to my brother, and expect the event.   [*Exit*]

⟨SCENE IV⟩

Enter Belfond Senior, Shamwell and Hackum.

CHEATLY I value not misfortune, so as I have my dear friend still within my arms.

SHAMWELL My dear, dear cousin! I will hug thee close to me; I feared to have lost thee.

BELFOND SENIOR How happy am I in the truest, the dearest friends that ever man enjoyed! Well, I was so afflicted for you, I was forced to make myself devilish boozy to comfort me.

CHEATLY Your brother has heard of this great match you are to-wards: she has to my knowledge, (for I do all her law business for her) £1500 a year jointure, and ten thousand pound in plate, money, and jewels; and this damned envious brother of yours will break it off, if you make not haste and prevent him.

BELFOND SENIOR My dear friends, you are in the right: never man met with such before. I'll disappoint the rogue my brother, and the old prig my father; adad, I'll do't instantly.

CHEATLY Come, squire, haste: captain, do you follow us. [*Exeunt*]

⟨SCENE V⟩

Scene changes to Mrs Termagant's fine lodgings

Enter Belfond Senior, Cheatly, Shamwell, Hackum, Parson;
Mrs Termagant and her Servants.

CHEATLY Madam, the time admits of no longer deliberation: if you take not this opportunity, my friend here will be ravished from us.

BELFOND SENIOR Aye, Madam, if you take me not now, you will lose me Madam, you will consider what you do.

MRS TERMAGANT Well, Mr Cheatly, you dispose of me as you please: I have ever been guided by your wise advice.

SHAMWELL Come, parson, do your office; have you your book about ye?

PARSON What, do you think I am without the tools of my trade?

CHEATLY Can't you come presently to the joining of hands, and leave out the rest of the formalities.

PARSON Aye, aye; come, stand forth. [*Belfond Senior and Mrs Termagant stand forth*]

Enter Belfond Junior, Truman, Constable, Serjeant, Musketeers.

BELFOND JUNIOR Here they are: seize them all.

CHEATLY Hell and damnation! We are all undone.

BELFOND SENIOR Hands off; let me alone: I am going to be married. You envious rascal to come just in the nick.

BELFOND JUNIOR Brother, be satisfied, there's nothing but honour meant to you: 'tis for your service.

MRS TERMAGANT O this accursed wretch, to come in this unlucky minute, and ruin all my fortune.

BELFOND SENIOR She has fifteen hundred a year jointure, and ten thousand pound in money, etc. and I had been married to her in three minutes.

BELFOND JUNIOR You have escaped the worst of ruins: resist not, for if you do, you shall be carried by head and heels. Your father will receive you, and be kind, and give you as good an allowance as ever I had.

SHAMWELL Where's your warrant?

CONSTABLE 'Tis here, from my lord Chief Justice.

BELFOND JUNIOR Let me see your bride that was to be. O Mrs Termagant! O horror! Horror! What a ruin have you escaped! This was my mistress, and still maintained by me: I have a child by her three years old.

MRS TERMAGANT Impudent villain! How dare you lie so basely?

BELFOND JUNIOR By heaven 'tis true.

MRS TERMAGANT I never saw him in my life before.

BELFOND JUNIOR Yes, often, to my plague. Brother, if I do not prove this, to you, believe me not in ought I e'er shall say. [⟨*Mrs*⟩ *Termagant goes to stab at Belfond Junior. Truman lays hold on her*]

TRUMAN Belfond, look to yourself.

BELFOND JUNIOR Ha! Disarm her. This is another show of her good nature. Brother, give me your hand, I'll wait on you; and you will thank me for your deliverance.

TRUMAN I am assured you will: you are delivered from the most infamous, and destructive villains, that ever yet took sanctuary here.

BELFOND JUNIOR And from two mischiefs you must have for ever sunk under, incest and beggary. Those three are only in the warrant with my brother; him I'll wait upon, bring you the rest. Hey! The cry is up; but we are provided. [*A great noise in the streets, and the horn blowing*; 'An arrest, an arrest.']

CHEATLY Undone, undone, all's lost!

SHAMWELL Ruined; for ever lost!

CAPTAIN HACKUM I am surprised, and cannot fight my way through.

BELFOND SENIOR What, are all these rogues? And that a whore? And am I cheated!

BELFOND JUNIOR Even so; come along; make ready musketeers. ⟨*to Truman*⟩ Do you take care of my brother, and conduct him with the rest to my uncle's house: I must go before, and carry my little mistress, to make up the business with her father.

TRUMAN I'll do it, I warrant you.

SERJEANT We are ready.			[*Exeunt all but Mrs Termagant*]

MRS TERMAGANT O vile misfortune! Had he but stayed six minutes, I had crowned all my revenge with one brave act, in marrying of his brother. Well, I have one piece of vengeance, which I will execute, or perish: besides, I'll have his blood, and then I'll die contented.

SCENE ⟨VI⟩

The street

Enter Belfond Junior, Cheatly, Shamwell, Hackum, Truman, Constable, Serjeant, Guards.

TRUMAN What do all these rabble here?

CONSTABLE Fire amongst 'em.

SERJEANT Present.

The debtors run up and down, some without their breeches, others without their coats; some out of balconies; some crying out, 'Oars, oars, sculler, five pound for a boat, ten pound for a boat, twenty pound for a boat.' The inhabitants all come out armed as before; but as soon as they see the musketeers they run, and everyone shifts for himself.

TRUMAN Hey how they run!			[*Exeunt*]

⟨SCENE VII⟩

Enter in Sir Edward's house, Sir Edward Belfond, and Attorney.

SIR EDWARD BELFOND This is the time I appointed my son to bring your daughter hither: the witness is a most malicious lying wench, and can never have credit. Besides, you know an action will sufficiently stop her mouth; for, were it true, she can never prove what she says.

ATTORNEY You say right, Sir: next to her being innocent, is the concealing of her shame.

Enter Belfond Junior and Lucia.

LUCIA And can I live to hear my fatal sentence of parting with you? Hold heart a little.

BELFOND JUNIOR It is with some convulsions I am torn from you; but I must marry, I cannot help it.

LUCIA And must I never see you more?

BELFOND JUNIOR As a lover, never: but your friend I'll be while I have breath.

LUCIA [*to herself*] Heart, do not swell so. This has awakened me, and made me see my crime: oh, that it had been sooner!

BELFOND JUNIOR Sir, I beg a thousand pardons, that I should attempt to injure your family, for it has gone no farther yet: for any fact, she's innocent; but 'twas no thanks to me, I am not so. [*aside*] If a lie be ever lawful, 'tis in this case.

SIR EDWARD BELFOND Come, pretty lady, let me present you to your father: though as my son says, she's innocent; yet, because his love had gone so far, I present her with £1500. My son and you shall be trustees for her: tomorrow you shall have the money.

BELFOND JUNIOR You are the best of all mankind.

ATTORNEY All the world speaks your praises justly.

LUCIA A thousand thanks, Sir, for your bounty: and if my father please to pardon me this slip, in which I was so far from fact, that I had scarce intention, I will hereafter outlive the strictest nun.

ATTORNEY Rise: I do pardon you.

SIR EDWARD BELFOND That's well: and if they be not kind to you, appeal to me. It will be fit for you to go from hence with the

least notice that can be: tomorrow I'll bring the money. Who are
the ladies you have entrusted me with, Ned?

                                     [Exeunt Attorney and Lucia]

BELFOND JUNIOR Scrapeall's niece and daughter! The niece my
father was to give £5000 for, for his son: if you will give me leave,
I shall marry her for nothing; and the other will take my friend –

SIR EDWARD BELFOND How Ned! She's a puritan?

BELFOND JUNIOR No more than you, Sir: she was bred otherwise, but was fain to comply for peace: she is beautiful, and witty
to a miracle; and I beg your consent, for I will die before I marry
without it.

SIR EDWARD BELFOND Dear Ned, thou hast it; but what hast
thou done with the Alsatians?

BELFOND JUNIOR I have the rogues in custody, and my brother
too; whom I rescued in the very minute he was going to be
married to a whore, to my whore who plagues me continually. I
see my father coming, pray prepare him, while I prepare my
brother for a meeting with him; he shall not see me.   *[Exit]*

Enter Sir William Belfond.

SIR WILLIAM BELFOND Your servant brother: no news of Ned
yet?

SIR EDWARD BELFOND Oh, yes; he has your son, and the three
rogues in custody, and will bring 'em hither: brother, pray resolve not to lose a son; but use him kindly, and forgive him.

SIR WILLIAM BELFOND I will, brother: and let him spend what
he will, I'll come up to London feast and revel, and never take a
minute's care while I breathe again.

Enter a Servant to Sir Edward.

SERVANT Sir, a young gentleman would speak with you.

SIR EDWARD BELFOND Bid him come in.

Enter Mrs Termagant in man's clothes.

MRS TERMAGANT If you be Sir Edward Belfond, I come to tell
you, what concerns your honour, and my love.

SIR EDWARD BELFOND I am he.

MRS TERMAGANT Know then, Sir, I am informed your brother,

Sir William Belfond's son, is to marry Isabella the niece of Mr Scrapeall.

SIR EDWARD BELFOND What then Sir?

MRS TERMAGANT Then he invades my right, I have been many months contracted to her, and as you are a man of honour, I must tell you, we have sealed that contract with mutual enjoyments.

SIR WILLIAM BELFOND How! What was my son to marry a whore? I'll to this damned fellow instantly, and make him give up my articles.

SIR EDWARD BELFOND Have patience; be not too rash.

SIR WILLIAM BELFOND Patience! What, to have my son marry a whore.

SIR EDWARD BELFOND Look you brother, you must stay a moment.

Enter Belfond Junior.

SIR WILLIAM BELFOND Oh, Ned, your brother has 'scaped a fine match: this same Isabella is contracted to, and has been enjoyed, by this gentleman, as he calls it: he had like to have married a whore.

BELFOND JUNIOR Yes, that he had; but I will cut the throat of him that affirms that of Isabella.

MRS TERMAGANT Sir, I demand the protection of your house.

SIR EDWARD BELFOND Hold, son.

MRS TERMAGANT [*aside*] What devil sent him hither at this time?

BELFOND JUNIOR I'll bring 'em to confront this rogue, what a devil's this? Have we another brother of that devil Termagant's here? [*Exit*]

SIR EDWARD BELFOND This is a very odd story.

SIR WILLIAM BELFOND Let me go, brother; 'tis true enough. But what makes Ned concerned?

SIR EDWARD BELFOND Let us examine yet farther.

Enter Belfond Junior with Isabella, Teresia, and Ruth and Truman.

SIR WILLIAM BELFOND Look, here they are all: how the devil comes this about?

MRS TERMAGANT O Madam, are you here! I claim your contract, which, I suppose, will not offend you.

ISABELLA What means this impudent fellow? I ne'er saw his face
before.

MRS TERMAGANT Yes Madam, you have seen, and more than
seen me often since we were contracted.

ISABELLA What instrument of villainy is this?

MRS TERMAGANT Nay, if you deny: friends come in.

*Enter two Alsatian affidavit men.**

Friends, do you know this gentlewoman.

1. WITNESS Yes, she is Mr Scrapeall's niece.

2. WITNESS We were both witnesses to a contract of marriage
between you too.

ISABELLA O impious wretches! What conspiracy is this!

SIR WILLIAM BELFOND Can anything be more plain? They
seem civil, grave, substantial men.

BELFOND JUNIOR Hold, hold, have I found ye? 'Tis she, it
could be no other devil but herself. [*he pulls off her peruke*]

SIR WILLIAM BELFOND A woman!

SIR EDWARD BELFOND Secure those witnesses.

BELFOND JUNIOR A woman! No: she has out-sinned her sex,
and is a devil. O devil, most complete devil! This is the lady I
have been so much of late obliged to.

ISABELLA This is she that told us the fine story today.

TERESIA I know her face again: most infamous lying creature!

MRS TERMAGANT I am become desperate: have at thee. [*she
snaps a pistol at Belfond, which only flashes in the pan, the ladies shriek*]

BELFOND JUNIOR Thank you Madam: are not you a devil?
'Twas loaden, 'twas well meant truly. [*takes the pistol from her*]

SIR EDWARD BELFOND Lay hold on her: I'll send her to a place
where she shall be tamed, I never yet heard of such malice:

SIR WILLIAM BELFOND Dear Ned, thou hast so obliged me;
thou meltest my heart: that thou shouldst steal away those ladies,
and save me £5000. Now, I hope, Madam, my son Tim shall be
your husband without bargain and sale.

ISABELLA No: I can assure you, Sir, I would never have performed

* *affidavit men*: men hired to make a false affidavit.

that bargain of my uncle's: we had determined to dispose of ourselves before that; and now are more resolved.

TERESIA We have broken prison, by the help of these gentlemen, and I think we must e'en take the authors of our liberty.

ISABELLA Will not that be a little hard, cousin, to take their liberty from them, who have given it to us?

SIR WILLIAM BELFOND Well, I am disappointed; but cannot blame thee, Ned. [*Truman goes to Teresia*]

Enter Belfond Senior.

SIR EDWARD BELFOND Your son: pray use him kindly.

BELFOND SENIOR I have been betrayed, cheated, and abused: upon my knees I beg your pardon, and never will offend you more; adad, I will not: I thought they had been the honestest, the finest gentlemen in England; and it seems they are rogues, cheats, and blockheads.

SIR WILLIAM BELFOND Rise Tim, I profess thou makest me weep, thou hast subdued me; I forgive thee, I see all human care is vain, I will allow thee £500 a year, and come, and live with ease and pleasure here: I'll feast, and revel, and wear myself with pain and care no more.

BELFOND SENIOR A thousand thanks: I'll ne'er displease you while I live again; adad I won't. ⟨*aside*⟩ Here's an alteration: I ne'er had good word from him before.

SIR WILLIAM BELFOND I would have married you to that pretty lady: but your brother has been too hard for you.

BELFOND SENIOR She's very pretty: but 'tis no matter. I am in no such haste, but I can stay and see the world first.

SIR EDWARD BELFOND Welcome dear nephew, to my house and me: and now my dear son be free, and before all this company let me know all the encumbrances you have upon you.

BELFOND JUNIOR That good natured lady is the only one that's heavy upon me, I have her child in my possession, which she says, is mine.

MRS TERMAGANT Has he my child; then I am undone for ever – O cursed misfortune!

SIR EDWARD BELFOND Look you Madam, I will settle an annuity of £100 a year, upon you so long as you shall not disturb my son: and for your child I'll breed her up and provide for her like a gentlewoman: but if you are not quiet you shall never see her more.

MRS TERMAGANT You speak like a noble gentleman: I'll strive to compose myself. I am at last subdued, but will not stay to see the triumphs – [*Exit hastily*]

SIR EDWARD BELFOND Well, dear Ned, dost owe any money?

BELFOND JUNIOR No, my dear father, no: you have been too bountiful for that: I have five hundred guineas in my cabinet.

SIR EDWARD BELFOND Now Madam, if you please to accept him for a husband, I will settle fifteen hundred pound a year on him in present, which shall be your jointure. Besides that, your own money shall be laid out in land and settled on you too. And at my death the rest of my estate.

ISABELLA You do me too much honour, you much out-bid my value.

BELFOND JUNIOR You best of fathers, and of all mankind, I throw myself thus at your feet; let me embrace your knees, and kiss those hands.

SIR EDWARD BELFOND Come rise, and kiss these hands.

BELFOND JUNIOR A long farewell to all the vanity and lewdness of youth: I offer myself at your feet as a sacrifice without a blemish now!

ISABELLA Rise, I beseech you, rise.

TERESIA Your offers, Sir, are better much than I could expect or can deserve.

TRUMAN That's impossible: the wealth of both the Indies could not buy you from me I am sure.

RUTH Come, come, I have been governess, I know their minds. Come give your hands where you have given your hearts. Here friend Truman: first take this.

TERESIA My governess will have it so.

SIR EDWARD BELFOND Joy Sir, be ever with you: please to make my house your own.

ISABELLA How can I be secure you will not fall to your old courses again?

BELFOND JUNIOR I have been so sincere in my confessions, you may trust me; but I call heaven to witness, I will hereafter be entirely yours. I look on marriage as the most solemn vow a man can make; and 'tis by consequence, the basest perjury to break it.

RUTH Come, come, I know your mind too: take him, take him.

ISABELLA If fate will have it so.

BELFOND JUNIOR Let me receive this blessing on my knees.

ISABELLA You are very devout of late.

SIR EDWARD BELFOND A thousand blessings on you both.

SIR WILLIAM BELFOND Perpetual happiness attend you both.

BELFOND SENIOR Brother and Madam! I wish you joy from my heart, adad I do: though between you and I brother, I intend to have my swing at whoring, and drinking, as you had, before I come to it though.

SIR EDWARD BELFOND Here! Bring in these rogues!

The Constable brings in Cheatly, Shamwell and Hackum.

SIR EDWARD BELFOND Come rascals, I shall take a care to see examples made of you:

CHEATLY We have substantial bail.

SIR EDWARD BELFOND I'll see it shall be substantial bail: it is my lord Chief Justice's warrant, returnable to none but him: but I will prosecute you, I assure you.

CHEATLY Squire, dear squire.

CAPTAIN HACKUM Good noble squire speak for us.

SHAMWELL Dear cousin!

BELFOND SENIOR O rogues! Cousin, you have cozened me: you made a put, a caravan, a bubble of me: I gave a judgment for £1600 and had but £250 but there's some goods they talk of; but if e'er I be catched again I'll be hanged.

SIR WILLIAM BELFOND Unconscionable villains! The Chancery shall relieve us.

SIR EDWARD BELFOND I'll rout this knot of most pernicious knaves, for all the privilege of your place. Was ever such impudence suffered in a government? Ireland's conquered: Wales subdued: Scotland united: but there are some few spots of ground in London, just in the face of the government, unconquered yet, that hold in rebellion still. Methinks 'tis strange, that places so near the king's palace should be no parts of his dominions: 'tis a shame to the societies of law to countenance such practices:

should any place be shut against the king's writ or *posse comitatus*?
Take them away and those two witnesses. [*the Constable and Watch
hales 'em away*]

BELFOND SENIOR Away with 'em, rogues! Rascals, damned
prigs.

SIR EDWARD BELFOND Come ladies, I have sent for some neighbours to rejoice with us. We have fiddles: let's dance a brisk
round or two, and then we'll make a collation.

In the flourish before the dance enter Scrapeall.

SCRAPEALL O Sir William, I am undone, ruined: the birds are
flown. Read the note they left behind 'em.

SIR WILLIAM BELFOND Peace, they are dancing, they have disposed of themselves.

SCRAPEALL O seed of serpents! Am I cheated then? I'll try a trick
of law, you frogs of the bottomless pit, I will and instantly – [*they
dance*] What dancing too? Then they are fallen indeed.

[*Exit Scrapeall hastily*]

SIR EDWARD BELFOND Come brother, now who has been in the
right, you or I?

SIR WILLIAM BELFOND You have: prithee do not triumph.

BELFOND JUNIOR Farewell ever all the vices of the age:
There is no peace but in a virtuous life,
Nor lasting joy but in a tender wife.

SIR EDWARD BELFOND You, that would breed your children
well, by kindness and liberality endear 'em to you: and teach
'em by example.
Severity spoils ten, for one it mends:
If you'd not have your sons desire your ends,
By gentleness and bounty make those sons your friends.

[*Exeunt Omnes*]

EPILOGUE

Spoken by Mrs Mountfort ⟨Isabella⟩

Ye mighty scourers of these narrow seas,
Who suffer not a bark to sail in peace,
But with your fire of culverins ye roar,
Bring 'em by th' lee, and rummage all their store;
Our poet ducked, and looked as if half-dead,
At every shot that whistled o'er his head.
Frequent engagements ne'er could make him bold,
He sneaked into a corner of the hold.
Since he submits, pray ease him of his fear,
And with a joint applause bid him appear,
Good critics don't insult and domineer.
He fears not sparks, who with brisk dress and mien,
Come not to hear or see, but to be seen.
Each prunes himself, and with a languishing eye,
Designs to kill a lady by the by.
Let each fantastic ugly beau and shape,
Little of man, and very much of ape,
Admire himself, and let the poet 'scape.
    Ladies, your anger most he apprehends,
And is grown past the age of making friends
Of any of the sex whom he offends.
No princess frowns, no hero rants and whines,
Nor is weak sense embroidered with strong lines:
No battles, trumpets, drums, not any die;
No mortal wounds, to please your cruelty;
Who like not any thing but tragedy.
With fond, unnatural extravagancies,
Stolen from the silly authors of romances.
Let such the chamber-maids' diversion be,
Pray be you reconciled to comedy.
For when we make you merry, you must own
You are much prettier than when you frown.
With charming smiles you use to conquer still,
The melancholy look's not apt to kill.

Our poet begs you who adorn this sphere,
This shining circle, will not be severe.
Here no chit-chat,★ here no tea-tables are.
The cant he hopes will not be long unknown,
'Tis almost grown the language of the Town.
For fops, who feel a wretched want of wit,
Still set up something that may pass for it.
He begs that you will often grace his play,
And lets you know Monday's† his visiting day.

★ chit-chat: the contrast between tea-tables and coffee-houses was between feminine and masculine interests.
† Monday: the third day, when the author received the profits.

NOTES

The copy text used is that of the first edition of 1688 in the Brotherton Collection, University of Leeds.

Abbreviations
  Q1 The first quarto edition, 1688
  Q2 The second quarto edition, 1692
  Q3 The third quarto edition, 1693

113.3   Whitefriars / Whitefryers Q1 VVhite-fryers Q3
121.23   Lieutenant's / Lieutenants Q1
122.26   scholars / scholar Q1
122.29   Godsookers Q2 / Goodsookers Q1
124.13   him in thy / him thy Q1
124.30   Godsookers / Gudzookers Q1
124.36   boozy / bowzy Q1 / bowsie Q3
127.2   what, my / what my Q1
131.16   'tis that / This that Q1
133.8   boozy / Bowsy Q1
136.16   him you have adopted Q2 / him Q1
136.30   monstrous Q2 / monsters Q1
139.5   looks, my / looks? My Q1
143.12   me! / me? Q1
145.4   and by Q2 / by Q1
146.30   Oh, oh / Oh Oh Q1
146.38   Oh, oh / Oh Oh Q1
147.2   I'll / i'll Q1
158.1   *All cry out* . . . is placed four lines earlier in Q1
158.7   *across / cross* Q1
159.13   an he be / an be Q1
160.8   *Belfond strikes up* . . . is placed after Sir Edward's 'Let me
         see' in Q1
161.35   Fleet Street. Thanks / *Fleetstreet*, thanks Q1
162.17   immediately when / immediately; when Q1
168.2   brother! Courage / Brother, Courage Q1
168.32   boozy / bowsy Q1 bowsie Q2 Q3
171.5   and a cock-bawd / and cock-bawd Q1 / and a cook-bawd Q3
174.4   in a chair / in Chair Q1

174.6   her!/her? Q1
174.16   No, young/No young Q1
174.16   you. What/you: What Q1
174.21   convinced. Go/convinced: Go Q1
175.29   poetry/poerry Q1
175.31   *s.d. she snatches* . . . Q1 places at end of previous speech
176.6   casements Q3/casement Q1
180.6   *Enter Truman* is placed after 'my friend' in Q1
194.37   tattle; here's/ *Tattle?* here's Q1
195.7   slave; but . . . smoky; I . . . you; I/slave, but . . .
          smoaky, I . . . you, I Q1
195.12   adad. Odsookers/adad; Odsookers Q1
196.10   rogues, dogs/Rogues Dogs Q1
196.18   lose/loose Q1
197.26   boozy/bowsie Q1
201.3   sovereign/sovereingen Q1
201.10   barber's/barbers Q1
207.9   boozy/bowsie Q1
209.12   'Even so . . . musketeers' is given to Belford Junior in Q1
          who is repeated for the next speech
211.5   father was/father, was Q1
211.27   I breathe/breath Q1

LOVE FOR LOVE
by William Congreve

INTRODUCTION

Congreve was born in Bardsey, a village north of Leeds, in 1670, but he grew up in Ireland. His father was in command of the garrison at Youghal, Co. Cork, moved to Carrickfergus, and then was transferred to Kilkenny, to the Duke of Ormonde's regiment. William was sent to Kilkenny College, an excellent school supported by the Ormonde family. From Kilkenny he went to Trinity College, Dublin, in 1686, becoming a pupil of St George Ashe, among whose other pupils was Jonathan Swift, three years Congreve's senior, who had also been to Kilkenny College. When Trinity College closed in 1688 because of the dangerous political situation, Congreve joined the many Irish Protestants who sought safety in England. He went to the family seat in Staffordshire, then to London, becoming a student of law at the Middle Temple in 1691 when, after the Williamite victories, his father returned to Ireland to become agent for Richard Boyle, Earl of Cork.

Congreve was, however, more attracted to drama than law: his classical knowledge and interest in translation impressed Dryden and he became a close friend of the older man, who included some of his poems and translations in *Examen Poeticum*, a collection of miscellaneous poems. Congreve tried his hand at novel writing with *Incognita* (1692) which was completed in the 'idler hours of a fortnight's time'. This novel, he asserted in the preface, followed dramatic models in the working out of its plot. His first play, *The Old Bachelor*, was finished in the same year and appealed greatly to Dryden who helped him to polish it into a form suitable for the stage. Thomas Southerne (another graduate of Trinity College, Dublin) and Arthur Mainwaring also helped. The play was first performed in January 1693 at the Theatre Royal. Anne Bracegirdle played the part of Araminta when she was just 'blooming to her maturity'. This role established her fame; she became 'the darling of the theatre'; and Congreve subsequently created his heroines with her in mind. He told his friend Keally that 'our friend Venus' (Mrs Bracegirdle played the part of Venus in his masque *The Judgment of Paris*) performed 'to a miracle' and he was obviously in love with her. Their friendship was close, despite his cousin Robert Leke, third Earl of Scarsdale, becoming infatuated with her, but

Congreve's writing 'False tho' you've been to me and love' indicates some stresses. Marriage was probably out of the question on account of the social gulf between a country gentleman's son and an actress – but they were close neighbours, Congreve living in Arundel Street and Anne Bracegirdle in Howard Street.

Her acting and that of Thomas Betterton as well as that of the rest of the cast, which included Elizabeth Barry, Mrs Mountford, Dogget, Bowen, Cave Underhill and Jack Verbruggen, assured the success of *The Old Bachelor*, and Congreve, now known as poet, translator, novelist and dramatist, followed it with another comedy in the same vein. This was *The Double-Dealer*, a sombre and powerful but over-complicated play, which did not impress the public. Congreve – and Dryden who tended to see the younger man as his successor – were obviously annoyed at the play's reception, but *Love for Love*, first staged in 1695 at the Lincoln's Inn Fields theatre, had a far better reception. This play opened the programme of the new theatre and the prologues were spoken by Betterton and Mrs Bracegirdle ('in man's clothes').

The company which performed *Love for Love* had Congreve and Vanbrugh as its managers, and Congreve was meant to write a new play for the company each year, a task he did not fulfil. His next play was a tragedy, *The Mourning Bride*, which proved highly popular when it was performed in 1697. The following year the Rev. Jeremy Collier's pamphlet, *A Short View of the Immorality and Profaneness of the English Stage together with the sense of Ambiguity upon this argument*, was published and Congreve was among those who replied to it. His *Amendments of Mr Collier's False and Imperfect Citations* was not persuasive, though it does contain many valid points.

The reason for the ineffectiveness of Congreve's reply was that the taste of the audiences had begun to change. He recognised this himself, and wrote of it in his Dedication in *The Way of the World* (1700). This play, his greatest achievement, was not as popular as might have been expected, and after completing a masque, *The Judgment of Paris*, the following year, and collaborating with Vanbrugh and Walsh in writing *Monsieur de Pourceaugnac or, Squire Trelooby*, he ceased to write for the theatre.

Congreve's career in the theatre was short: by thirty he had given up his role as dramatist and five years later he gave up his managership of the new company he and John Vanbrugh had established in 1704 which worked in the Haymarket or Queen's Theatre. He had begun another career, as a public servant, and held various official posts: a commissionership for licensing hackney coaches in 1695; the collectorship of customs at Poole from 1700 to 1702; a commissionership for wine licences in 1705; and then a post in customs in London and secretary of Jamaica. He sought a quiet life; his friendship for Mrs Bracegirdle seems to have diminished after 1700; he withdrew from a wide range of acquaintances which included Swift, Gay, Pope, Steele and Lady Mary Wortley Montague to a small circle of friends; and his health deteriorated. He became a close friend of Henrietta the second Duchess of Marlborough after 1705, and was probably the father of her daughter, later the Duchess of Leeds. He was seriously ill in 1726, seemed to have recovered, then fell ill again in 1728, and died in January 1729.

Congreve's comedies mark the high point of Restoration comedy. The audience was changing, and the managers – who sought to fill the larger theatres by giving the new middle class audience the kind of drama it preferred – affected what was written. Cynicism, the comedy of manners, the reaction against puritanism, had virtually had their day. And though we can regard *The Way of the World* as being the most polished and refined example of the genre it does contain new elements. Millamant, for instance, wants more than had apparently satisfied the Restoration heroine earlier. And this is true of *Love for Love* as well, even though it was written before Collier's animadversions had put publicly what was already being sensed by dramatists.

Love for Love is not as brilliant as *The Way of the World* but in many ways it is a better acting play. When first performed it ran for thirteen days consecutively. The cast was excellent, Thomas Betterton playing Valentine, and Anne Bracegirdle Angelica. Thomas Dogget was extremely successful as Ben. In the eighteenth century the play was more often played than *The Way of the World*, and towards the latter half of the century it was often revived for benefits. In the nineteenth century its popularity diminished but it has been frequently produced in the twentieth.

Love for Love has a clear, fast-moving plot with an abundance of absurdity. But genuine humour and satire are also there, as well as plenty of characterisation. Foresight, with his hypochondria, his passion for astrology, and his absurd credulity, is akin to one of Ben Jonson's examples of a person dominated by characteristics all pursued to excess. In the same way Sir Sampson Legend's insensitivity is excessive and merits his exposure both as dictatorial father and ludicrous lover.

All the usual ingredients of the comedy of manners are present: conflicts of youth and age; problems of inheritance and of debts; flippant views on marriage; intrigues pursued with intelligence; deceits; witty conversations; contrasts between sophisticated city and naive country ways. Beneath the persiflage, however, we can experience the author's disquiet about conventional views of life. There is a touch of tempered idealism in both Valentine and Angelica: more than witty gallantry is required as a basis for civilised marriage.

The reason for the play's continuing success is probably its highly skilled characterisation, as well as its satire. Thus Ben's language is nautical while Sir Foresight's interest in astrology marks him out equally clearly. Valentine's pretended madness gives Congreve scope for introducing many topics, and Sir Sampson's replies to him are excellent in their furious expostulations. Mrs Frail and Mrs Foresight can also handle language with sharpness and skill. The result is a rich pattern of speech and differentiated character set in a web of intrigue.

William Congreve

Love For Love

A COMEDY

Acted at the Theatre in Little Lincolns Inn Fields,
by His Majesty's Servants

Written by Mr Congreve

Nudus agris, nudus nummis paternis,
Insanire parat certa ratione modoque.*
Hor.

LONDON

Printed for Jacob Tonson, at the Judge's Head,
near the Inner Temple Gate in Fleet Street.
1695

* *Nudus . . . modoque*: This quotation is adapted from two lines of Horace, *Satires*, II, iii, 184 and 271: *Nudus agris, nudus nummis, insane, paternis?* and *insanire paret certa ratione modoque*. Bereft of lands, bereft of paternal coins, let him prepare to rage. The copy text alters *paret* to *parat*, omitting *insane*: this should be translated as 'prepares to rage'.

DEDICATION

TO THE
RIGHT HONOURABLE
CHARLES
EARL OF DORSET AND MIDDLESEX.

Lord Chamberlain of His Majesty's Household, and Knight of the
Most Noble Order of the Garter, &c.

My lord,

A young poet, is liable to the same vanity and indiscretion with a
young lover; and the great man that smiles upon one, and the fine
woman that looks kindly upon t'other, are each of 'em in danger of
having the favour published with the first opportunity.

But there may be a different motive, which will a little distinguish the offenders. For though one should have a vanity in ruining
another's reputation, yet the other may only have an ambition to
advance his own. And I beg leave, my lord, that I may plead the
latter, both as the cause and excuse of this dedication.

Whoever is king, is also the father of his country; and as no body
can dispute your lordship's monarchy in poetry; so all that are
concerned, ought to acknowledge your universal patronage: and it
is only presuming on the privilege of a loyal subject, that I have
ventured to make this my address of thanks, to your lordship; which
at the same time, includes a prayer for your protection.

I am not ignorant of the common form of poetical dedications,
which are generally made up of panegyrics, where the authors endeavour to distinguish their patrons, by the shining characters
they give them, above other men. But that, my lord, is not my
business at this time, nor is your lordship *now* to be distinguished. I
am contented with the honour I do myself in this epistle; without the
vanity of attempting to add to, or explain your lordship's character.

I confess it is not without some struggling, that I behave myself
in this case, as I ought: for it is very hard to be pleased with a subject, and yet forbear it. But I choose rather to follow Pliny's precept,
than his example, when in his panegyric to the Emperor Trajan,
he says,

Nec minus considerabo quid aures ejus pati
possint, quam quid virtutibus debeatur.★

I hope I may be excused the pedantry of a quotation, when it is so justly applied. Here are some lines in the print, (and which your lordship read before this play was acted) that were omitted on the stage; and particularly one whole scene in the third act, which not only helps the design forward with less precipitation, but also heightens the ridiculous character of Foresight, which indeed seems to be maimed without it. But I found myself in great danger of a long play, and was glad to help it where I could. Though notwithstanding my care, and the kind reception it had from the Town; I could heartily wish it yet shorter: but the number of different characters represented in it, would have been too much crowded in less room.

This reflection on prolixity, (a fault, for which scarce any one beauty will atone) warns me not to be tedious now, and detain your lordship any longer with the trifles of,

my lord,
your lordship's
most obedient
and most humble
servant,

WILL. CONGREVE.

★ *Nec minus . . . debeatur*: And I will regard no less what his ears can tolerate than what is owed to his virtues.

DRAMATIS PERSONAE

MEN

Sir Sampson Legend	Father to Valentine and Ben.
Valentine	Fallen under his father's displeasure by his expensive way of living, in love with Angelica.
Scandal	His friend, a free speaker.
Tattle	A half-witted beau, vain of his amours, yet valuing himself for secrecy.
Ben	Sir Sampson's younger son, half home-bred, and half sea-bred, designed to marry Miss Prue.
Foresight	An illiterate old fellow, peevish and positive, superstitious, and pretending to understand astrology, palmistry, physiognomy, omens, dreams, &c. Uncle to Angelica.
Jeremy	Servant to Valentine.
Trapland	A scrivener.
Buckram	A lawyer.

WOMEN

Angelica	Niece to Foresight, of a considerable fortune in her own hands.
Mrs Foresight	Second wife to Foresight.
Mrs Frail	Sister to Mrs Foresight, a woman of the Town.
Miss Prue	Daughter to Foresight by a former wife, a silly, awkward, country girl.
Nurse	to Miss ⟨Prue⟩
Jenny	Maid to Angelica.

A Steward, Officers, Sailors, and several Servants.

The scene in London.

A PROLOGUE

For the opening of the new play-house, proposed to be
spoken by Mrs Bracegirdle ⟨Angelica⟩ in man's clothes

Sent from an unknown hand.

Custom, which everywhere bears mighty sway,
Brings me to act the orator today:
But women, you will say, are ill at speeches,
'Tis true, and therefore I appear in breeches:
Not for example to you City-wives;
That by prescription's settled for your lives.
Was it for gain the husband first consented?
O yes, their gains are mightily augmented:
And yet, methinks, it must have cost [*making horns
    with her hands over her head*] some strife:
A passive husband, and an active wife!
'Tis awkward, very awkward, by my life.
But to my speech, assemblies of all nations
Still are supposed to open with orations:
Mine shall begin, to show our obligations.
To you, our benefactors, lowly bowing,
Whose favours have prevented our undoing;
A long Egyptian bondage we endured,
Till freedom, by your justice we procured:
Our taskmasters were grown such very Jews,
We must at length have played in wooden shoes,
Had not your bounty taught us to refuse.
Freedoms of English growth, I think, alone;
What for lost English freedom can atone?
A free-born player loathes to be compelled;
Our rulers tyrannized, and we rebelled.
Freedom! The wise man's wish, the poor man's wealth;
Which you, and I, and most of us enjoy by stealth;
The soul of pleasure, and the sweet of life,
The woman's charter, widow, maid or wife,
This they'd have cancelled, and thence grew the strife.

But you perhaps, would have me here confess
How we obtained the favour; – can't you guess?
Why then I'll tell you, (for I hate a lie)
By bribery, errant bribery, let me die:
I was their agent, but by Jove I swear
No honourable member had a share
Though young and able members bid me fair:
I chose a wiser way to make you willing,
Which has not cost the house a single shilling;
Now you suspect at least I went a-billing.
You see I'm young, and to that air of youth,
Some will add beauty, and a little truth;
These powerful charms, improved by powerful arts,
Prevailed to captivate your opening hearts.
Thus furnished, I preferred my poor petition,
And bribed ye to commiserate our condition:
I laughed, and sighed, and sung, and leered upon ye;
With roguish loving looks, and that way won ye:
The young men kissed me, and the old I kissed,
And luringly, I led them as I list.
The ladies in mere pity took our parts,
Pity's the darling passion of their hearts.
Thus bribing, or thus bribed, fear no disgraces;
For thus you may take bribes, and keep your places.

PROLOGUE

The husbandman in vain renews his toil,
To cultivate each year a hungry soil;
And fondly hopes for rich and generous fruit,
When what should feed the tree, devours the root;
Th' unladen boughs, he sees, bode certain dearth,
Unless transplanted to more kindly earth.
So, the poor husbands of the stage, who found
Their labours lost upon the ungrateful ground,
This last and only remedy have proved;
And hope new fruit from ancient stocks removed.
Well may they hope, when you so kindly aid,
And plant a soil which you so rich have made.
As nature gave the world to man's first age,
So from your bounty, we receive this stage;
The freedom man was born to, you've restored,
And to our world, such plenty you afford,
It seems like Eden, fruitful of its own accord.
But since in Paradise frail flesh gave way,
And when but two were made, both went astray;
Forbear your wonder, and the fault forgive,
If in our larger family we grieve
One falling Adam, and one tempted Eve.
We who remain, would gratefully repay
What our endeavours can, and bring this day,
The first-fruit offering, of a virgin play.
We hope there's something that may please each taste,
And though of homely fare we make the feast,
Yet you will find variety at least.
There's humour, which for cheerful friends we got,
And for the thinking party there's a plot.
We've something too, to gratify ill nature,
(If there be any here) and that is satire.
Though satire scarce dares grin, 'tis grown so mild;

Or only shows its teeth, as if it smiled.
As asses thistles, poets mumble wit,
And dare not bite, for fear of being bit.
They hold their pens, as swords are held by fools,
And are afraid to use their own edge-tools.
Since *The Plain-Dealer's*★ scenes of manly rage,
Not one has dared to lash this crying age.
This time, the poet owns the bold essay,
Yet hopes there's no ill-manners in his play:
And he declares by me, he has designed
Affront to none, but frankly speaks his mind.
And should the ensuing scenes not chance to hit,
He offers but this one excuse, 'twas writ
Before your late encouragement of wit.

★ *The Plain Dealer's*: Wycherley's play of that name.

ACT ONE

SCENE I

Valentine in his chamber reading. Jeremy waiting.
Several books upon the table.

VALENTINE Jeremy.

JEREMY Sir.

VALENTINE Here, take away; I'll walk a turn, and digest what I have read –

JEREMY [*aside, and taking away the books*] You'll grow devilish fat upon this paper diet.

VALENTINE And d'ye hear, go you to breakfast – There's a page doubled down in Epictetus,* that is a feast for an emperor.

JEREMY Was Epictetus a real cook, or did he only write receipts?

VALENTINE Read, read, sirrah, and refine your appetite; learn to live upon instruction; feast your mind, and mortify your flesh; read, and take your nourishment in at your eyes; shut up your mouth; and chew the cud of understanding. So Epictetus advises.

JEREMY O Lord! I have heard much of him, when I waited upon a gentleman at Cambridge: pray what was that Epictetus?

VALENTINE A very rich man. – Not worth a groat.

JEREMY Humph, and so he has made a very fine feast, where there is nothing to be eaten.

VALENTINE Yes.

JEREMY Sir, you're a gentleman, and probably understand this fine feeding: but if you please, I had rather be at board-wages. Does your Epictetus, or your Seneca† here, or any of these poor, rich rogues, teach you how to pay your debts without money? Will they shut up the mouths of your creditors? Will Plato‡ be bail for you? Or Diogenes,§ because he understands confinement,

* Epictetus: Greek stoic philosopher who lived *c.* A.D. 55–135 and who taught that the universe is the work of God and that divine Providence manifests itself in its order and unity.

† Seneca: Lucius Annaeus Seneca (*d.* A.D. 65), philosopher who was Nero's tutor. He wrote nine tragedies and works on moral philosophy.

‡ Plato: Plato (*c.* 427–348 B.C.), Greek philosopher, pupil and admirer of Socrates, author of the theory of ideas.

§ Diogenes: Diogenes the Cynic, a Greek philosopher (*b.c.* 412 B.C.).

and lived in a tub, go to prison for you? S'life, Sir, what do you mean, to mew yourself up here with three or four musty books, in commendation of starving and poverty?

VALENTINE Why, sirrah, I have no money, you know it; and therefore resolve to rail at all that have: and in that I but follow the examples of the wisest and wittiest men in all ages; these poets and philosophers whom you naturally hate, for just such another reason; because they abound in sense, and you are a fool.

JEREMY Aye, Sir, I am a fool, I know it: and yet, heaven help me, I'm poor enough to be a wit – But I was always a fool, when I told you what your expenses would bring you to; your coaches and your liveries; your treats and your balls; your being in love with a lady, that did not care a farthing for you in your prosperity; and keeping company with wits, that cared for nothing but your prosperity; and now when you are poor, hate you as much as they do one another.

VALENTINE Well; and now I am poor, I have an opportunity to be revenged on 'em all; I'll pursue Angelica with more love than ever, and appear more notoriously her admirer in this restraint, than when I openly rivalled fops, that made court to her; so shall my poverty be a mortification to her pride, and perhaps, make her compassionate that love, which has principally reduced me to this lowness of fortune. And for the wits, I'm sure I'm in a condition to be even with them –

JEREMY Nay, your condition is pretty even with theirs, that's the truth on't.

VALENTINE I'll take some of their trade out of their hands.

JEREMY Now heaven of mercy continue the tax upon paper; you don't mean to write!

VALENTINE Yes, I do; I'll write a play.

JEREMY Hem! – Sir, if you please to give me a small certificate of three lines – only to certify those whom it may concern; that the bearer hereof, Jeremy Fetch by name, has for the space of seven years truly and faithfully served Valentine Legend Esq; and that he is not now turned away for any misdemeanour; but does voluntarily dismiss his master from any future authority over him –

VALENTINE No, sirrah, you shall live with me still.

JEREMY Sir, it's impossible – I may die with you, starve with you, or be damned with your works: but to live even three days, the life of a play, I no more expect it, than to be canonized for a muse after my decease.

VALENTINE You are witty, you rogue, I shall want your help; – I'll have you learn to make couplets, to tag the ends of acts: d'ye hear, get the maids to crambo in an evening, and learn the knack of rhyming; you may arrive at the height of a song, sent by an unknown hand, or a chocolate-house lampoon.

JEREMY But Sir, is this the way to recover your father's favour? Why Sir Sampson will be irreconcilable. If your younger brother should come from sea, he'd never look upon you again. You're undone, Sir; you're ruined; you won't have a friend left in the world, if you turn poet – Ah pox confound that Will's coffee-house,* it has ruined more young men than the Royal Oak lottery† – Nothing thrives that belongs to't. The man of the house would have been an alderman by this time with half the trade, if he had set up in the City – For my part, I never sit at the door, that I don't get double the stomach that I do at a horse-race. The air upon Banstead Downs‡ is nothing to it for a whetter; yet I never see it, but the spirit of famine appears to me; sometimes like a decayed porter, worn out with pimping, and carrying *billet-doux* and songs; not like other porters for hire, but for the jest's sake. Now like a thin chairman, melted down to half his proportion, with carrying a poet upon tick, to visit some great fortune; and his fare to be paid him like the wages of sin, either at the day of marriage, or the day of death.

VALENTINE Very well, Sir; can you proceed?

JEREMY Sometimes like a bilked bookseller, with a meagre ter-rified countenance, that looks as if he had written for himself, or were resolved to turn author, and bring the rest of his brethren into the same condition. And lastly, in the form of a worn-out punk, with verses in her hand, which her vanity had preferred to settlements, without a whole tatter to her tail, but as ragged as one of the muses; or as if she were carrying her linen to the paper-mill, to be converted into folio books, of warning to all young

---

* Will's coffee-house: in Bow Street, Covent Garden.
† Royal Oak lottery: one of many schemes for raising public money.
‡ Banstead Downs: a racing track in Surrey.

maids, not to prefer poetry to good sense; or lying in the arms of
a needy wit, before the embraces of a wealthy fool.

Enter Scandal.

SCANDAL What, Jeremy holding forth?

VALENTINE The rogue has (with all the wit he could muster up)
been declaiming against wit.

SCANDAL Aye? Why then I'm afraid Jeremy has wit: for wherever
it is, it's always contriving its own ruin.

JEREMY Why so I have been telling my master, Sir: Mr Scandal,
for heaven's sake, Sir, try if you can dissuade him from turning
poet.

SCANDAL Poet! He shall turn soldier first, and rather depend upon
the outside of his head, than the lining. Why, what the devil?
Has not your poverty made you enemies enough? Must you needs
show your wit to get more?

JEREMY Aye, more indeed; for who cares for anybody that has
more wit than himself?

SCANDAL Jeremy speaks like an oracle. Don't you see how worth-
less great men, and dull rich rogues, avoid a witty man of small
fortune? Why, he looks like a writ of enquiry into their titles and
estates; and seems commissioned by heaven to seize the better
half.

VALENTINE Therefore I would rail in my writings, and be revenged.

SCANDAL Rail? At whom? The whole world? Impotent and vain!
Who would die a martyr to sense in a country where the religion
is folly? You may stand at bay for a while; but when the full cry
is against you, you won't have fair play for your life. If you can't
be fairly run down by the hounds, you will be treacherously shot
by the huntsmen. – No, turn pimp, flatterer, quack, lawyer,
parson, be chaplain to an atheist, or stallion to an old woman,
anything but poet; a modern poet is worse, more servile, timorous, and fawning, than any I have named: without you could
retrieve the ancient honours of the name, recall the stage of Athens,
and be allowed the force of open honest satire.

VALENTINE You are as inveterate against our poets, as if your character had been lately exposed upon the stage. – Nay, I am not violently bent upon the trade. – [*one knocks*] Jeremy, see who's there. [*Exit Jeremy*] But tell me what you would have me do? – What do the world say of me, and my forced confinement?

SCANDAL The world behaves itself, as it used to do on such occasions; some pity you, and condemn your father: others excuse him, and blame you; only the ladies are merciful, and wish you well, since love and pleasurable expense, have been your greatest faults.

Enter Jeremy.

VALENTINE How now?

JEREMY Nothing new, Sir; I have dispatched some half a dozen duns with as much dexterity, as a hungry judge does causes at dinner-time.

VALENTINE What answer have you given 'em?

SCANDAL Patience, I suppose, the old receipt.

JEREMY No, faith Sir; I have put 'em off so long with patience and forbearance, and other fair words; that I was forced now to tell 'em in plain downright English –

VALENTINE What?

JEREMY That they should be paid.

VALENTINE When?

JEREMY Tomorrow.

VALENTINE And how the devil do you mean to keep your word?

JEREMY Keep it? Not at all; it has been so very much stretched, that I reckon it will break of course by tomorrow, and nobody be surprised at the matter – [*knocking*] – Again! Sir, if you don't like my negotiation, will you be pleased to answer these yourself.

VALENTINE See who they are.   [*Exit Jeremy*]
By this, Scandal, you may see what it is to be great; secretaries of state, presidents of the council, and generals of an army lead just such a life as I do; have just such crowds of visitants in a morning, all soliciting of past promises; which are but a civiler sort of duns, that lay claim to voluntary debts.

SCANDAL And you, like a true great man, having engaged their attendance, and promised more than ever you intend to perform; are more perplexed to find evasions, than you would be to invent the honest means of keeping your word, and gratifying your creditors.

VALENTINE Scandal, learn to spare your friends, and do not provoke your enemies; this liberty of your tongue, will one day bring a confinement on your body, my friend.

Re-enter Jeremy.

JEREMY O Sir, there's Trapland the scrivener, with two suspicious fellows like lawful pads,* that would knock a man down with pocket tipstaves, – And there's your father's steward, and the nurse with one of your children from Twitnam.†

VALENTINE Pox on her, could she find no other time to fling my sins in my face: here, give her this, [*gives money*] and bid her trouble me no more; a thoughtless two-handed whore, she knows my condition well enough and might have overlaid the child a fortnight ago, if she had had any forecast in her.

SCANDAL What, is it bouncing Margery, and my godson?

JEREMY Yes, Sir.

SCANDAL My blessing to the boy, with this token [*gives money*] of my love. And d'ye hear, bid Margery put more flocks in her bed, shift twice a week, and not work so hard, that she may not smell so vigorously. – I shall take the air shortly.

VALENTINE Scandal, don't spoil my boy's milk: – Bid Trapland come in. If I can give that Cerberus a sop, I shall be at rest for one day. [*Exit Jeremy*]

Enter Trapland and Jeremy.

O Mr Trapland! My old friend! Welcome. Jeremy, a chair quickly: a bottle of sack and a toast – fly – a chair first.

TRAPLAND A good morning to you Mr Valentine, and to you Mr Scandal.

SCANDAL The morning's a very good morning, if you don't spoil it.

VALENTINE Come sit you down, you know his way.

TRAPLAND [*sits*] There is a debt, Mr Valentine, of fifteen hundred pounds of pretty long standing. –

* lawful pads: bailiffs arresting persons on the streets.
† Twitnam: Twickenham, Middlesex.

VALENTINE I cannot talk about business with a thirsty palate. –
Sirrah the sack. –

TRAPLAND And I desire to know what course you have taken for
the payment?

VALENTINE Faith and troth, I am heartily glad to see you, –
my service to you, – fill, fill, to honest Mr Trapland, fuller.

TRAPLAND Hold, sweetheart. – This is not to our business; –
my service to you Mr Scandal – [*drinks*] – I have forborne as long. –

VALENTINE T'other glass, and then we'll talk. Fill, Jeremy.

TRAPLAND No more, in truth. – I have forborne, I say –

VALENTINE Sirrah, fill when I bid you. – And how does your
handsome daughter. – Come a good husband to her. [*drinks*]

TRAPLAND Thank you – I have been out of this money. –

VALENTINE Drink first. Scandal, why do you not drink? [*they
drink*]

TRAPLAND And in short, I can be put off no longer.

VALENTINE I was much obliged to you for your supply: it did
me signal service in my necessity. But you delight in doing good.
– Scandal, drink to me, my friend Trapland's health. An honester
man lives not, nor one more ready to serve his friend in distress,
though I say it to his face. Come, fill each man his glass.

SCANDAL What, I know Trapland has been a whoremaster, and
loves a wench still. You never knew a whoremaster, that was not an
honest fellow.

TRAPLAND Fie, Mr Scandal, you never knew –

SCANDAL What don't I know? – I know the buxom black widow
in the Poultry* – eight hundred pounds a year jointure, and
twenty thousand pounds in money. Ahah! Old Trap.

VALENTINE Say you so, i'faith: come, we'll remember the widow:
I know whereabouts you are: come, to the widow –

TRAPLAND No more indeed.

VALENTINE What, the widow's health; give it him – off with it:
[*they drink*] a lovely girl, i'faith, black sparkling eyes, soft pouting
ruby lips! Better sealing there, than a bond for a million, hah!

TRAPLAND No, no, there's no such thing, we'd better mind our
business. – You're a wag.

VALENTINE No faith, we'll mind the widow's business, fill again.

    * the Poultry: a street connecting Cheapside and Cornhill.

– Pretty round heaving breasts, – a Barbary shape, and a jut with her bum, would stir an anchorite: and the prettiest foot! O if a man could but fasten his eyes to her feet, as they steal in and out, and play at Bo-peep under her petticoats, ah! Mr Trapland?

TRAPLAND Verily, give me a glass, – you're a wag, – and here's to the widow. [*Drinks*]

SCANDAL He begins to chuckle; – ply him close, or he'll relapse into a dun.

Enter Officer.

OFFICER By your leave, gentlemen, – Mr Trapland, if we must do our office, tell us. – We have half a dozen gentlemen to arrest in Pall Mall and Covent Garden; and if we don't make haste, the chairmen will be abroad, and block up the chocolate-houses,* and then our labour's lost.

TRAPLAND Udso that's true. Mr Valentine I love mirth, but business must be done, are you ready to –

JEREMY Sir, your father's steward says he comes to make proposals concerning your debts.

VALENTINE Bid him come in: Mr Trapland, send away your officer, you shall have an answer presently.

TRAPLAND Mr Snap stay within call. [*Exit Officer*]

Enter Steward and whispers Valentine.

SCANDAL Here's a dog now, a traitor in his wine, sirrah refund the sack: Jeremy fetch him some warm water, or I'll rip up his stomach, and go the shortest way to his conscience.

TRAPLAND Mr Scandal, you are uncivil; I did not value your sack; but you cannot expect it again, when I have drank it.

SCANDAL And how do you expect to have your money again, when a gentleman has spent it?

VALENTINE You need say no more, I understand the conditions; they are very hard, but my necessity is very pressing, I agree to 'em. Take Mr Trapland with you, and let him draw the writing – Mr Trapland, you know this man, he shall satisfy you.

TRAPLAND Sincerely, I am loath to be thus pressing, but my necessity.

* e.g. the men who carried sedan chairs would impede arrests.

VALENTINE No apology, good Mr Scrivener, you shall be paid.

TRAPLAND I hope you forgive me, my business requires –

[*Exeunt Steward, Trapland and Jeremy*]

SCANDAL He begs pardon like a hangman at an execution.

VALENTINE But I have got a reprieve.

SCANDAL I am surprised; what, does your father relent?

VALENTINE No; he has sent me the hardest conditions in the world: you have heard of a booby brother of mine, that was sent to sea three years ago? This brother, my father hears is landed; whereupon he very affectionately sends me word; if I will make a deed of conveyance of my right to his estate after his death, to my younger brother, he will immediately furnish me with four thousand pound to pay my debts, and make my fortune. This was once proposed before, and I refused it; but the present impatience of my creditors for their money, and my own impatience of confinement, and absence from Angelica, force me to consent.

SCANDAL A very desperate demonstration of your love to Angelica: and I think she has never given you any assurance of hers.

VALENTINE You know her temper; she never gave me any great reason either for hope or despair.

SCANDAL Women of her airy temper, as they seldom think before they act, so they rarely give us any light to guess at what they mean: but you have little reason to believe that a woman of this age, who has had an indifference for you in your prosperity, will fall in love with your ill fortune; besides, Angelica has a great fortune of her own; and great fortunes either expect another great fortune, or a fool.

Enter Jeremy.

JEREMY More misfortunes, Sir.

VALENTINE What, another dun?

JEREMY No Sir, but Mr Tattle is come to wait upon you.

VALENTINE Well, I can't help it, – you must bring him up; he knows I don't go abroad.   [*Exit Jeremy*]

SCANDAL Pox on him, I'll be gone.

VALENTINE No, prithee stay: Tattle and you should never be asunder; you are light and shadow, and show one another; he is perfectly thy reverse both in humour and understanding; and as you set up for defamation, he is a mender of reputations.

SCANDAL A mender of reputations? Aye, just as he is a keeper of secrets, another virtue that he sets up for in the same manner. For the rogue will speak aloud in the posture of a whisper; and deny a woman's name, while he gives you the marks of her person: he will forswear receiving a letter from her, and at the same time show you her hand upon the superscription: and yet perhaps he has counterfeited the hand too; and sworn to a truth; but he hopes not to be believed; and refuses the reputation of a lady's favour, as a doctor says, 'No', to a bishopric, only that it may be granted him. – In short, he is a public professor of secrecy, and makes proclamation that he holds private intelligence. – He's here.

Enter Tattle.

TATTLE Valentine good-morrow, Scandal I am yours, – that is, when you speak well of me.

SCANDAL That is, when I am yours; for while I am my own, or anybody's else, that will never happen.

TATTLE How inhumane!

VALENTINE Why Tattle, you need not be much concerned at anything that he says: for to converse with Scandal, is to play at losing loadum;* you must lose a good name to him, before you can win it for yourself.

TATTLE But how barbarous that is, and how unfortunate for him, that the world shall think the better of any person for his calumniation! – I thank heaven, it has always been a part of my character to handle the reputation of others very tenderly.

SCANDAL Aye, such rotten reputations as you have to deal with, are to be handled tenderly indeed.

TATTLE Nay, but why rotten? Why should you say rotten, when you know not the persons of whom you speak? How cruel that is?

SCANDAL Not know 'em? Why, thou never hadst to do with anybody that did not stink to all the Town.

TATTLE Ha, ha, ha; nay, now you make a jest of it indeed. For there is nothing more known, than that nobody knows anything

* losing loadum: a card game in which the winner takes no cards.

of that nature of me: as I hope to be saved, Valentine, I never exposed a woman, since I knew what woman was.

VALENTINE And yet you have conversed with several.

TATTLE To be free with you, I have – I don't care if I own that – Nay more (I'm going to say a bold word now) I never could meddle with a woman, that had to do with anybody else.

SCANDAL How!

VALENTINE Nay, faith, I'm apt to believe him – except her husband, Tattle.

TATTLE O that –

SCANDAL What think you of that noble commoner, Mrs Drab?

TATTLE Pooh, I know Madam Drab has made her brags in three or four places, that I said this and that, and writ to her, and did I know not what – But, upon my reputation, she did me wrong – Well, well, that was malice – But I know the bottom of it. She was bribed to that by one that we all know – a man too. Only to bring me into disgrace with a certain woman of quality –

SCANDAL Whom we all know.

TATTLE No matter for that – Yes, yes, everybody knows – No doubt on't, everybody knows my secrets – But I soon satisfied the lady of my innocence; for I told her – Madam, says I, there are some persons who make it their business to tell stories, and say this and that of one and t'other, and everything in the world; and, says I, if your grace –

SCANDAL Grace!

TATTLE O Lord, what have I said? My unlucky tongue!

VALENTINE Ha, ha, ha.

SCANDAL Why, Tattle, thou hast more impudence than one can in reason expect: I shall have an esteem for thee, well, and ha, ha, ha, well, go on, and what did you say to her grace?

VALENTINE I confess this is something extraordinary.

TATTLE Not a word, as I hope to be saved; an errant *lapsus linguae* – Come, let's talk of something else.

VALENTINE Well, but how did you acquit yourself?

TATTLE Pooh, pooh, nothing at all, I only rallied with you – a woman of ordinary rank was a little jealous of me, and I told her something or other, faith – I know not what – Come, let's talk of something else. [*hums a song*]

SCANDAL Hang him, let him alone, he has a mind we should enquire.

TATTLE Valentine, I supped last night with your mistress, and her uncle old Foresight: I think your father lies at Foresight's.

VALENTINE Yes.

TATTLE Upon my soul Angelica's a fine woman – and so is Mrs Foresight, and her sister Mrs Frail.

SCANDAL Yes, Mrs Frail is a very fine woman, we all know her.

TATTLE O that is not fair.

SCANDAL What?

TATTLE To tell.

SCANDAL To tell what? Why, what do you know of Mrs Frail?

TATTLE Who I? Upon honour I don't know whether she be man or woman; but by the smoothness of her chin, and roundness of her lips.

SCANDAL No!

TATTLE No.

SCANDAL She says otherwise.

TATTLE Impossible!

SCANDAL Yes faith. Ask Valentine else.

TATTLE Why then, as I hope to be saved, I believe a woman only obliges a man to secrecy, that she may have the pleasure of telling herself.

SCANDAL No doubt on't. Well, but has she done you wrong, or no? You have had her? Ha?

TATTLE Though I have more honour than to tell first; I have more manners than to contradict what a lady has declared.

SCANDAL Well, you own it?

TATTLE I am strangely surprised! Yes, yes, I can't deny't, if she taxes me with it.

SCANDAL She'll be here by and by, she sees Valentine every morning.

TATTLE How!

VALENTINE She does me the favour – I mean of a visit sometimes. I did not think she had granted more to anybody.

SCANDAL Nor I faith – But Tattle does not use to belie a lady; it is contrary to his character – How one may be deceived in a woman, Valentine?

TATTLE Nay, what do you mean, gentlemen?

SCANDAL I'm resolved I'll ask her.

TATTLE O barbarous! Why, did you not tell me –

SCANDAL No; you told us.

TATTLE And bid me ask Valentine.

VALENTINE What did I say? I hope you won't bring me to confess an answer, when you never asked me the question.

TATTLE But, gentlemen, this is the most inhumane proceeding –

VALENTINE Nay, if you have known Scandal thus long, and cannot avoid such a palpable decoy as this was; the ladies have a fine time, whose reputations are in your keeping.

Enter Jeremy.

JEREMY Sir, Mrs Frail has sent to know if you are stirring.

VALENTINE Show her up, when she comes.   [*Exit Jeremy*]

TATTLE I'll be gone.

VALENTINE You'll meet her.

TATTLE Have you not a back way?

VALENTINE If there were, you have more discretion, than to give Scandal such an advantage; why, your running away will prove all that he can tell her.

TATTLE Scandal, you will not be so ungenerous – Oh, I shall lose my reputation of secrecy for ever – I shall never be received but upon public days; and my visits will never be admitted beyond a drawing-room: I shall never see a bed-chamber again, never be locked in a closet, nor run behind a screen, or under a table: never be distinguished among the waiting-women by the name of trusty Mr Tattle more – You will not be so cruel.

VALENTINE Scandal, have pity on him; he'll yield to any conditions.

TATTLE Any, any terms.

SCANDAL Come then, sacrifice half a dozen women of good reputation to me presently – Come, where are you familiar – And see that they are women of quality too, the first quality –

TATTLE 'Tis very hard – Won't a baronet's lady pass?

SCANDAL No, nothing under a right honourable.

TATTLE O inhumane! You don't expect their names.

SCANDAL No, their titles shall serve.

TATTLE Alas, that's the same thing: pray spare me their titles; I'll describe their persons.

SCANDAL Well, begin then: but take notice, if you are so ill a painter, that I cannot know the person by your picture of her, you must be condemned, like other bad painters, to write the name at the bottom.

TATTLE Well, first then –

Enter Mrs Frail.

O unfortunate! she's come already; will you have patience till another time – I'll double the number.

SCANDAL Well, on that condition – Take heed you don't fail me.

MRS FRAIL Hey day! I shall get a fine reputation, by coming to see fellows in a morning. Scandal, you devil, are you here too? O Mr Tattle, everything is safe with you, we know.

SCANDAL Tattle.

TATTLE Mum – O Madam, you do me too much honour.

VALENTINE Well Lady Galloper, how does Angelica?

MRS FRAIL Angelica? Manners!

VALENTINE What you will allow an absent lover –

MRS FRAIL No, I'll allow a lover present with his mistress to be particular – But otherwise I think his passion ought to give place to his manners.

VALENTINE But what if he have more passion than manners?

MRS FRAIL Then let him marry and reform.

VALENTINE Marriage indeed may qualify the fury of his passion, but it very rarely mends a man's manners.

MRS FRAIL You are the most mistaken in the world; there is no creature perfectly civil, but a husband. For in a little time he grows only rude to his wife, and that is the highest good breeding, for it begets his civility to other people. Well, I'll tell you news; but I suppose you hear your brother Benjamin is landed. And my brother Foresight's daughter is come out of the country – I assure you, there's a match talked of by the old people – Well, if he be but as great a sea-beast, as she is a land-monster, we shall have a most amphibious breed – The progeny will be all otters: he has been bred at sea, and she has never been out of the country.

VALENTINE Pox take 'em, their conjunction bodes no good, I'm sure.

MRS FRAIL Now you talk of conjunction, my brother Foresight has cast both their nativities, and prognosticates an admiral and an eminent justice of the peace to be the issue-male of their two bodies; 'tis the most superstitious old fool! He would have persuaded me, that this was an unlucky day, and would not let me come abroad: but I invented a dream, and sent him to Artemodorus★ for interpretation, and so stole out to see you. Well, and what will you give me now? Come, I must have something.

VALENTINE Step into the next room – and I'll give you something.

SCANDAL Aye, we'll all give you something.

MRS FRAIL Well, what will you all give me?

VALENTINE Mine's a secret.

MRS FRAIL I thought you would give me something, that would be a trouble to you to keep.

VALENTINE And Scandal shall give you a good name.

MRS FRAIL That's more than he has for himself. And what will you give me, Mr Tattle?

TATTLE I? My soul, Madam.

MRS FRAIL Pooh, no thank you, I have enough to do to take care of my own. Well; but I'll come and see you one of these mornings; I hear you have a great many pictures.

TATTLE I have a pretty good collection at your service, some originals.

SCANDAL Hang him, he has nothing but the *Seasons* and the *Twelve Caesars*, paltry copies; and the *Five Senses*,† as ill represented as they are in himself: and he himself is the only original you will see there.

MRS FRAIL Aye, but I hear he has a closet of beauties.

SCANDAL Yes, all that have done him favours, if you will believe him.

MRS FRAIL Aye, let me see those, Mr Tattle.

TATTLE O Madam, those are sacred to love and contemplation.

★ Artemodorus: Artemidorus Daldianus of Ephesus (of the late second century A.D.), an interpreter of dreams who wrote a treatise on the subject.

† *Seasons* . . . *Twelve Caesars* . . . *Five Senses*: prints fashionable at the time.

No man but the painter and myself was ever blessed with the sight.

MRS FRAIL Well, but a woman –

TATTLE Nor woman, till she consented to have her picture there too – for then she is obliged to keep the secret.

SCANDAL No, no; come to me if you would see pictures.

MRS FRAIL You?

SCANDAL Yes faith, I can show you your own picture, and most of your acquaintance to the life, and as like as at Kneller's.*

MRS FRAIL O lying creature – Valentine, does not he lie? – I can't believe a word he says.

VALENTINE No indeed, he speaks truth now: for as Tattle has pictures of all that have granted him favours, he has the pictures of all that have refused him; if satires, descriptions, characters and lampoons are pictures.

SCANDAL Yes, mine are most in black and white. – And yet there are some set out in their true colours, both men and women. I can show you pride, folly, affection, wantonness, inconstancy, covetousness, dissimulation, malice, and ignorance, all in one piece. Then I can show you lying, foppery, vanity, cowardice, bragging, lechery, impotence and ugliness in another piece; and yet one of these is a celebrated beauty, and t'other a professed beau. I have paintings too, some pleasant enough.

MRS FRAIL Come, let's hear 'em.

SCANDAL Why, I have a beau in a bagnio, cupping for a complexion, and sweating for a shape.

MRS FRAIL So.

SCANDAL Then I have a lady burning of brandy in a cellar with a hackney-coachman.

MRS FRAIL O devil! Well, but that story is not true.

SCANDAL I have some hieroglyphics too; I have a lawyer with a hundred hands, two heads, and but one face; a divine with two faces, and one head; and I have a soldier with his brains in his belly, and his heart where his head should be.

MRS FRAIL And no head?

SCANDAL No head.

MRS FRAIL Pooh, this is all invention. Have you ne'er a poet?

* Kneller's: a reference to the painter Sir Godfrey Kneller (1646–1723).

SCANDAL Yes, I have a poet weighing words, and selling praise for praise, and a critic picking his pocket. I have another large piece too, representing a school; where there are huge proportioned critics, with long wigs, laced coats, Steinkirk cravats,★ and terrible faces; with cat-calls in their hands, and horn-books about their necks. I have many more of this kind, very well painted, as you shall see.

MRS FRAIL Well, I'll come, if it be only to disprove you.

Enter Jeremy.

JEREMY Sir, here's the steward again from your father.

VALENTINE I'll come to him – will you give me leave, I'll wait on you again presently.

MRS FRAIL No, I'll be gone. Come, who squires me to the Exchange, I must call my sister Foresight there.

SCANDAL I will; I have a mind to your sister.

MRS FRAIL Civil!

TATTLE I will; because I have a tender for your ladyship.

MRS FRAIL That's somewhat the better reason, to my opinion.

SCANDAL Well, if Tattle entertains you, I have the better opportunity to engage your sister.

VALENTINE Tell Angelica, I am about making hard conditions to come abroad, and be at liberty to see her.

SCANDAL I'll give an account of you, and your proceedings. If indiscretion be a sign of love, you are the most a lover of anybody that I know: you fancy that parting with your estate, will help you to your mistress. – In my mind he is a thoughtless adventurer,

Who hopes to purchase wealth, by selling land;

Or win a mistress, with a losing hand.   [*Exeunt*]

★ Steinkirk cravats: cravats popular after the battle of Steenkerke, 1692.

ACT TWO

SCENE I

A room in Foresight's house

Foresight and Servant.

FORESIGHT Hey day! What are all the women of my family abroad? Is not my wife come home? Nor my sister, nor my daughter?

SERVANT No, Sir.

FORESIGHT Mercy on us, what can be the meaning of it? Sure the moon is in all her fortitudes;* is my niece Angelica at home?

SERVANT Yes, Sir.

FORESIGHT I believe you lie, Sir.

SERVANT Sir?

FORESIGHT I say you lie, Sir. It is impossible that anything should be as I would have it; for I was born, Sir, when the Crab† was ascending, and all my affairs go backward.

SERVANT I can't tell indeed, Sir.

FORESIGHT No, I know you can't, Sir: but I can tell, Sir, and foretell, Sir.

Enter Nurse.

Nurse, where's your young mistress?

NURSE Wee'st heart, I know not, they're none of 'em come home yet; poor child, I warrant she's fond o'seeing the Town, – marry, pray heaven they ha' given her any dinner, – good lack-a-day, ha, ha, ha, O strange; I'll vow and swear now, ha, ha, ha, marry and did you ever see the like!

FORESIGHT Why how now, what's the matter?

NURSE Pray heaven send your worship good luck, marry and amen with all my heart, for you have put on one stocking with the wrong side outward.

FORESIGHT Ha, how? Faith and troth I'm glad of it, and so I have, that may be good luck in troth, in troth it may, very good

* moon . . . fortitudes: the inconstant moon at the height of its influence.
† the Crab: one of the signs of the Zodiac.

luck; nay I have had some omens; I got out of bed backwards too
this morning, without premeditation; pretty good that too; but
then I stumbled coming down stairs, and met a weasel; bad
omens those: some bad, some good, our lives are checkered, mirth
and sorrow, want and plenty, night and day, make up our time, –
But in troth I am pleased at my stocking. Very well pleased at
my stocking – O here's my niece! –

Enter Angelica.

Sirrah, go tell Sir Sampson Legend, I'll wait on him, if he's at
leisure. – 'Tis now three o'clock, a very good hour for business,
Mercury governs this hour.   [*Exit Servant*]
ANGELICA Is not it a good hour for pleasure too? Uncle, pray lend
me your coach, mine's out of order.
FORESIGHT What, would you be gadding too? Sure all females
are mad today – It is of evil portent, and bodes mischief to the
master of a family – I remember an old prophecy written by
Messehalah* the Arabian, and thus translated by a reverend
Buckinghamshire bard.
When housewifes all the house forsake,
And leave good man to brew and bake,
Withouten guile, then be it said,
That house doth stand upon its head;
And when the head is set in grond,†
Ne marl,‡ if it be fruitful fond.§
Fruitful, the head fruitful, that bodes horns; the fruit of the head
is horns – Dear niece, stay at home – For by the head of the house
is meant the husband; the prophecy needs no explanation.
ANGELICA Well, but I can neither make you a cuckold, uncle, by
going abroad; nor secure you from being one, by staying at home.
FORESIGHT Yes, yes; while there's one woman left, the prophecy
is not in full force.
ANGELICA But my inclinations are in force, I have a mind to go
abroad; and if you won't lend me your coach, I'll take a hackney,
or a chair, and leave you to erect a scheme, and find who's in
conjunction with your wife. Why don't you keep her at home, if

★ Messehalah: a ninth-century Jewish astrologer.   † grond: ground.
‡ Ne marl: no wonder.   § fond: found.

you're jealous when she's abroad? You know my aunt is a little retrograde (as you call it) in her nature. Uncle, I'm afraid you are not lord of the ascendant,* ha, ha, ha.

FORESIGHT Well, jill-flirt, you are very pert – and always ridiculing that celestial science.

ANGELICA Nay uncle, don't be angry – If you are, I'll reap up all your false prophecies, ridiculous dreams, and idle divinations. I'll swear you are a nuisance to the neighbourhood – What a bustle did you keep against the last invisible eclipse, laying in provision as 'twere for a siege? What a world of fire and candle, matches and tinderboxes did you purchase! One would have thought we were ever after to live under ground, or at least making a voyage to Greenland, to inhabit all the dark season.

FORESIGHT Why, you malapert slut –

ANGELICA Will you lend me your coach, or I'll go on – Nay, I'll declare how you prophesied popery was coming, only because the butler had mislaid some of the apostles' spoons, and thought they were lost. Away went religion and spoon-meat together – Indeed, uncle, I'll indite you for a wizard.

FORESIGHT How hussy! Was there ever such a provoking minx?

NURSE O merciful father, how she talks!

ANGELICA Yes, I can make oath of your unlawful midnight practices; you and the old nurse there –

NURSE Marry heaven defend – I at midnight practices – O Lord, what's here to do? – I in unlawful doings with my master's worship – Why, did you ever hear the like now – Sir, did ever I do anything of your midnight concerns – but warm your bed, and tuck you up, and set the candle, and your tobacco-box, and your urinal by you, and now and then rub the soles of your feet? – O Lord, I! –

ANGELICA Yes, I saw you together, through the key-hole of the closet, one night, like Saul and the witch of Endor, turning the sieve and shears, and pricking your thumbs, to write poor innocent servants' names in blood, about a little nutmeg-grater,

* lord of the ascendant: conditions being such that an astrologer could make a successful prediction, the lord of the ascendant being the easternmost star in the sign of the Zodiac under which the person whose horoscope was being cast was born.

which she had forgot in the caudle-cup★ – Nay, I know something worse, if I would speak of it –

FORESIGHT I defy you, hussy; but I'll remember this, I'll be revenged on you, cockatrice; I'll hamper you – You have your fortune in your own hands – But I'll find a way to make your lover, your prodigal spendthrift gallant, Valentine, pay for all, I will.

ANGELICA Will you? I care not, but all shall out then – Look to it, nurse; I can bring witness that you have a great unnatural teat under your left arm, and he another; and that you suckle a young devil in the shape of a tabby cat, by turns, I can.

NURSE A teat, a teat, I an unnatural teat! O the false slanderous thing; feel, feel here, if I have anything but like another Christian, [*crying*] or any teats, but two that han't given suck this thirty years.

FORESIGHT I will have patience, since it is the will of the stars I should be thus tormented – This is the effect of the malicious conjunctions and oppositions in the third house† of my nativity; there the curse of kindred was foretold – But I will have my doors locked up – I'll punish you, not a man shall enter my house.

ANGELICA Do uncle, lock 'em up quickly before my aunt come home – You'll have a letter for alimony tomorrow morning – But let me be gone first, and then let no mankind come near the house, but converse with spirits and the celestial signs, the Bull, and the Ram, and the Goat. Bless me! There are a great many horned beasts among the twelve signs, uncle. But cuckolds go to heaven.

FORESIGHT But there's but one Virgin among the twelve signs, spitfire, but one Virgin.

ANGELICA Nor there had not been that one, if she had had to do with anything but astrologers, uncle. That makes my aunt go abroad.

FORESIGHT How? How? Is that the reason? Come, you know something; tell me, and I'll forgive you; do, good niece – Come, you shall have my coach and horses – Faith and troth you shall – Does my wife complain? Come, I know women tell one another – She is young and sanguine, has a wanton hazel eye, and was born under Gemini, which may incline her to society; she has a mole

★ caudle-cup: a warm drink.
† third house: one of the twelve parts of the heavens.

upon her lip, with a moist palm, and an open liberality on the mount of Venus.

ANGELICA Ha, ha, ha.

FORESIGHT Do you laugh? – Well gentlewoman, I'll – But come, be a good girl, don't perplex your poor uncle, tell me – won't you speak? Odd I'll –

Enter Servant.

SERVANT Sir Sampson is coming down to wait upon you –

ANGELICA Goodbye uncle – ⟨*to servant*⟩ Call me a chair – I'll find out my aunt, and tell her, she must not come home.

[*Exeunt Angelica and Servant*]

FORESIGHT I'm so perplexed and vexed, I am not fit to receive him; I shall scarce recover myself before the hour be past: go nurse, tell Sir Sampson I'm ready to wait on him.   [*Exit*]

NURSE Yes, Sir.

FORESIGHT Well – Why, if I was born to be a cuckold, there's no more to be said – he's here already.

Enter Sir Sampson Legend with a paper.

SIR SAMPSON Nor no more to be done, old boy; that's plain – here 'tis, I have it in my hand, old Ptolemy;* I'll make the ungracious prodigal know who begat him; I will, old Nostrodamus.† What, I warrant my son thought nothing belonged to a father, but forgiveness and affection; no authority, no correction, no arbitrary power; nothing to be done, but for him to offend, and me to pardon. I warrant you, if he danced till doomsday, he thought I was to pay the piper. Well, but here it is under black and white, *Signatum, Sigillatum,* and *Deliberatum*;‡ that as soon as my son Benjamin is arrived, he is to make over to him his right of inheritance. Where's my daughter that is to be – hah! Old Merlin! Body o'me, I'm so glad I'm revenged on this undutiful rogue.

---

* old Ptolemy: Ptolemaeus Alexandrinus, an astrologer of the second century A.D., whose *Almagest* was a standard work on astronomy for several centuries.
† old Nostrodamus: Michel de Notredame, a famous sixteenth-century fortune-teller.
‡ *Signatum* . . . *Deliberatum*: the equivalent of signed, sealed and delivered.

FORESIGHT Odso, let me see; let me see the paper – Aye, faith and troth, here 'tis, if it will but hold – I wish things were done, and the conveyance made – When was this signed, what hour? Odso, you should have consulted me for the time. Well, but we'll make haste –

SIR SAMPSON Haste, aye, aye; haste enough, my son Ben will be in Town tonight – I have ordered my lawyer to draw up writings of settlement and jointure – All shall be done tonight – No matter for the time; prithee, brother Foresight, leave superstition – Pox o'th' time; there's no time but the time present, there's no more to be said of what's past, and all that is to come will happen. If the sun shine by day, and the stars by night, why, we shall know one another's faces without the help of a candle, and that's all the stars are good for.

FORESIGHT How, how? Sir Sampson, that all? Give me leave to contradict you, and tell you, you are ignorant.

SIR SAMPSON I tell you I am wise; and *sapiens dominabitur astris*;* there's Latin for you to prove it, and an argument to confound your Ephemeris† – Ignorant! – I tell you, I have travelled old Fircu,‡ and know the globe. I have seen the Antipodes, where the sun rises at midnight, and sets at noon-day.

FORESIGHT But I tell you, I have travelled, and travelled in the celestial spheres, know the signs and planets, and their houses. Can judge of motions direct and retrograde, of sextiles, quadrates, trines and oppositions, fiery trigons and aquatical trigons. Know whether life shall be long or short, happy, or unhappy, whether diseases are curable or incurable. If journeys shall be prosperous, undertakings successful; or goods stolen recovered, I know –

SIR SAMPSON I know the length of the Emperor of China's foot; have kissed the great Mogul's slipper, and rid a-hunting upon an elephant with the Cham of Tartary, – Body of me, I have made a cuckold of a king, and the present majesty of Bantam§ is the issue of these loins.

* *sapiens dominabitur astris*: a wise man will be governed by the stars.
† Ephemeris: an astronomical diary.
‡ Fircu: a name applied to a witch's familiar, or the name of an astrologer.
§ Bantam: an area of Java.

FORESIGHT I know when travellers lie or speak truth, when they don't know it themselves.

SIR SAMPSON I have known an astrologer made a cuckold in the twinkling of a star; and seen a conjurer, that could not keep the devil out of his wife's circle.

FORESIGNT [*aside*] What does he twit me with my wife too, I must be better informed of this, – Do you mean my wife, Sir Sampson? Though you made a cuckold of the King of Bantam, yet by the body of the sun –

SIR SAMPSON By the horns of the moon, you would say, brother Capricorn.*

FORESIGHT Capricorn in your teeth, thou modern Mandevil;† Ferdinand Mendez Pinto‡ was but a type of thee, thou liar of the first magnitude. Take back your paper of inheritance; send your son to sea again. I'll wed my daughter to an Egyptian mummy, e'er she shall incorporate with a contemner of sciences, and a defamer of virtue.

SIR SAMPSON Body o' me, I have gone too far; – I must not provoke honest Albumazar,§ – an Egyptian mummy is an illustrious creature, my trusty hieroglyphic; and may have significations of futurity about him; odsbuds, I would my son were an Egyptian mummy for thy sake. What, thou art not angry for a jest, my good Haly‖ – I reverence the sun, moon and stars with all my heart. – What, I'll make thee a present of a mummy: now I think on't, body of me, I have a shoulder of an Egyptian king, that I purloined from one of the pyramids, powdered with hieroglyphics, thou shalt have it sent home to thy house, and make an entertainment for all the philomaths, and students in physic and astrology in and about London.

FORESIGHT But what do you know of my wife, Sir Sampson?

SIR SAMPSON Thy wife is a constellation of virtues; she's the

* Capricorn: the sign of the goat.
† Mandevil: from Jean de Bourgogne's *Travels of Sir John Mandeville*, translated into English in 1377. These are largely imaginary but Sir John made astronomical observations in the course of them.
‡ Ferdinand Mendez Pinto: a Portuguese adventurer of the sixteenth century.
§ Albumazar: an Arab astrologer who lived in Baghdad in the ninth century.
‖ Haly: probably Ali ibn Younis (*d.* A.D. 1008), an astronomer born in Cairo who made most of his observations there.

moon, and thou art the man in the moon: nay, she is more illustrious than the moon; for she has her chastity without her inconstancy, s'bud I was but in jest.

Enter Jeremy.

How now, who sent for you? Ha! What would you have?

FORESIGHT Nay, if you were but in jest. – Who's that fellow?
I don't like his physiognomy.

SIR SAMPSON ⟨*to Jeremy*⟩ My son, Sir; what son, Sir? My son
Benjamin, hoh?

JEREMY No, Sir, Mr Valentine, my master, – 'tis the first time he
has been abroad since his confinement, and he comes to pay his
duty to you.

SIR SAMPSON Well, Sir.

Enter Valentine.

JEREMY He is here, Sir.

VALENTINE Your blessing, Sir.

SIR SAMPSON You've had it already, Sir, I think I sent it you
today in a bill of four thousand pound: a great deal of money,
brother Foresight.

FORESIGHT Aye indeed, Sir Sampson, a great deal of money for a
young man, I wonder what he can do with it!

SIR SAMPSON Body o'me, so do I. – Hark ye, Valentine, if there
is too much, refund the superfluity; do'st hear boy?

VALENTINE Superfluity, Sir, it will scarce pay my debts, – I hope
you will have more indulgence, than to oblige me to those hard
conditions, which my necessity signed to.

SIR SAMPSON Sir, how I beseech you, what were you pleased to
intimate, concerning indulgence?

VALENTINE Why, Sir, that you would not go to the extremity of
the conditions, but release me at least from some part –

SIR SAMPSON O Sir, I understand you, – that's all, ha?

VALENTINE Yes, Sir, all that I presume to ask. – But what you,
out of fatherly fondness, will be pleased to add, shall be doubly
welcome.

SIR SAMPSON No doubt of it, sweet Sir, but your filial piety, and
my fatherly fondness would fit like two tallies. – Here's a rogue,

brother Foresight, makes a bargain under hand and seal in the morning, and would be released from it in the afternoon; here's a rogue, dog, here's conscience and honesty; this is your wit now, this is the morality of your wits! You are a wit, and have been a beau, and may be a – Why sirrah, is it not here under hand and seal – Can you deny it?

VALENTINE　Sir, I don't deny it. –

SIR SAMPSON　Sirrah, you'll be hanged: I shall live to see you go up Holborn Hill,* – has he not a rogue's face? – Speak, brother, you understand physiognomy, a hanging-look to me; – of all my boys the most unlike me; a has a damned Tyburn† face, without the benefit o' the clergy.

FORESIGHT　Hum – truly I don't care to discourage a young man, – he has a violent death in his face; but I hope no danger of hanging.

VALENTINE　Sir, is this usage for your son? – For that old, weather-headed fool, I know how to laugh at him; but you, Sir –

SIR SAMPSON　You Sir; and you Sir: – why, who are you Sir?

VALENTINE　Your son, Sir.

SIR SAMPSON　That's more than I know, Sir, and I believe not.

VALENTINE　Faith, I hope not.

SIR SAMPSON　What, would you have your mother a whore! Did you ever hear the like! Did you ever hear the like! Body o' me –

VALENTINE　I would have an excuse for your barbarity and unnatural usage.

SIR SAMPSON　Excuse! Impudence! Why sirrah, mayn't I do what I please? Are not you my slave? Did not I beget you? And might not I have chosen whether I would have begot you or no? Oons who are you? Whence came you? What brought you into the world? How came you here, Sir? Here, to stand here upon those two legs, and look erect with that audacious face, hah? Answer me that? Did you come a volunteer into the world? Or did I beat up for you with the lawful authority of a parent, and press you to the service?

VALENTINE　I know no more why I came, than you do why you

---

* Holborn Hill: on the way from Newgate Prison to Tyburn.

† Tyburn: where criminals were executed.

called me. But here I am, and if you don't mean to provide for me, I desire you would leave me as you found me.

SIR SAMPSON With all my heart: come, uncase, strip, and go naked out of the world as you came into't.

VALENTINE My clothes are soon put off: – but you must also deprive me of reason, thought, passions, inclinations, affections, appetites, senses, and the huge train of attendants that you begot along with me.

SIR SAMPSON Body o'me, what a many-headed monster have I propagated?

VALENTINE I am of myself, a plain easy simple creature; and to be kept at small expense; but the retinue that you gave me are craving and invincible; they are so many devils that you have raised, and will have employment.

SIR SAMPSON Oons, what had I to do to get children, – can't a private man be born without all these followers: – why nothing under an emperor should be born with appetites, – why at this rate a fellow that has but a groat in his pocket, may have a stomach capable of a ten shilling ordinary.★

JEREMY Nay, that's as clear as the sun; I'll make oath of it before any justice in Middlesex.

SIR SAMPSON Here's a cormorant too, – s'heart this fellow was not born with you? – I did not beget him, did I? –

JEREMY By the provision that's made for me, you might have begot me too: – nay, and to tell your worship another truth, I believe you did, for I find I was born with those same whoreson appetites too; that my master speaks of.

SIR SAMPSON Why look you there now, – I'll maintain it, that by the rule of right reason, this fellow ought to have been born without a palate. – S'heart, what should he do with a distinguishing taste? – I warrant now he'd rather eat a pheasant, than a piece of poor John;† and smell, now, why I warrant he can smell, and loves perfumes above a stink. – Why there's it; and music, don't you love music scoundrel?

JEREMY Yes, I have a reasonable good ear, Sir, as to jigs and

★ ten shilling ordinary: an eating-place where an expensive meal cost ten shillings.
† poor John: dried fish.

country dances; and the like; I don't much matter your solos or sonatas, they give me the spleen.

SIR SAMPSON The spleen, ha, ha, ha, a pox confound you – solos and sonatas? Oons whose son are you? How were you engendered, muckworm?

JEREMY I am by my father, the son of a chair-man, my mother sold oysters in winter, and cucumbers in summer; and I came up-stairs into the world; for I was born in a cellar.

FORESIGHT By your looks, you should go upstairs out of the world too, friend.

SIR SAMPSON And if this rogue were anatomized now, and dis-sected, he has his vessels of digestion and concoction, and so forth, large enough for the inside of a cardinal, this son of a cucumber. – These things are unaccountable and unreasonable, – body o' me, why was not I a bear? That my cubs might have lived upon suck-ing their paws; nature has been provident only to bears and spiders; the one has its nutriment in his own hands; and t'other spins his habitation out of his entrails.

VALENTINE Fortune was provident enough to supply all the necessities of my nature; if I had my right of inheritance.

SIR SAMPSON Again! Oons han't you four thousand pound – If I had it again, I would not give thee a groat, – what would'st thou have me turn pelican, and feed thee out of my own vitals? – S'heart, live by your wits, – You were always fond of the wits, – Now let's see, if you have wit enough to keep yourself? – Your brother will be in Town tonight, or tomorrow morning, and then look you perform covenants, and so your friend and servant. – Come brother Foresight.

[Exeunt Sir Sampson and Foresight]

JEREMY I told you what your visit would come to.

VALENTINE 'Tis as much as I expected – I did not come to see him: I came to Angelica; but since she was gone abroad, it was easily turned another way; and at least looked well on my side: what's here? Mrs Foresight and Mrs Frail, they are earnest, – I'll avoid 'em, – come this way, and go and enquire when Angelica will return. ⟨*Exeunt*⟩

Enter Mrs Foresight and Mrs Frail.

MRS FRAIL What have you to do to watch me? – S'life I'll do what I please.

MRS FORESIGHT You will?

MRS FRAIL Yes marry will I – A great piece of business to go to Covent Garden Square in a hackney-coach, and take a turn with one's friend.

MRS FORESIGHT Nay, two or three turns, I'll take my oath.

MRS FRAIL Well, what if I took twenty – I warrant if you had been there, it had been only innocent recreation. – Lord, where's the comfort of this life, if we can't have the happiness of conversing where we like.

MRS FORESIGHT But can't you converse at home? – I own it, I think there's no happiness like conversing with an agreeable man; I don't quarrel at that, nor I don't think but your conversation was very innocent; but the place is public, and to be seen with a man in a hackney-coach is scandalous: what if anybody else should have seen you alight as I did? – How can anybody be happy, while they're in perpetual fear of being seen and censured? – Besides it would not only reflect upon you, sister, but me.

MRS FRAIL Pooh, here's a clutter – Why should it reflect upon you? – I don't doubt but you have thought yourself happy in a hackney-coach before now. – If I had gone to Knightsbridge, or to Chelsea, or to Spring Garden,* or Barn Elms† with a man alone – something might have been said.

MRS FORESIGHT Why, was I ever in any of these places? What do you mean sister?

MRS FRAIL Was I? What do you mean?

MRS FORESIGHT You have been at a worse place.

MRS FRAIL I at a worse place, and with a man!

MRS FORESIGHT I suppose you would not go alone to the World's End.‡

MRS FRAIL The World's End! What do you mean to banter me?

MRS FORESIGHT Poor innocent! You don't know that there's a place called the World's End? I'll swear you can keep your

---

* Spring Garden: public gardens on the south bank of the Thames, laid out in 1661, and closed in 1859: they were frequently known as Vauxhall Gardens.
† Barn Elms: a village near Fulham, on the Thames.
‡ the World's End: a tavern in Chelsea.

countenance purely, you'd make an admirable player.

MRS FRAIL I'll swear you have a great deal of impudence, and in my mind too much for the stage.

MRS FORESIGHT Very well, that will appear who has most, you never were at the World's End?

MRS FRAIL No.

MRS FORESIGHT You deny it positively to my face.

MRS FRAIL Your face, what's your face?

MRS FORESIGHT No matter for that, it's as good a face as yours.

MRS FRAIL Not by a dozen years' wearing. – But I do deny it positively to your face then.

MRS FORESIGHT I'll allow you now to find fault with my face; – for I'll swear your impudence has put me out of countenance: – but look you here now, – where did you lose this gold bodkin? – O sister, sister!

MRS FRAIL My bodkin!

MRS FORESIGHT Nay, 'tis yours, look at it.

MRS FRAIL Well, if you go to that, where did you find this bodkin? – O sister, sister! – Sister every way.

MRS FORESIGHT [*aside*] O devil on't, that I could not discover her, without betraying myself.

MRS FRAIL I have heard gentlemen say, sister; that one should take great care, when one makes a thrust in fencing, not to lie open oneself.

MRS FORESIGHT It's very true, sister: well since all's out, and as you say, since we are both wounded, let us do that is often done in duels, take care of one another, and grow better friends than before.

MRS FRAIL With all my heart, ours are but slight flesh-wounds, and if we keep 'em from air, not at all dangerous: well, give me your hand in token of sisterly secrecy and affection.

MRS FORESIGHT Here 'tis with all my heart.

MRS FRAIL Well, as an earnest of friendship and confidence: I'll acquaint you with a design that I have: to tell truth, and speak openly one to another; I'm afraid the world have observed us more than we have observed one another. You have a rich husband, and are provided for, I am at a loss, and have no great stock either of fortune or reputation; and therefore must look sharply about

me. Sir Sampson has a son that is expected tonight; and by the
account I have heard of his education, can be no conjurer: the
estate you know is to be made over to him: – now if I could
wheedle him, sister, ha? You understand me?

MRS FORESIGHT I do; and will help you to the utmost of my
power – And I can tell you one thing that falls out luckily enough;
my awkward daughter-in-law,* who you know is designed for his
wife, is grown fond of Mr Tattle; now if we can improve that, and
make her have an aversion for the booby, it may go a great way
towards his liking of you. Here they come together; and let us
contrive some way or other to leave 'em together.

Enter Tattle, and Miss Prue.

MISS PRUE Mother, mother, mother, look you here.

MRS FORESIGHT Fie, fie, Miss, how you bawl – besides, I have
told you, you must not call me mother.

MISS PRUE What must I call you then, are not you my father's wife?

MRS FORESIGHT Madam; you must say Madam – By my soul, I
shall fancy myself old indeed, to have this great girl call me
mother – Well, but miss, what are you so overjoyed at?

MISS PRUE Look you here, Madam then, what Mr Tattle has given
me – Look you here, cousin, here's a snuff-box; nay, there's snuff
in't; – here, will you have any – O good! How sweet it is – Mr
Tattle is all over sweet, his peruke is sweet, and his gloves are
sweet, – and his handkerchief is sweet, pure sweet, sweeter than
roses – Smell him mother, Madam, I mean – He gave me this ring
for a kiss.

TATTLE O fie Miss, you must not kiss and tell.

MISS PRUE Yes; I may tell my mother – And he says he'll give
me something to make me smell so – O pray lend me your handkerchief – Smell cousin; he says, he'll give me something that will
make my smocks smell this way – Is not it pure? – It's better
than lavender mun – I'm resolved I won't let nurse put any more
lavender among my smocks – ha, cousin?

MRS FRAIL Fie, Miss; amongst your linen, you must say – You
must never say smock.

MISS PRUE Why, it is not bawdy, is it cousin?

* daughter-in-law: step-daughter.

TATTLE O Madam; you are too severe upon Miss; you must not find fault with her pretty simplicity, it becomes her strangely – pretty Miss, don't let 'em persuade you out of your innocency.

MRS FORESIGHT Oh, demn you toad – I wish you don't persuade her out of her innocency.

TATTLE Who I, Madam? – O Lord, how can your ladyship have such a thought – sure you don't know me?

MRS FRAIL Ah devil, sly devil – He's as close, sister, as a confessor – He thinks we don't observe him.

MRS FORESIGHT A cunning cur; how soon he could find out a fresh harmless creature; and left us, sister, presently.

TATTLE Upon reputation. –

MRS FORESIGHT They're all so, sister, these men – they love to have the spoiling of a young thing, they are as fond of it, as of being first in the fashion, or of seeing a new play the first day, – I warrant it would break Mr Tattle's heart, to think that anybody else should be beforehand with him.

TATTLE O Lord, I swear I would not for the world –

MRS FRAIL O hang you; who'll believe you? – You'd be hanged before you'd confess – we know you – she's very pretty! – Lord, what pure red and white! – she looks so wholesome; – ne'er stir, I don't know, but I fancy, if I were a man –

MISS PRUE How you love to jeer one, cousin.

MRS FORESIGHT Hark'ee, sister – by my soul the girl is spoiled already – d'ye think she'll ever endure a great lubberly tarpaulin – Gad I warrant you, she won't let him come near her, after Mr Tattle.

MRS FRAIL O' my soul, I'm afraid not – eh! – Filthy creature, that smells all of pitch and tar – Devil take you, you confounded toad – why did you see her, before she was married?

MRS FORESIGHT Nay, why did we let him – my husband will hang us – He'll think we brought 'em acquainted.

MRS FRAIL Come, faith let us be gone – If my brother Foresight should find us with them; – he'd think so, sure enough.

MRS FORESIGHT So he would – but then leaving 'em together is as bad – and he's such a sly devil, he'll never miss an opportunity.

MRS FRAIL I don't care; I won't be seen in't.

MRS FORESIGHT Well, if you should, Mr Tattle, you'll have a

world to answer for, remember I wash my hands of it. I'm thoroughly innocent.

[*Exeunt Mrs Foresight and Mrs Frail*]

MISS PRUE What makes 'em go away, Mr Tattle? What do they mean, do you know?

TATTLE Yes, my dear – I think I can guess – But hang me if I know the reason of it.

MISS PRUE Come, must not we go too?

TATTLE No, no they don't mean that.

MISS PRUE No! What then? What shall you and I do together?

TATTLE I must make love to you, pretty miss; will you let me make love to you.

MISS PRUE Yes, if you please.

TATTLE [*aside*] Frank, egad at least. What a pox does Mrs Foresight mean by this civility? Is it to make a fool of me? Or does she leave us together out of good morality, and do as she would be done by – Gad I'll understand it so.

MISS PRUE Well; and how will you make love to me – Come, I long to have you begin; – must I make love too? You must tell me how.

TATTLE You must let me speak Miss, you must not speak first; I must ask you questions, and you must answer.

MISS PRUE What, is it like the catechism? – Come then ask me.

TATTLE D'ye think you can love me?

MISS PRUE Yes.

TATTLE Pooh, pox, you must not say yes already; I shan't care a farthing for you then in a twinkling.

MISS PRUE What must I say then?

TATTLE Why you must say no, or you believe not, or you can't tell –

MISS PRUE Why, must I tell a lie then?

TATTLE Yes, if you would be well-bred. All well-bred persons lie – Besides, you are a woman, you must never speak what you think: your words must contradict your thoughts; but your actions may contradict your words. So, when I ask you, if you can love me, you must say no, but you must love me too – If I tell you you are handsome, you must deny it, and say I flatter you – But you must think yourself more charming than I speak you: – and like me, for the beauty which I say you have, as much as if I had it myself – If I ask you to kiss me, you must be angry, but you must not refuse me. If I ask you for more, you must be more angry, – but more complying; and as soon as ever I make you say you'll cry out, you must be sure to hold your tongue.

MISS PRUE O Lord, I swear this is pure, – I like it better than our old fashioned country way of speaking one's mind; – and must not you lie too?

TATTLE Hum – Yes – But you must believe I speak truth.

MISS PRUE O Gemini! Well, I always had a great mind to tell lies – but they frighted me, and said it was a sin.

TATTLE Well, my pretty creature; will you make me happy by giving me a kiss?

MISS PRUE No, indeed; I'm angry at you. – [*runs and kisses him*]

TATTLE Hold, hold, that's pretty well, – but you should not have given it me, but have suffered me to take it.

MISS PRUE Well, we'll do it again.

TATTLE With all my heart, – now then my little angel. [*kisses her*]

MISS PRUE Pish.

TATTLE That's right, – again my charmer. [*kisses again*]

MISS PRUE O fie, nay, now I can't abide you.

TATTLE Admirable! That was as well as if you had been born and bred in Covent Garden, all the days of your life; – and won't you show me, pretty Miss, where your bed-chamber is?

MISS PRUE No, indeed won't I: but I'll run there, and hide myself from you behind the curtains.

TATTLE I'll follow you.

MISS PRUE Ah, but I'll hold the door with both hands, and be angry; – and you shall push me down before you come in.

TATTLE No, I'll come in first, and push you down afterwards.

MISS PRUE Will you? Then I'll be more angry, and more complying.

TATTLE Then I'll make you cry out.

MISS PRUE O but you shan't, for I'll hold my tongue. –

TATTLE O my dear, apt scholar.

MISS PRUE Well, now I'll run and make more haste than you.

[*Exit Miss Prue*]

TATTLE You shall not fly so fast, as I'll pursue. [*Exit after her*]

ACT THREE

SCENE I

Enter Nurse.

NURSE Miss, Miss, Miss Prue – Mercy on me, marry and amen: why, what's become of the child? – Why Miss, Miss Foresight – Sure she has not locked herself up in her chamber, and gone to sleep, or to prayers; Miss, Miss, I hear her – Come to your father, child: open the door – Open the door Miss – I hear you cry husht – O Lord, who's there? [*peeps*] What's here to do? – O the Father! A man with her! – Why, Miss I say, God's my life, here's fine doings towards – O Lord, we're all undone – O you young harlotry [*knocks*] Ods my life, won't you open the door? I'll come in the back way. [*Exit*]

Tattle and Miss ⟨Prue⟩ at the door.

MISS PRUE O Lord, she's coming – and she'll tell my father, what shall I do now?

TATTLE Pox take her; if she had stayed two minutes longer, I should have wished for her coming.

MISS PRUE O dear, what shall I say? Tell me, Mr Tattle, tell me a lie.

TATTLE There's no occasion for a lie; I could never tell a lie to no purpose – But since we have done nothing, we must say nothing, I think. I hear her – I'll leave you together, and come off as you can. [*thrusts her in, and shuts the door*]

Enter Valentine, Scandal, and Angelica.

ANGELICA You can't accuse me of inconstancy; I never told you, that I loved you.

VALENTINE But I can accuse you of uncertainty, for not telling me whether you did or no.

ANGELICA You mistake indifference for uncertainty; I never had concern enough to ask myself the question.

SCANDAL Nor good nature enough to answer him that did ask you: I'll say that for you, Madam.

ANGELICA What, are you setting up for good nature?

SCANDAL Only for the affectation of it, as the women do for ill nature.

ANGELICA Persuade your friend, that it is all affectation.

VALENTINE I shall receive no benefit from the opinion: for I know no effectual difference between continued affectation and reality.

TATTLE [*coming up, aside to Scandal*] Scandal, are you in private discourse, anything of secrecy?

SCANDAL Yes, but I dare trust you; we were talking of Angelica's love for Valentine; you won't speak of it.

TATTLE No, no, not a syllable – I know that's a secret, for it's whispered everywhere.

SCANDAL Ha, ha, ha.

ANGELICA What is, Mr Tattle? I heard you say something was whispered everywhere.

SCANDAL Your love of Valentine.

ANGELICA How!

TATTLE No, Madam, his love for your ladyship – Gad take me, I beg your pardon – for I never heard a word of your ladyship's passion, till this instant.

ANGELICA My passion! And who told you of my passion, pray Sir?

SCANDAL Why, is the devil in you? Did not I tell it you for a secret?

TATTLE Gad so; but I thought she might have been trusted with her own affairs.

SCANDAL Is that your discretion? Trust a woman with herself?

TATTLE You say true, I beg your pardon; – I'll bring all off – It was impossible, Madam, for me to imagine, that a person of your ladyship's wit and gallantry, could have so long received the passionate addresses of the accomplished Valentine, and yet remain insensible; therefore you will pardon me, if from a just weight of his merit, with your ladyship's good judgment, I formed the balance of a reciprocal affection.

VALENTINE O the devil, what damned costive poet has given thee this lesson of fustian to get by rote?

ANGELICA I dare swear you wrong him, it is his own – And Mr Tattle only judges of the success of others, from the effects of his own merit. For certainly Mr Tattle was never denied anything in his life.

TATTLE O Lord! Yes indeed, Madam, several times.

ANGELICA I swear I don't think 'tis possible.

TATTLE Yes, I vow and swear I have: Lord, Madam, I'm the most unfortunate man in the world, and the most cruelly used by the ladies.

ANGELICA Nay, now you're ungrateful.

TATTLE No, I hope not – 'tis as much ingratitude to own some favours, as to conceal others.

VALENTINE There, now it's out.

ANGELICA I don't understand you now. I thought you had never asked anything, but what a lady might modestly grant, and you confess.

SCANDAL So faith, your business is done here; now you may go brag somewhere else.

TATTLE Brag! O heavens! Why, did I name anybody?

ANGELICA No; I suppose that is not in your power; but you would if you could, no doubt on't.

TATTLE Not in my power, Madam! What does your ladyship mean, that I have no woman's reputation in my power?

SCANDAL ⟨*aside*⟩ Oons, why you won't own it, will you?

TATTLE Faith, Madam, you're in the right; no more I have, as I hope to be saved; I never had it in my power to say anything to a lady's prejudice in my life – For as I was telling you Madam, I have been the most unsuccessful creature living, in things of that nature; and never had the good fortune to be trusted once with a lady's secret, not once.

ANGELICA No.

VALENTINE Not once, I dare answer for him.

SCANDAL And I'll answer for him; for I'm sure if he had, he would have told me; I find, Madam, you don't know Mr Tattle.

TATTLE No indeed, Madam, you don't know me at all, I find: for sure my intimate friends would have known –

ANGELICA Then it seems you would have told, if you had been trusted.

TATTLE O pox, Scandal, that was too far put – Never have told particulars, Madam. Perhaps I might have talked as of a third person – or have introduced an amour of my own, in conversation, by way of novel: but never have explained particulars.

ANGELICA But whence comes the reputation of Mr Tattle's secrecy, if he was never trusted?

SCANDAL Why thence it arises – The thing is proverbially spoken; but may be applied to him – As if we should say in general terms, he only is secret who never was trusted; a satirical proverb upon our sex – There's another upon yours – As she is chaste, who was never asked the question. That's all.

VALENTINE A couple of very civil proverbs, truly. 'Tis hard to tell whether the lady or Mr Tattle be the more obliged to you. For you found her virtue, upon the backwardness of the men; and his secrecy, upon the mistrust of the women.

TATTLE Gad, it's very true, Madam, I think we are obliged to acquit ourselves – And for my part – But your ladyship is to speak first –

ANGELICA Am I? Well, I freely confess I have resisted a great deal of temptation.

TATTLE And egad, I have given some temptation that has not been resisted.

VALENTINE Good.

ANGELICA I cite Valentine here, to declare to the court, how fruitless he has found his endeavours, and to confess all his solicitations and my denials.

VALENTINE I am ready to plead, not guilty for you; and guilty, for myself.

SCANDAL So, why this is fair, here's demonstration with a witness.

TATTLE Well, my witnesses are not present – But I confess I have had favours from persons – But as the favours are numberless, so the persons are nameless.

SCANDAL Pooh, pox, this proves nothing.

TATTLE No? I can show letters, lockets, pictures and rings; and if there be occasion for witnesses, I can summon the maids at the chocolate-houses, all the porters of Pall Mall and Covent Garden, the door-keepers at the playhouse, the drawers at Locket's,* Pontack's,† the Rummer,‡ Spring Garden; my own landlady and

---

* Locket's: a tavern in Charing Cross.   † Pontack's: a French eating-house.
‡ the Rummer: a tavern between Whitehall and Charing Cross, kept by the uncle of Matthew Prior.

valet de chambre; all who shall make oath, that I receive more letters than the secretary's office; and that I have more vizor-masks to enquire for me, than ever went to see the hermaphrodite, or the naked prince.★ And it is notorious, that in a country church, once, an enquiry being made, who I was, it was answered, I was the famous Tattle, who had ruined so many women.

VALENTINE It was there, I suppose, you got the nick-name of the Great Turk.

TATTLE True; I was called Turk-Tattle all over the parish – The next Sunday all the old women kept their daughters at home, and the parson had not half his congregation. He would have brought me into the spiritual court, but I was revenged upon him, for he had a handsome daughter whom I initiated into the science. But I repented it afterwards, for it was talked of in Town – And a lady of quality that shall be nameless, in a raging fit of jealousy, came down in her coach and six horses, and exposed herself upon my account; Gad, I was sorry for it with all my heart – You know whom I mean – You know where we raffled –

SCANDAL Mum, Tattle.

VALENTINE S'death, are not you ashamed?

ANGELICA O barbarous! I never heard so insolent a piece of vanity – Fie, Mr Tattle – I'll swear I could not have believed it – Is this your secrecy?

TATTLE Gad so, the heat of my story carried me beyond my discretion, as the heat of the lady's passion hurried her beyond her reputation – But I hope you don't know whom I mean; for there were a great many ladies raffled – Pox on't, now could I bite off my tongue.

SCANDAL No, don't; for then you'll tell us no more – Come, I'll recommend a song to you upon the hint of my two proverbs, and I see one in the next room that will sing it.   [*Goes to the door*]

TATTLE For heaven's sake, if you do guess, say nothing; gad, I'm very unfortunate.

Re-enter Scandal, with one to sing.

SCANDAL Pray sing the first song in the last new play.

★ the naked prince: Giolo, a South Sea islander whose tattooings roused much interest in London.

SONG
Set by Mr John Eccles.★
A nymph and a swain to Apollo once prayed,
The swain had been jilted, the nymph been betrayed,
Their intent was to try if his oracle knew
E'er a nymph that was chaste, or a swain that was true.

2

Apollo was mute, and had like t' have been posed,
But sagely at length he this secret disclosed:
He alone won't betray in whom none will confide,
And the nymph may be chaste that has never been tried.

Enter Sir Sampson, Mrs Frail, Miss ⟨Prue⟩, and Servant.

SIR SAMPSON Is Ben come? Odso, my son Ben come? Odd, I'm
glad on't: where is he? I long to see him. Now, Mrs Frail, you
shall see my son Ben – Body o'me, he's the hopes of my family – I
han't seen him these three years – I warrant he's grown – Call
him in, bid him make haste – I'm ready to cry for joy. [*Exit Servant*]
MRS FRAIL Now Miss, you shall see your husband.
MISS PRUE [*aside to Mrs Frail*] Pish, he shall be none of my
husband.
MRS FRAIL Hush: well he shan't, leave that to me – I'll beckon
Mr Tattle to us.
ANGELICA Won't you stay and see your brother?
VALENTINE We are the twin stars, and cannot shine in one sphere;
when he rises I must set – Besides, if I should stay, I don't know
but my father in good nature may press me to the immediate
signing the deed of conveyance of my estate, and I'll defer it as
long as I can – Well, you'll come to a resolution.
ANGELICA I can't. Resolution must come to me, or I shall never
have one.
SCANDAL Come, Valentine, I'll go with you; I've something in
my head to communicate to you.   [*Exeunt Valentine and Scandal*]

★ John Eccles: (*d.* 1738) wrote music for forty-six plays and became Master of
the King's Music in 1704. The song is based on Scandal's two proverbs (*see*
p. 276) and was sung by Mr Pate.

SIR SAMPSON What, is my son Valentine gone? What, is he sneaked off, and would not see his brother? There's an unnatural whelp! There's an ill-natured dog! What, were you here too, Madam, and could not keep him! Could neither love, nor duty, nor natural affection oblige him. Odsbud, Madam, have no more to say to him; he is not worth your consideration. The rogue has not a dram of generous love about him: all interest, all interest; he's an undone scoundrel, and courts your estate: body o'me, he does not care a doit* for your person.

ANGELICA I'm pretty even with him, Sir Sampson; for if ever I could have liked anything in him, it should have been his estate too: but since that's gone, the bait's off, and the naked hook appears.

SIR SAMPSON Odsbud, well spoken; and you are a wiser woman than I thought you were: for most young women nowadays are to be tempted with a naked hook.

ANGELICA If I marry, Sir Sampson, I'm for a good estate with any man, and for any man with a good estate: therefore if I were obliged to make a choice, I declare I'd rather have you than your son.

SIR SAMPSON Faith and troth you're a wise woman, and I'm glad to hear you say so; I was afraid you were in love with the reprobate; odd, I was sorry for you with all my heart: hang him, mongrel; cast him off; you shall see the rogue show himself, and make love to some desponding Cadua† of fourscore for sustenance. Odd, I love to see a young spendthrift forced to cling to an old woman for support, like ivy round a dead oak: faith I do; I love to see 'em hug and cotton together, like down upon a thistle.

Enter Ben Legend and Servant.

BEN Where's father?
SERVANT There, Sir, his back's toward you.
SIR SAMPSON My son Ben! Bless thee my dear boy; body o' me, thou art heartily welcome.
BEN Thank you father, and I'm glad to see you.
SIR SAMPSON Odsbud, and I'm glad to see thee, kiss me boy, kiss me again and again, dear Ben. [*kisses him*]

* doit: a trifle. † Cadua: a wanton harridan, probably elderly.

BEN So, so, enough father – Mess,* I'd rather kiss these gentle-women.

SIR SAMPSON And so thou shalt, – Mrs Angelica, my son Ben.

BEN Forsooth an you please – [*salutes her*] Nay mistress, I'm not for dropping anchor here; about ship i'faith – [*kisses Mrs Frail*] Nay, and you too, my little cock-boat – so – [*kisses Miss Prue*]

TATTLE Sir, you're welcome ashore.

BEN Thank you, thank you friend.

SIR SAMPSON Thou hast been many a weary league Ben, since I saw thee.

BEN Aye, aye, been! Been far enough, an that be all – well father, and how do all at home? How does brother Dick, and brother Val?

SIR SAMPSON Dick, body o'me, Dick has been dead these two years; I writ you word, when you were at Leghorn.

BEN Mess, and that's true: marry I had forgot. Dick's dead as you say – well, and how? I have a many questions to ask you; well, you be'nt married again, father, be you?

SIR SAMPSON No, I intend you shall marry, Ben; I would not marry for thy sake.

BEN Nay, what does that signify? – an you marry again – Why then, I'll go to sea again, so there's one for t'other, an that be all – Pray don't let me be your hindrance; e'en marry a God's name an the wind fit that way. As for my part, mayhap I have no mind to marry.

MRS FRAIL That would be pity, such a handsome young gentle-man.

BEN Handsome! He, he, he, nay forsooth, an you be for joking, I'll joke with you, for I love my jest, an the ship were sinking, as we sayn at sea. But I'll tell you why I don't much stand towards matrimony. I love to roam about from port to port, and from land to land: I could never abide to be port-bound as we call it: now a man that is married, has as it were, d'ye see, his feet in the bilboes,† and mayhap mayn't get 'em out again when he would.

SIR SAMPSON Ben's a wag.

BEN A man that is married, d'ye see, is no more like another man, than a galley-slave is like one of us free sailors, he is chained to an

* Mess: by the mass.   † bilboes: stocks.

oar all his life; and mayhap forced to tug a leaky vessel into the bargain.

SIR SAMPSON A very wag, Ben's a very wag; only a little rough, he wants a little polishing.

MRS FRAIL Not at all; I like his humour mightily, it's plain and honest, I should like such a humour in a husband extremely.

BEN Say'n you so forsooth? Marry and I should like such a handsome gentlewoman for a bedfellow hugely, how say you mistress, would you like going to sea? Mess you're a tight vessel, and well rigged, an you were but as well manned.

MRS FRAIL I should not doubt that, if you were master of me.

BEN But I'll tell you one thing, an you come to sea in a high wind, or that lady. – You mayn't carry so much sail o' your head – Top and top-gallant by the mess.

MRS FRAIL No, why so?

BEN Why an you do, you may run the risk to be overset, and then you'll carry your keels above water, he, he, he.

ANGELICA I swear, Mr Benjamin is the verriest wag in nature; an absolute sea-wit.

SIR SAMPSON Nay, Ben has parts, but as I told you before, they want a little polishing: you must not take anything ill, Madam.

BEN No, I hope the gentlewoman is not angry; I mean all in good part: for if I give a jest, I'll take a jest: and so forsooth you may be as free with me.

ANGELICA I thank you, Sir, I am not at all offended; – but methinks Sir Sampson, you should leave him alone with his mistress. Mr Tattle, we must not hinder lovers.

TATTLE [*aside to Miss Prue*] Well Miss, I have your promise.

SIR SAMPSON Body o'me, Madam, you say true: – look you Ben; this is your mistress, – come Miss, you must not be shamefaced, we'll leave you together.

MISS PRUE I can't abide to be left alone, mayn't my cousin stay with me?

SIR SAMPSON No, no. Come let's away.

BEN Look you father, mayhap the young woman mayn't take a liking to me. –

SIR SAMPSON I warrant thee boy, come, come, we'll be gone; I'll venture that.   [*Exeunt all but Ben and Miss Prue*]

BEN Come mistress, will you please to sit down, for an you stand astern a that'n, we shall never grapple together, – come, I'll haul a chair; there, an you please to sit, I'll sit by you.

MISS PRUE You need not sit so near one, if you have anything to say, I can hear you farther off, I an't deaf.

BEN Why, that's true as you say, nor I an't dumb, I can be heard as far as another, – I'll heave off to please you. [*sits further off*] An we were a league asunder, I'd undertake to hold discourse with you, and 'twere not a main high wind indeed, and full in my teeth. Look you forsooth, I am as it were, bound for the land of matrimony; 'tis a voyage d'ye see that was none of my seeking, I was commanded by father, and if you like of it, mayhap I may steer into your harbour. How say you mistress? The short of the thing is this, that if you like me, and I like you, we may chance to swing in a hammock together.

MISS PRUE I don't know what to say to you, nor I don't care to speak with you at all.

BEN No, I'm sorry for that. – But pray why are you so scornful.

MISS PRUE As long as one must not speak one's mind, one had better not speak at all, I think, and truly I won't tell a lie for the matter.

BEN Nay, you say true in that, it's but a folly to lie: for to speak one thing, and to think just the contrary way; is as it were, to look one way, and to row another. Now, for my part d'ye see, I'm for carrying things above board, I'm not for keeping anything under hatches, – so that if you ben't as willing as I, say so a God's name, there's no harm done; mayhap you may be shamefaced, some maidens tho'f they love a man well enough, yet they don't care to tell'n so to's face: if that's the case, why silence gives consent.

MISS PRUE But I'm sure it is not so, for I'll speak sooner than you should believe that; and I'll speak truth, though one should always tell a lie to a man; and I don't care, let my father do what he will; I'm too big to be whipped, so I'll tell you plainly, I don't like you, nor love you at all, nor never will, that's more: so, there's your answer for you; and don't trouble me no more, you ugly thing.

BEN Look you young woman, you may learn to give good words

however. I spoke you fair d'ye see, and civil. – As for your love or your liking, I don't value it of a rope's end; – And mayhap I like you a little as you do me: – what I said was in obedience to father; gad I fear a whipping no more than you do. But I tell you one thing, if you should give such language at sea, you'd have a cat o' nine-tails laid cross your shoulders. Flesh who are you? You heard t'other handsome young woman speak civilly to me, of her own accord: whatever you think of yourself, Gad I don't think you are any more to compare to her, than a can of small beer to a bowl of punch.

MISS PRUE Well, and there's a handsome gentleman, and a fine gentleman, and a sweet gentleman, that was here that loves me, and I love him; and if he sees you speak to me any more, he'll thrash your jacket for you, he will, you great sea-calf.

BEN What, do you mean that fair-weather spark that was here just now? Will he thrash my jacket? – Let'n, – let'n, – But an he comes near me, mayhap I may giv'n a salt eel for's supper, for all that. What does father mean to leave me alone as soon as I come home, with such a dirty dowdy. – Sea-calf? I an't calf enough to lick your chalked face, you cheese-curd you, – marry thee! Oons I'll marry a Lapland witch as soon, and live upon selling of contrary winds, and wracked vessels.

MISS PRUE I won't be called names nor I won't be abused thus, so I won't. – If I were a man, – [*cries*] – You durst not talk at this rate – No you durst not, you stinking tar-barrel.

Enter Mrs Foresight and Mrs Frail.

MRS FORESIGHT They have quarrelled just as we could wish.

BEN Tar-barrel? Let your sweetheart there call me so, if he'll take your part, your Tom Essence,* and I'll say something to him; Gad I'll lace his musk-doublet for him, I'll make him stink; he shall smell more like a weasel than a civet cat, afore I ha' done with 'en.

MRS FORESIGHT Bless me, what's the matter, Miss? What does she cry? – Mr Benjamin, what have you done to her?

BEN Let her cry: the more she cries, the less she'll – she has been

* Tom Essence: the leading character in Thomas Rawlinson's play of that name of 1676.

gathering foul weather in her mouth, and now it rains out at her eyes.

MRS FORESIGHT Come, Miss, come along with me, and tell me, poor child.

MRS FRAIL Lord, what shall we do, there's my brother Foresight, and Sir Sampson coming. Sister, do you take Miss down into the parlour, and I'll carry Mr Benjamin into my chamber, for they must not know that they are fallen out. – Come, Sir, will you venture yourself with me? [*looks kindly on him*]

BEN Venture, Mess, and that I will, though 'twere to sea in a storm. [*Exeunt*]

Enter Sir Sampson and Foresight.

SIR SAMPSON I left 'em together here; what are they gone? Ben's a brisk boy: he has got her into a corner, father's own son faith, he'll tousle her, and mousle her: the rogue's sharp set, coming from sea, if he should not stay for saying grace, old Foresight, but fall too without the help of a parson, ha? Odd if he should I could not be angry with him; 'twould be but like me, a chip of the old block. Ha! Thou'rt melancholy old prognostication. As melancholy as if thou hadst spilt the salt, or pared thy nails of a Sunday: – come, cheer up, look about thee: look up old star-gazer. Now is he poring upon the ground for a crooked pin, or an old horse-nail, with the head towards him.

FORESIGHT Sir Sampson, we'll have the wedding tomorrow morning.

SIR SAMPSON With all my heart.

FORESIGHT At ten o'clock, punctually at ten.

SIR SAMPSON To a minute, to a second; thou shall set thy watch, and the bridegroom shall observe its motions; they shall be married to a minute, go to bed to a minute; and when the alarm strikes, they shall keep time like the figures of St Dunstan's clock, and *consummatum est* shall ring all over the parish.

Enter Scandal.

SCANDAL Sir Sampson, sad news.

FORESIGHT Bless us!

SIR SAMPSON Why, what's the matter?

SCANDAL Can't you guess at what ought to afflict you and him, and all of us, more than anything else.

SIR SAMPSON Body o'me, I don't know any universal grievance, but a new tax, and the loss of the Canary fleet. Without popery should be landed in the west, or the French fleet were at anchor at Blackwall.*

SCANDAL No. Undoubtedly Mr Foresight knew all this, and might have prevented it.

FORESIGHT 'Tis no earthquake!

SCANDAL No, not yet; nor whirlwind. But we don't know what it may come to – But it has had a consequence already that touches us all.

SIR SAMPSON Why, body o'me, out with't.

SCANDAL Something has appeared to your son Valentine – He's gone to bed upon't, and very ill – He speaks little, yet says he has a world to say. Asks for his father and the wise Foresight; talks of Raymond Lully,† and the ghost of Lilly.‡ He has secrets to impart I suppose to you two. I can get nothing out of him but sighs. He desires he may see you in the morning, but would not be disturbed tonight, because he has some business to do in a dream.

SIR SAMPSON Hoity toity, what have I to do with his dreams or his divination – Body o'me, this is a trick to defer signing the conveyance. I warrant the devil will tell him in a dream, that he must not part with his estate: but I'll bring him a parson to tell him, that the devil's a liar – Or if that won't do, I'll bring a lawyer that shall out-lie the devil. And so I'll try whether my blackguard or his shall get the better of the day.   [*Exit*]

SCANDAL Alas, Mr Foresight, I'm afraid all is not right – You are a wise man, and a conscientious man; a searcher into obscurity and futurity; and if you commit an error, it is with a great deal of consideration, and discretion, and caution –

FORESIGHT Ah, good Mr Scandal –

SCANDAL Nay, nay, 'tis manifest; I do not flatter you – But Sir

---

* the loss . . . French fleet: England was at war with France (the war of the League of Augsburg 1688–97); the French twice attempted to invade England. In 1694 Lord Russell failed to find the French fleet at sea.
† Lully: a Catalan philosopher poet (*c.* 1236–1315).
‡ Lilly: William Lilly (1602–81), an English astrologer.

Sampson is hasty, very hasty; – I'm afraid he is not scrupulous enough, Mr Foresight – He has been wicked, and heaven grant he may mean well in his affair with you – But my mind gives me, these things cannot be wholly insignificant. You are wise, and should not be over-reached; methinks you should not –

FORESIGHT Alas, Mr Scandal – *Humanum est errare.*

SCANDAL You say true, man will err; mere man will err – but you are something more – There have been wise men; but they were such as you – Men who consulted the stars, and were observers of omens – Solomon was wise, but how? – By his judgment in astrology – So says Pineda* in his third book and eighth chapter –

FORESIGHT You are learned, Mr Scandal –

SCANDAL A trifler – but a lover of art – And the wise men of the East owed their instruction to a star, which is rightly observed by Gregory the Great† in favour of astrology! And Albertus Magnus‡ makes it the most valuable science, because, says he, it teaches us to consider the causation of causes, in the causes of things.

FORESIGHT I protest I honour you, Mr Scandal – I did not think you had been read in these matters – few young men are inclined –

SCANDAL I thank my stars that have inclined me – But I fear this marriage and making over this estate, this transferring of a rightful inheritance, will bring judgments upon us. I prophesy it, and I would not have the fate of Cassandra, not to be believed. Valentine is disturbed, what can be the cause of that? And Sir Sampson is hurried on by an unusual violence – I fear he does not act wholly from himself; methinks he does not look as he used to do.

FORESIGHT He was always of an impetuous nature – But as to this marriage I have consulted the stars; and all appearances are prosperous –

SCANDAL Come, come, Mr Foresight, let not the prospect of worldly lucre carry you beyond your judgment, nor against your

---

* Pineda: Joannes de Pineda (1558–1637) who wrote a commentary *De Rebus Salomonis Regis.*

† Gregory the Great: Pope (*c.* 540–604) under whom the mission to England commenced.

‡ Albertus Magnus: St Albert of Cologne (*c.* 1200–80), a distinguished theologian, philosopher and natural scientist.

conscience – You are not satisfied that you act justly.

FORESIGHT How!

SCANDAL You are not satisfied, I say – I am loath to discourage you – But it is palpable that you are not satisfied.

FORESIGHT How does it appear, Mr Scandal, I think I am very well satisfied.

SCANDAL Either you suffer yourself to deceive yourself; or you do not know yourself.

FORESIGHT Pray explain yourself.

SCANDAL Do you sleep well o'nights?

FORESIGHT Very well.

SCANDAL Are you certain? You do not look so.

FORESIGHT I am in health, I think.

SCANDAL So was Valentine this morning; and looked just so.

FORESIGHT How! Am I altered any way? I don't perceive it.

SCANDAL That may be, but your beard is longer than it was two hours ago.

FORESIGHT Indeed! Bless me.

Enter Mrs Foresight.

MRS FORESIGHT Husband, will you go to bed? It's ten o'clock. Mr Scandal, your servant –

SCANDAL Pox on her, she has interrupted my design – But I must work her into the project. You keep early hours, Madam.

MRS FORESIGHT Mr Foresight is punctual, we sit up after him.

FORESIGHT My dear, pray lend me your glass, your little looking-glass.

SCANDAL Pray lend it him, Madam – I'll tell you the reason. [*she gives him the glass: Scandal and she whisper*] My passion for you is grown so violent: – that I am no longer master of myself – I was interrupted in the morning, when you had charity enough to give me your attention, and I had hopes of finding another opportunity of explaining myself to you – but was disappointed all this day; and the uneasiness that has attended me ever since, brings me now hither at this unseasonable hour –

MRS FORESIGHT Was there ever such impudence, to make love to me before my husband's face? I'll swear I'll tell him.

SCANDAL Do, I'll die a martyr, rather than disclaim my passion.

But come a little farther this way, and I'll tell you what project I
had to get him out of the way; that I might have an opportunity
of waiting upon you. [*whisper*]

FORESIGHT [*looking in the glass*] I do not see any revolution here; –
methinks I look with a serene and benign aspect – pale, a little
pale – but the roses of these cheeks have been gathered many
years; – ha! I do not like that sudden flushing – gone already! –
Hem, hem, hem! Faintish. My heart is pretty good; yet it beats;
and my pulses ha! – I have none – Mercy on me – hum – Yes, here
they are – Gallop, gallop, gallop, gallop, gallop, gallop, hey!
Whither will they hurry me? – Now they're gone again – And
now I'm faint again; and pale again, and hem! And my hem! –
Breath, hem! – grows short; hem! Hem! He, he, hem!

SCANDAL It takes, pursue it in the name of love and pleasure.

MRS FORESIGHT How do you do, Mr Foresight?

FORESIGHT Hum, not so well as I thought I was. Lend me your
hand.

SCANDAL Look you there now – your lady says your sleep has
been unquiet of late.

FORESIGHT Very likely.

MRS FORESIGHT Oh, mighty restless, but I was afraid to tell him
so – He has been subject to talking and starting.

SCANDAL And did not use to be so.

MRS FORESIGHT Never, never; till within these three nights; I
cannot say that he has once broken my rest, since we have been
married.

FORESIGHT I will go to bed.

SCANDAL Do so, Mr Foresight, and say your prayers; – He looks
better than he did.

MRS FORESIGHT [*calls*] Nurse, nurse!

FORESIGHT Do you think so, Mr Scandal?

SCANDAL Yes, yes, I hope this will be gone by morning, taking it
in time. –

FORESIGHT I hope so.

Enter Nurse.

MRS FORESIGHT Nurse; your master is not well; put him to bed.

SCANDAL I hope you will be able to see Valentine in the morning,

– you had best take a little diacodion* and cowslip water, and lie upon your back, maybe you may dream.

FORESIGHT I thank you Mr Scandal, I will – Nurse, let me have a watch-light, and lay *The Crums of Comfort*† by me. –

NURSE Yes, Sir.

FORESIGHT And – hem, hem! I am very faint. –

SCANDAL No, no, you look much better.

FORESIGHT Do I? And d'ye hear – bring me, let me see – within a quarter of twelve – hem – he, hem! – Just upon the turning of the tide, bring me the urinal; – and I hope, neither the lord of my ascendant, nor the moon will be combust;‡ and then I may do well.

SCANDAL I hope so – Leave that to me; I will erect a scheme; and I hope I shall find both Sol and Venus in the sixth house.

FORESIGHT I thank you, Mr Scandal, indeed that would be a great comfort to me. Hem, hem! Good night.   [*Exit*]

SCANDAL Goodnight, good Mr Foresight – and I hope Mars and Venus will be in conjunction; – while your wife and I are together.

MRS FORESIGHT Well; and what use do you hope to make of this project? You don't think, that you are ever like to succeed in your design upon me.

SCANDAL Yes, faith I do; I have a better opinion both of you and myself, than to despair.

MRS FORESIGHT Did you ever hear such a toad – hark'ee devil; do you think any woman honest?

SCANDAL Yes, several, very honest; – they'll cheat a little at cards, sometimes, but that's nothing.

MRS FORESIGHT Pshaw! But virtuous, I mean.

SCANDAL Yes, faith, I believe some women are virtuous too; but 'tis as I believe some men are valiant, through fear – For why should a man court danger, or a woman shun pleasure.

MRS FORESIGHT O monstrous! What are conscience and honour?

SCANDAL Why, honour is a public enemy; and conscience a domestic thief; and he that would secure his pleasure, must pay a

---

* diacodion: a syrup made of poppy heads, used as an opiate.
† *The Crums of Comfort*: a seventeenth-century devotional manual.
‡ combust: burned by the sun. A planet was thought to be without influence when close to the sun. (8°30′)

tribute to one, and go halves with the t'other. As for honour, that you have secured, for you have purchased a perpetual opportunity for pleasure.

MRS FORESIGHT An opportunity for pleasure!

SCANDAL Aye, your husband, a husband is an opportunity for pleasure, so you have taken care of honour, and 'tis the least I can do to take care of conscience.

MRS FORESIGHT And so you think we are free for one another?

SCANDAL Yes faith, I think so; I love to speak my mind.

MRS FORESIGHT Why then I'll speak my mind. Now as to this affair between you and me. Here you make love to me; why, I'll confess it does not displease me. Your person is well enough, and your understanding is not amiss.

SCANDAL I have no great opinion of myself; – yet I think, I'm neither deformed, nor a fool.

MRS FORESIGHT But you have a villainous character; you are a libertine in speech, as well as practice.

SCANDAL Come, I know what you would say, – you think it more dangerous to be seen in conversation with me, than to allow some other men the last favour; you mistake, the liberty I take in talking, is purely affected, for the service of your sex. He that first cries out 'stop thief,' is often he that has stolen the treasure. I am a juggler, that act by confederacy; and if you please, we'll put a trick upon the world.

MRS FORESIGHT Aye: but you are such an universal juggler, – that I'm afraid you have a great many confederates.

SCANDAL Faith, I'm sound.

MRS FORESIGHT Oh, fie – I'll swear you're impudent.

SCANDAL I'll swear you're handsome.

MRS FORESIGHT Pish, you'd tell me so, though you did not think so.

SCANDAL And you'd think so, though I should not tell you so: and now I think we know one another pretty well.

MRS FORESIGHT O Lord, who's here?

Enter Mrs Frail and Ben.

BEN Mess, I love to speak my mind – Father has nothing to do with me – Nay, I can't say that neither; he has something to do with me. But what does that signify? If so be, that I ben't minded to be steered by him; 'tis as tho'f he should strive against wind and tide.

MRS FRAIL Aye, but my dear, we must keep it secret, till the estate be settled; for you know, marrying without an estate, is like sailing in a ship without ballast.

BEN He, he, he; why that's true; just so for all the world it is indeed, as like as two cable ropes.

MRS FRAIL And though I have a good portion; you know one would not venture all in one bottom.

BEN Why that's true again; for mayhap one bottom may spring a leak. You have hit it indeed, Mess you've nicked the channel.

MRS FRAIL Well, but if you should forsake me after all, you'd break my heart.

BEN Break your heart? I'd rather the *Marigold* should break her cable in a storm, as well as I love her. Flesh, you don't think I'm false-hearted, like a land-man. A sailor will be honest, though mayhap he has never a penny of money in his pocket – Mayhap I may not have so fair a face, as a citizen or a courtier; but for all that, I've as good blood in my veins, and a heart as sound as a biscuit.

MRS FRAIL And will you love me always?

BEN Nay, an I love once, I'll stick like pitch; I'll tell you that. Come, I'll sing you a song of a sailor.

MRS FRAIL Hold, there's my sister, I'll call her to hear it.

MRS FORESIGHT Well; I won't go to bed to my husband tonight; because I'll retire to my own chamber, and think of what you have said.

SCANDAL Well; you'll give me leave to wait upon you to your chamber-door; and leave you my last instructions?

MRS FORESIGHT Hold, here's my sister coming toward us.

MRS FRAIL If it won't interrupt you, I'll entertain you with a song.

BEN The song was made upon one of our ships-crew's wife; our boatswain made the song, mayhap you may know her, Sir. Before she was married, she was called buxom Joan of Deptford.

SCANDAL I have heard of her.

BEN [*sings*]

BALLAD
Set by Mr John Eccles.

A soldier and a sailor,
A tinker, and a tailor,
Had once a doubtful strife, Sir,
To make a maid a wife, Sir,
    Whose name was buxom Joan.
For now the time was ended,
When she no more intended,
To lick her lips at men, Sir,
And gnaw the sheets in vain, Sir,
    And lie o' nights alone.

2
The soldier swore like thunder,
He loved her more than plunder;
And showed her many a scar, Sir,
That he had brought from far, Sir.
    With fighting for her sake.
The tailor thought to please her,
With offering her his measure.
The tinker too with metal,
Said he could mend her kettle,
    And stop up every leak.

3
But while these three were prating,
The sailor slyly waiting,
Thought if it came about, Sir,
That they should all fall out, Sir:
    He then might play his part.
And just e'en as he meant, Sir,
To loggerheads they went, Sir,
And then he let fly at her,
A shot 'twixt wind and water,
    That won this fair maid's heart.

BEN If some of our crew that came to see me, are not gone; you shall see, that we sailors can dance sometimes, as well as other folks. [*whistles*] I warrant that brings 'em, an' they be within hearing.

Enter Seamen.

O here they be – And fiddles along with 'em; come, my lads, let's have a round, and I'll make one. [*dance*] We're merry folk, we sailors, we han't much to care for. Thus we live at sea; eat biscuit, and drink flip;* put on a clean shirt once a quarter – Come home and lie with our landladies once a year, get rid of a little money; and then put off with the next fair wind. How d'ye like us?

MRS FRAIL Oh, you are the happiest, merriest men alive.

MRS FORESIGHT We're beholding to Mr Benjamin for this entertainment. I believe it's late.

BEN Why, forsooth, an you think so, you had best go to bed. For my part, I mean to toss a can, and remember my sweetheart, afore I turn in; mayhap I may dream of her.

MRS FORESIGHT Mr Scandal, you had best go to bed and dream too.

SCANDAL Why faith, I have a good lively imagination; and can dream as much to the purpose as another, if I set about it: but dreaming is the poor retreat of a lazy, hopeless, and imperfect lover; 'tis the last glimpse of love to worn-out sinners, and the faint dawning of a bliss to wishing girls, and growing boys.
There's nought but willing, waking love, that can
Make blessed the ripened maid, and finished man.   [*Exeunt*]

---

* flip: a sweetened heated mixture of beer and spirit.

ACT FOUR

SCENE I

Valentine's lodging

Enter Scandal, and Jeremy.

SCANDAL Well, is your master ready; does he look madly, and
talk madly?

JEREMY Yes, Sir; you need make no great doubt of that; he that
was so near turning poet yesterday morning, can't be much to
seek in playing the madman today.

SCANDAL Would he have Angelica acquainted with the reason of
his design?

JEREMY No, Sir, not yet; – he has a mind to try, whether his
playing the madman, won't make her play the fool, and fall in
love with him; or at least own that she has loved him all this
while, and concealed it.

SCANDAL I saw her take coach just now with her maid; and think
I heard her bid the coachman drive hither.

JEREMY Like enough, Sir, for I told her maid this morning, my
master was run stark mad only for love of her mistress; I hear a
coach stop; if it should be she, Sir, I believe he would not see her,
till he hears how she takes it.

SCANDAL Well, I'll try her – 'tis she, here she comes.

Enter Angelica with Jenny.

ANGELICA Mr Scandal, I suppose you don't think it a novelty, to
see a woman visit a man at his own lodgings in a morning.

SCANDAL Not upon a kind occasion, Madam. But when a lady
comes tyrannically to insult a ruined lover, and make manifest the
cruel triumphs of her beauty; the barbarity of it, something sur-
prises me.

ANGELICA I don't like raillery from a serious face – pray tell me
what is the matter.

JEREMY No strange matter, Madam; my master's mad, that's all:
I suppose your ladyship has thought him so a great while.

ANGELICA How d'ye mean, mad?

JEREMY Why faith, Madam, he's mad for want of his wits, just as he was for want of money; his head is e'en as light as his pockets; and anybody that has a mind to a bad bargain, can't do better than to beg him for his estate.

ANGELICA If you speak truth, your endeavouring at wit is very unseasonable –

SCANDAL [*aside*] She's concerned, and loves him.

ANGELICA Mr Scandal, you can't think me guilty of so much inhumanity, as not to be concerned for a man I must own myself obliged to – pray tell me truth.

SCANDAL Faith, Madam, I wish telling a lie would mend the matter. But this is no new effect of an unsuccessful passion.

ANGELICA [*aside*] I know not what to think – Yet I should be vexed to have a trick put upon me – May I not see him?

SCANDAL I'm afraid the physician is not willing you should see him yet – Jeremy, go in and enquire.   [*Exit Jeremy*]

ANGELICA ⟨*aside*⟩ Ha! I saw him wink and smile – I fancy 'tis a trick – I'll try – ⟨*to Scandal*⟩ I would disguise to all the world a failing, which I must own to you – I fear my happiness depends upon the recovery of Valentine. Therefore I conjure you, as you are his friend, and as you have compassion upon one fearful of affliction, to tell me what I am to hope for – I cannot speak – But you may tell me, tell me, for you know what I would ask?

SCANDAL So, this is pretty plain – Be not too much concerned, Madam; I hope his condition is not desperate: an acknowledgment of love from you, perhaps, may work a cure; as the fear of your aversion occasioned his distemper.

ANGELICA [*aside*] Say you so; nay, then I'm convinced: and if I don't play trick for trick, may I never taste the pleasure of revenge – ⟨*to Scandal*⟩ Acknowledgment of love I find you have mistaken my compassion, and think me guilty of a weakness I am a stranger to. But I have too much sincerity to deceive you, and too much charity to suffer him to be deluded with vain hopes. Good nature and humanity oblige me to be concerned for him; but to love is neither in my power nor inclination; and if he can't be cured without I suck the poison from his wounds, I'm afraid he won't recover his senses till I lose mine.

SCANDAL Hey, brave woman, i'faith – Won't you see him then, if he desire it?

ANGELICA What signify a madman's desires? Besides, 'twould make me uneasy – If I don't see him, perhaps my concern for him may lessen – If I forget him, 'tis no more than he has done by himself: and now the surprise is over, methinks I am not half so sorry for him as I was –

SCANDAL So, faith good nature works apace; you were confessing just now an obligation to his love.

ANGELICA But I have considered that passions are unreasonable and involuntary; if he loves, he can't help it; and if I don't love, I can't help it; no more than he can help his being a man, or I my being a woman; or no more than I can help my want of inclination to stay longer here – Come, Jenny.

[Exeunt Angelica and Jenny]

SCANDAL Humh! – An admirable composition, faith, this same womankind.

Enter Jeremy.

JEREMY What, is she gone, Sir?

SCANDAL Gone; why she was never here, nor anywhere else; nor I don't know her if I see her; nor you neither.

JEREMY Good lack! What's the matter now? Are any more of us to be mad? Why, Sir, my master longs to see her; and is almost mad in good earnest, with the joyful news of her being here.

SCANDAL We are all under a mistake – Ask no questions, for I can't resolve you; but I'll inform your master. In the meantime, if our project succeed no better with his father, than it does with his mistress, he may descend from his exaltation of madness into the road of commonsense, and be content only to be made a fool with other reasonable people. I hear Sir Sampson, you know your cue; I'll to your master. *[Exit]*

Enter Sir Sampson Legend with a Lawyer.

SIR SAMPSON D'ye see, Mr Buckram, here's the paper signed with his own hand.

BUCKRAM Good, Sir. And the conveyance is ready drawn in this box, if he be ready to sign and seal.

SIR SAMPSON Ready, body o'me, he must be ready; his sham-sickness shan't excuse him – Oh, here's his scoundrel. Sirrah, where's your master?

JEREMY Ah, Sir, he's quite gone.

SIR SAMPSON Gone! What, he is not dead?

JEREMY No, Sir, not dead.

SIR SAMPSON What, is he gone out of Town, run away, ha! Has he tricked me? Speak, varlet.

JEREMY No, no, Sir; he's safe enough, Sir, an he were but as sound, poor gentleman. He is indeed here, Sir, and not here, Sir.

SIR SAMPSON Hey day, rascal, do you banter me? Sirrah, d'ye banter me – Speak Sirrah, where is he, for I will find him.

JEREMY Would you could, Sir; for he has lost himself. Indeed, Sir, I have almost broke my heart about him – I can't refrain tears when I think of him, Sir; I'm as melancholy for him as a passing-bell, Sir; or a horse in a pound.

SIR SAMPSON A pox confound your similitudes, Sir – Speak to be understood, and tell me in plain terms what the matter is with him, or I'll crack your fool's skull.

JEREMY Ah, you've hit it, Sir; that's the matter with him, Sir; his skull's cracked, poor gentleman; he's stark mad, Sir.

SIR SAMPSON Mad!

BUCKRAM What, is he *non compos*?

JEREMY Quite *non compos*, Sir.

BUCKRAM Why then all's obliterated, Sir Sampson, if he be *non compos mentis*, his act and deed will be of no effect, it is not good in law.

SIR SAMPSON Oons, I won't believe it; let me see him, Sir – Mad, I'll make him find his senses.

JEREMY Mr Scandal is with him, Sir; I'll knock at the door.

Goes to the scene, which opens and discovers Valentine upon a couch disorderly dressed, Scandal by him.

SIR SAMPSON How now, what's here to do? –

VALENTINE [*starting*] Ha! Who's that?

SCANDAL For heaven's sake softly, Sir, and gently; don't provoke him.

VALENTINE Answer me; who is that? And that?

SIR SAMPSON Gads bobs, does he not know me? Is he mischievous? I'll speak gently – Val, Val, do'st thou not know me, boy? Not know thy own father, Val! I am thy own father, and this is honest Brief Buckram the lawyer.

VALENTINE It may be so – I did not know you – the world is full – There are people that we do know, and people that we do not know; and yet the sun shines upon all alike – There are fathers that have many children; and there are children that have many fathers – 'tis strange! But I am Truth, and come to give the world the lie.

SIR SAMPSON Body o' me, I know not what to say to him.

VALENTINE Why, does that lawyer wear black? – Does he carry his conscience withoutside? – Lawyer, what art thou? Dost thou know me?

BUCKRAM O Lord, what must I say? – Yes, Sir.

VALENTINE Thou liest, for I am Truth. 'Tis hard I cannot get a livelihood amongst you. I have been sworn out of Westminster Hall the first day of every term – Let me see – No matter how long – But I'll tell you one thing; it's a question that would puzzle an arithmetician, if you should ask him, whether the Bible saves more souls in Westminster Abbey, or damns more in Westminster Hall: for my part, I am Truth, and can't tell; I have very few acquaintance.

SIR SAMPSON Body o' me, he talks sensibly in his madness – Has he no intervals?

JEREMY Very short, Sir.

BUCKRAM Sir, I can do you no service while he's in this condition: here's your paper, Sir – He may do me a mischief if I stay – The conveyance is ready, Sir. If he recover his senses.   [*Exit*]

SIR SAMPSON Hold, hold, don't you go yet.

SCANDAL You'd better let him go, Sir; and send for him if there be occasion; for I fancy his presence provokes him more.

VALENTINE Is the lawyer gone? 'Tis well, then we may drink about without going together by the ears – Heigh ho! What o'clock is't? My father here! Your blessing, Sir?

SIR SAMPSON He recovers – Bless thee, Val – How do'st thou do, boy?

VALENTINE Thank you, Sir, pretty well – I have been a little out of order; won't you please to sit, Sir?

SIR SAMPSON Aye, boy – Come, thou shalt sit down by me.

VALENTINE Sir, 'tis my duty to wait.

SIR SAMPSON No, no, come, come, sit you down, honest Val. How do'st thou do? Let me feel thy pulse – Oh, pretty well now, Val: body o' me, I was sorry to see thee indisposed: but I'm glad thou'rt better, honest Val.

VALENTINE I thank you, Sir.

SCANDAL [*aside*] Miracle! The monster grows loving.

SIR SAMPSON Let me feel thy hand again, Val: it does not shake – I believe thou can'st write, Val: ha, boy? Thou can'st write thy name, Val? – [*in whisper to Jeremy*] – Jeremy, step and overtake Mr Buckram, bid him make haste back with the conveyance – quick – quick [*Exit Jeremy*]

SCANDAL [*aside*] That ever I should suspect such a heathen of any remorse!

SIR SAMPSON Do'st thou know this paper, Val: I know thou'rt honest, and wilt perform articles. [*shows him the paper, but holds it out of his reach*]

VALENTINE Pray let me see it, Sir. You hold it so far off, that I can't tell whether I know it or no.

SIR SAMPSON See it, boy? Aye, aye, why thou do'st see it – 'Tis thy own hand, Val. Why, let me see, I can read it as plain as can be: look you here [*reads*] 'The condition of this obligation' – Look you, as plain as can be, so it begins – And then at the bottom – 'As witness my hand, VALENTINE LEGEND,' in great letters. Why, 'tis as plain as the nose in one's face: what, are my eyes better than thine? I believe I can read it farther off yet – let me see. [*stretches his arm as far as he can*]

VALENTINE Will you please to let me hold it, Sir?

SIR SAMPSON Let thee hold it, say'st thou – Aye, with all my heart – What matter is it who holds it? What need anybody hold it? – I'll put it up in my pocket, Val: and then nobody need hold it. [*puts the paper in his pocket*] There Val: it's safe enough, boy – But thou shalt have it as soon as thou hast set thy hand to another paper, little Val.

Re-enter Jeremy with Buckram.

VALENTINE What, is my bad genius here again! O no, 'tis the
lawyer with an itching palm; and he's come to be scratched –
My nails are not long enough – Let me have a pair of red hot
tongues quickly, quickly, and you shall see me act St Dunstan,*
and lead the devil by the nose.

BUCKRAM O Lord, let me be gone; I'll not venture myself with a
madman.   [*Exit Buckram*]

VALENTINE Ha, ha, ha; you need not run so fast, honesty will not
overtake you – Ha, ha, ha, the rogue found me out to be *in forma
pauperis*† presently.

SIR SAMPSON Oons! What a vexation is here! I know not what
to do, or say, nor which way to go.

VALENTINE Who's that, that's out of his way? – I am Truth, and
can set him right – Hark'ee, friend, the straight road is the worst
way you can go – He that follows his nose always, will very often
be led into a stink. *Probatum est*. But what are you for? Religion or
politics? There's a couple of topics for you, no more like one
another than oil and vinegar; and yet those two beaten together
by a state-cook, make sauce for the whole nation.

SIR SAMPSON What the devil had I to do, ever to beget sons? Why
did I ever marry?

VALENTINE Because thou wer't a monster; old boy? – The two
greatest monsters in the world are a man and a woman? What's
thy opinion?

SIR SAMPSON Why, my opinion is, that those two monsters
joined together, make yet a greater, that's a man and his wife.

VALENTINE Aha! Old truepenny, say'st thou so? Thou hast
nicked it – But it's wonderful strange, Jeremy!

JEREMY What is, Sir?

VALENTINE That grey hairs should cover a green head – and I
make a fool of my father.

Enter Foresight, Mrs Foresight, and Mrs Frail.

---

* St Dunstan: Archbishop of Canterbury (924–88) who was reputed to have
seized the devil in the form of a woman by the nose with a pair of red-hot tongs.
† *in forma pauperis*: every poor man was entitled by law (II Hen. 7, c. 12) to have
writs according to the nature of the case without paying fees for them and the
judge could assign counsel and solicitors who acted gratis.

What's here! Erra Pater?⋆ Or a bearded Sybil? If prophecy comes, truth must give place.   [*Exit with Jeremy*]

FORESIGHT What says he? What, did he prophesy? Ha, Sir Sampson, bless us! How are we?

SIR SAMPSON Are we? Ah pox o' your prognostication – Why, we are fools as we use to be – Oons, that you could not foresee that the moon would predominate, and my son be mad – Where's your oppositions, your trines, and your quadrates? – What did your Cardan† and your Ptolemy tell you? Your Messahalah and your Longomontanus,‡ your harmony of chiromancy with astrology. Ah! Pox on't, that I that know the world, and men and manners, that don't believe a syllable in the sky and stars, and sun and almanacs, and trash, should be directed by a dreamer, an omen-hunter, and defer business in expectation of a lucky hour. When, body o'me, there never was a lucky hour after the first opportunity.   [*Exit Sir Sampson*]

FORESIGHT Ah, Sir Sampson, heaven help your head – This is none of your lucky hour; *nemo omnibus horis sapit.*§ What, is he gone, and in contempt of science! Ill stars and unconverted ignorance attend him.

SCANDAL You must excuse his passion, Mr Foresight; for he has been heartily vexed – His son is *non compos mentis*, and thereby incapable of making any conveyance in law; so that all his measures are disappointed.

FORESIGHT Ha! say you so?

MRS FRAIL [*aside to Mrs Foresight*] What, has my sea-lover lost his anchor of hope then?

MRS FORESIGHT O sister, what will you do with him?

MRS FRAIL Do with him, send him to sea again in the next foul weather – He's used to an inconstant element, and won't be surprised to see the tide turned.

FORESIGHT [*considers*] Wherein was I mistaken, not to foresee this?

SCANDAL [*aside to Mrs Foresight*] Madam, you and I can tell

⋆ Erra Pater: the assumed name of the author of an almanac of 1535.

† Cardan: Geronimo Cardano (1501–76), Italian physician and astrologer.

‡ Longomontanus: Christian Severin (1562–1647), born in Longberg (Longomontanus), Denmark, an astrologer who worked with Tycho Brahe.

§ *nemo . . . sapit*: Pliny, *Nat. Hist.* VII, ix, 'no man is wise at all times'.

him something else, that he did not foresee, and more particularly relating to his own fortune.

MRS FORESIGHT What do you mean? I don't understand you.

SCANDAL Hush, softly – the pleasures of last night, my dear, too considerable to be forgot so soon.

MRS FORESIGHT Last night! And what would your impudence infer from last night? Last night was like the night before, I think.

SCANDAL S'death do you make no difference between me and your husband?

MRS FORESIGHT Not much, – he's superstitious; and you are mad in my opinion.

SCANDAL You make me mad – You are not serious – Pray recollect yourself.

MRS FORESIGHT O yes, now I remember, you were very impertinent and impudent, – and would have come to bed to me.

SCANDAL And did not?

MRS FORESIGHT Did not! With that face can you ask the question?

SCANDAL This I have heard of before, but never believed. I have been told she had that admirable quality of forgetting to a man's face in the morning, that she had lain with him all night, and denying favours with more impudence, than she could grant 'em.– Madam, I'm your humble servant, and honour you. – You look pretty well, Mr Foresight; – How did you rest last night?

FORESIGHT Truly Mr Scandal, I was so taken up with broken dreams and distracted visions, that I remember little.

SCANDAL 'Twas a very forgetting night. – But would you not talk with Valentine, perhaps you may understand him; I'm apt to believe there is something mysterious in his discourses, and sometimes rather think him inspired than mad.

FORESIGHT You speak with singular good judgment, Mr Scandal, truly, – I am inclining to your Turkish opinion in this matter, and do reverence a man whom the vulgar think mad. Let us go in to him.

MRS FRAIL Sister, do you stay with them; I'll find out my lover, and give him his discharge, and come to you. O' my conscience here he comes.   [*Exeunt Foresight, Mrs Foresight and Scandal*]

Enter Ben.

BEN All mad, I think – Flesh, I believe all the calentures★ of the sea are come ashore, for my part.

MRS FRAIL Mr Benjamin in choler!

BEN No, I'm pleased well enough, now I have found you, – Mess, I've had such a hurricane upon your account yonder. –

MRS FRAIL My account, pray what's the matter?

BEN Why, father came and found me squabbling with yon chitty faced thing, as he would have me marry, – so he asked what was the matter. – He asked in a surly sort of way – (It seems brother Val is gone mad, and so that put'n into a passion; but what did I know that, what's that to me?) – So he asked in a surly sort of manner, – and Gad I answered 'n as surlily, – What tho'f he be my father, I an't bound prentice to 'en: – so faith I told 'n in plain terms, if I were minded to marry, I'd marry to please myself, not him; and for the young woman that he provided for me, I thought it more fitting for her to learn her sampler, and make dirt-pies, than to look after a husband; for my part I was none of her man. – I had another voyage to make, let him take it as he will.

MRS FRAIL So then you intend to go to sea again?

BEN Nay, nay, my mind run upon you, – but I would not tell him so much. – So he said he'd make my heart ache; and if so be that he could get a woman to his mind, he'd marry himself. Gad, says I, an you play the fool and marry at these years, there's more danger of your head's aching than my heart. – He was woundy angry when I gav'n that wipe. – He hadn't a word to say, and so I left'n, and the green girl together; – mayhap the bee may bite, and he'll marry her himself, with all my heart.

MRS FRAIL And were you this undutiful and graceless wretch to your father?

BEN Then why was he graceless first, – if I am undutiful and grace-less, why did he beget me so? I did not get myself.

MRS FRAIL O impiety! How have I been mistaken! What an inhuman merciless creature have I set my heart upon? O I am happy to have discovered the shelves and quicksands that lurk beneath that faithless smiling face.

★ calentures: diseases or fevers afflicting sailors in the tropics.

BEN Hey toss! What's the matter now? Why you ben't angry, be you?

MRS FRAIL O see me no more, – for thou wert born amongst rocks, suckled by whales, cradled in a tempest, and whistled to by winds; and thou art come forth with fins and scales, and three rows of teeth, a most outrageous fish of prey.

BEN O Lord, O Lord, she's mad, poor young woman, love has turned her senses, her brain is quite overset. Well-a-day, how shall I do to set her to rights.

MRS FRAIL No, no, I am not mad, monster, I am wise enough to find you out. – Had'st thou the impudence to aspire at being a husband with that stubborn and disobedient temper? – You that know not how to submit to a father, presume to have a sufficient stock of duty to undergo a wife? I should have been finely fobbed indeed, very finely fobbed.

BEN Hark'ee forsooth; if so be that you are in your right senses, d'ye see; for ought as I perceive I'm like to be finely fobbed, – if I have got anger here upon your account, and you are tacked about already. – What d'ye mean, after all your fair speeches, and stroking my cheeks, and kissing and hugging, what would you sheer off so? Would you, and leave me aground?

MRS FRAIL No, I'll leave you adrift, and go which way you will.

BEN What, are you false-hearted then?

MRS FRAIL Only the wind's changed.

BEN More shame for you, – the wind's changed? – It's an ill wind blows nobody good, – mayhap I have good riddance on you, if these be your tricks, – what d'ye mean all this while, to make a fool of me?

MRS FRAIL Any fool, but a husband.

BEN Husband! Gad I would not be your husband, if you would have me; now I know your mind, tho'f you had your weight in gold and jewels, and though I loved you never so well.

MRS FRAIL Why canst thou love, porpoise?

BEN No matter what I can do? Don't call names, – I don't love you so well as to bear that, whatever I did, – I'm glad you show yourself, mistress: – Let them marry you, as don't know you: – Gad I know you too well, by sad experience; – I believe he that marries you will go to sea in a hen-pecked frigate. – I believe that, young woman – and mayhap may come to an anchor at Cuckold's Point;* so there's a dash for you, take it as you will, mayhap you may holla after me when I won't come too.   [*Exit*]

MRS FRAIL Ha, ha, ha, no doubt on't. [*sings*]
'My true love is gone to sea.' –

Enter Mrs Foresight.

O sister, had you come a minute sooner, you would have seen the resolution of a lover, – honest Tar and I are parted; – and with the same indifference that we met: – O' my life I am half-vexed at the insensibility of a brute that I despised.

MRS FORESIGHT What then, he bore it most heroically?

MRS FRAIL Most tyrannically, – for you see he has got the start of me; and I the poor forsaken maid am left complaining on the shore. But I'll tell you a hint that he has given me; Sir Sampson is enraged, and talks desperately of committing matrimony himself. – If he has a mind to throw himself away, he can't do it more effectually than upon me, if we could bring it about.

MRS FORESIGHT O hang him old fox, he's too cunning, besides he hates both you and me. – But I have a project in my head for you, and I have gone a good way towards it. I have almost made a bargain with Jeremy, Valentine's man, to sell his master to us.

MRS FRAIL Sell him, how?

MRS FORESIGHT Valentine raves upon Angelica, and took me for her, and Jeremy says will take anybody for her that he imposes on him. – Now I have promised him mountains; if in one of his mad fits he will bring you to him in her stead, and get you married together, and put to bed together; and after consummation, girl, there's no revoking. And if he should recover his senses, he'll be glad at least to make you a good settlement. – Here they come, stand aside a little, and tell me how you like the design.

Enter Valentine, Scandal, Foresight, and Jeremy.

SCANDAL [*to Jeremy*] And have you given your master a hint of their plot upon him?

JEREMY Yes, Sir; he says he'll favour it, and mistake her for Angelica.

* Cuckold's Point: a headland on the Thames, below Rotherhithe.

SCANDAL It may make sport.

FORESIGHT Mercy on us!

VALENTINE Husht – Interrupt me not – I'll whisper prediction to thee, and thou shalt prophesy; – I am Truth, and can teach thy tongue a new trick, – I have told thee what's past, – Now I tell what's to come; – Dost thou know what will happen tomorrow? – Answer me not – for I will tell thee. Tomorrow, knaves will thrive through craft, and fools through fortune; and honesty will go as it did, frost-nipped in a summer suit. Ask me questions concerning tomorrow?

SCANDAL Ask him, Mr Foresight.

FORESIGHT Pray what will be done at Court?

VALENTINE Scandal will tell you; – I am truth, I never come there.

FORESIGHT In the City?

VALENTINE Oh, prayers will be said in empty churches, at the usual hours. Yet you will see such zealous faces behind counters, as if religion were to be sold in every shop. O things will go methodically in the City, the clocks will strike twelve at noon, and the horned herd buzz in the Exchange★ at two. Wives and husbands will drive distinct trades, and care and pleasure separately occupy the family. Coffee-houses will be full of smoke and stratagem. And the cropped prentice, that sweeps his master's shop in the morning, may ten to one, dirty his sheets before night. But there are two things that you will see very strange; which are wanton wives, with their legs at liberty, and tame cuckolds, with chains about their necks. But hold, I must examine you before I go further; you look suspiciously. Are you a husband?

FORESIGHT I am married.

VALENTINE Poor creature! Is your wife of Covent Garden parish?

FORESIGHT No; St Martins in the Fields.

VALENTINE Alas, poor man; his eyes are sunk, and his hands shrivelled; his legs dwindled, and his back bowed, pray, pray, for a metamorphosis – Change thy shape, and shake off age; get thee Medea's kettle,† and be boiled anew, come forth with labouring callous hands, a chine of steel, and Atlas shoulders. Let

★ Exchange: the New Exchange in the Strand.
† Medea's kettle: Medea could restore youth with her cauldron, and did this for Jason's father.

Taliacotius* trim the salves of twenty chairmen, and make thee
pedestals to stand erect upon, and look matrimony in the face.
Ha, ha, ha! That a man should have a stomach to a wedding
supper, when the pigeons† ought rather to be laid to his feet, ha,
ha, ha.

FORESIGHT His frenzy is very high now, Mr Scandal.

SCANDAL I believe it is a spring tide.

FORESIGHT Very likely truly; you understand these matters –
Mr Scandal, I shall be very glad to confer with you about these
things which he has uttered. – His sayings are very mysterious and
hieroglyphical.

VALENTINE Oh, why would Angelica be absent from my eyes so
long?

JEREMY She's here, Sir.

MRS FORESIGHT Now, sister.

MRS FRAIL O Lord, what must I say?

SCANDAL Humour him, Madam, by all means.

VALENTINE Where is she? O I see her – she comes, like riches,
health, and liberty at once, to a despairing, starving, and abandoned wretch. O welcome, welcome.

MRS FRAIL How d'ye Sir? Can I serve you?

VALENTINE Hark'ee; – I have a secret to tell you – Endymion‡
and the moon shall meet us upon Mount Latmos, and we'll be
married in the dead of night. – But say not a word. Hymen shall
put his torch into a dark lanthorn, that it may be secret; and Juno
shall give her peacock poppy-water, that he may fold his ogling
tail, and Argos's hundred eyes be shut, ha?§ Nobody shall know,
but Jeremy.

MRS FRAIL No, no, we'll keep it secret, it shall be done presently.

VALENTINE The sooner the better – Jeremy, come hither – closer
– that none may overhear us; – Jeremy, I can tell you news; –
Angelica is turned nun; and I am turning friar, and yet we'll

---

* Taliacotius: Gaspare Tagliacozzi (1546–99), a famous surgeon.
† pigeons: a remedy for plague.
‡ Endymion: a shepherd boy with whom the moon goddess fell in love when
she saw him asleep on Mount Latmos: he was given eternal youthfulness
through eternal sleep.
§ Juno . . . eyes: Juno shall give her peacock an opiate. Since Argos's hundred
eyes were placed in the peacock's tail, all will be secret.

marry one another in spite of the Pope – Get me a cowl and beads, that I may play my part, – for she'll meet me two hours hence in black and white, and a long veil to cover the project, and we won't see one another's faces, till we have done something to be ashamed of; and then we'll blush once for all.

Enter Tattle, and Angelica.

JEREMY I'll take care, and –

VALENTINE Whisper.

ANGELICA Nay, Mr Tattle, if you make love to me, you spoil my design, for I intended to make you my confident.

TATTLE But, Madam, to throw away your person, such a person! And such a fortune, on a madman!

ANGELICA I never loved him till he was mad; but don't tell anybody so.

SCANDAL How's this! Tattle making love to Angelica!

TATTLE Tell, Madam! Alas you don't know me – I have much ado to tell your ladyship, how long I have been in love with you – but encouraged by the impossibility of Valentine's making any more addresses to you, I have ventured to declare the very inmost passion of my heart. Oh, Madam, look upon us both. There you see the ruins of a poor decayed creature – Here, a complete and lively figure, with youth and health, and all his five senses in perfection, Madam, and to all this, the most passionate lover –

ANGELICA O fie for shame, hold your tongue, a passionate lover, and five senses in perfection! When you are as mad as Valentine, I'll believe you love me, and the maddest shall take me.

VALENTINE It is enough. Ha! Who's here?

MRS FRAIL [*to Jeremy*] O Lord, her coming will spoil all.

JEREMY No, no, Madam, he won't know her, if he should, I can persuade him.

VALENTINE Scandal, who are all these? Foreigners? If they are, I'll tell you what I think – [*whisper*] Get away all the company but Angelica, that I may discover my design to her.

SCANDAL [*whisper*] I will, – I have discovered something of Tattle, that is of a piece with Mrs Frail. He courts Angelica, if we could contrive to couple 'em together – Hark'ee –

MRS FORESIGHT He won't know you, cousin, he knows no-body.

FORESIGHT But he knows more than anybody, – O niece, he knows things past and to come, and all the profound secrets of time.

TATTLE Look you, Mr Foresight, it is not my way to make many words of matters, and so I shan't say much, – but in short, d'ye see, I will hold you a hundred pound now, that I know more secrets than he.

FORESIGHT How! I cannot read that knowledge in your face, Mr Tattle – Pray, what do you know?

TATTLE Why d'ye think I'll tell you, Sir! Read it in my face? No, Sir, 'tis written in my heart. And safer there, Sir, than letters writ in juice of lemon, for no fire can fetch it out. I am no blab, Sir.

VALENTINE [*to Scandal*] Acquaint Jeremy with it, he may easily bring it about, – They are welcome, and I'll tell 'em so myself. What do you look strange upon me? – Then I must be plain. [*coming up to them*] I am Truth, and hate an old acquaintance with a new face. [*Scandal goes aside with Jeremy*]

TATTLE Do you know me, Valentine?

VALENTINE You? Who are you? No, I hope not.

TATTLE I am Jack Tattle, your friend.

VALENTINE My friend, what to do? I am no married man, and thou can'st not lie with my wife? I am very poor, and thou can'st not borrow money of me; then what employment have I for a friend.

TATTLE Hah! A good open speaker, and not to be trusted with a secret.

ANGELICA Do you know me, Valentine?

VALENTINE O very well.

ANGELICA Who am I?

VALENTINE You're a woman, – one to whom Heaven gave beauty, when it grafted roses on a briar. You are the reflection of heaven in a pond, and he that leaps at you is sunk. You are all white, a sheet of lovely spotless paper, when you first are born; but you are to be scrawled and blotted by every goose's quill. I know you; for I loved a woman, and loved her so long, that I found out a strange thing: I found out what a woman was good for.

TATTLE Aye, prithee, what's that?

VALENTINE Why to keep a secret.

TATTLE O Lord!

VALENTINE O exceeding good to keep a secret: for though she should tell, yet she is not to be believed.

TATTLE Hah! Good again, faith.

VALENTINE I would have music – Sing me the song that I like –

SONG

*Set by Mr Finger.**

I tell thee, Charmion, could I time retrieve,
And could again begin to love and live,
To you I should my earliest offering give;
    I know my eyes would lead my heart to you,
    And I should all my vows and oaths renew,
    But to be plain, I never would be true.

2

For by our weak and weary truth, I find,
Love hates to centre in a point assigned,
But runs with joy the circle of the mind.
    Then never let us chain what should be free,
    But for relief of either sex agree,
    Since women love to change, and so do we.

VALENTINE [*walks musing*] No more, for I am melancholy.

JEREMY [*to Scandal*] I'll do't, Sir.

SCANDAL Mr Foresight, we had best leave him. He may grow outrageous, and do mischief.

FORESIGHT I will be directed by you.

JEREMY [*to Mrs Frail*] You'll meet, Madam; – I'll take care everything shall be ready.

MRS FRAIL Thou shalt do what thou wilt, have what thou wilt, in short I will deny thee nothing.

TATTLE [*to Angelica*] Madam, shall I wait upon you?

    * Mr Finger: Godfrey Finger, a contemporary composer.

ANGELICA No, I'll stay with him – Mr Scandal will protect me. Aunt, Mr Tattle desires you would give him leave to wait on you.

TATTLE Pox on't, there's no coming off, now she has said that – Madam, will you do me the honour?

MRS FORESIGHT Mr Tattle might have used less ceremony.

[*Exeunt Foresight, Mrs Foresight, Tattle, Mrs Frail, Jeremy*]

SCANDAL Jeremy, follow Tattle.

ANGELICA Mr Scandal, I only stay till my maid comes, and because I had a mind to be rid of Mr Tattle.

SCANDAL Madam, I am very glad that I overheard a better reason, which you gave to Mr Tattle; for his impertinence forced you to acknowledge a kindness for Valentine, which you denied to all his sufferings and my solicitations. So I'll leave him to make use of the discovery; and your ladyship to the free confession of your inclinations.

ANGELICA O Heavens! You won't leave me alone with a madman?

SCANDAL No, Madam; I only leave a madman to his remedy.

[*Exit Scandal*]

VALENTINE Madam, you need not be very much afraid, for I fancy I begin to come to myself.

ANGELICA [*aside*] Aye, but if I don't fit you, I'll be hanged.

VALENTINE You see what disguises love makes us put on; gods have been in counterfeited shapes for the same reason; and the divine part of me, my mind, has worn this mask of madness, and this motley livery, only as the slave of love, and menial creature of your beauty.

ANGELICA Mercy on me, how he talks! Poor Valentine!

VALENTINE Nay faith, now let us understand one another, hypocrisy apart, – The comedy draws toward an end, and let us think of leaving acting, and be ourselves; and since you have loved me, you must own I have at length deserved you should confess it.

ANGELICA [*sighs*] I would I had loved you – for heaven knows I pity you; and could I have foreseen the sad effects, I would have striven; but that's too late.

VALENTINE What sad effects? – What's too late? My seeming madness has deceived my father, and procured me time to think of means to reconcile me to him; and preserve the right of my inheritance to his estate; which otherwise by articles, I must this morning have resigned: and this I had informed you of today, but you were gone, before I knew you had been here.

ANGELICA How! I thought your love of me had caused this transport in your soul; which, it seems, you only counterfeited; for mercenary ends and sordid interest.

VALENTINE Nay, now you do me wrong; for if any interest was considered, it was yours; since I thought I wanted more than love, to make me worthy of you.

ANGELICA Then you thought me mercenary – But how am I deluded by this interval of sense, to reason with a madman?

VALENTINE Oh, 'tis barbarous to misunderstand me longer.

Enter Jeremy.

ANGELICA O here's a reasonable creature – Sure he will not have the impudence to persevere – Come, Jeremy, acknowledge your trick, and confess your master's madness counterfeit.

JEREMY Counterfeit, Madam! I'll maintain him to be as absolutely and substantially mad, as any freeholder in Bethlehem;* nay, he's as mad as any projector, fanatic, chemist, lover, or poet in Europe.

VALENTINE Sirrah, you lie; I am not mad.

ANGELICA Ha, ha, ha, you see he denies it.

JEREMY O Lord, Madam, did you ever know any madman mad enough to own it?

VALENTINE Sot, can't you apprehend?

ANGELICA Why he talked very sensibly just now.

JEREMY Yes, Madam; he has intervals: but you see he begins to look wild again now.

VALENTINE Why you thick-skulled rascal, I tell you the farce is done, and I will be mad no longer. [*beats him*]

ANGELICA Ha, ha, ha, is he mad, or no, Jeremy?

JEREMY Partly I think – for he does not know his mind two hours – I'm sure I left him just now, in a humour to be mad: and I think I have not found him very quiet at this present. [*one knocks*] Who's there?

---

* Bethlehem: Bedlam, the hospital of St Mary of Bethlehem, the lunatic hospital in London.

VALENTINE Go see, you sot. I'm very glad that I can move your mirth, though not your compassion.   [*Exit Jeremy*]

ANGELICA I did not think you had apprehension enough to be exceptious: but madmen show themselves most, by over-pretending to a sound understanding; as drunken men do by overacting sobriety; I was half inclining to believe you, till I accidentally touched upon your tender part: but now you have restored me to my former opinion and compassion.

Enter Jeremy.

JEREMY Sir, your father has sent to know if you are any better yet – Will you please to be mad, Sir, or how?

VALENTINE Stupidity! You know the penalty of all I'm worth must pay for the confession of my senses; I'm mad, and will be mad to everybody but this lady.

JEREMY So – Just the very backside of truth, – But lying is a figure of speech, that interlards the greatest part of my conversation – Madam, your ladyship's woman.   [*Goes to the door*]

Enter Jenny.

ANGELICA Well, have you been there? – Come hither.

JENNY Yes, Madam, [*aside to Angelica*] Sir Sampson will wait upon you presently.

VALENTINE You are not leaving me in this uncertainty?

ANGELICA Would anything, but a madman complain of uncertainty? Uncertainty and expectation are the joys of life. Security is an insipid thing, and the overtaking and possessing of a wish, discovers the folly of the chase. Never let us know one another better; for the pleasure of a masquerade is done, when we come to show faces; but I'll tell you two things before I leave you; I am not the fool you take me for; and you are mad and don't know it.   [*Exeunt Angelica and Jenny*]

VALENTINE From a riddle, you can expect nothing but a riddle. There's my instruction, and the moral of my lesson.

Re-enter Jeremy.

JEREMY What, is the lady gone again, Sir? I hope you understood one another before she went.

VALENTINE Understood! She is harder to be understood than a piece of Egyptian antiquity, or an Irish manuscript; you may pore till you spoil your eyes, and not improve your knowledge.

JEREMY I have heard 'em say, Sir, they read hard Hebrew books backwards; may be you begin to read at the wrong end.

VALENTINE They say so of a witch's prayer, and dreams and Dutch almanacs are to be understood by contraries. But there's regularity and method in that; she is a medal without a reverse or inscription; for indifference has both sides alike. Yet while she does not seem to hate me, I will pursue her, and know her if it be possible, in spite of the opinion of my satirical friend, Scandal, who says,

That women are like tricks by slight of hand,
Which, to admire, we should not understand.

[*Exeunt*]

ACT FIVE

SCENE I

A room in Foresight's house

Enter Angelica and Jenny.

ANGELICA Where is Sir Sampson? Did you not tell me, he would be here before me?

JENNY He's at the great glass in the dining-room, Madam, setting his cravat and wig.

ANGELICA How! I'm glad on't – If he has a mind I should like him, it's a sign he likes me; and that's more than half my design.

JENNY I hear him, Madam.

ANGELICA Leave me, and d'ye hear, if Valentine should come, or send, I am not to be spoken with. [*Exit Jenny*]

Enter Sir Sampson.

SIR SAMPSON I have not been honoured with the commands of a fair lady, a great while – Odd, Madam, you have revived me – Not since I was five and thirty.

ANGELICA Why you have no great reason to complain, Sir Sampson, that is not long ago.

SIR SAMPSON Zooks, but it is, Madam, a very great while; to a man that admires a fine woman, as much as I do.

ANGELICA You're an absolute courtier, Sir Sampson.

SIR SAMPSON Not at all, Madam; odsbud you wrong me; I am not so old neither, to be a bare courtier, only a man of words. Odd, I have warm blood about me yet, I can serve a lady anyway – Come, come, let me tell you, you women think a man old too soon, faith and troth you do – Come, don't despise fifty; odd fifty, in a hale constitution, is no such contemptible age.

ANGELICA Fifty a contemptible age! Not at all, a very fashionable age I think – I assure you I know very considerable beaus, that set a good face upon fifty, fifty! I have seen fifty in a side box by candle-light, out-blossom five and twenty.

SIR SAMPSON O pox, outsides, outsides; a pize take'em, mere outsides. Hang your side-box beaus; no, I'm none of those, none of

your forced trees, that pretend to blossom in the fall; and bud
when they should bring forth fruit. I am of a long lived race, and
inherit vigour, none of my family married till fifty; yet they begot
sons and daughters till fourscore. I am of your patriarchs, I, a
branch of one of your antediluvian families, fellows, that the
Flood could not wash away. Well, Madam, what are your commands? Has any young rogue affronted you, and shall I cut his
throat? Or –

ANGELICA No, Sir Sampson, I have no quarrel upon my hands – I
have more occasion for your conduct than your courage at this
time. To tell you the truth, I'm weary of living single, and want a
husband.

SIR SAMPSON [*aside*] Odsbud, and 'tis pity you should – Odd,
would she would like me, then I should hamper my young rogues:
odd, would she would; faith and troth she's devilish handsome.
⟨*to Angelica*⟩ Madam, you deserve a good husband, and 'twere
pity you should be thrown away upon any of these young idle
rogues about the Town. Odd, there's ne'er a young fellow worth
hanging – that is a very young fellow – Pize on 'em, they never
think beforehand of anything; – and if they commit matrimony,
'tis as they commit murder; out of a frolic: and are ready to hang
themselves, or to be hanged by the law, the next morning. –
Odso, have a care, Madam.

ANGELICA Therefore I ask your advice, Sir Sampson: I have fortune enough to make any man easy that I can like; if there were
such a thing as a young agreeable man, with a reasonable stock of
good nature and sense – For I would neither have an absolute wit,
nor a fool.

SIR SAMPSON Odd, you are hard to please, Madam; to find a
young fellow that is neither a wit in his own eye, nor a fool in the
eye of the world, is a very hard task. But, faith and troth you
speak very discreetly; for I hate both a wit and a fool.

ANGELICA She that marries a fool, Sir Sampson, commits the
reputation of her honesty or understanding to the censure of the
world: and she that marries a very witty man, submits both to
the severity and insolent conduct of her husband. I should like a
man of wit for a lover, because I would have such an one in my
power; but I would no more be his wife, than his enemy. For his

malice is not a more terrible consequence of his aversion, than his jealousy is of his love.

SIR SAMPSON None of old Foresight's Sybils ever uttered such a truth. Odsbud, you have won my heart: I hate a wit; I had a son that was spoiled among 'em; a good hopeful lad, till he learned to be a wit – And might have risen in the state – But, a pox on't, his wit run him out of his money, and now his poverty has run him out of his wits.

ANGELICA Sir Sampson, as your friend, I must tell you, you are very much abused in that matter; he's no more mad than you are.

SIR SAMPSON How, Madam! Would I could prove it.

ANGELICA I can tell you how that may be done – But it is a thing that would make me appear to be too much concerned in your affairs.

SIR SAMPSON [*aside*] Odsbud I believe she likes me. – ⟨*to her*⟩ Ah, Madam, all my affairs are scarce worthy to be laid at your feet; and I wish, Madam, they stood in a better posture, that I might make a more becoming offer to a lady of your incomparable beauty and merit. – If I had Peru in one hand, and Mexico in t'other, and the Eastern empire under my feet; it would make me only a more glorious victim to be offered at the shrine of your beauty.

ANGELICA Bless me, Sir Sampson, what's the matter?

SIR SAMPSON Odd, Madam, I love you – And if you would take my advice in a husband –

ANGELICA Hold, hold, Sir Sampson. I asked your advice for a husband, and you are giving me your consent – I was indeed thinking to propose something like it in a jest, to satisfy you about Valentine: for if a match were seemingly carried on, between you and me, it would oblige him to throw off his disguise of madness, in apprehension of losing me: for you know he has long pretended a passion for me.

SIR SAMPSON Gadzooks, a most ingenious contrivance – If we were to go through with it. But why must the match only be seemingly carried on? – Odd, let it be a real contract.

ANGELICA O fie, Sir Sampson, what would the world say?

SIR SAMPSON Say, they would say, you were a wise woman, and

I a happy man. Odd, Madam, I'll love you as long as I live; and leave you a good jointure when I die.

ANGELICA Aye; but that is not in your power, Sir Sampson; for when Valentine confesses himself in his senses; he must make over his inheritance to his younger brother.

SIR SAMPSON Odd, you're cunning, a wary baggage! Faith and troth I like you the better – But, I warrant you, I have a proviso in the obligation in favour of myself – Body o'me, I have a trick to turn the settlement upon the issue male of our two bodies begotten. Odsbud, let us find children, and I'll find an estate.

ANGELICA Will you? Well, do you find the estate, and leave the t'other to me –

SIR SAMPSON O rogue! But I'll trust you. And will you consent? Is it a match then?

ANGELICA Let me consult my lawyer concerning this obligation; and if I find what you propose practicable; I'll give you my answer.

SIR SAMPSON With all my heart; – Come in with me, and I'll lend you the bond, – You shall consult your lawyer, and I'll consult a parson; Odzooks I'm a young man: Odzooks I'm a young man, and I'll make it appear – Odd, you're devilish handsome; faith and troth, you're very handsome and I'm very young, and very lusty – Odsbud, hussy, you know how to choose, and so do I; – Odd, I think we are very well met; – Give me your hand. Odd let me kiss it; 'tis as warm and as soft – as what? – Odd, as t'other hand – give me t'other hand, and I'll mumble 'em, and kiss 'em till they melt in my mouth.

ANGELICA Hold, Sir Sampson – You're profuse of your vigour before your time: you'll spend your estate before you come to it.

SIR SAMPSON No, no, only give you a rent-roll of my possessions – Ah! Baggage – I warrant you; for little Sampson: Odd, Sampson's a very good name for an able fellow: your Sampsons were strong dogs from the beginning.

ANGELICA Have a care, and don't over-act your part – If you remember, the strongest Sampson of your name, pulled an old house over his head at last.

SIR SAMPSON Say you so, hussy? – Come let's go then; Odd, I long to be pulling down too, come away – Odso, here's somebody coming. [*Exeunt*]

Enter Tattle and Jeremy.

TATTLE Is not that she, gone out just now?

JEREMY Aye, Sir, she's just going to the place of appointment. Ah Sir, if you are not very faithful and close in this business, you'll certainly be the death of a person that has a most extraordinary passion for your honour's service.

TATTLE Aye, who's that?

JEREMY Even my unworthy self, Sir – Sir, I have had an appetite to be fed with your commands a great while; – and now, Sir, my former master, having much troubled the fountain of his under-standing; it is a very plausible occasion for me to quench my thirst at the spring of your bounty – I thought I could not recom-mend myself better to you, Sir, than by the delivery of a great beauty and fortune into your arms, whom I have heard you sigh for.

TATTLE I'll make thy fortune; say no more – Thou art a pretty fellow, and canst carry a message to a lady, in a pretty soft kind of phrase, and with a good persuading accent.

JEREMY Sir, I have the seeds of rhetoric and oratory in my head – I have been at Cambridge.

TATTLE Aye; 'tis well enough for a servant to be bred at an university: but the education is a little too pedantic for a gentle-man. I hope you are secret in your nature, private, close, ha?

JEREMY O Sir, for that Sir, 'tis my chief talent; I'm as secret as the head of Nilus.

TATTLE Aye? Who's he, though? A Privy Counsellor?

JEREMY [aside] O ignorance! ⟨to him⟩ A cunning Egyptian, Sir, that with his arms would overrun the country, yet nobody could ever find out his headquarters.

TATTLE Close dog! A good whoremaster, I warrant him – The time draws nigh, Jeremy. Angelica will be veiled like a nun; and I must be hooded like a friar; ha, Jeremy?

JEREMY Aye, Sir, hooded like a hawk, to seize at first sight upon the quarry. It is the whim of my master's madness to be so dres-sed; and she is so in love with him, she'll comply with anything to please him. Poor lady, I'm sure she'll have reason to pray for me, when she finds what a happy exchange she has made, between a madman and so accomplished a gentleman.

TATTLE Aye faith, so she will, Jeremy: you're a good friend to her, poor creature – I swear I do it hardly so much in consideration of myself, as compassion to her.

JEREMY 'Tis an act of charity, Sir, to save a fine woman with thirty thousand pound, from throwing herself away.

TATTLE So 'tis, faith – I might have saved several others in my time; but egad I could never find in my heart to marry anybody before.

JEREMY Well, Sir, I'll go and tell her my master's coming; and meet you in half a quarter of an hour, with your disguise, at your own lodgings. You must talk a little madly, she won't distinguish the tone of your voice.

TATTLE No, no, let me alone for a counterfeit; – I'll be ready for you.

Enter Miss Prue.

MISS PRUE O Mr Tattle, are you here! I'm glad I have found you; I have been looking up and down for you like anything, till I'm as tired as anything in the world.

TATTLE [*aside*] O pox, how shall I get rid of this foolish girl?

MISS PRUE O I have pure news, I can tell you pure news – I must not marry the seaman now – my father says so. Why won't you be my husband? You say you love me, and you won't be my husband. And I know you may be my husband now if you please.

TATTLE O fie, Miss; who told you so, child?

MISS PRUE Why, my father – I told him that you loved me.

TATTLE O fie, Miss, why did you do so? And who told you so, child?

MISS PRUE Who? Why you did; did not you?

TATTLE O pox, that was yesterday, Miss, that was a great while ago, child. I have been asleep since; slept a whole night, and did not so much as dream of the matter.

MISS PRUE Pshaw, O but I dreamed that it was so though.

TATTLE Aye, but your father will tell you that dreams come by contraries, child – O fie; what, we must not love one another now – Pshaw, that would be a foolish thing indeed – Fie, fie, you're a woman now, and must think of a new man every morning, and forget him every night – No, no, to marry, is to be a child again, and play with the same rattle always: O fie, marrying is a paw* thing.

MISS PRUE Well, but don't you love me as well as you did last night then?

TATTLE No, no, child, you would not have me.

MISS PRUE No? Yes but I would though.

TATTLE Pshaw, but I tell you, you would not – You forget you're a woman, and don't know your own mind.

MISS PRUE But here's my father, and he knows my mind.

Enter Foresight.

FORESIGHT Oh, Mr Tattle, your servant, you are a close man; but methinks your love to my daughter was a secret I might have been trusted with, – or had you a mind to try if I could discover it by my art – Hum, ha! I think there is something in your physiognomy, that has a resemblance of her; and the girl is like me.

TATTLE And so you would infer, that you and I are alike – [*aside*] What does the old prig mean? I'll banter him, and laugh at him, and leave him. ⟨*to Foresight*⟩ I fancy you have a wrong notion of faces.

FORESIGHT How? What? A wrong notion! How so?

TATTLE In the way of art: I have some taking features, not obvious to vulgar eyes; that are indications of a sudden turn of good fortune, in the lottery of wives; and promise a great beauty and great fortune reserved alone for me, by a private intrigue of destiny, kept secret from the piercing eye of perspicuity; from all astrologers, and the stars themselves.

FORESIGHT How! I will make it appear that what you say is impossible.

TATTLE Sir, I beg your pardon, I'm in haste –

FORESIGHT For what?

TATTLE To be married, Sir, married.

FORESIGHT Aye, but pray take me along with you, Sir –

TATTLE No, Sir; 'tis to be done privately – I never make confidents.

* paw: improper, naughty or obscene.

FORESIGHT Well; but my consent I mean – You won't marry my daughter without my consent?

TATTLE Who I, Sir? I'm an absolute stranger to you and your daughter, Sir.

FORESIGHT Hey day! What time of the moon is this?

TATTLE Very true, Sir, and desire to continue so. I have no more love for your daughter, than I have likeness of you; and I have a secret in my heart, which you would be glad to know, and shan't know; and yet you shall know it too, and be sorry for't afterwards. I'd have you to know, Sir, that I am as knowing as the stars, and as secret as the night. – And I'm going to be married just now, yet did not know of it half an hour ago; and the lady stays for me, and does not know of it yet – There's a mystery for you, – I know you love to untie difficulties – Or if you can't solve this; stay here a quarter of an hour, and I'll come and explain it to you. [*Exit*]

MISS PRUE O father, why will you let him go? Won't you make him be my husband?

FORESIGHT Mercy on us, what do these lunacies portend? Alas! He's mad, child, stark wild.

MISS PRUE What, and must not I have e'er a husband then? What, must I go to bed to nurse again, and be a child as long as she's an old woman? Indeed but I won't: for now my mind is set upon a man, I will have a man some way or other. Oh! Methinks I'm sick when I think of a man; and if I can't have one, I would go to sleep all my life: for when I'm awake, it makes me wish and long, and I don't know for what – And I'd rather be always a-sleeping, than sick with thinking.

FORESIGHT O fearful! I think the girl's influenced too, – hussy you shall have a rod.

MISS PRUE A fiddle of a rod, I'll have a husband; and if you won't get me one, I'll get one for myself: I'll marry our Robin the butler, he says he loves me, and he's a handsome man, and shall be my husband: I warrant he'll be my husband and thank me too, for he told me so.

Enter Scandal, Mrs Foresight, and Nurse.

FORESIGHT Did he so – I'll dispatch him for't presently; rogue! Oh, nurse, come hither.

NURSE What is your worship's pleasure?

FORESIGHT Here, take your young mistress, and lock her up presently, till further orders from me – not a word hussy – Do what I bid you, no reply, away. And bid Robin make ready to give an account of his plate and linen, d'ye hear, begone when *I* bid you.   [*Exeunt Nurse and Miss Prue*]

MRS FORESIGHT What's the matter, husband?

FORESIGHT 'Tis not convenient to tell you now – Mr Scandal, heaven keep us all in our senses – I fear there is a contagious frenzy abroad. How does Valentine?

SCANDAL O I hope he will do well again – I have a message from him to your niece Angelica.

FORESIGHT I think she has not returned, since she went abroad with Sir Sampson.

Enter Ben.

MRS FORESIGHT Here's Mr Benjamin, he can tell us if his father be come home.

BEN Who, Father? Aye, he's come home with a vengeance.

MRS FORESIGHT Why, what's the matter?

BEN Matter! Why he's mad.

FORESIGHT Mercy on us, I was afraid of this.

BEN And there's the handsome young woman, she, as they say, brother Val went mad for, she's mad too, I think.

FORESIGHT O my poor niece, my poor niece, is she gone too? Well, I shall run mad next.

MRS FORESIGHT Well, but how mad? How d'ye mean?

BEN Nay, I'll give you leave to guess – I'll undertake to make a voyage to Antegoa* – No, hold, I mayn't say so neither – But I'll sail as far as Ligorn,† and back again, before you shall guess at the matter, and do nothing else; Mess you may take in all the points of the compass, and not hit right.

MRS FORESIGHT Your experiment will take up a little too much time.

BEN Why then I'll tell you, there's a new wedding upon the stocks; and they two are a-going to be married to rights.

* Antegoa: Antigua, in the West Indies.
† Ligorn: Leghorn, in north-west Italy.

SCANDAL Who?

BEN Why father and – the young woman. I can't hit of her name.

SCANDAL Angelica?

BEN Aye, the same.

MRS FORESIGHT Sir Sampson and Angelica, impossible!

BEN That may be – but I'm sure it is as I tell you.

SCANDAL S'death it's a jest. I can't believe it.

BEN Look you, friend, it's nothing to me, whether you believe it or no. What I say is true; d'ye see, they are married, or just going to be married, I know not which.

FORESIGHT Well, but they are not mad, that is, not lunatic?

BEN I don't know what you may call madness – But she's mad for a husband, and he's horn-mad, I think, or they'd ne'er make a match together – Here they come.

Enter Sir Sampson, Angelica, with Buckram.

SIR SAMPSON Where is this old soothsayer? This uncle of mine elect? Aha, old Foresight, uncle Foresight, wish me joy uncle Foresight, double joy, both as uncle and astrologer; here's a conjunction that was not foretold in all your Ephemeris – The brightest star in the blue firmament – is shot from above, in a jelly of love, and so forth; and I'm lord of the ascendant. Odd, you're an old fellow, Foresight; uncle I mean, a very old fellow, uncle Foresight; and yet you shall live to dance at my wedding; faith and troth you shall. Odd we'll have the music of the spheres for thee, old Lilly, that we will, and thou shalt lead up a dance in *Via Lactea.*★

FORESIGHT I'm thunderstruck! You are not married to my niece?

SIR SAMPSON Not absolutely married, uncle; but very near it, within a kiss of the matter, as you see. [*kisses Angelica*]

ANGELICA 'Tis very true indeed, uncle; I hope you'll be my father, and give me.

SIR SAMPSON That he shall, or I'll burn his globes – Body o'me, he shall be thy father, I'll make him thy father, and thou shalt make me a father, and I'll make thee a mother, and we'll beget sons and daughters enough to put the weekly bills out of countenance.

★ *Via Lactea*: the Milky Way.

SCANDAL Death and hell! Where's Valentine?   [*Exit Scandal*]

MRS FORESIGHT This is so surprising –

SIR SAMPSON How! What does my aunt say? Surprising, aunt? Not at all, for a young couple to make a match in winter? Not at all – It's a plot to undermine cold weather; and destroy that usurper of a bed called a warming-pan.

MRS FORESIGHT I'm glad to hear you have so much fire in you, Sir Sampson.

BEN Mess, I fear his fire's little better than tinder; mayhap it will only serve to light up a match for somebody else. The young woman's a handsome young woman, I can't deny it: but, father, if I might be your pilot in this case, you should not marry her. It's just the same thing, as if so be you should sail so far as the Straights without provision.

SIR SAMPSON Who gave you authority to speak, sirrah? To your element, fish, be mute, fish, and to sea, rule your helm, sirrah, don't direct me.

BEN Well, well, take you care of your own helm, or you mayn't keep your own vessel steady.

SIR SAMPSON Why you impudent tarpaulin! Sirrah, do you bring your forecastle jests upon your father? But I shall be even with you, I won't give you a groat. Mr Buckram is the conveyance so worded, that nothing can possibly descend to this scoundrel? I would not so much as have him have the prospect of an estate; though there were no way to come to it, but by the North-East passage.

BUCKRAM Sir, it is drawn according to your directions; there is not the least cranny of the law unstopped.

BEN Lawyer, I believe there's many a cranny and leak unstopped in your conscience – If so be that one had a pump to your bosom, I believe we should discover a foul hold. They say a witch will sail in a sieve – But I believe the devil would not venture aboard o' your conscience. And that's for you.

SIR SAMPSON Hold your tongue, sirrah. How now, who's there?

Enter Tattle and Mrs Frail.

MRS FRAIL Oh, sister, the most unlucky accident!

MRS FORESIGHT What's the matter?

TATTLE Oh, the two most unfortunate poor creatures in the world we are.

FORESIGHT Bless us! How so?

MRS FRAIL Ah Mr Tattle and I, poor Mr Tattle and I are – I can't speak it out.

TATTLE Nor I – But poor Mrs Frail and I are –

MRS FRAIL Married.

MRS FORESIGHT Married! How?

TATTLE Suddenly – before we knew where we were – that villain Jeremy, by the help of disguises, tricked us into one another.

FORESIGHT Why, you told me just now, you went hence in haste to be married.

ANGELICA But I believe Mr Tattle meant the favour to me, I thank him.

TATTLE I did, as I hope to be saved, Madam, my intentions were good – But this is the most cruel thing, to marry one does not know how, nor why, nor wherefore – The devil take me if ever I was so much concerned at anything in my life.

ANGELICA 'Tis very unhappy, if you don't care for one another.

TATTLE The least in the world – That is for my part, I speak for myself. Gad, I never had the least thought of serious kindness – I never liked anybody less in my life. Poor woman! Gad I'm sorry for her too; for I have no reason to hate her neither; but I believe I shall lead her a damned sort of a life.

MRS FORESIGHT [*aside to Mrs Frail*] He's better than no husband at all – though he's a coxcomb.

MRS FRAIL [*to her*] Aye, aye, it's well it's no worse – Nay, for my part I always despised Mr Tattle of all things; nothing but his being my husband could have made me like him less.

TATTLE Look you there, I thought as much – pox on't, I wish we could keep it secret, why I don't believe any of this company would speak of it.

MRS FRAIL But, my dear, that's impossible; the parson and that rogue Jeremy will publish it.

TATTLE Aye, my dear, so they will as you say.

ANGELICA O you'll agree very well in a little time; custom will make it easy to you.

TATTLE Easy! Pox on't, I don't believe I shall sleep tonight.

SIR SAMPSON Sleep quotha! No, why you would not sleep o'
your wedding night? I'm an older fellow than you, and don't mean
to sleep.

BEN Why there's another match now, as tho'f a couple of privateers
were looking for a prize, and should fall foul of one another. I'm
sorry for the young man with all my heart. Look you, friend, if I
may advise you, when she's going, for that you must expect, I
have experience of her, when she's going, let her go. For no
matrimony is tough enough to hold her, and if she can't drag her
anchor along with her, she'll break her cable, I can tell you that.
Who's here? The madman?

Enter Valentine dressed, Scandal and Jeremy.

VALENTINE No; here's the fool; and if occasion be, I'll give it
under my hand.

SIR SAMPSON How now?

VALENTINE Sir, I'm come to acknowledge my errors, and ask your
pardon.

SIR SAMPSON What, have you found your senses at last then? In
good time, Sir.

VALENTINE You were abused, Sir, I never was distracted.

FORESIGHT How! Not mad! Mr Scandal.

SCANDAL No really, Sir; I'm his witness, it was all counterfeit.

VALENTINE I thought I had reasons – But it was a poor contrivance, the effect has shown it such.

SIR SAMPSON Contrivance, what to cheat me? To cheat your
father! Sirrah, could you hope to prosper?

VALENTINE Indeed, I thought, Sir, when the father endeavoured
to undo the son, it was a reasonable return of nature.

SIR SAMPSON Very good, Sir – Mr Buckram, are you ready? –
Come, Sir, will you sign and seal?

VALENTINE If you please, Sir; but first I would ask this lady one
question.

SIR SAMPSON Sir, you must ask my leave first; that lady, no, Sir;
you shall ask that lady no questions, till you have asked her
blessing, Sir; that lady is to be my wife.

VALENTINE I have heard as much, Sir; but I would have it from
her own mouth.

SIR SAMPSON That's as much as to say, I lie, Sir, and you don't believe what I say.

VALENTINE Pardon me, Sir. But I reflect that I very lately counterfeited madness; I don't know but the frolic may go round.

SIR SAMPSON Come, chuck, satisfy him, answer him; – Come, come, Mr Buckram, the pen and ink.

BUCKRAM Here it is, Sir, with the deed, all is ready.

Valentine goes to Angelica.

ANGELICA 'Tis true, you have a great while pretended love to me; nay, what if you were sincere? Still you must pardon me, if I think my own inclinations have a better right to dispose of my person, than yours.

SIR SAMPSON Are you answered now, Sir?

VALENTINE Yes, Sir.

SIR SAMPSON Where's your plot, Sir? And your contrivance now, Sir? Will you sign, Sir? Come, will you sign and seal?

VALENTINE With all my heart, Sir.

SCANDAL S'death, you are not mad indeed, to ruin yourself?

VALENTINE I have been disappointed of my only hope; and he that loses hope may part with anything. I never valued fortune, but as it was subservient to my pleasure; and my only pleasure was to please this lady: I have made many vain attempts, and find at last, that nothing but my ruin can effect it: which, for that reason, I will sign to – Give me the paper.

ANGELICA [*aside*] Generous Valentine!

BUCKRAM Here is the deed, Sir.

VALENTINE But where is the bond, by which I am obliged to sign this?

BUCKRAM Sir Sampson you have it.

ANGELICA No, I have it; and I'll use it, as I would everything that is an enemy to Valentine. [*tears the paper*]

SIR SAMPSON How now!

VALENTINE Ha!

ANGELICA [*to Valentine*] Had I the world to give you, it could not make me worthy of so generous and faithful a passion: here's my hand, my heart was always yours, and struggled very hard to make this utmost trial of your virtue.

VALENTINE Between pleasure and amazement, I am lost – But on my knees I take the blessing.

SIR SAMPSON Oons, what is the meaning of this?

BEN Mess, here's the wind changed again. Father, you and I may make a voyage together now.

ANGELICA Well, Sir Sampson, since I have played you a trick, I'll advise you, how you may avoid such another. Learn to be a good father, or you'll never get a second wife. I always loved your son, and hated your unforgiving nature. I was resolved to try him to the utmost; I have tried you too, and know you both. You have not more faults than he has virtues; and 'tis hardly more pleasure to me, that I can make him and myself happy, than that I can punish you.

VALENTINE If my happiness could receive addition, this kind surprise would make it double.

SIR SAMPSON Oons you're a crocodile.

FORESIGHT Really, Sir Sampson, this is a sudden eclipse –

SIR SAMPSON You're an illiterate fool, and I'm another, and the stars are liars; and if I had breath enough, I'd curse them and you, myself and everybody – Oons, culled, bubbled, jilted, woman-bobbed at last – I have not patience.   [*Exit Sir Sampson*]

TATTLE If the gentleman is in his disorder for want of a wife, I can spare him mine. [*to Jeremy*] O are you there, Sir? I'm indebted to you for my happiness.

JEREMY Sir, I ask you ten thousand pardons, 'twas an errant mistake – You see, Sir, my master was never mad, nor anything like it – Then how could it be otherwise?

VALENTINE Tattle, I thank you, you would have interposed between me and heaven; but providence laid purgatory in your way – You have but justice.

SCANDAL I hear the fiddles that Sir Sampson provided for his own wedding; methinks 'tis pity they should not be employed when the match is so much mended. Valentine, though it be morning, we may have a dance.

VALENTINE Anything, my friend, everything that looks like joy and transport.

SCANDAL Call 'em, Jeremy.

ANGELICA I have done dissembling now, Valentine; and if that coldness which I have always worn before you, should turn to an extreme fondness, you must not suspect it.

VALENTINE I'll prevent that suspicion – For I intend to dote on at that immoderate rate, that your fondness shall never distinguish itself enough, to be taken notice of. If ever you seem to love too much, it must be only when I can't love enough.

ANGELICA Have a care of large promises; you know you are apt to run more in debt than you are able to pay.

VALENTINE Therefore I yield my body as your prisoner, and make your best on't.

SCANDAL The music stays for you.

Dance.

SCANDAL Well, Madam, you have done exemplary justice, in punishing an inhuman father, and rewarding a faithful lover: but there is a third good work, which I, in particular, must thank you for; I was an infidel to your sex; and you have converted me – For now I am convinced that all women are not like fortune, blind in bestowing favours, either on those who do not merit, or who do not want 'em.

ANGELICA 'Tis an unreasonable accusation, that you lay upon our sex: you tax us with injustice, only to cover your own want of merit. You would all have the reward of love; but few have the constancy to stay till it becomes your due. Men are generally hypocrites and infidels, they pretend to worship but have neither zeal nor faith: how few, like Valentine, would persevere even unto martyrdom, and sacrifice their interest to their constancy! In admiring me, you misplace the novelty.

The miracle today is, that we find

A lover true: not that a woman's kind.

[*Exeunt Omnes*]

EPILOGUE

Spoken at the opening of the new house, by
Mrs Bracegirdle ⟨Angelica⟩

Sure Providence at first, designed this place
To be the player's refuge in distress;
For still in every storm, they all run hither,
As to a shed, that shields 'em from the weather.
But thinking of this change which last befell us,
It's like what I have heard our poets tell us:
For when behind our scenes their suits are pleading,
To help their love, sometimes they show their reading;
And wanting ready cash to pay for hearts,
They top their learning on us, and their parts.
Once of philosophers they told us stories,
Whom, as I think they called – *Py – Pythagories*,
I'm sure 'tis some such Latin name they give 'em,
And we, who know no better, must believe 'em.
Not to these men (say they) such souls were given,
That after death, ne'er went to hell, nor heaven,
But lived, I know not how, in beasts; and then
When many years were past, in men again.
Methinks, we players resemble such a soul,
That, does from bodies, we from houses stroll.
Thus Aristotle's soul, of old that was,
May now be damned to animate an ass;
Or in this very house, for ought we know,
Is doing painful penance in some beau,
And this our audience, which did once resort
To shining theatres to see our sport,
Now find us tossed into a tennis court.*
These walls but t'other day were filled with noise
Of roaring gamesters, and your Damme Boys.†
Then bounding balls and rackets they encompassed,

---

* tennis court: the Lincoln's Inn Fields theatre was converted from a tennis court.
† Damme Boys: roisterers.

And now they're filled with jests, and flights, and bombast!
I vow, I don't much like this transmigration,
Strolling from place to place, by circulation.
Grant heaven, we don't return to our first station.
I know not what these think, but for my part,
I can't reflect without an aching heart,
How we should end in our original, a cart.*
But we can't fear, since you're so good to save us,
That you have only set us up, to leave us.
Thus from the past, we hope for future grace,
I beg it –
And some here know I have a begging face.
Then pray continue this your kind behaviour,
For a clear stage† won't do, without your favour.

* a cart: Thespis according to tradition sang ballads from a cart.
† a clear stage: one free from control, and from debt.

NOTES

The copy text used is that of the first edition of 1695 in the Brotherton Collection, University of Leeds.

Abbreviations

Q1   The first quarto edition, 1695
Q2   The 'second edition', quarto, 1695
Q3   Another quarto edition, 1695
Q4   The 'third edition', quarto, 1697
W   The Works, 1710

An italic 'I' has been replaced by roman 'I' in parts of the text. Because of the copy text's inconsistency, the initial M of 'Miss' has been capitalized throughout and Buckram is spelled thus rather than Buckrum throughout. Similarly, 'Mrs' has been added to Frail, and 'Oons, Ouns, Oo'ns and Ou'ns have been amended to Oons throughout. Ods so has been altered to Odso.

244.16   What, is / What is Q1
245.34   ruby lips / Ruby-lips Q1
246.15   that's true. Mr / that's true, Mr Q1
246.31   to 'em. Take / to 'em, take Q1
247.6   what, does / what does Q1
251.3   Why, did / Why did Q1
251.32   you familiar W / your familiar Q1
258.17   apostles' / Apostle's Q1
260.17   said - he's here already W / said - Q1
262.18   o' / of Q1
266.14   body o'me / body of me Q1
277.29   No, don't Q4 W / No doubt on't Q1
278.26   me Q3 / one Q1
283.33   matter, Miss? What Q2 / matter? *Miss*, what Q1
286.29   stars Q4 W / Science Q1
288.21   Oh, mighty / O' mighty Q1
293.12   Oh, you / O' you Q1
297.14   almost / a most Q1
299.4   Val. / *Val*: Q1
299.34   it. [. . . *Pocket*] / it [. . . *Pocket*.] Q1

303.13   answered' n / answer'd' n Q1 / answer'd' en W
303.34   inhuman / inhumane Q1
304.10   mad, monster / mad Monster Q1
310.24   *s.p.* Valentine / Q1 omits
312.5   for mercenary / for by, mercinary Q1 / for by mercenary
           Q3 W
315.3   *s.d.* room / Rome Q1
317.34   ingenious / ingenuous Q1
330.8   able to pay Q1 / able pay Q1
330.14   inhuman / inhumane Q1

LOVE'S LAST SHIFT
by Colley Cibber

INTRODUCTION

Colley Cibber (1671–1757), the son of a sculptor who came to England from Holstein, was educated at Grantham in Lincolnshire, and became an actor before he was twenty. He married at twenty-two. He achieved some success in *The Double Dealer* when Kynaston was ill, and as a result of his good performance Congreve got his salary raised from fifteen to twenty shillings a week. He extended his career to include the writing of plays, and *Love's Last Shift*, his first comedy, was produced in 1696. His acting was not fully appreciated till that year when he continued his success as Sir Novelty in his own play by playing Lord Foppington in Vanbrugh's *The Relapse*. Then adding theatre management to his activities, Cibber became, in 1709, one of the three managers of Drury Lane.

Appointed Poet Laureate in 1730, Cibber suffered some fierce attacks from other writers, notably Pope, who made him the hero of *The Dunciad*. In 1732 he sold his interest in the theatre, and eight years later published his autobiography, his *Apology for the life of Mr Colley Cibber, Comedian*.

As a playwright Cibber was well aware of the taste of the audience. He sensed a change gradually building up in the theatre-going public and in his first play – in which the hero was 'lewd for above four acts' – conformed to the accepted mode of Restoration comedy while genuflecting in the direction of morality by making the hero reform in the fifth act. The conversion, however, was over-sudden to be convincing and received Cibber's own somewhat wry comment in the epilogue:

'For faith, he knew, when once he'd changed his fortune,
And reformed his vice, 'twas time – to drop the curtain.'
In 1700 he added sententious material at the end of *Love makes a Man*, another play which attempted to have it both ways by moving from lubricity to propriety, though with less of a jolt. *The Careless Husband*, acted four years later, was far more effective than the earlier plays in dealing with human failings.

Love's Last Shift provides us with an admirable coxcomb in Sir Novelty Fashion, a part played by Cibber himself, who, as we are told in the life included in *The Dramatic Works* (1757), 'excelled in the walk of fops and feeble old men in comedy, in the former of which he does not appear ever to have been excelled in any period before him, or nearly equalled in any sense'. Sir Novelty is deeply concerned that Worthy has appeared in a coat with buttons no bigger than nut-megs, his own being 'not above three inches diameter', while his sleeves reach his knuckles. He regards his main triumph as a beau as that of making fashion: 'In short, Madam, the cravat-string, the garter, the sword-knot, the centurine, bardash, the steinkirk, the large button, the long sleeve, the plume, and full peruke were all created, cried down, or revived by me . . .' He shows off his coach and equipage naively; he takes pain to preserve a public reputation. When he decides he would like to marry Narcissa, Sir William Wisewoud's daughter, a wealthy heiress, he is rejected firmly by Sir William, to whom he seems to be 'the offspring of more than one man's labour; for certainly no less than a dancing, singing and fenc-ing-master, with a tailor, milliner, perfumer, peruke-maker and a French *valet de chambre*', could be at his begetting. When he finally pays off his mistress, Mrs Flareit, he boasts he has paid her three hundred pounds a year for life and says, in reply to a comment that this is an excessive settlement, he did it 'to be the first man should raise their price'.

Sir Novelty's absurd character remains constant, unlike that of Loveless, who having left his wife and his debts, now returns 'in a very mean condition' to England. He thinks his long-suffering loyal wife Amanda is dead. Young Worthy tells her he has returned and suggests the stratagem which finally brings him back to married bliss.

The play is firmly concerned with the question of money. As Young Worthy, very conscious of Sir William Wisewoud's daughter being an heiress, remarks:

'The wise, and grave, may tell us of strange *chimaeras* called virtues in a woman, and that they alone are the best dowry; but, faith, we younger brothers are of another mind.

Women are changed from what they were of old:

Therefore let lovers still this maxim hold,

She's only worth that brings her weight in gold.'

The love affairs of the two Worthies are skilfully intermingled with the reclamation of Loveless, and the play is generally well made. The comedy of Snap's falling into the cellar with Amanda's woman provides a farcical slapstick element, as an anti-masque to the encounter of Loveless and Amanda. The irony of what happens to Amanda's woman after she has been listening at the door is presaged by Snap's drunken remark that since his master is provided for, it is time for him to take care of himself. Then Sir William is gulled in the usual way, but is placated, once the financial side of matters has been suitably cleared up. And the play ends on a note of general content.

Colley Cibber

Love's Last Shift

or

The Fool in Fashion

A COMEDY

As it is Acted at the
Theatre Royal by His Majesty's Servants

Written by C. Cibber

Fuit haec sapientia quondam,
Concubitu prohibere vago, dare jura maritis★
Horace, de Arte Poetica.

LONDON

Printed for H. Rhodes, in Fleet Street; R. Parker at
the Royal Exchange, and S. Briscoe, the corner
shop of Charles Street, in Russell Street, Covent Garden.

1696

★ *Fuit . . . maritis*: once this was wisdom, to prohibit copulation, and to propound laws for married people. The title usually given to Horace's discussion of poetry (*Epistula ad Pisones*) is *Ars Poetica*. This title was first used by Quintilian, 8, 3, 60.

DEDICATION

To
Richard Norton,
of Southwick, Esq;*

Sir,

Though I can't without ingratitude, conceal the exceeding favours, which the Town have shown this piece; yet they must give me leave to own, that even my vanity lay hushed, quite stifled in my fears, till I had securely fixed its good fortune, by publishing your approbation of it: an advantage, which as it will confirm my friends in their favourable opinion, so it must in some measure, qualify the severity of the malicious. After this declaration; let the world imagine, how difficult it is for me, not to launch into your character: but since the smoothness of your temper, and depth of judgment, are my chief protection, I am loath to discompose you, by an ungrateful repetition of those virtues, which only please you in the practice: the world as little wants the knowledge of 'em, as you desire the recital.

'Tis your happiness, Sir, that your fortune has fixed you above the need of praise, or friends, yet both are equally unavoidable: for even to your solitude, praise will follow you, and grows fonder of you for your coldness; she loves you for your choice of pleasures, those noble pleasures of a sweet retirement, from which nothing but the consideration of your country's weal could draw you.

But as no man can properly be made a patron, whose virtues have not in some sort qualified him for such a care: so, Sir, it is sufficient for me, that your life and conversation are the best heralds of your power, and my safety.

Here, Sir, I must beg leave to clear myself from what the ill wishes of some would have the world believe, that what I now offer you is spurious, and not the product of my own labour: and though I am pleased, that this report seems to allow it some beauties, yet I am sorry, it has made a discovery of some persons, who think me worth their malice. This dedication were little better than an affront,

* Richard Norton: a playwright, author of *Pausanias, the Betrayer of his Country* (1696).

unless I could with all sincerity assure you, Sir, that the fable is entirely my own; nor is there a line or thought, throughout the whole, for which I am wittingly obliged either to the dead, or living; for I could no more be pleased with a stolen reputation, than with a mistress, who yielded only upon the intercession of my friend: it satisfies me, Sir, that you believe it mine, and I hope what others say to the contrary, is rather owing to an unreasonable disgust, than their real opinion. I am not ignorant of those oversights I have committed, nor have the dissecting critics much discouraged me: for 'tis their diversion to find fault; and to have none, is to them an unpardonable disappointment; no man can expect to go free, while they don't spare one another: but as I write not in defiance of their censure; so, after having diverted you, Sir, I shall not trouble myself for a defensive preface. Had it not succeeded, I should have had modesty enough to impute it to my own want of merit: for certainly the Town can take no pleasure in decrying any man's labours, when 'tis their interest to encourage 'em; every guest is the best judge of his own palate, and a poet ought no more to impose good sense upon the galleries, than dull farce upon the undisputed judges. I first considered who my guests were, before I prepared my entertainment, and therefore I shall only add this as a general answer to all objections, that it has every way exceeded mine, and hitherto has not wronged the house's expectation; that Mr Southerne's★ good nature (whose own works best recommend his judgment,) engaged his reputation for the success, which its reception, and your approbation, Sir, has since redeemed to the entire satisfaction of

SIR,
your most devoted,
humble servant,
Colley Cibber.

Febr. 7.
1696.

★ Mr Southerne: Thomas Southerne (1659–1746), a friend of Dryden and author of several comedies and two tragedies, *The Fatal Marriage* and *Oroonoko*, both founded on novels by Mrs Behn.

DRAMATIS PERSONAE

MEN

Sir Will Wisewoud   A rich old gentleman, that fancies himself a great master of his passion, which he only is in trivial matters.

Loveless   Of a debauched life, grew weary of his wife in six months, left her, and the Town, for debts he did not care to pay; and having spent the last part of his estate beyond the sea, returns to England in a very mean condition.

Sir Novelty Fashion   A coxcomb that loves to be the first in all foppery.

Elder Worthy   A sober gentleman of a fair estate in love with Hillaria.

Young Worthy   His brother of a looser temper, lover to Narcissa.

Snap   Servant to Loveless.

Sly   Servant to Young Worthy.

A lawyer.

WOMEN

Amanda   A woman of strict virtue, married to Loveless very young, and forsaken by him.

Narcissa   Daughter to Will Wisewoud, a fortune.

Hillaria   His niece.

Mrs Flareit   A kept mistress of Sir Novelty's.

Woman to Amanda.

Maid to Flareit.

Servants, Sentinels, Porters, Bullies and Music.

PROLOGUE

By a FRIEND

Spoken by Mr Verbruggen ⟨Loveless⟩

Wit bears so thin a crop this duller age,
We're forced to clean it from the barren stage.
Even players fledged by nobler pens, take wing
Themselves, and their own rude composures sing.
Nor need our young one dread a shipwreck here;
Who trades without a stock has nought to fear.
In every smile of yours, a prize he draws,
And if you damn him, he's but where he was.
Yet where's the reason for the critic crew,
With killing blasts, like winter, to pursue
The tender plant, that ripens but for you?
Nature in all her works requires time,
Kindness, and years, 'tis makes the virgin climb,
And shoot, and hasten to the expected prime;
And then, if untaught fancy fail to please,
T'instruct the willing pupil by degrees;
By gentle lessons you your joys improve
And mould her awkward passion into love.
Even folly has its growth: few fools are made,
You drudge, and sweat for't, as it were a trade.
'Tis half the labour of your trifling age,
To fashion you fit subjects for the stage.
Well! If our author fail to draw you like,
In the first draft, you're not to expect Vandyke.
What, though no master-stroke in this appears;
Yet some may find features resembling theirs.
Nor do the bad alone his colours share;
Neglected virtue is at least shown fair;
And that's enough o' conscience for a player.
But if you'd have him take a bolder flight,
And draw your pictures by a truer light,
You must yourselves, by follies yet unknown,

Inspire his pencil, and divert the Town.
Nor judge by this, his genius at a stand;
For Time, that makes new fools, may mend his hand.

ACT ONE

SCENE ⟨I⟩

The Park

Enter Loveless, and Snap (his servant).

LOVELESS Sirrah! Leave your preaching – your counsel's like an ill clock, either stands still, or goes too slow – you ne'er thought my extravagancies amiss, while you had your share of 'em; and now I want money to make myself drunk, you advise me to live sober, you dog – They that will hunt pleasure, as I ha' done, rascal, must never give over in a fair chase.

SNAP Nay, I knew you would never rest, till you had tired your dogs – ah Sir! What a fine pack of guineas have you had! And yet you would make them run till they were quite spent. – Would I were fairly turned out of your service – here we have been three days in Town, and I can safely swear I have lived upon picking a hollow tooth ever since.

LOVELESS Why don't you eat then, sirrah?

SNAP Even, because I don't know where, Sir.

LOVELESS Then stay till I eat, hangdog, ungrateful rogue! To murmur at a little fasting with me, when thou hast been an equal partner of my good fortune.

SNAP Fortune! – It makes me weep to think what you have brought yourself and me to! How well might you ha' lived, Sir, had you been a sober man – Let me see! I ha' been in your service just ten years – In the first you married, and grew weary of your wife; in the second you whored, drank, gamed, run in debt, mortgaged your estate, and was forced to leave the kingdom; in the third, fourth, fifth, sixth and seventh, you made the tour of Europe, with the state and equipage of a French court favourite, while your poor wife at home broke her heart for the loss of you. In the eighth and ninth you grew poor, and little the wiser, and now in the tenth you are resolved I shall starve with you.

LOVELESS Despicable rogue, can'st not thou bear the frowns of a common strumpet fortune?

SNAP – S'bud I never think of the pearl necklace you gave that damned Venetian strumpet, but I wish her hanged in't!

LOVELESS Why sirrah! I knew I could not have her without it, and I had a night's enjoyment of her, was worth a Pope's revenue for't.

SNAP Ah! You had better ha' laid out your money here in London; I'll undertake you might have had the whole Town over and over, for half the price – Beside, Sir, what a delicate creature was your wife! She was the only celebrated beauty in Town; I'll undertake there were more fops and fools run mad for her, odsbud she was more plagued with 'em, and more talked of, than a good actress with a maidenhead! Why the devil could not she content you?

LOVELESS No sirrah! The world to me is a garden, stocked with all sorts of fruit, where the greatest pleasure we can take, is in the variety of taste: but a wife is an eternal apple tree, after a pull or two you are sure to set your teeth on edge.

SNAP And yet I warrant you grudged another man a bit of her, though you valued her no more, than you would a half-eaten pippin, that had lain a week a-sunning in a parlour window. – But see, Sir, who's this – for methinks I long to meet with an old acquaintance!

LOVELESS Ha! Egad he looks like one, and may be necessary as the case stands with me –

SNAP Pray heaven he do but invite us to dinner!

Enter Young Worthy.

LOVELESS Dear Worthy! Let me embrace thee, the sight of an old friend warms me, beyond that of a new mistress.

YOUNG WORTHY S'death, what bully's this? Sir, your pardon I don't know you!

LOVELESS Faith Will, I am a little out of repairs at present: but I am all that's left of honest Ned Loveless.

YOUNG WORTHY Loveless! I am amazed! What means this metamorphosis? – Faith Ned, I am glad to find thee amongst the living, however – How long hast thou been in Town?

LOVELESS About three days – But prithee Will, how goes the world?

YOUNG WORTHY Why like a bowl, it runs on at the old rate, interest is still the jack it aims at, and while it rolls, you know, it must of necessity be often turned upside down – But I doubt friend, you have bowled out of the green, have lived a little too fast, [*surveying his dress*] like one that has lost all his ready money, and are forced to be an idle spectator – Prithee what brought thee at last to England?

LOVELESS Why my last hopes faith, which were to persuade Sir Will. Wisewoud, (if he be alive) to whom I mortgaged my estate, to let me have five hundred pounds more upon it, or else to get some honest friend to redeem the mortgage, and share the overplus! Beside, I thought that London might now be a place of uninterrupted pleasure, for I hear my wife is dead; and to tell you the truth 'twas the staleness of her love, was the main cause of my going over.

YOUNG WORTHY [*aside*] His wife dead, ha! I'm glad he knows no other, I won't undeceive him lest the rogue should go and rifle her, of what she has. ⟨*to Loveless*⟩ Yes faith I was at her burial, and saw her take possession of her long home, and am sorry to tell you, Ned, she died with grief! Your wild courses broke her heart.

LOVELESS Why faith! She was a good natured fool! That's the truth on't, well! Rest her soul.

SNAP Now, Sir, you are a single man indeed; for you have neither wife, nor estate.

YOUNG WORTHY But how hast thou improved thy money beyond sea? What hast thou brought over?

LOVELESS Oh! A great deal of experience.

YOUNG WORTHY And no money?

SNAP Not a souse,* faith, Sir, as my belly can testify.

LOVELESS But I have a great deal more wit than I had!

SNAP Not enough to get your estate again, or to know where we shall dine today. – [*aside*] O Lord he don't ask us yet!

YOUNG WORTHY Why your rogue's witty, Ned, where did'st thou pick him up?

LOVELESS Don't you remember Snap? Formerly your pimp in ordinary: but he is much improved in his calling I assure you, Sir.

YOUNG WORTHY I don't doubt it, considering who has been his master.

SNAP Yes, Sir, I was an humble servant of yours, and am still, Sir, and should be glad to stand behind your chair at dinner, Sir. [*bows*]

YOUNG WORTHY Oh! Sir, that you may do another time: but

* souse: a sol or sou, a very small coin.

today I am engaged upon business, however, there's a meal's meat for you? [*throws him a guinea*]

SNAP Bless my eyesight, a guinea – Sir! Is there e'er a whore you would have kicked, any old bawd's windows you would have broken, shall I beat your tailor for disappointing you? Or your surgeon that would be paid for a clap of two years' standing? If you have occasion, you may command your humble servant –

YOUNG WORTHY Sweet Sir, I am obliged to you! But at present am so happy, as to have no occasion for your assistance – But hark you Ned! Prithee what hast thou done with thy estate?

LOVELESS I pawned it to buy pleasure, that is, old wine, young whores, and the conversation of brave fellows, as mad as myself; pox! If a man has appetites, they are torments, if not indulged! I shall never complain, as long as I have health, and vigour; and as for my poverty, why the devil should I be ashamed of that, since a rich man won't blush at his knavery.

YOUNG WORTHY Faith Ned, I am as much in love with wickedness, as thou can'st be, but I am for having it at a cheaper rate, than my ruin! Don't it grate you a little to see your friends blush for you?

LOVELESS 'Tis very odd, that people should be more ashamed of others' faults, than their own; I never yet could meet with a man that offered me counsel; but had more occasion for it himself.

YOUNG WORTHY So far you may be in the right: for indeed good counsel is like a home jest, which every busy fool is offering to his fellow, and yet won't take himself.

LOVELESS Right – thus have I known a jolly red-nosed parson, at three o'clock in the morning, belch out invectives against late hours, and hard drinking: and a canting hypocritical sinner, protest against fornication, when the rogue was himself just crawling out of a flux.

YOUNG WORTHY Though these are truths friend, yet I don't see any advantage you can draw from them. Prithee how will you live now, all your money's gone?

LOVELESS Live! How dost thou live? Thou art but a younger brother I take it.

YOUNG WORTHY Oh! Very well, Sir, though faith my father left me but three thousand pounds, one of which I gave for a place at

Court, that I still enjoy; the other two are gone after pleasure, as thou say'st. But beside this, I am supplied by the continual bounty of an indulgent brother; now I am loath to load his good nature too much, and therefore have e'en thought fit, like the rest of my raking brotherhood, to purge out my wild humours with matrimony: by the way I have taken care to see the dose well sweetened, with a swinging portion.

LOVELESS Ah! Will, you'll find marrying to cure lewdness, is like surfeiting to cure hunger: for all the consequence is, you loathe what you surfeit on; and are only chaste to her you marry – but prithee, friend, what is thy wife that must be?

YOUNG WORTHY Why faith, since I believe the matter is too far gone for any man to postpone me, (at least, I am sure, thou wilt not do me an injury to do thyself no good) I'll tell thee – you must know, my mistress is the daughter of that very knight to whom you mortgaged your estate, Sir William Wisewoud.

LOVELESS Why, she's an heiress, and has a thousand pounds a year in her own hands, if she be of age: but I suppose the old man knows nothing of your intentions. Therefore prithee how have you had opportunities of promoting your love?

YOUNG WORTHY Why thus – you must know, Sir William (being very well acquainted with the largeness of my brother's estate,) designs this daughter for him, and to encourage his passion offers him, out of his own pocket, the additional blessing of five thousand pounds. This offer, my brother, knowing my inclinations, seems to embrace; but at the same time, is really in love with his niece, who lives with him in the same house, and therefore to hide my design from the old gentleman, I pretend visits to his daughter, as an intercessor for my brother only, and thus he has given me daily opportunities of advancing my own interest. – Nay, and I have so contrived it, that I design to have the five thousand pounds too.

LOVELESS How is that possible, since I see no hopes of the old man's consent for you?

YOUNG WORTHY Have a day's patience, and you'll see the effects on't; in a word, 'tis so sure, that nothing but delays can hinder my success; therefore I am very earnest with my mistress that to-morrow may be the day: but a pox on't, I have two women to prevail with, for my brother quarrels every other day with his mistress, and while I am reconciling him, I lose ground in my own amour.

LOVELESS Why, has not your mistress told you her mind yet?

YOUNG WORTHY She will I suppose, as soon as she knows it herself, for within this week, she has changed it as often, as her linen, and keeps it as secret too; for she would no more own her love before my face, than she would shift herself before my face.

LOVELESS Pshaw! She shows it the more, by striving to conceal it.

YOUNG WORTHY Nay, she does give me some proofs indeed, for she will suffer nobody but herself to speak ill of me, is always uneasy till I am sent for, never pleased when I am with her, and still jealous when I leave her.

LOVELESS Well! Success to thee Will; I will send the fiddles to release you from your first night's labour.

YOUNG WORTHY But hark you! Have a care of disobliging the bride, though – Ha! Yonder goes my brother! I am afraid his walking so early proceeds from some disturbance in his love; I must after him, and set him right – Dear Ned you'll excuse me; shall I see you at the Blue Posts between five and six this afternoon?

LOVELESS With all my heart – but d'ye hear – can'st not thou lend me the fellow to that same guinea you gave my man? I'll give you my bond if you mistrust me.

YOUNG WORTHY O Sir! Your necessity is obligation enough – there 'tis, and all I have faith. When I see you at night, you may command me farther – Adieu, at six at farthest.

[*Exit Young Worthy*]

LOVELESS Without fail – so! Now rascal, you are an hungry, are you? Thou deservest never to eat again – Rogue! Grumble before fortune had quite forsaken us!

SNAP Ah! Dear Sir, the thoughts of eating again, have so transported me, I am resolved to live and die with you.

LOVELESS Look ye, sirrah, here's that will provide us of a dinner and a brace of whores into the bargain, at least as guineas and whores go now.

SNAP Ah! Good Sir! No whores before dinner I beseech you.

LOVELESS Well, for once I'll take your advice, for to say truth, a

man is as unfit to follow love with an empty stomach, as business
with an empty head: therefore I think a bit and a bottle won't be
amiss first.
The gods of wine, and love, were ever friends;
For by the help of wine, love gains his ends.   [*Exeunt*]

Enter Elder Worthy with a letter.

ELDER WORTHY How hard is it to find that happiness which our
short-sighted passions hope from woman? 'Tis not their cold disdain, or cruelty should make a faithful lover curse his stars, that is
but reasonable; 'tis the shadow in our pleasure's picture! Without
it love could ne'er be heightened! No 'tis their pride, and vain
desire of many lovers, that robs our hope of its imagined rapture:
the blind are only happy! For if we look through reason's never
erring perspective, we then survey their souls, and view the
rubbish we were chaffering for: and such I find, Hillaria's mind is
made of. This letter is an order for the knocking off my fetters, and
I'll send it her immediately.

Enter to him Young Worthy.

YOUNG WORTHY Morrow brother! [*seeing the letter*] What! Is
your fit returned again? What beau's box has Hillaria taken snuff
from? What fool has led her from the box to her coach? What fop
has she suffered to read a play or novel to her? Or whose money
has she indiscreetly won at basset* – come, let's see the ghastly
wound she has made in your quiet, that I may know how much
claret to prescribe you?
ELDER WORTHY I have my wound, and cure from the same person I'll assure you; the one from Hillaria's wit and beauty, the
other from her pride and vanity.
YOUNG WORTHY That's what I could ne'er yet find her guilty of:
are you angry at her loving you?
ELDER WORTHY I am angry at myself, for believing she e'er did.
YOUNG WORTHY Have her actions spoke the contrary? Come
you know she loves.
ELDER WORTHY Indeed she gave a great proof on't last night
here in the Park, by fastening upon a fool, and caressing him

* basset: a card game resembling faro.

before my face, when she might have so easily avoided him.

YOUNG WORTHY What! And I warrant interrupted you in the middle of your sermon; for I don't question but you were preaching to her. But prithee who was the fool she fastened upon?

ELDER WORTHY One that heaven intended for a man; but the whole business of his life is to make the world believe, he is of another species. A thing that affects mightily to ridicule himself; only to give others a kind of necessity of praising him. I can't say he's a slave to every new fashion, for he pretends to be the master of it, and is ever reviving some old, or advancing some new piece of foppery; and though it don't take, is still as well pleased, because it then obliges the Town to take the more notice of him: he's so fond of a public reputation, that he is more extravagant in his attempts to gain it, than the fool that fired Diana's temple, to immortalize his name.

YOUNG WORTHY You have said enough to tell me his name is Sir Novelty Fashion.

ELDER WORTHY The same; but that which most concerns me, is that he has the impudence to address to Hillaria, and she vanity enough to discard him.

YOUNG WORTHY Is this all? Why thou art as hard to please in a wife, as thy mistress in a new gown: how many women have you took in hand, and yet can't please yourself at last!

ELDER WORTHY I had need to have the best goods, when I offer so great a price as marriage for them: Hillaria has some good qualities, but not enough to make a wife of.

YOUNG WORTHY She has beauty!

ELDER WORTHY Granted.

YOUNG WORTHY And money.

ELDER WORTHY Too much: enough to supply her vanity.

YOUNG WORTHY She has sense.

ELDER WORTHY Not enough to believe I am no fool.

YOUNG WORTHY She has wit.

ELDER WORTHY Not enough to deceive me.

YOUNG WORTHY Why then you are happy, if she can't deceive you.

ELDER WORTHY Yet she has folly enough to endeavour it: I'll see her no more, and this shall tell her so.

YOUNG WORTHY Which in an hour's time you'll repent, as much as ever.

ELDER WORTHY As ever I should marrying her.

YOUNG WORTHY You'll have a damned sneaking look, when you are forced to ask her pardon, for your ungenerous suspicion, and lay the fault upon excess of love.

ELDER WORTHY I am not so much in love as you imagine.

YOUNG WORTHY Indeed, Sir, you are in love, and that letter tells her so.

ELDER WORTHY Read it, you'll find the contrary.

YOUNG WORTHY Prithee I know what's in't, better than thou dost: you say, 'tis to take your leave of her; but I say 'tis in hopes of a kind excusive answer: but faith you mistake her and yourself too; she is too high-spirited not to take you at your word; and you are too much in love, not to ask her pardon.

ELDER WORTHY Well then, I'll not be too rash: but will show my resentment in forbearing my visits.

YOUNG WORTHY Your visits! Come, I shall soon try what a man of resolution you are – for yonder she comes – now, let's see if you have power to move.

ELDER WORTHY I'll soon convince you of that – farewell. [*Exit*]

YOUNG WORTHY Ha! Gone! I don't like that? I am sorry to find him so resolute: but I hope Hillaria has taken too fast hold of his heart, to let this fit shake him off: I must to her, and make up this breach: for while his amour stands still I have no hopes of advancing my own.   [*Exit*]

Enter Hillaria, Narcissa, and Amanda, in mourning.

HILLARIA Well, dear Amanda, thou art the most constant wife I ever heard of: not to shake off the memory of an ill husband, after eight or ten years' absence; nay, to mourn for ought you know for the living too, and such an husband, that though he were alive, would never thank you for't: why d'ye persist in such a hopeless grief?

AMANDA Because 'tis hopeless! For if he be alive, he is dead to me; his dead affections not virtue's self can e'er retrieve; would I were with him, though in his grave!

HILLARIA In my mind, you are much better where you are! The

grave! Young widows use to have warmer wishes. But methinks the death of a rich old uncle, should be a cordial to your sorrows.

AMANDA That adds to 'em; for he was the only relation I had left, and was as tender of me, as the nearest! He was a father to me.

HILLARIA He was better than some fathers to you; for he died, just when you had occasion for his estate.

NARCISSA I have an old father, and the deuce take me, I think he only lives to hinder me of my occasions; but Lord bless me, Madam, how can you be unhappy with two thousand pounds a year in your own possession?

HILLARIA For my part, the greatest reason I think you have to grieve, is that you are not sure your husband's dead, for were that confirmed, then indeed there were hopes, that one poison might drive out another, you might marry again.

AMANDA All the comfort of my life is, that I can tell my conscience, I have been true to virtue.

HILLARIA And to an extravagant husband, that cares not a farthing for you. But come let's leave this unseasonable talk, and pray give me a little of your advice! What shall I do with this Mr Worthy? Would you advise me to make a husband of him?

AMANDA I am but an ill judge of men; the only one I thought myself secure of, most cruelly deceived me?

HILLARIA A losing gamester is fittest to give counsel; what d'ye think of him?

AMANDA Better than of any man I know: I read nothing in him but what is some part of a good man's character.

HILLARIA He's jealous.

AMANDA He's a lover.

HILLARIA He taxes me with a fool!

AMANDA He would preserve your reputation, and a fool's love ends only in the ruin of it.

HILLARIA Methinks he's not handsome.

AMANDA He's a man, Madam.

HILLARIA Why then e'en let him make a woman of me.

NARCISSA [*smiling*] Pray, Madam, what d'ye think of his brother?

AMANDA I would not think of him.

NARCISSA O dear, why pray?

AMANDA He puts me in mind of a man too like him, one that had beauty, wit, and falsehood! –

NARCISSA You have hit some part of his character, I must confess Madam; but as to his truth, I'm sure he loves only me.

AMANDA I don't doubt but he tells you so, nay, and swears it too.

NARCISSA O Lord! Madam, I hope I may without vanity believe him.

AMANDA But you will hardly without magic secure him.

NARCISSA I shall use no spells, or charms, but this poor face, Madam.

AMANDA And your fortune, Madam.

NARCISSA [*aside*] Senseless malice! ⟨*to Amanda*⟩ I know he'd marry me without a groat.

AMANDA Then he's not the man I take him for.

NARCISSA Why pray – what do you take him for?

AMANDA A wild young fellow, that loves everything he sees.

NARCISSA [*peevishly*] He never loved you yet.

AMANDA I hope, Madam, he never saw anything in me to encourage him.

NARCISSA In my conscience you are in the right on't, Madam, I dare swear he never did, nor e'er would, though he gazed till doomsday.

AMANDA I hope, Madam, your charms will prevent his putting himself to the trial, and I wish he may never –

NARCISSA Nay, dear, Madam, no more railing at him, unless you would have me believe you love him.

HILLARIA Indeed ladies you are both in the wrong, you, cousin, in being angry at what you desired, her opinion of your lover; and you, Madam, for speaking truth against the man she resolves to love.

NARCISSA Love him! Prithee, cousin, no more of that old stuff.

HILLARIA Stuff! Why? Don't you own you are to marry him this week – Here he comes, I suppose you'll tell him another thing in his ear.

Enter Young Worthy.

HILLARIA Mr Worthy, your servant! You look with the face of business, what's the news, pray?

YOUNG WORTHY Faith, Madam, I have news for you all, and
private news too: but that of the greatest consequence is with this
lady: your pardon ladies, I'll whisper with you all, one after
another.

NARCISSA Come, cousin, will you walk, the gentleman has business, we shall interrupt him.

HILLARIA Why really, cousin, I don't say positively you love Mr
Worthy, but I vow this looks very like jealousy.

NARCISSA Pish! Lord! Hillaria, you are in a very odd humour today. But to let you see I have no such weak thoughts about me,
I'll wait as unconcerned as yourself. [*aside*] I'll rattle him.

AMANDA Not unpleasing say you? Pray, Sir, unfold yourself, for
I have long despaired of welcome news.

YOUNG WORTHY Then in a word, Madam, your husband Mr
Loveless is in Town, and has been these three days. I parted with
him not an hour ago.

AMANDA In Town, you amaze me! For heaven's sake go on.

YOUNG WORTHY Faith, Madam, considering Italy, and those
parts have furnished him with nothing but an improvement of
that lewdness he carried over; I can't properly give you joy of his
arrival: besides, he is so very poor, that you would take him for
an inhabitant of that country. And when I confirmed your being
dead, he only shook his head, and called you good natured fool,
or to that effect: nay, though I told him his unkindness broke your
heart.

AMANDA Barbarous man! Not shed a tear upon my grave? But
why did you tell him I was dead?

YOUNG WORTHY Because, Madam, I thought you had no mind,
to have your house plundered, and for another reason, which if
you dare listen to me, perhaps you'll not dislike. In a word 'tis
such a stratagem that will either make him ashamed of his folly,
or in love with your virtue.

AMANDA Can there be a hope, when even my death could not
move him to a relenting sigh! Yet pray instruct me, Sir.

YOUNG WORTHY You know, Madam, 'twas not above four or
five months after you were married, but (as most young husbands do) he grew weary of you: now I am confident 'twas more
an affectation of being fashionably vicious, than any reasonable

dislike, he could either find in your mind or person: therefore
could you by some artifice, pass upon him, as a new mistress, I
am apt to believe you would find none of the wonted coldness in
his love; but a younger heat, and fierce desire.

AMANDA Suppose this done! What would be the consequence!

YOUNG WORTHY O your having then a just occasion to reproach
him with his broken vows, and to let him see the weakness of his
deluded fancy, which even in a wife, while unknown, could find
those real charms, which his blind, ungrateful lewdness would
ne'er allow her to be mistress of. After this, I'd have you seem,
freely to resign him to those fancied raptures, which he denied
were in a virtuous woman: who knows but this with a little submissive eloquence, may strike him with so great sense of shame,
as may reform his thoughts, and fix him yours?

AMANDA You have revived me, Sir: but how can I assure myself
he'll like me as a mistress?

YOUNG WORTHY From your being a new one – Leave the management of all to me; I have a trick shall draw him to your bed,
and when he's there, faith e'en let him cuckold himself. I'll engage he likes you as a mistress, though he could not as a wife.
[*aside*] At least she'll have the pleasure of knowing the difference
between a husband and a lover, without the scandal of the former.

AMANDA You have obliged me, Sir, if I succeed, the glory shall
be yours.

YOUNG WORTHY I'll wait on you at your lodging, and consult
how I may be farther serviceable to you: but you must put this in
a speedy execution, lest he should hear of you, and prevent your
designs. In the meantime, 'tis a secret to all the world, but yourself and me.

AMANDA I'll study to be grateful, Sir.

YOUNG WORTHY [*to Hillaria*] Now for you, Madam.

NARCISSA [*aside*] So! I am to be last served: very well!

YOUNG WORTHY My brother, Madam, confesses he scattered
some rough words last night, and I have taken the liberty to tell
you, you gave him some provocation.

HILLARIA That may be; but I'm resolved to be mistress of my
actions before marriage, and no man shall usurp a power over me,
till I give it him.

YOUNG WORTHY At least, Madam, consider what he said, as the effects of an impatient passion, and give him leave this afternoon to set all right again.

HILLARIA Well, if I don't find myself out of order after dinner, perhaps I may step into the garden: but I won't promise you neither.

YOUNG WORTHY I dare believe you without it – Now, Madam, [*to Narcissa*] I am your humble servant.　　　⟨*Hillaria walks off*⟩

NARCISSA And everybody's humble servant.

YOUNG WORTHY Why, Madam, I am come to tell you –

NARCISSA What success you have had with that lady, I suppose, I don't mind intrigues, Sir.

YOUNG WORTHY I like this jealousy however, though I scarce know how to appease it. 'Tis business of moment, Madam, and may be done in a moment.

NARCISSA Yours is done with me, Sir, but my business is not so soon done as you imagine.

YOUNG WORTHY In a word, I have very near reconciled my brother, and your cousin, and I don't doubt but tomorrow will be the day, if I were but as well assured of your consent for my happiness too!

NARCISSA First tell me your discourse with that lady; and afterwards if you can, look me in the face – O are you studying, Sir?

YOUNG WORTHY ⟨*aside*⟩ S'death! I must not trust her with it, she'll tell it the whole Town for a secret – Pox, ne'er a lie!

NARCISSA You said it was of the greatest consequence too!

YOUNG WORTHY [*aside*] A good hint faith. ⟨*to Narcissa*⟩ Why, Madam, since you will needs force it from me, 'twas to desire her to advance my interest with you: but all my entreaties could not prevail: for she told me I was unworthy of you: was not this of consequence, Madam?

NARCISSA Nay, now I must believe you, Mr Worthy, and I ask your pardon, for she was just railing against you for a husband, before you came.

YOUNG WORTHY Oh! Madam, a favoured lover like a good poem, for the malice of some few, makes the generous temper more admire it.

NARCISSA Nay, what she said, I must confess, had much the same effects as the coffee critics ridiculing Prince Arthur,★ for I found a pleasing disappointment in my reading you, and till I see your beauty's equalled, I shan't dislike you for a few faults.

YOUNG WORTHY Then, Madam, since you have blessed me with your good opinion, let me beg of you, before these ladies, to complete my happiness tomorrow. Let this be the last night of your lying alone.

NARCISSA What d'ye mean?

YOUNG WORTHY To marry you tomorrow, Madam.

NARCISSA Marry me! Who put that in your head?

YOUNG WORTHY Some small encouragement which my hopes have formed, Madam.

NARCISSA Hopes! O insolence! If it once comes to that I don't question but you have been familiar with me in your imagination. Marry you! What lie in a naked bed with you! Trembling by your side, like a tame lamb for sacrifice! D'ye think I can be moved to love a man, to kiss him, toy with him, and so forth!

YOUNG WORTHY [*aside*] Egad! I find nothing but downright impudence will do with her. ⟨*to Narcissa*⟩ No, Madam, 'tis the man must kiss, and toy with you, and so forth! Come my dear angel, pronounce the joyful word, and draw the scene of my eternal happiness. Ah! Methinks I'm there already, eager and impatient of approaching bliss! Just laid within the bridal bed, our friends retired, the curtains close drawn around us, no light but Cælia's eyes, no noise but her soft trembling words, and broken sighs, that plead in vain for mercy: and now a trickling tear steals down her glowing cheek, which tells the rushing lover at length she yields: yet vows she'd rather die. [*embracing her*] But still submits to the unexperienced joy.

Re-enter Hillaria.

HILLARIA What raptures Mr Worthy!

YOUNG WORTHY Only the force of love in imagination, Madam.

NARCISSA O Lord! Dear cousin! And Madam! Let's be gone, I vow he grows rude! Oh! For heaven's sake, I shan't shake off my

★ *Prince Arthur*: a reference to the play of that name (1695) by Sir Richard Blackmore.

fright these ten days, O Lord! I will not stay – Begone! For I
declare I loathe the sight of you.   [_Exit_]

YOUNG WORTHY I hope you'll stand my friend, Madam.

HILLARIA I'll get her into the garden after dinner.   [_Exit_]

YOUNG WORTHY I find there's nothing to be done with my lady
before company, 'tis a strange affected piece – But there's no
fault in her thousand pounds a year, and that's the loadstone that
attracts my heart – The wise, and grave, may tell us of strange
chimaeras called virtues in a woman, and that they alone are the
best dowry; but faith we younger brothers are of another mind.
Women are changed from what they were of old:
Therefore let lovers still this maxim hold,
She's only worth that brings her weight in gold.

                                                                      [_Exit_]

ACT TWO

SCENE ⟨I⟩

A garden belonging to Sir William Wisewoud's house

Enter Narcissa, Hillaria, and Sir Novelty Fashion.

HILLARIA Oh! For heaven's sake! No more of this gallantry Sir Novelty: for I know you say the same to every woman you see.

SIR NOVELTY Everyone that sees you, Madam, must say the same. Your beauty, like the rack forces every beholder to confess his crime – of daring to adore you.

NARCISSA ⟨*aside*⟩ Oh! I han't patience to hear all this! If he be blind I'll open his eyes – I vow Sir Novelty, you men of amour are strange creatures: you think no woman worth your while, unless you walk over a rival's ruin to her heart; I know nothing has encouraged your passion to my cousin more, than her engagement to Mr Worthy.

HILLARIA [*aside*] Poor creature now is she angry, she han't the address of a fop I nauseate!

SIR NOVELTY Oh! Madam, as to that, I hope the lady will easily distinguish the sincerity of her adorers. Though I must allow Mr Worthy is infinitely the handsomer person!

NARCISSA Oh! Fie Sir Novelty, make not such a preposterous comparison!

SIR NOVELTY Oh! Ged! Madam, there is no comparison.

NARCISSA Pardon me Sir! He's an unpolished animal!

SIR NOVELTY Why does your ladyship really think me tolerable?

HILLARIA [*aside*] So! She has snapped his heart already.

SIR NOVELTY Pray Madam, how do I look today? What, cursedly? I warrant with a more hellish complexion, than any stale actress at a rehearsal – I don't know Madam – 'tis true – the Town does talk of me indeed – but the devil take me, in my mind I am a very ugly fellow!

NARCISSA Now you are too severe, Sir Novelty!

SIR NOVELTY Not I, burn me. – For heaven's sake deal freely with me, Madam, and if you can, tell me – one tolerable thing about me?

HILLARIA [*aside*] T'would pose me, I'm sure.

NARCISSA O! Sir Novelty this is unanswerable; 'tis hard to know the brightest part of a diamond.

SIR NOVELTY You'll make me blush, stop my vitals, Madam – [*aside*] Egad I always said she was a woman of sense. Strike me dumb, I am in love with her – I'll try her farther – ⟨*to Narcissa*⟩ But Madam, is it possible I may vie with Mr Worthy – not that he is any rival of mine, Madam, for I can assure you my inclinations lie, where perhaps your ladyship little thinks.

HILLARIA [*aside*] So! Now I am rid of him.

SIR NOVELTY But pray tell me, Madam: for I really love a severe critic, I am sure you must believe he has a more happy genius in dress: for my part I am but a sloven.

NARCISSA He a genius! Unsufferable! Why he dresses worse than a captain of the militia: but you Sir Novelty are a true original, the very pink of fashion; I'll warrant there's not a milliner in Town, but has got an estate by you?

SIR NOVELTY I must confess Madam, I am for doing good, to my country: for you see this suit, Madam, – I suppose you are not ignorant what a hard time the ribbon weavers have had since the late mourning: now my design is to set the poor rogues up again, by recommending this sort of trimming: the fancy is pretty well for second mourning, – By the way, Madam, I had fifteen hundred guineas laid in my hand as a gratuity to encourage it: but egad I refused 'em being too well acquainted with the consequence of taking a bribe, in a national concern!

HILLARIA A very charitable fashion indeed Sir Novelty; but how if it should not take?

NARCISSA Ridiculous! Take! I warrant you in a week the whole Town will have it: though perhaps Mr Worthy will be one of the last of 'em: he's a mere *valet de chambre* to all fashion; and never is in any till his betters have left them off.

SIR NOVELTY Nay Ged now I must laugh, for the devil take me, if I did not meet him, not above fortnight ago, in a coat with buttons no bigger than nutmegs.

HILLARIA There I must confess you out-do him, Sir Novelty.

SIR NOVELTY O dear, Madam, why mine are not above three inches diameter.

HILLARIA But methinks, Sir Novelty, your sleeve is a little too extravagant.

SIR NOVELTY Nay, Madam, there you wrong me, mine does but just reach my knuckles. But my Lord Overdo's covers his diamond ring.

HILLARIA Nay, I confess, the fashion may be very useful to you, gentlemen, that make campaigns; for should you unfortunately lose an arm, or so, that sleeve might be very convenient to hide the defect on't.

SIR NOVELTY [*hiding his hand in his sleeve*] Ha! I think your ladyship's in the right on't, Madam.

NARCISSA Oh! Such an air! So becoming a negligence! Upon my soul, Sir Novelty, you'll be the envy of the *beau monde*!

HILLARIA Mr Worthy! A good fancy were thrown away upon him! But you, Sir, are an ornament to your clothes.

SIR NOVELTY Then your ladyship really thinks they are – *bien entendu!*

HILLARIA *A merveille, Monsieur!*

SIR NOVELTY She has almost as much wit as her cousin – I must confess, Madam, this coat has had a universal approbation: for this morning I had all the eminent tailors about Town at my levee, earnestly petitioning for the first measure of it: now, Madam, if you thought 'twould oblige Mr Worthy, I would let his tailor have it before any of 'em.

NARCISSA See here he comes, and the deuce take me, I think 'twould be a great piece of good nature; for I declare he looks as rough as a Dutch corporal – Prithee, Sir Novelty let's laugh at him!

SIR NOVELTY O Ged! No, Madam, that were too cruel: why you know he can't help it – Let's take no notice of him.

HILLARIA [*aside*] Wretched coxcomb.

Enter Elder Worthy.

ELDER WORTHY ⟨*aside*⟩ I find my resolution is but vain, my feet have brought me hither 'gainst my will: but sure I can command my tongue, which I'll bite off, ere it shall seek a reconciliation. Still so familiar there! But 'tis no matter, I'll try if I can wear indifference, and seem as careless in my love, as she is of her honour, which she can never truly know the worth of, while she persists to let a fool thus play with it. – Ladies, your humble servant.

HILLARIA [*aside*] Now can't I forbear fretting his spleen a little. ⟨*to Worthy*⟩ Oh! Mr Worthy, we are admiring Sir Novelty, and his new suit, did you ever see so sweet a fancy? He is as full of variety as a good play.

ELDER WORTHY He's a very pleasant comedy indeed, Madam, and dressed with a great deal of good satire, and no doubt may oblige both the stage and the Town, especially the ladies.

HILLARIA [*aside*] So! There's for me. –

SIR NOVELTY O Ged! Nay prithee, Tom, you know my humour, – Ladies! Stop my vitals! I don't believe there are five hundred in Town that ever took any notice of me.

ELDER WORTHY Oh, Sir, there are some that take so much notice of you, that the Town takes notice of them for't.

HILLARIA [*aside*] It works rarely.

SIR NOVELTY How of them, Tom upon my account! O Ged, I would not be the ruin of any lady's reputation for the world: stop my vitals, I am very sorry for't; prithee name but one, that has a favourable thought of me, and to convince you that I have no design upon her, I'll instantly visit her in an unpowdered periwig.

ELDER WORTHY Nay, she, I mean, is a woman of sense too.

SIR NOVELTY Phoo! Prithee, pox, don't banter me: 'tis impossible! What can she see in me?

ELDER WORTHY Oh, a thousand taking qualities! This lady will inform you – [*pulls him*] come, I'll introduce you.

SIR NOVELTY O Ged no! Prithee! – Hark you in your ear – I am off of her! Demme if I ben't, I am, stop my vitals!

ELDER WORTHY [*aside*] Wretched rogue! ⟨*to Sir Novelty*⟩ Pshaw! No matter, I'll reconcile you. Come, come, Madam.

HILLARIA Sir!

ELDER WORTHY This gentleman humbly begs to kiss your hands.

HILLARIA He needs not your recommendation, Sir.

ELDER WORTHY True! A fool recommends himself to your sex, and that's the reason men of common sense live unmarried.

HILLARIA A fool without jealousy, is better than a wit with ill-nature.

ELDER WORTHY A friendly office, seeing your fault is ill-nature.

HILLARIA Believing more than we have is pitiful, – You know I hate this wretch, loathe, and scorn him.

ELDER WORTHY Fools have a secret art of pleasing women: if he did not delight you, you would not hazard your reputation, by encouraging his love.

HILLARIA Dares he wrong my reputation?

ELDER WORTHY He need not; the world will do it for him, while you keep him company.

HILLARIA I dare answer it to the world.

ELDER WORTHY Then why not to me?

HILLARIA To satisfy you, were a fondness, I never should forgive myself.

ELDER WORTHY To persist in it, is what I'll ne'er forgive.

HILLARIA Insolence! Is it come to this? Never see me more.

ELDER WORTHY [*as Hillaria is going off*] I have lost the sight of you already; there hangs a cloud of folly between you, and the woman I once thought you.

Enter Young Worthy.

YOUNG WORTHY What to ourselves in passion we propose,
The passion ceasing does the purpose lose:
Madam, therefore pray let me engage you to stay a little till your fury is over, that you may see whether you have reason to be angry or no.

SIR NOVELTY [*to Narcissa*] Pray, Madam, who is that gentleman?

NARCISSA Mr Worthy's brother, Sir, a gentleman of no mean parts, I can assure you.

SIR NOVELTY I don't doubt it, Madam, – He has a very good walk.

HILLARIA To be jealous of me with a fool, is an affront to my understanding.

YOUNG WORTHY Tamely to resign your reputation to the merciless vanity of a fool, were no proof of his love.

HILLARIA 'Tis questioning my conduct.

YOUNG WORTHY Why you let him kiss your hand last night before his face.

HILLARIA The fool diverted me, and I gave him my hand, as I would lend my money, fan, or handkerchief to a legerdemain, that I might see him play all his tricks over.

YOUNG WORTHY O Madam! No juggler is so deceitful as a fop; for while you look his folly in the face, he steals away your reputation, with more ease, than the other picks your pocket.

HILLARIA Some fools indeed are dangerous.

YOUNG WORTHY I grant you, your design is only to laugh at him: but that's more than he finds out: therefore you must expect he will tell the world another story: and 'tis ten to one, but the consequence makes you repent of your curiosity.

HILLARIA You speak like an oracle: I tremble at the thoughts on't.

YOUNG WORTHY Here's one shall reconcile your fears – Brother I have done your business: Hillaria is convinced of her indiscretion, and has a pardon ready for your asking it.

ELDER WORTHY She's the criminal, I have no occasion for it.

YOUNG WORTHY See she comes toward you, give her a civil word at least.

HILLARIA Mr Worthy, I'll not be behind-hand in the acknowledgment I owe you: I freely confess my folly, and forgive your harsh construction of it: nay, I'll not condemn your want of good nature, in not endeavouring, (as your brother has done), by mild arguments to convince me of my error.

ELDER WORTHY Now you vanquish me! I blush to be outdone in generous love! I am your slave, dispose of me as you please.

HILLARIA No more, from this hour be you the master of my actions, and my heart.

ELDER WORTHY This goodness gives you the power, and I obey with pleasure.

YOUNG WORTHY So! I find I han't preached to no purpose! Well Madam if you find him guilty of love, even let tomorrow be his execution day, make a husband of him, and there's the extent of love's law.

ELDER WORTHY Brother I am indebted to you.

YOUNG WORTHY Well I'll give you a discharge, if you will but leave me but half an hour in private with that lady.

HILLARIA How will you get rid of Sir Novelty?

YOUNG WORTHY I'll warrant you, leave him to me.

HILLARIA Come, Mr Worthy, as we walk, I'll inform you, how I intend to sacrifice that wretch to your laughter.

ELDER WORTHY Not, Madam, that I want revenge on so contemptible a creature: but, I think, you owe this justice to your-self, to let him see (if possible) you never took him for any other, than what he really is.

YOUNG WORTHY Well! Pox of your politics, prithee consult of 'em within.

HILLARIA We'll obey you Sir.   [*Exeunt Elder Worthy and Hillaria*]

YOUNG WORTHY Pray, Madam, give me leave to beg a word in private with you; [*to Sir Novelty who is taking snuff*] Sir if you please –

SIR NOVELTY Aye Sir, with all my heart.

YOUNG WORTHY Sir. –

SIR NOVELTY [*offering his box*] Nay, 'tis right, I'll assure you.

YOUNG WORTHY Aye Sir – but now the lady would be alone.

SIR NOVELTY Sir!

YOUNG WORTHY The lady would be alone, Sir.

SIR NOVELTY I don't hear her say any such thing.

YOUNG WORTHY Then I tell you so, and I would advise you to believe me.

SIR NOVELTY I shall not take your advice, Sir: but if you really think the lady would be alone, why – you had best leave her.

YOUNG WORTHY In short, Sir, your company is very unseason-able at present.

SIR NOVELTY I can tell you, Sir, if you have no more wit, than manners, the lady will be but scurvily entertained.

NARCISSA O fie, gentlemen, no quarrelling before a woman, I beseech you. Pray let me know the business.

SIR NOVELTY My business is love, Madam.

NARCISSA And yours, Sir!

YOUNG WORTHY What, I hope you are no stranger to, Madam: as for that spark you need take no care of him, for if he stays much longer I will do his business myself.

NARCISSA ⟨*aside*⟩ Well, I vow love's a pleasant thing, when the men come to cutting of throats once: O Gad! I'd fain have them fight a little – Methinks Narcissa would sound so great in an expiring lover's mouth – Well, I am resolved Sir Novelty shall not go yet; for I will have the pleasure of hearing myself praised a little, though I don't marry this month for't – Come, gentlemen, since you both say love's your business, even plead for yourselves, and he that speaks the greater passion, shall have the fairest return.

YOUNG WORTHY ⟨*aside*⟩ Oh, the devil! Now is she wrapped with the hopes of a little flattery! There's no remedy but patience. S'death, what piece have I to work upon!

NARCISSA Come gentlemen, one at a time, Sir Novelty what have you to say to me?

SIR NOVELTY In the first place, Madam, I was the first person in England that was complimented with the name of beau, which is a title I prefer before Right Honourable: for that may be inherited: but this I extorted from the whole nation, by my surprising *mien*, and unexampled gallantry.

NARCISSA So, Sir!

SIR NOVELTY Then another thing, Madam, it has been observed, that I have been eminently successful in those fashions, I have recommended to the Town, and I don't question, but this very suit will raise as many ribbon-weavers, as ever the clipping, or melting trade did goldsmiths.

NARCISSA ⟨*aside*⟩ Pish! What does the fool mean! He says nothing of me yet.

SIR NOVELTY In short Madam, the cravat-string, the garter, the sword-knot, the centurine,* the bardash, the steinkirk,† the large button, the long sleeve, the plume, and full peruke, were all created, cried down, or revived by me; in a word Madam, there has never been anything particularly taking, or agreeable for these ten years past, but your humble servant was the author of it.

YOUNG WORTHY ⟨*aside*⟩ Where the devil will this end?

NARCISSA This is all extravagant, Sir Novelty; but what have you to say to me Sir?

SIR NOVELTY I'll come to you presently Madam, I have just done: then you must know my coach, and equipage are as well known, as myself; and since the conveniency of two playhouses I have a better opportunity of showing them: for between every act – whisk – I am gone from one to th'other – Oh! What pleasure 'tis at a good play, to go out before half an act's done!

NARCISSA Why at a good play?

SIR NOVELTY Oh! Madam it looks particular, and gives the

* centurine: cincture.
† steinkirk: a neckcloth in the steinkirk style, with lace ends, called after the French victory at Steenkerke, 1692.

whole audience an opportunity of turning upon me at once: then do they conclude I have some extraordinary business, or a fine woman to go to at least: and then again it shows my contempt of what the dull Town think their chiefest diversion: but if I do stay a play out, I always sit with my back to the stage.

NARCISSA Why so Sir?

SIR NOVELTY Then everybody will imagine I have been tired with it before; or that I am jealous who talks to who in the King's box. And thus, Madam, do I take more pains to preserve a public reputation, than ever any lady took after the smallpox, to recover her complexion.

NARCISSA Well but to the point, what have you to say to me, Sir Novelty?

YOUNG WORTHY ⟨*aside*⟩ Now does she expect some compliment shall out-flatter her glass.

SIR NOVELTY To you Madam, – Why I have been saying all this to you.

NARCISSA To what end, Sir?

SIR NOVELTY Why all this have I done for your sake.

NARCISSA What kindness is it to me?

SIR NOVELTY Why, Madam don't you think it more glory to be beloved by one eminently particular person, whom all the Town knows and talks of; than to be adored by five hundred dull souls, that have lived *incognito*?

NARCISSA That I must confess is a prevailing argument, but still you han't told me why you love me?

YOUNG WORTHY That's a task he has left for me, Madam.

SIR NOVELTY 'Tis a province I never undertake, I must confess, I think 'tis sufficient if I tell a lady why she should love me?

NARCISSA ⟨*aside*⟩ Hang him! He's too conceited, he's so in love with himself, he won't allow a woman the bare comfort of a cold compliment: – Well Mr Worthy?

YOUNG WORTHY Why, Madam, I have observed several particular qualities in your ladyship, that I have perfectly adored you for, as the majestic toss of your head – [*what he speaks she imitates in dumb show*] – your obliging bowed curtsey – your satirical smile – your blushing laugh – your demure look – the careless tie of your hood – the genteel flirt of your fan – the designed accident in your letting fall, and your agreeable manner of receiving it from him that takes it up. [*they both offer to take her fan, and in striving Young Worthy pushes Sir Novelty on his back*]

SIR NOVELTY [*adjusting himself*] I hope your ladyship will excuse my disorder, Madam, – How now?

Enter a Footman to Sir Novelty.

FOOTMAN Oh! Sir, Mrs Flareit –

SIR NOVELTY Ha! Speak lower, what of her?

FOOTMAN By some unlucky accident has discovered your being here, and raves like a madwoman: she's at your lodging Sir, and had broke you above forty pounds' worth of china before I came away; she talked of following hither, and if you don't make haste, I'm afraid will be here before you can get through the house, Sir.

SIR NOVELTY This woman is certainly the devil; her jealousy is implacable, I must get rid of her, though I give her more for a separate maintenance, than her conscience demanded for a settlement before enjoyment. – See the coach ready, and if you meet her, be sure you stop her with some pretended business, till I am got away from hence – Madam, I ask your ladyship ten thousand pardons: there's a person of quality expects me at my lodging upon extraordinary business.

NARCISSA What, will you leave us, Sir Novelty?

SIR NOVELTY As unwillingly as the soul the body: but this is an irresistible occasion! – Madam your most devoted slave. – Sir your most humble servant. – Madam, I kiss your hands. – [*Young Worthy sees him to the door*] – O Ged, no farther dear Sir, upon my soul I won't stir if you do. –   [*Exit Sir Novelty*]

YOUNG WORTHY Nay then Sir, your humble servant: so! This was a lucky deliverance.

NARCISSA I overheard the business. – You see, Mr Worthy, a man must be a slave to a mistress sometimes, as well as a wife; yet all can't persuade your sex to a favourable opinion of poor marriage.

YOUNG WORTHY I long, Madam, for an opportunity to convince you of your error; and therefore give me leave to hope tomorrow you will free me from the pain of farther expectation, and make an husband of me – Come I'll spare your blushes, and believe I have already named the day.

NARCISSA Had not we better consider a little?

YOUNG WORTHY No, let's avoid consideration, 'tis an enemy both to love and courage; they that consider much, live to be old bachelors, and young fighters. No! no! We shall have time enough to consider after marriage – But why are you so serious, Madam?

NARCISSA Not but I do consent tomorrow shall be the day, Mr Worthy. But I'm afraid you have not loved me long enough to make our marriage be the Town-talk: for 'tis the fashion now to be the Town-talk, and you know one had as good be out of the world, as out of the fashion.

YOUNG WORTHY I don't know, Madam, what you call Town-talk, but it has been in the news-letters above a fortnight ago, that we were already married. Beside, the last song I made of you, has been sung at the music meeting; and you may imagine, Madam, I took no little care to let the ladies and the beaux know who 'twas made on.

NARCISSA Well, and what said the ladies?

YOUNG WORTHY What was most observable, Madam, was that while it was singing my Lady Manlove went out in a great passion.

NARCISSA Poor jealous animal! On my conscience that charitable creature has such a fund of kind compliance for all young fellows, whose love lies dead upon their hands, that she has been as great a hindrance to us virtuous women, as ever the Bank of England was to City goldsmiths.

YOUNG WORTHY The reason of that is Madam, because you virtuous ladies pay no interest: I must confess the principal, our health, is a little securer with you.

NARCISSA Well, and is not that an advantage worth entering into bonds for? Not but I vow we virtuous devils do love to insult a little; and to say truth, it looks too credulous, and easy in a woman to encourage a man before he has sighed himself to a skeleton.

YOUNG WORTHY But heaven be thanked, we are pretty even with you in the end: for the longer you hold us off before marriage, the sooner we fall off after it.

NARCISSA What then, you take marriage to be a kind of Jesuits' powder,* that infallibly cures the fever of love?

* Jesuits' powder: powdered Peruvian bark, used to cure malaria and fevers of malarial type.

YOUNG WORTHY 'Tis indeed a Jesuits' powder; for the priests first invented it: and only abstained from it, because they knew it had a better taste: then gilded it over with a pretended blessing, and so palmed it upon the unthinking laity.

NARCISSA Prithee don't screw your wit beyond the compass of good manners – D'ye think I shall be tuned to matrimony by your railing against it? If you have so little stomach to it, I'll even make you fast a week longer.

YOUNG WORTHY Aye, but let me tell you, Madam, 'tis no policy to keep a lover at a thin diet in hopes to raise his appetite on the wedding night, for then

We come like starving beggars to a feast,

Where unconfined we feed with eager haste,

Till each repeated morsel palls the taste.

Marriage gives prodigals a boundless treasure,

Who squander that, which might be lasting pleasure,

And women think they ne'er have over measure.

ACT THREE

SCENE ⟨I⟩

Sir William Wisewoud's house

Enter Amanda and Hillaria meeting.

AMANDA My dear, I have news for you.

HILLARIA I guess at it: and would be fain satisfied of the particulars: your husband is returned, and I hear knows nothing of your being alive: Young Worthy has told me of your design upon him.

AMANDA 'Tis that I wanted your advice in; what think you of it?

HILLARIA Oh! I admire it: next to forgetting your husband, 'tis the best counsel was ever given you; for under the disguise of mistress, you may now take a fair advantage of indulging your love, and the little experience you have had of it already, has been just enough not to let you be afraid of a man.

AMANDA Will you never leave your mad humour?

HILLARIA Not till my youth leaves me: why should women affect ignorance among themselves, when we converse with men indeed? Modesty and good breeding oblige us not to understand, what sometimes we can't help thinking of.

AMANDA Nay I don't think the worse of you for what you say: for 'tis observed that a bragging lover, and an over-shy lady, are the farthest from what they would seem; the one is as seldom known to receive a favour, as the other to resist an opportunity.

HILLARIA Most women have a wrong sense of modesty, as some men of courage; if you don't fight with all you meet, or run from all you see, you are presently thought a coward, or an ill woman.

AMANDA You say true, and 'tis as hard a matter nowadays for a woman to know how to converse with men, as for a man to know, when to draw his sword: for many times both sexes are apt to over-act their parts: to me the rules of virtue have been ever sacred; and I am loath to break 'em by an unadvised understanding: therefore, dear Hillaria, help me, for I am at a loss – Can I justify, think you, my intended design upon my husband?

HILLARIA As how, prithee?

AMANDA Why, if I court and conquer him, as a mistress, am not I accessary to his violating the bonds of marriage? For though I am his wife, yet while he loves me not as such, I encourage an unlawful passion; and though the act be safe, yet his intent is criminal: how can I answer this?

HILLARIA Very easily, for if he don't intrigue with you, he will with somebody else in the meantime, and I think you have as much right to his remains as anyone.

AMANDA Aye! But I am assured the love he will pretend to me is vicious: and 'tis uncertain, that I shall prevent his doing worse elsewhere.

HILLARIA 'Tis true, a certain ill ought not to be done for an uncertain good. But then again of two evils choose the least; and sure 'tis less criminal to let him love you as a mistress, than to let him hate you as a wife: if you succeed I suppose you will easily forgive your guilt in the undertaking.

AMANDA To say truth, I find no argument yet strong enough to conquer my inclination to it. But is there no danger think you of his knowing me?

HILLARIA Not the least, in my opinion: in the first place he confidently believes you are dead: then he has not seen you these eight or ten years: besides you were not above sixteen when he left you: this with the alteration the smallpox have made in you, (though not for the worse), I think are sufficient disguises to secure you from his knowledge.

AMANDA Nay and to this I may add the considerable amendment of my fortune; for when he left me I had only my bare jointure for a subsistence: beside my strange manner of receiving him.

HILLARIA That's what I would fain be acquainted with.

AMANDA I expect further instructions from Young Worthy every moment; then you shall know all, my dear.

HILLARIA Nay he will do you no small service: for a thief is the best thief-catcher.

Enter a Servant.

SERVANT [*to Amanda*] Madam, your servant is below, who says young Mr Worthy's man waits at your lodgings with earnest business from his master. ⟨*Exit*⟩

AMANDA 'Tis well – Come, my dear I must have your assistance too.

HILLARIA With all my heart, I love to be at the bottom of a

secret: for they say the confident of any amour, has sometimes more pleasure in the observation, than the parties concerned in the enjoyment: but methinks, you don't look with a good heart upon the business.

AMANDA I can't help a little concern in a business of such moment: for though my reason tells me my design must prosper; yet my fears say 'twere happiness too great. – Oh! To reclaim the man I'm bound by heaven to love, to expose the folly of a roving mind in pleasing him with what he seemed to loathe, were such a sweet revenge for slighted love, so vast a triumph of rewarded constancy, as might persuade the looser part of womankind even to forsake themselves and fall in love with virtue.

Re-enter the Servant.

SERVANT [*to Hillaria*] Sir Novelty Fashion is below in his coach, Madam, and enquires for your ladyship, or Madam Narcissa.

HILLARIA You know my cousin is gone out with my Lady Tattletongue: I hope you did not tell him I was within!

SERVANT No, Madam, I did not know if your ladyship would be spoke with, and therefore came to see.

HILLARIA Then tell him I went with her.

SERVANT I shall, Madam.   [*Exit Servant*]

HILLARIA You must know, my dear, I have sent to that fury Mrs Flareit, whom this Sir Novelty keeps, and have stung her to some purpose with an account of his passion for my cousin: I owed him a quarrel for that he made between Mr Worthy and me, and I hope her jealousy will severely revenge it; therefore I sent my cousin out of the way, because unknown to her, her name is at the bottom of my design. – Here he comes, prithee, my dear, let's go down the back-stairs, and take coach from the garden. –
                              [*Exeunt Amanda and Hillaria*]

Re-enter the Servant conducting Sir Novelty.

SIR NOVELTY Both the ladies abroad say you? Is Sir William within?

SERVANT Yes Sir, if you please to walk in, I'll acquaint him that you expect him here.
                                                              [*Exit*]

SIR NOVELTY Do so prithee – and in the meantime let me consider what I have to say to him – Hold! In the first place his daughter is in love with me! Would I marry her? Noh! Demn it, 'tis mechanical to marry the woman you love: men of quality should always marry those they never saw – But I hear Young Worthy marries her tomorrow! Which if I prevent not, will spoil my design upon her? Let me see! – I have it – I'll persuade the old fellow, that I would marry her myself! Upon which he immediately rejects Young Worthy, and gives me free access to her! Good! What follows upon that? Opportunity, importunity, – resistance, force, entreaty, persisting! – Doubting, swearing, lying – blushes, yielding, victory, pleasure! – Indifference. Oh! Here he comes *in ordine ad.* –

Enter Sir William Wisewoud.

SIR WILLIAM Sir Novelty, your servant, have you any commands for me, Sir?

SIR NOVELTY I have some proposals to make, Sir, concerning your happiness and my own, which perhaps will surprise you. In a word Sir, I am upon the very brink of matrimony.

SIR WILLIAM 'Tis the best thing you can pursue, Sir, considering you have a good estate.

SIR NOVELTY But whom do you think I intend to marry?

SIR WILLIAM I can't imagine. Dear Sir, be brief, lest your delay transport me into a crime I would avoid, which is impatience. Sir, pray go on.

SIR NOVELTY In fine, Sir, 'tis to your very daughter, the fair Narcissa.

SIR WILLIAM Humh! Pray, Sir, how long have you had this in your head?

SIR NOVELTY Above these two hours, Sir.

SIR WILLIAM Very good! Then you han't slept upon't?

SIR NOVELTY No! Nor shan't sleep, for thinking on't; did not I tell you I would surprise you?

SIR WILLIAM Oh! You have indeed, Sir, I am amazed! I am amazed!

SIR NOVELTY Well, Sir, and what think you of my proposal?

SIR WILLIAM Why truly, Sir, I like it not: but if I did, 'tis now too late; my daughter is disposed of to a gentleman, that she and I like very well; at present, Sir, I have a little business, if this be all, your humble servant, I am in haste.

SIR NOVELTY Demme! What an insensible blockhead's this? Hold, Sir, d'ye hear – is this all the acknowledgment you make for the honour I designed you?

SIR WILLIAM Why truly, Sir, 'tis an honour, that I am not ambitious of: in plain terms, I do not like you for a son-in-law.

SIR NOVELTY Now you speak to the purpose, Sir: but prithee what are thy exceptions to me?

SIR WILLIAM Why in the first place, Sir, you have too great a passion for your own person to have any for your wife's: in the next place you take such an extravagant care in the clothing your body, that your understanding goes naked for't: had I a son so dressed, I should take the liberty to call him an egregious fop.

SIR NOVELTY Egad thou art a comical old gentleman, and I'll tell thee a secret: understand then, Sir, from me, that all young fellows hate the name of fop, as women do the name of whore: but egad they both love the pleasure of being so: nay faith, and 'tis as hard a matter for some men to be fops, as you call 'em, as 'tis for some women to be whores.

SIR WILLIAM That's pleasant, i'faith, can't any man be a fop, or any woman be a whore, that has a mind to't?

SIR NOVELTY No faith, Sir; for let me tell you, 'tis not the cold-ness of my Lady Freelove's inclination: but her age and wrinkles that won't let her cuckold her husband: and again, 'tis not Sir John Wouldlook's aversion to dress; but his want of a fertile genius, that won't let him look like a gentleman: therefore in vindication of all well-dressed gentlemen, I intend to write a play; where my chiefest character shall be a down-right English booby, that affects to be a beau, without either genius, or foreign education, and to call it in imitation of another famous comedy, *He would if he could*,★ and now, I think, you are answered, Sir; have you any exceptions to my birth, or family, pray Sir?

SIR WILLIAM Yes, Sir, I have. You seem to me the offspring of more than one man's labour: for certainly no less, than a dancing,

★ *He would if he could*: probably a reference to Etherege's *She Would If She Could* (1668).

singing, and fencing-master, with a tailor, milliner, perfumer, peruke-maker, and French *valet de chambre*, could be at the begetting of you.

SIR NOVELTY All these have been at the finishing of me since I was made.

SIR WILLIAM That is, heaven made you a man, and they have made a monster of you: and so farewell to ye! [*is going*]

SIR NOVELTY Hark ye Sir, am I to expect no farther satisfaction in the proposals I made you?

SIR WILLIAM Sir – Nothing makes a man lose himself like passion: now I presume you are young, and consequently rash upon a disappointment, therefore to prevent any difference that may arise by repeating my refusal of your suit; I do not think it convenient to hold any farther discourse with you.

SIR NOVELTY Nay faith thou shalt stay to hear a little more of my mind first.

SIR WILLIAM Since you press me, Sir, I will rather bear than resist you.

SIR NOVELTY I doubt, old gentleman, you have such a torrent of philosophy running through your *pericranium*, that it has washed your brains away.

SIR WILLIAM Pray, Sir, why do you think so?

SIR NOVELTY Because you choose a beggarly unaccountable sort of younger brotherish rake-hell for your son-in-law, before a man of quality, estate, good parts and breeding, demme.

SIR WILLIAM Truly, Sir I know neither of the persons to whom these characters belong, if you please to write their names under 'em, perhaps I may tell you, if they be like or no.

SIR NOVELTY Why then, in short, I would have been your son-in-law, and you, it seems, prefer Young Worthy before me. Now are your eyes open?

SIR WILLIAM Had I been blind, Sir, you might have been my son-in-law, and if you were not blind you would not think, that I design my daughter for Young Worthy – His brother, I think, may deserve her.

SIR NOVELTY Then you are not jealous of Young Worthy! Humh!

SIR WILLIAM No really, Sir, nor of you neither.

SIR NOVELTY Give me thy hand, thou art very happy: stop my

vitals: for thou dost not see thou art blind: not jealous of Young Worthy? Ha! Ha! How now!

Enter Sir Novelty's Servant with a Porter.

SERVANT Sir, here's a porter with a letter for your honour.

PORTER I was ordered to give it into your own hands, Sir, and expect an answer.

SIR NOVELTY [*reads*] 'Excuse my dear Sir Novelty the forced indifference I have shown you, and let me recompence your past sufferings with an hour's conversation, after the play at Rosamond's Pond, where you will find an hearty welcome to the arms of your Narcissa!' Unexpected happiness! The arms of your Narcissa! Egad and when I am there, I'll make myself welcome! Faith I did not think she was so far gone neither! But I don't question there are five hundred more in her condition. – I have a good mind not to go faith! Yet hang it, I will though only, to be revenged of this old fellow! Nay, I'll have the pleasure of making it public too: for I will give her the music and draw all the Town to be witness of my triumph [*to the Porter*] Where is the lady –

PORTER In a hackney coach at the corner of the street.

SIR NOVELTY Enough, tell her I will certainly be there –

[*Exit Porter*]

Well, old gentleman then you are resolved I shall be no kin to you? Your daughter is disposed of: humh!

SIR WILLIAM You have your answer, Sir, you shall be no kin to me.

SIR NOVELTY Farewell old philosophy: and d'ye hear, I would advise you to study nothing but the art of patience: you may have an unexpected occasion for it. Hark you! Would not it nettle you damnably to hear my son call you grandfather?

SIR WILLIAM Sir – notwithstanding this provocation, I am calm; but were I like other men, a slave to passion, should not forbear calling you impertinent! How I swell with rising vexation – Leave me, leave me; go Sir, go, get you out of my house. [*angrily*]

SIR NOVELTY Oh! Have a care of passion, dear Diogenes. Ha! Ha! Ha! He!

SIR WILLIAM So! [*sighing*] At last I have conquered it; pray Sir oblige me with your absence [*taking off his hat*], I protest I am tired with you, [*submissively*] pray leave my house.

SIR NOVELTY Damn your house, your family, your ancestors, your generation, and your eternal posterity. [*Exit*]

SIR WILLIAM Ah! – A fair riddance; how I bless myself, that it was not in this fool's power to provoke me beyond that serenity of temper, which a wise man ought to be master of: how near are men to brutes, when their unruly passions break the bounds of reason? And of all passions, anger is the most violent, which often puts me in mind of that admirable saying,
He that strives not to stem his anger's tide,
Does a mad horse without a bridle ride.

SCENE ⟨II⟩

Changes to St James's Park

Enter Young Worthy and Loveless as from the tavern – Snap following.

YOUNG WORTHY What a sweet evening 'tis – Prithee Ned, let's walk a little – Look how lovingly the trees are joined, since thou wert here, as if nature had designed this walk for the private shelter of forbidden love. [*several crossing the stage*] Look here are some for making use of the conveniency.

LOVELESS But, hark ye friend, are the women as tame and civil as they were before I left the Town? Can they endure the smell of tobacco, or vouchsafe a man a word with a dirty cravat on?

YOUNG WORTHY Aye, that they will; for keeping is almost out of fashion: so that now an honest fellow with a promising back need not fear a night's lodging for bare good fellowship.

LOVELESS If whoring be so poorly encouraged, methinks the women should turn honest in their own defence.

YOUNG WORTHY Faith I don't find there's a whore the less for it; the pleasure of fornication is still the same; all the difference is, lewdness is not so barefaced, as heretofore, – virtue is as much debased as our money; for maidenheads are as scarce as our milled half-crowns; and faith, *Dei gratia* is as hard to be found in a girl of sixteen, as round the brims of an old shilling.

LOVELESS Well, I find, in spite of law and duty, the flesh will get the better of the spirit. But I see no game yet. – Prithee Will, let's go and take t'other bumper to enliven assurance that we may come downright to the business.

YOUNG WORTHY No, no; what we have in our bellies already, by the help of a little fresh air, will soon be in our *pericraniums*, and work us to a right pitch, to taste the pleasures of the night.

LOVELESS The day thou mean'st; my day always breaks at sunset. We wise fellows, that know the use of life, know too that the moon lights men to more pleasures than the sun, – the sun was meant for dull soul of business, and poor rogues that have a mind to save candles.

YOUNG WORTHY Nay, the night was always a friend to pleasure, and that made Diana run a-whoring by the light of her own horns.

LOVELESS Right: and, prithee what made Daphne run away from Apollo, but that he wore so much daylight about his ears?

YOUNG WORTHY Ha! Look out Ned, there's the enemy before you!

LOVELESS Why then, as Cæsar said, come follow me.

[Exit Loveless]

YOUNG WORTHY I hope 'tis his wife, whom I desired to meet me here, that she might take a view of her soldier before she new-mounted him. *[Exit]*

Enter Mrs Flareit and her maid.

MAID I wonder, Madam, Sir Novelty don't come yet: I am so afraid he should see Narcissa, and find out the trick of your letter.

MRS FLAREIT No! No! Narcissa is out of the way: I am sure he won't be long; for, I heard the *hautbois*,* as they passed by me, mention his name; I suppose to make the intrigue more fashionable, he intends to give me the music.

MAID Suppose he do take you for Narcissa, what advantage do you propose by it?

MRS FLAREIT I shall then have a just occasion to quarrel with him for his perfidiousness, and so force his pocket to make his peace with me: beside, my jealousy will not let me rest till I am revenged.

MAID Jealousy! Why, I have often heard you say, you loathed him!

MRS FLAREIT 'Tis my pride, not love, that makes me jealous:

* hautbois: oboe, hence oboe players.

for, though I don't love him, yet I am incensed to think he dares love another.

MAID See! Madam, here he is, and the music with him.

MRS FLAREIT Put on your mask, and leave me. [*They mask*]

Enter Sir Novelty with the Music.

SIR NOVELTY Here, gentlemen, place yourselves on this spot, and pray oblige me with a trumpet *sonata* [*the Music prepare to play*]. – This taking a man at his first word, is a very new way of preserving reputation, stop my vitals, – nay, and secure one too; for now may we enjoy and grow weary of one another, before the Town can take any notice of us. [*Mrs Flareit making towards him*] Ha! This must be she. – I suppose, Madam, you are no stranger to the contents of this letter.

MRS FLAREIT Dear Sir, this place is too public for my acknowledgment, if you please to withdraw to a more private conveniency. [*Exeunt*]

The Music prepare to play, and all sorts of people gather about it. Enter at one door Narcissa, Hillaria, Amanda, Elder Worthy, and Young Worthy; at another Loveless and Snap, who talk to the Masks.

ELDER WORTHY What say you ladies, shall we walk homewards? It begins to be dark.

YOUNG WORTHY Prithee don't be so impatient, it's light enough to hear the music, I'll warrant ye.

AMANDA Mr Worthy, you promised me a sight I long for: is Mr Loveless among all those?

YOUNG WORTHY That's he, Madam, a-surveying that masked lady.

AMANDA Ha! Is't possible! Methinks I read his vices in his person! Can he be insensible, even to the smart of pinching poverty? Pray, Sir, your hand, – I find myself disordered. It troubles me to think I dare not speak to him after so long an absence.

YOUNG WORTHY Madam, your staying here may be dangerous, therefore let me advise you to go home, and get all things in order to receive him: about an hour hence will be a convenient time to set my design a-going; till when let me beg you to have a little patience: give me leave, Madam, to see you to your coach.

AMANDA I'll not trouble you, Sir, yonder's my cousin Welbred, I'll beg his protection.   [*Exit*]

The Music plays, after which Narcissa speaks.

NARCISSA I vow it's very fine, considering what dull souls our nation are: I find 'tis an harder matter to reform their manners than their government, or religion.

ELDER WORTHY Since the one has been so happily accomplished, I know no reason why we should despair of the other: I hope in a little time to see our youth return from travel big with praises of their own country. But come, ladies, the music's done I suppose, shall we walk?

NARCISSA Time enough, why you have no taste of the true pleasure of the Park: I'll warrant you hate as much to ridicule others, as to hear yourself praised: for my part, I think a little harmless railing's half the pleasure of one's life.

ELDER WORTHY I don't love to create myself enemies by observing the weakness of other people; I have more faults of my own than I know how to mend.

NARCISSA Protect me! How can you see such a medley of human stuffs as here is, without venting your spleen? – Why look there now, is not it comical to see that wretched creature there with her autumnal face, dressed in all the colours of the spring?

ELDER WORTHY Pray, who is she Madam?

NARCISSA A thing that won't believe herself out of date, though she was a known woman at the Restoration.

YOUNG WORTHY Oh! I know her, 'tis Mrs Holdout, one that is proud of being an original of fashionable fornication, and values herself mightily for being one of the first mistresses that ever kept her coach publicly in England.

HILLARIA Pray who's that impudent young fellow there?

ELDER WORTHY Oh, that's an eternal fan-tearer, and a constant persecuter of womankind: he had a great misfortune lately.

NARCISSA Pray, what was it?

ELDER WORTHY Why, impudently presuming to cuckold a Dutch officer, he had his fore-teeth kicked out.

OMNES Ha, ha, ha!

NARCISSA There's another too, Mr Worthy, do you know him?

YOUNG WORTHY That's Beau Noisy, one that brags of favours from my lady, though refused by her woman: that sups with my lord, and borrows his club of his footman; that beats the watch, and is kicked by his companions; that is one day at Court, and the next in jail; that goes to church without religion, is valiant without courage, witty without sense, and drunk without measure.

ELDER WORTHY A very complete gentleman.

HILLARIA Prithee cousin, who's that over-shy lady there, that won't seem to understand what that brisk young fellow says to her?

NARCISSA Why, that's my Lady Slylove: that other ceremonious gentleman is her lover: she is so overmodest, that she makes a scruple of shifting herself before her woman, but afterwards makes none of doing it before her gallant.

YOUNG WORTHY Hang her, she's a jest to the whole Town: for, though she has been the mother of two byblows, endeavours to appear as ignorant in all company as if she did not know the distinction of sexes.

NARCISSA Look, look! Mr Worthy, I vow there's the Countess of Incog out of her *dishabille*, in a high head, I protest!

YOUNG WORTHY 'Tis as great a wonder to see her out of an hackney coach, as out of debt or –

NARCISSA Or out of countenance.

YOUNG WORTHY That, indeed, she seldom changes; for she is never out of a mask, and is so well known in't, that when she has a mind to be private, she goes barefaced.

NARCISSA But come, cousin, now let's see what monsters the next walk affords.

ELDER WORTHY With all my heart, 'tis in our way home.

YOUNG WORTHY Ladies, I must beg your pardon for a moment, yonder comes one I have a little business with. I'll dispatch it immediately, and follow you.

HILLARIA No, no; we'll stay for you.

NARCISSA You may, if you please, cousin; but, I suppose, he will hardly thank you for't.

HILLARIA What, then you conclude 'tis a woman's business, by his promising a quick dispatch!

YOUNG WORTHY Madam, in three minutes you shall know the

business, if it displease you, condemn me to an eternal absence.

ELDER WORTHY Come, Madam, let me be his security.

NARCISSA I dare take your word, Sir –

[*Exeunt Elder Worthy, Hillaria and Narcissa*]

Enter Sly, Servant to Young Worthy.

YOUNG WORTHY Well! How go matters, is she in a readiness to receive him?

SLY To an hair, Sir, every servant has his cue, and all are impatient till the comedy begins.

YOUNG WORTHY Stand aside a little, and let us watch our opportunity.

SNAP [*to a Mask*] Enquire about half an hour hence for Number Two, at the Gridiron.

MASK Tomorrow with all my heart, but tonight I am engaged to the chaplain of Colonel Thunder's regiment.

SNAP What, will you leave me for a mutton-chop, for that's all he'll give you, I'm sure.

MASK You are mistaken, faith he keeps me.

SNAP Not to himself, I'll engage him: yet he may too, if nobody likes you no better than I do. Hark you child, prithee when was your smock washed?

MASK Why dost thou pretend to fresh linen, that never wore a clean shirt but of thy mother's own washing?   [*Goes from him*]

LOVELESS What, no adventure, no game, Snap?

SNAP None, none, Sir, I can't prevail with any from the point head-cloths to the horse-guard-whore.

LOVELESS What a pox! Sure the whores can't smell an empty pocket.

SNAP No, no, that's certain, Sir, they must see it in our faces.

SLY [*to Loveless*] My dear boy, how is't? Egad I am glad thou art come to Town: my lady expected you above an hour ago, and I am overjoyed I ha' found thee: come, come, come along, she's impatient till she sees you.

SNAP Odsbud, Sir, follow him, he takes you for another.

LOVELESS Egad, it looks with the face of an intrigue – I'll humour him: – Well, what, shall we go now?

SLY Aye, aye, now it's pure and dark, you may go undiscovered.

LOVELESS That's what I would do.

SLY Odsheart, she longs to see thee, and she is a curious fine creature, ye rogue! Such eyes! Such lips! – And such a tongue between em! Ah, the tip of it will set a man's soul on fire!

LOVELESS [*aside*] The rogues make me impatient!

SLY Come, come, the key, the key, the key, you dear rogue!

SNAP [*aside*] O Lord, the key, the key!

LOVELESS The key: why sh—— sh—— sh—— should yo——
yo—— you have it?

SLY Aye, aye! Quickly, give's it!

LOVELESS Why – what the devil – sure I han't lost it; – oh! No
Gad, it is not there; – what the devil shall we do?

SLY Oons, ne'er stand fumbling; if you have lost it we must shoot
the lock I think.

LOVELESS Egad, and so we must, for I han't it.

SLY Come, come along, follow me.

LOVELESS Snap, stand by me, you dog.

SNAP Aye, aye, Sir.   [*Exeunt Sly, Loveless and Snap*]

YOUNG WORTHY Ha, ha! The rogue managed him most dex-
terously; how greedily he chopped at the bait? What the event
will be, heaven knows; but thus far 'tis pleasant; and since he is
safe, I'll venture to divert my company with the story. Poor
Amanda, thou well deservest a better husband: thou wert never
wanting in thy endeavours to reclaim him: and, faith, considering how a long despair has worn thee,

'Twere pity now thy hopes should not succeed;

This new attempt is love's last shift indeed.

ACT FOUR

⟨SCENE I⟩

The Scene continues

Enter two Bullies, and Sir William Wisewoud observing them.

FIRST BULLY Damme! Jack, let's after him, and fight him; 'tis not to be put up.

SECOND BULLY No! Damn him! Nobody saw the affront, and what need we take notice of it?

FIRST BULLY Why that's true! – But damme! I have much ado to forbear cutting his throat.

SIR WILLIAM Pray gentlemen, what's the matter? Why are you in such a passion?

FIRST BULLY What's that to you, Sir? What would you have?

SIR WILLIAM I hope, Sir, a man may ask a civil question.

FIRST BULLY Damme! Sir, we are men of honour, we dare answer any man.

SIR WILLIAM But why are you angry, gentlemen? Have you received any wrong?

SECOND BULLY We have been called rascals, Sir, have had the lie given us, and had like to have been kicked.

SIR WILLIAM But I hope, you were not kicked, gentlemen.

SECOND BULLY How, Sir! We kicked!

SIR WILLIAM Nor do I presume, that you are rascals!

FIRST BULLY Blood! And thunder! Sir, let any man say it that wears an head! We rascals!

SIR WILLIAM Very good! Since then you are not rascals, he rather was one, who maliciously called you so: – Pray take my advice, gentlemen; never disturb yourselves, for any ill your enemy says of you; for from an enemy the world will not believe it: now you must know, gentlemen, that a flea-bite is to me more offensive, than the severest affront any man can offer me!

FIRST BULLY What, and so you would have us put it up! Damme! Sir, don't preach cowardice to us, we are men of valour: you won't find us cowards, Sir.

SECOND BULLY No, Sir! We are no cowards, though you are.

FIRST BULLY Hang him, let him alone, I see a coward in his face.

SIR WILLIAM If my face make any reflection, Sir, 'tis against my will.

SECOND BULLY Prithee Tom, let's affront him, and raise his spleen a little.

SIR WILLIAM Raise my spleen! That's more than any man could ever boast of.

FIRST BULLY You lie.

SIR WILLIAM I am not angry yet, therefore I do not lie, Sir: now one of us must lie, I do not lie, *ergo* –

FIRST BULLY Damme! Sir, have a care! Don't give me the lie, I shan't take it, Sir.

SIR WILLIAM I need not, Sir! You give it yourself.

FIRST BULLY Well, Sir, what then? If I make bold with myself, every old puppy shall not pretend to do it.

SIR WILLIAM Ha! Ha! Ha! Ha! Ha!

FIRST BULLY Damme, Sir, what do you laugh at!

SIR WILLIAM To let you see, that I am no puppy, Sir, for puppies are brutes, now brutes have not risibility: but I laugh, therefore I am no puppy. Ha! Ha!

FIRST BULLY Blood and thunder, Sir! Dare you fight?

SIR WILLIAM Not in cool blood, Sir, and I confess 'tis impossible to make me angry.

SECOND BULLY I'll try that! Hark ye, don't you know you are a snivelling old cuckold?

SIR WILLIAM No, really, Sir.

SECOND BULLY Why then I know you to be one.

SIR WILLIAM Look you, Sir, my reason weighs this injury, which is so light, it will not raise my anger in the other scale.

FIRST BULLY Oons! What a tame old prig's this? I'll give you better weight then, I know who got all your children.

SIR WILLIAM Not so well as my wife I presume – Now she tells me, 'twas myself, and I believe her too.

FIRST BULLY She tells you so, because the poor rogue that got 'em is not able to keep 'em.

SIR WILLIAM Then my keeping them is charity.

FIRST BULLY Blood and thunder, Sir, this is an affront to us, not to be angry after all these provocations – Damme! Jack, let's souse him in the canal. [*as they lay hold on him*]

Enter Elder Worthy, Young Worthy, Narcissa and Hillaria.

YOUNG WORTHY S'death, what's here? Sir William in the rogues' hands that affronted the ladies – Oh, forbear, forbear – [*strikes them*]

ELDER WORTHY So, gentlemen, I thought you had fair warning before, now you shall pay for't.

Enter three or four sentinels.

Heark you, honest soldiers, pray do me the favour to wash these rascals in the canal, and there's a guinea for your trouble.

BULLIES Damme, Sir! We shall expect satisfaction.

[*Exeunt dragging the bullies*]

SIR WILLIAM O dear gentlemen, I am obliged to you, for I was just going to the canal myself, if you had not come as you did.

ELDER WORTHY Pray, Sir, what had you done to 'em?

SIR WILLIAM Why, hearing the music from my parlour window, and being invited by the sweetness of the evening, I even took a walk to see if I could meet with you, when the first objects that presented themselves were these bullies, threatening to cut somebody's throat: now, I endeavouring to allay their fury, occasioned their giving me scurrilous language: and finding they could not make me as angry as themselves, they offered to fling me into the water.

ELDER WORTHY I am glad we stepped to your deliverance.

SIR WILLIAM Oh, I thank you, gentlemen. – I'll e'en go home, and recover my fright. Good night, good night to you all.   [*Exit*]

ELDER WORTHY [*to his servant*] Harry, see Sir William safe to his lodging. Well, ladies, I believe it's time for us to be walking too.

HILLARIA No, pray let me engage you to stay a little longer: yonder comes Sir Novelty and his mistress, in pursuance of the design I told you of; pray have a little patience, and you will see the effect on't.

ELDER WORTHY With all my heart, Madam.   [*They stand aside*]

Enter Sir Novelty embracing Mrs Flareit (masked).

SIR NOVELTY Generous creature! This is an unexampled condescension to meet my passion with such early kindness: thus let me pay my soft acknowledgments. [*kisses her hand*]

HILLARIA You must know he has mistaken her for another.

MRS FLAREIT For heaven's sake let me go, if Hillaria should be at home before me, I am ruined forever.

NARCISSA Hillaria! What does she mean?

SIR NOVELTY Narcissa's reputation shall be ever safe, while my life and fortune can protect it.

NARCISSA O Gad let me go, does the impudent creature take my name upon her – I'll pull off her head-cloths.

HILLARIA Oh! Fie! Cousin, what an ungenteel revenge would that be! Have a little patience.

NARCISSA [*throwing back her hood*] Oh! I am in a flame.

MRS FLAREIT But will you never see that common creature Flareit more?

SIR NOVELTY Never! Never! Feed on such homely fare after so rich a banquet?

MRS FLAREIT Nay, but you must hate her too.

SIR NOVELTY That I did long ago for her stinking breath! 'Tis true, I have been led away; but I detest a strumpet: I am informed she keeps a fellow under my nose, and for that reason, I would not make the settlement I lately gave her some hopes of: but e'en let her please herself for now I am wholly yours.

MRS FLAREIT Oh, now you charm me! But will you love me ever?

SIR NOVELTY Will you be ever kind?

MRS FLAREIT Be sure you never see Flareit more.

SIR NOVELTY When I do, may this soft hand revenge my perjury.

MRS FLAREIT So it shall, villain! [*strikes him a box on the ear, and unmasks*]

OMNES Ha! Ha! Ha!

SIR NOVELTY Flareit, the devil!

MRS FLAREIT What, will nothing but a maidenhead go down with you! Thou miserable conceited wretch – Foh! My breath stinks does it! I'm a homely puss! A strumpet, not worth your notice! Devil, I'll be revenged.

SIR NOVELTY [*holding his cheek*] Damn your revenge, I'm sure I feel it.

NARCISSA Really, Sir Novelty, I am obliged to you, for your kind thoughts of me, and your extraordinary care of my reputation.

SIR NOVELTY S'death, she here! Exposed to half the Town! –
Well, I must brazen it out however! [*walks unconcerned*]

MRS FLAREIT What! No pretence! No evasion now!

SIR NOVELTY There's no occasion for any, Madam.

MRS FLAREIT Come come, swear you knew me all this while.

SIR NOVELTY No, faith, Madam, I did not know you: for if I had,
you would not have found me so furious a lover.

MRS FLAREIT Furies and hell! Dares the monster own his guilt!
This is beyond all sufferance! Thou wretch, thou thing, thou
animal, that I (to the everlasting forfeiture of my sense and understanding) have made a man. For till thou knewest me, 'twas
doubted if thou wert of human kind. And dost thou think I'll
suffer such a worm as thee to turn against me! No! When I do,
may I be cursed to thy embraces all my life, and never know a
joy beyond thee.

SIR NOVELTY Why – wh—— wh—— what will your ladyship's
fury do, Madam?

MRS FLAREIT Only change my lodging, Sir.

SIR NOVELTY I shall keep mine, Madam, that you may know
where to find me when your fury is over – You see I am good
natured. [*walks by her*]

MRS FLAREIT [*aside*] This bravery's affected: I know he loves
me, and I'll pierce him to the quick: I have yet a surer way to
fool him.

HILLARIA Methinks the knight bears it bravely.

NARCISSA I protest the lady weeps.

YOUNG WORTHY She knows what she does, I'll warrant you.

ELDER WORTHY Aye, aye, the fox is a better politician than the lion.

MRS FLAREIT [*aside*] Now woman. [*with tears in her eyes*] Sir
Novelty, pray Sir, let me speak with you.

SIR NOVELTY Aye, Madam.

MRS FLAREIT Before we part (for I find I have irrecoverably lost
your love) let me beg of you, that from this hour, you ne'er will
see me more, or make any new attempts to deceive my easy temper: for I find my nature's such, I shall believe you, though to
my utter ruin.

SIR NOVELTY [*aside*] Pray heaven she be in earnest.

MRS FLAREIT One thing more, Sir; since our first acquaintance, you have received several letters from me; I hope you will be so much a gentleman as to let me have 'em again: those I have of yours shall be returned tomorrow morning. And now, Sir, wishing you as much happiness in her love, as you once pretended I could give you – I take of you my everlasting leave – Farewell, and may your next mistress love you till I hate you. [*is going*]

SIR NOVELTY So! Now must I seem to persuade her. Nay, prithee my dear! Why do you struggle so? Whither would you go?

MRS FLAREIT [*crying*] Pray, Sir, give me leave to pass, I can't bear to stay.

SIR NOVELTY What is't that frightens you?

MRS FLAREIT Your barbarous usage: pray let me go.

SIR NOVELTY Nay, if you are resolved, Madam, I won't press you against your will: your humble servant. [*leaves her*] And a happy riddance, stop my vitals.

MRS FLAREIT [*looks back*] Ha! Not move to call me back! So unconcerned! Oh! I could tear my flesh, stab every feature in this dull, decaying face, that wants a charm to hold him! Damn him! I loathe him too! But shall my pride now fall from such an height, and bear the torture unrevenged? No! My very soul's on fire, and nothing but the villain's blood shall quench it. Devil, have at thee. [*snatches Young Worthy's sword, and runs at him ⟨Sir Novelty⟩*]

YOUNG WORTHY Have a care, Sir.

SIR NOVELTY Let her alone, gentlemen, I'll warrant you. [*draws, and stands upon his guard. Young Worthy takes the sword from her, and holds her*]

MRS FLAREIT [*raving*] Prevented! Oh! I shall choke with boiling gall. Oh! Oh! Uumh! Let me go; I'll have his blood, his blood, his blood!

SIR NOVELTY Let her come, let her come, gentlemen!

MRS FLAREIT Death and vengeance, am I become his sport! He's pleased, and smiles to see me rage the more! But he shall find no fiend in hell can match the fury of a disappointed woman! – Scorned! Slighted! Dismissed without a parting pang! O torturing thought! May all the racks mankind e'er gave our easy sex, neglected love, decaying beauty, and hot raging lust light on me, if e'er I cease to be the eternal plague of his remaining life, nay, after death:

– When his, his black soul lies howling in despair,
I'd plunge to hell, and be his torment there.   [*Exit in a fury*]

ELDER WORTHY Sure Sir Novelty, you never loved this lady, if you are so indifferent at parting.

SIR NOVELTY Why faith Tom, to tell you the truth, her jealousy has been so very troublesome and expensive to me of late, that I have these three months sought an opportunity to leave her; but faith I had always more respect to my life, than to let her know it before.

HILLARIA Methinks, Sir Novelty, you had very little respect to her life, when you drew upon her.

SIR NOVELTY Why what would you have had me done, Madam? Complimented her with my naked bosom! No! No! Look ye, Madam, if she had made any advances, I could have disarmed her in *seconde*★ at the very first pass. – But come, ladies, as we walk, I'll beg your judgments in a particular nice fancy, that I intend to appear in, the very first week the Court is quite out of mourning.

ELDER WORTHY With all my heart, Sir Novelty. – Come ladies, considering how little rest you'll have tomorrow night, I think 'twere charity not to keep you up any longer.

YOUNG WORTHY Nay as for that matter, the night before a wedding is as unfit to sleep in, as the night following: imagination's a very troublesome bedfellow:– your pardon, ladies, I only speak for myself.

ELDER WORTHY [*to his servant*] See the coaches ready at St James's Gate.   [*Exeunt*]

SCENE ⟨II⟩

Amanda's house

Enter two Servants.

FIRST SERVANT Come, come, make haste; is the supper, and the music ready?

SECOND SERVANT It is, it is: well! Is he come?

FIRST SERVANT Aye, aye, I came before to tell my lady the news; that rogue Sly managed him rarely, he has been this half

★ *seconde*: the second of the eight parries recognised in second play.

hour pretending to pick the lock of the garden door: well poor lady! I wish her good luck with him: for she's certainly the best mistress living. Hark ye, is the wine strong, as she ordered it? Be sure you ply him home: for he must have two or three bumpers to qualify him for her design. See here he comes: away to your post.

Enter Loveless, conducted by Sly, Snap stealing after them.

LOVELESS Where the devil will this fellow lead me – Nothing but silence, and darkness! – Sure the house is haunted, and he has brought me to face the spirit at his wonted hour!

SLY There, there, in in, – slip on your night-gown, and refresh yourself, in the meantime I'll acquaint my lady, that you are here.
                                                                    [*Exit*]

LOVELESS Snap.

SNAP Aye, aye, Sir, I'll warrant you.   [*Exeunt*]

SCENE ⟨III⟩

Changes to an antechamber, a table, a light, a night-gown, and a periwig lying by

They re-enter.

LOVELESS Ha! What sweet lodgings are here? Where can this end?

SNAP Egad, Sir, I long to know. – Pray heaven we are not deluded hither to be starved. – Methinks I wish I had brought the remnants of my dinner with me.

LOVELESS Hark! I hear somebody coming! Hide yourself, rascal; I would not have you seen.

SNAP Well Sir, I'll line this trench in case of your being in danger. [*gets under the table*]

LOVELESS Ha! This night-gown and peruke don't lie here for nothing. – I'll make myself agreeable. [*puts 'em on*] – I have baulked many a woman in my time, for want of a clean shirt. –

Enter servants with a supper, after them, a man; a woman.

LOVELESS Ha! A supper! Heaven send it be no vision! If the meat be real, I shall believe the lady may prove flesh and blood. –

Now am I damnably puzzled to know whether this be she, or not?
Madam – [*bows*]

WOMAN Sir, my lady begs your pardon for a moment.

LOVELESS Humh! Her lady! Good! –

WOMAN She's unfortunately detained by some female visitors,
which she will despatch with all the haste imaginable; in the meantime, be pleased to refresh yourself with what the house affords.
– Pray Sir sit down.

LOVELESS Not alone; Madam, you must bear me company!

WOMAN To oblige you, Sir, I'll exceed my commission.

SNAP [*under the table*] Was there ever so unfortunate a dog! What
the devil put it in my head to hide myself before supper; why
this is worse than being locked into a closet, while another man's
abed with my wife! I suppose my master will take as much care
of me too, as I should of him, if I were in his place.

WOMAN Sir, my humble service to you. [*drinks*]

LOVELESS Madam, your humble servant: I'll pledge you. [*aside
to Snap*] Snap, when there's any danger I'll call you; in the meantime lie still, d'ye hear.

SNAP Egad I'll shift for myself then: [*snatches a flask unseen*] so, now
I am armed, defiance to all danger.

LOVELESS Madam, your lady's health.

SNAP Aye, aye, let it go round, I say. [*drinks*]

WOMAN Well really Sir my lady's very happy, that she has got
loose from her relations: for they were always teasing her about
you: but she defies 'em all now. – Come Sir, success to both your
wishes. [*drinks*]

LOVELESS Give me a glass; methinks this health inspires me – My
heart grows lighter for the weight of wine; – Here, Madam, –
prosperity to the man, that ventures most to please her.

WOMAN What think you of a song to support this gaiety?

LOVELESS With all my heart.

A song here.

LOVELESS You have obliged me, Madam; egad I like this girl! She
takes off her glass so feelingly, I am half persuaded she's of a
thirsty love: if her lady don't make a little haste, I find I shall
present my humble service to her.

Enter a Servant, who whispers Amanda's woman.

WOMAN Sir I ask your pardon, my lady has some commands for me, I will return immediately.

LOVELESS Your servant. – Methinks this is a very new method of intriguing!

SNAP Pray heaven it be new! For the old way commonly ended in a good beating: but a pox of danger I say, and so here's good luck to you, Sir.

LOVELESS Take heed, rogue, you don't get drunk, and discover yourself.

SNAP It must be with a fresh flask then; for this is expired *supernaculum*.*

LOVELESS Lie close, you dog; I hear somebody coming: I am impatient till I see this creature. This wine has armed me against all thoughts of danger! Pray heaven she be young, for then she can't want beauty. Ha! Here she comes! Now! Never-failing impudence assist me.

Enter Amanda loosely dressed.

AMANDA Where's my love? Oh, let me fly into his arms, and live forever there.

LOVELESS My life, my soul! [*runs and embraces her*] By heaven a tempting creature! Melting, soft, and warm – as my desire – Oh, that I could hide my face for ever thus, that undiscovered I might reap the harvest of a ripe desire, without the lingering pains of growing love. [*kisses her hand*]

AMANDA Look up, my lord, and bless me with a tender look, and let my talking eyes inform thee how I have languished for thy absence.

LOVELESS Let's retire, and chase away our fleeting cares with the raptures of untired love.

AMANDA Bless me! Your voice is strangely altered! Ha! Defend me! Who's this? Help! Help! Within there?

LOVELESS So! I am discovered! A pox on my tattling! That I could not hold my tongue till I got to her bed-chamber.

* *supernaculum*: a reference to the practice of turning up an emptied glass or cup on the left thumbnail to show that the liquor had been completely drunk, hence, to the last drop completely.

Enter Sly, and other Servants.

SLY Did your ladyship call help, Madam, what's the matter?

AMANDA Villain! Slave! Who's this? What ruffian have you brought me here – Dog, I'll have you murdered!

SLY [*looks in his face*] Bless me! O Lord! Dear Madam, I beg your pardon, as I hope to be saved, Madam; 'tis a mistake, I took him for Mr –

AMANDA Be dumb! Eternal blockhead – Here! Take this fellow, toss him in a blanket, and let him be turned out of my doors immediately.

SLY O pray! Dear Madam, for heaven's sake, I am a ruined man –

SNAP Ah! Snap, what will become of thee? Thou art fallen into the hands of a tigress that has lost her whelp; I have no hopes, but in my master's impudence! Heaven strengthen it!

AMANDA I'll hear no more! Away with him!

[*Exeunt the Servants with Sly*]

Now, Sir, for you; I expected –

LOVELESS A man, Madam, did you not?

AMANDA Not a stranger, Sir; but one that has a right and title to that welcome, which by mistake has been given to you.

LOVELESS Not an husband, I presume! He would not have been so privately conducted to your chamber, and in the dark too!

AMANDA Whoever it was, Sir, is not your business to examine: but if you would have civil usage, pray begone.

LOVELESS To be used civilly, I must stay, Madam: there can be no danger with so fair a creature!

AMANDA I doubt you are mad, Sir.

LOVELESS While my senses have such luscious food before 'em, no wonder if they are in some confusion, each striving to be foremost at the banquet, and sure my greedy eyes will starve the rest. [*approaching her*]

AMANDA Pray, Sir, keep your distance, lest your feeling too be gratified.

SNAP O Lord! Would I were a hundred leagues off at sea!

LOVELESS Then briefly thus, Madam, know I like and love you: now if you have so much generosity as to let me know, what title my pretended rival has to your person, or your inclinations: perhaps the little hopes I then may have of supplanting him, may make me leave your house. If not, my love shall still pursue you, though to the hazard of my life, which I shall not easily resign, while this sword can guard it, Madam.

AMANDA [*aside*] Oh, were this courage shown but in a better cause, how worthy were the man that owned it! ⟨*to Loveless*⟩ What is it, Sir, that you propose by this unnecessary trifling? Know then, that I did expect a lover, a man perhaps more brave than you: one, that if present, would have given you a shorter answer to your question.

LOVELESS I am glad to hear he's brave, however; it betrays no weakness in your choice: but if you'd still preserve, or raise the joys of love, remove him from your thoughts a moment, and in his room receive a warmer heart, a heart that must admire you more than he, because my passion's of a fresher date.

AMANDA What d'ye take me for?

LOVELESS A woman, and the most charming of your sex; one whose pointed eyes declare you formed for love, and though your words are flinty, your every look and motion all confess there's a secret fire within you, which must sparkle, when the steel of love provokes it. Come, now pull away your hand, and make me hold it faster.

AMANDA Nay, now you are rude, Sir.

LOVELESS If love be rudeness, let me be impudent: when we are familiar, rudeness will be love. No woman ever thought a lover rude after she had once granted him the favour.

AMANDA Pray Sir, forbear.

LOVELESS How can I? When my desire's so violent: oh, let me snatch the rosy dew from those distilling lips, and as you see your power to charm, so chide me with your pity. Why do you thus cruelly turn away your face? I own the blessing's worth an age's expectation, but if refused till merited, 'tis esteemed a debt. Would you oblige your lover, let loose your early kindness.

AMANDA I shall not take your counsel, Sir, while I know a woman's early kindness is as little sign of her generosity, as her generosity is a sign of her discretion: nor would I have you believe I am so ill provided for, that I need listen to any man's first addresses.

LOVELESS Why, Madam, would not you drink the first time you had a thirst?

AMANDA Yes; but not before I had.

LOVELESS If you can't drink, yet you may kiss the cup, and that may give you inclination.

AMANDA Your pardon, Sir, I drink out of nobody's glass but my own; as the man I love confines himself to me, so my inclination keeps me true to him.

LOVELESS That's a cheat imposed upon you, by your own vanity; for, when your back's turned, your very chambermaid sips of your leavings, and becomes your rival. Constancy in love is all a cheat, women of your understanding know it: the joys of love are only great when they are new, and to make 'em lasting, we must often change.

AMANDA Suppose 'twere a fresh lover I now expected.

LOVELESS Why then, Madam, your expectation's answered; for, I must confess I don't take you for an old acquaintance, though somewhere I have seen a face not much unlike you. Come, your arguments are vain; for they are so charmingly delivered, they but inspire me the more, as blows in battle raise the brave man's courage. Come, everything pleads for me, your beauty, wit, time, place, opportunity, and my own excess of raging passion.

AMANDA Stand off: distant as the globes of heaven and earth, that like a falling star I may shoot with greater force into your arms, and think it heaven to lie expiring there. [*runs into his arms*]

SNAP Ah! Ah! Ah! Rogue, the day's our own.

LOVELESS Thou sweetest, softest creature heaven e'er formed; thus let me twine myself about thy beauteous limbs, till struggling with the pangs of painful bliss, motionless and mute we yield to conquering love, both vanquished, and both victors.

AMANDA [*aside*] Can all this heat be real? Oh, why has hateful vice such power to charm? While poor abandoned virtue lies neglected.

LOVELESS Come, let us surfeit on our new-born raptures, let's waken sleeping nature with delight, till we may justly say, 'Now! Now! We live!'

AMANDA Come on, let's indulge the transports of our present bliss, and bid defiance to our future change of fate. Who waits here?

Enter Amanda's Woman.

AMANDA Bring me word immediately if my apartment's ready, as
I ordered it. ⟨*Exit Woman*⟩ Oh, I am charmed, I have found the
man to please me now: one that can, and dares maintain the noble
rapture of a lawless love: I own myself a libertine, a mortal foe to
that dull thing called virtue, that mere disease of sickly nature.
Pleasure's the end of life, and while I'm mistress of myself, and
fortune, I will enjoy it to the height. Speak freely then, (not
that I love like other women the nauseous pleasure of a little
flattery) but answer me like a man that scorns a lie: does my face
invite you, Sir? May I from what you see of me, propose a pleasure
to myself in pleasing you?

LOVELESS By heaven you may; I have seen all beauties that the
sun shines on, but never saw the sun out-shined before: I have
measured half the world in search of pleasure: but not returning
home, had ne'er been happy.

AMANDA [*aside*] Spoken like the man I wish might love me – Pray
heaven his words prove true. – ⟨*to Loveless*⟩ Be sure you never
flatter me, and when my person tires you, confess it freely: for
change whene'er you will, I'll change as soon: but while we
chance to meet still let it be with raging fire: no matter how
soon it dies, provided the small time it lasts, it burn the
fiercer.

LOVELESS Oh! Would the blinded world, like us, agree to change,
how lasting might the joys of love be? For thus beauty, though
stale to one, might somewhere else be new; and while this man
were blessed in leaving what he loathed, another were new
ravished in receiving what he ne'er enjoyed.

Re-enter Amanda's Woman.

WOMAN Madam, everything is according to your order.

LOVELESS Oh! Lead me to the scene of unsupportable delight,
rack me with pleasures never known before, till I lie gasping with
convulsive passion: this night let us be lavish to our unbounded
wishes.

> Give all our stock at once to raise the fire,
> And revel to the height of loose desire.   [*Exeunt*]

WOMAN Ah! What an happy creature's my lady now? There's many an unsatisfied wife about Town, would be glad to have her husband as wicked as my master, upon the same terms my lady has him. Few women I'm afraid would grudge an husband the laying out his stock of love, that could receive such considerable interest for it! Well – Now shan't I take one wink of sleep for thinking how they'll employ their time tonight – Faith, I must listen if I were to be hanged for't. [*listens at the door*]

SNAP So! My master's provided for, therefore 'tis time for me to take care of myself: I have no mind to be locked out of my lodging: I fancy there's room for two in the maid's bed, as well as my lady's – This same flask was plaguey strong wine – I find I shall storm, if she don't surrender fairly. By your leave, damsel.

WOMAN Bless me! Who's this? O Lord! What would you have? Who are you?

SNAP One that has a right and title to your body, my master having already taken possession of your lady's.

WOMAN Let me go, or I'll cry out.

SNAP Ye lie, ye dare not disturb your lady: but the better to secure you, thus I stop your mouth. [*kisses her*]

WOMAN Humh! – Lord bless me, is the devil in you, tearing one's things!

SNAP Then show me your bed-chamber.

WOMAN The devil shall have you first.

SNAP A shall have us both together then: here will I fix, [*takes her about the neck*] just in this posture till tomorrow morning: in the meantime when you find your inclination stirring, prithee give me a call, for at present I am very sleepy. [*seems to sleep*]

WOMAN Foh! How he stinks. [*he belches*] Ah! What a whiff was there – The rogue's as drunk as a sailor with a twelve months arrears in his pocket; or a Jacobite upon a day of ill news. I'll ha' nothing to say to him – Let me see, how shall I get rid of him – Oh! I have it! I'll soon make him sober I'll warrant him: so ho! Mr What d'ye call'um, where do you intend to lie tonight?

SNAP Humh. Why, where you lay last night, unless you change your lodging.

WOMAN Well, for once I'll take pity of you – Make no noise, but put out the candles, and follow me softly, for fear of disturbing my lady.

SNAP I'll warrant ye! There's no fear of spoiling her music, while we are playing the same tune.

SCENE ⟨IV⟩
Changes to a dark entry

They re-enter.

WOMAN Where are you? Lend me your hand.

SNAP Here! Here! Make haste, my dear concupiscence.

WOMAN Hold! Stand there a little, while I open the door gently without waking the footmen. [*she feels about, and opens a trap door*]

WOMAN Come along softly this way!

SNAP Whereabouts are you?

WOMAN Here, here, come straight forward. [*he goes forward, and falls into the cellar*]

SNAP O Lord! O Lord! I have broke my neck.

WOMAN I am glad to hear him say so, however I should be loath to be hanged for him. How d'ye, Sir?

SNAP D'ye, Sir! I am a league under ground.

WOMAN Whereabouts are you?

SNAP In hell, I think.

WOMAN No! No! You are but in the road to it, I dare say: ah dear! Why will you follow lewd women at this rate, when they lead you to the very gulf of destruction? I knew you would be swallowed up at last. Ha! Ha! Ha! Ha!

SNAP Ah, ye sneering whore!

WOMAN Shall I fetch you a Prayer Book, Sir? To arm you against the temptations of the flesh!

SNAP No! You need but show your own damned ugly face to do that – Hark ye, either help me out, or I'll hang myself, and swear you murdered me.

WOMAN Nay, if you are so bloody-minded, good night to ye, Sir. [*she offers to shut the door over him, and he catches hold on her*]

SNAP Ah! Ah! Ah! Have I caught you! Egad we'll pig together now.

WOMAN O Lord! Pray let me go, and I'll do anything.

SNAP And so you shall before I part with you. [*pulls her in to him*] And now, master, my humble service to you. [*he pulls the door over them*]

ACT FIVE

SCENE ⟨I⟩

Sir William Wisewoud's house

Enter Elder Worthy, Young Worthy, and a Lawyer with writing.

ELDER WORTHY Are the ladies ready?

YOUNG WORTHY Hillaria is just gone up to hasten her cousin, and Sir William will be here immediately.

ELDER WORTHY But hark you, brother! I have considered of it, and pray let me oblige you not to pursue your design upon his five thousand pound: for in short, 'tis no better than a cheat, and what a gentleman should scorn to be guilty of. Is not it sufficient that I consent to your wronging him of his daughter?

YOUNG WORTHY Your pardon, brother, I can't allow that a wrong: for his daughter loves me, her fortune, you know, he has nothing to do with; and it's a hard case a young woman shall not have the disposal of her heart. Love's a fever of the mind, which nothing but our own wishes can assuage, and I don't question but we shall find marriage a very cooling cordial. – And as to the five thousand pound, 'tis no more than what he has endeavoured to cheat his niece of.

ELDER WORTHY What d'ye mean, I take him for an honest man!

YOUNG WORTHY Oh! Very honest! As honest as an old agent to a new-raised regiment – No faith, I'll say that for him, he will not do an ill thing unless he gets by it. In a word, this so very honest Sir William, as you take him to be, has offered me the refusal of your mistress; and upon condition I will secure him five thousand pound upon my day of marriage with her, he will secure me her person, and ten thousand pound, the remaining part of her fortune! There's a guardian for ye! What think ye now, Sir?

ELDER WORTHY Why I think he deserves to be served in the same kind! I find age, and avarice are inseparable! Therefore even make what you can of him, and I will stand by you. But hark you, Mr Forge, are you sure it will stand good in law if Sir William signs the bond?

LAWYER In any court in England, Sir.

ELDER WORTHY Then there's your fifty pieces, and if it

succeeds, here are as many more in the same pocket to answer 'em: but mum – here comes Sir William and the ladies.

Enter Sir William Wisewoud, Hillaria, and Narcissa.

SIR WILLIAM Good morrow gentlemen! Mr Worthy, give you joy! Odso! If my heels were as light as my heart, I should ha' much ado to forbear dancing – Here, here, take her, man, [*gives him Narcissa's hand*] she's yours, and so is her thousand pound a year, and my five thousand pound shall be yours too .

YOUNG WORTHY [*aside*] You must ask me leave first.

SIR WILLIAM Odso! Is the lawyer come?

ELDER WORTHY He is, and all the writings are ready, Sir.

SIR WILLIAM Come, come, let's see man! What's this! Odd! This law is a plaguey troublesome thing; for nowadays it won't let a man give away his own, without repeating the particulars five hundred times over: when in former times a man might have held his title to twenty thousand pound a year, in the compass of an horn-book.

LAWYER That is, Sir, because there are more knaves nowadays and this age is more treacherous and distrustful than heretofore.

SIR WILLIAM That is, Sir, because there are more lawyers than heretofore: but come, what's this, prithee?

LAWYER These are the old writings of your daughter's fortune; this is Mr Worthy's settlement upon her, – and this, Sir, is your bond for five thousand pound to him: there wants nothing but filling up the blanks with the parties' names; if you please, Sir, I'll do't immediately.

SIR WILLIAM Do so.

LAWYER May I crave your daughter's Christian name, the rest I know, Sir.

SIR WILLIAM Narcissa! Prithee make haste –

YOUNG WORTHY [*aside to the Lawyer*] You know your business –

LAWYER I'll warrant you, Sir. [*sits to write*]

SIR WILLIAM Mr Worthy, methinks your brother does not relish your happiness as he should do; poor man! I'll warrant he wishes himself in his brother's condition!

YOUNG WORTHY Not I, I'll assure you, Sir.

SIR WILLIAM Niece! Niece! Have you no pity? Prithee look

upon him a little! Odd! He's a pretty young fellow – I am sure he loves you, or he would not have frequented my house so often! D'ye think his brother could not tell my daughter his own story without his assistance! Pshaw! Waw! I tell you, you were the beauty that made him so assiduous: come, come, give him your hand, and he'll soon creep into your heart, I'll warrant you: come, say the word, and make him happy.

HILLARIA What, to make myself miserable, Sir, marry a man without an estate?

SIR WILLIAM Hang an estate! True love's beyond all riches! 'Tis all dirt – mere dirt! – Beside han't you fifteen thousand pound to your portion?

HILLARIA I doubt, Sir, you would be loath to give him your daughter, though her fortune's larger.

SIR WILLIAM Odd, if he loved her but half so well, as he loves you, he should have her for a word speaking.

HILLARIA But, Sir, this asks some consideration –

NARCISSA You see, Mr Worthy, what an extraordinary kindness my father has for you!

YOUNG WORTHY Aye, Madam, and for your cousin too: but I hope with a little of your assistance we shall be both able very shortly to return it.

NARCISSA Nay, I was always ready to serve Hillaria; for heaven knows I only marry to revenge her quarrel to my father: I cannot forgive his offering to sell her.

YOUNG WORTHY Oh, you need not take such pains, Madam, to conceal your passion for me; you may own it without a blush upon your wedding-day.

NARCISSA My passion! When did you hear me acknowledge any? If I thought you could believe me guilty of such a weakness, though after I had married you, I would never look you in the face.

YOUNG WORTHY [aside] A very pretty humour, this faith! What a world of unnecessary sins have we two to answer for? For she has told more lies to conceal her love, than I have sworn false oaths to promote it. Well, Madam, at present I'll content myself with your giving me leave to love.

NARCISSA Which if I don't give, you'll take I suppose.

HILLARIA Well, uncle, I won't promise you, but I'll go to church and see them married; when we come back 'tis ten to one but I surprise you where you least think on.

SIR WILLIAM Why, that's well said! – Mr Worthy, now! Now's your time; Odd! I have so fired her, 'tis not in her power to deny you, man – To her! To her! I warrant her thy own, boy! You'll keep your word, five thousand pound upon the day of marriage.

YOUNG WORTHY I'll give you my bond upon demand, Sir.

SIR WILLIAM Oh! I dare take your word, Sir. – Come, lawyer, have you done? Is all ready?

LAWYER All, Sir! This is your bond to Mr Worthy: will you be pleased to sign that first, Sir?

SIR WILLIAM Aye, aye; let's see! [*reads*] 'The condition of this obligation'. Hum um – Come, lend me the pen. – There – Mr Worthy, I deliver this as my act and deed to you, and heaven send you a good bargain – Niece, will you witness it? [*which she does*] – Come, lawyer, your fist too. [*Lawyer witnesses it*]

LAWYER Now, Sir, if you please to sign the jointure.

ELDER WORTHY Come on – Sir William, I deliver this to you for the use of your daughter. Madam, will you give yourself the trouble once more? [*Hillaria sets her hand*] Come, Sir – [*the Lawyer does the same*] So, now let a coach be called as soon as you please, Sir.

SIR WILLIAM You may save that charge, I saw your own at the door.

ELDER WORTHY Your pardon, Sir, that would make our business too public; for which reason, Sir William, I hope you will excuse our not taking you along with us.   [*Exit a Servant*]

SIR WILLIAM Aye, aye, with all my heart, the more privacy the less expense. But pray, what time may I expect you back again? For Amanda has sent to me for the writings of her husband's estate: I suppose she intends to redeem the mortgage, and I am afraid she will keep me there till dinner-time.

YOUNG WORTHY Why, about that time she has obliged me to bring some of her nearest friends to be witnesses of her good or evil fortune with her husband: methinks I long to know her success; if you please, Sir William, we'll meet you there.

SIR WILLIAM With all my heart –

Enter a Servant.

Well! Is the coach come?

SERVANT It is at the door, Sir.

SIR WILLIAM Come, gentlemen, no ceremony; your time's short.

ELDER WORTHY Your servant, Sir William.

    [*Exeunt Elder Worthy, Young Worthy, Narcissa and Hillaria*]

SIR WILLIAM So! Here's five thousand pounds got with a wet finger! This 'tis to read mankind! I knew a young lover would never think he gave too much for his mistress! Very well! If I don't suddenly meet with some misfortune, I shall never be able to bear this tranquillity of mind.   [*Exit*]

SCENE ⟨II⟩

Changes to Amanda's house

Enter Amanda sola.

AMANDA Thus far my hopes have all been answered, and my disguise of vicious love has charmed him even to a madness of impure desire: – But now I tremble to pull off the mask, lest barefaced virtue should fright him from my arms for ever. Yet sure there are charms in virtue, nay, stronger, and more pleasing far, than hateful vice can boast of! Else why have holy martyrs perished for its sake? While lewdness ever gives severe repentance, and unwilling death. – Good heaven inspire my heart, and hang upon my tongue the force of truth and eloquence, that I may lure this wandering falcon back to love and virtue – He comes, and now my dreaded task begins!

Enter Loveless in new clothes.

AMANDA How fare you, Sir? D'ye not already think yourself confined? Are you not tired with my easy love?

LOVELESS Oh! Never! Never! You have so filled my thoughts with pleasures past, that but to reflect on 'em is still new rapture to my soul, and the bliss must last while I have life or memory.

AMANDA No flattery, Sir! I loved you for your plain-dealing; and to preserve my good opinion, tell me, what think you of the grape's persuading juice! Come, speak freely, would not the next tavern-bush put all this out of your head?

LOVELESS Faith, Madam, to be free with you, I am apt to think
you are in the right on't: for though love and wine are two very
fine tunes, yet they make no music, if you play them both together, separately they ravish us: thus the mistress ought to
make room for the bottle, the bottle for the mistress, and both
to wait the call of inclination.

AMANDA That's generously spoken – I have observed, Sir, in all
your discourse you confess something of a man, that has thoroughly
known the world! – Pray give me leave to ask you, of what condition you are, and whence you came?

LOVELESS Why, in the first place, Madam, – by birth, I am a
gentleman; by ill friends, good wine, and false dice, almost a
beggar: but by your servants mistaking me, the happiest man,
that ever love and beauty smiled on.

AMANDA One thing more, Sir! Are you married? – [*aside*] Now
my fears.

LOVELESS I was, but very young.

AMANDA What was your wife?

LOVELESS A foolish loving thing, that built castles in the air, and
thought it impossible for a man to forswear himself when he
made love.

AMANDA Was she not virtuous?

LOVELESS Uumh! Yes faith, I believe she might, I was ne'er
jealous of her.

AMANDA Did you ne'er love her?

LOVELESS Ah! Most damnably at first, for she was within two
women of my maidenhead.

AMANDA What's become of her?

LOVELESS Why, after I had been from her beyond sea, about seven
or eight years, like a very loving fool she died of the pip, and
civilly left me the world free to range in.

AMANDA Why did you leave her?

LOVELESS Because she grew stale, and I could not whore in quiet
for her: besides she was always exclaiming against my extravagancies, particularly my gaming; which she so violently opposed,
that I fancied a pleasure in it, which since I never found; for in
one month I lost between eight and ten thousand pound, which
I had just before called in to pay my debts. This misfortune made

my creditors come so thick upon me, that I was forced to mortgage the remaining part of my estate to purchase new pleasure,
which I knew I could not do on this side the water, amidst the
clamours of insatiate duns, and the more hateful noise of a complaining wife.

AMANDA Don't you wish you had taken her counsel though?

LOVELESS Not I, faith, Madam.

AMANDA Why so?

LOVELESS Because 'tis to no purpose: I am master of more philosophy, than to be concerned at what I can't help – But now,
Madam, – pray give me leave to inform myself as far in your
condition.

AMANDA In a word, Sir, till you know me throughly, I must own
myself a perfect riddle to you.

LOVELESS Nay, nay, I know you are a woman: but in what circumstances? Wife, or widow?

AMANDA A wife, Sir; a true, a faithful, and a virtuous wife.

LOVELESS Humh! Truly, Madam, your story begins something
like a riddle! A virtuous wife say you! What, and was you never
false to your husband!

AMANDA I never was by heaven! For him, and only him I still
love above the world.

LOVELESS Good again! Pray, Madam, don't your memory fail
you sometimes? Because I fancy you don't remember what you do
overnight!

AMANDA I told you, Sir, I should appear a riddle to you: but if
my heart will give me leave, I'll now unloose your fettered
apprehension – But I must first amaze you more – Pray, Sir,
satisfy me in one particular – 'tis this – What are your undissembled thoughts of virtue? Now, if you can, shake off your
loose unthinking part, and summon all your force of manly reason
to resolve me.

LOVELESS Faith, Madam, methinks this is a very odd question for
a woman of your character. I must confess you have amazed
me.

AMANDA It ought not to amaze you! Why should you think I
make a mock of virtue? But last night you allowed my understanding greater than is usual in our sex: if so, can you believe I

have no farther sense of happiness than what this empty, dark and barren world can yield me! No, I have yet a prospect of a sublimer bliss, an hope, that carries me to the bright regions of eternal day.

LOVELESS ⟨*aside*⟩ Humh! I thought her last night's humour was too good to hold. I suppose by and by she will ask me to go to church with her – Faith, Madam, in my mind this discourse is a little out of the way. You told me I should be acquainted with your condition, and at present that's what I had rather be informed of.

AMANDA Sir, you shall: but first, this question must be answered; your thoughts of virtue, Sir? – By all my hopes of bliss hereafter, your answering this pronounces half my good, or evil fate forever: but on my knees I beg you do not speak till you have weighed it well – Answer me with the same truth, and sincerity, as you would answer heaven at your latest hour.

LOVELESS Your words confound me, Madam; some wondrous secret sure lies ripened in your breast, and seems to struggle for its fatal birth! What is it I must answer you?

AMANDA Give me your real thoughts of virtue, Sir; can you believe there ever was a woman truly mistress of it, or is it only notion?

LOVELESS Let me consider, Madam. [*aside*] What can this mean? Why is she so earnest in her demands, and begs me to be serious, as if her life depended on my answer – I will resolve her, as I ought, as truth, and reason, and the strange occasion seems to press me. – ⟨*to Amanda*⟩ Most of your sex confound the very name of virtue; for they would seem to live without desires, which could they do, that were not virtue but the defect of unperforming nature, and no praise to them: for who can boast a victory when they have no foe to conquer? Now she alone gives the fairest proofs of virtue, whose conscience and whose force of reason can curb her warm desires, when opportunity would raise 'em: that such a woman may be found I dare believe.

AMANDA May I believe that from your soul you speak this undissembled truth?

LOVELESS Madam, you may. But still you rack me with amazement! Why am I asked so strange a question?

AMANDA I'll give you ease immediately. – Since then you have allowed a woman may be virtuous – How will you excuse the man who leaves the bosom of a wife, so qualified, for the abandoned pleasures of deceitful prostitutes! Ruins her fortune! Condemns her counsel! Loathes her bed, and leaves her to the lingering miseries of despair and love: while in return of all these wrongs, she his poor forsaken wife meditates no revenge, but what her piercing tears, and secret vows to heaven for his conversion yield her: yet still loves on, is constant and unshaken to the last! Can you believe, that such a man can live without the stings of conscience, and yet be master of his senses! Conscience! Did you ne'er feel the checks of it! Did it never, never tell you of your broken vows?

LOVELESS That you should ask me this, confounds my reason – And yet your words are uttered with such a powerful accent, they have awaked my soul, and strike my thoughts with horror and remorse – [*stands in a fixed posture*]

AMANDA Then let me strike you nearer, deeper yet: – but arm your mind with gentle pity first, or I am lost for ever.

LOVELESS I am all pity, all faith, expectation, and confused amazement: be kind, be quick, and ease my wonder.

AMANDA Look on me well: revive your dead remembrance: and oh! for pity's sake [*kneels*] hate me not for loving long, faithfully forgive this innocent attempt of a despairing passion, and I shall die in quiet.

LOVELESS Hah! Speak on!

AMANDA It will not be! – The word's too weighty for my faltering tongue, and my soul sinks beneath the fatal burden. Oh! [*falls on the ground*]

LOVELESS Ha! She faints! Look up fair creature! Behold a heart that bleeds for your distress, and fain would share the weight of your oppressing sorrows! Oh! Thou hast raised a thought within me, that shocks my soul.

AMANDA 'Tis done! [*rising*] The conflict's passed, and heaven bids me speak undaunted. Know then, even all the boasted raptures of your last night's love you found in your Amanda's arms – I am your wife.

LOVELESS Hah!

AMANDA Forever blessed or miserable, as your next breath shall sentence me.

LOVELESS My wife! Impossible! Is she not dead! How shall I believe thee?

AMANDA How time and my afflictions may have altered me I know not: but here's an indelible confirmation. [*bares her arm*] These speaking characters, which in their cheerful bloom our early passions mutually recorded.

LOVELESS Hah! 'Tis here – 'Tis no illusion, but my real name; which seems to unbraid me as a witness of my perjured love – O I am confounded with my guilt, and tremble to behold thee – Pray give me leave to think. [*turns from her*]

AMANDA I will. [*kneels*] But you must look upon me. For only eyes can hear the language of the eyes, and mine have sure the tenderest tale of love to tell, that ever misery, at the dawn of rising-hope could utter.

LOVELESS I have wronged you. Oh! Rise! Basely wronged you! And can I see your face?

AMANDA One kind, one pitying look cancels those wrongs for ever: and oh! forgive my fond presuming passion; for from my soul I pardon and forgive you all: all, all but this, the greatest, your unkind delay of love.

LOVELESS Oh! Seal my pardon with thy trembling lips, while with this tender grasp of fond reviving love I seize my bliss and stifle all thy wrongs forever. [*embraces her*]

AMANDA No more; I'll wash away their memory in tears of flowing joy.

LOVELESS O thou hast roused me from my deep lethargy of vice! For hitherto my soul has been enslaved to loose desires, to vain deluding follies, and shadows of substantial bliss: but now I wake with joy to find my rapture real. – Thus let me kneel and pay my thanks to her, whose conquering virtue has at last subdued me. Here will I fix, thus prostrate sigh my shame, and wash my crimes in never ceasing tears of penitence.

AMANDA O rise! This posture heaps new guilt on me! Now you over-pay me.

LOVELESS Have I not used thee like a villain! For almost ten long years deprived thee of my love, and ruined all thy fortune! But I

will labour, dig, beg or starve, to give new proofs of my unfeigned affection.

AMANDA Forbear this tenderness, lest I repent of having moved
your soul so far: you shall not need to beg. Heaven has provided
for us beyond its common care. 'Tis now near two years since
my Uncle Sir William Wealthy sent you the news of my pretended death. Knowing the extravagance of your temper he
thought it fit you should believe no other of me; and about a
month after he had sent you that advice, poor man, he died, and
left me in the full possession of two thousand pounds a year, which
I now cannot offer as a gift, because my duty, and your lawful
right, makes you the undisputed master of it.

LOVELESS How have I laboured for my own undoing, while in
despite of all my follies, kind heaven resolved my happiness.

Enter a Servant.

SERVANT [*to Amanda*] Madam, Sir William Wisewoud has sent
your ladyship the writings you desired him, and says he'll wait
upon you immediately.

AMANDA Now Sir, if you please to withdraw awhile, you may
inform yourself how fair a fortune you are master of.

LOVELESS None, none that can outweigh a virtuous mind, while
in my arms I thus can circle thee, I grasp more treasure, than in a
day the posting sun can travel o'er. Oh! Why have I so long been
blind to the perfections of thy mind and person! Not knowing thee
a wife, I found thee charming beyond the wishes of luxurious
love. Is it then a name, a word, shall rob thee of thy worth? Can
fancy be a surer guide to happiness than reason? Oh! I have wan-
dered like a benighted wretch, and lost myself in life's unpleasing
journey.
'Twas heedless fancy first, that made me stray,
But reason now breaks forth, and lights me on my way.   [*Exeunt*]

SCENE ⟨III⟩

Changes to an entry

Enter three or four Servants.

FIRST SERVANT Prithee Tom make haste below there; my lady has ordered dinner at half an hour after one precisely: look out some of the red that came in last.

Two of the Servants haul Snap and Amanda's Woman out of the cellar.

SECOND SERVANT Come Sir, come out here, and show your face.

WOMAN O I am undone; ruined!

SECOND SERVANT Pray Sir, who are you, and what was your business, and how in the devil's name came you in here?

SNAP Why truly, Sir, the flesh led me to the cellar-door; but I believe the devil pushed me in – that gentlewoman can inform you better.

THIRD SERVANT Pray Mrs Anne how came you two together in the cellar?

WOMAN [*sobbing*] Why he – he – pu—— pu—— pulled me in.

THIRD SERVANT But how the devil came he in?

WOMAN He fe—— fe—— fe—— fell in.

SECOND SERVANT How came he into the house?

WOMAN I don—— do—— don't know.

SECOND SERVANT Ah! You are a crocodile; I thought what was the reason I could never get a good word from you! What, in a cellar too! But come, Sir, we will take care of you however. Bring him along, we will first carry him before my lady; and then toss him in a blanket.

SNAP Nay but gentlemen! Dear gentlemen.   [*Exeunt*]

Enter Loveless, Amanda, Elder Worthy, Young Worthy,
Narcissa and Hillaria.

ELDER WORTHY This is indeed a joyful day, we must all congratulate your happiness.

AMANDA Which while our lives permit us to enjoy, we must still reflect with gratitude on the generous author of it: Sir, we owe you more than words can pay you.

LOVELESS Words are indeed too weak; therefore let my gratitude be dumb till it can speak in actions.

YOUNG WORTHY The success of the design I thought on, sufficiently rewards me.

HILLARIA When I reflect upon Amanda's past afflictions, I could almost weep to think of his unexpected change of fortune.

ELDER WORTHY Methinks her fair example should persuade all constant wives ne'er to repine at unrewarded virtue. Nay even my brother being the first promoter of it, has atoned for all the looseness of his character.

LOVELESS I never can return his kindness.

NARCISSA In a short time Sir, I suppose you'll meet with an opportunity, if you can find a receipt to preserve love after his honeymoon's over.

LOVELESS The receipt is easily found, Madam; love's a tender plant, which cannot live out of a warm bed: you must take care with undissembled kindness to keep him from the northern blast of jealousy.

NARCISSA But I have heard your experienced lovers make use of coldness, and that's more agreeable to my inclination.

LOVELESS Coldness, Madam, before marriage, like throwing a little water upon a clear fire, makes it burn the fiercer: but after marriage you must still take care to lay on fresh fuel.

NARCISSA O fie, Sir! How many examples have we of men's hating their wives for being too fond of 'em?

LOVELESS No wonder Madam: you may stifle a flame by heaping on too great a load.

NARCISSA Nay Sir, if there be no other way of destroying his passion; for me he may love till Doomsday.

ELDER WORTHY Humph! Don't you smell powder, gentlemen? Sir Novelty is not far off.

LOVELESS What not our fellow collegian, I hope, that was expelled the university for beating the proctor.

ELDER WORTHY The same.

LOVELESS Does that weed grow still?

ELDER WORTHY Aye faith, and as rank as ever, as you shall see, for here he comes.

Enter Sir Novelty.

SIR NOVELTY Ladies your humble servant; dear Loveless let me embrace thee, I am o'erjoyed at thy good fortune: stop my vitals – the whole Town rings of it already – my Lady Tattletongue has tired a pair of horses in spreading the news about. Hearing gentlemen that you were all met upon an extraordinary good occasion, I could not resist this opportunity of joining my joy with yours: for you must know I am –

NARCISSA Married, Sir!

SIR NOVELTY To my liberty, Madam, I am just parted from my mistress.

NARCISSA And pray Sir, how do you find yourself after it?

SIR NOVELTY The happiest man alive, Madam. Pleasant! Easy! Gay! Light! And free as air: hah; [*capers*] I beg your ladyship's pardon, Madam, but upon my soul I cannot confine my rapture.

NARCISSA Are you so indifferent Sir?

SIR NOVELTY Oh! Madam she's engaged already to a Temple beau! I saw 'em in a coach together so fond! And bore it with as unmoved a countenance as Tom Worthy does a thundering jest in a comedy when the whole house roars at it.

YOUNG WORTHY Pray Sir, what occasioned your separation?

SIR NOVELTY Why this Sir, – you must know she being still possessed with a brace of implacable devils, called revenge and jealousy, dogged me this morning to the chocolate-house, where I was obliged to leave a letter for a young foolish girl, that – (you will excuse me Sir) which I had no sooner delivered to the maid of the house; but whip! She snatches it out of her hand, flew at her like a dragon, tore off her head-clothes, flung down three or four sets of lemonade-glasses, dashed my Lord Whiffle's chocolate in his face, cut him over the nose, and had like to have strangled me in my own steinkirk.

LOVELESS Pray Sir, how did this end?

SIR NOVELTY Comically, stop my vitals! For in the cloud of powder, that she had battered out of the beaux' periwigs I stole away: after which I sent a friend to her, with an offer, which she readily accepted: three hundred pound a year during life, provided she would renounce all claims to me, and resign my person to my own disposal.

ELDER WORTHY Methinks, Sir Novelty, you were a little too extravagant in your settlement, considering how the price of women is fallen.

SIR NOVELTY Therefore I did it – to be the first man should raise their price: for the devil take me, but the women of the Town now come down so low, that my very footman, while he kept my place t'other day at the playhouse, carried a mask out of the side-box with him, and stop my vitals, the rogue is now taking physic for't.

Enter the Servants with Snap.

FIRST SERVANT Come bring him along there.

LOVELESS How now! Hah! Snap in hold: pray let's know the business; release him gentlemen.

FIRST SERVANT Why, an't please you, Sir, this fellow was taken in the cellar with my lady's woman! She says he kept her in by force, and was rude to her: she stands crying here without, and begs her ladyship to do her justice.

AMANDA Mr Loveless, we are both the occasion of this misfortune, and for the poor girl's reputation-sake, something should be done.

LOVELESS Snap, answer me directly, have you lain with this poor girl?

SNAP Why, truly Sir, imagining you were doing little less with my lady, I must confess, I did commit familiarity with her, or so Sir!

LOVELESS Then you shall marry her, Sir! No reply unless it be your promise.

SNAP Marry her? O Lord, Sir! After I have lain with her? Why, Sir! How the devil can you think a man can have any stomach to his dinner, after he has had three or four slices off of the spit?

LOVELESS Well sirrah! To renew your appetite, and because thou hast been my old acquaintance, I'll give thee a hundred pounds with her, and thirty pound a year during life, to set up in some honest employment.

SNAP Ah! Sir, now I understand you, the Lord reward you! Well

Sir, I partly find that the genteel scenes of our lives are pretty well over; and I thank heaven, that I have so much grace left, that I can repent, when I have no more opportunities of being wicked, – come spouse! [*she enters*] Here's my hand, the rest of my body shall be forthcoming, ah! Little did my master and I think last night that we were robbing our own orchards! Look ye child, you must not expect me to be over-troublesome tonight; for faith and troth.
I'm afraid that the height of my pleasure is over;
I must drudge like an husband, for being too lavish a lover.

[Exeunt 〈Snap and Woman〉]

ELDER WORTHY Brother, stand upon your guard! Here comes Sir William.

Enter Sir William Wisewoud.

SIR WILLIAM Joy, joy to you all! Madam, I congratulate your good fortune. Well, my dear rogue must not I give thee joy too? Ha!

YOUNG WORTHY If you please, Sir: but I confess, I have more than I deserve already.

SIR WILLIAM And art thou married?

YOUNG WORTHY Yes Sir, I am married!

SIR WILLIAM Odso, I am glad on't: I dare swear, thou dost not grudge me the five thousand pounds.

YOUNG WORTHY Not I really Sir: you have given me all my soul could wish for, but the addition of a father's blessing. [*kneels with Narcissa*]

SIR WILLIAM Humh! What dost thou mean? I am none of thy father.

YOUNG WORTHY This lady is your daughter, Sir, I hope.

SIR WILLIAM Prithee get up! Prithee get up! Thou art stark mad! True, I believe she may be my daughter: well, and so Sir!

YOUNG WORTHY If she be not, I'm certain she's my wife, Sir.

SIR WILLIAM Humh! Mr Worthy, pray Sir do me the favour to help me to understand your brother a little – do you know anything of his being married?

ELDER WORTHY Then without any abuse, Sir William, he married your daughter this very morning, not an hour ago, Sir.

SIR WILLIAM Pray Sir whose consent had you, who advised you to it?

YOUNG WORTHY Our mutual love and your consent Sir, which these writings, entitling her to a thousand pound a year, and this bond, whereby you have obliged yourself to pay me five thousand pound upon our day of marriage, are sufficient proofs of.

SIR WILLIAM He, he! I gave your brother such a bond, Sir.

YOUNG WORTHY You did so! But the obligation is to me; look there Sir.

SIR WORTHY Very good! This is my hand, I must confess Sir: and what then?

YOUNG WORTHY Why then I expect my five thousand pound, Sir: pray Sir, do you know my name?

SIR WILLIAM I am not drunk Sir, I am sure it was Worthy, and Jack, or Tom, or Dick, or something.

YOUNG WORTHY No Sir, I'll show you – 'tis William, look you there Sir; you should have taken more care of the lawyer Sir, that filled up the blank.

ELDER WORTHY So now his eyes are open!

SIR WILLIAM And have you married my daughter against my consent, and tricked me out of five thousand pounds Sir?

HILLARIA His brother, Sir, has married me too with my consent, and I am not tricked out of five thousand pounds.

SIR WILLIAM Insulting witch! Look ye Sir! I never had a substantial cause to be angry in my life before: but now I have reason on my side, I will indulge my indignation most immoderately: I must confess, I have not patience to wait the slow redress of a tedious law-suit! Therefore am resolved to right myself the nearest way – Draw, draw Sir, you must not enjoy my five thousand pound, though I sling as much more after it in procuring a pardon for killing you. [*they hold him*] Let me come at him, I'll murder him! I'll cut him! I'll tear him! I'll broil him! And eat him! A rogue! A dog! A cursed dog! A cut-throat, murdering dog!

ELDER WORTHY O fie, Sir William, how monstrous is this passion?

SIR WILLIAM You have disarmed me, but I shall find a time to poison him.

LOVELESS Think better on't Sir William, your daughter has

married a gentleman; and one whose love entitles him to her person.

SIR WILLIAM Aye, but the five thousand pounds Sir! Why, the very report of his having such a fortune, will ruin him, I warrant you. Within this week he will have more duns at his chamber in a morning, than a gaming lord after a good night at the Groom Porters, or a poet upon the fourth day of his new play. I shall never be pleased with paying it against my own consent, Sir.

HILLARIA Yet you would have had me done it Sir William: but however I heartily wish you would as freely forgive Mr Worthy, as I do you Sir.

SIR WILLIAM I must confess this girl's good nature makes me ashamed of what I have offered: but Mr Worthy I did not expect such usage from a man of your character: I always took you for a gentleman.

ELDER WORTHY You shall find me no other, Sir: brother a word with you!

LOVELESS Sir William, I have some obligations to this gentleman, and have so great a confidence in your daughter's merit, and his love; that I here promise to return you your five thousand pounds if after the expiration of one year, you are then dissatisfied in his being your son-in-law.

YOUNG WORTHY But see brother, he has forestalled your purpose.

ELDER WORTHY Mr Loveless, you have been beforehand with me, but you must give me leave to offer Sir William my joint-security for what you have promised him.

LOVELESS With all my heart Sir! Dare you take our bonds, Sir William?

YOUNG WORTHY Hold gentlemen! I should blush to be obliged to that degree: therefore Sir William, as the first proof of that respect and duty I owe a father, I here unasked return your bond, and will henceforth expect nothing from you, but as my conduct shall deserve it.

AMANDA This is indeed a generous act, methinks 'twere pity it should go unrewarded.

SIR WILLIAM Nay, now you vanquish me! After this I can't suspect your future conduct: there Sir! 'Tis yours, I acknowledge the bond, and with you all the happiness of a bridal bed. Heaven's blessing on you both. Now rise my boy! And let the world know 'twas I set you upon your legs again.

YOUNG WORTHY I'll study to deserve your bounty, Sir.

LOVELESS Now Sir William, you have shown yourself indeed a father. This prudent action has secured your daughter from the usual consequence of a stolen marriage; a parent's curse. Now she must be happy in her love, while you have such a tender care on't.

AMANDA This is indeed a happy meeting, we all of us have drawn our several prizes in the lottery of human life: therefore I beg our joys may be united: not one of us must part this day. The ladies I'll entreat my guests.

LOVELESS The rest are mine, and I hope will often be so.

AMANDA 'Tis yet too soon to dine: therefore to divert us in the meantime, what think you of a little music, the subject perhaps not improper to this occasion!

ELDER WORTHY 'Twill oblige us, Madam, we are all lovers of it.

A song, set by Mr Frank

Cupid is seated on a throne, attended with
a Chorus.

FAME   Hail! hail! Victorious love!
              To whom all hearts below,
              With no less pleasure bow,
              Than to the thundering Jove,
              The happy souls above.

CHORUS   Hail, &c.

Enter Reason.

REASON   Cease, cease fond fools your empty noise,
              And follow not such fleeting toys,
              Love gives you but a short-lived bliss,
              But I bestow immortal happiness.

CUPID   Rebellious Reason, talk no more,
              Of all my slaves, I thee abhor:
              But thou, alas! dost strive in vain
              To free the lover from a pleasing chain,

In spite of reason, love shall live and reign.

CHORUS   In spite, &c.

                                 [*A martial symphony*]

                Enter Honour.

HONOUR   What wretch would follow love's alarms,
            When honour's trumpet sounds to arms:
            Hark! How the warlike notes inspire
            In every breast a glowing fire.

CUPID   Hark how it swells with love and desire.

HONOUR   Behold, behold the married state
            By thee too soon betrayed,
            Repenting now too late.

         Enter Marriage with his yoke.

MARRIAGE Oh! Tell me cruel god of love,
            Why didst thou my thoughts possess
            With an eternal round of happiness,
            And yet alas! I lead a wretched life,
            Doomed to this galling yoke – the emblem of a wife.

CUPID   Ungrateful wretch! How dar'st thou love upbraid?
            I gave thee raptures in the bridal-bed.

MARRIAGE Long since alas! The airy vision's fled.
            And I with wandring flames my passion feed.
            Oh! Tell me powerful god
            Where I shall find
            My former peace of mind!

CUPID   Where first I promised thee a happy life,
            There thou shalt find it in a virtuous wife.

CUPID ⎫ Go home unhappy wretch, and mourn
AND   ⎬ For all thy guilty passion past,
FAME ⎭ There thou shalt those joys return,
            Which shall for ever, ever last.

                            [*End with the first chorus*]

LOVELESS 'Twas generously designed, and all my life to come shall show how I approve the moral. Oh! Amanda! Once more receive me to thy arms; and while I am there, let all the world

confess my happiness. By my example taught let every man, whose fate has bound him to a married life, beware of letting loose his wild desires: for if experience may be allowed to judge, I must proclaim the folly of a wandering passion: the greatest happiness we can hope on earth,
And sure the nearest to the joys above,
Is the chaste rapture of a virtuous love.

⟨*Exeunt*⟩

EPILOGUE

Spoken by Miss Cross, who sung Cupid

Now gallants, for the author: first to you
Kind City-gentlemen, o'th' middle-row:
He hopes you nothing to his charge can lay,
There's not one cuckold made in all his play,
Nay, you must own, if you'll believe your eyes,
He draws his pen against your enemies:
For he declares today, he merely strives
To maul the beaux – because they maul your wives.
Now, Sirs, to you, whose sole religion's drinking,
Whoring, roaring, without the pain of thinking;
He fears h'as made a fault, you'll ne'er forgive,
A crime, beyond the hopes of a reprieve;
An honest rake forego the joys of life!
His whores, and wine! T'embrace a dull cast wife;
Such out of fashion stuff! But then again!
He's lewd for above four acts, gentlemen!
For faith he knew, when once he'd changed his fortune,
And reformed his vice, 'twas time – to drop the curtain:
Four acts for your coarse palates was designed
But then the ladies' taste is more refined,
They for Amanda's sake will sure be kind.
Pray let this figure once your pity move,
Can you resist the pleading god of love!
In vain my prayers the other sex pursue,
Unless your conquering smiles their stubborn hearts subdue.

NOTES

The copy text used is that of the first edition of 1696 in the Brotherton Collection, University of Leeds.

Abbreviations
Q1   The first quarto edition, 1696
DW   Dramatic Works, 4 vols, 1760
'Mrs' has been added to Flareit throughout. An italic '*I*' has been replaced by roman 'I' in parts of the text.

349.2   Scene: The/SCENE *The* Q1
349.22   lived/liv'd Q1
352.4   kicked,/kick'd Q1/kick'd? DW
352.22   than/then Q1
352.37   Sir, though . . . pounds, one/Sir, (though . . . *l.*) one Q1
354.23   man? I'll/man, I'll Q1
354.26   faith. When/faith, when Q1
355.20   beau's/beaux Q1
355.28   vanity./vanity? Q1
355.30   you?/you. Q1
355.31   e'er/ere Q1/ever DW
357.4   sneaking DW/meaking Q1
358.33   handsome./handsom Q1
360.15   days. I/days, I Q1
361.28   designs. In/designs in Q1
362.8   ⟨Hillaria *walks off*⟩/Q1 places [*walks off*] after Narcissa's 'humble servant'
363.34   off/of Q1
364.4   [*Exit*]/[*Exeunt*] Q1
365.2   Scene: a/*Scene* a Q1
365.18   I nauseate DW/inauseate Q1
365.29   any/an Q1
365.31   me, in/me in Q1
367.16   *entendu*/*entendue* Q1 DW
367.34   I'll/Ill Q1
368.30   you. Come/you, Come Q1
370.19   ),/,) Q1

372.20	Centurine, the Q1 / Centurine, Bardash DW
373.5	sit DW / set Q1
373.7	everybody / Every Body Q1 / every one DW
373.32	Mr Worthy? / Mr Worthy, Q1
374.7	Mrs Flareit– / Mrs Flareit. – Q1
374.11	pounds' / Pounds Q1
375.27	health, is / health is Q1
376.5	your wit DW / your, wit Q1
377.21	over-shy lady / over shy-Lady Q1
378.22	),/,) Q1
378.32	[*to* Amanda] / Q1 places after *Enter a Servant*
379.14	[*to* Hillaria] / Q1 places after *Re-enter the Servant*
380.12	Indifference. / Indifference, Q1
380.23	imagine. Dear / imagine, dear Q1
381.12	wife's DW / wives Q1
381.35	have. You / have, you Q1
382.7	ye / yee Q1
382.8	ye / yee Q1
383.22	no DW / on Q1
383.33	Diogenes. / Diogenes, Q1
383.36	*hat*], I / *Hat*) I Q1
386.7	*sonata* / *sonata*, Q1
388.31	with. I'll / with, I'll Q1
390.13	Oons / Oon's Q1
392.19	puppy. Ha / puppy, ha Q1
392.29	Oons / Oon's Q1
394.11	*hood* / *hoads* Q1
397.15	in *seconde* / in second Q1 DW
398.17	*table, a light* / *table light* Q1
398.31	*s.d.* man; a woman / man; woman Q1
405.35	your DW / you Q1
413.16	circumstances? / Circumstances! Q1
413.16	Widow? / Widdow. Q1
414.23	Madam. DW / Madam, Q1
415.27	It will not be DW / I wo'not be Q1
417.7	death. Knowing / death, knowing Q1
417.23	travel DW / travail Q1
419.34	off DW / of Q1

420.15   Madam. Pleasant / Madam, pleasant Q1
422.1   genteel DW / gentile Q1
424.5   you. Within / you, within Q1
425.2   both. Now / both, now Q1
425.19   *Cupid* / Love Q1
425.32   *s.p.* CUPID / Love Q1
426.5   alarms, / alarms. Q1
426.9   *s.p.* CUPID / love Q1
426.19   *s.p.* CUPID / love Q1
426.26   *s.p.* CUPID / love Q1
426.28   *s.p.* CUPID / love Q1

THE RELAPSE
by Sir John Vanbrugh

INTRODUCTION

Sir John Vanbrugh (1664–1726) came of a Flemish family, his grandfather having fled from Ghent to avoid religious persecution.
Vanbrugh's father was a sugar-baker in Chester. Nothing is known
of John's education, and presumably this took place in Chester. He
held a commission in the Earl of Huntingdon's Foot Regiment, but
only briefly, from January to August 1686. In 1688 he was arrested
in France as a suspected spy and was in prison in Calais, Vincennes
and finally the Bastille. He returned to England in 1692. His military career continued in 1696 with a commission in Lord Berkeley's
Marine Regiment of Foot, until it was disbanded in 1698, and then
he became a captain in 1702, in a regiment raised by the Earl of
Huntingdon, under whom he had first served. This captaincy,
however, does not seem to have involved him in any further military service. He was a playwright and an architect, the latter career
the more rewarding financially.

Vanbrugh was a member of the Kit Cat Club where he met not
only his fellow authors, Addison, Steele, Garth, Congreve and Pope,
but also many powerful Whig politicians who helped his career. In
1702 he became Comptroller of the Board of Works, the next year
Carlisle Herald and the next Clarenceux King-of-Arms. In 1705 he
was appointed surveyor for the building of Blenheim Palace, the
reward for Marlborough's victory at Blenheim in 1704. This led to
many difficulties and he resigned his surveyorship in 1716 after
fierce quarrels with the Duchess of Marlborough, and long disputes
over payment. Vanbrugh was even shut out when he brought his
wife to see the Palace, his greatest work. Among the many other fine
houses he designed are Castle Howard in Yorkshire, Grimsthorpe
Castle in Lincolnshire and Kimbolton. His architecture exhibits a
sense of grandeur and also a flair for placing houses superbly in
suitable surroundings.

He was knighted by George I in 1714, and five years later, at the
age of fifty-five, he married a Yorkshire girl, Henrietta Maria Yar-
borough. Virtually a professional bachelor, he feared marriage like
one of his stage gallants and less than three weeks before the ceremony wrote quizzically, from Castle Howard, that there 'has now
fallen a snow up to one's neck . . . In short, 'tis so bloody cold, I

have almost a mind to marry to keep myself warm.' The marriage was successful and he wrote gaily to Jacob Tonson:

I am now two boys strong in the nursery but am forbid getting any more this season for fear of killing my wife. A reason; that in Kit Cat days, would have been stronger for it, than against it: but let her live, for she's special good, as far as I know of the matter.

He died of quinzy in 1726, and left an unfinished play, *A Journey to London*, which Cibber took in hand and entitled *The Provok'd Husband*. Throughout his life Vanbrugh had been, in Rowe's words, 'a most sweet-natured gentleman, and pleasant'.

Vanbrugh's dramatic writing began when he was in the Bastille, where he drafted a comedy. Later, when he was a needy soldier, he became friendly with Sir Thomas Skipwith, a patentee of the Theatre Royal, who lent him money and he repaid this by writing. When the leading actor of the day, Thomas Betterton, left the Theatre Royal with many of the company to work at the Lincoln's Inn Fields Theatre, Vanbrugh joined in assisting what remained of the Theatre Royal Company. Colley Cibber wrote *Love's Last Shift* for them in 1696 and Vanbrugh gave the company *The Relapse, or Virtue in Danger*, first produced in November 1696. This was followed by his *Aesop* in December of the same year. By forgoing his profits on these plays Vanbrugh was able, opportunely, to repay his debts owed to Sir Thomas Skipworth.

The Relapse was intended as a sequel to Cibber's *Love's Last Shift* in which a new twist had been given to the comedy of manners. Loveless, who had dodged his debts and deserted his wife, returned to England to find his wife Amanda forgiving and wealthy. The sentimentality of Cibber was there for Vanbrugh to refute. It was not a difficult task. Cibber's reformed rake Loveless was full of remorse: but only after being 'lewd for above four acts'. However, Cibber's plot had elements in it that Vanbrugh could use, and the same actors and actresses appeared in *The Relapse* as in *Love's Last Shift*, Cibber himself playing Lord Foppington (who had been Sir Novelty Fashion in his own play) and Verbruggen Loveless.

Vanbrugh shows Loveless and Berinthia, Amanda's friend and cousin, involved in lust while Amanda is pursued by Worthy. And Worthy and Berinthia were made associates so that complications could be woven into the plot, in which Loveless shows the instability and inconstancy of his affections. Amanda herself becomes a deeper character in Vanbrugh's treatment of her. As Jeremy Collier remarked, however, the Loveless-Berinthia-Amanda plot has much less zest and is less important than the sub-plot dealing with Young Fashion in which the action moves to the country and presents the problem of younger brothers in the person of Young Fashion himself who captures the young heiress Hoyden, while his elder brother Lord Foppington fails to conquer Amanda and is cheated of Hoyden by his brother. The part of Young Fashion was initially played by Mrs Kent *en travestie*.

Hoyden is a lively girl with her ambitions set on the town, her nurse is obsessed with the physical side of life, Coupler the homosexual is depraved, and Sir Tunbelly Clumsy is gross and insensitive, interested only in what he can buy with Hoyden and her dowry. In other words, there is a considerable variety of characterization, and the spelling he uses to mirror Foppington's eccentric speech is equally eccentric and amusing.

The play's lapses into blank verse are puzzling to modern readers; emotional scenes seem to engender this irregular blank verse which may perhaps have been written down by Vanbrugh in the way he spoke the words. Actors certainly found his speeches very easy to memorize and even in many of the emotive scenes the speech though sometimes formal is not stilted or unnatural. Vanbrugh brought to his plays commonsense, a capacity to create very diverse individuals (Sir Tunbelly Clumsy and Lord Foppington are classic comic characters), a realisation of the struggle between man's animality and desire for reason, and a shrewd awareness of the comic capacity of many men and women for self-deception, though he could also draw virtue convincingly.

The play held the stage for half a century, being staged nearly every year, but after the middle of the eighteenth century it lost its popularity, though there were two early adaptations of the play – John Lee's *The Man of Quality* (1773) and Sheridan's *A Trip to Scarborough* (1777).

Sir John Vanbrugh

The Relapse

or

Virtue in Danger

Being the Sequel of

The Fool in Fashion

A COMEDY

Acted at the Theatre Royal in Drury Lane

Printed for Samuel Briscoe at the corner of
Charles Street in Russell Street, Covent Garden.
1697

THE PREFACE

To go about to excuse half the defects this abortive brat is come into the world with, would be to provoke the Town with a long useless preface, when 'tis, I doubt, sufficiently soured already, by a tedious play.

I do therefore (with all the humility of a repenting sinner) confess, it wants everything but length; and in that, I hope the severest critic, will be pleased to acknowledge, I have not been wanting. But my modesty will sure atone for everything, when the world shall know it is so great, I am even to this day insensible of those two shining graces in the play (which some part of the Town is pleased to compliment me with) blasphemy and bawdy.

For my part, I cannot find 'em out. If there was any obscene expressions upon the stage, here they are in the print; for I have dealt fairly, I have not sunk a syllable, that could (though by racking of mysteries) be ranged under that head; and yet I believe with a steady faith, there is not one woman of a real reputation in Town, but when she has read it impartially over in her closet, will find it so innocent, she'll think it no affront to her prayer book, to lay it upon the same shelf. So to them, (with all manner of deference), I entirely refer my cause, and I'm confident they'll justify me, against those pretenders to good manners, who at the same time, have so little respect for the ladies, they would extract a bawdy jest from an ejaculation, to put 'em out of countenance. But I expect to have these well-bred persons always my enemies, since I'm sure I shall never write anything lewd enough, to make 'em my friends.

As for the Saints (your thorough-paced ones I mean, with screwed faces and wry mouths) I despair of them, for they are friends to nobody. They love nothing, but their altars and themselves. They have too much zeal to have any charity: they make debauches in piety, as sinners do in wine; and are as quarrelsome in their religion, as other people are in their drink: so I hope nobody will mind what they say. But if any man (with flat plod shoes, a little band, greasy hair, and a dirty face, who is wiser than I, at the expense of being forty years older) happens to be offended at a story of a cock and a bull, and a priest and a bulldog: I beg his pardon with all my heart, which I hope I shall obtain, by eating my words, and making this public recantation. I do therefore for his satisfaction, acknowledge, I lied, when I said, they never quit their hold, for in that little time I have lived in the world, I thank God I have seen 'em forced to't, more than once; but next time I'll speak with more caution and truth; and only say, they have very good teeth.

If I have offended any honest gentlemen of the Town, whose friendship or good word is worth the having, I am very sorry for it; I hope they'll correct me as gently as they can, when they consider I have had no other design, in running a very great risk, than to divert (if possible) some part of their spleen, in spite of their wives and their taxes.

One word more about the bawdy, and I have done. I own the first night this thing was acted, some indecencies had like to have happened, but 'twas not my fault.

The fine gentleman⋆ of the play, drinking his mistress's health in Nantes brandy, from six in the morning, to the time he waddled on upon the stage in the evening, had toasted himself up, to such a pitch of vigour, I confess I once gave Amanda for gone, and I am since (with all due respect to Mrs Rogers) very sorry she escaped; for I am confident a certain lady, (let no one take it to herself that's handsome) who highly blames the play, for the barrenness of the conclusion would then have allowed it, a very natural close.

⋆ The fine gentleman: the actor George Powell who was a heavy drinker.

DRAMATIS PERSONAE

MEN
Sir Novelty Fashion, newly created Lord Foppington.
Young Fashion, his brother.
Loveless, husband to Amanda.
Worthy, a gentleman of the Town.
Sir Tunbelly Clumsey, a country gentleman.
Sir John Friendly, his neighbour.
Coupler, a matchmaker.
Bull, chaplain to Sir Tunbelly.
Seringe, a surgeon.
Lory, servant to young Fashion.
Shoemaker, Tailor, Periwig-maker, &c.

WOMEN
Amanda, wife to Loveless.
Berinthia, her cousin, a young widow.
Miss Hoyden, a great fortune, daughter to Sir Tunbelly.
Nurse, her gouvernante.

FIRST PROLOGUE

Spoken by Mrs Cross* ⟨Hoyden⟩

Ladies, this play in too much haste was writ,
To be o'ercharged with either plot or wit;
'Twas got, conceived and born in six weeks' space,
And wit, you know, is as slow in growth – as grace.
Sure it can ne'er be ripened to your taste,
I doubt 'twill prove, our author bred too fast.
For mark 'em well, who with the Muses marry,
They rarely do conceive, but they miscarry.
'Tis the hard fate of those wh'are big with rhyme,
Still to be brought to bed before their time.
Of our late poets, nature few has made,
The greatest part – are only so by trade.
Still want of something, brings the scribbling fit,
For want of money, some of 'em have writ,
And others do't you see – for want of wit.
Honour, they fancy, summons 'em to write,
So out they lug in resty† nature's spite,
As some of you spruce beaux do – when you fight.
Yet let the ebb of wit be ne'er so low,
Some glimpse of it, a man may hope to show,
Upon a theme, so ample – as a beau.
So, howsoe'er true courage may decay,
Perhaps there's not one smock-face‡ here today,
But's bold as Cæsar – to attack a play.
Nay, what's yet more, with an undaunted face
To do the thing with more heroic grace,
'Tis six to four, y'attack the strongest place.
You are such Hotspurs, in this kind of venture,
Where there's no breach, just there you needs must enter.
But be advised.
E'en give the hero, and the critic o'er,
For nature sent you on another score,
She formed her beau, for nothing but her whore.

* Mrs Cross: she was about fourteen at the time.
† resty: impatient.   ‡ smock-face: effeminate.

THE PROLOGUE ON THE THIRD DAY

Spoken by Mrs Verbruggen ⟨Berinthia⟩

Apologies for plays, experience shows,
Are things almost as useless – as the beaux.
Whate'er we say (like them) we neither move,
Your friendship, pity, anger, nor your love,
'Tis interest turns the globe: let us but find,
The way to please you, and you'll soon be kind:
But to expect you'd for our sakes approve,
Is just as though you for their sakes should love,
And that, we do confess, we think a task,
Which (though they may impose) we never ought to ask.

This is an age where all things we improve,
But, most of all, the art of making love.
In former days, women were only won,
By merit, truth, and constant service done,
But lovers now are much more expert grown.
They seldom wait, t'approach, by tedious form,
They're for dispatch, for taking you by storm,
Quick are their sieges, furious are their fires,
Fierce their attacks, and boundless their desires.
Before the play's half ended, I'll engage,
To show you beaux, come crowding on the stage,
Who with so little pains, have always sped,
They'll undertake to look a lady dead.
How I have shook, and trembling stood with awe,
When here, behind the scenes, I've seen 'em draw
– A comb: that dead-doing weapon to the heart;
And turn each powdered hair into a dart.
When I have seen 'em sally on the stage,
Dressed to the war, and ready to engage,
I've mourned your destiny – yet more their fate,
To think, that after victories so great,
It should so often prove, their hard mishap,

To sneak into a lane – and get a clap.
But, hush; they're here already, I'll retire,
And leave 'em to you ladies to admire.
They'll show you twenty thousand airs and graces,
They'll entertain you with their soft grimaces,
Their snuff-box, awkward bows – and ugly faces.
In short, they're after all so much your friends,
That lest the play should fail the author's ends,
They have resolved to make you some amends.
Between each act (performed by nicest rules)
They'll treat you – with an interlude of fools:
Of which, that you may have the deeper sense,
The entertainment's – at their own expense.

ACT ONE

SCENE I

Enter Loveless reading.

LOVELESS How true is that philosophy, which says,
  Our heaven is seated in our minds?
  Through all the roving pleasures of my youth,
  (Where nights and days seemed all consumed in joy,
  Where the false face of luxury
  Displayed such charms,
  As might have shaken the most holy hermit,
  And made him totter at his altar;)
  I never knew one moment's peace like this.
  Here – in this little soft retreat,
  My thoughts unbent from all the cares of life,
  Content with fortune,
  Eased from the grating duties of dependence,
  From envy free, ambition under foot,
  The raging flame of wild destructive lust
  Reduced to a warm pleasing fire of lawful love,
  My life glides on, and all is well within.

Enter Amanda.

LOVELESS [*meeting her kindly*] How does the happy cause of my content,
  My dear Amanda?
  You find me musing on my happy state,
  And full of grateful thoughts to heaven, and you.
AMANDA Those grateful offerings heaven can't receive
  With more delight than I do:
  Would I could share with it as well
  The dispensations of its bliss,
  That I might search its choicest favours out,
  And shower 'em on your head for ever.
LOVELESS The largest boons that Heaven thinks fit to grant,
  To things it has decreed shall crawl on earth,
  Are in the gift of women formed like you,

Perhaps, when time shall be no more,
When the aspiring soul shall take its flight,
And drop this pond'rous lump of clay behind it,
It may have appetites we know not of,
And pleasures as refined as its desires –
But till that day of knowledge shall instruct me,
The utmost blessing that my thought can reach,

[taking her in his arms]

Is folded in my arms, and rooted in my heart.

AMANDA There let it grow for ever.

LOVELESS Well said, Amanda – let it be for ever –
Would heaven grant that –

AMANDA 'Twere all the heaven I'd ask.
But we are clad in black mortality,
And the dark curtain of eternal night,
At last must drop between us.

LOVELESS It must:
That mournful separation we must see,
A bitter pill it is to all; but doubles its ungrateful taste,
When lovers are to swallow it.

AMANDA Perhaps, that pain may only be my lot,
You possibly may be exempted from it;
Men find out softer ways to quench their fires.

LOVELESS Can you then doubt my constancy, Amanda?
You'll find 'tis built upon a steady basis –
The rock of reason now supports my love
On which it stands so fixed,
The rudest hurricane of wild desire
Would, like the breath of a soft slumbring babe,
Pass by, and never shake it.

AMANDA Yet still 'tis safer to avoid the storm;
The strongest vessels, if they put to sea,
May possibly be lost.
Would I could keep you here, in this calm port, for ever!
Forgive the weakness of a woman,
I am uneasy at your going to stay so long in Town,
I know its false insinuating pleasures;
I know the force of its delusions;

I know the strength of its attacks;
I know the weak defence of nature;
I know you are a man – and I – a wife.
LOVELESS You know then all that needs to give you rest,
For wife's the strongest claim that you can urge.
When you would plead your title to my heart,
On this you may depend; therefore be calm,
Banish your fears, for they are traitors to your peace;
Beware of 'em,
They are insinuating busy things that gossip to and fro,
And do a world of mischief where they come:
But you shall soon be mistress of 'em all,
I'll aid you with such arms for their destruction,
They never shall erect their heads again.
You know the business is indispensable,
That obliges me to go for London;
And you have no reason, that I know of,
To believe I'm glad of the occasion;
For my honest conscience is my witness.
I have found a due succession of such charms
In my retirement here with you;
I have never thrown one roving thought that way;
But since, against my will, I'm dragged once more
To that uneasy theatre of noise;
I am resolved to make such use on't,
As shall convince you, 'tis an old-cast* mistress,
Who has been so lavish of her favours,
She's now grown bankrupt of her charms,
And has not one allurement left to move me.
AMANDA Her bow, I do believe, is grown so weak,
Her arrows (at this distance) cannot hurt you,
But in approaching 'em, you give 'em strength;
The dart that has not far to fly, will put
The best of armour to a dangerous trial.
LOVELESS That trial past, and y'are at ease for ever;
When you have seen the helmet proved,
You'll apprehend no more, for him that wears it.
                * old-cast: discarded.

Therefore to put a lasting period to your fears,
I am resolved, this once, to launch into temptation,
I'll give you an essay of all my virtues,
My former boon companions of the bottle
Shall fairly try what charms are left in wine:
I'll take my place amongst 'em,
They shall hem me in,
Sing praises to their god, and drink his glory.
Turn wild enthusiasts★ for his sake,
And beasts to do him honour,
Whilst I a stubborn atheist,
Sullenly look on,
Without one reverend glass to his divinity,
That for my temperance,
Then for my constancy. –

AMANDA Aye, there take heed.

LOVELESS Indeed the danger's small,

AMANDA And yet my fears are great.

LOVELESS Why are you so timorous?

AMANDA Because you are so bold.

LOVELESS My courage should disperse your apprehensions.

AMANDA My apprehensions should alarm your courage.

LOVELESS Fie, fie, Amanda, it is not kind thus to distrust me.

AMANDA And yet my fears are founded on my love.

LOVELESS Your love then, is not founded as it ought,
For if you can believe 'tis possible,
I should again relapse to my past follies;
I must appear to you a thing,
Of such an undigested composition,
That but to think of me with inclination,
Would be a weakness in your taste,
Your virtue scarce could answer.

AMANDA 'Twould be a weakness in my tongue;
My prudence could not answer,
If I should press you farther with my fears,
I'll therefore trouble you no longer with 'em.

LOVELESS Nor shall they trouble you much longer,

★ enthusiasts: religious fanatics.

A little time shall show you they were groundless
This winter shall be the fiery trial of my virtue;
Which when it once has passed,
You'll be convinced, 'twas of no false allay,★
There all your cares will end. –
AMANDA Pray heaven they may.

[Exeunt hand in hand]

SCENE ⟨II⟩
Whitehall

Enter Young Fashion, Lory and Waterman.

YOUNG FASHION Come, pay the waterman, and take the portmantle.

LORY Faith Sir, I think the waterman had as good take the portmantle and pay himself.

YOUNG FASHION Why sure there's something left in't!

LORY But a solitary old waistcoat, upon honour, Sir.

YOUNG FASHION Why, what's become of the blue coat, sirrah?

LORY Sir, 'twas eaten at Gravesend, the reckoning came to thirty shillings, and your privy purse was worth but two half-crowns.

YOUNG FASHION 'Tis very well.

WATERMAN Pray master will you please to dispatch me?

YOUNG FASHION Aye, here, a – can'st thou change me a guinea?

LORY *[aside]* Good.

WATERMAN Change a guinea, master; ha, ha, your honour's pleased to compliment.

YOUNG FASHION Egad I don't know how I shall pay thee then, for I have nothing but gold about me.

LORY *[aside]* Hum, hum.

YOUNG FASHION What dost thou expect, friend?

WATERMAN Why master, so far against wind and tide, is richly worth half a piece.†

YOUNG FASHION Why, faith, I think thou art a good conscion-

★ allay: alloy.   † half a piece: half a guinea approximately.

able fellow. Egad I begin to have so good an opinion of thy honesty, I care not if I leave my portmantle with thee, till I send thee thy money.

WATERMAN Ha! God bless your honour; I should be as willing to trust you, master, but that you are, as a man may say, a stranger to me, and these are nimble times. There are a great many sharpers stirring. [*taking up the portmantle*] Well master, when your worship sends the money, your portmantle shall be forthcoming; my name's Tugg; my wife keeps a brandy-shop in Drab Alley at Wapping.*

YOUNG FASHION Very well; I'll send for't tomorrow.

[*Exit Waterman*]

LORY So – Now Sir, I hope you'll own yourself a happy man, you have outlived all your cares,

YOUNG FASHION How so, Sir?

LORY Why, you have nothing left to take care of.

YOUNG FASHION Yes sirrah, I have myself and you to take care of still.

LORY Sir, if you could but prevail with somebody else to do that for you, I fancy we might both fare the better for't.

YOUNG FASHION Why if thou can'st tell me where to apply myself I have at present so little money and so much humility about me, I don't know but I may follow a fool's advice.

LORY Why then, Sir, your fool advises you to lay aside all animosity, and apply to Sir Novelty your elder brother.

YOUNG FASHION Damn my elder brother.

LORY With all my heart, but get him to redeem your annuity however.

YOUNG FASHION My annuity? S'death he's such a dog, he would not give his powder puff† to redeem my soul. –

LORY Look you, Sir, you must wheedle him, or you must starve.

YOUNG FASHION Look you, Sir, I will neither wheedle him, nor starve.

LORY Why? What will you do then?

YOUNG FASHION I'll go into the army.

LORY You can't take the oaths; you are a Jacobite.

* Wapping: a Thames port downstream from London.
† powder puff: for a wig.

YOUNG FASHION Thou may'st as well say I can't take orders because I'm an atheist.

LORY Sir, I ask your pardon, I find I did not know the strength of your conscience, so well as I did the weakness of your purse.

YOUNG FASHION Methinks, Sir, a person of your experience should have known that the strength of the conscience proceeds from the weakness of the purse.

LORY Sir, I am very glad to find you have a conscience, able to take care of us, let it proceed from what it will; but I desire you'll please to consider, that the army alone will be but a scanty maintenance for a person of your generosity, (at least, as rents* now are paid) I shall see you stand in damnable need of some auxiliary guineas, for your _menus plaisirs_, I will therefore turn fool once more for your service, and advise you to go directly to your brother.

YOUNG FASHION Art thou then so impregnable a blockhead, to believe he'll help me with a farthing?

LORY Not if you treat him, _de haut en bas_, as you used to do.

YOUNG FASHION Why, how would'st have me treat him?

LORY Like a trout, tickle him.

YOUNG FASHION I can't flatter. –

LORY Can you starve?

YOUNG FASHION Yes. –

LORY I can't; goodbye t'ye Sir – [_going_]

YOUNG FASHION Stay, thou wilt distract me. What would'st thou have me say to him?

LORY Say nothing to him, apply yourself to his favourites, speak to his periwig, his cravat, his feather, his snuff-box, and when you are well with them, – desire him to lend you a thousand pounds. I'll engage you prosper.

YOUNG FASHION S'death and furies, why was that coxcomb thrust into the world before me? O Fortune – Fortune – Thou art a bitch by gad –

[_Exeunt_]

---

* rents: money, here an army officer's pay.

SCENE ⟨III⟩

A dressing-room

*Enter Lord Foppington in his nightgown.**

LORD FOPPINGTON Page. –

Enter Page.

PAGE Sir.

LORD FOPPINGTON Sir, pray Sir do me the favour to teach your tongue the title the King has thought fit to honour me with.

PAGE I ask your lordship's pardon, my lord.

LORD FOPPINGTON Oh, you can pronounce the word then, I thought it would have choked you – D'ye hear?

PAGE My lord.

LORD FOPPINGTON Call La Vérole,† I would dress – [*Exit page*] [*solus*] Well, 'tis an unspeakable pleasure to be a man of quality – Strike me dumb – my lord – your lordship – my Lord Foppington – *Ah c'est quelque chose de beau, que le diable m'emporte.* – Why the ladies were ready to puke at me, whilst I had nothing but Sir Navelty to recommend me to 'em – Sure whilst I was but a knight, I was a very nauseous fellow – Well, 'tis ten thousand pawnd‡ well given – stap my vitals –

Enter La Vérole.

LA VÉROLE Me lord, de shoemaker, de tailor, de hosier, de semp-stress, de barber, be all ready, if your lordship please to be dress.

LORD FOPPINGTON 'Tis well, admit 'em.

LA VÉROLE Hey, *messieurs, entrez.*

Enter Tailor, &c.

LORD FOPPINGTON So gentlemen, I hope you have all taken pains to show yourselves masters in your professions.

* nightgown: dressing gown.   † La Vérole: syphilis in French.
‡ ten thousand pawnd: about the amount paid for peerages (which were virtually for sale) under James I; the practice had ceased by the time of this play.

TAILOR I think I may presume to say, Sir, –

LA VÉROLE My lord – you clawn you.

TAILOR Why, is he made a lord – My lord, I ask your lordship's pardon my lord; I hope my lord, your lordship will please to own, I have brought your lordship as accomplished a suit of clothes, as ever peer of England trod the stage in; my lord; will your lordship please to try 'em now.

LORD FOPPINGTON Aye, but let my people dispose the glasses so, that I may see myself before and behind, for I love to see myself all raund. –

Whilst he puts on his clothes, enter Young Fashion and Lory.

YOUNG FASHION Hey-day, what the devil have we here? Sure my gentleman's grown a favourite at Court, he has got so many people at his levee.

LORY Sir, these people come in order to make him a favourite at Court, they are to establish him with the ladies.

YOUNG FASHION Good God, to what an ebb of taste, are women fallen, that it should be in the power of a laced coat to recommend a gallant to 'em –

LORY Sir, tailors and periwig-makers are now become the bawds of the nation, 'tis they debauch all the women.

YOUNG FASHION Thou say'st true, for there's that fop now, has not by nature wherewithal to move a cook-maid, and by that time these fellows have done with him, egad he shall melt down a countess. – But now for my reception, I'll engage it shall be as cold a one, as a courtier's to his friend, who comes to put him in mind of his promise.

LORD FOPPINGTON [*to his Tailor*] Death and eternal tartures, Sir, I say the packet's too high by a foot.

TAILOR My lord, if it had been an inch lower, it would not have held your lordship's pocket-handkerchief.

LORD FOPPINGTON Rat my pocket-handkerchief, have not I a page to carry it? You may make him a packet up to his chin a purpose for it: but I will not have mine come so near my face.

TAILOR 'Tis not for me to dispute your lordship's fancy.

YOUNG FASHION [*to Lory*] His lordship; Lory, did you observe that?

LORY Yes Sir, I always thought 'twould end there. Now I hope you'll have a little more respect for him.

YOUNG FASHION Respect, damn him for a coxcomb; now has he ruined his estate to buy a title, that he may be a fool of the first rate: But let's accost him. – [*to Lord Foppington*] Brother, I'm your humble servant.

LORD FOPPINGTON O Lard Tam, I did not expect you in England; brother, I am glad to see you. – [*turning to his Tailor*] Look you Sir, I shall never be reconciled to this nauseous packet, therefore pray get me another suit with all manner of expedition, for this is my eternal aversion; Mrs Callicoe, are not you of my mind?

SEMPSTRESS Oh, directly my lord, it can never be too low. –

LORD FOPPINGTON You are positively in the right on't, for the packet becomes no part of the body but the knee.

SEMPSTRESS I hope your lordship is pleased with your steinkirk.*

LORD FOPPINGTON In love with it, stap my vitals; bring your bill, you shall be paid tomarrow. –

SEMPSTRESS I humbly thank your honour –   [*Exit Sempstress*]

LORD FOPPINGTON Hark thee, shoemaker, these shoes an't ugly but they don't fit me.

SHOEMAKER My lord, my thinks they fit you very well.

LORD FOPPINGTON They hurt me just below the instep.

SHOEMAKER [*feeling his foot*] My lord, they don't hurt you there.

LORD FOPPINGTON I tell thee they pinch me execrably.

SHOEMAKER My lord, if they pinch you, I'll be bound to be hanged, that's all.

LORD FOPPINGTON Why wilt thou undertake to persuade me I cannot feel.

SHOEMAKER Your lordship may please to feel what you think fit; but that shoe does not hurt you; I think I understand my trade. –

LORD FOPPINGTON Now by all that's great and powerful, thou art an incomprehensible coxcomb; but thou makest good shoes, and so I'll bear with thee.

SHOEMAKER My lord, I have worked for half the people of quality

* steinkirk: a cravat with tiny studs, named after the attire of French cavalry at the battle of Steenkerke (1692).

in Town, these twenty years; and 'twere very hard I should not
know when a shoe hurts, and when it don't.

LORD FOPPINGTON Well, prithee begone about thy business. –

[*Exit Shoemaker*]

[*to the Hosier*] Mr Mendlegs, a word with you; the calves of these
stockings are thickened a little too much. They make my legs
look like a chairman's.*

MENDLEGS My lord, my thinks they look mighty well.

LORD FOPPINGTON Aye, but you are not so good a judge of these
things as I am, I have studied 'em all my life; therefore pray let the
next be the thickness of a crawn-piece less – [*aside*] If the Town
takes notice my legs are fallen away, 'twill be attributed to the
violence of some new intrigue. [*to the periwig-maker*] Come, Mr
Foretop, let me see what you have done, and then the fatigue of
the marning will be over.

FORETOP My lord, I have done what I defy any prince in Europe
t' outdo; I have made you a periwig so long, and so full of hair, it
will serve you for hat and cloak in all weathers.

LORD FOPPINGTON Then thou hast made me thy friend to eternity; come, comb it out.

YOUNG FASHION Well, Lory, what dost think on't? A very
friendly reception from a brother after three years' absence.

LORY Why, Sir, it's your own fault. We seldom care for those that
don't love what we love; if you would creep into his heart, you
must enter into his pleasures – Here have you stood ever since
you came in, and have not commended any one thing that belongs
to him.

YOUNG FASHION Nor never shall, whilst they belong to a coxcomb.

LORY Then, Sir, you must be content to pick a hungry bone.

YOUNG FASHION No, Sir, I'll crack it, and get to the marrow
before I have done.

LORD FOPPINGTON Gad's curse; Mr Foretop, you don't intend
to put this upon me for a full periwig?

FORETOP Not a full one, my lord? I don't know what your lordship may please to call a full one, but I have crammed twenty
ounces of hair into it.

* chairman's: like the muscular legs of a sedan-chair carrier.

LORD FOPPINGTON What it may be by weight, Sir, I shall not dispute, but by tale, there are not nine hairs of a side.

FORETOP O Lord! O Lord! O Lord! Why, as Gad shall judge me, your honour's side-face is reduced to the tip of your nose.

LORD FOPPINGTON My side-face may be in eclipse for aught I know; but I'm sure, my full-face is like the full moon.

FORETOP Heavens bless my eye-sight – [*rubbing his eyes*] Sure I look through the wrong end of the perspective,* for by my faith, an't please your honour, the broadest place I see in your face, does not seem to me to be two inches diameter.

LORD FOPPINGTON If it did, it would be just two inches too broad; far a periwig to a man, should be like a mask to a woman, nothing should be seen but his eyes –

FORETOP My lord, I have done; if you please to have more hair in your wig, I'll put it in.

LORD FOPPINGTON Passitively, yes.

FORETOP Shall I take it back now, my lord?

LORD FOPPINGTON Noh: I'll wear it today, though it show such a manstrous pair of cheeks: stap my vitals, I shall be taken for a trumpeter.

[*Exit Foretop*]

YOUNG FASHION Now your people of business are gone, brother, I hope I may obtain a quarter of an hour's audience of you.

LORD FOPPINGTON Faith, Tam; I must beg you'll excuse me at this time, for I must away to the House of Lards immediately; my Lady Teaser's case is to come on today, and I would not be absent for the salvation of mankind. Hey page, is the coach at the door?

PAGE Yes, my lord.

LORD FOPPINGTON You'll excuse me, brother. [*going*]

YOUNG FASHION Shall you be back at dinner?

LORD FOPPINGTON As Gad shall jidge me, I can't tell; for 'tis passible I may dine with some of aur House at Lacket's.†

YOUNG FASHION Shall I meet you there? For I must needs talk with you.

LORD FOPPINGTON That I'm afraid mayn't be so praper; far

* perspective: telescope.
† Lacket's: Locket's, the famous tavern near Charing Cross.

the lards I commonly eat with, are people of a nice conversation, and you know, Tam, your education has been a little at large; but if you'll stay here, you'll find a family-dinner. Hey fellow! What is there for dinner? There's beef; I suppose, my brother will eat beef. Dear Tom, I'm glad to see thee in England, stap my vitals.

[Exit with his equipage]

YOUNG FASHION Hell and furies, is this to be borne?

LORY Faith, Sir, I could almost have given him a knock o'th' pate myself.

YOUNG FASHION 'Tis enough; I will now show thee the excess of my passion by being very calm: come, Lory, lay your logger-head to mine, and in cool blood let us contrive his destruction.

LORY Here comes a head, Sir, would contrive it better than us both, if he would but join in the confederacy.

Enter Coupler.

YOUNG FASHION By this light, old Coupler alive still; why, how now, matchmaker, art thou here still to plague the world with matrimony? You old bawd, how have you the impudence to be hobbling out of your grave twenty years after you are rotten!

COUPLER When you begin to rot, sirrah, you'll go off like a pippin; one winter will send you to the devil. What mischief brings you home again? Ha! You young lascivious rogue you. Let me put my hand in your bosom, sirrah.

YOUNG FASHION Stand off, old Sodom.

COUPLER Nay, prithee now don't be so coy.

YOUNG FASHION Keep your hands to yourself, you old dog you, or I'll wring your nose off.

COUPLER Hast thou then been a year in Italy, and brought home a fool at last? By my conscience, the young fellows of this age profit no more by their going abroad, than they do by their going to church. Sirrah, sirrah, if you are not hanged before you come to my years, you'll know a cock from a hen. But come, I'm still a friend to thy person, though I have a contempt of thy under-standing; and therefore I would willingly know thy condition, that I may see whether thou stand'st in need of my assistance, for widows swarm, my boy, the Town's infected with 'em.

YOUNG FASHION I stand in need of anybody's assistance, that will help me to cut my elder brother's throat, without the risk of being hanged for him.

COUPLER Egad, sirrah, I could help thee to do him almost as good a turn, without the danger of being burned in the hand for't.*

YOUNG FASHION Sayest thou so, old Satan? Show me but that, and my soul is thine.

COUPLER Pox o'thy soul, give me thy warm body, sirrah; I shall have a substantial title to't when I tell thee my project.

YOUNG FASHION Out with it then, dear dad, and take possession as soon as thou wilt.

COUPLER Say'st thou so my Hephestion?† Why then thus lies the scene, but hold; who's that? If we are heard we are undone.

YOUNG FASHION What, have you forgot Lory?

COUPLER Who, trusty Lory, is it thee?

LORY At your service, Sir.

COUPLER Give me thy hand, old boy, egad I did not know thee again, but I remember thy honesty, though I did not thy face; I think thou had'st like to have been hanged once or twice for thy master.

LORY Sir, I was very near once having that honour.

COUPLER Well, live and hope, don't be discouraged, eat with him, and drink with him, and do what he bids thee, and it may be thy reward at last, as well as another's. [*to Young Fashion*] Well, Sir, you must know I have done you the kindness to make up a match for your brother.

YOUNG FASHION Sir, I am very much beholding to you, truly.

COUPLER You may be, sirrah, before the wedding-day yet, the lady is a great heiress; fifteen hundred pound a year, and a great bag of money; the match is concluded, the writings are drawn, and the pipkin's to be cracked‡ in a fortnight – Now you must know, stripling, (with respect to your mother) your brother's the son of a whore.

YOUNG FASHION Good.

---

* burned in the hand: a punishment for thieves who were not sentenced to be hanged.
† Hephestion: Alexander the Great's favourite.
‡ the pipkin's to be cracked: the marriage consummated.

COUPLER He has given me a bond of a thousand pounds for helping him to this fortune, and has promised me as much more in ready money upon the day of marriage, which I understand by a friend, he ne'er designs to pay me; if therefore you will be a generous young dog, and secure me five thousand pounds, I'll be a covetous old rogue, and help you to the lady.

YOUNG FASHION Egad, if thou canst bring this about, I'll have thy statue cast in brass. But don't you dote, you old pander, you? When you talk at this rate?

COUPLER That your youthful parts shall judge of; this plump partridge that I tell you of, lives in the country, fifty miles off, with her honoured parents, in a lonely old house which nobody comes near; she never goes abroad, nor sees company at home: to prevent all misfortunes, she has her breeding within doors, the parson of the parish teaches her to play upon the bass-viol, the clerk to sing, her nurse to dress, and her father to dance: in short, nobody can give you admittance there but I, nor can I do it any other way, than by making you pass for your brother.

YOUNG FASHION And how the devil wilt thou do that?

COUPLER Without the devil's aid, I warrant thee. Thy brother's face, not one of the family ever saw, the whole business has been managed by me, and all the letters go through my hands: the last that was writ to Sir Tunbelly Clumsey (for that's the old gentleman's name), was to tell him, his lordship would be down in a fortnight to consummate. Now you shall go away immediately, pretend you writ that letter only to have the romantic pleasure of surprising your mistress; fall desperately in love, as soon as you see her; make that your plea, for marrying her immediately, and when the fatigue of the wedding night's over, you shall send me a swinging purse of gold, you dog you.

YOUNG FASHION Egad, old dad, I'll put my hand in thy bosom now. –

COUPLER Ah, you young hot lusty thief, let me muzzle you – [*kissing*] – Sirrah, let me muzzle you.

YOUNGFASHION [*aside*] Pshaw, the old lecher –

COUPLER Well, I'll warrant thou hast not a farthing of money in thy pocket now, no; one may see it in thy face –

YOUNG FASHION Not a souse,* by Jupiter.

COUPLER Must I advance then – well sirrah, be at my lodgings in half an hour, and I'll see what may be done; we'll sign and seal, and eat a pullet, and when I have given thee some farther instructions, thou sha't hoist sail and begone. – [*kissing*] – T'other buss and so adieu.

YOUNG FASHION U'm, P'sha.

COUPLER Ah, you young warm dog you, what a delicious night will the bride have on't.   [*Exit Coupler*]

YOUNG FASHION So Lory. Providence thou see'st at last, takes care of men of merit. We are in a fair way to be great people.

LORY Aye, Sir, if the devil don't step between the cup and the lip, as he uses to do.

YOUNG FASHION Why faith he has played me many a damned trick to spoil my fortune, and egad I'm almost afraid he's at work about it again now, but if I should tell thee how, thou'dst wonder at me.

LORY Indeed, Sir, I should not.

YOUNG FASHION How dost know. –

LORY Because, Sir, I have wondered at you so often, I can wonder at you no more.

YOUNG FASHION No; what wouldst thou say, if a qualm of conscience should spoil my design.

LORY I would eat my words, and wonder more than ever.

YOUNG FASHION Why faith Lory, though I am a young rakehell, and have played many a roguish trick; this is so full grown a cheat, I find I must take pains to come up to't, I have scruples –

LORY They are strong symptoms of death; if you find they increase, pray Sir make your will.

YOUNG FASHION No, my conscience shan't starve me neither. But thus far I will harken to it; before I execute this project. I'll try my brother to the bottom, I'll speak to him with the temper of a philosopher, my reasons, (though they press him home), shall yet be clothed with so much modesty, not one of all the truths they urge, shall be so naked to offend his sight; if he has yet so much humanity about him, as to assist me, (though with a moderate aid), I'll drop my project at his feet, and show him I

* souse: a small coin.

can – do for him, much more than what I ask, he'd do for me;
this one conclusive trial of him I resolve to make. –
Succeed or no, still victory's my lot,
If I subdue his heart, 'tis well; if not
I shall subdue my conscience to my plot.   [*Exeunt*]

ACT TWO

SCENE I

Enter Loveless and Amanda.

LOVELESS How do you like these lodgings, my dear? For my part I am so well pleased with 'em, I shall hardly remove whilst we stay in Town, if you are satisfied.

AMANDA I am satisfied with everything that pleases you; else I had not come to Town at all.

LOVELESS Oh, a little of the noise and bustle of the world, sweetens the pleasure of retreat: we shall find the charms of our retirement doubled, when we return to it.

AMANDA That pleasing prospect, will be my chiefest entertainment, whilst (much against my will) I am obliged to stand surrounded with these empty pleasures, which 'tis so much the fashion to be fond of.

LOVELESS I own most of 'em are indeed but empty; nay, so empty, that one would wonder by what magic power they act, when they induce us to be vicious for their sakes. Yet some there are we may speak kindlier of; there are delights, (of which a private life is destitute) which may divert an honest man, and be a harmless entertainment to a virtuous woman. The conversation of the Town is one; and truly, (with some small allowances) the plays, I think, may be esteemed another.

AMANDA The plays, I must confess, have some small charms, and would have more, would they restrain that loose obscene encouragement to vice, which shocks, if not the virtue of some women, at least the modesty of all.

LOVELESS But till that reformation can be made, I would not leave the wholsome corn, for some intruding tares that grow amongst it. Doubtless, the moral of a well-wrought scene, is of prevailing force. – Last night there happened one, that moved me strangely.

AMANDA Pray, what was that?

LOVELESS Why 'twas about – but 'tis not worth repeating.

AMANDA Yes, pray let me know it.

LOVELESS No, I think 'tis as well let alone.

AMANDA Nay, now you make me have a mind to know.

LOVELESS 'Twas a foolish thing: you'd perhaps grow jealous, should I tell it you, though without cause heaven knows.

AMANDA I shall begin to think I have cause, if you persist in making it a secret.

LOVELESS I'll then convince you, you have none, by making it no longer so. Know then, I happened in the play to find my very character, only with the addition of a relapse; which struck me so, I put a sudden stop to a most harmless entertainment, which till then, diverted me between the acts. 'Twas to admire the workmanship of nature, in the face of a young lady, that sat some distance from me, she was so exquisitely handsome.

AMANDA So exquisitely handsome?

LOVELESS Why do you repeat my words, my dear?

AMANDA Because you seemed to speak 'em with such pleasure, I thought I might oblige you with their echo.

LOVELESS Then you are alarmed, Amanda?

AMANDA It is my duty to be so, when you are in danger.

LOVELESS You are too quick in apprehending for me; all will be well when you have heard me out. I do confess I gazed upon her; nay, eagerly I gazed upon her.

AMANDA Eagerly? That's with desire.

LOVELESS No, I desired her not; I viewed her with a world of admiration, but not one glance of love.

AMANDA Take heed of trusting to such nice distinctions.

LOVELESS I did take heed; for observing in the play that he who seemed to represent me there, was by an accident like this, unwarily surprised into a net, in which he lay a poor entangled slave, and brought a train of mischiefs on his head; I snatched my eyes away: they pleaded hard for leave to look again, but I grew absolute, and they obeyed.

AMANDA Were they the only things that were inquisitive? Had I been in your place, my tongue, I fancy, had been curious too; I should have asked her name, and where she lived, (yet still without design): – Who was she pray?

LOVELESS Indeed I cannot tell.

AMANDA You will not tell.

LOVELESS By all that's sacred then, I did not ask.

AMANDA Nor do you know what company was with her?

LOVELESS I do not.

AMANDA Then I am calm again.

LOVELESS Why were you disturbed?

AMANDA Had I then no cause?

LOVELESS None certainly.

AMANDA I thought I had.

LOVELESS But you thought wrong, Amanda: for turn the case, and let it be your story: should you come home and tell me you had seen a handsome man, should I grow jealous, because you had eyes?

AMANDA But should I tell you, he were exquisitely so: that I had gazed on him with admiration: that I had looked with eager eyes upon him, should you not think 'twere possible I might go one step farther, and enquire his name?

LOVELESS [*aside*] She has reason on her side: I have talked too much: but I must turn it off another way. [*to Amanda*] Will you then make no difference, Amanda, between the language of our sex and yours? There is a modesty restrains your tongues, which makes you speak by halves when you commend; but roving flattery gives a loose to ours, which makes us still speak double what we think: you should not therefore in so strict a sense take what I said to her advantage.

AMANDA Those flights of flattery, Sir, are to our faces only: when women once are out of hearing, you are as modest in your commendations as we are. But I shan't put you to the trouble of farther excuses, if you please this business shall rest here. Only give me leave to wish both for your peace and mine, that you may never meet this miracle of beauty more.

LOVELESS I am content.

Enter Servant.

SERVANT Madam, there's a young lady at the door in a chair, desires to know whether your ladyship sees company. I think her name is Berinthia.

AMANDA O dear! 'Tis a relation I have not seen these five years. Pray her to walk in. [*Exit Servant*]
[*to Loveless*] Here's another beauty for you. She was young when I saw her last; but I hear she's grown extremely handsome.

LOVELESS Don't you be jealous now; for I shall gaze upon her too.

Enter Berinthia.

LOVELESS [*aside*] Ha! By heavens the very woman.

BERINTHIA [*saluting Amanda*] Dear Amanda, I did not expect to meet with you in Town.

AMANDA Sweet cousin, I'm overjoyed to see you. [*to Loveless*] Mr Loveless, here's a relation and a friend of mine, I desire you'll be better acquainted with.

LOVELESS [*saluting Berinthia*] If my wife never desires a harder thing, Madam, her request will be easily granted.

BERINTHIA [*to Amanda*] I think, Madam, I ought to wish you joy.

AMANDA Joy! Upon what?

BERINTHIA Upon your marriage: you were a widow★ when I saw you last.

LOVELESS You ought rather, Madam, to wish me joy upon that, since I am the only gainer.

BERINTHIA If she has got so good a husband as the world reports, she has gained enough to expect the compliments of her friends upon it.

LOVELESS If the world is so favourable to me, to allow I deserve that title, I hope 'tis so just to my wife to own I derive it from her.

BERINTHIA Sir, it is so just to you both, to own you are, (and deserve to be) the happiest pair that live in it.

LOVELESS I'm afraid we shall lose that character, Madam, whenever you happen to change your condition.

Enter Servant.

SERVANT Sir, my Lord Foppington presents his humble service to you, and desires to know how you do. He but just now heard you were in Town. He's at the next door; and if it be not inconvenient, he'll come and wait upon you.

LOVELESS Lord Foppington? – I know him not.

BERINTHIA Not his dignity, perhaps, but you do his person. 'Tis Sir Novelty; he has bought a barony in order to marry a

★ a widow: a reference to Amanda as she supposed herself to be in Cibber's *Love's Last Shift* I, iii.

great fortune: his patent has not been passed eight and forty hours, and he has already sent how-do-ye's to all the Town, to make 'em acquainted with his title.

LOVELESS Give my service to his Lordship, and let him know, I am proud of the honour he intends me. [*Exit* ⟨*Servant*⟩] Sure this addition of quality, must have so improved his coxcomb, he can't but be very good company for a quarter of an hour.

AMANDA Now it moves my pity more than my mirth, to see a man whom nature has made no fool, be so very industrious to pass for an ass.

LOVELESS No, there you are wrong, Amanda; you should never bestow your pity upon those who take pains for your contempt. Pity those whom nature abuses, but never those who abuse nature.

BERINTHIA Besides, the Town would be robbed of one of its chief diversions, if it should become a crime to laugh at a fool.

AMANDA I could never yet perceive the Town inclined to part with any of its diversions, for the sake of their being crimes; but I have seen it very fond of some, I think had little else to recommend 'em.

BERINTHIA I doubt, Amanda, you are grown its enemy, you speak with so much warmth against it.

AMANDA I must confess I am not much its friend.

BERINTHIA Then give me leave to make you mine, by not engaging in its quarrel.

AMANDA You have many stronger claims than that, Berinthia, whenever you think fit to plead your title.

LOVELESS You have done well to engage a second, my dear; for here comes one will be apt to call you to an account for your country principles.

Enter Lord Foppington.

LORD FOPPINGTON [*to Loveless*] Sir, I am your most humble servant.

LOVELESS I wish you joy, my lord.

LORD FOPPINGTON O Lard, Sir – Madam, your ladyship's welcome to Tawn.

AMANDA I wish your lordship joy.

LORD FOPPINGTON O heavens, Madam –

LOVELESS My lord this young lady is a relation of my wife's.

LORD FOPPINGTON [*saluting her*] The beautifull'st race of people upon earth: rat me. Dear Loveless, I'm overjoyed to see you have braught your family to Tawn again; I am, stap my vitals – [*aside*] Far I design to lie with your wife. [*to Amanda*] Far Gad's sake, Madam, haw has your ladyship been able to subsist thus long, under the fatigue of a country life?

AMANDA My life has been very far from that, my lord; it has been a very quiet one.

LORD FOPPINGTON Why, that's the fatigue I speak of Madam: for 'tis impossible to be quiet, without thinking: now thinking is to me, the greatest fatigue in the world.

AMANDA Does not your lordship love reading then?

LORD FOPPINGTON Oh, passionately, Madam – but I never think of what I read.

BERINTHIA Why, can your lordship read without thinking?

LORD FOPPINGTON O Lard – Can your ladyship pray without devotion – Madam?

AMANDA Well, I must own I think books the best entertainment in the world.

LORD FOPPINGTON I am so much of your ladyship's mind; Madam; that I have a private gallery (where I walk sometimes) is furnished with nothing but books and looking-glasses. Madam, I have gilded 'em, and ranged 'em so prettily, before Gad, it is the most entertaining thing in the world to walk and look upon 'em.

AMANDA Nay, I love a neat library too; but 'tis I think the inside of the book, should recommend it most to us.

LORD FOPPINGTON That I must confess I am nat altogether so fand of. Far to mind the inside of a book, is to entertain oneself with the forced product of another man's brain. Naw I think a man of quality and breeding, may be much better diverted with the natural sprauts of his own. But to say the truth, Madam, let a man love reading never so well, when once he comes to know this Tawn, he finds so many better ways of passing the four and twenty hours, that 'twere ten thousand pities he should consume his time in that. Far example, Madam, my life: my life, Madam, is a perpetual stream of pleasure, that glides through such a variety of entertainments, I believe the wisest of our ancestors never had the least conception of any of 'em. I rise, Madam, about ten a-clack. I don't rise sooner, because 'tis the worst thing in the world for the complexion; nat that I pretend to be a beau: but a man must endeavour to look wholesome, lest he make so nauseous a figure in the side-bax, the ladies should be compelled to turn their eyes upon the play. So at ten a-clack I say I rise. Naw if I find 'tis a good day, I resalve to take a turn in the Park, and see the fine women: so huddle on my clothes, and get dressed by one. If it be nasty weather, I take a turn in the chocolate-hause; where, as you walk Madam, you have the prettiest prospect in the world; you have looking-glasses all round you. – But I'm afraid I tire the company?

BERINTHIA Not at all. Pray go on.

LORD FOPPINGTON Why then, ladies, from thence I go to dinner at Lacket's; where you are so nicely and delicately served, that, stap my vitals, they shall compose you a dish no bigger than a saucer, shall come to fifty shillings. Between eating my dinner, (and washing my mauth, ladies) I spend my time, 'till I go to the play;* where, 'till nine a-clack, I entertain myself with looking upon the company; and usually dispose of one hour more in leading 'em aut. So there's twelve of the four and twenty pretty well over. The other twelve, Madam, are disposed of in two articles: in the first four, I toast myself drunk, and in t'other eight, I sleep myself sober again. Thus, ladies, you see my life is an eternal raund O of delights.

LOVELESS 'Tis a heavenly one, indeed.

AMANDA But I thought, my lord, you beaux spent a great deal of your time in intrigues: you have given us no account of them yet.

LORD FOPPINGTON [*aside*] Soh; she would enquire into my amours – that's jealousy – she begins to be in love with me. [*to Amanda*] Why, Madam – as to time for my intrigues, I usually make detachments of it from my other pleasures, according to the exigency: far your ladyship may please to take notice, that those who intrigue with women of quality, have rarely occasion far above half an hour at a time: people of that rank being under those

---

* the play: plays generally commenced before six o'clock at this period.

decorums, they can seldom give you a langer view than will just serve to shoot 'em flying. So that the course of my other pleasures, is not very much interrupted by my amours.

LOVELESS But your lordship is now become a pillar of the state: you must attend the weighty affairs of the nation.

LORD FOPPINGTON Sir – as to weighty affairs. – I leave them to weighty heads. I never intend mine shall be a burthen to my body.

LOVELESS O but you'll find the House will expect your attendance.

LORD FOPPINGTON Sir you'll find the House will compound★ for my appearance.

LOVELESS But your friends will take it ill if you don't attend their particular causes.

LORD FOPPINGTON Not, Sir, if I come time enough, to give 'em my particular vote.

BERINTHIA But pray, my lord, how do you dispose of yourself on Sundays, for that, methinks, is a day should hang wretchedly upon your hands.

LORD FOPPINGTON Why faith, Madam, – Sunday – is a vile day I must confess. I intend to move for leave to bring in a bill, that the players may work upon it, as well as the hackney coaches. Though this I must say for the government, it leaves us the churches to entertain us – But then again, they begin so abominable early, a man must rise by candlelight to get dressed by the psalm.†

BERINTHIA Pray which church does your lordship most oblige with your presence?

LORD FOPPINGTON Oh, Saint James's,‡ Madam, – There's much the best company.

AMANDA Is there good preaching too?

LORD FOPPINGTON Why faith, Madam, – I can't tell. A man must have very little to do there, that can give an account of the sermon.

BERINTHIA You can give us an account of the ladies at least?

★ compound: agree mutually.
† the psalm: the time the psalm was sung in the morning service.
‡ Saint James's: a fashionable church, recently built in Piccadilly.

LORD FOPPINGTON Or I deserve to be excommunicated. – There is my Lady Tattle, my Lady Prate, my Lady Titter, my Lady Leer, my Lady Giggle, and my Lady Grin. These sit in the front of the boxes, and all church time, are the prettiest company in the world, stap my vitals. [*to Amanda*] Mayn't we hope for the honour to see your ladyship added to our society, Madam?

AMANDA Alas, my lord, I am the worst company in the world at church: I'm apt to mind the prayers or the sermon, or –

LORD FOPPINGTON One is indeed strangely apt at church, to mind what one should not do. But I hope, Madam, at one time or other, I shall have the honour to lead your ladyship to your coach there. [*aside*] Methinks she seems strangely pleased with everything I say to her. – 'Tis a vast pleasure to receive encouragement from a woman, before her husband's face – I have a good mind to pursue my conquest, and speak the thing plainly to her at once. – Egad I'll do't, and that in so cavalier a manner, she shall be surprised at it. Ladies I'll take my leave, I'm afraid I begin to grow troublesome with the length of my visit.

AMANDA Your lordship's too entertaining to grow troublesome anywhere.

LORD FOPPINGTON [*aside*] That now was as much as if she had said – 'Pray lie with me'. I'll let her see I'm quick of apprehension. [*to Amanda*] O Lard, Madam, I had like to have forgot a secret, I must needs tell your ladyship. [*to Loveless*] Ned you must not be so jealous now as to listen.

LOVELESS Not I, my lord, I am too fashionable a husband to pry into the secrets of my wife.

LORD FOPPINGTON [*to Amanda squeezing her hand*] I am in love with you, to desperation, strike me speechless.

AMANDA [*giving him a box o'th'ear*] Then thus I return your passion; an impudent fool.

LORD FOPPINGTON Gad's curse Madam, I'm a peer of the realm.

LOVELESS Hey, what the devil do you affront my wife, Sir, nay then – [*they draw and fight*]

AMANDA Ah! What has my folly done? Help, murder, help: part 'em for heaven's sake. [*the women run shrieking for help*]

LORD FOPPINGTON [*falling back, and leaning upon his sword*] Ah – quite through the body – stap my vitals.

Enter Servants.

LOVELESS [*running to him*] I hope I han't killed the fool however. –
Bear him up! Where's your wound?

LORD FOPPINGTON Just through the guts.

LOVELESS Call a surgeon there: unbutton him quickly.

LORD FOPPINGTON Aye pray make haste.

LOVELESS This mischief you may thank yourself for.

LORD FOPPINGTON I may so. Love's the devil indeed, Ned.

Enter Seringe and Servant.

SERVANT Here's Mr Seringe, Sir, was just going by the door.

LORD FOPPINGTON He's the welcomest man alive.

SERINGE Stand by, stand by, stand by. Pray gentlemen stand by.
Lord have mercy upon us, did you never see a man run through the
body before? Pray stand by.

LORD FOPPINGTON Ah Mr Seringe – I'm a dead man.

SERINGE A dead man and I by – I should laugh to see that, egad.

LOVELESS Prithee don't stand prating, but look upon his wound.

SERINGE Why, what if I won't look upon his wound this hour Sir?

LOVELESS Why then he'll bleed to death, Sir.

SERINGE Why, then I'll fetch him to life again, Sir.

LOVELESS S'life he's run through the guts I tell thee.

SERINGE Would he were run through the heart, I should get the
more credit by his cure. Now I hope you're satisfied? – Come,
now let me come at him; now let me come at him. [*viewing his
wound*] Oons, what a gash is here? – Why, Sir, a man may drive
a coach and six horses into your body.

LORD FOPPINGTON Ho –

SERINGE Why, what the devil, have you run the gentleman
through with a scythe. – [*aside*] A little prick, between the skin
and the ribs, that's all.

LOVELESS Let me see his wound.

SERINGE Then you shall dress it, Sir, for if anybody looks upon it,
I won't.

LOVELESS Why, thou art the veriest coxcomb I ever saw.

SERINGE Sir, I am not master of my trade for nothing.

LORD FOPPINGTON Surgeon.

SERINGE Well, Sir.

LORD FOPPINGTON Is there any hopes?

SERINGE Hopes? – I can't tell. – What are you willing to give for your cure?

LORD FOPPINGTON Five hundred paunds with pleasure.

SERINGE Why then perhaps there may be hopes, but we must avoid farther delay. Here: help the gentleman into a chair, and carry him to my house presently, that's the properest place, [*aside*] to bubble★ him out of his money. Come, a chair, a chair quickly – there, in with him. [*they put him into a chair*]

LORD FOPPINGTON Dear Loveless, – adieu. If I die – I forgive thee, and if I live – I hope thou'lt do as much by me. I'm very sorry you and I should quarrel; but I hope here's an end on't, for if you are satisfied – I am.

LOVELESS I shall hardly think it worth my prosecuting any farther, so you may be at rest, Sir.

LORD FOPPINGTON Thou art a generous fellow, strike me dumb. [*aside*] But thou hast an impertinent wife, stap my vitals.

SERINGE So, carry him off, carry him off, we shall have him prate himself into a fever by and by, carry him off.

[*Exit Seringe with Lord Foppington*]

AMANDA Now on my knees, my dear, let me ask your pardon for my indiscretion, my own I never shall obtain.

LOVELESS Oh! There's no harm done: you served him well.

AMANDA He did indeed deserve it. But I tremble to think how dear my indiscreet resentment might have cost you.

LOVELESS O no matter, never trouble yourself about that.

BERINTHIA For heaven's sake, what was't he did to you?

AMANDA O nothing; he only squeezed me kindly by the hand, and frankly offered me a coxcomb's heart. I know I was to blame to resent it as I did; since nothing but a quarrel could ensue. But the fool so surprised me with his insolence, I was not mistress of my fingers.

BERINTHIA Now I dare swear, he thinks you had 'em at great command, they obeyed you so readily.

Enter Worthy.

★ bubble: cheat.

WORTHY Save you, save you good people: I'm glad to find you all alive, I met a wounded peer carrying off: for heaven's sake what was the matter?

LOVELESS O a trifle: he would have lain with my wife before my face, so she obliged him with a box o'th' ear, and I run him through the body: that was all.

WORTHY Bagatelle on all sides. But, pray Madam, how long has this noble lord been an humble servant of yours?

AMANDA This is the first I have heard on't. So I suppose 'tis his quality more than his love, has brought him into this adventure. He thinks his title an authentic passport to every woman's heart, below the degree of a peeress.

WORTHY He's coxcomb enough to think anything. But I would not have you brought into trouble for him: I hope there's no danger of his life?

LOVELESS None at all: he's fallen into the hands of a roguish surgeon, who, I perceive designs to frighten a little money out of him. But I saw his wound, 'tis nothing; he may go to the play tonight if he pleases.

WORTHY I am glad you have corrected him without farther mischief. And now, Sir, if these ladies have no farther service for you, you'll oblige me if you can go to the place, I spoke to you of t'other day.

LOVELESS With all my heart. [*aside*] Though I could wish methinks, to stay and gaze a little longer on that creature. Good gods! How beautiful she is – But what have I to do with beauty? I have already had my portion, and must not covet more. [*to Worthy*] Come, Sir, when you please.

WORTHY Ladies your servant.

AMANDA Mr Loveless, pray one word with you before you go.

LOVELESS [*to Worthy*] I'll overtake you, Sir, what would my dear.

[*Exit Worthy*]

AMANDA Only a woman's foolish question. How do you like my cousin here?

LOVELESS Jealous already, Amanda?

AMANDA Not at all; I ask you for another reason.

LOVELESS [*aside*] Whate'er her reason be, I must not tell her true. [*to Amanda*] Why, I confess she's handsome. But you must not think I slight your kinswoman, if I own to you, of all the women who may claim that character, she is the last would triumph in my heart.

AMANDA I'm satisfied.

LOVELESS Now tell me why you asked?

AMANDA At night I will. Adieu.

LOVELESS I'm yours. [*kissing her*]

AMANDA [*aside*] I'm glad to find he does not like her; for I have a great mind to persuade her to come and live with me. [*to Berinthia*] Now dear Berinthia, let me enquire a little into your affairs: for I do assure you I am enough your friend, to interest myself in everything that concerns you.

BERINTHIA You formerly have given me such proofs on't, I should be very much to blame to doubt it. I am sorry I have no secrets to trust you with, that I might convince you how entire a confidence I durst repose in you.

AMANDA Why is it possible, that one so young and beautiful as you should live and have no secrets?

BERINTHIA What secrets do you mean?

AMANDA Lovers.

BERINTHIA O twenty; but not one secret one amongst 'em. Lovers in this age have too much honour to do anything underhand; they do all above board.

AMANDA That now methinks would make me hate a man.

BERINTHIA But the women of the Town are of another mind: for by this means a lady may (with the expense of a few coquette glances) lead twenty fools about in a string, for two or three years together. Whereas, if she should allow 'em greater favours, and oblige 'em to secrecy, she would not keep one of 'em a fortnight.

AMANDA There's something indeed in that to satisfy the vanity of a woman, but I can't comprehend how the men find their account in it.

BERINTHIA Their entertainment I must confess is a riddle to me. For there's very few of 'em ever get farther, than a bow and an ogle. I have half a score for my share, who follow me all over the Town; and at the play, the park, and the church, do (with their eyes) say the violent'st things to me – But I never hear any more of 'em.

AMANDA What can be the reason of that?

BERINTHIA One reason is, they don't know how to go farther. They have had so little practice they don't understand the trade. But besides their ignorance, you must know there is not one of my half score lovers but what follows half a score mistresses. Now their affections being divided amongst so many, are not strong enough for anyone to make 'em pursue her to the purpose. Like a young puppy in a warren, they have a flirt at all, and catch none.

AMANDA Yet they seem to have a torrent of love to dispose of.

BERINTHIA They have so: but 'tis like the rivers of a modern philosopher* (whose works, though a woman, I have read) it sets out with a violent stream, splits in a thousand branches, and is all lost in the sands.

AMANDA But do you think this river of love runs all its course without doing any mischief? Do you think it overflows nothing.

BERINTHIA O yes, 'tis true it never breaks into anybody's ground that has the least fence about it; but it overflows all the commons that lie in its way. And this is the utmost achievement of those dreadful champions in the field of love – the beaux.

AMANDA But prithee, Berinthia, instruct me a little farther, for I'm so great a novice, I am almost ashamed on't. My husband's leaving me whilst I was young and fond, threw me into that depth of discontent, that ever since I have led so private and recluse a life, my ignorance is scarce conceivable. I therefore fain would be instructed: not (heaven knows) that what you call intrigues have any charms for me; my love and principles are too well fixed. The practical part of all unlawful love is –

BERINTHIA O 'tis abominable: but for the speculative; that we must all confess is entertaining. The conversation of all the virtuous women in the Town, turns upon that and new clothes.

AMANDA Pray be so just then to me, to believe, 'tis with a world of innocency I would enquire, whether you think those women we call women of reputation, do really 'scape all other men, as they do those shadows of 'em, the beaux.

BERINTHIA O no Amanda; there are a sort of men make dreadful

* a modern philosopher: according to Curt A. Zimansky, in his edition of 1969, Thomas Burnet's *Sacred Theory of the Earth* (1684) is alluded to here.

work amongst 'em: men that may be called, the beaux' antipathy,
for they agree in nothing but walking upon two legs.
These have brains,
The beau has none.
These are in love with their mistress,
The beau with himself.
They take care of her reputation,
He's industrious to destroy it.
They are decent,
He's a fop.
They are sound,
He's rotten.
They are men,
He's an ass.

AMANDA If this be their character, I fancy we had here e'en now
a pattern of 'em both.

BERINTHIA His lordship and Mr Worthy?

AMANDA The same.

BERINTHIA As for the lord, he's eminently so: and for the other
I can assure you, there's not a man in Town who has a better
interest with the women, that are worth having an interest with.
But 'tis all private: he's like a back-stair minister at Court, who,
whilst the reputed favorites are sauntering in the bed-chamber, is
ruling the roost in the closet.

AMANDA He answers then the opinion I had ever of him. Heavens!
What a difference there is between a man like him, and that vain
nauseous fop, Sir Novelty. [*taking her hand*] I must acquaint you
with a secret, cousin. 'Tis not that fool alone, has talked to me of
love. Worthy has been tampering too: 'tis true, he has done't in
vain: not all his charms or art have power to shake me: my love,
my duty, and my virtue, are such faithful guards, I need not fear
my heart should e'er betray me. But what I wonder at is this. I
find I did not start at his proposal; as when it came from one
whom I condemned. I therefore mention his attempt, that I may
learn from you, whence it proceeds; that vice (which cannot
change its nature) should so far change at least its shape, as that
the self-same crime proposed from one shall seem a monster
gaping at your ruin; when from another it shall look so kind; as

though it were your friend, and never meant to harm you. Whence think you can this difference proceed, for 'tis not love, heaven knows.

BERINTHIA O no; I would not for the world believe it were. But possibly, should there a dreadful sentence pass upon you, to undergo the rage of both their passions; the pain you'd apprehend from one, might seem so trivial to the other; the danger would not quite so much alarm you.

AMANDA Fie, fie, Berinthia, you would indeed alarm me, could you incline me to a thought, that all the merit of mankind combined, could shake that tender love I bear my husband: no, he sits triumphant in my heart, and nothing can dethrone him.

BERINTHIA But should he abdicate again, do you think you should preserve the vacant throne ten tedious winters more in hopes of his return?

AMANDA Indeed I think I should. Though I confess, after those obligations he has to me, should he abandon me once more, my heart would grow extremely urgent with me to root him thence, and cast him out for ever.

BERINTHIA Were I that thing they call a slighted wife, somebody should run the risk of being that thing they call – a husband.

AMANDA O fie, Berinthia, no revenge should ever be taken against a husband: but to wrong his bed is a vengeance which of all vengeance –

BERINTHIA Is the sweetest, ha, ha, ha. Don't I talk madly?

AMANDA Madly indeed.

BERINTHIA Yet I'm very innocent.

AMANDA That I dare swear you are. I know how to make allowances for your humour: you were always very entertaining company; but I find since marriage and widowhood have shown you the world a little, you are very much improved.

BERINTHIA [aside] Alack-a-day, there has gone more than that to improve me, if she knew all.

AMANDA For heaven's sake, Berinthia, tell me what way I shall take to persuade you to come and live with me?

BERINTHIA Why, one way in the world there is; – and but one.

AMANDA Pray which is that?

BERINTHIA It is, to assure me – I shall be very welcome.

AMANDA If that be all, you shall e'en lie here tonight.

BERINTHIA Tonight?

AMANDA Yes, tonight.

BERINTHIA Why, the people where I lodge will think me mad.

AMANDA Let 'em think what they please.

BERINTHIA Say you so, Amanda? Why then they shall think what they please: for I'm a young widow, and I care not what anybody thinks. Ah, Amanda, it's a delicious thing to be a young widow.

AMANDA You'll hardly make me think so.

BERINTHIA Phu, because you are in love with your husband: but that is not every woman's case.

AMANDA I hope 'twas yours, at least.

BERINTHIA Mine, say ye? – Now have I a great mind to tell you a lie, but I should do it so awkwardly, you'd find me out.

AMANDA Then e'en speak the truth.

BERINTHIA Shall I? – Then after all I did love him, Amanda as a nun does penance.

AMANDA Why did not you refuse to marry him then?

BERINTHIA Because my mother would have whipped me.

AMANDA How did you live together?

BERINTHIA Like man and wife, asunder.
He loved the country, I the Town.
He hawks and hounds, I coaches and equipage.
He eating and drinking, I carding and playing.
He the sound of a horn, I the squeak of a fiddle.
We were dull company at table, worse abed.
Whenever we met, we gave one another the spleen.
And never agreed but once, which was about lying alone.

AMANDA But tell me one thing, truly and sincerely.

BERINTHIA What's that?

AMANDA Notwithstanding all these jars, did not his death at last – extremely trouble you?

BERINTHIA O yes: not that my present pangs were so very violent, but the after-pains were intolerable. I was forced to wear a beastly widow's band★ a twelvemonth for't.

AMANDA Women I find have different inclinations.

★ band: a head band.

BERINTHIA Women I find keep different company. When your husband ran away from you, if you had fallen into some of my acquaintance, 'twould have saved you many a tear. But you go and live with a grandmother, a bishop, and an old nurse; which was enough to make any woman break her heart for her husband. Pray, Amanda, if ever you are a widow again, keep yourself so as I do.

AMANDA Why do you then resolve you'll never marry?

BERINTHIA Oh, no; I resolve I will.

AMANDA How so?

BERINTHIA That I never may.

AMANDA You banter me.

BERINTHIA Indeed I don't. But I consider I'm a woman, and form my resolutions accordingly.

AMANDA Well, my opinion is, form what resolution you will, matrimony will be the end on't.

BERINTHIA Faith it won't.

AMANDA How do you know?

BERINTHIA I'm sure on't.

AMANDA Why, do you think 'tis impossible for you to fall in love?

BERINTHIA No.

AMANDA Nay, but to grow so passionately fond, that nothing but the man you love can give you rest?

BERINTHIA Well, what then?

AMANDA Why, then you'll marry him.

BERINTHIA How do you know that?

AMANDA Why what can you do else?

BERINTHIA Nothing – but sit and cry.

AMANDA Psha.

BERINTHIA Ah, poor Amanda; you have led a country life: but if you'll consult the widows of this Town, they'll tell you, you should never take a lease of a house you can hire for a quarter's warning.* [*Exeunt*]

* a quarter's warning: three months' notice.

ACT THREE

⟨SCENE I⟩

Enter Lord Foppington and Servant.

LORD FOPPINGTON Hey, fellow, let the coach come to the door.

SERVANT Will your lordship venture so soon to expose yourself to the weather?

LORD FOPPINGTON Sir, I will venture as soon as I can, to expose myself to the ladies, though give me my cloak however; for in that side-box, what between the air that comes in at the door on one side, and the intolerable warmth of the masks* on t'other: a man gets so many heats and colds, 'twould destroy the canstitution of a harse.

SERVANT [*putting on his cloak*] I wish your lordship would please to keep house a little longer, I'm afraid your honour does not well consider your wound.

LORD FOPPINGTON My wound? – I would not be in eclipse another day, though I had as many wounds in my guts as I have had in my heart.

Enter Young Fashion.

YOUNG FASHION Brother, your servant, how do you find yourself today?

LORD FOPPINGTON So well, that I have ardered my coach to the door: so there's no great danger of death this baut Tam.

YOUNG FASHION I'm very glad of it.

LORD FOPPINGTON [*aside*] That I believe's a lie. ⟨*to Young Fashion*⟩ Prithee, Tam, tell me one thing. Did nat your heart cut a caper up to your mouth, when you heard I was run through the bady?

YOUNG FASHION Why do you think it should?

LORD FOPPINGTON Because I remember mine did so, when I heard my father was shat through the head.

YOUNG FASHION It then did very ill.

LORD FOPPINGTON Prithee, why so?

YOUNG FASHION Because he used you very well.

* masks: probably prostitutes in masks.

LORD FOPPINGTON Well? – Naw strike me dumb he starved me. He has let me want a thausand women, for want of a thausand paund.

YOUNG FASHION Then he hindered you from making a great many ill bargains, for I think no woman is worth money, that will take money.

LORD FOPPINGTON If I were a younger brother, I should think so too.

YOUNG FASHION Why, is it possible you can value a woman that's to be bought.

LORD FOPPINGTON Prithee, why not as well as a pad-nag?*

YOUNG FASHION Because a woman has a heart to dispose of; a horse has none.

LORD FOPPINGTON Look you Tam, of all things that belang to a woman, I have an aversion to her heart: far when once a woman has given you her heart – you can never get rid of the rest of her body.

YOUNG FASHION This is strange doctrine: but pray in your amours how is it with your own heart?

LORD FOPPINGTON Why, my heart in my amours – is like my heart aut of my amours: *à la glace*. My bady Tam is a watch; and my heart is the pendulum to it; whilst the finger runs raund to every hour in the circle, that still beats the same time.

YOUNG FASHION Then you are seldom much in love?

LORD FOPPINGTON Never, stap my vitals.

YOUNG FASHION Why then did you make all this bustle about Amanda?

LORD FOPPINGTON Because she was a woman of an insolent virtue, and I thought myself picked in honour to debauch her.

YOUNG FASHION Very well. [*aside*] Here's a rare fellow for you, to have the spending of five thousand pounds a year. But now for my business with him. [*to Lord Foppington*] Brother, though I know to talk to you of business (especially of money) is a theme not quite so entertaining to you as that of the ladies: my necessities are such, I hope you'll have patience to hear me.

LORD FOPPINGTON The greatness of your necessities Tam, is the worst argument in the world for your being patiently heard. I do

* pad-nag: an easy-going horse.

believe you are going to make me a very good speech, but, strike me dumb, it has the worst beginning of any speech I have heard this twelvemonth.

YOUNG FASHION I'm very sorry you think so.

LORD FOPPINGTON I do believe thau art. But come, let's know thy affair quickly, far 'tis a new play, and I shall be so rumpled and squeezed with pressing through the crawd, to get to my servant, the women will think I have lain all night in my clothes.

YOUNG FASHION Why then (that I may not be the author of so great a misfortune) my case in a word is this. The necessary expenses of my travels have so much exceeded the wretched income of my annuity, that I have been forced to mortgage it for five hundred pounds, which is spent; so that unless you are so kind to assist me in redeeming it, I know no remedy, but to go take a purse. *

LORD FOPPINGTON Why, faith Tam – to give you my sense of the thing, I do think taking a purse the best remedy in the world; for if you succeed, you are relieved that way; if you are taken – you are relieved t'other.

YOUNG FASHION I'm glad to see you are in so pleasant a humour, I hope I shall find the effects on't.

LORD FOPPINGTON Why, do you then really think it a reasonable thing I should give you five hundred paunds?

YOUNG FASHION I do not ask it as a due, brother, I am willing to receive it as a favour.

LORD FOPPINGTON Thau art willing to receive it anyhaw, strike me speechless. But these are damned times to give money in, taxes are so great, repairs so exorbitant, tenants such rogues, and periwigs so dear, that the devil take me I am reduced to that extremity in my cash, I have been forced to retrench in that one article of sweet pawder, till I have braught it dawn to five guineas a manth. Naw judge, Tam, whether I can spare you five hundred paunds.

YOUNG FASHION If you can't, I must starve, that's all. [*aside*] Damn him.

LORD FOPPINGTON All I can say is, you should have been a better husband.†

---

* take a purse: become a highwayman.   † husband: manager of your resources.

YOUNG FASHION Oons if you can't live upon five thousand a year, how do you think I should do't upon two hundred?

LORD FOPPINGTON Don't be in a passion Tam, far passion is the most unbecoming thing in the world – to the face. Look you, I don't love to say anything to you to make you melancholy; but upon this occasion I must take leave to put you in mind, that a running horse★ does require more attendance than a coach-horse. Nature has made some difference 'twixt you and I.

YOUNG FASHION Yes, she has made you older. [*aside*] Pox take her.

LORD FOPPINGTON That is nat all, Tam.

YOUNG FASHION Why, what is there else?

LORD FOPPINGTON [*looking first upon himself, then upon his brother*] – Ask the ladies.

YOUNG FASHION Why, thou essence-bottle,† thou musk-cat, dost thou then think thou hast any advantage over me, but what fortune has given thee.

LORD FOPPINGTON I do – stap my vitals.

YOUNG FASHION Now, by all that's great and powerful, thou art the prince of coxcombs.

LORD FOPPINGTON Sir, – I am praud of being at the head of so prevailing a party.

YOUNG FASHION Will nothing then provoke thee? – Draw coward.

LORD FOPPINGTON Look you, Tam, you know I have always taken you for a mighty dull fellow, and here is one of the foolishest plats broke out, that I have seen a long time. Your paverty makes your life so burthensome to you, you would provoke me to a quarrel, in hopes either to slip through my lungs into my estate, or to get yourself run through the guts, to put an end to your pain: but I will disappoint you in both your designs; far with the temper of a philasapher, and the discretion of a statesman, – I will go to the play with my sword in my scabbard.

[*Exit Lord Foppington*]

YOUNG FASHION Soh, farewell snuff-box. And now, conscience, I defy thee.

★ a running horse: a racehorse.   † essence-bottle: scent bottle.

Enter Lory.

LORY Sir.

YOUNG FASHION Here's rare news, Lory: his lordship has given me a pill has purged off all my scruples.

LORY Then my heart's at ease again: for I have been in a lamentable fright, Sir, ever since your conscience had the impudence to intrude into your company.

YOUNG FASHION Be at peace: it will come there no more: my brother has given it a wring by the nose, and I have kicked it downstairs. So run away to the inn; get the horses ready quickly, and bring 'em to old Coupler's without a moment's delay.

LORY Then, Sir, you are going straight about the fortune?

YOUNG FASHION I am; away; fly, Lory.

LORY The happiest day I ever saw. I'm upon the wing already.

[*Exeunt several ways*]

SCENE ⟨II⟩

A garden

Enter Loveless and Servant.

LOVELESS Is my wife within?

SERVANT No, Sir, she has been gone out this half hour.

LOVELESS 'Tis well; leave me.   ⟨*Exit Servant*⟩

[*solus*] Sure fate has yet some business to be done,
Before Amanda's heart and mine must rest:
Else, why amongst those legions of her sex,
Which throng the world,
Should she pick out for her companion
The only one on earth,
Whom nature has endowed for her undoing.
Undoing was't, I said? – Who shall undo her?
Is not her empire fixed? Am I not hers?
Did she not rescue me, a grovelling slave?
When chained and bound by that black tyrant vice,
I laboured in his vilest drudgery,
Did she not ransom me, and set me free?
Nay more: when by my follies sunk

To a poor tattered despicable beggar,
Did she not lift me up to envied fortune?
Give me herself, and all that she possessed?
Without a thought of more return,
Than what a poor repenting heart might make her.
Han't she done this? And if she has,
Am I not strongly bound to love her for it?
To love her! – Why, do I not love her then?
By earth and heaven I do.
Nay, I have demonstration that I do:
For I would sacrifice my life to serve her.
Yet hold: – if laying down my life
Be demonstration of my love,
What is't I feel in favour of Berinthia?
For should she be in danger, methinks I could incline
To risk it for her service too; and yet I do not love her.
How then subsists my proof? –
– Oh, I have found it out.
What I would do for one, is demonstration of my love; and if I'd
do as much for t'other: it there is demonstration of my friend-
ship – Aye – it must be so. I find I'm very much her friend. –
Yet let me ask myself one puzzling question more. Whence springs
this mighty friendship all at once? For our acquaintance is of
later date. [*musing*] Now friendship's said to be a plant of tedious
growth; its root composed of tender fibres, nice in their taste,
cautious in spreading, checked with the least corruption in the
soil; long ere it take, and longer still ere it appear to do so:
whilst mine is in a moment shot so high, and fixed so fast, it
seems beyond the power of storms to shake it. I doubt it thrives
too fast.

Enter Berinthia.

Ha, she here! – Nay, then take heed my heart, for there are
dangers towards.

BERINTHIA What makes you look so thoughtful Sir? I hope you
are not ill?

LOVELESS I was debating, Madam, whether I was so or not; and
that was it which made me look so thoughtful.

BERINTHIA Is it then so hard a matter to decide? I thought all people had been acquainted with their own bodies, though few people know their own minds.

LOVELESS What, if the distemper, I suspect, be in the mind?

BERINTHIA Why, then I'll undertake to prescribe you a cure.

LOVELESS Alas, you undertake you know not what.

BERINTHIA So far at least then allow me to be a physician.

LOVELESS Nay, I'll allow you so yet farther: for I have reason to believe, should I put myself into your hands, you would increase my distemper.

BERINTHIA Perhaps I might have reasons from the College⋆ not to be too quick in your cure; but 'tis possible I might find ways to give you often ease, Sir.

LOVELESS Were I but sure of that, I'd quickly lay my case before you.

BERINTHIA Whether you are sure of it or no, what risk do you run in trying?

LOVELESS Oh, a very great one.

BERINTHIA How?

LOVELESS You might betray my distemper to my wife.

BERINTHIA And so lose all my practice.

LOVELESS Will you then keep my secret?

BERINTHIA I will, if it don't burst me.

LOVELESS Swear.

BERINTHIA I do.

LOVELESS By what?

BERINTHIA By woman.

LOVELESS That's swearing by my deity. Do it by your own, or I shan't believe you.

BERINTHIA By man, then.

LOVELESS I'm satisfied. Now hear my symptoms, and give me your advice. The first were these:
When 'twas my chance to see you at the play,
A random glance you threw, at first alarmed me,
I could not turn my eyes from whence the danger came:
I gazed upon you, 'till you shot again,
And then my fears came on me.

⋆ the College: the College of Physicians.

My heart began to pant, my limbs to tremble,
My blood grew thin; my pulse beat quick,
My eyes grew hot and dim, and all the frame of nature
Shook with apprehension.
'Tis true, some small recruits of resolution,
My manhood brought to my assistance,
And by their help I made a stand a while,
But found at last your arrows flew so thick,
They could not fail to pierce me;
So left the field,
And fled for shelter to Amanda's arms.
What think you of these symptoms, pray.

BERINTHIA Feverish every one of 'em. But what relief pray did your wife afford you?

LOVELESS Why, instantly she let me blood;
Which for the present much assuaged my flame.
But when I saw you, out it burst again,
And raged with greater fury than before.
Nay, since you now appear, 'tis so increased,
That in a moment if you do not help me,
I shall, whilst you look on, consume to ashes. [*taking hold of her hand*]

BERINTHIA [*breaking from him*] O Lard, let me go: 'tis the plague, and we shall all be infected.

LOVELESS [*catching her in his arms and kissing her*] Then we'll die together, my charming angel.

BERINTHIA O Ged – the devil's in you. Lord, let me go, here's somebody coming.

Enter Servant.

SERVANT Sir, my lady's come home, and desires to speak with you: she's in her chamber.

LOVELESS Tell her I'm coming.   [*Exit Servant*]
[*to Berinthia*] But before I go, one glass of nectar more to drink her health.

BERINTHIA Stand off, or I shall hate you, by heavens.

LOVELESS [*kissing her*] In matters of love, a woman's oath is no more to be minded than a man's.

BERINTHIA Um –

Enter Worthy.

WORTHY Ha! What's here? My old mistress, and so close, i'faith?
I would not spoil her sport for the universe.   [*He retires*]

BERINTHIA O Ged – Now do I pray to heaven,

                                         [*Exit Loveless running*]
With all my heart and soul, that the devil in hell may take me, if
ever – I was better pleased in my life – This man has bewitched
me, that's certain. [*sighing*] Well, I am condemned; but thanks to
heaven I feel myself each moment more and more prepared for
my execution. Nay, to that degree, I don't perceive I have the
least fear of dying. No, I find, let the – executioner be but a man,
and there's nothing will suffer with more resolution than a
woman. Well, I never had but one intrigue yet: but I confess I
long to have another. Pray heaven it end as the first did though,
that we may both grow weary at a time, for 'tis a melancholy
thing for lovers to outlive one another.

Enter Worthy.

WORTHY [*aside*] This discovery's a lucky one, I hope to make a
happy use on't. That gentlewoman there is no fool; so I shall be
able to make her understand her interest. [*to Berinthia*] Your
servant Madam, I need not ask you how you do, you have got so
good a colour.

BERINTHIA No better than I used to have I suppose?

WORTHY A little more blood in your cheeks.

BERINTHIA The weather's hot.

WORTHY If it were not, a woman may have a colour.

BERINTHIA What do you mean by that?

WORTHY Nothing.

BERINTHIA Why do you smile then?

WORTHY Because the weather's hot.

BERINTHIA You'll never leave roguing, I see that.

WORTHY [*putting his finger to his nose*] You'll never leave – I see that.

BERINTHIA Well, I can't imagine what you drive at. Pray tell
me what you mean?

WORTHY Do you tell me, it's the same thing?

BERINTHIA I can't.

WORTHY Guess!

BERINTHIA I shall guess wrong.

WORTHY Indeed you wont.

BERINTHIA Psha! Either tell, or let it alone.

WORTHY Nay, rather than let it alone, I will tell. But first I must put you in mind, that after what has passed 'twixt you and I, very few things ought to be secrets between us.

BERINTHIA Why what secrets do we hide? I know of none.

WORTHY Yes, there are two; one I have hid from you, and t'other you would hide from me. You are fond of Loveless, which I have discovered: and I am fond of his wife –

BERINTHIA Which I have discovered.

WORTHY Very well, now I confess your discovery to be true: what do you say to mine?

BERINTHIA Why, I confess – I would swear 'twere false, if I thought you were fool enough to believe me.

WORTHY Now am I almost in love with you again. Nay, I don't know but I might be quite so, had I made one short campaign with Amanda. Therefore if you find 'twould tickle your vanity, to bring me down once more to your lure, e'en help me quickly to dispatch her business, that I may have nothing else to do, but to apply myself to yours.

BERINTHIA Do you then think, Sir, I am old enough to be a bawd?

WORTHY No, but I think you are wise enough to –

BERINTHIA To do what?

WORTHY To hoodwink Amanda with a gallant, that she mayn't see who is her husband's mistress.

BERINTHIA [*aside*] He has reason: the hint's a good one.

WORTHY Well, Madam, what think you on't?

BERINTHIA I think you are so much a deeper politician in these affairs than I am; that I ought to have a very great regard to your advice.

WORTHY Then give me leave to put you in mind, that the most easy, safe, and pleasant situation for your own amour, is the house in which you now are; provided you keep Amanda from any sort of suspicion. That the way to do that is to engage her in an intrigue of her own, making yourself her confident. And the way to bring her to intrigue, is to make her jealous of her husband in a wrong place; which the more you foment, the less you'll be suspected. This is my scheme, in short; which if you follow as you should do (my dear Berinthia) we may all four pass the winter very pleasantly.

BERINTHIA Well, I could be glad to have nobody's sins to answer for but my own. But where there is a necessity –

WORTHY Right as you say, where there is a necessity, a Christian is bound to help his neighbour. So good Berinthia, lose no time, but let us begin the dance as fast as we can.

BERINTHIA Not till the fiddles are in tune, pray Sir. Your lady's strings will be very apt to fly, I can tell you that, if they are wound up too hastily. But if you'll have patience to screw 'em to their pitch by degrees, I don't doubt but she may endure to be played upon.

WORTHY Aye, and will make admirable music too, or I'm mistaken; but have you had no private closet discourse with her yet about males and females, and so forth, which may give you hopes in her constitution; for I know her morals are the devil against us.

BERINTHIA I have had so much discourse with her, that I believe were she once cured of her fondness to her husband, the fortress of her virtue would not be so impregnable as she fancies.

WORTHY What? She runs I'll warrant you into that common mistake of fond wives, who conclude themselves virtuous, because they can refuse a man they don't like, when they have got one they do.

BERINTHIA True, and therefore I think 'tis a presumptuous thing in a woman, to assume the name of virtuous; till she has heartily hated her husband, and been soundly in love with somebody else. Whom, if she has withstood – then – much good may it do her.

WORTHY Well, so much for her virtue. Now, one word of her inclinations, and every one to their post. What opinion do you find she has of me?

BERINTHIA What you could wish; she thinks you handsome and discreet.

WORTHY Good, that's thinking half-seas over.* One tide more brings us into port.

* half-seas over: half-way there in thought, or half-drunk.

BERINTHIA Perhaps it may, though still remember, there's a difficult bar to pass.

WORTHY I know there is, but I don't question I shall get well over it, by the help of such a pilot.

BERINTHIA You may depend upon your pilot, she'll do the best she can; so weigh anchor and be gone as soon as you please.

WORTHY I'm under sail already. Adieu.   [*Exit Worthy*]

BERINTHIA Bon voyage. [*sola*] So, here's fine work. What a business have I undertaken, I'm a very pretty gentlewoman truly; but there was no avoiding it: he'd have ruined me if I had refused him. Besides, faith, I begin to fancy there may be as much pleasure in carrying on another body's intrigue, as one's own. This at least is certain, it exercises almost all the entertaining faculties of a woman. For there's employment for hypocrisy, invention, deceit, flattery, mischief, and lying.

Enter Amanda, her Woman following her.

WOMAN If you please, Madam, only to say, whether you'll have me buy 'em or not?

AMANDA Yes, no, go fiddle; I care not what you do: prithee leave me.

WOMAN I have done.   [*Exit Woman*]

BERINTHIA What in the name of Jove's the matter with you?

AMANDA The matter Berinthia, I'm almost mad, I'm plagued to death.

BERINTHIA Who is it that plagues you?

AMANDA Who do you think should plague a wife, but her husband?

BERINTHIA O ho, is it come to that? We shall have you wish yourself a widow by and by.

AMANDA Would I were anything but what I am; a base ungrateful man, after what I have done for him, to use me thus!

BERINTHIA What, he has been ogling now I'll warrant you?

AMANDA Yes, he has been ogling.

BERINTHIA And so you are jealous? Is that all?

AMANDA That all! Is jealousy then nothing?

BERINTHIA It should be nothing, if I were in your case.

AMANDA Why, what would you do?

BERINTHIA I'd cure myself.

AMANDA How?

🔖 BERINTHIA Let blood in the fond vein: care as little for my husband, as he did for me.

AMANDA That would not stop his course.

BERINTHIA Nor nothing else, when the wind's in the warm corner. Look you, Amanda, you may build castles in the air, and fume, and fret, and grow thin and lean, and pale and ugly, if you please. But I tell you, no man worth having, is true to his wife, or can be true to his wife, or ever was, or ever will be so.

AMANDA Do you then really think he's false to me? For I did but suspect him.

BERINTHIA Think so? I know he's so.

AMANDA Is it possible? Pray tell me what you know?

BERINTHIA Don't press me then to name names; for that I have sworn I won't do.

AMANDA Well I won't; but let me know all you can without perjury.

BERINTHIA I'll let you know enough to prevent any wise woman's dying of the pip; and I hope you'll pluck up your spirits, and show upon occasion, you can be as good a wife as the best of 'em.

AMANDA Well, what a woman can do I'll endeavour.

BERINTHIA Oh, a woman can do a great deal, if once she sets her mind to it. Therefore pray don't stand trifling any longer, and teasing yourself with this and that, and your love and your virtue, and I know not what. But resolve to hold up your head, get a-tiptoe, and look over 'em all; for to my certain knowledge your husband is a-pickeering* elsewhere.

AMANDA You are sure on't?

BERINTHIA Positively; he fell in love at the play.

AMANDA Right, the very same; do you know the ugly thing?

BERINTHIA Yes, I know her well enough; but she's no such an ugly thing neither.

AMANDA Is she very handsome?

BERINTHIA Truly I think so.

AMANDA Hey ho.

---

* a-pickeering: scouting or skirmishing, a military term adapted to amorous dallying.

BERINTHIA What do you sigh for now?

AMANDA O my heart.

BERINTHIA [*aside*] Only the pangs of nature; she's in labour of her love, heaven send her a quick delivery, I'm sure she has a good midwife.

AMANDA I'm very ill, I must go to my chamber. Dear Berinthia, don't leave me a moment.

BERINTHIA No, don't fear. [*aside*] I'll see you safe brought to bed, I'll warrant you.

[*Exeunt Amanda leaning upon Berinthia*]

SCENE ⟨III⟩

A country house

Enter Young Fashion and Lory.

YOUNG FASHION So, here's our inheritance, Lory, if we can but get into possession. But methinks the seat of our family looks like Noah's ark, as if the chief part on't were designed for the fowls of the air, and the beasts of the field.

LORY Pray, Sir, don't let your head run upon the orders* of building here; get but the heiress, let the devil take the house.

YOUNG FASHION Get but the house, let the devil take the heiress, I say, at least if she be as old Coupler describes her. But come we have no time to squander. Knock at the door. [*Lory knocks two or three times*] What the devil have they got no ears in this house: knock harder.

LORY Egad, Sir, this will prove some enchanted castle; we shall have the giant come out by and by with his club, and beat our brains out. [*knocks again*]

YOUNG FASHION Hush; they come.

⟨SERVANT⟩ [*from within*] Who is there?

LORY Open the door and see: is that your country breeding?

⟨SERVANT⟩ [*within*] Aye, but two words to a bargain: Tummas, is the blunderbuss primed?

* the orders: the orders of architecture, Doric, Ionic and Corinthian.

YOUNG FASHION Oons give 'em good words, Lory, we shall be shot here a-fortune-catching.

LORY Egad, Sir, I think y'are in the right on't. Ho, Mr What-d'ye-call-'um.

SERVANT [*appears at the window with a blunderbuss*] Weall, naw what's yare business?

YOUNG FASHION Nothing, Sir, but to wait upon Sir Tunbelly, with your leave.

SERVANT To weat upon Sir Tunbelly? Why, you'll find that's just as Sir Tunbelly pleases.

YOUNG FASHION But will you do me the favour, Sir, to know whether Sir Tunbelly pleases or not?

SERVANT Why, look you, do you see, with good words much may be done. Ralph, go thy weas, and ask Sir Tunbelly if he pleases to be waited upon. And do'st hear. Call to Nurse, that she may lock up Miss Hoyden before the geats open.

YOUNG FASHION D'ye hear that Lory?

LORY Aye, Sir, I'm afraid we shall find a difficult job on't. Pray heaven that old rogue Coupler han't sent us to fetch milk out of the gunroom.

YOUNG FASHION I'll warrant thee all will go well: see, the door opens.

*Enter Sir Tunbelly, with his Servants, armed, with guns, clubs,
pitchforks, scythes, &c.*

LORY [*running behind his master*] O Lord, O Lord, O Lord, we are both dead men.

YOUNG FASHION Take heed, fool, thy fear will ruin us.

LORY My fear, Sir, s'death, Sir, I fear nothing. [*aside*] Would I were well up to the chin in a horsepond.

SIR TUNBELLY Who is it here has any business with me?

YOUNG FASHION Sir, 'tis I, if your name be Sir Tunbelly Clumsey.

SIR TUNBELLY Sir, my name is Sir Tunbelly Clumsey, whether you have any business with me or not. So you see I am not ashamed of my name; – nor my face neither.

YOUNG FASHION Sir, you have no cause, that I know of.

SIR TUNBELLY Sir, if you have no cause neither, I desire to know who you are; for till I know your name, I shall not ask you to come into my house; and when I know your name; – 'tis six to four I don't ask you neither.

YOUNG FASHION [*giving him a letter*] Sir, I hope you'll find this letter an authentic passport.

SIR TUNBELLY Cod's my life, I ask your lordship's pardon ten thousand times. [*to his Servants*] Here, run in a-doors quickly: get a Scotch coal fire in the great parlour; set all the Turkey-work★ chairs in their places; get the great brass candlesticks out, and be sure stick the sockets full of laurel, run. [*turning to Young Fashion*] My lord, I ask your lordship's pardon. [*to other servants*] And do you hear, run away to Nurse, bid her let Miss Hoyden loose again, and if it was not shifting-day,† let her put on a clean tucker quick. [*Exeunt Servants confusedly*] [*to Young Fashion*] I hope your honour will excuse the disorder of my family, we are not used to receive men of your lordship's great quality every day; pray where are your coaches, and servants, my lord?

YOUNG FASHION Sir, that I might give you and your fair daughter a proof how impatient I am to be nearer a kin to you, I left my equipage to follow me, and came away post, with only one servant.

SIR TUNBELLY Your lordship does me too much honour, it was exposing your person to too much fatigue and danger, I protest it was, but my daughter shall endeavour to make you what amends she can; and though I say it, that should not say it – Hoyden has charms.

YOUNG FASHION Sir, I am not a stranger to them, though I am to her, common fame has done her justice.

SIR TUNBELLY My lord, I am common fame's very grateful humble servant. My lord – my girl's young, Hoyden is young, my lord; but this I must say for her, what she wants in art, she has by nature; what she wants in experience, she has in breeding; and what's wanting in her age, is made good in her constitution. So pray, my lord, walk in; pray my lord, walk in.

YOUNG FASHION Sir, I wait upon you. [*Exeunt*]

★ Turkey-work: with Turkish tapestries, or with material imitating them.
† shifting-day: a day for changing clothes.

⟨SCENE IV⟩

MISS HOYDEN [*sola*] Sure never nobody was used as I am. I know well enough what other girls do, for all they think to make a fool of me; it's well I have a husband a-coming, or ecod I'd marry the baker, I would so. Nobody can knock at the gate, but presently I must be locked up, and here's the young greyhound bitch can run loose about the house all day long she can, 'tis very well.

NURSE [*without, opening the door*] Miss Hoyden, miss, miss, miss; Miss Hoyden.

Enter Nurse.

MISS Well, what do you make such a noise for, ha? What do you din a body's ears for? Can't one be at quiet for you?

NURSE What do I din your ears for? Here's one come will din your ears for you.

MISS What care I who's come; I care not a fig who comes, nor who goes, as long as I must be locked up like the ale cellar.

NURSE That, miss, is for fear you should be drank, before you are ripe.

MISS O don't you trouble your head about that, I'm as ripe as you, though not so mellow.

NURSE Very well; now have I a good mind to lock you up again, and not let you see my lord tonight.

MISS My lord? Why is my husband come?

NURSE Yes marry is he, and a goodly person too.

MISS [*hugging Nurse*] O my dear nurse, forgive me this once, and I'll never misuse you again; no, if I do, you shall give me three thumps on the back, and a great pinch by the cheek.

NURSE Ah the poor thing, see how it melts, it's as full of good nature, as an egg's full of meat.

MISS But, my dear nurse, don't lie now, is he come by your troth?

NURSE Yes, by my truly, is he.

MISS O Lord! I'll go put on my laced smock, though I'm whipped 'till the blood run down my heels for't.   [*Exit running*]

NURSE Eh – the Lord succour thee, how thou art delighted.

[*Exit after her*]

⟨SCENE V⟩

Enter Sir Tunbelly, and Young Fashion. A servant with wine.

SIR TUNBELLY My lord, I am proud of the honour to see your lordship within my doors; and I humbly crave leave to bid you welcome, in a cup of sack wine.★

YOUNG FASHION Sir, to your daughter's health. [*drinks*]

SIR TUNBELLY Ah poor girl, she'll be scared out of her wits on her wedding night; for, honestly speaking, she does not know a man from a woman, but by his beard, and his breeches.

YOUNG FASHION Sir, I don't doubt but she has a virtuous education, which with the rest of her merit, makes me long to see her mine. I wish you would dispense with the canonical hour, and let it be this very night.

SIR TUNBELLY O not so soon neither, that's shooting my girl before you bid her stand. No, give her fair warning, we'll sign and seal tonight, if you please; and this day seven-night – let the jade look to her quarters.

YOUNG FASHION This day sennight? – Why, what do you take me for a ghost, Sir? S'life, Sir, I'm made of flesh and blood, and bones and sinews, and can no more live a week without your daughter – [*aside*] – than I can live a month with her.

SIR TUNBELLY Oh, I'll warrant you my hero, young men are hot I know, but they don't boil over at that rate, neither, besides, my wench's wedding gown is not come home yet.

YOUNG FASHION O, no matter Sir, I'll take her in her shift. [*aside*] A pox of this old fellow, he'll delay the business 'till my damned star finds me out, and discovers me. [*to Sir Tunbelly*] Pray, Sir, let it be done without ceremony, 'twill save money.

SIR TUNBELLY Money? – Save money when Hoyden's to be married? Udswoons I'll give my wench a wedding-dinner, though I go to grass with the King of Assyria† for't; and such a dinner it shall be, as is not to be cooked in the poaching of an egg. Therefore, my noble lord, have a little patience, we'll go and look over our deeds and settlements immediately; and as for your bride, though you may be sharp set before she's quite ready, I'll engage for my girl, she stays your stomach at last.   [*Exeunt*]

★ sack wine: sherry.
† King of Assyria: a reference to Nebuchadnezzar, King of Babylon.

ACT FOUR

SCENE I

Enter Miss Hoyden, and Nurse.

NURSE Well miss, how do you like your husband that is to be?

MISS O Lord, nurse, I'm so overjoyed, I can scarce contain myself.

NURSE O but you must have a care of being too fond, for men nowadays, hate a woman that loves 'em.

MISS Love him? Why do you think I love him, nurse? Ecod I would not care if he were hanged, so I were but once married to him – No – that which pleases me, is to think what work I'll make when I get to London; for when I am a wife and a lady both nurse, ecod I'll flaunt it with the best of 'em.

NURSE Look, look, if his honour be not coming again to you; now if I were sure you would behave yourself handsomely, and not disgrace me that have brought you up, I'd leave you alone together.

MISS That's my best nurse, do as you would be done by; trust us together this once, and if I don't show my breeding from the head to the foot of me, may I be twice married, and die a maid.

NURSE Well, this once I'll venture you, but if you disparage me –

MISS Never fear, I'll show him my parts I'll warrant him.

[*Exit Nurse*]

[*sola*] These old women are so wise when they get a poor girl in their clutches, but e'er it be long, I shall know what's what, as well as the best of 'em.

Enter Young Fashion.

YOUNG FASHION Your servant, Madam, I'm glad to find you alone, for I have something of importance to speak to you about.

MISS Sir, (my lord, I meant,) you may speak to me about what you please, I shall give you a civil answer.

YOUNG FASHION You give me so obliging a one, it encourages me to tell you in few words, what I think both for your interest, and mine. Your father, I suppose you know, has resolved to make me happy in being your husband, and I hope I may depend upon your consent, to perform what he desires.

MISS Sir, I never disobey my father in anything, but eating of green gooseberries.

YOUNG FASHION So good a daughter must needs make an admirable wife, I am therefore impatient till you are mine; and hope you will so far consider the violence of my love, that you won't have the cruelty to defer my happiness, so long as your father designs it.

MISS Pray, my lord, how long is that?

YOUNG FASHION Madam, a thousand year – a whole week.

MISS A week – why I shall be an old woman by that time.

YOUNG FASHION And I an old man, which you'll find a greater misfortune than t'other.

MISS Why I thought 'twas to be tomorrow morning, as soon as I was up; I'm sure nurse told me so.

YOUNG FASHION And it shall be tomorrow morning still, if you'll consent?

MISS If I'll consent? Why I thought I was to obey you as my husband?

YOUNG FASHION That's when we are married, 'till then, I am to obey you.

MISS Why then if we are to take it by turns, it's the same thing, I'll obey you now, and when we are married, you shall obey me.

YOUNG FASHION With all my heart, but I doubt we must get nurse on our side, or we shall hardly prevail with the chaplain.

MISS No more we shan't indeed, for he loves her better than he loves his pulpit, and would always be a-preaching to her by his good will.

YOUNG FASHION Why then my dear little bedfellow, if you'll call her hither, we'll try to persuade her presently.

MISS O Lord, I can tell you a way how to persuade her to anything.

YOUNG FASHION How's that?

MISS Why tell her she's a wholesome comely woman – and give her half a crown.

YOUNG FASHION Nay, if that will do, she shall have half a score of 'em.

MISS O Gemini,★ for half that, she'd marry you herself; I'll run and call her.   [*Exit Miss*]

★ Gemini: not the heavenly twins, but an expletive probably of low Dutch origin, and probably blasphemous.

YOUNG FASHION [*solus*] So, matters go swimmingly, this is a rare girl, i'faith, I shall have a fine time on't with her at London; I'm much mistaken, if she don't prove a March hare all the year round; what a scampering chase will she make on't, when she finds the whole kennel of beaux at her tail; hey to the park, and the play, and the church, and the devil; she'll show 'em sport I'll warrant 'em. But no matter, she brings an estate will afford me a separate maintenance.

Enter Miss, and Nurse.

YOUNG FASHION How do you do, good mistress nurse; I desired your young lady would give me leave to see you, that I might thank you for your extraordinary care and conduct in her education; pray accept of this small acknowledgment for it at present, and depend upon my farther kindness, when I shall be that happy thing her husband.

NURSE [*aside*] Gold by makings, your honour's goodness is too great; alas, all I can boast of is, I gave her pure good milk, and so your honour would have said, an you had seen how the poor thing sucked it – Eh God's blessing on the sweet face on't, how it used to hang at this poor tit, and suck and squeeze, and kick and sprawl it would, 'till the belly on't was so full, it would drop off like a leech.

MISS [*to Nurse, taking her angrily aside*] Pray one word with you; prithee nurse don't stand ripping up old stories, to make one ashamed before one's love; do you think such a fine proper gentleman as he, cares for a fiddlecome* tale of a draggle-tailed girl; if you have a mind to make him have a good opinion of a woman; don't tell him what one did then, tell him what one can do now. [*to Young Fashion*] I hope your honour will excuse my mismanners to whisper before you, it was only to give some orders about the family.

YOUNG FASHION O everything, Madam, is to give way to business; besides, good housewifery is a very commendable quality in a young lady.

MISS Pray Sir, are the young ladies good housewives at London town, do they darn their own linen?

* fiddlecome: nonsensical.

YOUNG FASHION O no, they study how to spend money, not to save it.

MISS Ecod I don't know but that may be better sport than t'other, ha, nurse.

YOUNG FASHION Well, you shall have your choice when you come there.

MISS Shall I? – Then by my troth I'll get there as fast as I can. [*to Nurse*] His honour desires you'll be so kind, as to let us be married tomorrow.

NURSE Tomorrow, my dear Madam?

YOUNG FASHION Yes, tomorrow sweet nurse; privately; young folks you know are impatient, and Sir Tunbelly would make us stay a week for a wedding-dinner. Now all things being signed, and sealed, and agreed, I fancy there could be no great harm in practising a scene or two of matrimony in private, if it were only to give us the better assurance when we come to play it in public.

NURSE Nay, I must confess stolen pleasures are sweet, but if you should be married now, what will you do when Sir Tunbelly calls for you to be wed?

MISS Why then we'll be married again.

NURSE What, twice my child?

MISS Ecod I don't care how often I'm married, not I.

YOUNG FASHION Pray nurse don't you be against your young lady's good, for by this means she'll have the pleasure of two wedding-days.

MISS [*to Nurse softly*] And of two wedding-nights too, nurse.

NURSE Well, I'm such a tender-hearted fool, I find I can refuse nothing; so you shall e'en follow your own inventions.

MISS Shall I? [*aside*] O Lord, I could leap over the moon.

YOUNG FASHION Dear nurse, this goodness of yours shan't go unrewarded; but now you must employ your power with Mr Bull the chaplain, that he may do us his friendly office too, and then we shall all be happy; do you think you can prevail with him?

NURSE Prevail with him? – Or he shall never prevail with me, I can tell him that.

MISS My lord, she has had him upon the hip this seven year.

YOUNG FASHION I'm glad to hear it; however, to strengthen your interest with him, you may let him know I have several fat livings in my gift, and that the first that falls shall be in your disposal.

NURSE Nay, then I'll make him marry more folks than one, I'll promise him.

MISS Faith do nurse, make him marry you too, I'm sure he'll do't for a fat living, for he loves eating, more than he loves his Bible; and I have often heard him say, a fat living was the best meat in the world.

NURSE Aye, and I'll make him commend the sauce too, or I'll bring his gown to a cassock,★ I will so.

YOUNG FASHION Well nurse, whilst you go and settle matters with him, then your lady and I will go take a walk in the garden.

NURSE I'll do your honour's business in the catching up of a garter.   [*Exit Nurse*]

YOUNG FASHION [*giving her his hand*] Come, Madam, dare you venture yourself alone with me?

MISS O dear, yes, Sir, I don't think you'll do anything to me I need be afraid on.   [*Exeunt*]

⟨SCENE II⟩

Enter Amanda, and Berinthia.

A SONG
I
'I smile at love, and all its arts,'
    The charming Cynthia cried;
'Take heed, for love has piercing darts',
    A wounded swain replied.
'Once free and blest as you are now,
    I trifled with his charms,
I pointed at his little bow,
    And sported with his arms:
Till urged too far, "Revenge" he cries,
    A fatal shaft he drew,
It took its passage through your eyes,
    And to my heart it flew.'

★ his gown to a cassock: possibly tear his gown down to the cassock underneath, or else to make him live single as a priest.

II

'To tear it thence, I tried in vain,
   To strive, I quickly found,
Was only to increase the pain
   And to enlarge the wound.
Ah! Much too well I fear you know
   What pain I'm to endure,
Since what your eyes alone could do,
   Your heart alone can cure.
And that (grant heaven I may mistake)
   I doubt is doomed to bear
A burden for another's sake,
   Who ill rewards its care.'

AMANDA Well, now Berinthia I'm at leisure to hear what 'twas you had to say to me.

BERINTHIA What I had to say, was only to echo the sighs and groans of a dying lover.

AMANDA Phu, will you never learn to talk in earnest of anything?

BERINTHIA Why this shall be in earnest, if you please; for my part, I only tell you matter of fact, you may take it which way you like best, but if you'll follow the women of the Town, you'll take it both ways; for when a man offers himself to one of them, first she takes him in jest, and then she takes him in earnest.

AMANDA I'm sure there's so much jest and earnest in what you say to me, I scarce know how to take it; but I think you have bewitched me, for I don't find it possible to be angry with you, say what you will.

BERINTHIA I'm very glad to hear it, for I have no mind to quarrel with you, for more reasons than I'll brag of; but quarrel or not, smile or frown, I must tell you what I have suffered upon your account.

AMANDA Upon my account?

BERINTHIA Yes, upon yours; I have been forced to sit still and hear you commended for two hours together, without one compliment to myself; now don't you think a woman had a blessed time of that?

AMANDA Alas! I should have been unconcerned at it, I never knew where the pleasure lay of being praised by the men; but pray who was this that commended me so?

BERINTHIA One you have a mortal aversion to. Mr Worthy, he used you like a text, he took you all to pieces, but spoke so learnedly upon every point, one might see the spirit of the church was in him; if you are a woman, you'd have been in an ecstasy to have heard how feelingly he handled your hair, your eyes, your nose, your mouth, your teeth, your tongue, your chin, your neck, and so forth. Thus he preached for an hour, but when he came to use an application, he observed that all these without a gallant were nothing – Now consider of what has been said, and heaven give you grace to put it in practice.

AMANDA Alas! Berinthia, did I incline to a gallant, (which you know I do not) do you think a man so nice as he, could have the least concern for such a plain unpolished thing as I am? It is impossible!

BERINTHIA Now have you a great mind to put me upon commending you.

AMANDA Indeed that was not my design.

BERINTHIA Nay, if it were, it's all one, for I won't do't, I'll leave that to your looking-glass. But to show you I have some good nature left, I'll commend him, and may be that may do as well.

AMANDA You have a great mind to persuade me I am in love with him.

BERINTHIA I have a great mind to persuade you, you don't know what you are in love with.

AMANDA I am sure I am not in love with him, nor never shall be, so let that pass; but you were saying something you would commend him for.

BERINTHIA O you'd be glad to hear a good character of him however.

AMANDA Pshaw.

BERINTHIA Pshaw, – Well 'tis a foolish undertaking for women in these kind of matters, to pretend to deceive one another – have not I been bred a woman as well as you?

AMANDA What then?

BERINTHIA Why then I understand my trade so well, that when ever I am told of a man I like, I cry psha; but that I may spare you the pains of putting me a second time in mind to commend him, I'll proceed, and give you this account of him; that though 'tis possible he may have had women with as good faces as your ladyship's (no discredit to it neither) yet you must know your cautious behaviour, with that reserve in your humour, has given him his death's wound; he mortally hates a coquette; he says 'tis impossible to love where we cannot esteem; and that no woman can be esteemed by a man who has sense, if she makes herself cheap in the eye of a fool. That pride to a woman, is as necessary as humility to a divine; and that far-fetched, and dear-bought, is meat for gentlemen, as well as for ladies – in short, that every woman who has beauty, may set a price upon herself, and that by underselling the market, they ruin the trade. This is his doctrine, how do you like it?

AMANDA So well, that since I never intend to have a gallant for myself, if I were to recommend one to a friend, he should be the man.

Enter Worthy.

Bless me! he's here, pray heaven he did not hear me.

BERINTHIA If he did, it won't hurt your reputation; your thoughts are as safe in his heart, as in your own.

WORTHY I venture in at an unseasonable time of night, ladies; I hope if I'm troublesome, you'll use the same freedom in turning me out again.

AMANDA I believe it can't be late, for Mr Loveless is not come home yet, and he usually keeps good hours.

WORTHY Madam, I'm afraid he'll transgress a little tonight, for he told me about half an hour ago, he was going to sup with some company, he doubted would keep him out till three or four o'clock in the morning, and desired I would let my servant acquaint you with it, that you might not expect him; but my fellow's a blunderhead, so lest he should make some mistake, I thought it my duty to deliver the message myself.

AMANDA I'm very sorry he should give you that trouble, Sir, but –

BERINTHIA But since he has, will you give me leave, Madam, to keep him to play at ombre* with us?

AMANDA Cousin, you know you command my house.

WORTHY [*to Berinthia*] And, Madam, you know you command me, though I'm a very wretched gamester.

BERINTHIA O you play well enough to lose your money, and that's all the ladies require, so without anymore ceremony, let us go into the next room, and call for the cards.

AMANDA With all my heart.   [*Exit Worthy leading Amanda*]

BERINTHIA [*sola*] Well, how this business will end, heaven knows; but she seems to me to be in as fair a way – as a boy is to be a rogue, when he's put clerk to an attorney.   [*Exit Berinthia*]

SCENE ⟨III⟩

Berinthia's Chamber

Enter Loveless cautiously in the dark.

LOVELESS So, thus far all's well, I'm got into her bed-chamber, and I think nobody has perceived me steal into the house; my wife don't expect me home till four o'clock, so if Berinthia comes to bed by eleven, I shall have a chase of five hours; let me see, where shall I hide myself? Under her bed? No: we shall have her maid searching there for something or other, her closet's a better place, and I have a master key will open it. I'll e'en in there, and attack her just when she comes to her prayers, that's the most likely to prove her critical minute, for then the devil will be there to assist me. [*he opens the closet, goes in, and shuts the door after him*]

Enter Berinthia with a candle in her hand.

BERINTHIA Well, sure I am the best-natured woman in the world. I that love cards so well (there is but one thing upon earth I love better), have pretended letters to write, to give my friends – a *tête à tête*; however, I'm innocent, for picquet is the game I set 'em to; at her own peril be it, if she ventures to play with him at any other. But now what shall I do with myself, I don't know how

* ombre: a three-handed card game.

in the world to pass my time. Would Loveless were here to *badiner* a little; well, he's a charming fellow, I don't wonder his wife's so fond of him; what if I should sit down and think of him till I fall asleep, and dream of the Lord knows what; O but then if I should dream we were married, I should be frightened out of my wits. [*seeing a book*] What's this book? I think I had best go read. O *splénétique*! It's a sermon; well, I'll go into my closet, and read *The Plotting Sisters*.★ [*she opens the closet, sees Loveless, and shrieks out*] O Lord, a ghost, a ghost, a ghost, a ghost.

Enter Loveless running to her.

LOVELESS Peace, my dear, it's no ghost, take it in your arms, you'll find 'tis worth a hundred of 'em.

BERINTHIA Run in again, here's somebody coming.

Enter her Maid.

MAID Lord, Madam, what's the matter?

BERINTHIA O heavens! I'm almost frighted out of my wits, I thought verily I had seen a ghost, and 'twas nothing but the white curtain, with a black hood pinned up against it; you may be gone again, I am the fearful'st fool.   [*Exit Maid*]

Re-enter Loveless.

LOVELESS Is the coast clear?

BERINTHIA The coast clear! I suppose you are clear,† you'd never play such a trick as this else.

LOVELESS I'm very well pleased with my trick thus far, and shall be so 'till I have played it out, if it be'nt your fault; where's my wife?

BERINTHIA At cards.

LOVELESS With whom?

BERINTHIA With Worthy.

LOVELESS Then we are safe enough.

BERINTHIA Are you so? Some husbands would be of another mind if he were at cards with their wives.

★ *The Plotting Sisters*: Thomas Durfey's *A Fond Husband, or The Plotting Sisters* (1677).

† you are clear: are drunk.

LOVELESS And they'd be in the right on't too. But I dare trust mine – Besides, I know he's in love in another place, and he's not one of those who court half a dozen at a time.

BERINTHIA Nay, the truth on't is, you'd pity him if you saw how uneasy he is at being engaged with us, but 'twas my malice, I fancied he was to meet his mistress somewhere else, so did it to have the pleasure of seeing him fret.

LOVELESS What says Amanda to my staying abroad so late?

BERINTHIA Why she's as much out of humour as he, I believe they wish one another at the devil.

LOVELESS Then I'm afraid they'll quarrel at play, and soon throw up the cards; [*offering to pull her into the closet*] Therefore my dear charming angel, let us make a good use of our time.

BERINTHIA Heavens, what do you mean?

LOVELESS Pray what do you think I mean?

BERINTHIA I don't know.

LOVELESS I'll show you.

BERINTHIA You may as well tell me.

LOVELESS No, that would make you blush worse than t'other.

BERINTHIA Why, do you intend to make me blush?

LOVELESS [*pulling her*] Faith I can't tell that, but if I do, it shall be in the dark.

BERINTHIA O heavens! I would not be in the dark with you for all the world.

LOVELESS I'll try that. [*puts out the candles*]

BERINTHIA O Lord! Are you mad, what shall I do for light?

LOVELESS You'll do as well without it.

BERINTHIA Why, one can't find a chair to sit down?

LOVELESS Come into the closet, Madam, there's moonshine upon the couch.

BERINTHIA Nay, never pull, for I will not go.

LOVELESS [*carrying her*] Then you must be carried.

BERINTHIA [*very softly*] Help, help, I'm ravished, ruined, undone. O Lord, I shall never be able to bear it. [*Exeunt*]

SCENE ⟨IV⟩

Sir Tunbelly's house

Enter Miss Hoyden, Nurse, Young Fashion, and Bull.

YOUNG FASHION This quick dispatch of yours, Mr Bull, I take so kindly, it shall give you a claim to my favour as long as I live, I do assure you.

MISS And to mine too, I promise you.

BULL I most humbly thank your honours, and I hope, since it has been my lot, to join you in the holy bands of wedlock, you will so well cultivate the soil, which I have craved a blessing on, that your children may swarm about you, like bees about a honeycomb.

MISS Ecod with all my heart, the more the merrier, I say; ha, Nurse?

Enter Lory taking his master hastily aside.

LORY One word with you for heaven's sake.

YOUNG FASHION What the devil's the matter?

LORY Sir, your fortune's ruined; and I don't think your life's worth a quarter of an hour's purchase: yonder's your brother arrived with two coaches and six horses, twenty footmen and pages, a coat worth fourscore pound, and a periwig down to his knees, so judge what will become of your lady's heart.

YOUNG FASHION Death and furies, 'tis impossible.

LORY Fiends and spectres, Sir, 'tis true.

YOUNGFASHION Is he in the house yet?

LORY No, they are capitulating with him at the gate; the porter tells him, he's ome to run away with Miss Hoyden, and has cocked the blunderbuss at him; your brother swears Gad damme, they are a parcel of clawns, and he has a good mind to break off the match; but they have given the word for Sir Tunbelly, so I doubt all will come out presently. Pray Sir resolve what you'll do this moment, for egad they'll maul you.

YOUNG FASHION Stay a little. [*to Miss*] My dear, here's a troublesome business my man tells me of, but don't be frightened, we shall be too hard for the rogue. Here's an impudent fellow at the gate (not knowing I was come hither *incognito*) has taken my name upon him, in hopes to run away with you.

MISS O the brazen-faced varlet, it's well we are married, or maybe we might never a been so.

YOUNG FASHION [*aside*] Egad, like enough: prithee, dear doctor, run to Sir Tunbelly, and stop him from going to the gate, before I speak with him.

BULL I fly, my good lord –   [*Exit Bull*]

NURSE An't please your honour, my lady and I had best lock ourselves up 'till the danger be over.

YOUNG FASHION Aye, by all means.

MISS Not so fast, I won't be locked up any more. I'm married.

YOUNG FASHION Yes, pray my dear do, till we have seized this rascal.

MISS Nay, if you pray me, I'll do anything.

                              [*Exeunt Miss and Nurse*]

YOUNG FASHION Oh! Here's Sir Tunbelly coming. [*to Lory*] Hark you, sirrah, things are better than you imagine; the wedding's over.

LORY The devil it is, Sir.

YOUNG FASHION Not a word, all's safe: but Sir Tunbelly don't know it, nor must not yet; so I am resolved to brazen the business out, and have the pleasure of turning the impostor upon his lordship, which I believe may easily be done.

Enter Sir Tunbelly, Chaplain and Servants armed.

YOUNG FASHION Did you ever hear, Sir, of so impudent an undertaking?

SIR TUNBELLY Never, by the mass, but we'll tickle him I'll warrant him.

YOUNG FASHION They tell me, Sir, he has a great many people with him disguised like servants.

SIR TUNBELLY Aye, aye, rogues, enough; but I'll soon raise the posse upon 'em.

YOUNG FASHION Sir, if you'll take my advice, we'll go a shorter way to work; I find whoever this spark is, he knows nothing of my being privately here; so if you pretend to receive him civilly, he'll enter without suspicion; and as soon as he is within the gate, we'll whip up the drawbridge upon his back, let fly the blunderbuss to disperse his crew, and so commit him to gaol.

SIR TUNBELLY Egad, your lordship is an ingenious person, and a very great general; but shall we kill any of 'em or not?

YOUNG FASHION No, no, fire over their heads only to fright 'em, I'll warrant the regiment scours★ when the colonel's a prisoner.

SIR TUNBELLY Then come along my boys, and let your courage be great – for your danger is but small.   [*Exeunt*]

SCENE ⟨V⟩
The gate

Enter Lord Foppington and Followers.

LORD FOPPINGTON A pax of these bumkinly people, will they open the gate, or do they desire I should grow at their moat-side like a willow? [*to the Porter*] Hey, fellow – Prithee do me the favour, in as few words as thou can'st find to express thyself, to tell me whether thy master will admit me or not, that I may turn about my coach and be gone?

PORTER Here's my master himself now at hand; he's of age, he'll give you his answer.

Enter Sir Tunbelly, and Servants.

SIR TUNBELLY My most noble lord, I crave your pardon, for making your honour wait so long, but my orders to my servants have been to admit nobody, without my knowledge; for fear of some attempt upon my daughter, the times being full of plots and roguery.

LORD FOPPINGTON Much caution, I must confess, is a sign of great wisdom: but stap my vitals, I have got a cold enough to destroy a porter, – he, hem –

SIR TUNBELLY I am very sorry for't, indeed, my lord; but if your lordship please to walk in, we'll help you to some brown sugar-candy. My lord, I'll show you the way.

LORD FOPPINGTON Sir, I follow you with pleasure.   [*Exeunt*]

★ scours: flees.

*As Lord Foppington's Servants go to follow him in, they clap
the door against La Vérole.*

SERVANTS [*within*] Nay, hold you me there, Sir.
LA VÉROLE *Jernie die, qu'est ce que veut dire ça?*★
SIR TUNBELLY [*within*] – Fire, porter.
PORTER [*fires*] – Have among ye, my masters.
LA VÉROLE *Ah je suis mort* –   [*The Servants all run off*]
PORTER Not one soldier left, by the mass.

SCENE ⟨VI⟩

Changes to the hall

*Enter Sir Tunbelly, the Chaplain and
Servants, with Lord Foppington disarmed.*

SIR TUNBELLY Come, bring him along, bring him along.
LORD FOPPINGTON What the pax do you mean, gentlemen, is it fair time, that you are all drunk before dinner?
SIR TUNBELLY Drunk, sirrah? Here's an impudent rogue for you; drunk or sober, bully, I'm a justice of the peace, and know how to deal with strollers.†
LORD FOPPINGTON Strollers!
SIR TUNBELLY Aye, strollers; come give an account of yourself, what's your name, where do you live? Do you pay scot and lot?‡ Are you a Williamite, or a Jacobite? Come.
LORD FOPPINGTON And why dost thou ask me so many impertinent questions?
SIR TUNBELLY Because I'll make you answer 'em before I have done with you, you rascal you.
LORD FOPPINGTON Before Gad, all the answer I can make thee to 'em, is, that thou art a very extraordinary old fellow; stap my vitals –

★ *Jernie die: je renie dieu*, literally 'I renounce God': 'My God what does this mean?'
† strollers: vagabonds.
‡ scot and lot: a local parish tax assessed on ability to pay.

SIR TUNBELLY Nay, if you are for joking with Deputy-Lieu-
tenants, we'st know how to deal with you: here, draw a warrant
for him immediately.

LORD FOPPINGTON A warrant – what the devil is't thou would'st
be at, old gentleman?

SIR TUNBELLY I would be at you, sirrah, (if my hands were not
tied as a magistrate) and with these two double fists, beat your
teeth down your throat, you dog you.

LORD FOPPINGTON And why would'st thou spoil my face at
that rate?

SIR TUNBELLY For your design to rob me of my daughter, villain.

LORD FOPPINGTON Rab thee of thy daughter – Now do I begin
to believe I am abed and asleep, and that all this is but a dream, –
If it be, 'twill be an agreeable surprise enough, to waken by and
by; and instead of the impertinent company of a nasty country
justice, find myself, perhaps, in the arms of a woman of quality.
[*to Sir Tunbelly*] – Prithee, old father, wilt thou give me leave to
ask thee one question?

SIR TUNBELLY I can't tell whether I will or not, 'till I know what
it is.

LORD FOPPINGTON Why, then it is, whether thou didst not write
to my Lord Foppington to come down and marry thy daughter?

SIR TUNBELLY Yes marry did I; and my Lord Foppington is
come down, and shall marry my daughter before she's a day older.

LORD FOPPINGTON Now give me thy hand, dear dad, I thought
we should understand one another at last.

SIR TUNBELLY This fellow's mad – here, bind him hand and
foot. [*they bind him down*]

LORD FOPPINGTON Nay, prithee, knight, leave fooling, thy jest
begins to grow dull.

SIR TUNBELLY Bind him, I say, he's mad – Bread and water, a
dark room and a whip, may bring him to his senses again.

LORD FOPPINGTON [*aside*] Egad, if I don't waken quickly, by
all I can see, this is like to prove one of the most impertinent
dreams that ever I dreamed in my life.

Enter Miss and Nurse.

MISS [*going up to him*] Is this he that would have run away with me?

Fough, how he stinks of sweets: pray, father, let him be dragged through the horse-pond.

LORD FOPPINGTON [*aside*] This must be my wife by her natural inclination to her husband.

MISS Pray, father, what do you intend to do with him, hang him?

SIR TUNBELLY That, at least, child.

NURSE Aye, and it's e'en too good for him too.

LORD FOPPINGTON [*aside*] *Madame la gouvernante*, I presume; hitherto this appears to me, to be one of the most extraordinary families that ever man of quality matched into.

SIR TUNBELLY What's become of my lord, daughter?

MISS He's just coming, Sir.

LORD FOPPINGTON [*aside*] My lord – What does he mean by that, now?

Enter Young Fashion, and Lory.

[*seeing him*] Stap my vitals Tam, now the dream's out.

YOUNG FASHION Is this the fellow, Sir, that designed to trick me of your daughter?

SIR TUNBELLY This is he, my lord, how do you like him? Is not he a pretty fellow to get a fortune?

YOUNG FASHION I find by his dress, he thought your daughter might be taken with a beau.

MISS O Gemini! Is this a beau? Let me see him again, – ha! I find a beau's no such an ugly thing neither.

YOUNG FASHION Egad, she'll be in love with him presently; I'll e'en have him sent away to gaol. [*to Lord Foppington*] Sir, though your undertaking shows you are a person of no extraordinary modesty, I suppose you han't confidence enough to expect much favour from me?

LORD FOPPINGTON Strike me dumb, Tam, thou art a very impudent fellow.

NURSE Look if the varlet has not the frontery to call his lordship plain Thomas.

BULL The business is, he would feign himself mad, to avoid going to gaol.

LORD FOPPINGTON [*aside*] That must be the chaplain, by his unfolding of mysteries.

SIR TUNBELLY Come, is the warrant writ?

CLERK Yes, Sir.

SIR TUNBELLY Give me the pen, I'll sign it – So, now constable away with him.

LORD FOPPINGTON Hold one moment. – Pray, gentlemen; my Lord Foppington, shall I beg one word with your lordship?

NURSE O ho, it's my lord with him now; see how afflictions will humble folks.

MISS Pray, my lord, don't let him whisper too close, lest he bite your ear off.

LORD FOPPINGTON I am not altogether so hungry, as your ladyship is pleased to imagine. [*to Young Fashion*] Look you, Tam, I am sensible I have not been so kind to you as I ought, but I hope you'll forget what's past, and accept of the five thousand pounds I offer; thou may'st live in extreme splendour with it; stap my vitals.

YOUNG FASHION It's a much easier matter to prevent a disease than to cure it; a quarter of that sum would have secured your mistress; twice as much won't redeem her. [*leaving him*]

SIR TUNBELLY Well, what says he?

YOUNG FASHION Only the rascal offered me a bribe to let him go.

SIR TUNBELLY Aye, he shall go with a pox to him: lead on, constable.

LORD FOPPINGTON One word more, and I have done.

SIR TUNBELLY Before Gad, thou art an impudent fellow, to trouble the court at this rate, after thou art condemned; but speak once for all.

LORD FOPPINGTON Why then once for all, I have at last luckily called to mind, that there is a gentleman of this country, who, I believe cannot live far from this place, and (if he were here) would satisfy you, I am Navelty, Baron of Foppington, with five thousand pounds a year, and that fellow there, a rascal not worth a groat.

SIR TUNBELLY Very well; now who is this honest gentleman you are so well acquainted with. [*to Young Fashion*] Come, Sir, we shall hamper him.

LORD FOPPINGTON 'Tis Sir John Friendly.

SIR TUNBELLY So; he lives within half a mile, and came down into the country but last night; this bold-faced fellow thought he had been at London still, and so quoted him; now we shall display him in his colours: I'll send for Sir John immediately: here, fellow, away presently, and desire my neighbour he'll do me the favour to step over, upon an extraordinary occasion; and in the meanwhile you had best secure this sharper in the gate house.

CONSTABLE An't please your worship, he may chance to give us the slip thence: if I were worthy to advice, I think the dog-kennel's a surer place.

SIR TUNBELLY With all my heart, anywhere.

LORD FOPPINGTON Nay, for heaven's sake, Sir, do me the favour to put me in a clean room, that I mayn't daub my clothes.

SIR TUNBELLY O when you have married my daughter, her estate will afford you new ones: away with him.

LORD FOPPINGTON A dirty country justice, is a barbarous magistrate; stap my vitals. –

[*Exit Constable with Lord Foppington*]

YOUNG FASHION [*aside*] Egad, I must prevent this knight's coming, or the house will grow soon too hot to hold me. [*to Sir Tunbelly*] Sir, I fancy 'tis not worth while to trouble Sir John upon this impertinent fellow's desire: I'll send and call the messenger back. –

SIR TUNBELLY Nay, with all my heart: for to be sure he thought he was far enough off, or the rogue would never have named him.

Enter Servant.

SERVANT Sir, I met Sir John just lighting at the gate, he's come to wait upon you.

SIR TUNBELLY Nay, then it happens as one could wish.

YOUNG FASHION [*aside*] The devil it does: Lory, you see how things are, here will be a discovery presently, and we shall have our brains beat out; for my brother will be sure to swear he don't know me, therefore run into the stable, take the two first horses you can light on, I'll slip out at the back door, and we'll away immediately.

LORY What, and leave your lady, Sir?

YOUNG FASHION There's no danger in that, as long as I have

taken possession, I shall know how to treat with 'em well enough, if once I am out of their reach: away, I'll steal after thee.

[*Exit Lory, his master follows him out at one door, as Sir John enters at t'other*]

Enter Sir John.

SIR TUNBELLY Sir John, you are the welcomest man alive, I had just sent a messenger to desire you'd step over, upon a very extraordinary occasion – we are all in arms here.

SIR JOHN How so?

SIR TUNBELLY Why you must know – a finical sort of a tawdry fellow here (I don't know who the devil he is, not I) hearing I suppose, that the match was concluded between my Lord Foppington, and my girl Hoyden, comes impudently to the gate, with a whole pack of rogues in liveries, and would have passed upon me for his lordship; but what does I? I comes up to him boldly at the head of his guards, takes him by the throat, strikes up his heels, binds him hand and foot, dispatches a warrant, and commits him prisoner to the dog-kennel.

SIR JOHN So, but how do you know but this was my lord? For I was told he set out from London the day before me, with a very fine retinue, and intended to come directly hither.

SIR TUNBELLY Why now to show you how many lies people raise in that damned Town, he came two nights ago post, with only one servant, and is now in the house with me, but you don't know the cream of the jest yet; this same rogue (that lies yonder neck and heels among the hounds) thinking you were out of the country, quotes you for his acquaintance, and said if you were here, you'd justify him to be Lord Foppington, and I know not what.

SIR JOHN Pray will you let me see him?

SIR TUNBELLY Aye, that you shall presently – here, fetch the prisoner.

[*Exit Servant*]

SIR JOHN I wish there be'nt some mistake in this business. Where's my lord, I know him very well?

SIR TUNBELLY He was here just now; see for him, doctor, tell him Sir John is here to wait upon him.   [*Exit Chaplain*]

SIR JOHN I hope, Sir Tunbelly, the young lady is not married yet.

SIR TUNBELLY No, things won't be ready this week, but why do you say you hope she is not married?

SIR JOHN Some foolish fancies only, perhaps I'm mistaken.

Re-enter Chaplain.

BULL Sir, his lordship is just rid out to take the air.

SIR TUNBELLY To take the air! Is that his London breeding to go take the air, when gentlemen come to visit him?

SIR JOHN 'Tis possible he might want it, he might not be well, some sudden qualm perhaps.

Enter Constable, &c. with Lord Foppington.

LORD FOPPINGTON Stap my vitals, I'll have satisfaction.

SIR JOHN [*running to him*] My dear Lord Foppington.

LORD FOPPINGTON Dear Friendly thou art come in the critical minute, strike me dumb.

SIR JOHN Why, I little thought I should have found you in fetters.

LORD FOPPINGTON Why truly the world must do me the justice to confess I do use to appear a little more *dégagé*; but this old gentleman, not liking the freedom of my air, has been pleased to skewer down my arms like a rabbit.

SIR TUNBELLY Is it then possible that this should be the true Lord Foppington at last?

LORD FOPPINGTON Why what do you see in his face to make you doubt of it? Sir, without presuming to have any extraordinary opinion of my figure, give me leave to tell you, if you had seen as many lords as I have done, you would not think it impossible a person of a worse *taille*★ than mine, might be a modern man of quality.

SIR TUNBELLY Unbind him, slaves: my lord, I'm struck dumb, I can only beg pardon by signs; but if a sacrifice will appease you, you shall have it? Here, pursue this tartar, bring him back – away, I say, a dog – Oons – I'll cut off his ears, and his tail, I'll draw out all his teeth, pull his skin over his head – and – and what shall I do more?

SIR JOHN He does indeed deserve to be made an example of.

★ *taille*: figure.

LORD FOPPINGTON He does deserve to be *châtré*,* stap my vitals.

SIR TUNBELLY May I then hope I have your honour's pardon?

LORD FOPPINGTON Sir, we courtiers do nothing without a bribe, that fair young lady might do miracles.

SIR TUNBELLY Hoyden, come hither Hoyden.

LORD FOPPINGTON Hoyden is her name, Sir?

SIR TUNBELLY Yes, my lord.

LORD FOPPINGTON The prettiest name for a song I ever heard.

SIR TUNBELLY My lord – here's my girl, she's yours, she has a wholesome body, and a virtuous mind, she's a woman complete both in flesh and in spirit; she has a bag of milled crowns,† as scarce as they are, and fifteen hundred a year stitched fast to her tail, so go thy ways Hoyden.

LORD FOPPINGTON Sir, I do receive her like a gentleman.

SIR TUNBELLY Then I'm a happy man, I bless heaven, and if your lordship will give me leave, I will like a good Christian at Christmas, be very drunk by way of thanksgiving; come, my noble peer, I believe dinner's ready. If your honour pleases to follow me, I'll lead you on to the attack of a venison pasty.

[Exit Sir Tunbelly]

LORD FOPPINGTON Sir, I wait upon you, will your ladyship do me the favour of your little finger, Madam?

MISS My lord, I'll follow you presently, I have a little business with my nurse.

LORD FOPPINGTON Your ladyship's most humble servant; come Sir John, the ladies have *des affaires*.

[Exeunt Lord Foppington and Sir John]

MISS So nurse, we are finely brought to bed, what shall we do now?

NURSE [*crying*] Ah dear miss, we are all undone; Mr Bull, you were used to help a woman to a remedy.

BULL Alack-a-day, but it's past my skill now, I can do nothing.

NURSE Who would have thought that ever your invention should have been drained so dry.

---

* *châtré*: castrated, an emendation by A. E. H. Swain of the original *chartre*, probably a misreading of Vanbrugh's *chastre*.

† milled crowns: milled silver coins had existed since 1663: hammered coins were called in after 1696, so there was a great scarcity of silver coins at the time, owing to slowness in replacing the hammered coins.

MISS Well, I have often thought old folks fools, and now I'm sure they are so; I have found a way myself to secure us all.

NURSE Dear lady what's that?

MISS Why, if you two will be sure to hold your tongues, and not say a word of what's passed, I'll e'en marry this lord too.

NURSE What! Two husbands, my dear?

MISS Why you have had three, good nurse, you may hold your tongue.

NURSE Aye, but not all together, sweet child.

MISS Pshaw, if you had, you'd ne'er a thought much on't.

NURSE O but 'tis a sin – sweeting.

BULL Nay that's my business to speak to, nurse; I do confess, to take two husbands for the satisfaction of the flesh, is to commit the sin of exorbitancy, but to do it for the peace of the spirit, is no more than to be drunk by way of physic; besides, to prevent a parent's wrath, is to avoid the sin of disobedience; for when the parent's angry, the child is froward. So that upon the whole matter, I do think, though Miss should marry again, she may be saved.

MISS Ecod and I will marry again then, and so there's an end of the story. *[Exeunt]*

ACT FIVE

SCENE ⟨I⟩

London

Enter Coupler, Young Fashion, and Lory.

COUPLER Well, and so Sir John coming in –

YOUNG FASHION And so Sir John coming in, I thought it might be manners in me to go out, which I did, and getting on horseback as fast as I could, rid away as if the devil had been at the rear of me; what has happened since, heaven knows.

COUPLER Egad sirrah, I know as well as heaven.

YOUNG FASHION What do you know?

COUPLER That you are a cuckold.

YOUNG FASHION The devil I am? By who?

COUPLER By your brother.

YOUNG FASHION My brother! Which way?

COUPLER The old way, he has lain with your wife.

YOUNG FASHION Hell and furies, what dost thou mean?

COUPLER I mean plainly, I speak no parable.

YOUNG FASHION Plainly! Thou do'st not speak common sense, I cannot understand one word thou say'st.

COUPLER You will do soon, youngster. In short, you left your wife a widow, and she married again.

YOUNG FASHION It's a lie.

COUPLER Ecod if I were a young fellow, I'd break your head, sirrah.

YOUNG FASHION Dear dad don't be angry, for I'm as mad as Tom of Bedlam.

COUPLER When I had fitted you with a wife, you should have kept her.

YOUNG FASHION But is it possible the young strumpet could play me such a trick?

COUPLER A young strumpet, Sir – can play twenty tricks.

YOUNG FASHION But prithee instruct me a little farther, whence comes thy intelligence?

COUPLER From your brother, in this letter, there you may read it.

YOUNG FASHION [*reads*] 'Dear Coupler, [*pulling off his hat*]★ I have only time to tell thee in three lines, or thereabouts, that here has been the devil, that rascal Tam having stole the letter thou hadst formerly writ for me to bring to Sir Tunbelly, formed a damnable design upon my mistress, and was in a fair way of success when I arrived. But after having suffered some indignities, (in which I have all daubed my embroidered coat) I put him to flight. I sent out a party of horse after him, in hopes to have made him my prisoner, which if I had done, I would have qualified him for the seraglio, stap my vitals.

'The danger I have thus narrowly 'scaped, has made me fortify myself against further attempts, by entering immediately into an association with the young lady, by which we engage to stand by one another, as long as we both shall live.

'In short, the papers are sealed, and the contract is signed, so the business of the lawyer is *achevé*, but I defer the divine part of the thing 'till I arrive at London; not being willing to consummate in any other bed but my own.

'Postscript.

' 'Tis possible I may be in Tawn as soon as this letter, far I find the lady is so violently in love with me, I have determined to make her happy with all the dispatch that is practicable, without disardering my coach-harses.'

So, here's rare work, i' faith.

LORY Egad Miss Hoyden has laid about her bravely.

COUPLER I think my country girl has played her part as well, as if she had been born and bred in St James's parish.

YOUNG FASHION That rogue the chaplain.

LORY And then that jade the nurse, Sir.

YOUNG FASHION And then that drunken sot Lory, Sir, that could not keep himself sober, to be a witness to the marriage.

LORY Sir – with respect – I know very few drunken sots that do keep themselves sober.

YOUNG FASHION Hold your prating sirrah, or I'll break your

★ This stage direction is set left beside the first two lines of Young Fashion's speech in the copy text, but the action intended by it is not clear. It may be that Young Fashion raises his hat to Coupler as he reads the letter or that Coupler is intended to raise his hat on hearing himself addressed.

head; dear Coupler what's to be done?

COUPLER Nothing's to be done, 'till the bride and bridegroom come to Town.

YOUNG FASHION Bride, and bridegroom? Death and furies, I can't bear that thou should'st call 'em so.

COUPLER Why what shall I call 'em, dog and cat?

YOUNG FASHION Not for the world, that sounds more like man and wife than t'other.

COUPLER Well, if you'll hear of 'em in no language, we'll leave 'em for the nurse and the chaplain.

YOUNG FASHION The devil and the witch.

COUPLER When they come to Town –

LORY We shall have stormy weather.

COUPLER Will you hold your tongues gentlemen, or not?

LORY Mum.

COUPLER I say when they come, we must find what stuff they are made of, whether the churchman be chiefly composed of the flesh, or the spirit; I presume the former – For as chaplains now go, 'tis probable he eats three pound of beef to the reading of one chapter – This gives him carnal desires, he wants money, preferment, wine, a whore; therefore we must invite him to supper, give him fat capons, sack and sugar, a purse of gold, and a plump sister. Let this be done, and I'll warrant thee, my boy, he speaks truth like an oracle.

YOUNG FASHION Thou art a profound statesman I allow it, but how shall we gain the nurse?

COUPLER O never fear the nurse, if once you have got the priest, for the devil always rides the hag. Well, there's nothing more to be said of the matter at this time, that I know of; so let us go and enquire, if there's any news of our people yet, perhaps they may be come. But let me tell you one thing by the way, sirrah, I doubt you have been an idle fellow, if thou had'st behaved thyself as thou should'st have done, the girl would never have left thee. [*Exeunt*]

SCENE ⟨II⟩

Berinthia's apartment

Enter her Maid passing the stage, followed by Worthy.

WORTHY Hem, Mrs Abigail, is your mistress to be spoken with?
ABIGAIL By you, Sir, I believe she may.
WORTHY Why 'tis by me I would have her spoken with.
ABIGAIL I'll acquaint her, Sir.   [*Exit Abigail*]
WORTHY [*solus*] One lift more I must persuade her to give me, and
  then I'm mounted. Well, a young bawd and a handsome one for
  my money, 'tis they do the execution; I'll never go to an old one,
  but when I have occasion for a witch. Lewdness looks heavenly
  to a woman, when an angel appears in its cause; but when a hag
  is advocate, she thinks it comes from the devil. An old woman has
  something so terrible in her looks, that whilst she is persuading
  your mistress to forget she has a soul, she stares hell and damnation full in her face.

Enter Berinthia.

BERINTHIA Well Sir, what news bring you?
WORTHY No news, Madam, there's a woman going to cuckold her
  husband.
BERINTHIA Amanda?
WORTHY I hope so.
BERINTHIA Speed her well.
WORTHY Aye, but there must be more than a God-speed, or your
  charity won't be worth a farthing.
BERINTHIA Why han't I done enough already?
WORTHY Not quite.
BERINTHIA What's the matter?
WORTHY The lady has a scruple still, which you must remove.
BERINTHIA What's that?
WORTHY Her virtue – she says.
BERINTHIA And do you believe her?
WORTHY No, but I believe it's what she takes for her virtue, it's

some relics of lawful love; she is not yet fully satisfied her husband
has got another mistress, which unless I can convince her of, I
have opened the trenches in vain, for the breach must be wider,
before I dare storm the town.

BERINTHIA And so I'm to be your engineer?

WORTHY I'm sure you know best how to manage the battery.

BERINTHIA What think you of springing a mine? I have a thought
just now come into my head, how to blow her up at once.

WORTHY That would be a thought indeed.

BERINTHIA Faith I'll do't, and thus the execution of it shall be.
We are all invited to my Lord Foppington's tonight to supper;
he's come to Town with his bride, and makes a ball with an
entertainment of music. Now you must know, my undoer here,
Loveless, says he must needs meet me about some private business (I don't know what 'tis) before we go to the company. To
which end, he has told his wife one lie, and I have told her another.
But to make her amends, I'll go immediately, and tell her a solemn
truth.

WORTHY What's that?

BERINTHIA Why, I'll tell her, that to my certain knowledge, her
husband has a rendezvous with his mistress this afternoon; and
that if she'll give me her word, she'll be satisfied with the discovery, without making any violent inquiry after the woman,
I'll direct her to a place, where she shall see 'em meet. Now,
friend; this I fancy may help you to a critical minute. For home
she must go again to dress. You (with your good breeding) come
to wait upon us to the ball. Find her all alone: her spirit en-
flamed against her husband for his treason; and her flesh in a
heat from some contemplations upon the treachery: her blood on
a fire; her conscience in ice; a lover to draw, and the devil to
drive – Ah poor Amanda.

WORTHY [*kneeling*] Thou angel of light, let me fall down and adore
thee?

BERINTHIA Thou minister of darkness, get up again, for I hate to
see the devil at his devotions.

WORTHY Well, my incomparable Berinthia – How I shall requite
you –

BERINTHIA O ne'er trouble yourself about that: virtue is its own reward: there's a pleasure in doing good, which sufficiently pays itself. Adieu.

WORTHY Farewell, thou best of women.   [*Exeunt several ways*]*

Enter Amanda, meeting Berinthia.

AMANDA Who was that went from you?

BERINTHIA A friend of yours.

AMANDA What does he want?

BERINTHIA Something you might spare him, and be ne'er the poorer.

AMANDA I can spare him nothing but my friendship; my love already's all disposed of. Though, I confess, to one ungrateful to my bounty.

BERINTHIA Why there's the mystery: you have been so bountiful, you have cloyed him. Fond wives do by their husbands, as barren wives do by their lap-dogs; cram 'em with sweet-meats 'till they spoil their stomachs.

AMANDA Alas! Had you but seen how passionately fond he has been since our last reconciliation; you would have thought it were impossible, he ever should have breathed an hour without me.

BERINTHIA Aye, but there you thought wrong again Amanda, you should consider, that in matters of love, men's eyes are always bigger than their bellies. They have violent appetites, 'tis true: but they have soon dined.

AMANDA Well; there's nothing upon earth astonishes me more, than men's inconstancy.

BERINTHIA Now there's nothing upon earth astonishes me less, when I consider what they and we are composed of. For nature has made them children, and us babies.† Now, Amanda; how we used our babies, you may remember. We were mad to have 'em, as soon as we saw 'em; kissed 'em to pieces, as soon as we got 'em. Then pulled off their clothes, saw 'em naked, and so threw 'em away.

AMANDA But do you think all men are of this temper?

* This stage direction probably intends that Berinthia should begin to leave the stage at the same time as Worthy, but in the opposite direction since Amanda meets her when she herself enters.
† babies: dolls.

BERINTHIA All but one.

AMANDA Who is that?

BERINTHIA Worthy.

AMANDA Why he's weary of his wife too, you see.

BERINTHIA Aye, that's no proof.

AMANDA What can be a greater?

BERINTHIA Being weary of his mistress.

AMANDA Don't you think 'twere possible he might give you that too?

BERINTHIA Perhaps he might, if he were my gallant; not if he were yours.

AMANDA Why do you think he should be more constant to me, than he would to you? I'm sure I'm not so handsome.

BERINTHIA Kissing goes by favour; he likes you best.

AMANDA Suppose he does? That's no demonstration he would be constant to me.

BERINTHIA No, that I'll grant you: but there are other reasons to expect it: for you must know after all, Amanda, the inconstancy we commonly see in men of brains, does not so much proceed from the uncertainty of their temper, as from the misfortunes of their love. A man sees perhaps a hundred women he likes well enough for an intrigue, and away. But possibly, through the whole course of his life, does not find above one, who is exactly what he could wish her; now her, 'tis a thousand to one, he never gets. Either she is not to be had at all, (though that seldom happens you'll say) or he wants those opportunities that are necessary to gain her. Either she likes somebody else much better than him, or uses him like a dog, because he likes nobody so well as her: still something or other fate claps in the way between them and the woman they are capable of being fond of: and this makes them wander about, from mistress to mistress, like a pilgrim from town to town, who every night must have a fresh lodging, and's in haste to be gone in the morning.

AMANDA 'Tis possible there may be something in what you say; but what do you infer from it, as to the man we were talking of?

BERINTHIA Why, I infer; that you being the woman in the world, the most to his humour; 'tis not likely he would quit you for one that is less.

AMANDA That is not to be depended upon, for you see Mr Loveless does so.

BERINTHIA What does Mr Loveless do?

AMANDA Why? He runs after something for variety; I'm sure he does not like so well as he does me.

BERINTHIA That's more than you know, Madam.

AMANDA No, I'm sure on't: I'm not very vain, Berinthia; and yet I'd lay my life, if I could look into his heart, he thinks I deserve to be preferred to a thousand of her.

BERINTHIA Don't be too positive in that neither; a million to one, but she has the same opinion of you. What would you give to see her?

AMANDA Hang her, dirty trull; though I really believe she's so ugly, she'd cure me of my jealousy.

BERINTHIA All the men of sense about Town, say she's handsome.

AMANDA They are as often out in those things as any people.

BERINTHIA Then I'll give you farther proof – All the women about Town, say, she's a fool: now I hope you're convinced?

AMANDA Whate'er she be, I'm satisfied he does not like her well enough, to bestow anything more, than a little outward gallantry upon her.

BERINTHIA Outward gallantry? – [*aside*] I can't bear this. [*to Amanda*] Don't you think she's a woman to be fobbed off so. Come, I'm too much your friend, to suffer you should be thus grossly imposed upon, by a man who does not deserve the least part about you, unless he knew how to set a greater value upon it. Therefore in one word, to my certain knowledge, he is to meet her; now within a quarter of an hour, somewhere about that Babylon of wickedness, Whitehall. And if you'll give me your word, that you'll be content with seeing her masked in his hand, without pulling her head-cloths off, I'll step immediately to the person, from whom I have my intelligence, and send you word whereabouts you may stand to see 'em meet. My friend and I'll watch 'em from another place, and dodge 'em to their private lodging: but don't you offer to follow 'em, lest you do it awkwardly, and spoil all. I'll come home to you again, as soon as I have earthed★ 'em, and give you an account, in what corner of the

★ earthed: run them to earth.

house, the scene of their lewdness lies.

AMANDA If you can do this, Berinthia; he's a villain.

BERINTHIA I can't help that, men will be so.

AMANDA Well! I'll follow your directions; for I shall never rest till I know the worst of this matter.

BERINTHIA Pray, go immediately, and get yourself ready then. Put on some of your woman's clothes, a great scarf and a mask, and you shall presently receive orders. [*calls within*] Here, who's there? Get me a chair quickly.

SERVANT ⟨*off stage*⟩ There are chairs at the door, Madam.

BERINTHIA 'Tis well, I'm coming.

AMANDA But pray, Berinthia, before you go; tell me how I may know this filthy thing, if she should be so forward, (as I suppose she will) to come to the rendezvous first, for methinks I would fain view her a little.

BERINTHIA Why she's about my height; and very well shaped.

AMANDA I thought she had been a little crooked?

BERINTHIA O no, she's as straight as I am. But we lose time, come away.   [*Exeunt*]

⟨SCENE III⟩

Enter Young Fashion, meeting Lory.

YOUNG FASHION Well, will the doctor come?

LORY Sir I sent a porter to him as you ordered me. He found him with a pipe of tobacco and a great tankard of ale, which he said he would dispatch while I could tell three, and be here.

YOUNG FASHION He does not suspect 'twas I that sent for him?

LORY Not a jot, Sir; he divines as little for himself, as he does for other folks.

YOUNG FASHION Will he bring nurse with him?

LORY Yes.

YOUNG FASHION That's well; where's Coupler?

LORY He's half way up the stairs taking breath; he must play his bellows a little, before he can get to the top.

Enter Coupler.

YOUNG FASHION O here he is. Well old Phthisic?* The doctor's coming.

COUPLER Would the pox had the doctor – I'm quite out of wind. [*to Lory*] Set me a chair, sirrah. Ah – [*sits down*] [*to Young Fashion*] Why the plague can'st not thou lodge upon the ground floor.

YOUNG FASHION Because I love to lie as near heaven as I can.

COUPLER Prithee let heaven alone; ne'er affect tending that way: thy centre's downwards.

YOUNG FASHION That's impossible. I have too much ill luck in this world, to be damned in the next.

COUPLER Thou art out in thy logic. Thy major is true, but thy minor is false; for thou art the luckiest fellow in the universe.

YOUNG FASHION Make out that.

COUPLER I'll do't: last night the devil ran away with the parson of Fatgoose living.

YOUNG FASHION If he had run away with the parish too, what's that to me?

COUPLER I'll tell thee what it's to thee. This living is worth five hundred pound a year, and the presentation of it is thine, if thou can'st prove thyself a lawful husband to Miss Hoyden.

YOUNG FASHION Say'st thou so, my protector? Then egad I shall have a brace of evidences here presently.

COUPLER The nurse and the doctor?

YOUNG FASHION The same: the devil himself won't have interest enough to make 'em withstand it.

COUPLER That we shall see presently: here they come.

Enter Nurse and Chaplain: they start back, seeing Young Fashion.

NURSE Ah goodness, Roger, we are betrayed.

YOUNG FASHION [*laying hold on 'em*] Nay, nay, ne'er flinch for the matter; for I have you safe. Come, to your trials immediately: I have no time to give you copies of your indictment. There sits your judge.

BOTH [*kneeling*] Pray, Sir, have compassion on us.

NURSE I hope, Sir, my years will move your pity, I am an aged woman.

COUPLER That is a moving argument indeed.

* Phthisic: asthmatic, or consumptive.

BULL I hope, Sir, my character will be considered; I am heaven's ambassador.

COUPLER [*to Bull*] Are not you a rogue of sanctity?

BULL Sir, (with respect to my function) I do wear a gown.

COUPLER Did not you marry this vigorous young fellow, to a plump young buxom wench?

NURSE [*to Bull*] Don't confess, Roger, unless you are hard put to it indeed.

COUPLER Come, out with't – Now is he chewing the cud of his roguery, and grinding a lie between his teeth.

BULL Sir – I cannot positively say – I say, Sir – positively I cannot say –

COUPLER Come, no equivocations; no Roman turns upon us. Consider thou standest upon Protestant ground, which will slip from under thee, like a Tyburn cart; for in this country, we have always ten hangmen for one Jesuit.★

BULL [*to Young Fashion*] Pray, Sir, then will you but permit me to speak one word in private with nurse.

YOUNG FASHION Thou art always for doing something in private with nurse.

COUPLER But pray let his betters be served before him for once. I would do something in private with her myself: Lory take care of this reverend gownman in the next room a little. Retire priest.

                                        [*Exit Lory with Bull*]

Now, virgin, I must put the matter home to you a little: do you think it might not be possible to make you speak truth.

NURSE Alas! Sir, I don't know what you mean by truth.

COUPLER Nay, 'tis possible thou may'st be a stranger to it.

YOUNG FASHION Come, nurse, you and I were better friends when we saw one another last; and I still believe, you are a very good woman in the bottom. I did deceive you and your young lady, 'tis true, but I always designed to make a very good husband to her, and to be a very good friend to you. And 'tis possible in the end, she might have found herself happier, and you richer, than ever my brother will make you.

NURSE Brother! Why is your worship then his lordship's brother?

★ equivocations . . . Jesuit: the use of words to say one thing while meaning another, ascribed to Roman Catholics and particularly Jesuits at this period.

YOUNG FASHION I am, which you should have known, if I durst have stayed to have told you; but I was forced to take horse a little in haste you know.

NURSE You were indeed, Sir, poor young man, how he was bound to scour for't. Now won't your worship be angry, if I confess the truth to you, when I found you were a cheat (with respect be it spoken) I verily believed, Miss had got some pitiful skip-jack* varlet or other to her husband; or I had ne'er let her think of marrying again.

COUPLER But where was your conscience all this while, woman? Did not that stare in your face, with huge saucer eyes, and a great horn upon the forehead? Did not you think you should be damned for such a sin? Ha?

YOUNG FASHION Well said, divinity, press that home upon her.

NURSE Why, in good truly Sir, I had some fearful thoughts on't, and could never be brought to consent, 'till Mr Bull said it was a peckadilla,† and he'd secure my soul, for a tithe pig.

YOUNG FASHION There was a rogue for you.

COUPLER And he shall thrive accordingly: he shall have a good living. Come, honest nurse, I see you have butter in your compound; you can melt. Some compassion you can have of this handsome young fellow.

NURSE I have indeed, Sir.

YOUNG FASHION Why then I'll tell you, what you shall do for me. You know what a warm living here is fallen; and that it must be in the disposal of him, who has the disposal of Miss. Now if you and the doctor will agree to prove my marriage, I'll present him to it, upon condition he makes you his bride.

NURSE Naw the blessing of the Lord follow your good worship both by night and by day. Let him be fetched in by the ears; I'll soon bring his nose to the grindstone.

COUPLER [*aside*] Well said old white-leather.‡ Hey; bring in the prisoner there.

Enter Lory with Bull.

---

* skip-jack: a deceiver.   † peckadilla: peccadillo.
‡ white-leather: specially treated leather, probably used to indicate Nurse's transformed attitude as well as her complexion.

COUPLER Come, advance holy man: here's your duck, does not think fit to retire with you into the chancel at this time: but she has a proposal to make to you, in the face of the congregation. Come, nurse, speak for yourself; you are of age.

NURSE Roger, are not you a wicked man, Roger, to set your strength against a weak woman; and persuade her it was no sin to conceal Miss's nuptials? My conscience flies in my face for it, thou priest of Baal; and I find by woeful experience, thy absolution, is not worth an old cassock. Therefore I am resolved to confess the truth to the whole world, though I die a beggar for it. But his worship overflows with his mercy and his bounty: he is not only pleased to forgive us our sins, but designs thou shalt squat thee down in Fatgoose living, and which is more than all; has prevailed with me, to become the wife of thy bosom.

YOUNG FASHION All this I intend for you, doctor. What you are to do for me; I need not tell you.

BULL Your worship's goodness is unspeakable: yet there is one thing, seems a point of conscience: and conscience is a tender babe. If I should bind myself, for the sake of this living, to marry nurse, and maintain her afterwards, I doubt it might be looked on as a kind of simony.

COUPLER [*rising up*] If it were sacrilege, the living's worth it: therefore no more words, good doctor. But with the [*giving Nurse to him*] parish – here – take the parsonage house. 'Tis true, 'tis a little out of repair; some dilapidations there are to be made good; the windows are broke, the wainscot is warped; the ceilings are peeled, and the walls are cracked; but a little glazing, painting, whitewash and plaster, will make it last thy time.

BULL Well, Sir, if it must be so, I shan't contend: what providence orders, I submit to.

NURSE And so do I, with all humility.

COUPLER Why, that now was spoke like good people: come my turtle doves, let us go help this poor pigeon to his wandering mate again; and after institution and induction, you shall all go a-cooing together. [*Exeunt*]

⟨SCENE IV⟩

Enter Amanda in a scarf, &c. as just returned, her Woman following her.

AMANDA Prithee what care I who has been here.

WOMAN Madam, 'twas my Lady Bridle, and my Lady Tiptoe.

AMANDA My Lady Fiddle, and my Lady Faddle. What do'st stand troubling me with the visits of a parcel of impertinent women, when they are well seamed with the smallpox, they won't be so fond of showing their faces – there are more coquettes about this town.

WOMAN Madam, I suppose they only came to return your ladyship's visit, according to the custom of the world.

AMANDA Would the world were on fire, and you in the middle on't. Begone; leave me.   [*Exit Woman*]

[*sola*] At last I am convinced, My eyes are testimonies
Of his falsehood. The base, ungrateful, perjured villain –
Good gods – What slippery stuff are men composed of?
Sure, the account of their creation's false,
And 'twas the woman's rib that they were formed of;
But why am I thus angry?
This poor relapse should only move my scorn.
'Tis true: the roving flights of his unfinished youth,
Had strong excuse, from the plea of nature;
Reason had thrown the reins loose on his neck,
And slipped him to unlimited desire.
If therefore he went wrong, he had a claim
To my forgiveness, and I did him right.
But since the years of manhood, rein him in,
And reason well digested into thought,
Has pointed out the course he ought to run;
If now he strays?
'Twould be as weak, and mean in me to pardon,
As it has been in him t'offend.
But hold:
'Tis an ill cause indeed, where nothing's to be said for't.
My beauty possibly is in the wane;
Perhaps sixteen has greater charms for him:

Yes, there's the secret: but let him know,
My quiver's not entirely emptied yet,
I still have darts, and I can shoot 'em too;
They're not so blunt, but they can enter still,
The want's not in my power, but in my will.
Virtue's his friend, or through another's heart,
I yet could find the way, to make his smart.

Going off she meets Worthy.

Ha! He here? Protect me heaven, for this looks ominous.

WORTHY You seem disordered, Madam; I hope there's no misfortune happened to you?

AMANDA None that will long disorder me, I hope.

WORTHY Whate'er it be disturbs you; I would to heaven 'twere
in my power to bear the pain, 'till I were able to remove the cause.

AMANDA I hope ere long it will remove itself.
At least, I have given it warning to be gone.

WORTHY Would I durst ask, where 'tis the thorn torments you?
Forgive me, if I grow inquisitive?
'Tis only with desire to give you ease.

AMANDA Alas! 'tis in a tender part.
It can't be drawn, without a world of pain:
Yet out it must;
For it begins to fester in my heart.

WORTHY If 'tis the sting of unrequited love,
Remove it instantly:
I have a balm will quickly heal the wound.

AMANDA You'll find the undertaking difficult:
The surgeon, who already has attempted it,
Has much tormented me.

WORTHY I'll aid him with a gentler hand.
– If you will give me leave.

AMANDA How soft soe'er the hand may be,
There still is terror in the operation.

WORTHY Some few preparatives would make it easy,
Could I persuade you to apply 'em.
Make home reflections, Madam, on your slighted love.
Weigh well, the strength and beauty of your charms:

Rouse up that spirit women ought to bear,
And slight your god; if he neglects his angel.
With arms of ice, receive his cold embraces,
And keep your fire, for those who come in flames:
Behold a burning lover at your feet,
His fever raging in his veins.
See how he trembles, how he pants;
See how he glows, how he consumes:
Extend the arms of mercy to his aid;
His zeal may give him title to your pity,
Although his merit cannot claim your love.

AMANDA Of all my feeble sex, sure I must be the weakest,
Should I again presume to think on love.
[*sighing*] – Alas! My heart has been too roughly treated.

WORTHY 'Twill find the greater bliss, in softer usage.

AMANDA But where's that usage to be found?

WORTHY 'Tis here, within this faithful breast, which if you doubt,
I'll rip it up before your eyes;
Lay all its secrets open to your view:
And then, you'll see 'twas sound.

AMANDA With just such honest words as these:
The worst of men deceived me.

WORTHY He therefore merits,
All revenge can do; his fault is such,
The extent and stretch of vengeance, cannot reach it.
O make me but your instrument of justice:
You'll find me execute it with such zeal,
As shall convince you, I abhor the crime.

AMANDA The rigour of an executioner,
Has more the face of cruelty than justice:
And he who puts the cord about the wretch's neck,
Is seldom known to exceed him in his morals.

WORTHY What proof then can I give you of my truth?

AMANDA There is on earth, but one.

WORTHY And is that in my power?

AMANDA It is:
And one that would so thoroughly convince me,
I should be apt, to rate your heart so high;

I possibly might purchase 't with a part of mine.

WORTHY Then heaven thou art my friend, and I am blessed;
For if 'tis in my power, my will I'm sure
Will reach it. No matter what the terms may be,
When such a recompense is offered.
O tell me quickly what this proof must be:
What is it, will convince you of my love?

AMANDA I shall believe you love me as you ought,
If, from this moment, you forbear to ask
Whatever is unfit for me to grant –
You pause upon it, Sir – I doubt, on such hard terms,
A woman's heart is scarcely worth the having.

WORTHY A heart like yours, on any terms is worth it;
'Twas not on that I paused. But I was thinking, [*drawing nearer
to her*]
Whether some things there may not be,
Which women cannot grant without a blush,
And yet which men may take without offence. [*taking her hand*]
Your hand, I fancy, may be of the number:
O pardon me, if I commit a rape
Upon it, [*kissing it eagerly*] and thus devour it with my kisses.

AMANDA O heavens! Let me go.

WORTHY Never whilst I have strength to hold you here. [*forcing
her to sit down on a couch*]
My life, my soul, my goddess – O forgive me?

AMANDA O whither am I going? Help, heaven, or I am lost.

WORTHY Stand neuter, gods, this once I do invoke you.

AMANDA Then save me, virtue, and the glory's thine.

WORTHY Nay, never strive.

AMANDA I will; and conquer too.
My forces rally bravely to my aid, [*breaking from him*]
And thus I gain the day.

WORTHY Then mine as bravely double their attack; [*seizing her
again*]
And thus I wrest it from you. Nay struggle not;
For all's in vain: or death or victory; I am determined.

AMANDA And so am I. [*rushing from him*]
Now keep your distance, or we part for ever.

WORTHY [*offering again*] For heaven's sake –
AMANDA [*going*] Nay, then farewell.
WORTHY [*kneeling and holding by her clothes*]
  O stay, and see the magic force of love:
  Behold this raging lion at your feet,
  Struck dead with fear, and tame as charms can make him.
  What must I do to be forgiven by you?
AMANDA Repent, and never more offend.
WORTHY Repentance for past crimes, is just and easy;
  But sin no more's a task too hard for mortals.
AMANDA Yet those who hope for heaven,
  Must use their best endeavours to perform it.
WORTHY Endeavours we may use but flesh and blood
  Are got in t'other scale;
  And they are ponderous things.
AMANDA What e'er they are;
  There is a weight in resolution
  Sufficient for their balance. The soul I do confess,
  Is usually so careless of its charge,
  So soft, and so indulgent to desire,
  It leaves the reins in the wild hand of nature,
  Who like a Phaeton, drives the fiery chariot,
  And sets the world on flame.
  Yet still the sovereignty is in the mind,
  Whene'er it pleases to exert its force.
  Perhaps you may not think it worth your while,
  To take such mighty pains for my esteem,
  But that I leave to you.
  You see the price I set upon my heart,
  Perhaps 'tis dear: but spite of all your art,
  You'll find on cheaper terms, we ne'er shall part. [*Exit Amanda*]
WORTHY [*solus*] Sure there's divinity about her;
  And sh'as dispensed some portion on't to me.
  For what but now was the wild flame of love,
  Or (to dissect that specious term)
⅄ The vile, the gross desires of flesh and blood,
  Is in a moment turned to adoration.
  The coarser appetite of nature's gone,

And 'tis methinks the food of angels I require,
How long this influence may last, heaven knows.
But in this moment of my purity,
I could on her own terms, accept her heart.
Yes, lovely woman; I can accept it.
For now 'tis doubly worth my care.
Your charms are much increased, since thus adorned.
When truth's extorted from us, then we own
The robe of virtue is a graceful habit.
Could women but our secret councils scan,
Could they but reach the deep reserves of man,
They'd wear it on, that that of love might last,
For when they throw off one, we soon the other cast.
Their sympathy is such –
The fate of one, the other scarce can fly;
They live together, and together die.   [*Exit*]

⟨SCENE V⟩

⟨Lord Foppington's house⟩

Enter Miss and Nurse.

MISS But is it sure and certain, say you, he's my lord's own brother?
NURSE As sure, as he's your lawful husband.
MISS Ecod if I had known that in time, I don't know but I might have kept him: for between you and I nurse, he'd have made a husband worth two of this I have. But which do you think you should fancy most, nurse?
NURSE Why truly, in my poor fancy, Madam, your first husband is the prettier gentleman.
MISS I don't like my lord's shapes, nurse.
NURSE Why in good truly, as a body may say, he is but a slam.*
MISS What do you think now he puts me in mind of? Don't you remember, a long, loose, shambling sort of a horse my father called Washy?

* slam: an ungainly ill-shaped person.

NURSE As like as two twin brothers.

MISS Ecod, I have thought so a hundred times: faith I'm tired of him.

NURSE Indeed, Madam, I think you had e'en as good stand to your first bargain.

MISS O but, nurse, we han't considered the main thing yet. If I leave my lord, I must leave my lady too; and when I rattle about the streets in my coach, they'll only say, there goes Mistress – Mistress – Mistress what? What's this man's name, I have married, nurse?

NURSE Squire Fashion.

MISS Squire Fashion is it? – Well squire, that's better than nothing: do you think one could not get him made a knight, nurse?

NURSE I don't know but one might, Madam, when the King's in a good humour.

MISS Ecod, that would do rarely. For then he'd be as good a man as my father, you know?

NURSE By'r Lady, and that's as good as the best of 'em.

MISS So 'tis, faith; for then I shall be my lady, and your ladyship at every word, and that's all I have to care for. Ha, nurse, but hark you me; one thing more, and then I have done. I'm afraid, if I change my husband again, I shan't have so much money to throw about, nurse?

NURSE Oh, enough's as good as a feast: besides, Madam, one don't know, but as much may fall to your share with the younger brother as with the elder. For though these lords have a power of wealth indeed: yet, as I have heard say, they give it all to their sluts and their trulls, who joggle it about in their coaches, with a murrain to 'em, whilst poor Madam, sits sighing and wishing, and knotting and crying, and has not a spare half crown, to buy her a *Practice of Piety*.★

MISS Oh, but for that, don't deceive yourself, nurse. For this I must say for my lord, and a – [*snapping her fingers*] for him. He's as free as an open house at Christmas. For this very morning, he told me, I should have two hundred a year to buy pins. Now, nurse, if he gives me two hundred a year to buy pins; what do you think he'll give me to buy fine petticoats?

★ *Practice of Piety*: a popular work of piety by Lewis Bayley.

NURSE Ah, my dearest, he deceives thee faully; and he's no better than a rogue for his pains. These Londoners have got a gibberidge with 'em, would confound a gypsy. That which they call pin-money, is to buy their wives everything in the varsal* world, dawn to their very shoe-ties: nay, I have heard folks say, that some ladies, if they will have gallants, as they call 'um; are forced to find them out of their pin-money too.

MISS Has he served me so, say ye? – Then I'll be his wife no longer, so that's fixed. Look, here he comes with all the fine folk at's heels. Ecod, nurse, these London ladies will laugh 'till they crack again, to see me slip my collar, and run away from my husband. But d'ye hear? Pray take care of one thing: when the business comes to break out; be sure you get between me and my father, for you know his tricks; he'll knock me down.

NURSE I'll mind him, ne'er fear, Madam.

Enter Lord Foppington, Loveless, Worthy, Amanda, and Berinthia.

LORD FOPPINGTON Ladies and gentlemen, you are all welcome. [*to Loveless*] Loveless – that's my wife; prithee do me the favour to salute her: and do'st hear, [*aside to him*] if thau hast a mind to try thy fartune, to be revenged of me? I won't take it ill, stap my vitals.

LOVELESS You need not fear, Sir, I'm too fond of my own wife, to have the least inclination to yours. [*all salute Miss*]

LORD FOPPINGTON [*aside*] I'd give you a thousand paund he would make love to her, that he may see she has sense enough to prefer me to him, though his own wife has not. [*viewing him*] – He's a very beastly fellow in my opinion.

MISS [*aside*] What a power of fine men there are in this London? He that kissed me first, is a goodly gentleman, I promise you: sure those wives have a rare time on't, that live here always?

Enter Sir Tunbelly with Musicians, Dancers, &c.

SIR TUNBELLY Come; come in, good people, come in, come tune your fiddles, tune your fiddles. [*to the Hautboys*] Bag-pipes, make ready there. Come strike up.
[*Sings*] For this is Hoyden's wedding-day,

* varsal: an illiterate abbreviation of universal, only used in this phrase.

And therefore we keep holiday,
And come to be merry.
Ha! There's my wench i'faith: touch and take, I'll warrant her:
she'll breed like a tame rabbit.

MISS [*aside*] Ecod, I think my father's gotten drunk before supper!

SIR TUNBELLY [*to Lord Foppington and Worthy*] Gentlemen, you
are welcome. [*saluting Amanda and Berinthia*] Ladies by your leave.
Ha – they bill like turtles. Udsookers, they set my old blood a-fire;
I shall cuckold somebody before morning.

LORD FOPPINGTON [*to Sir Tunbelly*] Sir, you being master of the
entertainment; will you desire the company to sit?

SIR TUNBELLY Oons, Sir, – I'm the happiest man on this side the
Ganges.

LORD FOPPINGTON [*aside*] This is a mighty unaccountable old
fellow. [*to Sir Tunbelly*] I said, Sir, it would be convenient to ask
the company to sit.

SIR TUNBELLY Sit? – With all my heart: come, take your places,
ladies, take your places, gentlemen: come sit down, sit down; a
pox of ceremony, take your places. [*they sit, and the Masque begins*]

Dialogue between Cupid and Hymen.

I

CUPID Thou bane to my empire, thou spring of contest,
Thou source of all discord, thou period to rest;
Instruct me, what wretches in bondage can see,
That the aim of their life is still pointed to thee.

2

HYMEN Instruct me, thou little impertinent god,
From whence all thy subjects have taken the mode,
To grow fond of a change, to whatever it be,
And I'll tell thee why those would be bound, who are free.

CHORUS For change, we're for change, to whatever it be,
We are neither contented with freedom nor thee.
Constancy's an empty sound,
Heaven and earth, and all go round,

All the works of nature move,
And the joys of life and love
    Are in variety.

3

CUPID Were love the reward of a painstaking life,
       Had a husband the art to be fond of his wife,
       Were virtue so plenty, a wife could afford,
       These very hard times, to be true to her lord,
       Some specious account, might be given of those
       Who are tied by the tail, to be led by the nose.

4

But since 'tis the fate of a man and his wife,
To consume all their days in contention and strife:
Since whatever the bounty of heaven may create her,
He's morally sure, he shall heartily hate her,
I think 'twere much wiser to ramble at large,
And the volleys of love on the herd to discharge.

5

HYMEN Some colour of reason, thy counsel might bear,
      Could a man have no more, than his wife to his share:
      Or were I a monarch so cruelly just,
      To oblige a poor wife, to be true to her trust;
      But I have not pretended, for many years past,
      By marrying of people, to make 'em grow chaste.

6

I therefore advise thee to let me go on,
Thou'lt find I'm the strength and support of thy throne;
For hadst thou but eyes, thou wouldst quickly perceive it,
        How smoothly the dart
        Slips into the heart
        Of a woman that's wed;
        Whilst the shivering maid,
Stands trembling, and wishing, but dare not receive it.

CHORUS For change &c.

The Masque ended, enter Young Fashion, Coupler, and Bull.

SIR TUNBELLY So, very fine, very fine i'faith, this is something like a wedding, now if supper were but ready, I'd say a short grace, and if I had such a bedfellow as Hoyden tonight – I'd say as short prayers. [*seeing Young Fashion*] How now? – What have we got here? A ghost? Nay it must be so, for his flesh and his blood could never have dared to appear before me. [*to him*] Ah rogue –

LORD FOPPINGTON Stap my vitals, Tam again.

SIR TUNBELLY My lord, will you cut his throat? Or shall I?

LORD FOPPINGTON Leave him to me, Sir, if you please. Prithee Tam be so ingenuous now, as to tell me what thy business is here?

YOUNG FASHION 'Tis with your bride.

LORD FOPPINGTON Thau art the impudent'st fellow that nature has yet spawned into the warld, strike me speechless.

YOUNG FASHION Why you know my modesty would have starved me, I sent it a-begging to you, and you would not give it a groat.

LORD FOPPINGTON And dost thau expect by an excess of assurance, to extart a maintenance fram me?

YOUNG FASHION [*taking Miss by the hand*] I do intend to extort your mistress from you, and that I hope will prove one.

LORD FOPPINGTON I ever thaught Newgate or Bedlam would be his fartune, and naw his fate's decided. Prithee Loveless dost know of ever a mad-doctor hard by?

YOUNG FASHION There's one at your elbow will cure you presently. [*to Bull*] Prithee Doctor take him in hand quickly.

LORD FOPPINGTON Shall I beg the favour of you, Sir, to pull your fingers out of my wife's hand.

YOUNG FASHION His wife! Look you there, now I hope you are all satisfied he's mad?

LORD FOPPINGTON Naw is it nat possible far me to penetrate what species of fally it is thau art driving at.

SIR TUNBELLY Here, here, here, let me beat out his brains, and that will decide all.

LORD FOPPINGTON No, pray Sir hold, we'll destray him presently, according to law.

YOUNG FASHION [*to Bull*] Nay, then advance doctor; come, you are a man of conscience, answer boldly to the questions I shall ask; did not you marry me to this young lady, before ever that gentleman there saw her face?

BULL Since the truth must out, I did.

YOUNG FASHION Nurse, sweet nurse, were not you a witness to it?

NURSE Since my conscience bids me speak – I was.

YOUNG FASHION [*to Miss*] Madam, am not I your lawful husband?

MISS Truly I cannot tell, but you married me first.

YOUNG FASHION Now I hope you are all satisfied?

SIR TUNBELLY [*offering to strike him, is held by Loveless and Worthy*] Oons and thunder you lie.

LORD FOPPINGTON Pray Sir, be calm, the battle is in disarder, but requires more canduct than courage to rally our forces. Pray dactar one word with you. [*to Bull aside*] Look you, Sir, though I will not presume to calculate your notions of damnation, fram the description you give us of hell, yet since there is at least a possibility, you may have a pitchfark thrust in your backside, methinks it should not be worth your while to risk your saul in the next warld, far the sake of a beggarly yaunger brather, who is nat able to make your lady happy in this.

BULL Alas! My lord, I have no worldly ends, I speak the truth, heaven knows.

LORD FOPPINGTON Nay prithee never engage heaven in the matter, for by all I can see, 'tis like to prove a business for the devil.

YOUNG FASHION Come, pray Sir, all above-board, no corrupting of evidences, if you please, this young lady is my lawful wife, and I'll justify it in all the courts of England; so your lordship (who always had a passion for variety) may go seek a new mistress if you think fit.

LORD FOPPINGTON I am struck dumb with his impudence, and cannot passitively tell whether ever I shall speak again or nat.

SIR TUNBELLY Then let me come and examine the business a little, I'll jerk the truth out of 'em presently; here, give me my dog-whip.

YOUNG FASHION Look you, old gentleman, 'tis in vain to make a noise, if you grow mutinous, I have some friends within call, have swords by their sides, above four foot long, therefore be calm, hear the evidence patiently, and when the jury have given their verdict, pass sentence according to law; here's honest Coupler shall be foreman, and ask as many questions as he pleases.

COUPLER All I have to ask is, whether nurse persists in her evidence? The parson I dare swear will never flinch from his.

NURSE [*to Sir Tunbelly kneeling*] I hope in heaven your worship will pardon me, I have served you long and faithfully, but in this thing I was over-reached, your worship however was deceived as well, as I, and if the wedding-dinner had been ready, you had put Madam to bed to him with your own hands.

SIR TUNBELLY But how durst you do this, without acquainting of me?

NURSE Alas! If your worship had seen how the poor thing begged, and prayed, and clung and twined about me, like ivy to an old wall, you would say, I who had suckled it, and swaddled it, and nursed it both wet and dry, must have had a heart of adamant to refuse it.

SIR TUNBELLY Very well.

YOUNG FASHION Foreman, I expect your verdict.

COUPLER Ladies, and gentlemen, what's your opinions?

ALL A clear case, a clear case.

COUPLER Then my young folks, I wish you joy.

SIR TUNBELLY [*to Young Fashion*] Come hither stripling, if it be true then that thou hast married my daughter, prithee tell me who thou art?

YOUNG FASHION Sir, the best of my condition is, I am your son-in-law; and the worst of it is, I am brother to that noble peer there.

SIR TUNBELLY Art thou brother to that noble peer? – Why then that noble peer and thee, and thy wife, and the nurse, and the priest – may all go and be damned together. [*Exit Sir Tunbelly*]

LORD FOPPINGTON [*aside*] Now for my part, I think the wisest thing a man can do with an aching heart, is to put on a serene countenance, for a philosophical air is the most becoming thing in the world to the face of a person of quality, I will therefore bear my disgrace like a great man, and let the people see I am above an affront. [*to Young Fashion*] Dear Tam, since things are thus fallen aut, prithee give me leave to wish thee jay, I do it *de bon coeur*, strike me dumb. You have married a woman beautiful in her person, charming in her airs, prudent in her canduct, canstant in her inclinations, and of a nice marality, split my windpipe.

YOUNG FASHION Your lordship may keep up your spirits with your grimace if you please, I shall support mine with this lady, and two thousand pound a year. [*taking Miss*] Come, Madam.
We once again you see are man and wife,
And now perhaps the bargain's struck for life;
If I mistake, and we should part again,
At least you see you may have choice of men:
Nay, should the war★ at length such havoc make,
That lovers should grow scarce, yet for your sake,
Kind heaven always will preserve a beau,
[*pointing to Lord Foppington*] You'll find his lordship ready to come to.†

LORD FOPPINGTON Her ladyship shall stap my vitals if I do.

★ the war: from 1689–1697 England was at war on the continent.
† come to: reach a reconciliation.

EPILOGUE

Spoken by Lord Foppington

Gentlemen, and ladies,
   These people have regaled you here today
   (In my opinion) with a saucy play;
   In which the author does presume to show,
   That coxcomb, *ab origine* – was beau.
   Truly I think the thing of so much weight,
   That if some smart chastisement ben't his fate,
   Gad's curse it may in time destroy the state.
   I hold no one its friend, I must confess,
   Who would discauntenance your men of dress.
   Far give me leave t'abserve good clothes are things,
   Have ever been of great support to kings;
   All treasons come fram slovens, it is nat
   Within the reach of gentle beaux to plat.
   They have no gaul, no spleen, no teeth, no stings,
   Of all Gad's creatures the most harmless things.
   Through all recard, no prince was ever slain,
   By one who had a feather in his brain.
   They're men of too refined an education,
   To squabble with a court – for a vile dirty nation.
   I'm very pasitive, you never saw
   A through republican a finished beau.
   Nor truly shall you very often see
   A Jacobite much better dressed than he;
   In shart, through all the courts that I have been in,
   Your men of mischief – still are in faul linen.
   Did ever one yet dance the Tyburn jig,
   With a free air, ar a well pawdered wig?
   Did ever highwayman yet bid you stand,
   With a sweet bawdy snuff-bax in his hand;
   Ar do you ever find they ask your purse
   As men of breeding do? – Ladies Gad's curse,
   This author is a dag, and 'tis not fit
   You should allow him ev'n one grain of wit.

To which, that his pretence may ne'er be named,
My humble motion is – he may be damned.

NOTES

The copy text used is that of the first edition of 1697 in the Brotherton Collection, University of Leeds.

Abbreviations
    Q1 The first quarto edition, 1697
    Q2 The second quarto edition, 1698
    P   *Plays written by Sir John Vanbrugh,* 1719

The printer of the first edition seems to have been uncertain about setting various passages in prose or verse, notably where, in Jeremy Collier's phrase, Worthy talks prose to Amanda in metre in V.iv. The other scenes involved are I.i and III.iv. Some inconsistencies in the copy text (where Loveless is sometimes spelled Lovelace, stap spelled stop and Ecod varies in form) have been regularized.

445.2   Mrs Cross / Miss Cross Q1
445.31   must enter. / must enter Q1
446.28   draw / draw. Q1
446.32   engage, / engage. Q1
447.7   friends, / Friends Q1
447.10   rules) / Rules, Q1
447.11   fools : / Fools. Q1
450.1   more, / more. Q1
452.7   me in, / me in Q1
452.18   great. / great, Q1
452.20   bold. / bold, Q1
454.8   money, your / money. Your Q1
454.13   So / So' Q1
455.13   *menus* / *Menu* Q1
457.6   trod Q2 / trode Q1
459.23   fault. We / fault, we Q1
461.21   Q1 sets Coupler's speech as verse
462.14   what, have you forgot Lory? Q2 / What have you forgot, Lory Q1
462.32   mother) your / Mother. Your Q1
463.11   partridge Q2 / Patridge Q1
463.25   ), / ,) Q1

463.26	fortnight Q2/Forthnight Q1
464.11	merit. We/merit we Q1
464.34	),/,) Q1
464.37	),/,) Q1
467.25	play that/play. That Q1
469.21	If the P/I the Q1 ('Aye the' could possibly be intended as in Q2).
469.24	be)/be,) Q1
472.4	a-clack/a-Clock Q1
472.29	you beaux spent/you, *Beaux*, spent Q1
474.5	the world/the the world Q1
476.16	Sir./Sir, Q1
477.17	surgeon, who, I/Surgeon, I Q1
480.13	men,/men. Q1
481.11	no, he/No he Q1
485.29	picked/pickt Q1/prickt Q2/piqued P
488.21	[*Exit Servant*] Q1 omits
489.20	it there is P/If there is Q1
490.16	Whether P/Whither Q1
492.3	universe./Universe Q1
492.35	me, it's P/me its Q1
495.17	whether P/whither Q1
498.12	whether P/whethe Q1
499.9	laurel, run/laurel run Q1
502.12	flaunt/flant Q1
502.29	,)/,) Q1
503.35	Gemini P/Gimmini Q1
507.12	burden P/burthen Q1
507.33	AMANDA Upon Q2/*Ber.* Upon Q1
509.8	coquette; he/Coquett he Q1
510.22	it. I'll/it, I'll Q1
510.29	),/,) Q1
511.1	time. Would/time, would Q1
518.16	dream's/dreams Q1
518.23	Gemini/gimmeni Q1
518.26	*Lord Foppington* Q2/*L. Fash.* Q1
519.25	LORD FOPPINGTON Q2/*L. Fash.* Q1
519.31	place, and (if . . . /place, (if . . . Q1

521.33   business. Where's/business, where's Q1
523.1   *châtré* emendation of A. E. H. Swain; chatre Q1
523.18   ready. If/ready, if Q1
524.9   all together P/altogether Q1
525.28   When/Then Q1
528.4   Abigail/*Abigall* Q1
529.11   supper; he's/supper, he's
531.18   Amanda, the/Amanda; the Q1
532.37   earthed Q2/earth Q1
534.20   Hoyden./Hoyden? Q1
534.26   come./come? Q1
536.14   press 1730 ed. (cited by Curt A. Zimansky, op. cit.)/pass Q1
545.26   not./not, Q1
546.5   supper!/supper:
551.4   dumb. You/dumb, you Q1
551.17   come to./come to, Q1

THE PROVOKED WIFE
by Sir John Vanbrugh

INTRODUCTION

The Provoked Wife was probably written when Vanbrugh was a prisoner in the Bastille in 1692; it was first acted by Betterton's company at Lincoln's Inn Fields (probably in April) in 1697. The play, with Betterton as Sir John Brute, Mrs Barry as Lady Brute and Mrs Bracegirdle as Bellinda, was successful, and often performed. Others who played the part of Sir John Brute later were Keene, Quin, Cibber, Garrick and Macklin, while Lady Brute was played by Anne Oldfield, Susanna Cibber and Peg Woffington. The play was less popular towards the end of the eighteenth century and did not suit the nineteenth, although it was reprinted quite often. Surprisingly, *The Provoked Wife* has been played only a few times in the twentieth century.

The plot of *The Provoked Wife*, revolving around the unsatisfactory marriage of Sir John and Lady Brute, is not its strong point. As the name Brute suggests, Sir John is a largely unpleasant character, and the situation of a woman married to such a man was indeed sad, for she could not divorce him. Such a possibility is in fact discussed in the first scene of the first Act between Lady Brute and Bellinda: but it will be achieved only in 'a court of Chancery in heaven'. Marriage was still a solid institution: the remedies offered by comic writers for the unhappily matched were adulterous liaisons.

The play provides us with a somewhat episodic view of the roistering of gallants and their attacks upon citizens, and of the meeting for intrigues in the Spring Gardens in between the conversations of the characters. The subsidiary subjects – the lovers, the affected Lady Fanciful who longs for revenge, the relationship between Mademoiselle and Razor – are not closely linked with the main sad theme of the ill-assorted Brutes. But there is plenty of amusement here and there, notably in Mademoiselle's role, though Razor's repentance at the end of the play is hardly convincing.

For the dialogue Vanbrugh produces an easy, natural and occasionally witty prose relying on short conversational sentences which run well, and are realistic. Though Jeremy Collier denounced the play in 1698, and later, in 1701, the actors were indicted for speaking its profane language, and there are indeed passages that carry a sense that reform may be needed. Bellinda asks 'Why don't some reformer or other beat the poet for't?' and the Prologue suggests 'a venomed priest' may write against the author of plays. The play was announced 'with alterations' in 1706, but Colley Cibber categorically stated that when the play was prepared for the Drury Lane production of 11 January 1726, it was 'a comedy which while we found our account in keeping the stage clear of those loose liberties it had formerly too justly been charged with', we had 'laid aside for some years' (which was not quite accurate), and that Sir John Vanbrugh had been prevailed upon to write a new scene for the fourth act. As Cibber puts it, 'where the wantonness of his wit and humour had [originally] made a rake talk like a rake in the borrowed habit of a clergyman: to avoid which offence, he clapped the same debauchee into the undress of a woman of quality' (*An Apology for the Life of Colley Cibber*, 1889, II, 233). The altered scenes first appeared in a Dublin edition of 1743. But these are very minor points; the cynicism of the gallants and the realism of Lady Brute in her talks with Bellinda reveal a libertine looseness and, at times, a certain despair at the way life is ordered.

Mrs Anne Bracegirdle who played Bellinda in
the first performance of The Provoked Wife

The Provoked Wife

A COMEDY

As it is acted at the New Theatre,
in Little Lincolns Inn Fields

By the author of a new comedy called
The Relapse, or Virtue in Danger

LONDON

Printed by J. O. for R. Wellington, at the Lute in
St Paul's Church Yard, and Sam Briscoe in Covent Garden.
1697

DRAMATIS PERSONAE

⟨MEN⟩
Constant.
Heartfree.
Sir John Brute.
Treble, a singing master.
Razor, valet de chambre to Sir John Brute.
Justice of the Peace.
Lord Rake
Colonel Bully } companions to Sir John Brute.
Constable and Watch.

⟨WOMEN⟩
Lady Brute.
Bellinda her niece.
Lady Fanciful.
Mademoiselle.
Cornet
Pipe } servants to *Lady Brute.*

PROLOGUE

To *The Provoked Wife*, spoke by Mistress
Bracegirdle ⟨Bellinda⟩

Since 'tis the intent and business of the stage,
To copy out the follies of the age;
To hold to every man a faithful glass,
And show him of what species he's an ass.
I hope the next that teaches in the school,
Will show our author he's a scribbling fool.
And that the satire may be sure to bite,
Kind heaven! Inspire some venomed priest to write,
And grant some ugly lady may indite.
For I would have him lashed, by heavens! I would,
Till his presumption swam away in blood.
Three plays at once★ proclaims a face of brass,
No matter what they are! That's not the case,
To write three plays, even that's to be an ass.
But what I least forgive, he knows it too,
For to his cost he lately has known you.
Experience shows, to many a writer's smart
You hold a court where mercy ne'er had part;
So much of the old serpent's sting you have,
You love to damn, as heaven delights to save.
In foreign parts, let a bold volunteer,
For public good upon the stage appear,
He meets ten thousand smiles to dissipate his fear.
All tickle on, th' adventuring young beginner,
And only scourge th' incorrigible sinner;
They touch indeed his faults, but with a hand
So gentle, that his merit still may stand:
Kindly they buoy the follies of his pen,
That he may shun 'em when he writes again.
But 'tis not so, in this good-natured Town,
All's one, an ox, a poet, or a crown,
Old England's play was always knocking down.

★ Three plays at once: Vanbrugh's *The Relapse* and *Aesop* were staged earlier in
the 1696–97 season.

ACT ONE

SCENE ⟨I⟩

Sir John Brute's house

Enter Sir John, solus.

SIR JOHN What cloying meat is love, – when matrimony's the sauce to it. Two years' marriage has debauched my five senses. Everything I see, everything I hear, everything I feel, everything I smell, and everything I taste – methinks has wife in't. No boy was ever so weary of his tutor; no girl of her bib; no nun of doing penance nor old maid of being chaste, as I am of being married. Sure there's a secret curse entailed upon the very name of wife. My lady is a young lady, a fine lady, a witty lady, a virtuous lady – and yet I hate her. There is but one thing on earth I loathe beyond her: that's fighting. Would my courage come up but to a fourth part of my ill nature, I'd stand buff* to her relations, and thrust her out of doors. But marriage has sunk me down to such an ebb of resolution, I dare not draw my sword, though even to get rid of my wife. But here she comes.

Enter Lady Brute.

LADY BRUTE Do you dine at home today, Sir John?

SIR JOHN Why, do you expect I should tell you, what I don't know myself?

LADY BRUTE I thought there was no harm in asking you.

SIR JOHN If thinking wrong were an excuse for impertinence, women might be justified in most things they say or do.

LADY BRUTE I'm sorry I have said anything to displease you.

SIR JOHN Sorrow for things past, is of as little importance to me, as my dining at home or abroad ought to be to you.

LADY BRUTE My enquiry was only that I might have provided what you liked.

SIR JOHN Six to four you had been in the wrong there again, for what I liked yesterday I don't like today, and what I like today, 'tis odds I mayn't like tomorrow.

* stand buff: stand firm.

LADY BRUTE But if I had asked you what you liked?

SIR JOHN Why then there would have been more asking about it, than the thing was worth.

LADY BRUTE I wish I did but know how I might please you.

SIR JOHN Aye, but that sort of knowledge is not a wife's talent.

LADY BRUTE Whate'er my talent is, I'm sure my will has ever been to make you easy.

SIR JOHN If women were to have their wills, the world would be finely governed.

LADY BRUTE What reason have I given you to use me as you do of late? It once was otherwise: you married me for love.

SIR JOHN And you me for money: so you have your reward, and I have mine.

LADY BRUTE What is it that disturbs you?

SIR JOHN A parson.

LADY BRUTE Why, what has he done to you?

SIR JOHN He has married me.   [*Exit Sir John*]

LADY BRUTE [*sola*] The devil's in the fellow I think – I was told before I married him, that thus 'twould be; but I thought I had charms enough to govern him; and that where there was an estate, a woman must needs be happy; so my vanity has deceived me, and my ambition has made me uneasy. But some comfort still; if one would be revenged of him, these are good times; a woman may have a gallant, and a separate maintenance* too – The surly puppy – yet he's a fool for't: for hitherto he has been no monster: but who knows how far he may provoke me. I never loved him, yet I have been ever true to him; and that, in spite of all the attacks of art and nature upon a poor weak woman's heart, in favour of a tempting lover. Methinks so noble a defence as I have made, should be rewarded with a better usage – or who can tell – perhaps a good part of what I suffer from my husband may be a judgement upon me for my cruelty to my lover. – Lord with what pleasure could I indulge that thought, were there but a possibility of finding arguments to make it good. – And how do I know but there may – Let me see – What opposes? – My matrimonial vow? – Why, what did I vow: I think I promised to be

---

* separate maintenance: a woman divorced for adultery still was entitled to an allowance from her husband.

true to my husband. Well; and he promised to be kind to me. But he han't kept his word – Why then I'm absolved from mine – aye, that seems clear to me. The argument's good between the King and the people, why not between the husband and the wife? Oh, but that condition was not expressed. – No matter, 'twas understood. Well, by all I see, if I argue the matter a little longer with myself, I shan't find so many bugbears in the way, as I thought I should. Lord what fine notions of virtue do we women take up upon the credit of old foolish philosophers. Virtue's its own reward, virtue's this, virtue's that; – virtue's an ass, and a gallant's worth forty on't.

Enter Bellinda.

LADY BRUTE Good-morrow, dear cousin.

BELLINDA Good-morrow, Madam; you look pleased this morning.

LADY BRUTE I am so.

BELLINDA With what, pray?

LADY BRUTE With my husband.

BELLINDA Drown husbands; for yours is a provoking fellow: as he went out just now, I prayed him to tell me what time of day 'twas: and he asked me if I took him for the church clock, that was obliged to tell all the parish.

LADY BRUTE He has been saying some good obliging things to me too. In short, Bellinda, he has used me so barbarously of late, that I could almost resolve to play the downright wife, – and cuckold him.

BELLINDA That would be downright indeed.

LADY BRUTE Why, after all, there's more to be said for't than you'd imagine, child. I know according to the strict statute law of religion, I should do wrong: but if there were a Court of Chancery★ in heaven, I'm sure I should cast him.

BELLINDA If there were a House of Lords you might.

LADY BRUTE In either I should infallibly carry my cause. Why, he is the first aggressor. Not I.

BELLINDA Aye, but you know, we must return good for evil.

LADY BRUTE That may be a mistake in the translation – Prithee be of my opinion, Bellinda; for I'm positive I'm in the right; and

★ Court of Chancery: Chancery courts did not deal with divorce.

if you'll keep up the prerogative of a woman, you'll likewise be positive you are in the right, whenever you do anything you have a mind to. But I shall play the fool, and jest on till I make you begin to think I'm in earnest.

BELLINDA I shan't take the liberty, Madam, to think of anything that you desire to keep a secret from me.

LADY BRUTE Alas, my dear, I have no secrets. My heart could never yet confine my tongue.

BELLINDA Your eyes you mean; for I am sure I have seen them gadding, when your tongue has been locked up safe enough.

LADY BRUTE My eyes gadding? Prithee after who, child?

BELLINDA Why, after one that thinks you hate him, as much as I know you love him.

LADY BRUTE Constant you mean.

BELLINDA I do so.

LADY BRUTE Lord, what should put such a thing into your head?

BELLINDA That which puts things into most people's heads; observation.

LADY BRUTE Why, what have you observed, in the name of wonder?

BELLINDA I have observed you blush when you meet him; force yourself away from him; and then be out of humour with everything about you: in a word; never was poor creature so spurred on by desire, and so reined in with fear!

LADY BRUTE How strong is fancy!

BELLINDA How weak is woman.

LADY BRUTE Prithee, niece, have a better opinion of your aunt's inclinations.

BELLINDA Dear aunt, have a better opinion of your niece's understanding.

LADY BRUTE You'll make me angry.

BELLINDA You'll make me laugh.

LADY BRUTE Then you are resolved to persist?

BELLINDA Positively.

LADY BRUTE And all I can say –

BELLINDA Will signify nothing,

LADY BRUTE Though I should swear 'twere false –

BELLINDA I should think it true.

LADY BRUTE Then let us both forgive [*kissing her*] for we have both offended. I in making a secret, you in discovering it.

BELLINDA Good nature may do much: but you have more reason to forgive one, than I have to pardon t'other.

LADY BRUTE 'Tis true, Bellinda, you have given me so many proofs of your friendship, that my reserve has been indeed a crime: but that you may more easily forgive me, remember, child, that when our nature prompts us to a thing, our honour and religion have forbid us, we would (were't possible) conceal even from the soul itself, the knowledge of the body's weakness.

BELLINDA Well, I hope, to make your friend amends, you'll hide nothing from her for the future, though the body should still grow weaker and weaker.

LADY BRUTE No, from this moment I have no more reserve; and for a proof of my repentance, I own, Bellinda, I'm in danger. Merit and wit assault me from without: nature and love solicit me within; my husband's barbarous usage piques me to revenge; and Satan catching at the fair occasion, throws in my way that vengeance, which of all vengeance pleases women best.

BELLINDA 'Tis well Constant don't know the weakness of the fortifications; for o'my conscience he'd soon come on to the assault.

LADY BRUTE Aye, and I'm afraid carry the town too. But whatever you may have observed, I have dissembled so well as to keep him ignorant. So you see I'm no coquette, Bellinda: and if you'll follow my advice you'll never be one neither. 'Tis true, coquetry is one of the main ingredients in the natural composition of a woman, and I as well as others, could be well enough pleased to see a crowd of young fellows, ogling and glancing and watching all occasions to do forty foolish officious things: nay should some of 'em push on, even to hanging or drowning: why – faith – if I should let pure woman alone, I should e'en be but too well pleased with't.

BELLINDA I'll swear 'twould tickle me strangely.

LADY BRUTE But after all, 'tis a vicious practice in us, to give the least encouragement but where we design to come to a conclusion. For 'tis an unreasonable thing, to engage a man in a disease which we beforehand resolve we never will apply a cure to.

BELLINDA 'Tis true; but then a woman must abandon one of the supreme blessings of her life. For I am fully convinced, no man has half that pleasure in possessing a mistress, as a woman has in jilting a gallant.

LADY BRUTE The happiest woman then on earth must be our neighbour.

BELLINDA O the impertinent composition; she has vanity and affectation enough to make her a ridiculous original, in spite of all that art and nature ever furnished to any of her sex before her.

LADY BRUTE She concludes all men her captives; and whatever course they take, it serves to confirm her in that opinion.

BELLINDA If they shun her, she thinks 'tis modesty, and takes it for a proof of their passion.

LADY BRUTE And if they are rude to her, 'tis conduct, and done to prevent town talk.

BELLINDA When her folly makes 'em laugh, she thinks they are pleased with her wit.

LADY BRUTE And when her impertinence makes 'em dull, concludes they are jealous of her favours.

BELLINDA All their actions and their words, she takes for granted, aim at her.

LADY BRUTE And pities all other women, because she thinks they envy her.

BELLINDA Pray, out of pity to ourselves, let us find a better subject, for I am weary of this. Do you think your husband inclined to jealousy?

LADY BRUTE Oh, no; he does not love me well enough for that. Lord how wrong men's maxims are. They are seldom jealous of their wives, unless they are very fond of 'em; whereas they ought to consider the woman's inclinations, for there depends their fate. Well, men may talk; but they are not so wise as we – that's certain.

BELLINDA At least in our affairs.

LADY BRUTE Nay, I believe we should outdo 'em in the business of the state too: for methinks they do and undo, and make but mad work on't.

BELLINDA Why then don't we get into the intrigues of government as well as they?

LADY BRUTE Because we have intrigues of our own, that make us more sport, child. And so let's in and consider of 'em.   [*Exeunt*]

SCENE ⟨II⟩

A dressing room

Enter Lady Fanciful, Mademoiselle and Cornet.

LADY FANCIFUL How do I look this morning?

CORNET Your ladyship looks very ill, truly.

LADY FANCIFUL Lard how ill-natured thou art, Cornet, to tell me so, though the thing should be true. Don't you know that I have humility enough to be but too easily out of conceit with myself. Hold the glass; I dare swear that will have more manners than you have. Mademoiselle, let me have your opinion too.

MADEMOISELLE My opinion pe, Matam, dat your ladyship never look so well in your life.

LADY FANCIFUL Well, the French are the prettiest obliging people, they say the most acceptable, well-mannered things – and never flatter.

MADEMOISELLE Your ladyship say great justice inteed.

LADY FANCIFUL Nay everything's just in my house but Cornet. The very looking-glass gives her the *dementi*.★ [*looking affectedly in the glass*] But I'm almost afraid it flatters me, it makes me look so very engaging.

MADEMOISELLE Inteed, Matam, your face pe hansomer den all de looking-glass in tee world, *croyez moi*.

LADY FANCIFUL But is it possible my eyes can be so languishing – and so very full of fire?

MADEMOISELLE Matam, if de glass was burning glass, I believe your eyes set de fire in de house.

LADY FANCIFUL You may take that nightgown, Mademoiselle; get out of the room Cornet; I can't endure you. This wench methinks does look so unsufferably ugly.   [*Exit Cornet*]

MADEMOISELLE Everyting look ugly Matam, dat stand by your latiship.

★ the *dementi*: the lie.

LADY FANCIFUL No really, Mademoiselle, methinks you look mighty pretty.

MADEMOISELLE Ah Matam; de moon have no *eclat*, ven de sun appear.

LADY FANCIFUL O pretty expression. Have you ever been in love, Mademoiselle?

MADEMOISELLE [*sighing*] *Oui*, Matam.

LADY FANCIFUL And were you, beloved again?

MADEMOISELLE [*sighing*] No Matam.

LADY FANCIFUL O ye gods, what an unfortunate creature should I be in such a case. But nature has made me nice for my own defence; I'm nice, strangely nice, Mademoiselle; I believe were the merit of whole mankind bestowed upon one single person, I should still think the fellow wanted something, to make it worth my while to take notice of him: and yet I could love; nay fondly love, were it possible to have a thing made on purpose for me: for I'm not cruel, Mademoiselle, I'm only nice.

MADEMOISELLE Ah Matam, I wish I was fine gentleman for your sake. I do all de ting in de world to get leetel way into your heart. I make song, I make verse, I give you de serenade, I give great many present to Mademoiselle, I no eat, I no sleep, I be lean, I be mad, I hang myself, I drown myself? [*embracing her*] *Ah ma chère dame, que je vous aimerais.*

LADY FANCIFUL Well the French have strange obliging ways with 'em; you may take those two pair of gloves Mademoiselle.

MADEMOISELLE Me humbly tanke my sweet lady.

Enter Cornet.

CORNET Madam here's a letter for your ladyship by the penny-post.

LADY FANCIFUL Some new conquest I'll warrant you. For without vanity I looked extremely clear last night, when I went to the Park. O agreeable. Here's a new song made of me. And ready set too. O thou welcome thing. [*kissing it*] Call Pipe hither, she shall sing it instantly.

Enter Pipe.

Here, sing me this new song, Pipe.

SONG

I

Fly, fly, you happy shepherds, fly,
    Avoid Philira's charms;
The rigour of her heart denies
    The heaven that's in her arms.
Ne'er hope to gaze and then retire,
    Nor yielding, to be blessed:
Nature who formed her eyes of fire,
    Of ice composed her breast.

II

Yet, lovely maid, this once believe
    A slave, whose zeal you move:
The gods alas, your youth deceive;
    Their heaven consists in love.
In spite of all the thanks you owe,
    You may reproach 'em this,
That where they did their form bestow
    They have denied their bliss.

LADY FANCIFUL Well, there may be faults, Mademoiselle, but the design is so very obliging, 'twould be a matchless ingratitude in me to discover 'em.

MADEMOISELLE *Ma foi* Matam, I tink de gentelman's song tell you de trute. If you never love, you never be happy – *Ah – que j'aime l' amour moi.*

Enter Servant with another letter.

SERVANT Madam here's another letter for your ladyship.

LADY FANCIFUL 'Tis thus I am importuned every morning, Mademoiselle. Pray how do the French ladies when they are thus *accablées*?★

MADEMOISELLE Matam, dey never complain. *Au contraire.* When one Frense laty have got hundred lover – den she do all she can – to get hundred more.

★ *accablées*: overburdened.

LADY FANCIFUL Well, strike me dead, I think they have *le goût bon*. For 'tis an unutterable pleasure to be adored by all the men, and envied by all the women – Yet I'll swear I'm concerned at the torture I give 'em. Lard, why was I formed to make the whole creation uneasy? But let me read my letter. [*reads*] 'If you have a mind to hear of your faults, instead of being praised for your virtues, take the pains to walk in the Green Walk in St James's with your woman an hour hence. You'll there meet one, who hates you for some things, as he could love you for others, and therefore is willing to endeavour your reformation – If you come to the place I mention, you'll know who I am; if you don't, you never shall, so take your choice.' This is strangely familiar, Mademoiselle; now have I a provoking fancy to know who this impudent fellow is.

MADEMOISELLE Den take your scarf and your mask, and go to de rendezvous. De Frense laty do *justement comme ça*.

LADY FANCIFUL Rendezvous! What, rendezvous with a man; Mademoiselle.

MADEMOISELLE *Eh, pourquoi non?*

LADY FANCIFUL What? And a man perhaps I never saw in my life.

MADEMOISELLE *Tant mieux: c'est donc quelque chose de nouveau.*

LADY FANCIFUL Why, how do I know what designs he may have. He may intend to ravish me for ought I know.

MADEMOISELLE Ravish? – Bagatelle. I would fain see one impudent rogue ravish Mademoiselle; *oui, je le voudrais*.

LADY FANCIFUL O but my reputation, Mademoiselle, my reputation, *ah ma chère réputation.*

MADEMOISELLE Matam; – *Quand on l'a une fois perdue* – *On n'en est plus embarasseé.*

LADY FANCIFUL Fe Mademoiselle, fe: reputation is a jewel.

MADEMOISELLE *Qui coûte bien chère* Matam.

LADY FANCIFUL Why sure you would not sacrifice your honour to your pleasure?

MADEMOISELLE *Je suis philosophe.*

LADY FANCIFUL Bless me how you talk. Why what if honour be a burden, Mademoiselle, must it not be borne?

MADEMOISELLE *Chaqu'un à sa façon – quand quelque chose m'incommode moi, je m'en défais, vite.*

LADY FANCIFUL Get you gone you little naughty French woman you, I vow and swear I must turn you out of doors if you talk thus.

MADEMOISELLE Turn me out of doors? – Turn yourself out of doors and go see what de gentelman have to say to you – *Tenez. Voilà* [*giving her her things hastily*] *votre écharpe, voilà votre coiffe, voilà votre masque, voilà tout.* [*calling within*] Hey, *Mercure, Coquin*; call one chair for Matam, and one oder for me, *va t'en vite.* [*turning to her lady and helping her on hastily with her things*] *Allons*, Matam; *dépêchez vous donc. Mon dieu quelles scrupules.*

LADY FANCIFUL Well, for once, Mademoiselle, I'll follow your advice, out of the intemperate desire I have to know who this ill-bred fellow is. But I have too much *delicatesse*, to make a practice on it.

MADEMOISELLE *Belle chose vraiment que la delicatesse, lorsqu'il s' agit de se divertir. – à ça – vous voilà équipée partons. – He bien? – qu'avez vous donc?*

LADY FANCIFUL *J' ai peur.*

MADEMOISELLE *Je n'en ai point moi.*

LADY FANCIFUL I dare not go.

MADEMOISELLE *Demeurez donc.*

LADY FANCIFUL *Je suis poltrone.*

MADEMOISELLE *Tant pis pour vous.*

LADY FANCIFUL Curiosity's a wicked devil.

MADEMOISELLE *C'est une charmante sainte.*

LADY FANCIFUL It ruined our first parents.

MADEMOISELLE *Elle a bien diverti leurs enfants.*

LADY FANCIFUL *L'honneur est contre.*

MADEMOISELLE *Le plaisir est pour.*

LADY FANCIFUL Must I then go?

MADEMOISELLE Must you go? – Must you eat, must you drink, must you sleep, must you live? De nature bid you do one, de nature bid you do toder. *Vous me ferez enrager.*

LADY FANCIFUL But when reason corrects nature, Mademoiselle.

MADEMOISELLE *Elle est donc bien insolente. C'est sa soeur aînée.*

LADY FANCIFUL Do you then prefer your nature to your reason, Mademoiselle.

MADEMOISELLE *Oui da.*

LADY FANCIFUL *Pourquoi?*

MADEMOISELLE Because my nature make me merry, my reason make me mad.

LADY FANCIFUL *Ah la méchante française.*

MADEMOISELLE *Ah la belle anglaise.*   [*Forcing her lady off*]

ACT TWO

SCENE ⟨I⟩

St James's Park

Enter Lady Fanciful and Mademoiselle.

LADY FANCIFUL Well, I vow, Mademoiselle, I'm strangely impatient to know who this confident fellow is.

Enter Heartfree.

Look there's Heartfree. But sure it can't be him, he's a professed woman-hater. Yet who knows what my wicked eyes may have done?

MADEMOISELLE *Il nous approche*, Matam.

LADY FANCIFUL Yes, 'tis he: now will he be most intolerably cavalier, though he should be in love with me.

HEARTFREE Madam, I'm your humble servant: I perceive you have more humility and good-nature than I thought you had.

LADY FANCIFUL What you attribute to humility and good nature, Sir, may perhaps be only due to curiosity. I had a mind to know who 'twas had ill manners enough to write that letter. [*throwing him his letter*]

HEARTFREE Well, and now, I hope, you are satisfied.

LADY FANCIFUL I am so, Sir; goodbye to ye.

HEARTFREE Nay, hold there; though you have done your business, I han't done mine: by your ladyship's leave, we must have one moment's prattle together. Have you a mind to be the prettiest woman about Town, or not? How she stares upon me! What! This passes for an impertinent question with you now, because you think you are so already.

LADY FANCIFUL Pray Sir, let me ask you a question in my turn: by what right do you pretend to examine me?

HEARTFREE By the same right that the strong govern the weak, because I have you in my power; for you cannot get so quickly to your coach, but I shall have time enough to make you hear everything I have to say to you.

LADY FANCIFUL These are strange liberties you take, Mr Heartfree.

HEARTFREE They are so, Madam, but there's no help for it; for know, that I have a design upon you.

LADY FANCIFUL Upon me, Sir!

HEARTFREE Yes; and one that will turn to your glory and my comfort, if you will but be a little wiser than you use to be.

LADY FANCIFUL Very well, Sir.

HEARTFREE Let me see, – your vanity, Madam, I take to be about some eight degrees higher than any woman's in the Town, let t'other be who she will; and my indifference is naturally about the same pitch. Now, could you find the way to turn this indifference into fire and flames, methinks your vanity ought to be satisfied; and this, perhaps, you might bring about upon pretty reasonable terms.

LADY FANCIFUL And pray at what rate would this indifference be bought off, if one should have so depraved an appetite to desire it?

HEARTFREE Why, Madam, to drive a Quaker's bargain,* and make but one word with you, if I do part with it, – you must lay me down – your affectation.

LADY FANCIFUL My affectation, Sir!

HEARTFREE Why, I ask you nothing but what you may very well spare.

LADY FANCIFUL You grow rude, Sir. Come, Mademoiselle, 'tis high time to be gone.

MADEMOISELLE *Allons, allons, allons.*

HEARTFREE [*stopping 'em*] Nay, you may as well stand still for hear me, you shall, walk which way you please.

LADY FANCIFUL What mean you, sir?

HEARTFREE I mean to tell you, that you are the most ungrateful woman upon earth.

LADY FANCIFUL Ungrateful! To who?

HEARTFREE To nature.

LADY FANCIFUL Why, what has nature done for me?

HEARTFREE What you have undone by art. It made you handsome, it gave you beauty to a miracle, a shape without a fault, wit enough to make 'em relish, and so turned you loose to your

* a Quaker's bargain: a take-it-or-leave-it attitude.

own discretion; which has made such work with you, that you are become the pity of our sex, and the jest of your own. There is not a feature in your face, but you have found the way to teach it some affected convulsion; your feet, your hands, your very fingers' ends, are directed never to move without some ridiculous air or other; and your language is a suitable trumpet, to draw people's eyes upon the raree-show.★

MADEMOISELLE [*aside*] *Est ce qu'on fait l'amour en Angleterre comme ça?*

LADY FANCIFUL [*aside*] Now could I cry for madness, but that I know he'd laugh at me for it.

HEARTFREE How do you hate me for telling you the truth; but that's because you don't believe it is so: for were you once convinced of that; you'd reform for your own sake. But 'tis as hard to persuade a woman to quit anything that makes her ridiculous, as 'tis to prevail with a poet to see a fault in his own play.

LADY FANCIFUL Every circumstance of nice breeding must needs appear ridiculous to one who has so natural an antipathy to good manners.

HEARTFREE But suppose I could find the means to convince you, that the whole world is of my opinion, and that those who flatter and commend you, do it to no other intent, but to make you persevere in your folly, that they may continue in their mirth.

LADY FANCIFUL Sir, though you and all that world you talk of, should be so impertinently officious, as to think to persuade me, I don't know how to behave myself, I should still have charity enough for my own understanding, to believe myself in the right, and all you in the wrong.

MADEMOISELLE *Le voilà mort.*   [*Exeunt Lady Fanciful and Mademoiselle*]

HEARTFREE [*gazing after her*] There her single clapper has published the sense of the whole sex. Well, this once I have endeavoured to wash the blackamoor white; but henceforward I'll sooner undertake to teach sincerity to a courtier, generosity to an usurer, honesty to a lawyer, nay, humility to a divine, than discretion to a woman I see has once set her heart upon playing the fool.

★ raree-show: a peepshow, carried in a box.

Enter Constant.

'Morrow, Constant.

CONSTANT Good-morrow, Jack; what are you doing here this morning?

HEARTFREE Doing! Guess if thou canst. Why, I have been endeavouring to persuade my Lady Fanciful, that she's the foolishest woman about Town.

CONSTANT A pretty endeavour truly.

HEARTFREE I have told her in as plain English as I could speak, both what the Town says of her, and what I think of her. In short, I have used her as an absolute king would do Magna Charta.

CONSTANT And how does she take it?

HEARTFREE As children do pills; bite 'em, but can't swallow 'em.

CONSTANT But, prithee, what has put it in your head, of all mankind, to turn reformer?

HEARTFREE Why, one thing was, the morning hung upon my hands, I did not know what to do with myself. And another was, that as little as I care for women, I could not see with patience one that heaven had taken such wondrous pains about, be so very industrious, to make herself the jack-pudding of the creation.

CONSTANT Well, now could I almost wish to see my cruel mistress make the selfsame use of what heaven has done for her, that so I might be cured of a disease that makes me so very uneasy; for love, love is the devil, Heartfree.

HEARTFREE And why do you let the devil govern you?

CONSTANT Because I have more flesh and blood than grace and self-denial. My dear, dear mistress, s'death! That so genteel a woman should be a saint, when religion's out of fashion!

HEARTFREE Nay, she's much in the wrong truly; but who knows how far time and good example may prevail?

CONSTANT Oh! They have played their parts in vain already: 'tis now two years since that damned fellow her husband invited me to his wedding; and there was the first time I saw that charming woman, whom I have loved ever since, more than e'er a martyr did his soul; but she's cold, my friend, still cold as the Northern Star.

HEARTFREE So are all women by nature, which makes 'em so willing to be warmed.

CONSTANT Oh, don't profane the sex; prithee think 'em all angels for her sake, for she's virtuous, even to a fault.

HEARTFREE A lover's head is a good accountable thing truly: he adores his mistress for being virtuous, and yet is very angry with her, because she won't be lewd.

CONSTANT Well, the only relief I expect in my misery, is to see thee some day or other as deeply engaged as myself, which will force me to be merry in the midst of all my misfortunes.

HEARTFREE That day will never come, be assured, Ned: not but that I can pass a night with a woman, and for the time, perhaps, make myself as good sport as you can do. Nay, I can court a woman too, call her nymph, angel, goddess, what you please; but here's the difference 'twixt you and I: I persuade a woman she's an angel; she persuades you she's one. Prithee let me tell you how I avoid falling in love; that which serves me for prevention, may chance to serve you for a cure.

CONSTANT Well, use the ladies moderately then, and I'll hear you.

HEARTFREE That using 'em moderately undoes us all; but I'll use 'em justly, and that you ought to be satisfied with. I always consider a woman, not as the tailor, the shoe-maker, the tire-woman, the sempstress, and (which is more than all that) the poet makes her; but I consider her as pure nature has contrived her, and that more strictly than I should have done our old grandmother Eve, had I seen her naked in the garden; for I consider her turned inside out. Her heart well examined, I find there pride, vanity, covetousness, indiscretion, but above all things, malice; plots eternally a-forging, to destroy one another's reputations, and as honestly to charge the levity of men's tongues with the scandal; hourly debates how to make poor gentlemen in love with 'em, with no other intent, but to use 'em like dogs when they have done; a constant desire of doing more mischief, and an everlasting war waged against truth and good nature.

CONSTANT Very well, Sir, an admirable composition truly.

HEARTFREE Then for her outside, I consider it merely as an outside; she has a thin tiffany covering over just such stuff as you and I are made on. As for her motion, her mien, her airs, and all those tricks, I know they affect you mightily. If you should see your mistress at a coronation, dragging her peacock's train, with all her state and insolence about her, 'twould strike you with all the awful thoughts that heaven itself could pretend to from you; whereas I turn the whole matter into a jest, and suppose her strutting in the self-same stately manner, with nothing on but her stays, and her under scanty quilted petticoat.

CONSTANT Hold thy profane tongue, for I'll hear no more.

HEARTFREE What, you'll love on then?

CONSTANT Yes, to eternity.

HEARTFREE Yet you have no hopes at all.

CONSTANT None.

HEARTFREE Nay, the resolution may be discreet enough; perhaps you have found out some new philosophy, that love's like virtue, its own reward: so you and your mistress will be as well content at a distance, as others that have less learning are in coming together.

CONSTANT [*embracing him*] No; but if she should prove kind at last, my dear Heartfree.

HEARTFREE Nay, prithee don't take me for your mistress, for lovers are very troublesome.

CONSTANT Well, who knows what time may do?

HEARTFREE And just now he was sure time could do nothing.

CONSTANT Yet not one kind glance in two years, is somewhat strange.

HEARTFREE Not strange at all; she don't like you, that's all the business.

CONSTANT Prithee don't distract me.

HEARTFREE Nay, you are a good handsome young fellow, she might use you better: come, will you go see her? Perhaps she may have changed her mind; there's some hopes as long as she's a woman.

CONSTANT Oh, 'tis in vain to visit her: sometimes to get a sight of her, I visit that beast her husband, but she certainly finds some pretence to quit the room as soon as I enter.

HEARTFREE It's much she don't tell him you have made love to her too, for that's another good-natured thing usual amongst women, in which they have several ends. Sometimes 'tis to recommend their virtue, that they may be lewd with the greater security. Sometimes 'tis to make their husbands fight in hopes they may be killed, when their affairs require it should be so. But most commonly 'tis to engage two men in a quarrel, that they may have the credit of being fought for; and if the lover's killed in the business, they cry, 'Poor fellow! He had ill luck'. – And so they go to cards.

CONSTANT Thy injuries to women are not to be forgiven. Look to't if ever thou dost fall into their hands –

HEARTFREE They can't use me worse than they do you, that speak well of 'em. O ho! Here comes the knight.

Enter Sir John Brute.

HEARTFREE Your humble servant, Sir John.

SIR JOHN Servant, Sir.

HEARTFREE How does all your family?

SIR JOHN Pox o' my family.

CONSTANT How does your lady? I han't seen her abroad a good while.

SIR JOHN Do! I don't know how she does, not I; she was well enough yesterday; I ha'nt been at home tonight.

CONSTANT What! Were you out of Town!

SIR JOHN Out of Town! No, I was drinking.

CONSTANT You are a true Englishman; don't know your own happiness? If I were married to such a woman, I would not be from her a night for all the wine in France.

SIR JOHN Not from her? – Oons, – what a time should a man have of that!

HEARTFREE Why, there's no division, I hope?

SIR JOHN No; but there's a conjunction,* and that's worse; a pox o' the parson. – Why the plague don't you two marry? I fancy I look like the devil to you.

HEARTFREE Why, you don't think you have horns, do you?

SIR JOHN No; I believe my wife's religion will keep her honest.

HEARTFREE And what will make her keep her religion?

SIR JOHN Persecution; and therefore she shall have it.

HEARTFREE Have a care knight, women are tender things.

SIR JOHN And yet, methinks, 'tis a hard matter to break their hearts.

* conjunction: a conjunction of planets was considered malign.

CONSTANT Fie, fie; you have one of the best wives in the world, and yet you seem the most uneasy husband.

SIR JOHN Best wives! – The woman's well enough, she has no vice that I know of, but she's a wife, and – damn a wife; if I were married to a hogshead of claret, matrimony would make me hate it.

HEARTFREE Why did you marry then? You were old enough to know your own mind.

SIR JOHN Why did I marry! I married because I had a mind to lie with her, and she would not let me.

HEARTFREE Why did not you ravish her?

SIR JOHN Yes, and so have hedged myself into forty quarrels with her relations, besides buying my pardon: but more than all that, you must know, I was afraid of being damned in those days, for I kept sneaking cowardly company, fellows that went to church, said grace to their meat, and had not the least tincture of quality about 'em.

HEARTFREE But I think you are got into a better gang now.

SIR JOHN Zoons, Sir, my Lord Rake and I are hand and glove, I believe we may get our bones broke together tonight; have you a mind to share a frolic?

CONSTANT Not I truly, my talent lies to softer exercises.

SIR JOHN What? A down bed and a strumpet? A pox of venery, I say. Will you come and drink with me this afternoon?

CONSTANT I can't drink today, but we'll come and sit an hour with you if you will.

SIR JOHN Phugh, pox, sit an hour! Why can't you drink?

CONSTANT Because I'm to see my mistress.

SIR JOHN Who's that?

CONSTANT Why, do you use to tell?

SIR JOHN Yes.

CONSTANT So won't I.

SIR JOHN Why?

CONSTANT Because 'tis a secret.

SIR JOHN Would my wife knew it, 'twould be no secret long.

CONSTANT Why, do you think she can't keep a secret?

SIR JOHN No more than she can keep Lent.

HEARTFREE Prithee tell it her to try, Constant.

SIR JOHN No, prithee don't, that I mayn't be plagued with it.

CONSTANT I'll hold you a guinea you don't make her tell it you.

SIR JOHN I'll hold you a guinea I do.

CONSTANT Which way?

SIR JOHN Why I'll beg her not to tell it me.

HEARTFREE Nay, if anything does it, that will.

CONSTANT But do you think, Sir?

SIR JOHN Oons, Sir, I think a woman and a secret, are the two impertinentest themes in the universe. Therefore pray let's hear no more, of my wife nor your mistress. Damn 'em both with all my heart, and everything else that daggles a petticoat, except four generous whores, with Betty Sands at the head of 'em, who were drunk with my Lord Rake and I, ten times in a fortnight.

[Exit Sir John]

CONSTANT Here's a dainty fellow for you. And the veriest coward too. But his usage of his wife makes me ready to stab the villain.

HEARTFREE Lovers are short-sighted: all their senses run into that of feeling. This proceeding of his is the only thing on earth can make your fortune. If anything can prevail with her to accept of a gallant 'tis his ill usage of her; for women will do more for revenge than they'll do for the gospel. Prithee take heart, I have great hopes for you, and since I can't bring you quite off of her, I'll endeavour to bring you quite on; for a whining lover is the damnedest companion upon earth.

CONSTANT My dear friend, flatter me a little more with these hopes; for whilst they prevail I have heaven within me, and could melt with joy.

HEARTFREE Pray no melting yet: let things go farther first. This afternoon perhaps we shall make some advance. In the meanwhile, let's go dine at Locket's,★ and let hope get you a stomach.   *[Exeunt]*

★ Locket's: a fashionable tavern.

SCENE ⟨II⟩

Lady Fanciful's house

Enter Lady Fanciful and Mademoiselle.

LADY FANCIFUL Did you ever see anything so importune, Mademoiselle?

MADEMOISELLE Inteed Matam, to say de trute, he want leetel good breeding.

LADY FANCIFUL Good breeding? He wants to be caned, Mademoiselle: an insolent fellow. And yet let me expose my weakness, 'tis the only man on earth I could resolve to dispense my favours on, were he but a fine gentleman. Well, did men but know how deep an impression a fine gentleman makes on a lady's heart, they would reduce all their studies to that of good breeding alone.

Enter Cornet.

CORNET Madam here's Mr Treble. He has brought home the verses your ladyship made and gave him to set.

LADY FANCIFUL O let him come in by all means. Now, Mademoiselle, am I going to be unspeakably happy.

Enter Treble.

So Mr Treble, you have set my little dialogue?

TREBLE Yes, Madam, and I hope your ladyship will be pleased with it.

LADY FANCIFUL Oh, no doubt on't; for really Mr Treble, you set all things to a wonder: but your music is in particular heavenly, when you have my words to clothe in't.

TREBLE Your words themselves, Madam, have so much music in 'em they inspire me.

LADY FANCIFUL Nay, now you make me blush, Mr Treble; but pray let's hear what you have done.

TREBLE You shall, Madam.

A Song to be sung between a man and a woman.

MAN   Ah lovely nymph, the world's on fire:
                  Veil, veil those cruel eyes.

WOMAN   The world may then in flames expire,

And boast that so it dies.

MAN   But when all mortals are destroyed,
                Who then shall sing your praise?

WOMAN   Those who are fit to be employed:
                The gods shall altars raise.

TREBLE How does your ladyship like it, Madam?

LADY FANCIFUL Rapture, rapture, Mr Treble, I'm all rapture. O
wit and art, what power you have when joined. I must needs tell
you the birth of this little dialogue, Mr Treble. Its father was a
dream, and its mother was the moon. I dreamed, that by an
unanimous vote, I was chosen queen of that pale world. And that
the first time I appeared upon my throne, – all my subjects fell
in love with me. Just then I waked: and seeing pen, ink and paper
lie idle upon the table, I slid into my morning gown, and writ this
impromptu.

TREBLE So I guess the dialogue, Madam, is supposed to be between Your Majesty and your first Minister of State.

LADY FANCIFUL Just: he as minister advises me to trouble my
head about the welfare of my subjects; which I as sovereign, find
a very impertinent proposal. But is the Town so dull, Mr Treble,
it affords us never another new song?

TREBLE Madam, I have one in my pocket, came out but yesterday,
if your ladyship pleases to let Mrs Pipe sing it.

LADY FANCIFUL By all means. Here Pipe. Make what music you
can of this song, here.

SONG

⟨I⟩

Not an angel dwells above
Half so fair as her I love:
    Heaven knows how she'll receive me:
If she smiles, I'm blessed indeed
If she frowns, I'm quickly freed;
    Heaven knows, she ne'er can grieve me.

II

None can love her more than I,
Yet she ne'er shall make me die.

        If my flame can never warm her;
        Lasting beauty, I'll adore,
        I shall never love her more,
          Cruelty will so deform her.

LADY FANCIFUL Very well: this is Heartfree's poetry without question.

TREBLE Won't your ladyship please to sing yourself this morning?

LADY FANCIFUL O Lord, Mr Treble, my cold is still so barbarous, to refuse me that pleasure; he he hem.

TREBLE I'm very sorry for it, Madam: methinks all mankind should turn physicians for the cure on't.

LADY FANCIFUL Why truly to give mankind their due; there's few that know me, but have offered their remedy.

TREBLE They have reason, Madam, for I know nobody sings so near a cherubim as your ladyship.

LADY FANCIFUL What I do I owe chiefly to your skill and care, Mr Treble. People do flatter me indeed, that I have a voice and a *je ne sais quoi* in the conduct of it, that will make music of anything. And truly I begin to believe so, since what happened t'other night: would you think it, Mr Treble; walking pretty late in the Park, (for I often walk late in the Park, Mr Treble;) a whim took me to sing Chevy-Chase, and would you believe it? Next morning I had three copies of verses, and six *billet-doux* at my levee upon it.

TREBLE And without all dispute you deserved as many more, Madam, are there any further commands for your ladyship's humble servant?

LADY FANCIFUL Nothing more at this time, Mr Treble. But I shall expect you here every morning for this month, to sing my little matter there to me. I'll reward you for your pains.

TREBLE O Lord, Madam –

LADY FANCIFUL Good-morrow, sweet Mr Treble.

TREBLE Your ladyship's most obedient servant.   [*Exit Treble*]

Enter Servant.

SERVANT Will your ladyship please to dine yet?

LADY FANCIFUL Yes: let 'em serve. [*Exit servant*] Sure this Heart-free has bewitched me, Mademoiselle. You can't imagine how oddly he mixed himself in my thoughts during my rapture e'en now. I vow 'tis a thousand pities he is not more polished. Don't you think so?

MADEMOISELLE Matam, I tink it so great pity, dat if I was in your ladyship place, I take him home in my house, I lock him up in my closet, and I never let him go till I teach him everyting dat fine laty expect from fine gentelman.

LADY FANCIFUL Why truly I believe, I should soon subdue his brutality; for without doubt, he has a strange penchant to grow fond of me, in spite of his aversion to the sex, else he would ne'er have taken so much pains about me. Lord how proud would some poor creatures be of such a conquest? But I alas, I don't know how to receive as a favour, what I take to be so infinitely my due. But what shall I do to new-mould him, Mademoiselle? For till then he's my utter aversion.

MADEMOISELLE Matam, you must laugh at him in all de place dat you meet him, and turn into de ridicule all he say and all he do.

LADY FANCIFUL Why truly satire has been ever of wondrous use, to reform ill manners. Besides 'tis my particular talent to ridicule folks. I can be severe; strangely severe, when I will, Mademoiselle. – Give me the pen and ink: – I find myself whimsical – I'll write to him. [*sitting down to write*] – or I'll let it alone, and be severe upon him that way. [*rising up again*] – Yet active severity is better than passive. [*sitting down*] – 'Tis as good let alone too, for every lash I give him, perhaps he'll take for a favour. [*rising*] – Yet 'tis a thousand pities so much satire should be lost. [*sitting*] – But if it should have a wrong effect upon him 'twould distract me. [*rising*] – Well I must write though after all [*sitting*] – Or I'll let it alone which is the same thing. [*rising*]

MADEMOISELLE *La voilà determinée.* [*Exeunt*]

ACT THREE

SCENE ⟨I⟩

Opens. Sir John, Lady Brute and Bellinda rising from the table

SIR JOHN [*to a Servant*] Here; take away the things: I expect company. But first bring me a pipe: I'll smoke.

LADY BRUTE Lord, Sir John, I wonder you won't leave that nasty custom.

SIR JOHN Prithee don't be impertinent.

BELLINDA [*to Lady Brute*] I wonder who those are he expects this afternoon.

LADY BRUTE I'd give the world to know: perhaps 'tis Constant; he comes here sometimes; if it does prove him, I'm resolved I'll share the visit.

BELLINDA We'll send for our work and sit here.

LADY BRUTE He'll choke us with his tobacco.

BELLINDA Nothing will choke us, when we are doing what we have a mind to. Lovewell.*

Enter Lovewell.

LOVEWELL Madam.

LADY BRUTE Here; bring my cousin's work and mine hither.

[*Exit Lovewell and re-enters with their work*]

SIR JOHN Why; pox, can't you work somewhere else.

LADY BRUTE We shall be careful not to disturb you, Sir.

BELLINDA Your pipe would make you too thoughtful, uncle, if you were left alone; our prittle-prattle will cure your spleen.

SIR JOHN Will it so, Mrs Pert? Now I believe it will so increase it I shall take my own house for a paper-mill. [*sitting and smoking*]

LADY BRUTE [*to Bellinda aside*] Don't let's mind him; let him say what he will.

SIR JOHN A woman's tongue a cure for the spleen – Oons –

* Curt A. Zimansky, in his edition of 1969, suggests that as Q1 has a long space before 'Lovewell' it is possible that a speech prefix was dropped and that it was in fact Lady Brute who called her servant.

[*aside*] If a man had got the headache, they'd be for applying the same remedy.

LADY BRUTE You have done a great deal Bellinda since yesterday.

BELLINDA Yes, I have worked very hard; how do you like it?

LADY BRUTE O 'tis the prettiest fringe in the world. Well cousin you have the happiest fancy. Prithee advise me about altering my crimson petticoat.

SIR JOHN A pox o' your petticoat; here's such a prating a man can't digest his own thoughts for you.

LADY BRUTE [*aside*] Don't answer him. Well, what do you advise me.

BELLINDA Why really I would not alter it at all. Methinks 'tis very pretty as it is.

LADY BRUTE Aye that's true: but you know one grows weary of the prettiest things in the world, when one has had 'em long.

SIR JOHN Yes, I have taught her that.

BELLINDA Shall we provoke him a little?

LADY BRUTE With all my heart. Bellinda, don't you long to be married?

BELLINDA Why there are some things in't I could like well enough.

LADY BRUTE What do you think you should dislike?

BELLINDA My husband a hundred to one else.

LADY BRUTE O ye wicked wretch: sure you don't speak as you think.

BELLINDA Yes I do: especially if he smoked tobacco.

[*He ⟨Sir John⟩ looks earnestly at 'em*]

LADY BRUTE Why that many times takes off worse smells.

BELLINDA Then he must smell very ill indeed.

LADY BRUTE So some men will, to keep their wives from coming near 'em.

BELLINDA Then those wives should cuckold 'em at a distance.

He ⟨Sir John⟩ rises in a fury, throws his pipe at 'em and drives 'em out. As they run off, Constant and Heartfree enter. Lady Brute runs against Constant.

SIR JOHN Oons get you gone upstairs you confederating strumpets you, or I'll cuckold you with a vengeance.

LADY BRUTE O Lord he'll beat us, he'll beat us. Dear, dear Mr Constant save us. [*Exeunt*]

SIR JOHN I'll cuckold you with a pox.

CONSTANT Heavens, Sir John, what's the matter?

SIR JOHN Sure if woman had been ready created, the devil, instead of being kicked down into hell, had been married.

HEARTFREE Why what new plague have you found now?

SIR JOHN Why these two gentlewomen did but hear me say, I expected you here this afternoon; upon which, they presently resolved to take up the room, o'purpose to plague me and my friends.

CONSTANT Was that all? Why we should have been glad of their company.

SIR JOHN Then I should have been weary of yours. For I can't relish both together. They found fault with my smoking tobacco too; and said men stunk. But I have a good mind – to say something.

CONSTANT No, nothing against the ladies pray.

SIR JOHN Split the ladies. Come, will you sit down? Give us some wine, fellow: you won't smoke?

CONSTANT No nor drink neither at this time, I must ask your pardon.

SIR JOHN What, this mistress of yours runs in your head; I'll warrant it's some such squeamish minx as my wife, that's grown so dainty of late, she finds fault even with a dirty shirt.

HEARTFREE That a woman may do, and not be very dainty neither.

SIR JOHN Pox o' the women, let's drink. Come, you shall take one glass, though I send for a box of lozenges to sweeten your mouth after it.

CONSTANT Nay if one glass will satisfy you I'll drink it without putting you to that expense.

SIR JOHN Why that's honest. Fill some wine, sirrah: so, here's to you gentlemen – A wife's the devil. To your being both married. [*they drink*]

HEARTFREE O your most humble servant, Sir.

SIR JOHN Well? How do you like my wine?

CONSTANT 'Tis very good indeed.

HEARTFREE 'Tis admirable.

SIR JOHN Then give us t'other glass.

CONSTANT No pray excuse us now. We'll come another time, and then we won't spare it.

SIR JOHN This one glass and no more. Come: it shall be your mistresses' health: and that's a great compliment from me, I assure you.

CONSTANT And 'tis a very obliging one to me: so give us the glasses.

SIR JOHN So: let her live.

HEARTFREE And be kind. [*Sir John coughs in the glass*]

CONSTANT What's the matter? Does't go the wrong way?

SIR JOHN If I had love enough to be jealous, I should take this for an ill omen. For I never drank my wife's health in my life, but I puked in the glass.

CONSTANT O she's too virtuous to make a reasonable man jealous.

SIR JOHN Pox of her virtue. If I could but catch her adulterating I might be divorced from her by law.

HEARTFREE And so pay her a yearly pension, to be a distinguished cuckold.

Enter Servant.

SERVANT Sir, there's my Lord Rake, Colonel Bully, and some other gentlemen at the Blue Posts,⋆ desire your company.

SIR JOHN Cods so, we are to consult about playing the devil tonight.

HEARTFREE Well we won't hinder business.

SIR JOHN Methinks I don't know how to leave you though. But for once I must make bold – Or look you: maybe the conference mayn't last long; so if you'll wait here half an hour, or an hour; if I don't come then, – why then – I won't come at all.

HEARTFREE [*aside to Constant*] A good modest proposition truly:

CONSTANT But let's accept on't however. Who knows what may happen.

HEARTFREE Well Sir, to show you how fond we are of your company we'll expect your return as long as we can.

⋆ the Blue Posts: an inn in the Haymarket.

SIR JOHN Nay, maybe I mayn't stay at all: but business you know must be done. So your servant – Or hark you: if you have a mind to take a frisk with us, I have an interest with my lord, I can easily introduce you.

CONSTANT We are much beholding to you, but for my part I'm engaged another way.

SIR JOHN What? To your mistress I'll warrant. Prithee leave your nasty punk to entertain herself with her own lewd thoughts, and make one with us tonight.

CONSTANT Sir, 'tis business that is to employ me.

HEARTFREE And me; and business must be done you know.

SIR JOHN Aye; women's business, though the world were consumed for't.   *[Exit Sir John]*

CONSTANT Farewell beast: and now my dear friend, would my mistress be but as complaisant as some men's wives, who think it a piece of good breeding to receive the visits of their husband's friends in his absence.

HEARTFREE Why for your sake I could forgive her, though she should be so complaisant to receive something else in his absence. But what way shall we invent to see her.

CONSTANT O ne'er hope it: invention will prove as vain as wishes.

Enter Lady Brute and Bellinda.

HEARTFREE What do you think now, friend?

CONSTANT I think I shall swoon.

HEARTFREE I'll speak first then, whilst you fetch breath.

LADY BRUTE We think ourselves obliged gentlemen, to come and return you thanks for your knight-errantry. We were just upon being devoured by the fiery dragon.

BELLINDA Did not his fumes almost knock you down, gentlemen?

HEARTFREE Truly ladies, we did undergo some hardships, and should have done more, if some greater heroes than ourselves hard by had not diverted him.

CONSTANT Though I'm glad of the service, you are pleased to say we have done you; yet I'm sorry we could do it no other way, than by making ourselves privy, to what you would perhaps have kept a secret.

LADY BRUTE For Sir John's part, I suppose he designed it no

secret since he made so much noise. And for myself, truly I am not much concerned, since 'tis fallen only into this gentleman's hands and yours; who I have many reasons to believe, will neither interpret nor report anything to my disadvantage.

CONSTANT Your good opinion, Madam, was what I feared, I never could have merited.

LADY BRUTE Your fears were vain then, Sir, for I am just to everybody.

HEARTFREE Prithee, Constant, what is't you do to get the ladies' good opinions; for I'm a novice at it?

BELLINDA Sir, will you give me leave to instruct you?

HEARTFREE Yes, that I will with all my soul, Madam.

BELLINDA Why then you must never be slovenly, never be out of humour, fare well and cry roast-meat;* smoke tobacco, nor drink but when you are a-dry.

HEARTFREE That's hard.

CONSTANT Nay, if you take his bottle from him, you break his heart, Madam.

BELLINDA Why, is it possible the gentleman can love drinking?

HEARTFREE Only by way of antidote.

BELLINDA Against what, pray?

HEARTFREE Against love, Madam?

LADY BRUTE Are you afraid of being in love, Sir?

HEARTFREE I should, if there were any danger of it.

LADY BRUTE Pray why so?

HEARTFREE Because I always had an aversion to being used like a dog.

BELLINDA Why truly, men in love are seldom used better.

LADY BRUTE But was you never in love, Sir?

HEARTFREE No, I thank heaven, Madam.

BELLINDA Pray where got you your learning then?

HEARTFREE From other people's expense.

BELLINDA That's being a sponger, Sir, which is scarce honest; if you'd buy some experience with your own money, as 'twould be fairlier got, so 'twould stick longer by you.

Enter Footman.

* cry roast-meat: to boast about good fortune.

FOOTMAN Madam, here's my Lady Fanciful, to wait upon your ladyship.

LADY BRUTE Shield me, kind heaven, what an inundation of impertinence is here coming upon us!

Enter Lady Fanciful, who runs first to Lady Brute, then to Bellinda, kissing 'em.

LADY FANCIFUL My dear Lady Brute, and sweet Bellinda! Methinks 'tis an age since I saw you.

LADY BRUTE Yet 'tis but three days; sure you have passed your time very ill, it seems so long to you.

LADY FANCIFUL Why really, to confess the truth to you, I am so everlastingly fatigued with the addresses of unfortunate gentlemen, that were it not for the extravagancy of the example, I should e'en tear out these wicked eyes with my own fingers, to make both myself and mankind easy. What think you on't, Mr Heartfree, for I take you to be my faithful adviser?

HEARTFREE Why truly, Madam, – I think – every project that is for the good of mankind, ought to be encouraged.

LADY FANCIFUL Then I have your consent, Sir.

HEARTFREE To do whatever you please, Madam.

LADY FANCIFUL You had a much more limited complaisance this morning, Sir. Would you believe it, ladies? The gentleman has been so exceeding generous, to tell me of above fifty faults, in less time than it was well possible for me to commit two of 'em.

CONSTANT Why truly, Madam, my friend there is apt to be something familiar with the ladies.

LADY FANCIFUL He is indeed, Sir; but he's wondrous charitable with it; he has had the goodness to design a reformation, even down to my fingers' ends. 'Twas thus, I think, Sir, you would have had 'em stand. – [*opening her fingers in an awkward manner*] – My eyes too he did not like: how was't you would have directed 'em? Thus, I think. [*staring at him*] Then there was something amiss in my gait too, I don't know well how 'twas; but as I take it, he would have had me walk like him. Pray, Sir, do me the favour to take a turn or two about the room, that the company may see you. – He's sullen, ladies, and won't: but, to make short, and give you as true an idea as I can of the matter, I think 'twas much about this figure in general, he would have moulded me to: [*she walks awkwardly about, staring and looking ungainly, then changes on a sudden to the extremity of her usual affectation*] but I was an obstinate woman, and could not resolve to make myself mistress of his heart, by growing as awkward as his fancy.

HEARTFREE Just thus women do, when they think we are in love with 'em, or when they are so with us.

LADY FANCIFUL 'Twould however be less vanity for me to conclude the former, than you the latter, Sir.

HEARTFREE Madam, all I shall presume to conclude, is, that if I were in love, you'd find the means to make me soon weary on't.

LADY FANCIFUL Not by over-fondness, upon my word, Sir. But pray let's stop here, for you are so much governed by instinct, I know you'll grow brutish at last.

BELLINDA [*aside*] Now am I sure she's fond of him: I'll try to make her jealous. Well, for my part, I should be glad to find somebody would be so free with me, that I might know my faults, and mend 'em.

LADY FANCIFUL Then pray let me recommend this gentleman to you, I have known him some time, and will be surety for him, that upon a very limited encouragement on your side, you shall find an extended impudence on his.

HEARTFREE I thank you Madam, for your recommendation; but hating idleness, I'm unwilling to enter into a place where I believe there would be nothing to do. I was fond of serving your ladyship, because I knew you'd find me constant employment.

LADY FANCIFUL I told you he'd be rude, Bellinda.

BELLINDA Oh, a little bluntness is a sign of honesty, which makes me always ready to pardon it. So, Sir, if you have no other exceptions to my service, but the fear of being idle in't, you may venture to list yourself: I shall find you work I warrant you.

HEARTFREE [*offering to kiss her hand*] Upon those terms I engage, Madam, and this (with your leave) I take for earnest.

BELLINDA Hold there, Sir, I'm none of your earnest givers. But if I'm well served, I give good wages and pay punctually. [*Heartfree and Bellinda seem to continue talking familiarly*]

LADY FANCIFUL [*aside*] I don't like this jesting between 'em – methinks the fool begins to look as if he were in earnest –

but then he must be a fool indeed. Lard what a difference there is between me and her. [*looking at Bellinda scornfully*] How I should despise such a thing if I were a man. – What a nose she has – What a chin – What a neck. – Then her eyes – And the worst kissing lips in the universe – No no, he can never like her that's positive – Yet I can't suffer 'em together any longer. Mr Heartfree, do you know that you and I must have no quarrel for all this. I can't forbear being a little severe now and then: but women you know may be allowed anything.

HEARTFREE Up to a certain age, Madam.

LADY FANCIFUL Which I am not yet passed I hope.

HEARTFREE [*aside*] Nor never will, I dare swear.

LADY FANCIFUL [*to Lady Brute*] Come Madam; will your ladyship be witness to our reconciliation?

LADY BRUTE You agree then at last.

HEARTFREE [*slightingly*] We forgive.

LADY FANCIFUL [*aside*] That was a cold ill-natured reply.

LADY BRUTE Then there's no challenges sent between you?

HEARTFREE Not from me I promise. [*aside to Constant*] But that's more than I'll do for her, for I know she can as well be damned as forbear writing to me.

CONSTANT That I believe. But I think we had best be going lest she should suspect something, and be malicious.

HEARTFREE With all my heart.

CONSTANT Ladies we are your humble servants. I see Sir John is quite engaged, 'twould be in vain to expect him. Come Heartfree.

[*Exit*]

HEARTFREE Ladies your servant. [*to Bellinda*] I hope Madam you won't forget our bargain; I'm to say what I please to you.

[*Exit Heartfree*]

BELLINDA Liberty of speech entire, Sir.

LADY FANCIFUL [*aside*] Very pretty truly – But how the blockhead went out: languishing at her; and not a look toward me. – Well; churchmen may talk, but miracles are not ceased. For 'tis more than natural, such a rude fellow as he, and such a little impertinent as she, should be capable of making a woman of my sphere uneasy. But I can bear her sight no longer – methinks she's grown ten times uglier than Cornet. I must go home, and study revenge. [*to Lady Brute*] Madam your humble servant, I must take my leave.

LADY BRUTE What going already Madam?

LADY FANCIFUL I must beg you'll excuse me this once. For really I have eighteen visits to return this afternoon so you see I'm importuned by the women as well as the men.

BELLINDA [*aside*] And she's quits with 'em both.

LADY FANCIFUL [*going*] Nay you shan't go one step out of the room.

LADY BRUTE Indeed I'll wait upon you down.

LADY FANCIFUL No, sweet Lady Brute; you know I swoon at ceremony.

LADY BRUTE Pray give me leave.

LADY FANCIFUL You know I won't.

LADY BRUTE Indeed I must.

LADY FANCIFUL Indeed you shan't.

LADY BRUTE Indeed I will.

LADY FANCIFUL Indeed you shan't.

LADY BRUTE Indeed I will.

LADY FANCIFUL Indeed you shan't. Indeed indeed indeed you shan't.

[*Exit Lady Fanciful running. They follow*]

Re-enter Lady Brute, sola.

⟨LADY BRUTE⟩ This impertinent woman, has put me out of humour for a fortnight. – What an agreeable moment has her foolish visit interrupted – Lord how like a torrent love flows into my heart when once the sluice of desire is opened! Good gods what a pleasure there is in doing what we should not do!

Re-enter Constant.

Ha! Here again?

CONSTANT Though the renewing my visit may seem a little irregular, I hope I shall obtain your pardon for it, Madam, when you know I only left the room, lest the lady who was here should have been as malicious in her remarks, as she's foolish in her conduct.

LADY BRUTE He who has discretion enough to be tender of a

woman's reputation, carries a virtue about him may atone for a great many faults.

CONSTANT If it has a title to atone for any, its pretensions must needs be strongest, where the crime is love. I therefore hope I shall be forgiven the attempt I have made upon your heart, since my enterprise has been a secret to all the world but yourself.

LADY BRUTE Secrecy indeed in sins of this kind, is an argument of weight to lessen the punishment; but nothing's a plea, for a pardon entire, without a sincere repentance.

CONSTANT If sincerity in repentance, consist in sorrow for offending: no cloister ever enclosed, so true a penitent as I should be. But I hope it cannot be reckoned an offence to love, where 'tis a duty to adore.

LADY BRUTE 'Tis an offence, a great one, where it would rob a woman of all she ought to be adored for; her virtue.

CONSTANT Virtue? – Virtue alas is no more like the thing that's called so, than 'tis like vice itself. Virtue consists in goodness, honour, gratitude, sincerity and pity; and not in peevish, snarling straightlaced chastity. True virtue wheresoe'er it moves, still carries an intrinsic worth about it, and is in every place, and in each sex of equal value. So is not continence you see: that phantom of honour, which men in every age have so contemned, they have thrown it amongst the women to scrabble for.

LADY BRUTE If it be a thing of so very little value; why do you so earnestly recommend it to your wives and daughters?

CONSTANT We recommend it to our wives, Madam, because we would keep 'em to ourselves. And to our daughters, because we would dispose of 'em to others.

LADY BRUTE 'Tis then of some importance it seems, since you can't dispose of 'em without it.

CONSTANT That importance, Madam, lies in the humour of the country, not in the nature of the thing.

LADY BRUTE How do you prove that, Sir?

CONSTANT From the wisdom of a neighbouring nation in a contrary practice. In monarchies things go by whimsy, but commonwealths weigh all things in the scale of reason.

LADY BRUTE I hope we are not so very light a people to bring up fashions without some ground.

CONSTANT Pray what does your ladyship think of a powdered coat for deep mourning?

LADY BRUTE I think, Sir, your sophistry has all the effect that you can reasonably expect it should have: it puzzles, but don't convince.

CONSTANT I'm sorry for it.

LADY BRUTE I'm sorry to hear you say so.

CONSTANT Pray why?

LADY BRUTE Because if you expected more from it, you have a worse opinion of my understanding than I desire you should have.

CONSTANT [*aside*] I comprehend her: she would have me set a value upon her chastity, that I may think myself the more obliged to her, when she makes me a present of it. [*to her*] I beg you will believe I did but rally, Madam, I know you judge too well of right and wrong, to be deceived by arguments like those. I hope you'll have so favourable an opinion of my understanding too, to believe the thing called virtue has worth enough with me, to pass for an eternal obligation where'er 'tis sacrificed.

LADY BRUTE It is I think so great a one, as nothing can repay.

CONSTANT Yes; the making the man you love your everlasting debtor.

LADY BRUTE When debtors once have borrowed all we have to lend, they are very apt to grow very shy of their creditors' company.

CONSTANT That, Madam, is only when they are forced to borrow of usurers, and not of a generous friend. Let us choose our creditors, and we are seldom so ungrateful to shun 'em.

LADY BRUTE What think you of Sir John, Sir? I was his free choice.

CONSTANT I think he's married, Madam.

LADY BRUTE Does marriage then exclude men from your rule of constancy.

CONSTANT It does. Constancy's a brave, free, haughty, generous agent, that cannot buckle to the chains of wedlock. There's a poor sordid slavery in marriage, that turns the flowing tide of honour, and sinks us to the lowest ebb of infamy. 'Tis a corrupted soil; ill nature, avarice, sloth, cowardice and dirt, are all its product.

LADY BRUTE Have you no exceptions to this general rule, as well as to t'other?

CONSTANT Yes: I would (after all) be an exception to it myself if you were free, in power and will to make me so.

LADY BRUTE Compliments are well placed, where 'tis impossible to lay hold on 'em.

CONSTANT I would to heaven 'twere possible for you to lay hold on mine, that you might see it is no compliment at all. But since you are already disposed of beyond redemption, to one who does not know the value of the jewel you have put into his hands: I hope you would not think him greatly wronged, though it should sometimes be looked on by a friend, who knows how to esteem it as he ought.

LADY BRUTE If looking on't alone would serve his turn, the wrong perhaps might not be very great.

CONSTANT Why, what if he should wear it now and then a day, so he gave good security to bring it home again at night?

LADY BRUTE Small security I fancy might serve for that. One might venture to take his word.

CONSTANT Then where's the injury to the owner?

LADY BRUTE 'Tis an injury to him, if he think it one. For if happiness be seated in the mind, unhappiness must be so too.

CONSTANT Here I close with you, Madam, and draw my conclusive argument from your own position: if the injury lie in the fancy, there needs nothing but secrecy to prevent the wrong.

LADY BRUTE [*going*] A surer way to prevent it, is to hear no more arguments in its behalf.

CONSTANT [*following her*] But, Madam –

LADY BRUTE But, Sir, 'tis my turn to be discreet now, and not suffer too long a visit.

CONSTANT [*catching her hand*] By heaven you shall not stir, till you give me hopes that I shall see you again, at some more convenient time and place.

LADY BRUTE I give you just hopes enough – [*breaking from him*] to get loose from you: and that's all I can afford you at this time.

[*Exit running*]

CONSTANT [*solus*] Now by all that's great and good, she is a charming woman. In what ecstasy of joy she has left me. For she gave me hope; did she not say she gave me hope? – Hope? Aye; what hope? – Enough to make me let her go – Why that's enough in conscience. Or no matter how 'twas spoke; hope was the word: it came from her, and it was said to me.

Enter Heartfree.

Ha, Heartfree: thou hast done me noble service in prattling to the young gentlewoman without there; come to my arms, thou venerable bawd, and let me squeeze thee [*embracing him eagerly*] as a new pair of stays does a fat country girl, when she's carried to Court to stand for a maid of honour.

HEARTFREE Why what the devil's all this rapture for?

CONSTANT Rapture? There's ground for rapture, man, there's hopes, my Heartfree, hopes, my friend.

HEARTFREE Hopes? Of what?

CONSTANT Why hopes that my lady and I together, (for 'tis more than one body's work) should make Sir John a cuckold.

HEARTFREE Prithee what did she say to thee?

CONSTANT Say? What did she not say? She said that – says she – she said – Zoons I don't know what she said: but she looked as if she said everything I'd have her, and so if thou'lt go to the tavern, I'll treat thee with anything that gold can buy; I'll give all my silver amongst the drawers, make a bonfire before the door, say the plenipos, have signed the peace,* and the Bank of England's† grown honest. [*Exeunt*]

SCENE ⟨II⟩

Opens. ⟨The Blue Posts.⟩ Lord Rake,
Sir John, etc. at a table drinking

ALL Huzza.

LORD RAKE Come boys. Charge again. – So – Confusion to all order. Here's liberty of conscience.

ALL Huzza.

LORD RAKE I'll sing you a song I made this morning to this purpose.

---

* the peace: the Treaty of Ryswick, signed in September 1697.
† the Bank of England: founded in 1694, and not yet fully accepted.

SIR JOHN 'Tis wicked I hope.

COL. BULLY Don't my lord tell you he made it?

SIR JOHN Well then let's ha't.

LORD RAKE [*sings*]

I

What a pother of late
Have they kept in the state
   About setting our consciences free.★
A bottle has more
Dispensation in store,
   Than the king and the state can decree.

II

When my head's full of wine,
I o'erflow with design
   And know no penal laws† that can
                   curb me.
Whate'er I devise,
Seems good in my eyes,
   And religion ne'er dares to disturb me.

III

No fancy remorse
Intrudes in my course,
   Nor impertinent notions of evil:
So there's claret in store,
In peace I've my whore,
   And in peace I jog on to the devil.

ALL [*sing*] So there's claret, &c.

LORD RAKE [*repeats*] And in peace I jog on to the devil.
   Well, how do you like it, gentlemen?

ALL Oh, admirable.

SIR JOHN I would not give a fig for a song, that is not full of sin
   and impudence.

LORD RAKE Then my muse is to your taste. But drink away; the
   night steals upon us, we shall want time to be lewd in. Hey page,

★ setting . . . free: perhaps a reference to the Toleration Act of 1689.
† penal laws: against the practice of the Roman Catholic religion.

sally out, sirrah, and see what's doing in the camp, we'll beat up their quarters presently.

PAGE I'll bring your lordship an exact account.   [*Exit page*]

LORD RAKE Now let the spirit of clary★ go round. Fill me a brimmer. Here's to our forlorn hope. Courage knight; victory attends you.

SIR JOHN And laurels shall crown me. Drink away and be damned.

LORD RAKE Again boys; t'other glass, and damn morality.

SIR JOHN [*drunk*] Aye – damn morality – and damn the watch. And let the constable be married.

ALL Huzza.

Re-enter Page.

LORD RAKE How are the streets inhabited, sirrah?

PAGE My lord it's Sunday night, they are full of drunken citizens.

LORD RAKE Along then boys, we shall have a feast.

COL. BULLY Along noble knight.

SIR JOHN Aye – along Bully; and he that says Sir John Brute, is not as drunk and as religious, as the drunkenest citizen of 'em all – is a liar, and the son of a whore.

COL. BULLY Why that was bravely spoke, and like a free-born Englishman.

SIR JOHN What's that to you, Sir, whether I am an Englishman or a Frenchman?

COL. BULLY Zoons, you are not angry, Sir?

SIR JOHN Zoons I am angry, Sir, – for if I am a free-born Englishman, what have you to do, even to talk of my privileges.

LORD RAKE Why prithee knight don't quarrel here, leave private animosities to be decided by daylight, let the night be employed against the public enemy.

SIR JOHN My lord I respect you, because you are a man of quality: but I'll make that fellow know I am within a hair's breadth as absolute by my privileges, as the King of France is by his prerogative. He by his prerogative takes money where it is not his due; I, by my privilege refuse paying it, where I owe it. Liberty and property and old England, Huzza.   [*Exit Sir John reeling*]

ALL Huzza.   [*All following him*]

        ★ clary: wine with honey and spices.

SCENE ⟨III⟩

A bedchamber

Enter Lady Brute and Bellinda.

LADY BRUTE Sure it's late, Bellinda? I begin to be sleepy.

BELLINDA Yes 'tis near twelve. Will you go to bed?

LADY BRUTE To bed my dear? And by that time I'm fallen into a sweet sleep, (or perhaps a sweet dream which is better and better) Sir John will come home, roaring drunk, and be overjoyed he finds me in a condition to be disturbed.

BELLINDA O you need not fear him, he's in for all night. The servants say he's gone to drink with my Lord Rake.

LADY BRUTE Nay 'tis not very likely indeed, such suitable company should part presently. What hogs men turn, Bellinda, when they grow weary of women.

BELLINDA And what owls they are whilst they are fond of 'em.

LADY BRUTE But that we may forgive well enough, because they are so upon our accounts.

BELLINDA We ought to do so indeed: but 'tis a hard matter. For when a man is really in love, he looks so unsufferably silly; that though a woman liked him well enough before, she has then much ado, to endure the sight of him. And this I take to be the reason, why lovers are so generally ill used.

LADY BRUTE Well I own now, I'm well enough pleased to see a man look like an ass for me.

BELLINDA Aye, I'm pleased he should look like an ass too – That is I'm pleased with myself for making him look so.

LADY BRUTE Nay truly, I think if he'd find some other way to express his passion, 'twould be more to his advantage.

BELLINDA Yes; for then a woman might like his passion and him too.

LADY BRUTE Yet, Bellinda, after all, a woman's life would be but a dull business, if 'twere not for men; and men that can look like asses too. We should never blame fate, for the shortness of our days; our time would hang wretchedly upon our hands.

BELLINDA Why truly they do help us off with a good share on't. For were there no men in the world, o' my conscience I should be no longer a-dressing than I'm a-saying my prayers; nay though it were Sunday: for you know that one may go to church without stays on.

LADY BRUTE But don't you think emulation might do something; for every woman you see desires to be finer than her neighbour.

BELLINDA That's only that the men may like her better than her neighbour. No: if there were no men, adieu fine petticoats, we should be weary of wearing 'em.

LADY BRUTE And adieu plays, we should be weary of seeing 'em.

BELLINDA Adieu Hyde Park, the dust would choke us.

LADY BRUTE Adieu St James's, walking would tire us.

BELLINDA Adieu London, the smoke would stifle us.

LADY BRUTE And adieu going to church, for religion would ne'er prevail with us.

BOTH Ha, ha, ha, ha, ha.

BELLINDA Our confession is so very hearty, sure we merit absolution.

LADY BRUTE Not unless we go through with't, and confess all. So prithee, for the ease of our consciences, let's hide nothing.

BELLINDA Agreed.

LADY BRUTE Why then I confess, that I love to sit in the forefront of a box. For if one sits behind, there's two acts gone perhaps, before one's found out. And when I am there, if I perceive the men whispering and looking upon me, you must know I cannot for my life forbear thinking, they talk to my advantage. And that sets a thousand little tickling vanities on foot. –

BELLINDA Just my case for all the world; but go on.

LADY BRUTE I watch with impatience for the next jest in the play, that I may laugh and show my white teeth. If the poet has been dull, and the jest be long a-coming, I pretend to whisper one to my friend, and from thence fall into a little short discourse, in which I take occasion to show my face in all humours, brisk, pleased, serious, melancholy, languishing; – not that what we say to one another causes any of these alterations. But –

BELLINDA Don't trouble yourself to explain: for if I'm not mistaken, you and I have had some of these necessary dialogues before now, with the same intention.

LADY BRUTE Why I'll swear Bellinda, some people do give strange agreeable airs to their faces in speaking. Tell me true! – Did you never practice in the glass?

BELLINDA Why, did you?

LADY BRUTE Yes faith, many a time.

BELLINDA And I too, I own it. Both how to speak myself, and how to look when others speak; but my glass and I could never yet agree what face I should make, when they come blurt out, with a nasty thing in a play: for all the men presently look upon the women, that's certain; so laugh we must not, though our stays burst for't, because that's telling truth, and owning we understand the jest. And to look serious is so dull, when the whole house is a-laughing.

LADY BRUTE Besides, that looking serious, does really betray our knowledge in the matter, as much as laughing with the company would do. For if we did not understand the thing, we should naturally do like other people.

BELLINDA For my part I always take that occasion to blow my nose.

LADY BRUTE You must blow your nose half off then at some plays.

BELLINDA Why don't some reformer or other, beat the poet for't?

LADY BRUTE Because he is not so sure of our private approbation as of our public thanks. Well, sure there is not upon earth, so impertinent a thing, as women's modesty.

BELLINDA Yes; men's fantasque,* that obliges us to it. If we quit our modesty, they say we lose our charms, and yet they know that very modesty is affectation, and rail at our hypocrisy.

LADY BRUTE Thus one would think, 'twere a hard matter to please 'em, niece. Yet our kind mother nature has given us something, that makes amends for all. Let our weakness be what it will, mankind will still be weaker, and whilst there is a world, 'tis woman that will govern it. But prithee one word of poor Constant before we go to bed; if it be but to furnish matter for dreams; I dare swear he's talking of me now, or thinking of me at least, though it be in the middle of his prayers.

BELLINDA So he ought I think; for you were pleased to make him a good round advance today, Madam.

LADY BRUTE Why, I have e'en plagued him enough to satisfy

* fantasque: fancy.

any reasonable woman: he has besieged me these two years to no purpose.

BELLINDA And if he besieged you two years more, he'd be well enough paid, so he had the plundering of you at last.

LADY BRUTE That may be; but I'm afraid the town won't be able to hold out much longer; for to confess the truth to you, Bellinda, the garrison begins to grow mutinous.

BELLINDA Then the sooner you capitulate, the better.

LADY BRUTE Yet methinks I would fain stay a little longer, to see you fixed too, that we might start together, and see who could love longest. What think you if Heartfree should have a month's mind* to you?

BELLINDA Why faith I could almost be in love with him, for despising that foolish affected Lady Fanciful, but I'm afraid he's too cold ever to warm himself by my fire.

LADY BRUTE Then he deserves to be froze to death. [*kissing her*] Would I were a man for your sake, my dear rogue.

BELLINDA You'd wish yourself a woman again for your own, or the men are mistaken. But if I could make a conquest of this son of Bacchus, and rival his bottle: what should I do with him? He has no fortune; I can't marry him; and sure you would not have me commit fornication.

LADY BRUTE Why, if you did, child, 'twould be but a good friendly part; if 'twere only to keep me in countenance whilst I commit. – You know what.

BELLINDA Well, if I can't resolve to serve you that way, I may perhaps some other, as much to your satisfaction. But pray how shall we contrive to see these blades again quickly?

LADY BRUTE We must e'en have recourse to the old way; make 'em an appointment 'twixt jest and earnest, 'twill look like a frolic, and that you know's a very good thing to save a woman's blushes.

BELLINDA You advise well; but where shall it be?

LADY BRUTE In Spring Garden.† But they shan't know their women, till their women pull off their masks; for a surprise is the

---

* month's mind: a strong inclination.

† Spring Garden: the old Spring Garden was near Charing Cross, the new one was at Vauxhall.

most agreeable thing in the world: and I find myself in a very good humour, ready to do 'em any good turn I can think on.

BELLINDA Then pray write 'em the necessary billet, without farther delay.

LADY BRUTE Let's go into your chamber then, and whilst you say your prayers, I'll do it, child.   [*Exeunt*]

ACT FOUR

SCENE ⟨I⟩

Covent Garden

Enter Lord Rake, Sir John, etc. with swords drawn.

LORD RAKE Is the dog dead?

COL. BULLY No, damn him, I heard him wheeze.

LORD RAKE How the witch his wife howled!

COL. BULLY Aye, she'll alarm the watch presently.

LORD RAKE Appear, knight, then; come, you have a good cause to fight for, there's a man murdered.

SIR JOHN Is there? Then let his ghost be satisfied: for I'll sacrifice a constable to it presently; and burn his body upon his wooden chair.

Enter a Tailor, with a bundle under his arm.

COL. BULLY How now? What have we got here? A thief?

TAILOR No an't please you; I'm no thief.

LORD RAKE That we'll see presently: here, let the general examine him.

SIR JOHN Aye, aye; let me examine him; and I'll lay a hundred pound I find him guilty, in spite of his teeth - for he looks – like a – sneaking rascal. Come sirrah, without equivocation, or mental reservation, tell me of what opinion you are, and what calling; for by them – I shall guess at your morals.

TAILOR An't please you, I'm a dissenting journeyman tailor.

SIR JOHN Then sirrah, you love lying by your religion, and theft by your trade. And so, that your punishment may be suitable to your crimes, – I'll have you first gagged, – and then hanged.

TAILOR Pray good worthy gentlemen, don't abuse me; indeed I'm an honest man, and a good workman, though I say it, that should not say it.

SIR JOHN No words, sirrah, but attend your fate.

LORD RAKE Let me see what's in that bundle.

TAILOR An't please you, it's the doctor of the parish's gown.

LORD RAKE The doctor's gown! – Hark you, knight, you won't stick at abusing the clergy, will you?

SIR JOHN No, I'm drunk, and I'll abuse anything – but my wife; and her I name – with reverence.

LORD RAKE Then you shall wear this gown, whilst you charge the watch. That though the blows fall upon you, the scandal may light upon the church.

SIR JOHN A generous design – by all the gods – give it me. [*takes the gown and puts it on*]

TAILOR O dear gentlemen, I shall be quite undone, if you take the gown.

SIR JOHN Retire, sirrah; and since you carry off your skin – go home, and be happy.

TAILOR [*pausing*] I think I had e'en as good follow the gentleman's friendly advice. For if I dispute any longer, who knows but the whim may take him to case me.* These courtiers are fuller of tricks than they are of money; they'll sooner cut a man's throat, than pay his bill.   [*Exit Tailor*]

SIR JOHN So, how d'ye like my shapes now?

LORD RAKE This will do to a miracle; he looks like a bishop going to the Holy War. But to your arms, gentlemen, the enemy appears.

Enter Constable and Watch.

WATCHMAN Stand! Who goes there? Come before the constable.

SIR JOHN The constable's a rascal – and you are the son of a whore.

WATCHMAN A good civil answer for a parson, truly.

CONSTABLE Methinks Sir, a man of your coat, might set a better example.

SIR JOHN Sirrah, I'll make you know – there are men of my coat can set as bad examples – as you can do, you dog you. [*Sir John strikes the Constable. They knock him down, disarm him and seize him. Lord Rake etc. run away*]

CONSTABLE So, we have secured the parson however.

SIR JOHN Blood and blood – and blood.

WATCHMAN Lord have mercy upon us: how the wicked wretch raves of blood. I'll warrant he has been murdering somebody tonight.

SIR JOHN Sirrah, there's nothing got by murder but a halter: my talent lies towards drunkenness and simony.

* to case: to strip.

WATCHMAN Why that now was spoke like a man of parts, neighbours; it's pity he should be so disguised.

SIR JOHN You lie, – I am not disguised; for I am drunk barefaced.

WATCHMAN Look you there again, – This is a mad parson, Mr Constable; I'll lay a pot of ale upon's head, he's a good preacher.

CONSTABLE Come Sir, out of respect to your calling, I shan't put you into the roundhouse;* but we must secure you in our drawing-room till morning, that you may do no mischief. So, come along.

SIR JOHN You may put me where you will, sirrah, now you have overcome me; – but if I can't do mischief, I'll think of mischief – in spite of your teeth, you dog you.

[Exeunt]

SCENE ⟨II⟩

A bedchamber

Enter Heartfree, solus.

⟨HEARTFREE⟩ What the plague ails me? – Love? No, I thank you for that, my heart's rock still. – Yet 'tis Bellinda that disturbs me; that's positive. – Well, what of all that? Must I love her for being troublesome? At that rate, I might love all the women I meet, egad. But hold? – Though I don't love her for disturbing me, yet she may disturb me, because I love her – aye, that may be, faith. I have dreamed of her, that's certain – Well, so I have of my mother; therefore what's that to the purpose? Aye, but Bellinda runs in my mind waking – And so does many a damned thing, that I don't care a farthing for – Methinks though, I would fain be talking to her, and yet I have no business. – Well, am I the first man, that has had a mind to do an impertinent thing?

Enter Constant.

CONSTANT How now, Heartfree? What makes you up and dressed so soon? I thought none but lovers quarrelled with their beds; I expected to have found you snoring, as I used to do.

* roundhouse: the lock-up.

HEARTFREE Why, faith friend, 'tis the care I have of your affairs, that makes me so thoughtful; I have been studying all night, how to bring your matter about with Bellinda.

CONSTANT With Bellinda?

HEARTFREE With my lady, I mean: and faith I have mighty hopes on't. Sure you must be very well satisfied with her behaviour to you yesterday?

CONSTANT So well; that nothing but a lover's fears, can make me doubt of success. But what can this sudden change proceed from?

HEARTFREE Why, you saw her husband beat her, did you not?

CONSTANT That's true: a husband is scarce to be borne upon any terms, much less when he fights with his wife. Methinks she should e'en have cuckolded him upon the very spot, to show that after the battle, she was master of the field.

HEARTFREE A council of war to women, would infallibly have advised her to't. But, I confess, so agreeable a woman as Bellinda, deserves a better usage.

CONSTANT Bellinda again?

HEARTFREE My lady, I mean: what a pox makes me blunder so today? ⟨*aside*⟩ A plague of this treacherous tongue.

CONSTANT Prithee look upon me seriously, Heartfree – Now answer me directly! Is it my lady, or Bellinda, employs your careful thoughts thus?

HEARTFREE My lady, or Bellinda?

CONSTANT In love, by this light in love.

HEARTFREE In love?

CONSTANT Nay, ne'er deny it: for thou'lt do it so awkwardly, 'twill but make the jest sit heavier about thee. My dear friend, I give thee much joy.

HEARTFREE Why prithee, you won't persuade me to it, will you?

CONSTANT That she's mistress of your tongue, that's plain, and I know you are so honest a fellow, your tongue and heart always go together. But how? But how the devil? Pha, ha, ha, ha –

HEARTFREE Hey day: why sure you don't believe it in earnest?

CONSTANT Yes, I do; because I see you deny it in jest.

HEARTFREE Nay, but look you Ned, – a – deny in jest – a – gadzooks, you know I say – a – when a man denies a thing in jest – a –

CONSTANT Pha, ha, ha, ha, ha.

HEARTFREE Nay, then we shall have it: what, because a man stumbles at a word. Did you never make a blunder?

CONSTANT Yes, for I am in love, I own it.

HEARTFREE Then; so am I. – Now laugh till thy soul's glutted with mirth, [*embracing him*] but, dear Constant, don't tell the Town on't.

CONSTANT Nay, then 'twere almost pity to laugh at thee, after so honest a confession. But tell us a little, Jack. By what new-invented arms, has this mighty stroke been given?

HEARTFREE E'en by that unaccountable weapon, called, *je ne sais quoi*; for everything that can come within the verge of beauty, I have seen it with indifference.

CONSTANT So in few words then; the *je ne sais quoi*, has been too hard for the quilted petticoat.

HEARTFREE Egad, I think the *je ne sais quoi*, is in the quilted petticoat; at least, 'tis certain, I ne'er think on't without – a – a *je ne sais quoi* in every part about me.

CONSTANT Well, but have all your remedies lost their virtue, have you turned her inside-out yet?

HEARTFREE I dare not so much as think on't.

CONSTANT But don't the two years' fatigue, I have had, discourage you?

HEARTFREE Yes: I dread what I foresee; yet cannot quit the enterprise. Like some soldiers; whose courage dwells more in their honour, than their nature; on they go, though the body trembles, at what the soul makes it undertake.

CONSTANT Nay, if you expect your mistress will use you, as your profanations against her sex deserve, you tremble justly. But how do you intend to proceed, friend?

HEARTFREE Thou know'st I'm but a novice; be friendly and advise me.

CONSTANT Why look you then; I'd have you – serenade and a – write a song – go to church; look like a fool – be very officious: ogle, write and lead out; and who knows, but in a year or two's time, you may be – called a troublesome puppy, and sent about your business.

HEARTFREE That's hard.

CONSTANT Yet thus it oft falls out with lovers, Sir.

HEARTFREE Pox on me for making one of the number.

CONSTANT Have a care: say no saucy things: 'twill but augment your crime, and if your mistress hears on't, increase your punishment.

HEARTFREE Prithee say something then to encourage me. You know I helped you in your distress.

CONSTANT Why then to encourage you to perseverance, that you may be thoroughly ill used for your offences, I'll put you in mind, that even the coyest ladies of 'em all, are made up of desires, as well as we; and though they do hold out a long time, they will capitulate at last. For that thundering engineer, nature, does make such havoc in the town, they must surrender at long run, or perish in their own flames.

Enter a Footman.

⟨FOOTMAN⟩ Sir, there's a porter without with a letter; he desires to give it into your own hands.

CONSTANT Call him in.   ⟨*Exit Footman*⟩

Enter Porter.

CONSTANT What Jo; is it thee?

PORTER An't please you Sir, I was ordered to deliver this into your own hands, by two well-shaped ladies, at the New Exchange.* I was at your honour's lodgings, and your servants sent me hither.

CONSTANT 'Tis well, are you to carry any answer?

PORTER No, my noble master. They gave me my orders, and whip, they were gone, like a maidenhead at fifteen.

CONSTANT Very well; there. [*gives him money*]

PORTER God bless your honour.   [*Exit Porter*]

CONSTANT Now let's see, what honest trusty Jo has brought us. [*reads*] 'If you and your play-fellow, can spare time from your business and devotions, don't fail to be at Spring Garden about eight in the evening. You'll find nothing there but women, so you need bring no other arms than what you usually carry about

---

* New Exchange: an arcade with shops, on the south side of the Strand.

you.' So, playfellow: here's something to stay your stomach, till your mistress's dish is ready for you.

HEARTFREE Some of our old battered acquaintance. I won't go, not I.

CONSTANT Nay, that you can't avoid: there's honour in the case, 'tis a challenge, and I want a second.

HEARTFREE I doubt I shall be but a very useless one to you; for I'm so disheartened by this wound Bellinda has given me; I don't think I shall have courage enough to draw my sword.

CONSTANT Oh, if that be all, come along; I'll warrant you find sword enough for such enemies as we have to deal withal. [*Exeunt*]

⟨SCENE III⟩

⟨Street outside Justice's house⟩

Enter Constable, etc. with Sir John.

CONSTABLE Come along, Sir, I thought to have let you slip this morning, because you were a minister; but you are as drunk and as abusive as ever. We'll see what the Justice of the Peace will say to you.

SIR JOHN And you shall see what I'll say to the Justice of the Peace, sirrah. [*They knock at the door*]

Enter Servant.

CONSTABLE Pray acquaint his worship, we have got an unruly parson here: we are unwilling to expose him, but don't know what to do with him.

SERVANT I'll acquaint my master.   [*Exit Servant*]

SIR JOHN You - Constable – What damned Justice is this?

CONSTABLE One that will take care of you, I warrant you.

Enter Justice.

JUSTICE Well, Mr Constable; what's the disorder here?

CONSTABLE An't please your worship –

SIR JOHN Let me speak and be damned: I'm a divine, and can unfold mysteries better than you can do.

JUSTICE Sadness, sadness, a minister so overtaken. Pray Sir, give the constable leave to speak, and I'll hear you very patiently; I assure you Sir, I will.

SIR JOHN Sir, – you are a very civil magistrate. Your most humble servant.

CONSTABLE An't please your worship then; he has attempted to beat the watch tonight, and swore –

SIR JOHN You lie.

JUSTICE Hold, pray Sir, a little.

SIR JOHN Sir, your very humble servant.

CONSTABLE Indeed Sir, he came at us without any provocation, called us whores and rogues, and laid us on with a great quarter-staff. He was in my Lord Rake's company. They have been playing the devil tonight.

JUSTICE: Hem – hem – pray Sir – May you be chaplain to my lord?

SIR JOHN Sir – I presume – I may if I will.

JUSTICE My meaning Sir, is – are you so?

SIR JOHN Sir, – you mean very well.

JUSTICE He hem – hem – Under favour, Sir, pray answer me directly.

SIR JOHN Under favour, Sir – Do you use to answer directly when you are drunk?

JUSTICE Good lack, good lack: here's nothing to be got from him. Pray, Sir, may I crave your name?

SIR JOHN Sir, – my name's – [*he hiccups*] Hiccup, Sir.

JUSTICE Hiccup? Doctor Hiccup. I have known a great many country parsons of that name, especially down in the fens. Pray where do you live, Sir?

SIR JOHN Here – and there, Sir.

JUSTICE Why, what a strange man is this? Where do you preach, Sir? Have you any cure?

SIR JOHN Sir – I have – a very good cure – for a clap, at your service.

JUSTICE Lord have mercy upon us.

SIR JOHN [*aside*] This fellow does ask so many impertinent questions, I believe egad, 'tis the Justice's wife, in the Justice's clothes.

JUSTICE Mr Constable, I vow and protest, I don't know what to do with him.

CONSTABLE Truly, he has been but a troublesome guest to us all night.

JUSTICE I think I had e'en best let him go about his business, for I'm unwilling to expose him.

CONSTABLE E'en what your worship thinks fit.

SIR JOHN Sir, – not to interrupt Mr Constable, I have a small favour to ask.

JUSTICE Sir, I open both my ears to you.

SIR JOHN Sir, your very humble servant. I have a little urgent business calls upon me; and therefore I desire the favour of you, to bring matters to a conclusion.

JUSTICE Sir, if I were sure that business, were not to commit more disorders; I would release you.

SIR JOHN None, – by my priesthood.

JUSTICE Then, Mr Constable, you may discharge him.

SIR JOHN Sir, your very humble servant. If you please to accept of a bottle –

JUSTICE I thank you kindly, Sir; but I never drink in a morning. Good-bye to ye, Sir, good-bye to ye.

SIR JOHN Good-bye t'ye, good Sir.   [*Exit Justice*]
So – now, Mr Constable, shall you and I go pick up a whore together.

CONSTABLE No, thank you, Sir; my wife's enough to satisfy any reasonable man.

SIR JOHN [*aside*] He, he, he, he, he, – the fool is married then. Well, you won't go?

CONSTABLE Not I, truly.

SIR JOHN Then I'll go by myself; and you and your wife may be damned.   [*Exit Sir John*]

CONSTABLE [*gazing after him*] Why God-a-marcy parson. [*Exeunt*]

SCENE ⟨IV⟩

Spring Garden

Constant and Heartfree cross the stage. As they go off, enter
Lady Fanciful and Mademoiselle, masked and dogging 'em.

CONSTANT So: I think we are about the time appointed; let us
walk up this way. *[Exeunt]*

LADY FANCIFUL Good: thus far I have dogged 'em without being discovered. 'Tis infallibly some intrigue that brings them to
Spring Garden. How my poor heart is torn and wracked with fear
and jealousy. Yet let it be anything, but that flirt Bellinda, and
I'll try to bear it. But if it prove her, all that's woman in me shall
be employed to destroy her.

[Exeunt after Constant and Heartfree]

Re-enter Constant and Heartfree. Lady Fanciful and Mademoiselle
still following at a distance.

CONSTANT I see no females yet, that have anything to say to us.
I'm afraid we are bantered.

HEARTFREE I wish we were; for I'm in no humour to make either
them or myself merry.

CONSTANT Nay, I'm sure you'll make them merry enough; if I
tell 'em why you are dull. But prithee why so heavy and sad,
before you begin to be ill used?

HEARTFREE For the same reason, perhaps, that you are so brisk
and well pleased; because both pains and pleasures are generally
more considerable in prospect, than when they come to pass.

Enter Lady Brute and Bellinda, masked, and poorly dressed.

CONSTANT How now, who are these? Not our game I hope.

HEARTFREE If they are, we are e'en well enough served, to come
hunting here, when we had so much better game in chase elsewhere.

LADY FANCIFUL *[to Mademoiselle]* So, those are their ladies without doubt. But I'm afraid that doily* stuff is not worn for want of

---

* doily: lightweight woollen material named after Thomas Doyly.

better clothes. They are the very shape and size of Bellinda and her aunt.

MADEMOISELLE So day be inteed, Matam.

LADY FANCIFUL We'll slip into this close arbour, where we may hear all they say.   [*Exeunt Lady Fanciful and Mademoiselle*]

LADY BRUTE What, are you afraid of us, gentlemen?

HEARTFREE Why truly I think we may, if appearance don't lie.

BELLINDA Do you always find women what they appear to be, Sir?

HEARTFREE No forsooth; but I seldom find 'em better than they appear to be.

BELLINDA Then the outside's best, you think?

HEARTFREE 'Tis the honestest.

CONSTANT Have a care, Heartfree; you are relapsing again.

LADY BRUTE Why, does the gentleman use to rail at women?

CONSTANT He has done formerly.

BELLINDA I suppose he had very good cause for't: they did not use you so well, as you thought you deserved, Sir.

LADY BRUTE They made themselves merry at your expense, Sir.

BELLINDA Laughed when you sighed.

LADY BRUTE Slept while you were waking.

BELLINDA Had your porter beat.

LADY BRUTE And threw your *billet-doux* in the fire.

HEARTFREE Hey day, I shall do more than rail presently.

BELLINDA Why you won't beat us, will you?

HEARTFREE I don't know but I may.

CONSTANT What the devil's coming here? Sir John in a gown? – And drunk i'faith.

Enter Sir John.

SIR JOHN What a pox – here's Constant, Heartfree, – and two whores egad: – O you covetous rogues; what, have you never a spare punk for your friend? – But I'll share with you. [*he seizes both the women*]

HEARTFREE Why, what the plague have you been doing, knight.

SIR JOHN Why, I have been beating the watch, and scandalizing the clergy.

HEARTFREE A very good account, truly.

SIR JOHN And what do you think I'll do next?

CONSTANT Nay, that no man can guess.

SIR JOHN Why, if you'll let me sup with you, I'll treat both your strumpets.

LADY BRUTE [*aside*] O Lord, we are undone.

HEARTFREE No, we can't sup together, because we have some affairs elsewhere. But if you'll accept of these two ladies, we'll be so complaisant to you, to resign our right in 'em.

BELLINDA [*aside*] Lord, what shall we do?

SIR JOHN Let me see, their clothes are such damned clothes, they won't pawn for the reckoning.

HEARTFREE Sir John, your servant. Rapture attend you.

CONSTANT Adieu ladies, make much of the gentleman.

LADY BRUTE Why sure, you won't leave us in the hands of a drunken fellow to abuse us.

SIR JOHN Who do you call a drunken fellow, you slut you? I'm a man of quality; the King has made me a knight.

HEARTFREE Aye, aye, you are in good hands, adieu, adieu.

[*Heartfree runs off*]

LADY BRUTE The devil's hands: let me go, or I'll – for heaven's sake protect us. [*she breaks from him, runs to Constant, twitching off her mask and clapping it on again*]

SIR JOHN I'll devil you, you jade you. I'll demolish your ugly face.

CONSTANT Hold a little, knight, she swoons.

SIR JOHN I'll swoon her.

CONSTANT Hey, Heartfree.

Re-enter Heartfree. Bellinda runs to him and shows her face.

HEARTFREE O heavens! My dear creature, stand there a little.

CONSTANT Pull him off, Jack.

HEARTFREE Hold, mighty man; look you, Sir, we did but jest with you. These are ladies of our acquaintance, that we had a mind to frighten a little, but now you must leave us.

SIR JOHN Oons, I won't leave you, not I.

HEARTFREE Nay, but you must though; and therefore make no words on't.

SIR JOHN Then you are a couple of damned uncivil fellows. And I hope your punks will give you sauce to your mutton.

[*Exit Sir John*]

LADY BRUTE Oh, I shall never come to myself again, I'm so frightened.

CONSTANT 'Twas a narrow scape, indeed.

BELLINDA Women must have frolics, you see, whatever they cost 'em.

HEARTFREE This might have proved a dear one though.

LADY BRUTE You are the more obliged to us, for the risk we run upon your accounts.

CONSTANT And I hope you'll acknowledge something due to our knight-errantry, ladies. This is the second time we have delivered you.

LADY BRUTE 'Tis true; and since we see fate has designed you for our guardians, 'twill make us the more willing to trust ourselves in your hands. But you must not have the worse opinion of us for our innocent frolic.

HEARTFREE Ladies, you may command our opinions in everything that is to your advantage.

BELLINDA Then, Sir, I command you to be of opinion, that women are sometimes better than they appear to be.

Lady Brute and Constant talk apart.

HEARTFREE Madam, you have made a convert of me in everything. I'm grown a fool: I could be fond of a woman.

BELLINDA I thank you, Sir, in the name of the whole sex.

HEARTFREE Which sex nothing but yourself, could ever have atoned for.

BELLINDA Now has my vanity a devilish itch, to know in what my merit consists.

HEARTFREE In your humility, Madam, that keeps you ignorant it consists at all.

BELLINDA One other compliment with that serious face, and I hate you forever after.

HEARTFREE Some women love to be abused: is that it you would be at?

BELLINDA No, not that neither: but I'd have men talk plainly what's fit for women to hear; without putting 'em either to a real, or an affected blush.

HEARTFREE Why then, in as plain terms as I can find to express myself: I could love you even to – matrimony itself a'most egad.

BELLINDA Just as Sir John did her ladyship there. What think you? Don't you believe one month's time might bring you down to the same indifference, only clad in a little better manners, perhaps. Well, you men are unaccountable things, mad till you have your mistresses; and then stark mad till you are rid of 'em again. Tell me, honestly, is not your patience put to a much severer trial after possession, than before?

HEARTFREE With a great many, I must confess, it is, to our eternal scandal; but I – dear creature, do but try me.

BELLINDA That's the surest way indeed, to know, but not the safest. [*to Lady Brute*] Madam, are not you for taking a turn in the Great Walk: it's almost dark, nobody will know us.

LADY BRUTE Really I find myself something idle, Bellinda. Besides, I dote upon this little odd private corner. But don't let my lazy fancy confine you.

CONSTANT [*aside*] So, she would be left alone with me, that's well.

BELLINDA Well, we'll take one turn, and come to you again. [*to Heartfree*] Come, Sir, shall we go pry into the secrets of the garden. Who knows what discoveries we may make.

HEARTFREE Madam, I'm at your service.

CONSTANT [*aside to Heartfree*] Don't make too much haste back; for, d'ye hear – I may be busy.

HEARTFREE Enough. [*Exeunt Bellinda and Heartfree*]

LADY BRUTE Sure you think me scandalously free, Mr Constant. I'm afraid I shall lose your good opinion of me.

CONSTANT My good opinion, Madam, is like your cruelty, never to be removed.

LADY BRUTE But if I should remove my cruelty, then there's an end of your good opinion.

CONSTANT There is not so strict an alliance between 'em neither. 'Tis certain I should love you then better (if that be possible) than I do now; and where I love, I always esteem.

LADY BRUTE Indeed, I doubt you much: why suppose you had a wife, and she should entertain a gallant.

CONSTANT If I gave her just cause, how could I justly condemn her?

LADY BRUTE Ah; but you'd differ widely about just causes.

CONSTANT But blows can bear no dispute.

LADY BRUTE Nor ill manners much, truly.

CONSTANT Then no woman upon earth, has so just a cause as you have.

LADY BRUTE Oh, but a faithful wife, is a beautiful character.

CONSTANT To a deserving husband, I confess it is.

LADY BRUTE But can his faults release my duty?

CONSTANT In equity without doubt. And where laws dispense with equity; equity should dispense with laws.

LADY BRUTE Pray let's leave this dispute; for you men have as much witchcraft in your arguments, as women have in their eyes.

CONSTANT But whilst you attack me with your charms, 'tis but reasonable I assault you with mine.

LADY BRUTE The case is not the same. What mischief we do, we can't help, and therefore are to be forgiven.

CONSTANT Beauty soon obtains pardon, for the pain that it gives, when it applies the balm of compassion to the wound; but a fine face, and a hard heart, is almost as bad as an ugly face and a soft one: both very troublesome to many a poor gentleman.

LADY BRUTE Yes, and to many a poor gentlewoman too, I can assure you. But pray which of 'em is it, that most afflicts you?

CONSTANT Your glass and conscience will inform you, Madam. But for heaven's sake (for now I must be serious) if pity or if gratitude can move you, [*taking her hand*] if constancy and truth have power to tempt you; if love, if adoration can affect you, give me at least some hopes, that time may do, what you perhaps mean never to perform; 'twill ease my sufferings, though not quench my flame.

LADY BRUTE Your sufferings eased, your flame would soon abate; and that I would preserve, not quench it, Sir.

CONSTANT Would you preserve it, nourish it with favours; for that's the food, it naturally requires.

LADY BRUTE Yet on that natural food, 'twould surfeit soon, should I resolve to grant all that you would ask.

CONSTANT And in refusing all, you starve it. Forgive me therefore, since my hunger rages, if I at last grow wild, and in my frenzy force at least, this from you. [*kissing her hand*] Or if you'd have my flame, soar higher still, then grant me this, [*kissing first her hand, then her neck*] and this, and this, and thousands more; [*aside*] for now's the time, she melts into compassion.

LADY BRUTE [*aside*] Poor coward virtue, how it shuns the battle. O heavens! Let me go.

CONSTANT Aye, go, aye: where shall we go, my charming angel, – into this private arbour. – Nay, let's lose no time – Moments are precious.

LADY BRUTE And lovers wild. Pray let us stop here; at least for this time.

CONSTANT 'Tis impossible: he that has power over you, can have none over himself.

As he is forcing her into the arbour, Lady Fanciful and Mademoiselle bolt out upon them, and run over the stage.

LADY BRUTE Ah; I'm lost.

LADY FANCIFUL Fe, fe, fe, fe, fe.

MADEMOISELLE Fe, fe, fe, fe, fe.

CONSTANT Death and furies, who are these?

LADY BRUTE O heavens, I'm out of my wits; if they knew me, I'm ruined.

CONSTANT Don't be frightened; ten thousand to one they are strangers to you.

LADY BRUTE Whatever they are, I won't stay here a moment longer.

CONSTANT Whither will you go?

LADY BRUTE Home, as if the devil were in me. Lord where's this Bellinda now?

Enter Bellinda and Heartfree.

Oh! It's well you are come: I'm so frightened my hair stands on end. Let's be gone for heaven's sake.

BELLINDA Lord, what's the matter?

LADY BRUTE The devil's the matter, we are discovered. Here's a couple of women have done the most impertinent thing. Away, away, away, away, away.   [*Exit running ⟨The others follow⟩*]

Re-enter Lady Fanciful and Mademoiselle.

LADY FANCIFUL Well Mademoiselle, 'tis a prodigious thing, how women can suffer filthy fellows, to grow so familiar with 'em.

MADEMOISELLE Ah Matam, *il n'y a rien de si naturel*.

LADY FANCIFUL Fe, fe, fe. But O my heart; O jealousy, O torture. I'm upon the rack. What shall I do, my lover's lost, I ne'er shall see him mine. [*pausing*] But I may be revenged; and that's the same thing. Ah sweet revenge. Thou welcome thought, thou healing balsam, to my wounded soul. Be but propitious on this one occasion, I'll place my Heaven in thee, for all my life to come.
To woman how indulgent nature's kind.
No blast of fortune long disturbs her mind.
Compliance to her fate supports her still,
If love won't make her happy – mischief will.

                                                    [*Exeunt*]

ACT FIVE

SCENE ⟨I⟩

Lady Fanciful's house

Enter Lady Fanciful and Mademoiselle.

LADY FANCIFUL Well, Mademoiselle; did you dog the filthy things?

MADEMOISELLE *O que oui* Matam.

LADY FANCIFUL And where are they?

MADEMOISELLE *Au logis.*

LADY FANCIFUL What? Men and all?

MADEMOISELLE *Tous ensemble.*

LADY FANCIFUL O confidence! What, carry their fellows to their own house?

MADEMOISELLE *C'est que le mari n'y est pas.*

LADY FANCIFUL No, so I believe, truly. But he shall be there, and quickly too, if I can find him out. Well, 'tis a prodigious thing, to see when men and women get together, how they fortify one another in their impudence. But if that drunken fool, her husband, be to be found in e'er a tavern in Town, I'll send him amongst 'em. I'll spoil their sport.

MADEMOISELLE *En verité* Matam, *ce serait domage.*

LADY FANCIFUL 'Tis in vain to oppose it, Mademoiselle; therefore never go about it. For I am the steadiest creature in the world – when I have determined to do mischief. So, come along.

[*Exeunt*]

SCENE ⟨II⟩

Sir John Brute's house

Enter Constant, Heartfree, Lady Brute, Bellinda, and Lovewell.

LADY BRUTE But are you sure you don't mistake, Lovewell?

LOVEWELL Madam, I saw 'em all go into the tavern together, and my master was so drunk he could scarce stand.   ⟨*Exit*⟩

LADY BRUTE Then, gentlemen, I believe we may venture to let you stay and play at cards with us an hour or two; for they'll scarce part till morning.

BELLINDA I think 'tis pity they should ever part.

CONSTANT The company that's here, Madam.

LADY BRUTE Then, Sir, the company that's here, must remember to part itself, in time.

CONSTANT Madam, we don't intend to forfeit your future favours, by an indiscreet usage of this. The moment you give us the signal, we shan't fail to make our retreat.

LADY BRUTE Upon those conditions then, let us sit down to cards.

Enter Lovewell.

⟨LOVEWELL⟩ O Lord, Madam, here's my master just staggering in upon you; ye has been quarrelsome yonder, and they have kicked him out of the company.

LADY BRUTE Into the closet, gentlemen, for heaven's sake; I'll wheedle him to bed, if possible.

[*Constant and Heartfree run into the closet*]

Enter Sir John, all dirt and bloody.

LADY BRUTE Ah – ah – he's all over blood.

SIR JOHN What the plague, does the woman – squall for? Did you never see a man in pickle before?

LADY BRUTE Lord, where have you been?

SIR JOHN I have been at – cuffs.

LADY BRUTE I fear that is not all. I hope you are not wounded.

SIR JOHN Sound as a roach, wife.

LADY BRUTE I'm mighty glad to hear it.

SIR JOHN You know – I think you lie.

LADY BRUTE I know you do me wrong to think so, then. For heaven's my witness, I had rather see my own blood trickle down, than yours.

SIR JOHN Then will I be crucified.

LADY BRUTE 'Tis a hard fate, I should not be believed.

SIR JOHN 'Tis a damned atheistical age, wife.

LADY BRUTE I am sure I have given you a thousand tender proofs, how great my care is of you. Nay, spite of all your cruel thought, I'll still persist, and at this moment, if I can, persuade you to lie down, and sleep a little.

SIR JOHN Why, - do you think I am drunk – you slut, you?

LADY BRUTE Heaven forbid, I should: but I'm afraid you are feverish. Pray let me feel your pulse.

SIR JOHN Stand off and be damned.

LADY BRUTE Why, I see your distemper in your very eyes. You are all on fire. Pray go to bed; let me entreat you.

SIR JOHN – Come kiss me, then.

LADY BRUTE [*kissing him*] There: now go [*aside*] He stinks like poison.

SIR JOHN I see it goes damnably against your stomach – And therefore – Kiss me again.

LADY BRUTE Nay, now you fool me.

SIR JOHN Do't, I say.

LADY BRUTE [*aside*] Ah Lord have mercy upon me. Well; there; now will you go?

SIR JOHN Now wife, you shall see my gratitude. You give me two kisses – I'll give you – two hundred. [*kisses and tumbles her*]

LADY BRUTE O Lord: pray, Sir John, be quiet. Heavens, what a pickle am I in.

BELLINDA [*aside*] If I were in her pickle, I'd call my gallant out of the closet, and he should cudgel him soundly.

SIR JOHN So; now, you being as dirty and as nasty as myself, we may go pig together. [*going to the closet*] But first, I must have a cup of your cold tea, wife.

LADY BRUTE ⟨*aside*⟩ Oh, I'm ruined. There's none there, my dear.

SIR JOHN I'll warrant you, I'll find some, my dear.

LADY BRUTE You can't open the door, the lock's spoiled. I have been turning and turning the key this half hour to no purpose. I'll send for the smith tomorrow.

SIR JOHN There's ne'er a smith in Europe can open a door with more expedition than I can do – As for example, [*he bursts open the door with his foot*] – Pou. – How now? – What the devil have we got here? – Constant – Heartfree – And two whores again, egad. – This is the worst cold tea – that ever I met with in my life. –

Enter Constant and Heartfree.

LADY BRUTE [*aside*] O Lord, what will become of us?

SIR JOHN Gentlemen – I am your very humble servant – I give you many thanks – I see you take care of my family – I shall do all I can to return the obligation.

CONSTANT Sir, how oddly soever this business may appear to you, you would have no cause to be uneasy, if you knew the truth of all things; your lady is the most virtuous woman in the world, and nothing has passed, but an innocent frolic.

HEARTFREE Nothing else, upon my honour, Sir.

SIR JOHN You are both very civil gentlemen – and my wife, there, is a very civil gentlewoman; therefore I don't doubt but many civil things have passed between you. Your very humble servant.

LADY BRUTE [*aside to Constant*] Pray be gone; he's so drunk he can't hurt us tonight, and tomorrow morning you shall hear from us.

CONSTANT I'll obey you, Madam. Sir, when you are cool, you'll understand reason better. So then I shall take the pains to inform you. If not – I wear a sword, Sir, and so goodbye to you. Come along, Heartfree.

SIR JOHN – Wear a sword, Sir: – and what of all that, Sir? – He comes to my house; eats my meat; lies with my wife; dishonours my family; gets a bastard to inherit my estate. – And when I ask a civil account of all this – 'Sir,' says he, 'I wear a sword.' – 'Wear a sword, Sir?' 'Yes Sir', says he; 'I wear a sword'. – It may be a good answer at cross-purposes; but 'tis a damned one to a man in my whimsical circumstance – 'Sir,' says he, 'I wear a sword.' [*to Lady Brute*] And what do you wear now? Ha? Tell me. [*sitting down in a great chair*] What? You are modest and can't? – Why then I'll tell you, you slut you. You wear – an impudent lewd face. – A damned designing heart – And a tail – and a tail full of – [*he falls fast asleep, snoring*]

LADY BRUTE So; thanks to kind heaven, he's fast for some hours.

BELLINDA 'Tis well he is so, that we may have time to lay our story handsomely; for we must lie like the devil to bring ourselves off.

LADY BRUTE What shall we say, Bellinda?

BELLINDA [*musing*] – I'll tell you: it must all light upon Heartfree
and I. We'll say he has courted me some time, but for reasons unknown to us, has ever been very earnest the thing might be kept
from Sir John. That therefore hearing him upon the stairs, he run
into the closet, though against our will, and Constant with him,
to prevent jealousy. And to give this a good impudent face of
truth, (that I may deliver you from the trouble you are in:) I'll
e'en (if he pleases) marry him.

LADY BRUTE I'm beholding to you, cousin; but that would be
carrying the jest a little too far for your own sake: you know he's
a younger brother, and has nothing.

BELLINDA 'Tis true; but I like him, and have fortune enough to
keep above extremity: I can't say, I would live with him in a
cell upon love and bread and butter. But I had rather have the
man I love, and a middle state of life, than that gentleman in the
chair there, and twice your ladyship's splendour.

LADY BRUTE In truth, niece, you are in the right on't: for I am
very uneasy with my ambition. But perhaps, had I married as
you'll do, I might have been as ill used.

BELLINDA Some risk, I do confess, there always is; but if a man
has the least spark, either of honour or good nature, he can never
use a woman ill, that loves him and makes his fortune both. Yet
I must own to you, some little struggling I still have, with this
teasing ambition of ours. For pride, you know, is as natural to a
woman, as 'tis to a saint. I can't help being fond of this rogue;
and yet it goes to my heart to think I must never whisk to Hyde
Park, with above a pair of horses; have no coronet upon my coach,
nor a page to carry up my train. But above all – that business of
place – well; taking place, is a noble prerogative.

LADY BRUTE Especially after a quarrel.

BELLINDA Or of a rival. But pray say no more on't, for fear I
change my mind. For o' my conscience, were't not for your
affair in the balance, I should go near to pick up some odious man
of quality yet, and only take poor Heartfree for a gallant.

LADY BRUTE Then him you must have, however things go?

BELLINDA Yes.

LADY BRUTE Why we may pretend what we will; but 'tis a hard
matter to live without the man we love.

BELLINDA Especially when we are married to the man we hate. Pray tell me? Do the men of the Town ever believe us virtuous, when they see us do so?

LADY BRUTE Oh, no: nor indeed hardly, let us do what we will. They most of 'em think, there is no such thing as virtue considered in the strictest notions of it: and therefore when you hear 'em say, such a one is a woman of reputation, they only mean she's a woman of discretion. For they consider, we have no more religion than they have, nor so much morality; and between you and I, Bellinda, I'm afraid the want of inclination seldom protects any of us.

BELLINDA But what think you of the fear of being found out.

LADY BRUTE I think that never kept any woman virtuous long. We are not such cowards neither. No: let us once pass fifteen, and we have too good an opinion of our own cunning, to believe the world can penetrate, into what we would keep a secret. And so in short, we cannot reasonably blame the men for judging of us by themselves.

BELLINDA But sure we are not so wicked as they are, after all.

LADY BRUTE We are as wicked, child, but our vice lies another way: men have more courage than we, so they commit more bold, impudent sins. They quarrel, fight, swear, drink, blaspheme, and the like. Whereas we, being cowards, only backbite, tell lies, cheat at cards and so forth. But 'tis late. Let's end our discourse for tonight, and out of an excess of charity, take a small care, of that nasty drunken thing there – Do but look at him, Bellinda.

BELLINDA Ah – 'tis a savoury dish.

LADY BRUTE As savoury as 'tis, I'm cloyed with't. Prithee call the butler to take away.

BELLINDA Call the butler? – Call the scavenger. [*to a servant within*] Who's there? Call Razor! Let him take away his master, scour him clean with a little soap and sand, and so put him to bed.

LADY BRUTE Come Bellinda, I'll e'en lie with you tonight; and in the morning we'll send for our gentlemen to set this matter even.

BELLINDA With all my heart.

LADY BRUTE [*making a low curtsey ⟨to Sir John⟩*]   Good night, my dear.

BOTH Ha, ha, ha.   [*Exeunt*]

Enter Razor.

⟨RAZOR⟩ My lady there's a wag – My master there's a cuckold. Marriage is a slippery thing – women have depraved appetites: – My lady's a wag, I have heard all: I have seen all: I understand all, and I'll tell all; for my little Frenchwoman loves news dearly. This story'll gain her heart or nothing will. [*to his master*] Come, Sir, your head's too full of fumes at present, to make room for your jealousy; but I reckon we shall have rare work with you, when your pate's empty. Come; to your kennel, you cuckoldly drunken sot you. [*Carries him out upon his back*]

SCENE ⟨III⟩

Lady Fanciful's house

Enter Lady Fanciful and Mademoiselle.

LADY FANCIFUL But, why did not you tell me before, Mademoiselle, that Razor and you were fond?

MADEMOISELLE De modesty hinder me, Matam.

LADY FANCIFUL Why truly modesty does often hinder us from doing things we have an extravagant mind to. But does he love you well enough yet, to do anything you bid him? Do you think to oblige you he would speak scandal?

MADEMOISELLE Matam, to oblige your ladyship, he shall speak blasphemy.

LADY FANCIFUL Why then, Mademoiselle, I'll tell you what you shall do. You shall engage him to tell his master, all that passed at Spring Garden. I have a mind he should know what a wife and a niece he has got.

MADEMOISELLE *Il le fera*, Matam.

Enter a Footman, who speaks to Mademoiselle apart.

FOOTMAN Mademoiselle; yonder's Mr Razor desires to speak with you.

MADEMOISELLE Tell him, I come presently. [*Exit Footman*] Razor be dare, Matam.

LADY FANCIFUL That's fortunate: well, I'll leave you together.
And if you find him stubborn, Mademoiselle, – heark you – don't
refuse him a few little reasonable liberties, to put him into humour.
MADEMOISELLE *Laisez-moi faire.*   [*Exit Lady Fanciful*]

Razor peeps in; and seeing Lady Fanciful gone,
runs to Mademoiselle, takes her about the neck and kisses her.

MADEMOISELLE How now, confidence.
RAZOR How now, modesty.
MADEMOISELLE Who make you so familiar, sirrah?
RAZOR My impudence, hussy.
MADEMOISELLE Stand off, rogue-face.
RAZOR Ah – Mademoiselle – great news at our house.
MADEMOISELLE Wy wat be de matter?
RAZOR The matter? Why, uptails all's★ the matter.
MADEMOISELLE *Tu te mocque de moi.*
RAZOR Now do you long to know the particulars: the time when:
the place where: the manner how; but I won't tell you a word
more.
MADEMOISELLE Nay, den dou kill me, Razor.
RAZOR [*clapping his hands behind him*] Come, kiss me, then.
MADEMOISELLE Nay, pridee tell me.
RAZOR [*going*] Goodbye to ye.
MADEMOISELLE [*kissing him*] Hold, hold: I will kiss dee.
RAZOR So: that's civil: why now, my pretty pal; my goldfinch;
my little waterwagtail – you must know that – come, kiss me
again.
MADEMOISELLE I won't kiss dee no more.
RAZOR Good b'ye to ye.
MADEMOISELLE *Doucement:* [*kissing him*] dare: *es tu content?*
RAZOR So: now I'll tell thee all. Why the news is, that cuckoldom
in folio, is newly printed; and matrimony in quarto, is just going
into the press. Will you buy any books, Mademoiselle?
MADEMOISELLE *Tu parle comme un libraire,* de devil no understand
dee.
RAZOR Why then, that I may make myself intelligible to a waiting-

★ uptails all: an old song, here with sexual innuendo.

woman, I'll speak like a *valet de chambre*. My lady has cuckolded my master.

MADEMOISELLE *Bon.*

RAZOR Which we take very ill from her hands, I can tell her that.

MADEMOISELLE *N'importe.*

RAZOR But we can prove, that matter of fact had like to have been upon her.

MADEMOISELLE *Oui da.*

RAZOR For we have such bloody circumstances.

MADEMOISELLE *Sans doute.*

RAZOR That any man of parts, may draw tickling conclusions from 'em.

MADEMOISELLE *Fort bien.*

RAZOR We have found a couple of tight well-built gentlemen, stuffed into her ladyship's closet.

MADEMOISELLE *Le diable.*

RAZOR And I, in my particular person, have discovered a most damnable plot, how to persuade my poor master, that all this hide and seek, this will-in-the-wisp, has no other meaning than a Christian marriage for sweet Mrs Bellinda.

MADEMOISELLE *Une mariage? – Ah les drôlesses.*

RAZOR Don't you interrupt me, hussy; 'tis agreed, I say. And my innocent lady, to wriggle herself out at the back door of the business, turns marriage-bawd to her niece, and resolves to deliver up her fair body, to be tumbled and mumbled, by that young liquorish whipster, Heartfree. Now are you satisfied?

MADEMOISELLE No.

RAZOR Right woman; always gaping for more.

MADEMOISELLE Dis be all den, dat dou know?

RAZOR All? Aye, and a great deal too, I think.

MADEMOISELLE Dou be fool, dou know noting. *Écoute mon pauvre* Razor. Dou see des two eyes? – Des two eyes have see de devil.

RAZOR The woman's mad.

MADEMOISELLE In Spring Garden, dat rogue Constant, meet dy lady.

RAZOR *Bon.*

MADEMOISELLE – I'll tell dee no more.

RAZOR Nay, prithee, my swan.

MADEMOISELLE [*clapping her hands behind her, as he had done before*]
Come, kiss me den.

RAZOR I won't kiss you, not I.

MADEMOISELLE *Adieu.*

RAZOR Hold: [*gives her a hearty kiss*] – Now proceed.

MADEMOISELLE *À ça* – I hide myself in one cunning place, where
I hear all, and see all. First dy drunken master come *mal à propos*;
but de sot no know his own dear wife, so he leave her to her sport –

> *As she speaks, Razor still acts the man, and she the woman.*

Den de game begin.

De lover say soft ting.

De lady look upon de ground.

He take her by de hand.

She turn her head, one oder way.

Den he squeez very hard.

Den she pull – very softly.

Den he take her in his arm.

Den she give him, leetel pat.

Den he kiss her tetons.★

Den she say – Pish, nay see.

Den he tremble,

Den she – sigh.

Den he pull her into de arbour,

Den she pinch him.

RAZOR Aye, but not so hard, you baggage you.

MADEMOISELLE Den he grow bold.

She grow weak.

He tro her down.

Il tombe dessus,

Le diable assiste,

Il emporte tout:

[*Razor struggles with her, as if he would throw her down*]
Stand off, sirrah.

RAZOR You have set me afire, you jade you.

MADEMOISELLE Den go to de river and quench dyself.

★ tetons: breasts.

RAZOR What an unnatural harlot 'tis.

MADEMOISELLE [*looking languishingly on him*] Razor.

RAZOR Mademoiselle.

MADEMOISELLE Dou no love me.

RAZOR Not love thee! – More than a Frenchman does soup.

MADEMOISELLE Den dou will refuse noting dat I bid dee?

RAZOR Don't bid me be damned then:

MADEMOISELLE No, only tell dy master, all I have tell dee of dy laty.

RAZOR Why you little malicious strumpet, you; should you like to be served so?

MADEMOISELLE Dou dispute den? – *Adieu.*

RAZOR Hold – But why wilt thou make me be such a rogue, my dear?

MADEMOISELLE *Voilà un vrai Anglais: il est amoureux, et cependent il veut raisonner. Va-t-en au diable.*

RAZOR Hold once more: in hopes thou'lt give me up thy body, I resign thee up my soul.

MADEMOISELLE *Bon: écoute donc:* - if dou fail me – I never see dee more – if dou obey me – [*she takes him about the neck and gives him a smacking kiss*] *Je m'abandonne à toi.*   [*Exit Mademoiselle*]

RAZOR [*licking his lips*] Not be a rogue? – *Amor vincit omnia.*

[*Exit Razor*]

Enter Lady Fanciful and Mademoiselle.

LADY FANCIFUL Marry, say ye? Will the two things marry?

MADEMOISELLE *On le va faire,* Matam.

LADY FANCIFUL Look you, Mademoiselle, in short, I can't bear it – No; I find I can't – If once I see 'em a-bed together, I shall have ten thousand thoughts in my head will make me run distracted. Therefore run and call Razor back immediately, for something must be done to stop this impertinent wedding. If I can but defer it four and twenty hours, I'll make such work about Town, with that little pert slut's reputation. He shall as soon marry a witch.

MADEMOISELLE ⟨*aside*⟩ *La voilà bien intentionée.*   [*Exeunt*]

SCENE ⟨IV⟩

Constant's lodgings

Enter Constant and Heartfree.

CONSTANT But what dost think will come of this business?

HEARTFREE 'Tis easier to think what will not come on't.

CONSTANT What's that?

HEARTFREE A challenge. I know the knight too well for that. His dear body will always prevail upon his noble soul to be quiet.

CONSTANT But though he dare not challenge me, perhaps he may venture to challenge his wife.

HEARTFREE Not if you whisper him in the ear, you won't have him do't, and there's no other way left that I see. For as drunk as he was, he'll remember you and I were where we should not be; and I don't think him quite blockhead enough yet, to be persuaded we were got into his wife's closet, only to peep in her Prayer Book.

Enter Servant, with a letter.

SERVANT Sir, here's a letter, a porter brought it.

CONSTANT O ho, here's instructions for us. [*reads*] 'The accident that has happened has touched our invention to the quick. We would fain come off, without your help; but find that's impossible. In a word, the whole business must be thrown upon a matrimonial intrigue, between your friend and mine. But if the parties are not fond enough, to go quite through with the matter; 'tis sufficient for our turn, they own the design. We'll find pretences enough, to break the match. Adieu.' – Well, woman for invention: how long would my blockhead have been a-producing this. – Hey, Heartfree; what, musing man? Prithee be cheerful. What say'st thou, friend, to this matrimonial remedy?

HEARTFREE Why I say, it's worse than the disease.

CONSTANT Here's a fellow for you: there's beauty and money on her side, and love up to the ears on his; and yet –

HEARTFREE And yet, I think, I may reasonably be allowed to boggle at marrying the niece, in the very moment that you are a-debauching the aunt.

CONSTANT Why truly, there may be something in that. But have
not you a good opinion enough of your own parts, to believe you
could keep a wife to yourself?

HEARTFREE I should have, if I had a good opinion enough of hers,
to believe she could do as much by me. For to do 'em right, after
all, the wife seldom rambles, till the husband shows her the way.

CONSTANT 'Tis true; a man of real worth, scarce ever is a cuckold,
but by his own fault. Women are not naturally lewd, there must
be something to urge 'em to it. They'll cuckold a churl, out of
revenge; a fool, because they despise him; a beast because they
loathe him. But when they make bold with a man they once had
a well-grounded value for, 'tis because they first see themselves
neglected by him.

HEARTFREE Nay, were I well assured, that I should never grow
Sir John, I ne'er should fear Bellinda'd play my lady. But our
weakness, thou know'st, my friend, consists in that very change,
we so impudently throw upon (indeed) a steadier and more
generous sex.

CONSTANT Why faith we are a little impudent in that matter
that's the truth on't. But this is wonderful, to see you grown so
warm an advocate for those (but t'other day) you took so much
pains to abuse.

HEARTFREE All revolutions run into extremes, the bigot makes
the boldest atheist; and the coyest saint, the most extravagant
strumpet. But prithee advise me in this good and evil; this life
and death, this blessing and cursing, that is set before me. Shall I
marry – or die a maid?

CONSTANT Why faith, Heartfree, matrimony is like an army going
to engage. Love's the forlorn hope,* which is soon cut off; the
marriage-knot is the main body, which may stand buff a long
long time; and repentance is the rear-guard, which rarely gives
ground, as long as the main battle has a being.

HEARTFREE Conclusion then; you advise me to whore on, as
you do.

CONSTANT That's not concluded yet. For though marriage be a
lottery in which there are a wondrous many blanks; yet there is
one inestimable lot, in which the only heaven on earth is written.

* forlorn hope: advance guard.

Would your kind fate but guide your hand to that, though I
were wrapped in all that luxury itself could clothe me with, I still
should envy you.

HEARTFREE And justly too: for to be capable of loving one,
doubtless is better than to possess a thousand. But how far that
capacity's in me, alas I know not.

CONSTANT But you would know?

HEARTFREE I would so.

CONSTANT Matrimony will inform you. Come, one flight of
resolution carries you to the land of experience; where, in a very
moderate time, you'll know the capacity of your soul, and your
body both, or I'm mistaken.   [*Exeunt*]

SCENE ⟨V⟩

Sir John Brute's house

Enter Lady Brute and Bellinda.

BELLINDA Well, Madam, what answer have you from 'em?

LADY BRUTE That they'll be here this moment. I fancy 'twill
end in a wedding. I'm sure he's a fool if it don't. Ten thousand
pound, and such a lass as you are, is no contemptible offer to a
younger brother. But are not you under strange agitations?
Prithee how does your pulse beat?

BELLINDA High and low, I have much ado to be valiant, sure it
must feel very strange to go to bed to a man?

LADY BRUTE Um – it does feel a little odd at first, but it will
soon grow easy to you.

Enter Constant and Heartfree.

LADY BRUTE Good-morrow gentlemen: how have you slept
after your adventure?

HEARTFREE Some careful thoughts, ladies, on your accounts
have kept us waking.

BELLINDA And some careful thoughts on your own, I believe,
have hindered you from sleeping. Pray how does this matrimonial
project relish with you.

HEARTFREE Why faith e'en as storming towns does with soldiers, where the hopes of delicious plunder banishes the fear of being knocked on the head.

BELLINDA Is it then possible after all, that you dare think of downright lawful wedlock?

HEARTFREE Madam, you have made me so foolhardy, I dare do anything.

BELLINDA Then Sir, I challenge you; and matrimony's the spot where I expect you.

HEARTFREE 'Tis enough; I'll not fail. [*aside*] So, now I am in for Hob's voyage; a great leap in the dark.

LADY BRUTE Well, gentlemen, this matter being concluded then, have you got your lessons ready? For Sir John is grown such an atheist of late, he'll believe nothing upon easy terms.

CONSTANT We'll find ways to extend his faith, Madam. But pray how do you find him this morning?

LADY BRUTE Most lamentably morose, chewing the cud after last night's discovery; of which however he had but a confused notion e'en now. But I'm afraid his *valet de chambre* has told him all, for they are very busy together at this moment. When I told him of Bellinda's marriage, I had no other answer but a grunt: from which, you may draw what conclusions you think fit. But to your notes, gentlemen, he's here.

Enter Sir John and Razor.

CONSTANT Good-morrow, Sir.

HEARTFREE Good-morrow, Sir John. I'm very sorry my indiscretion should cause so much disorder in your family.

SIR JOHN Disorders generally come from indiscretions, Sir, 'tis no strange thing at all.

LADY BRUTE I hope, my dear, you are satisfied there was no wrong intended you.

SIR JOHN None, my dove.

BELLINDA If not, I hope my consent to marry Mr Heartfree will convince you. For as little as I know of amours, Sir, I can assure you, one intrigue is enough to bring four people together, without further mischief.

SIR JOHN And I know too, that intrigues tend to procreation of

more kinds than one. One intrigue will beget another as soon as
beget a son or a daughter.

CONSTANT I am very sorry, Sir, to see you still seem unsatisfied
with a lady, whose more than common virtue, I am sure, were she
my wife, should meet a better usage.

SIR JOHN Sir, if her conduct has put a trick upon her virtue, her
virtue's the bubble, but her husband's the loser.

CONSTANT Sir, you have received a sufficient answer already, to
justify both her conduct and mine. You'll pardon me for meddling
in your family affairs; but I perceive I am the man you are jealous
of, and therefore it concerns me.

SIR JOHN Would it did not concern me, and then I should not care
who it concerned.

CONSTANT Well, Sir, if truth and reason won't content you; I
know but one way more, which, if you think fit, you may take.

SIR JOHN Lord, Sir, you are very hasty: if I had been found at
prayers in your wife's closet, I should have allowed you twice as
much time to come to yourself in.

CONSTANT Nay, Sir, if time be all you want. We have no quarrel.
[*Sir John muses*]

HEARTFREE ⟨*aside to Constant*⟩ I told you how the sword would
work upon him.

CONSTANT Let him muse; however, I'll lay fifty pound our foreman brings us in, not guilty.

SIR JOHN [*aside*] 'Tis well – 'tis very well – In spite of that young
jade's matrimonial intrigue, I am a downright stinking cuckold –
Here they are – Boo – [*putting his hand to his forehead*] Methinks I
could butt with a bull. What the plague did I marry her for? I
knew she did not like me; if she had, she would have lain with
me; for I would have done so, because I liked her: but that's
passed, and I have her. And now, what shall I do with her –
If I put my horns in my pocket, she'll grow insolent. – If I don't;
that goat there, that stallion, is ready to whip me through the
guts. – The debate then is reduced to this; shall I die a hero? Or live
a rascal? – Why, wiser men than I, have long since concluded,
that a living dog is better than a dead lion. – [*to Constant and Heartfree*] Gentlemen, now my wine and my passion are governable,
I must own, I have never observed anything in my wife's course

of life, to back me in my jealousy of her: but jealousy's a mark of love; so she need not trouble her head about it, as long as I make no more words on't.

Lady Fanciful enters disguised, and addresses to Bellinda apart.

CONSTANT I am glad to see your reason rule at last. Give me your hand: I hope you'll look upon me as you are wont.

SIR JOHN Your humble servant. [*aside*] A wheedling son of a whore.

HEARTFREE And that I may be sure you are friends with me too, pray give me your consent to wed your niece.

SIR JOHN Sir, you have it with all my heart: damn me if you han't. [*aside*] 'Tis time to get rid of her; a young pert pimp; she'll make an incomparable bawd in a little time.

Enter a Servant, who gives Heartfree a letter.

BELLINDA ⟨*to Lady Fanciful*⟩ Heartfree your husband, say you? 'Tis impossible.

LADY FANCIFUL Would to kind heaven it were: but 'tis too true; and in the world there lives not such a wretch. I'm young; and either I have been flattered by my friends, as well as glass, or nature has been kind and generous to me. I had a fortune too, was greater far than he could ever hope for. But with my heart, I am robbed of all the rest. I'm slighted and I'm beggared both at once. [*weeping*] I have scarce a bare subsistence from the villain, yet dare complain to none; for he has sworn, if e'er 'tis known I am his wife, he'll murder me.

BELLINDA The traitor.

LADY FANCIFUL I accidentally was told he courted you; charity soon prevailed upon me to prevent your misery: [*weeping*] and as you see, I'm still so generous even to him, as not to suffer he should do a thing, for which the law might take away his life.*

BELLINDA ⟨*aside*⟩ Poor creature; how I pity her! [*they continue talking aside*]

HEARTFREE [*aside*] Death and damnation! – Let me read it again. [*reads*] 'Though I have a particular reason, not to let you know who I am till I see you; yet you'll easily believe 'tis a faithful

* law . . . life: bigamy was punishable by death until 1828.

friend that gives you this advice. – I have lain with Bellinda.'
(Good.) – 'I have a child by her,' (Better and better.) 'which is
now at nurse;' (Heaven be praised.) 'and I think the foundation
laid for another:' (Ha! – Old Trupenny!) – 'No rack could have
tortured this story from me; but friendship has done it. I heard
of your design to marry her, and could not see you abused. Make
use of my advice, but keep my secret till I ask you for't again.
Adieu.'

[Exit Lady Fanciful]

CONSTANT *[to Bellinda]* Come, Madam; shall we send for the
parson? I doubt here's no business for the lawyer: younger brothers have nothing to settle but their hearts, and that I believe
my friend here has already done, very faithfully.

BELLINDA *[scornfully]* Are you sure, Sir, there are no old mortgages
upon it.

HEARTFREE *[coldly]* If you think there are, Madam, it mayn't be
amiss to defer the marriage till you are sure they are paid off.

BELLINDA *[aside]* How the galled horse kicks! *[to Heartfree]* We'll
defer it as long as you please, Sir.

HEARTFREE The more time we take to consider on't, Madam, the
less apt we shall be to commit oversights; therefore, if you please,
we'll put it off, for just nine months.

BELLINDA Guilty consciences make men cowards: I don't wonder you want time to resolve.

HEARTFREE And they make women desperate: I don't wonder
you were so quickly determined.

BELLINDA What does the fellow mean?

HEARTFREE What does the lady mean?

SIR JOHN Zoons, what do you both mean?

[Heartfree and Bellinda walk chafing about]

RAZOR *[aside]* Here is so much sport going to be spoiled, it
makes me ready to weep again. A pox o'this impertinent Lady
Fanciful, and her plots, and her Frenchwoman too. She's a whimsical, ill-natured bitch, and when I have got my bones broke in her
service, 'tis ten to one but my recompence is a clap; I hear 'em
tittering without still. Ecod I'll e'en go lug 'em both in by the
ears, and discover the plot, to secure my pardon.   *[Exit Razor]*

CONSTANT Prithee explain, Heartfree.

HEARTFREE A fair deliverance; thank my stars and my friend.

BELLINDA ⟨*to Lady Brute*⟩ 'Tis well it went no farther. A base fellow.

LADY BRUTE What can be the meaning of all this?

BELLINDA What's his meaning, I don't know. But mine is; that if I had married him – I had had no husband.

HEARTFREE And what's her meaning, I don't know. But mine is; that if I had married her – I had had wife enough.

SIR JOHN Your people of wit, have got such cramp ways of expressing themselves, they seldom comprehend one another. Pox take you both, will you speak that you may be understood.

Enter Razor in sackcloth, pulling in Lady Fanciful and Mademoiselle.

RAZOR If they won't, here comes an interpreter.

LADY BRUTE Heavens, what have we here?

RAZOR A villain, – but a repenting villain. Stuff which saints in all ages have been made of.

ALL Razor.

LADY BRUTE What means this sudden metamorphose?

RAZOR Nothing: without my pardon.

LADY BRUTE What pardon do you want?

RAZOR *Imprimis*, your ladyship's; for a damnable lie made upon your spotless virtue, and set to the tune of Spring Garden. [*to Sir John*] Next, at my generous master's feet I bend, for interrupting his more noble thoughts with phantoms of disgraceful cuckoldom. [*to Constant*] Thirdly, I to this gentleman apply, for making him the hero of my romance. [*to Heartfree*] Fourthly, your pardon, noble Sir, I ask, for clandestinely marrying you, without either bidding of banns; bishop's licence, friend's consent – or your own knowledge. [*to Bellinda*] And lastly, to my good young lady's clemency I come, for pretending the corn was sowed in the ground, before ever the plough had been in the field.

SIR JOHN [*aside*] So that after all, 'tis a moot point, whether I am a cuckold or not.

BELLINDA Well Sir, upon condition you confess all, I'll pardon you myself, and try to obtain as much from the rest of the company. But I must know then, who 'tis has put you upon all this mischief?

RAZOR Satan, and his equipage. Woman tempted me, lust weakened me; – and so the devil overcame me: as fell Adam, so fell I.

BELLINDA Then pray, Mr Adam, will you make us acquainted with your Eve.

RAZOR [*to Mademoiselle*] Unmask, for the honour of France.

ALL Mademoiselle?

MADEMOISELLE Me ask ten tousand pardon of all de good company.

SIR JOHN Why this mystery thickens instead of clearing up. [*to Razor*] You son of a whore you, put us out of our pain.

RAZOR One moment brings sunshine. [*showing Mademoiselle*] 'Tis true; this is the woman, that tempted me. But this is the serpent, that tempted the woman; and if my prayers might be heard, her punishment for so doing, should be like the serpent's of old. [*pulls off Lady Fanciful's mask*] She should lie upon her face, all the days of her life.

ALL Lady Fanciful.

BELLINDA Impertinent.

LADY BRUTE Ridiculous.

ALL Ha, ha, ha, ha, ha.

BELLINDA I hope your ladyship will give me leave to wish you joy, since you have owned your marriage yourself. Mr Heartfree: I vow 'twas strangely wicked in you, to think of another wife, when you had one already so charming as her ladyship.

ALL Ha, ha, ha, ha, ha.

LADY FANCIFUL [*aside*] Confusion seize 'em as it seizes me.

MADEMOISELLE *Que le diable étouffe ce maraud de* Razor.

BELLINDA Your ladyship seems disordered: a breeding qualm, perhaps. Mr Heartfree: your bottle of Hungary water* to your lady. Why Madam, he stands as unconcerned as if he were your husband in earnest.

LADY FANCIFUL Your mirth's as nauseous as yourself Bellinda. You think you triumph o'er a rival now. *Hélas ma pauvre fille.* Where'er I'm rival, there's no cause for mirth. No, my poor wretch; 'tis from another principle I have acted. I knew that thing there would make so perverse a husband, and you so impertinent

* Hungary water: rosemary flowers infused in wine, used to revive those who had fainted.

a wife; that lest your mutual plagues should make you both run mad, I charitably would have broke the match. He, he, he, he, he.

[*Exit laughing affectedly. Mademoiselle following her*]

MADEMOISELLE He, he, he, he, he.

ALL Ha, ha, ha, ha, ha.

SIR JOHN [*aside*] Why now this woman will be married to somebody too.

BELLINDA Poor creature, what a passion she's in: but I forgive her.

HEARTFREE Since you have so much goodness for her, I hope you'll pardon my offence too, Madam.

BELLINDA There will be no great difficulty in that, since I am guilty of an equal fault.

HEARTFREE Then pardons being passed on all sides, pray let's to church to conclude the day's work.

CONSTANT But before you go, let me treat you pray with a song, a new married lady made within this week; it may be of use to you both.

SONG.

I

When yielding first to Damon's flame
    I sunk into his arms,
He swore he'd ever be the same,
    Then rifled all my charms.
But fond of what he'd long desired,
    Too greedy of his prey,
My shepherd's flame, alas, expired
    Before the verge of day.

2

My innocence in lovers' wars,
    Reproached his quick defeat.
Confused, ashamed, and bathed in tears,
    I mourned his cold retreat.
At length, 'Ah shepherdess', cried he,
    'Would you my fire renew,
Alas you must retreat like me,
    I'm lost if you pursue.'

HEARTFREE So Madam; now had the parson but done his business –

BELLINDA You'd be half weary of your bargain.

HEARTFREE No sure, I might dispense with one night's lodging.

BELLINDA I'm ready to try, Sir.

HEARTFREE Then let's to church: and if it be our chance, to disagree, –

BELLINDA Take heed: – the surly husband's fate you see.

EPILOGUE

By another Hand

Spoken by Lady Brute and Bellinda.

LADY BRUTE No Epilogue!

BELLINDA I swear I know of none.

LADY BRUTE Lord! How shall we excuse it to the Town?

BELLINDA Why, we must e'en say something of our own.

LADY BRUTE Our own! Aye, that must needs be precious stuff.

BELLINDA I'll lay my life they'll like well enough.
    Come faith begin –

LADY BRUTE Excuse me, after you.

BELLINDA Nay, pardon me for that, I know my cue.

LADY BRUTE O for the world, I would not have precedence.

BELLINDA O Lord!

LADY BRUTE I swear –

BELLINDA O fie!

LADY BRUTE I'm all obedience.
    First then, know all, before our doom is fixed,
    The third day is for us* –

BELLINDA Nay, and the sixth.

LADY BRUTE We speak not from the poet now, nor is it
    His cause – (I want a rhyme)

BELLINDA That we solicit.

LADY BRUTE Then sure you cannot have the hearts to be severe
    And damn us –

BELLINDA Damn us! Let 'em if they dare.

LADY BRUTE Why if they should, what punishment remains?

BELLINDA Eternal exile from behind our scenes.

LADY BRUTE But if they're kind, that sentence we'll recall,
    We can be grateful –

BELLINDA And have wherewithal.

LADY BRUTE But at grand treaties, hope not to be trusted,
    Before preliminaries are adjusted.

---

* the third day: traditionally the author's benefit, but Vanbrugh must have transferred it to the actors.

BELLINDA You know the time, and we appoint this place;
Where, if you please, we'll meet and sign the peace.★

★ the peace: an allusion to the Peace of Ryswick.

NOTES

The copy text used is that of the first edition of 1697 in the Brotherton Collection, University of Leeds.

Abbreviations
  Q1 The first quarto edition, 1697
  Q2 The second quarto edition, 1698
  Q3 The third quarto edition, 1709
  P   *Plays written by Sir John Vanbrugh*, 1719
  1776 An edition of 1776

The French of Mademoiselle (Madamoiselle in the original, but here regularized) has been modernized and normalized: her broken English has been left as it appeared in the first edition. Sir John Brute's oath 'zoons' has not been altered to 'zounds' throughout.

565.34 one, an/one an Q1
567.6   years'/years Q1
568.18 Lady Brute [*sola*]/enter Lady Brute *sola* Q1
571.9   us, we/us. We Q1
577.19 *Je n'en* Q3/I'n 'en Q1
578.5   *anglaise.*/anglaise, Q1
579.10 Matam/Madam Q1
583.21 and (which Q3/(and which Q1
589.15 *impromptu*/*in promptu* Q1
590.15 cherubim/cherubin Q1
590.35 *s.d.* [*Exit servant*]/Q1 places after 'to dine yet'.
591.3   Matam,/Matam. Q1
595.11 *s.d.* Sir John . . . /Q1 places after 'So, let her live'.
598.30 'em/em Q1
600.23 malicious/maliciou Q1
600.24 my heart/my my heart Q1
604.7   disposed of/disposed on Q1
607.8   t'other/to'ther Q1
607.13 LORD/*Lady* Q1
608.11 Rake./*Rake*? Q1
611.20 him? He/him, he Q1
618.6   me. You/me, you Q1
624.18 *s.d.* [Heartfree *runs off*]/Q1 places after 'made me a knight'.

626.14	Bellinda. Besides/Bellinda, besides Q1
628.28	on/an Q1
633.24	says he/says, he Q1
639.13	ground./ground Q1
639.25	pinch him./pinch him Q3
639.29	down./down Q1
642.15	Sir John, I/Sir John. I Q1
643.22	valiant, sure it must feel P/valiant feel Q1
644.28	SIR JOHN/*Const.* Q1
644.37	tend Q2/tends Q1
649.15	*off*/*of* Q1
649.27	*étouffe* 1776/e toute Q1
650.30	lovers'/lover's Q1